Current Psychotherapies

Second Edition

Current Psychotherapies

Raymond J. Corsini and Contributors

Second Edition

F. E. PEACOCK PUBLISHERS, INC.
ITASCA, ILLINOIS 60143

To My Teachers

Rudolf Dreikurs
J. L. Moreno
Carl Rogers

Contributors

JACOB A. ARLOW, M.D., Clinical Professor of Psychiatry, State University of New York, New York, N.Y.

DIANNE L. CHAMBLESS, Ph.D., Assistant Professor, Department of Psychology, University of Georgia, Athens, Georgia

JOHN M. DUSAY, M.D., Psychiatrist, Private Practice, San Francisco; Assistant Clinical Professor, University of California Medical School, San Francisco, California

KATHERINE MULHOLLAND DUSAY, M.A., California Licensed Marriage, Family and Child Counselor, Private Practice, San Francisco, California

ALBERT ELLIS, Ph.D., Executive Director, Institute for Advanced Study in Rational Psychotherapy, New York, N.Y.

LEON J. FINE, Ph.D., Clinical Professor of Psychiatry (Group Processes), University of Oregon Health Science Center, Portland, Oregon

VINCENT D. FOLEY, Ph.D., Department of Counselor Education, St. John's University, Jamaica, N.Y.

EUGENE T. GENDLIN, Ph.D., Associate Professor, Department of Psychology, University of Chicago, Chicago, Illinois

WILLIAM GLASSER, M.D., President, Institute for Reality Therapy and Educator Training Center, Los Angeles, California

ALAN GOLDSTEIN, Ph.D., Associate Professor, Temple University, Philadelphia, Pennsylvania

YORAM KAUFMANN, Ph.D., Private Practice, Psychotherapy, New York, N.Y.

JOHN H. MANN, Ph.D., Professor of Sociology, State University of New York, College of Geneseo, New York, N.Y.

BETTY D. MEADOR, Ph.D., Director, Center for Studies of the Person, La Jolla, California

HAROLD H. MOSAK, Ph.D., Private Practice, Psychotherapy, Chicago, Illinois

CARL R. ROGERS, Ph.D., Resident Fellow, Center for Studies of the Person, La Jolla, California

JAMES S. SIMKIN, Ph.D., Director, Simkin Training Center in Gestalt Therapy, Big Sur, California

LEONARD M. ZUNIN, M.D., Private Practice, Psychiatry; Director, Human Relations Consultants, Los Angeles, California

Table of Contents

Preface

The favorable reception given to the first edition of *Current Psychotherapies* has encouraged the publisher to attempt a second edition. Based on new developments in the field of psychotherapy, on comments by colleagues and students, but mostly on the basis of an in-depth questionnaire sent to professors who were using this book as a text, various changes in the content and the format have been made, hopefully making this edition even more useful than the first one.

Chapters have been shortened but some new materials, such as Case Readings, have been added. The outline is a bit more logical than it was for the first edition. Some chapters and some authors have been changed—all with the intention of making this book as authoritative, comprehensible, and readable as possible.

Generally, I have taken a conservative position and have given preference, all things considered, to well-established systems that have proven their validity through popularity and survival. Nevertheless, it is to be expected that some people will be disappointed by what has been put in and what has been left out. It is impossible for an editor to satisfy everyone, but I hope my choices of selections will be seen as a viable compromise.

Current Psychotherapies has a companion reader, *Great Cases in Psychotherapy* (Wedding and Corsini, Peacock, 1979), in which you will find further examples of reports of cases in the various systems included here plus some others as well.

I appreciate the assistance and cooperation of the authors of the various chapters, who generally complied with my demands for uniformity of presentation. I want to thank the many individuals, too numerous to mention, who helped me make decisions about format and content.

As with the first edition, this book is intended to advance further the art and science of psychotherapy in the hope that this will be of help in the alleviation of human misery.

RAYMOND J. CORSINI
Honolulu, 1978

ix

Outline of Book

	Psychoanalysis	Adlerian	Analytical	Person-Centered	Rational-Emotive	Behavioral	Gestalt	Reality	Experiential	Transactional Analysis	Psychodrama	Family Therapy	Human Potential
Overview (*Page*)	1	44	95	131	185	230	273	302	340	374	428	460	500
Basic Concepts	1	44	95	131	185	230	273	302	340	374	428	460	500
Other Systems	3	48	98	133	188	232	275	304	343	380	431	462	502
History	5	51	100	136	189	234	277	306	345	383	433	464	504
Precursors	5	51	100	136	189	234	277	306	345	383	433	464	504
Beginnings	6	53	101	137	191	235	278	307	347	385	434	465	505
Current Status	9	54	103	140	192	236	279	310	349	387	436	467	507
Personality	11	56	103	142	194	237	280	311	350	388	438	469	508
Theory of Personality	11	56	103	142	194	237	280	311	350	388	438	469	508
Variety of Concepts	12	61	107	145	199	239	282	313	352	397	439	471	510
Psychotherapy	17	62	110	151	202	242	284	316	353	399	442	474	512
Theory of Psychotherapy	17	62	110	151	202	242	284	316	353	399	442	474	512
Process of Psychotherapy	18	64	112	153	205	243	285	323		400	444	476	516
Mechanisms of Psychotherapy	20	71	116	164	212	255	287	326	360	408	447	481	518
Applications	22	73	118		213	256	288	327	361	409	448	483	521
Problems	22	73	118		213	256	288	327	361	409	448	483	521
Evaluation	25	74	119	172	214	257	288	329	362	412	449	484	522
Treatment	25	75	121	173	215	261	289	330	364	415	450	486	524
Management	30	77	122	174		262	291	332	365	418	451	489	525
Case Example	31	81	123	176	223	263	292	334	366	419	453	491	527
Summary	38	86	127	180	225	267	297	337	369	424	455	495	532
Annotated Bibliography	39	88	128	181	226	268	298	338	370	425	456	495	533
Case Readings	40	89	129	182	227	268	299	338	371	425	457	496	534
References	40	89	129	182	227	269	299	338	371	425	457	497	534

1

Psychoanalysis

JACOB A. ARLOW

OVERVIEW

Psychoanalysis is a system of psychology derived from the discoveries of Sigmund Freud. Originating as a method for treating certain psychoneurotic disorders, psychoanalysis has come to serve as the foundation for a general theory of psychology. Knowledge derived from the treatment of individual patients has led to insights into art, religion, social organization, child development, and education. In addition, by elucidating the influence of unconscious wishes and feelings on the physiology of the body, psychoanalysis has made it possible to understand and treat many psychosomatic illnesses.

Basic Concepts

Basically, psychoanalysis is a psychology of conflict. According to Ernst Kris (1950), psychoanalysis may be defined as human nature seen from the vantage point of conflict. Psychoanalysis views the functioning of the mind as the expression of conflicting forces. Some of these forces are conscious; others, perhaps the major ones, are unconscious. As a system of psychology and as a method of therapy, psychoanalysis emphasizes the importance of unconscious forces in mental life.

Conflict is an inexorable dimension of the human condition. It reflects the contradiction inherent in man's dual nature as a biological animal and a social being. In a few short years, each human infant has to be civilized and acculturated; he has to incorporate and integrate the ideals and values, the inhibitions and the taboos, of his particular society. The prime and immediate instrumentality in this process is the family. After the age of five, the more formalized institutions of society take over much of the responsibility for acculturating the individual. In this development, frustration, anger, disappointment, and conflict are inevitable.

From its inception, the functioning of the mind is related to events in the body. The physiology of the body is the substrate of all psychology, including psychoanalysis. The basic responses to stimuli in terms of pleasure and pain (or unpleasure) are part of man's biological inheritance. These responses, phylogenetically determined, undoubtedly were of evolutionary significance in the struggle of the species to survive. A fundamental principle of psychoanalytic theory is that human psychology is governed by a tendency to seek pleasure and to avoid pain. This is referred to as the *pleasure principle* (Freud, 1911). Although this principle is

1

operative throughout life, it is patently and overwhelmingly dominant in the first few years of existence. The earliest experiences of pleasure and pain (or one might say gratification and frustration) play a crucial role in shaping each individual's psychological structure. (The term *structure,* as used in psychoanalysis, pertains to the repetitive, relatively stable, organized forms of mental responses and functioning.) The impact of the earliest experiences is intensified in the case of the human infant, because in contrast to other animals, the human has a much longer period of dependence upon the adults in his environment. Without their care and solicitude over a period of several years, he could not survive. This fact of biology eventuates in an early and abiding attachment to others, a factor that comes to play a central role in what we know as human nature.

Freud's revolutionary perception of man's psychology represents a fusion of the most advanced humanistic and scientific ideas of the late nineteenth and early twentieth centuries. In psychoanalysis, he combined the liberal ideal of respect for the integrity of each individual with a rigorous attempt to establish a scientific method for studying the individual as a living, social entity. He emphasized that clinical observation is the foundation of psychoanalysis. Theory for Freud was a superstructure erected on clinical observation that could be altered by new findings. Accordingly, it was essential to establish an objective method by which reliable observations could be made. This prerequisite Freud met in his formulation of the psychoanalytic situation, a set of standard conditions governing the relationship between the patient and the analyst. The nature and the organization of the psychoanalytic situation are discussed below. Also, it is important to note that psycho-

analysis is at the same time a form of therapy and a method of investigation.

Of all the forms of psychotherapy, psychoanalysis is founded on the most extensive, inclusive, and comprehensive system of psychology. It encompasses man's inner experience and outer behavior, his biological nature and his social role, how he functions as an individual and how he functions as a member of the group. Many of the historical conflicts within the psychoanalytic movement may be understood as reflections of how various contributors at different times emphasized this or that particular aspect of psychoanalytic theory or practice, whether they placed greater or lesser emphasis on biological, psychological, social, economic, or historical forces in the development of the individual and his psychological conflicts.

Essentially, psychoanalysis continues the rationalist spirit of Greek philosophy in its command to "know thyself." Knowing one's self, however, is understood in quite a different way. It is not to be found in the pursuit of formal, logical analysis of thinking. As far as the individual is concerned, the sources of his neurotic illness and suffering are by their very nature "unknowable." They reside outside the realm of consciousness, having been barred from awareness by virtue of their painful, unacceptable quality. By enabling the patient to understand how his neurotic symptoms and behavior represent derivatives of unconscious conflicts, psychoanalysis permits the patient to make rational choices instead of responding automatically. Thus, self-knowledge of a very special kind strengthens the individual's ability to control his fate and his happiness. Psychoanalysis can accomplish this only to the extent that unhappiness and neurotic suffering are the outcome of the individual's unconscious conflicts. It can offer no magic key to universal happiness or individual salvation. Although much has been learned through psychoanalysis of group psychology and mass dynamics, it is an open question whether and how such rational insights can be applied. Whatever hopes and anticipations one entertains in these matters probably depends upon whether one is basically optimistic or pessimistic in one's outlook on life. For the successfully analyzed individual, however, freedom from neurotic inhibition and suffering is often experienced as a liberating, self-fulfilling transformation, which enables him not only to actualize his own potential but to contribute to the advancement and happiness of others. Thus, knowing one's self may have far-reaching social implications. It is important to bear this in mind, because even under the best of circumstances, because of practical difficulties, only a relatively small number of people at best can or will be analyzed.

Other Systems

Almost every form of modern psychotherapy owes some debt to psychoanalysis. As Leo Rangell (1973) has shown, most forms of psychotherapy now widely practiced are based on some element of psychoanalytic theory or technique. Usually some procedure or a particular concept is borrowed from psychoanalysis and used as the rationale for a particular treatment. This is not to imply that other forms of therapy are invalid or ineffectual. Quite the contrary. Although there are many ways to treat neuroses, there is but one way to understand them—psychoanalysis (Fenichel, 1945). It has been stated in many quarters that psychoanalysts believe their method is the only worthwhile form of treatment. This is not

true. There are many situations where a nonanalytic treatment is preferable to an analytic one. For many forms of mental illness, psychoanalysis is inadvisable or contraindicated. However, psychoanalysis is the only approach that makes clear what is going on in neurosis; it is the one theory that gives a scientific explanation to the effectiveness of all psychotherapies.

Historically, the line of descent of *Jungian analysis* and *Adlerian therapy* from psychoanalysis is clear. Both Carl Jung and Alfred Adler were students of Freud who broke with him early in the history of the psychoanalytic movement. Jung had serious differences with Freud concerning the nature of drives. His approach to the psychology of the individual places less emphasis on maturational and developmental processes. Beyond the vicissitudes of individual conflicts, Jung emphasized the significance of culturally determined, unconsciously transmitted symbolic representations of the principal themes of human existence. Behind the transformations of individual experience, Jung and his followers see the constant recurrence of mythic themes common to all mankind. The struggles in each individual's life eventuate from conflicting images, conflicting representations of the self and especially of the sexual role. Jung's concept of the transmission of unconscious fantasies through a collective unconscious has been criticized as being too mystical and too close to transcendent religious apprehension of the world. In some respects, Jung's views on the collective unconscious correspond to the Freudians' concept of primitive universal fantasy, but the latter regard these only as vehicles for derivatives of the instinctual drives of childhood rather than original determinants of behavior. They are secondary rather than primary factors in shaping personality. Some of Jung's concepts are particularly useful in elucidating the more regressed manifestations seen in schizophrenic patients (Jung, 1909).

Adler (Ansbacher & Ansbacher, 1956) made his departure from Freud on the basis of several considerations. He believed the role of social and political pressures was underestimated by Freudian psychoanalysts. At the time, in large measure, there was considerable validity to this criticism, analysts having concentrated primarily on the transformation of the derivatives of the energy of the sexual drive, the *libido*. To Adler, the cause of conflicts was more superficially determined by factors such as inferiority over social status, inadequate physical endowment, sexual weakness, and discrimination. Many of his concepts presaged later psychoanalytic contributions concerning the role of self-esteem, particularly in relation to the so-called narcissistic personality disorders.

Recent years have seen the burgeoning of many forms of therapy in which the central aspect of the treatment consists of self-expression, releasing emotion, overcoming inhibitions, and articulating in speech and behavior the fantasies or impulses previously suppressed. The *encounter movement* (Schutz, 1967; Burton, 1969) represents one such school. *Primal scream* is typical of another. These forms of treatment represent exaggerations and caricatures of the principle of emotional catharsis that Freud advanced in his early studies of hysteria (Freud, 1895). At that time, he thought that discharge of pent-up emotion could have a beneficial therapeutic effect. Subsequent experience with the treatment of neurotic patients, however, convinced Freud that this method was limited and, in the long run, ineffectual, since it did not give sufficient weight to the needs of self-punishment and the various defenses the ego uses to ward off anxiety. In the expressive forms of treatment, the group experience plays an enormous role in mitigating anxiety. Expressing in the presence of others what is ordinarily inexpressible can go far in ameliorating a sense of guilt. The burden of guilt, furthermore, is lightened by the knowledge that other members of the group admit to the same or similar feelings and impulses. Everyone's guilt is no one's guilt (Sachs, 1942). The effect of such treatment, however, depends to a large extent on the continuity of contact with the group experience. Since no essential insight or psychological restructuring has taken place, the tendency for relapse once the group experience is discontinued is very strong. Furthermore, there are cases in which the temptation and the opportunity to express derivatives of forbidden impulses is perceived as so overwhelming a danger by the individual that he is unable to cope with it. He may be overcome by uncontrollable panic and in some instances may suffer a psychotic break.

Mitigating the influence of the superego on the total psychological equilibrium seems to be the essential feature of the *rational-emotive system* of Albert Ellis (1970). Ellis attempts to get the patient to change his values, particularly in regard to sexuality, helping relieve the patient of irrational guilt that may have inhibited many aspects of his life and behavior. When this treatment is effective, it can be understood in terms of the patient having made an identification with the therapist, specifically with his personality and his values. The therapist comes to serve as an auxiliary superego that may, for a shorter or longer time, replace or alter the patient's patterns of judgment, self-evaluation and ideal aspirations. This is similar to what one observes in cases where individuals are "cured" of their difficulties through religious conversion, usually as the result of an attachment to some charismatic religious (sometimes political) figure.

As part of the psychoanalytic situation, the analyst listens patiently, sympathetically, uncritically, and receptively to the patient's productions. This aspect of psychoanalytic technique forms the core of treatments such as the nondirective listening of Carl R. Rogers (1951). In other forms of treatment, sympathetic listening may be combined with advice or counseling, or trying to guide the patient in a rational manner through the real and imaginary pitfalls of living. Otto Fenichel (1945) commented on the dynamics of these forms of therapy. He pointed out that verbalization of vaguely felt anxieties may bring relief since the individual can face concretized, verbalized ideas better than unclear, emotional sensations. The influence of transference also plays a role. The fact that a doctor, social worker, or other therapist spends time, interest, and sympathy on the patient reawakens echoes of previous situations of having been helped by friends or relatives. For lonely people it can be a substantial relief to have someone to talk to and not be scolded for their difficulties. When the patient can see some connection between his worries and other patterns of behavior, he feels an accession of strength in relation to the deeper unconscious forces within his personality. All the forms of therapy mentioned above make use of one or more of the fundamental features of psychoanalytic therapy, namely, a setting in which the patient can express his thoughts and feelings spontaneously and freely to an uncritical, receptive observer; the achievement of insight through interpretation; and finally, and perhaps most important, an awareness of the power of the transference relationship.

Other forms of therapy such as *Gestalt therapy* (Perls, 1951), *reality therapy* (Glasser, 1967), and *behavior therapy* (Wolpe, 1958) illustrate the principles just mentioned. Essentially, the therapist is unconsciously cast in the role of serving as a model or acting as the transference instrument in a desperate effort either to deny or project the effects of internal conflicts. The therapist unconsciously joins the patient in a pattern of playing out some derivative of the patient's childhood fantasies. Accordingly, such forms of therapy play into the tendency of patients to try to act out in reality expressions of their unconscious conflicts. For this reason, one can expect that such forms of therapy can have only limited usefulness and short-term effectiveness.

HISTORY

Precursors

Psychoanalysis, as originated by Sigmund Freud (1856–1939), represented an integration of the major European intellectual movements of his time. This was a period of unprecedented advance in the physical and biological sciences. A new liberal humanism was abroad, a humanism based on materialist philosophy and the free exercise of thought. These developments provided biologists with fresh concepts superseding the questionable theories of vitalism. The crucial issue of the day was Darwin's theory of evolution. A group of young biologists, deeply influenced by the teachings of Hermann Helmholtz (Berenfeld, 1944) took it as a matter of principle to explain biological phenomena solely in terms of physics and chemistry. One member of that group was Ernst Brücke (Jones, 1953), later chief of the biological research laboratories at the University of Vienna, where Freud went to pursue a career as a research biologist.

Models borrowed from physics, chemistry, and the theory of evolution recur regularly throughout Freud's writings but most strikingly in his early psychological works.

Freud came to psychoanalysis by way of his interest in neurology. During his formative years, great strides were being made in neurophysiology and neuropathology. Freud himself contributed to the advancement of the science. He did original work on the evolution of the elements of the central nervous system, on aphasia, cerebral palsy, and on the physiological functions of cocaine. In fact, he came very close to formulating the neurone theory (Jones, 1953). In *The Interpretation of Dreams,* he offered a model of the human mind based on the physiology of the reflex arc.

This was also the time when psychology separated from philosophy and began to emerge as an independent science. Freud was interested in both fields. He knew the works of "the association" school of psychologists (J. F. Herbart, Alexander Von Humboldt, and Wilhelm Wundt), and he had been impressed by the way Gustav Fechner (Freud, 1894) applied concepts of physics to problems of psychological research. Ernest Jones (1953) has suggested that the idea of using free association as a therapeutic technique may be traced to the influence of Herbart. There was, furthermore, an important field of investigation that bridged both neurology and psychiatry. In the midnineteenth century, there was great interest in states of split consciousness (Zilboorg & Henry, 1941). The French neuropsychiatrists had taken the lead in studying conditions such as somnambulism, multiple personalities, fugue states, and hysteria. Hypnotism was one of the principal methods used in studying these conditions. The leading

figures in this field of investigation were Jean Charcot, Pierre Janet, Hippolyte Bernheim, and Ambrose Liebault. Freud had the opportunity to work with several of them and he was particularly influenced by Charcot.

Beginnings

Freud wrote two essays on the history of psychoanalysis: *The History of the Psychoanalytic Movement* (1914a) and *An Autobiographical Study* (1925). Both works concerned primarily how Freud's theories evolved. In what follows, this evolution is traced in sketchy form by organizing the developments around Freud's major works. Six key points are delineated in this process.

1. *Studies on Hysteria* (1895)
2. *The Interpretation of Dreams* (1900)
3. *On Narcissism* (1914b)
4. *Papers on Metapsychology* (1915a, 1915b)
5. *Dual Instinct Theory* (1920)
6. *Structural Theory* (1923, 1926)

Studies on Hysteria. The history of psychoanalysis proper begins when Josef Breuer, a Viennese physician with research interests, told Freud about a remarkable experience he was having with a patient who seemed to be curing herself of the symptoms of hysteria by means of talking. Breuer had observed that when he placed his patient into an hypnotic trance and had her relate what was oppressing her mind, she would tell of some highly emotional fantasy or event in her life. If the telling of this material was accompanied by a massive outburst of emotion, the patient would be relieved of her symptoms. Once awake, the patient was totally unaware of the "traumatic event" she had related or of its connection to her disability. Freud tried the same procedure on other patients and was able to confirm Breuer's findings. They summarized their findings in a publication entitled *Studies on Hysteria* (1895), in which they reasoned that the symptoms of hysteria were the result of an undischarged quantity of emotion, connected with a very painful memory. These memories have been split off from their connection with the rest of the mind but they continue to exert a dynamic, instrusive effect in the form of symptoms. The task of therapy, accordingly, was to bring about recollection of the forgotten event together with a cathartic abreaction of the undischarged emotion. Working independently, Freud came to the conclusion that the traumatic events involved in causing hysteria took place in childhood and were regularly of a sexual nature. Since at the time it was generally believed that children before the age of puberty had no sexual drives, Freud was led to the conclusion that the patients he observed had all been seduced into some sexual experience by an older person. Further investigation demonstrated that this was not always true. Freud unknowingly had come upon the data that was to serve him as the basis for the discovery of childhood sexuality.

The Interpretation of Dreams and Its Implications (1900–1905). The second phase of Freud's discoveries concerned a solution to the riddle of the dream. The idea that dreams could be understood occurred to Freud when he observed how regularly they appeared in the associations of his neurotic patients. *Dreams* and *symptoms,* he came to realize, had a similar structure. They were both the end product of a compromise between two sets of conflicting forces in the mind, between unconscious childhood sexual wishes seeking discharge on the one hand,

and the repressive activity of the rest of the mind on the other. In effecting this compromise, an inner censor disguised and distorted the representation of the unconscious sexual wishes from childhood, and in a large measure, it is this process that makes dreams and symptoms unintelligible. The kind of wishes that entered into the formation of dreams were connected with the pleasurable sensations that children get from stimulating the mouth, anus, skin, and genitals, and resembled the various forms of overt sexual activity typical for the perversions.

The Interpretation of Dreams was at the same time a partial record of Freud's own self-analysis. In it Freud first described the Oedipus complex, perhaps the most striking of his many ideas that were destined to disturb the sleep of the world. In addition, in the concluding chapter of this work, Freud attempted to elaborate a theory of the human mind that would encompass dreaming, psychopathology, and normal functioning all at once. The central principle of this theory is that mental life represents an unrelenting conflict between the conscious and unconscious parts of the mind. The unconscious parts of the mind contain the biological, instinctual sexual drives, impulsively pressing for discharge. Opposed to these elements are those forces of the mind that are conscious or readily available to consciousness. This part of the mind functions at a logical, realistic, and adaptive level. Because the fundamental principle of this conceptualization of mental functioning concerned the depth or "layer" of an idea in relationship to consciousness, this theory was called the *topographic theory.*

In the ten years or so that followed the publication of *The Interpretation of Dreams,* Freud used the concepts of unconscious conflicts, infantile sexuality, and the Oedipus complex to attain new insights into the psychology of religion, art, character formation, mythology, and literature. These ideas were published in a group of major contributions: *The Psychopathology of Everyday Life* (1901), *Jokes and Their Relationship to the Unconscious* (1905a), *Three Essays on Sexuality* (1905b), and, somewhat later, *Totem and Taboo* (1913).

On Narcissism (1914b). The next phase in the development of Freud's concepts came when he attempted to apply methods of psychoanalysis to understanding the psychoses. Up to this point, Freud saw the major conflict in mental life as a struggle between the energy of the sexual drive, which he called *libido* and which was directed towards preserving the species, opposed by the energies of the *ego,* that is, the self-preservative drives. This frame of reference did not seem adequate to elucidate the symptoms of psychosis. These phenomena, Freud felt, could be understood much better in terms of a conflict between libidinal energies vested in the self in opposition to libidinal energies vested in the representation of objects of the external world. The concept of *narcissism* proved useful, in addition, in explaining such phenomena as falling in love, pride in one's own children, and group formation. (Freud 1914a, 1921)

The Metapsychological Papers (1915a). From his clinical observations, Freud came to recognize certain inconsistencies in the topographical model of the mind that he had formulated. He noted, for example, that many unconscious mental contents were, in fact, anti-instinctual and self-punitive; clearly, a strict qualitative differentiation of mental phenomena according to the single criterion of accessibility to consciousness was no longer tenable. In several papers, notably *Repression* (1915a) and *The Unconscious*

(1915b), Freud tried to synthesize his psychological concepts under the heading of *metapsychology.* By this term he meant "describing a mental process in all of its aspects—dynamic, topographic, and economic," that is, by understanding the interplay of the energies involved, the part of the psychic apparatus concerned, and the shifts of quantities of energies that take place. The papers written during this period represent a transitional phase in Freud's thinking before he embarked upon a major revision of his theory.

The Dual-Instinct Theory (1920). A whole series of clinical phenomena having in common the role of aggression in mental life convinced Freud that he had to revise his theory of drives. He observed how self-directed aggression operated in depression, masochism, and, generally, in the many ways people punish themselves. Individuals wrecked by success, persons who perform crimes out of a sense of guilt in the hope of being punished, and patients in therapy who respond negatively to the insight they achieve during treatment are typical of this category. In 1920, in his essay *Beyond the Pleasure Principle,* Freud extended his dualistic concept for the drives by putting forward the notion of two types of instincts, libido and aggression, both derived in turn from broader, all-pervading biological principles—instinct of love (*Eros*) and an instinct towards death and self-destruction (*Thanatos*).

The Structural Theory (1923). Having recognized that in the course of psychic conflict, conscience may operate at both a conscious and/or unconscious level, and having perceived that even the methods by which the mind protects itself from anxiety may be unconscious, Freud reformulated his theory in terms of a structural organization of the mind. Mental functions were grouped according to the role they played in conflict. The three major subdivisions of the psychic apparatus he called the ego, the id, and the superego. The *ego* comprises a group of functions that orient the individual toward the external world and mediates between it and the inner world. It acts, in effect, as an executant for the drives and correlates these demands with a proper regard for conscience and the world of reality. The *id* represents the organization of the sum total of the instinctual pressures on the mind, basically the sexual and aggressive impulses. The *superego* is a split-off portion of the ego, a residue of the early history of the individual's moral training and a precipitate of the most important childhood identifications and ideal aspirations. Under ordinary circumstances, there is no sharp demarcation among these three major components of the mind. Intrapsychic conflict, however, makes the differences and the demarcations stand out clearly.

One of the major functions of the ego is to protect the mind from internal dangers, that is, from the threat of a breakthrough into consciousness of conflict-laden impulses. The difference between mental health and illness depends upon how well the ego can succeed in this responsibility. In his monograph, *Inhibitions, Symptom and Anxiety* (1926), Freud detailed how this process functions. The key to the problem is the appearance of the unpleasant affective state of anxiety, perhaps the most common symptom of psychoneurosis. Anxiety, he demonstrated, serves as a warning signal alerting the ego against the danger of overwhelming anxiety or panic that may supervene if a repressed, unconscious wish emerges into consciousness. Once warned, the ego may undertake any of a wide array of defenses to protect itself. This new view had far-reaching implications for both theory and practice.

Current Status

Since Freud, developments in psychoanalysis have been many and varied. Under the leadership of Melanie Klein (1932), a so-called English school of psychoanalysis has emerged. It emphasizes the importance of primitive fantasies of loss (the *depressive* position) and persecution (the *paranoid* position) in the pathogenesis of mental illness. This school is particularly influential in Europe and South America.

When Nazi persecution forced many of the outstanding European analysts to migrate to this country, the United States became the strongest center for psychoanalysis in the world. The leading figures in this movement were Heinz Hartmann, Ernst Kris, and Rudolph Loewenstein. In a number of publications (1945, 1946, 1949) these three collaborators tried to establish psychoanalysis as the basis for a general psychology. They did so by extending Hartmann's concepts of the adaptive function of the ego (Hartmann, 1939) and clarifying fundamental working hypotheses concerning the nature of the drives and the maturation and development of the psychic apparatus. Their theories integrated the invaluable contributions of Anna Freud (1936, 1951) derived from the analysis of children and from studies of long-term child development. In the course of these investigations, several questions concerning the sense of self were posed. How and when does the sense of self develop and what are the consequences to the individual if the process miscarries? Edith Jacobson (1954), D. W. Winnicott (1953), and John Bowlby (1958) were among those who contributed to the clarification of the problem. The most cogent studies in the field, however, come from the meticulous clinical and developmental observations conducted by Margaret Mahler (1975) and her co-workers. All of these studies underline the importance of the early attachment to the mother and the vicissitudes of the processes of separation and individuation.

These early experiences seem to play a crucial role in the development of self-esteem. Considerations of self-esteem are central in the psychology of narcissistic character disorders and borderline personalities. Clinical and theoretical illumination of these conditions were offered in the writings of Annie Reich (1973) and have been extended in an original way by Heinz Kohut (1971) and Otto Kernberg (1968).

The more recent developments in the field are too numerous to describe. David Rapaport (1951) and several of his students have integrated psychoanalytic theories with broad psychological principles and findings. Jacob Arlow and Charles Brenner (1964) have attempted to synthesize newer clinical findings into the framework of the structural theory and other authors, critical of some of the propositions of psychoanalysis, are attempting to reformulate psychoanalytic theory in terms of communications theory (Peterfreund, 1971; Schafer, 1976) and neurophysiology (Rubinstein, 1967). Some authors have emphasized the importance of interpersonal relationships (Sullivan, 1953) and the role of identification and the transformations of the personality during the life cycle (Erikson, 1968). Karen Horney (1940) and Erich Fromm (1955) have stressed the social, political, and cultural factors in the development of the individual.

The American Psychoanalytic Association is the largest and the most prestigious of organized psychoanalytic societies in the United States. It consists of almost 2,500 members and affiliates. It is comprised of 33 affiliate societies and conducts centers for the professional training of psychoanalysts in 26 institutes around the country. With the exception of some recent changes, admission to training in affiliate institutes and to membership in the American Psychoanalytic Association is restricted to members of the medical profession. This condition does not hold in the other affiliate societies of the International Psychoanalytical Association. Standards for training in psychoanalysis are set by the Board on Professional Standards of the American Psychoanalytic Association. In addition to the requirement of an M.D. degree, a candidate must have had residency training in psychiatry. The course of study is from four to eight or more years and consists of three parts: (1) the training analysis, (2) formal courses in the literature and technique of psychoanalysis, and (3) the treatment of at least three or four patients under the supervision of a training analyst.

There are many other psychoanalytic organizations in the United States. The American Academy of Psychoanalysis is a scientific organization that has not in the past conducted programs of training. Although many of its members belong to the American Psychoanalytic Association, membership in the academy is not restricted to doctors of medicine. There are, in addition, several societies composed of physicians, psychologists, social workers, and other professionals who have received training at either the William Alanson White Institute or other centers for training in the United States. Perhaps the largest organization of these individuals is the National Psychological Association for Psychoanalysis.

Recent years have witnessed a rich burgeoning of the psychoanalytic literature. In addition to the long-standing major publications in the field, such as the

American Psychoanalytic Association Journal, the *International Journal of Psychoanalysis,* the *Psychoanalytic Quarterly, The Psychoanalytic Study of the Child,* the *Psychoanalytic Review,* and *Psychiatry,* many new books and journals have appeared, such as *The International Psychoanalytic Review, The Chicago Annual of Psychoanalysis, The International Journal of Psychoanalytic Psychotherapy, Psychoanalysis and the Contemporary Science,* and *Psychological Issues.*

The 24-volume *Standard Edition of the Complete Works of Sigmund Freud* is the basic source for theory and instruction in psychoanalysis. In 1945 Fenichel wrote *The Psychoanalytic Theory of Neurosis,* the closest work to a textbook in psychoanalysis. Unfortunately, this valuable source book has not been brought up to date. The 3-volume biography of Freud by Ernest Jones (1953–57) contains a comprehensive overview of Freud's contributions. The most concise, accurate, and readable statement of current psychoanalytic theory is to be found in Charles Brenner's (1973) *An Elementary Textbook of Psychoanalysis.* Alexander Grinstein (1971) has been editing *The Index of Psychoanalytic Writings.* Consisting of 14 volumes, it covers all the psychoanalytic literature up to and including the year 1969. Currently, under the auspices of the American Psychoanalytic Association, a cumulative index of all psychoanalytic writings is being prepared.

PERSONALITY

Theory of Personality

The psychoanalytic theory of personality is based on a number of fundamental principles. The first and foremost of these is the principle of *determinism.* Psychoanalytic theory assumes that events in the mind are not random, haphazard, accidental, unrelated phenomena. The thoughts, feelings, and impulses that come into awareness are events in a chain of causally related phenomena. They result from antecedent experiences in the life of the individual. Through appropriate methods of investigation, the connection between current mental experience and past events can be established. Many of these connections are unconscious.

The second principle of psychoanalytic personality theory is the *topographic* viewpoint. Every mental element is judged according to the criterion of its accessibility to consciousness. The process by which certain mental contents are barred from consciousness is called *repression.* This is an active process implying a persistent, repetitive effort on the part of the mind to keep certain thoughts out of awareness. In keeping with the pleasure principle, the motive for repression is to avoid pain or unpleasure. Psychoanalytic investigation of normal and pathological phenomena has demonstrated the important role unconscious forces play in the behavior of the individual. Some of the most important decisions in one's life may be determined in a decisive way by unconscious motives.

The third basic approach to psychoanalytic personality theory is the *dynamic* viewpoint. This pertains to the interaction of the forces that stimulate the mind to do work, to act, to change, that is, to the libidinal and aggressive impulses that are part of the human biological endowment. Because of their biological roots, these impulses have been loosely and inaccurately referred to as *instincts.* The correct term in psychoanalytic theory, translated from the German *Treib,* is *drives.* Since this has become common usage, *instinct* and *drive* will be used interchangeably in the rest of this chapter.

It is important to distinguish drives in the human from instinctive behavior in animals. *Instinct* in animals is a stereotyped response, usually with clear survival value evoked by specific stimuli in particular settings. As used in psychoanalysis, the *drive* is a state of central excitation in response to stimuli. This sense of central excitation, sometimes described as a need or a state of tension, impels the mind to activity, with the ultimate aim of bringing about a cessation of tension, a sense of gratification that is experienced as pleasurable. Although in a general way the appropriate motor activity response to the inner tension is biologically determined, drives in humans are capable of a wide variety of complex transformations. Drive theory in psychoanalysis is intended to account for the psychological findings gathered in the clinical setting. Biology supports many of the formulations regarding the libidinal drive. This is not so in the case of the aggressive drive, a concept founded almost exclusively on psychological data (Brenner, 1971).

The fourth approach to personality theory has been called the *genetic* viewpoint. This means the ability to trace the origins of later conflicts, character traits, neurotic symptoms, and psychological structure to the crucial events and wishes of childhood and the fantasies they generated. In contrast to the earlier concepts of determinism and the dynamic and topographic points of view, the genetic approach is not a theory; it is an empirical finding confirmed in every psychoanalysis. In effect, it states that in many ways, we never get over our childhood. We do not have a complete answer to the question why we fail to do so. One factor undoubtedly resides in the long period of biological dependence characteristic of the human infant. In addition, there seems to be a broad tendency in the higher forms of life for the earliest experiences to have a persistent and crucial effect on later development. Freud's observations about the crucial role of events in early childhood in shaping later behavior have been dramatically confirmed by ethologists in their studies of other forms of life (Lorenz, 1952; Tinbergern, 1951).

Personality evolves out of the interaction between inherent biological factors and the vicissitudes of experience. For any individual, given an average expectable environment, one may anticipate a more or less predictable sequence of events constituting the steps in the maturation of the drives and the other components of the psychic apparatus. Whatever happens to the individual—illness, accidents, deprivation, excess gratification, abuse, seduction, abandonment—in some way will alter and transform the native endowment and will contribute towards determining the ultimate personality structure.

The terminology used for describing the development of the drives originally applied only to the libidinal drives. This is so because Freud conceptualized them first and did not postulate an independent aggressive drive until later. Furthermore, the early phases of the libidinal drives are quite distinct and clearly related to specific zones of the body. The somatic substrate of aggression is not so clearly defined. Psychoanalysis postulates that whenever drive activity is involved, some mixture or fusion of the sexual and the aggressive drive energies has taken place. Ordinarily one of the component elements is more dominant than the other.

Variety of Concepts

Oral Phase. The earliest phase of instinctual life is the *oral phase*. It extends from birth to approximately eighteen months. It is so called because the chief source of libidinal gratification centers around feeding and the organs connected with that function—the mouth, the lips, and the tongue. Gratification of oral needs in the form of satiety brings about a state of freedom from tension and induces sleep. Many disturbances of sleep seem to be connected with unconscious fantasies of an oral libidinal nature (Lewin 1946, 1949). Biting and sucking are activities that serve both to gratify oral drives and to "explore" the world. During the oral phase, the basic orientation of the psychic apparatus is to take in what is pleasurable and therefore good and to expel what is unpleasant and therefore bad. According to Karl Abraham (1924), people whose early oral needs have been excessively frustrated constantly tend to anticipate disappointment. They turn out to be pessimists. On the other hand, individuals whose oral needs have been gratified tend to have a more optimistic view of the world.

Anal Phase. Between the ages of eighteen months to three years, the main source of pleasure and libidinal gratification comes from the activities connected with retaining and passing the feces. The fundamental instinctual orientation concerns what is to be retained and therefore valuable, and what is to be expelled, and which ultimately becomes worthless. During the *anal phase,* interest in the bodily processes, in smelling, touching, and playing with feces, are paramount. Regarded for a while as an extruded portion of one's self, the feces are considered as a particularly valuable and highly prized possession. The disgust that those who train the child evince and the shame the child is made to feel may contribute toward a lowered sense of self-esteem. In reaction, the child may respond by stubborn assertiveness, contrary rebelliousness, and by the determination to be in control of whatever happens to him. The latter may take the form of spiteful dilatoriness. Through a process known as *reaction formation,* the child may overcome his impulse to soil by becoming meticulously clean, excessively punctual, and quite parsimonious in handling his possessions (Freud, 1917).

Phallic Phase. After the third year, the main area of libidinal gratification shifts to the genitals. For both boys and girls, the penis becomes the principal object of interest in the *phallic phase.* It is at this time that the clitoris, embryologically an analogue of the penis, begins to be appreciated for the pleasurable sensations evoked by stimulation. Recent investigations indicate that some awareness of the pleasure potential of the vagina is present at this phase in many little girls (Greenacre, 1967). Also prominent in the phallic phase are the exhibitionistic and voyeuristic wishes. The former is connected with the pride and pleasure of showing off one's body and being admired; the latter involves the pleasure that comes from looking at the bodies of others.

By the time the child has reached the phallic phase, he has made marked advances in the complexity of his psychological structure. The basic orientation during this phase is therefore much more subtle and complicated. Although the child remains basically self-centered, his relations with others in the environment take on a rich texture. He loves and wants to possess those who give him pleasure; he hates and wants to annihilate those who stand in his way and frustrate him. He becomes curious about sexual differences and about the origin of life and in a primitive childlike way fashions his own answers to these important questions. He wants to love and to be loved, to be admired and to be like those he admires. He may overidealize himself or share a sense of power by feeling at one with those he idealizes. During this time, the child may entertain intensely hostile wishes with the penis serving as an instrument for aggression. This gives rise to intense fears of retaliation, usually directed against the penis. It is also the era of the discovery of the anatomical distinction between the sexes, a phase from which the fear of the female genital and envy of the male genital originate.

Three salient features in the development of the drives must be mentioned here. First is the concept of *autoerotism*. When gratification of a particular instinctual urge is not forthcoming from the usual source (mother, father, or other person who takes care of the child), it is always possible for the child to gratify himself by stimulating the appropriate zones of his body, combining such activities with appropriate fantasies. This evolves into the more common forms of childhood masturbation. Second, it should be noted that as the individual passes from one libidinal phase to another, the interest in the gratification of the preceding phase is not completely surrendered. It is only partially superseded by the succeeding libidinal gratification. When there is a particularly strong and persistent attachment to libidinal gratification from a particular object of infancy, one speaks of *fixation*. Fixations are usually unconscious and often serve, as we will presently see, as a focus for symptom formation later in life. A third feature of libidinal development is the potentiality for *regression,* that is, for the reactivation of or the return to an earlier mode of libidinal gratification. Regressive reactivation of earlier modes of mental functioning are common and not necessarily pathological. Under certain circumstances regression to earlier libidinal

wishes may occur. Usually the regression reactivates some childhood libidinal impulse that had been involved in the process of fixation.

For each of the aforementioned phases of development, there is a characteristic situation of danger, that is, a situation that can evoke intense unpleasure. During the oral phase, the greatest danger is that the mother will not be available. This is usually referred to as the danger of *loss of the* (need satisfying) *object.* During the anal phase, after the concept of the mother as an independent entity has crystallized, *losing the mother's love* constitutes the danger. Typical of the phallic phase is fear of retaliation or punishment for forbidden sexual and aggressive wishes. The kind of punishment usually fantasied by both boys and girls takes the form of injury to the body, specifically to the genitals. For this reason, the danger characteristic of the phallic phase is referred to as the *fear of castration.* Later in life, after external prohibitions and threats of punishment have been internalized into the personality in the form of the superego, *fear of conscience* takes its place among the danger situations. Each one of these situations evokes anxiety as a signal alerting the ego to set in motion various mental maneuvers whose purpose is to eliminate or minimize the danger. These maneuvers Anna Freud (1936) called the *mechanisms of defense,* because they protect the rest of the personality from the unpleasant affect of anxiety.

The combined influence on the mind of the libidinal and aggressive wishes constitute what is known in psychoanalytic theory as the id. The other components of the mind are the ego and the superego. It will be possible to present only a few observations on the development of these psychological structures. The earliest psychological experience of the infant is most likely one of global sensory impingement (Spitz, 1955). There is no differentiation between his self and the rest of the world, between what is in his body and what is outside of it. The inherent capacities of man to perceive, to move, and later to speak mature gradually. The concept of ` the self as an independent entity develops over a period of two to three years (Jacobson, 1954; Mahler, 1975). There is much evidence to suggest that for a certain period during the first year of life, the child is unable to distinguish between himself and the person who cares for him. Certain objects in the external world, for example, a blanket or a stuffed animal toy, may be experienced at times as being part of the self and at other times as part of the external world (Winnicott, 1953).

At first the instinctual drives center mainly on the self—a state called *narcissism*. As other persons come to be appreciated as sources of sustenance, protection, and gratification, some of the energy of the libidinal drive settles (is vested) on mental representations of others. Technically, these others are referred to as *love objects,* or *objects* for short. At its core, the human personality retains a considerable complement of childish self-centeredness. The capacity to need others, to love, to want to please, and to want to become like others is one of the most significant indicators of psychological maturity. In addition to constitutional factors, the quality of experience with objects during the early years is decisive in shaping the all-important capacity to love and identify with others. Disturbances in this process because of traumatic experiences or poor object relations contribute to the severe forms of pathology known as narcissistic character disorders, borderline states, and the psychoses.

Needing, wanting, and identifying with valued persons is fraught with the dangers of frustration, disappointment, and, inevitably, conflict. The imperious wishes of childhood can never be gratified in full. Inexorably, relations with the important objects become a mixture of love and hatred. They become ambivalent. Such feelings come to a climactic crisis with the Oedipus longings of the phallic phase. As a rule during the ages of three to six, the child develops intense erotic longings for the parent of the opposite sex and a hostile competitive orientation towards the parent of the same sex. Circumstances may induce enormous variations in this basic pattern, including a total inversion of the choice of sexual object. It is the responsibility of the ego as the executant agency of the total personality to deal with the conflicts of the Oedipus complex. Under favorable circumstances, the oedipal wishes are given up, that is, they are repressed. Like the rest of childhood sexuality, they become unconscious. They are, however, not totally obliterated but continue as a potential source of instinctual pressure in the form of unconscious fantasies. Disguised versions of these fantasies may persist in consciousness as the familiar daydreams of childhood. They continue to exert an important influence on nearly every aspect of mental life: on the forms and objects of adult sexuality; on creative, artistic, vocational, and other sublimated activity; on character formation; and on whatever neurotic symptoms the individual may develop later (Brenner, 1973).

Under favorable circumstances, the child relinquishes most of the hostile and neurotic impulses of the Oedipus complex and affects an identification with the parent of the same sex, especially with his moral standards and prohibitions. This is the matrix of the moral part of the personality called the superego. This agency observes the self and judges its thoughts and actions in terms of what it considers right and wrong. It may prescribe punishment, reparation, or repentance for wrongdoing or may reward the self with heightened esteem and affection for virtuous thought and action. The superego is the seed of the conscience and the source of guilt. Under certain conditions, its functioning may be as impulsive and demanding as any primitive instinctual wish of the id. This is particularly true in states of depression.

Latency Period. With the passing of the Oedipus complex and the consolidation of the superego, a relatively quiescent phase ensues, called the *latency period.* The child now can be socialized and he can direct his interests to the larger world where the process of education becomes a more formalized experience. This state prevails until the onset of *puberty and adolescence.* The transformations that take place during this period are crucial in establishing the adult identity. As a result of the physiological and psychological changes involved in assuming the adult role, the conflicts of childhood are evoked anew. Variations of fantasies that originally served as vehicles for the drives during childhood become the conscious concomitants of adolescent masturbation. The guilt over masturbation derives primarily from the unconscious wishes that find substitute expression in the masturbation fantasies. During the period of adolescence, a second attempt is made to master the conflicts arising from childhood wishes. (Through the successful resolution of these conflicts, the individual consolidates his adult identity about his sexual role, moral responsibility, and choice of work or profession.)

Conflicts stemming from some phase of life are part of normal human development. Uncontrolled expression of certain instinctual impulses could have calamitous consequences for the individual. Free expression of the drives represents a major confrontation with one's morality and could, under certain circumstances, provoke a severe superego response in the form of guilt or self-punishment. It falls upon the ego to mediate the demands made upon it by the id and the superego with due consideration for the exigent needs of reality. All of mental life represents a shifting balance, a tenuously stable equilibrium between the pressures of the id, the superego, and reality. Presumably, the most effective way to deal with a conflict would be to bar the impulse permanently from consciousness. When this occurs, one may speak of successful repression. In most instances, however, the victory is by no means one-sided. By their very nature, unconscious wishes remain dynamic and from time to time threaten to overcome the repression instituted to constrain them. Such intrusion may precipitate attacks of panic or, in lesser form, anxiety. Under such circumstances, the ego undertakes fresh measures to ward off the unpleasant affect of anxiety. If successful repression cannot be maintained, various compromises have to be affected by calling into play the different mechanisms of defense. Certain compromises affected by the use of defense mechanisms may become permanent features of the individual's character.

Unsuccessful resolution of intrapsychic conflicts eventuates in neurotic illness and neurotic character traits, inhibitions, sexual perversions, and patterns of behavior of a neurotic or self-defeating nature. In all these instances, the growth and development of the personality have been interfered with and a price has been paid in terms of suffering and restriction of the individual's capacities and freedom.

PSYCHOTHERAPY

Theory of Psychotherapy

The principles and techniques of psychoanalysis as therapy are based upon the psychoanalytic theory of neurosis. As the theory of neurosis changed, so did the technique of therapy. Originally, Freud felt that neurotic symptoms were the result of pent-up, undischarged emotional tension connected with the repressed memory of a traumatic childhood sexual trauma. At first, he used hypnosis to bring about emotional catharsis and abreaction of the trauma. Since many of his patients could not be hypnotized, he dropped hypnosis in favor of forced suggestion, a technique of recollection fostered by the insistent demanding pressure of the therapist. Among other things, this technique produced artifacts in the form of sexual fantasies about childhood, which the patient offered the therapist as if they were recollections of actual events. Taking advantage of his new operational concepts of the dynamic unconscious and the principle of strict psychic determinism, Freud reduced the element of suggestion to a minimum by a new technical procedure in which he asked his patients to report freely and without criticism whatever came into their minds. Thus, the technique of *free association* evolved.

During the period when the topographic model of the psychic apparatus was paramount in Freud's mind, the principal technical goal was to make the contents of the unconscious conscious. The patient's productions were interpreted according to principles very similar to those used in *The Interpretation of Dreams.* The most striking discovery Freud made during this period was the discovery of the *transference,* a very unique, highly emotional attitude the patient develops towards the analyst and which represents a repetition of the individual's fantasy wishes concerning objects of the past, now, however, foisted onto the person of the analyst. The discovery that the anti-instinctual forces of the mind, for example, the defense mechanisms, guilt, and self-punishment, could also operate at an unconscious level contributed to the elaboration of the structural theory. Applied to the technique of psychotherapy, the structural theory pointed to the need to analyze the functioning of the defense mechanisms and the self-punitive trends. Elucidating the nature of the unconscious danger and the quality of the anxiety attendant upon its appearance have since become central points of analytic technique.

In recent years, in an attempt to apply psychoanalytic therapy to types of cases that have heretofore been refractory to treatment, newer methods of technique have been suggested. Franz Alexander (1932) felt that since most patients had been traumatized by parental mismanagement during childhood, it was necessary for the analyst to arrange "a corrective emotional experience" that would counteract the effects of the original trauma. A more recent elaboration of these ideas has been proposed by E. R. Zetzel (1970) and Ralph Greenson (1967) who emphasized particular measures required to instill confidence to create a proper alliance between therapist and patient. Greenson in particular emphasizes the importance of the real personality of the analyst. Some analysts influenced by the ideas of Melanie Klein see in the analyst's emotional reaction a mirror of what the patient is experiencing consciously or unconsciously (Weigert, 1970; Racker, 1953). Heinz Kohut (1971) has suggested several technical innovations aimed at strengthening the self-esteem of patients with narcissistic personality disorders. In addition, the combination of psychoanalysis with other modalities of treatment such as drugs, group therapy, and family interaction have been advanced.

Onset of Neurosis. In the genesis of neurotic disorders, the conflicts of childhood are of critical importance. By far the most common and most significant conflicts are those that involve the wishes of the oedipal phase. All children have conflicts and most of them develop some kind of childhood neurosis. Usually *childhood neurosis* assumes the form of general apprehensiveness, nightmares, phobias, tics, mannerisms, or ritualistic practices. Most of the primary behavior disorders of children represent disguised forms of neurosis from which the element of manifest fear has disappeared. Phobia is probably the most frequent symptom of childhood neurosis. In most cases with the passage of the oedipal phase, the disturbances caused by the instinctual conflicts have been sufficiently ameliorated to permit the child to progress normally. In some cases, a childhood neurosis continues with relatively little change into adult life.

Neurosis in adults may develop anew when the balance between the pressures of the drives and the defensive forces of the ego is upset. There are three typical situations in which this may occur.

1. An individual may be unable to cope with the additional psychological burden that normal development places upon him. The unconscious significance of becoming an adult and assuming responsibilities of marriage and undertaking the competitive and aggressive challenges of maturity may prove too much for the ego.

2. Disappointment, defeat, loss of love, physical illness, or some other inevitable consequence of the human condition may lead an individual to turn away from current reality and unconsciously seek gratification in the world of fantasy. This usually involves a reactivation (regression) of the fantasy wishes of the oedipal phase. As these wishes are regressively reactivated, the conflicts and anxieties of childhood are revived and the process of symptom formation begins. The fantasy wishes that are regressively reactivated are the ones that earlier had been the subject of fixation.

3. By a combination of circumstances, an individual may find himself in adult life in a situation that corresponds in its essential features to some childhood trauma or conflict-laden fantasy. Current reality is then misperceived in terms of the childhood conflict and the individual responds as he did in childhood, by forming symptoms.

Process of Psychotherapy

The standard technical procedure of psychoanalysis for studying the functioning of the mind is known as the *psychoanalytic situation.* The patient is asked to assume a recumbent position on the couch, looking away from the analyst. As far as it is possible for him to do so, the patient is asked to express in words whatever thoughts, images, feelings, and so on come to mind. He is expected to express these elements as truthfully as he can without distortion, censorship, suppression, or prejudgment concerning the significance or insignificance of any particular idea. Seated behind the couch, the analyst listens in an uncritical, nonjudgmental fashion, in an attitude of benign curiosity. In keeping with the strict psychic determinism, any element of thought or behavior is observed and evaluated in the context of the patient's productions. The person of the analyst, his values, and his judgments are strictly excluded from the therapeutic interaction.

From time to time the analyst interrupts the free flow of the patient's associations to make connections among various items in the patient's productions. In doing so, he momentarily interferes with the patient's role as a passive reporter and makes him observe and reflect upon the significance and possible connections among his associations. The analyst's interventions momentarily change the patient's role from that of passive reporter to that of active observer and, at times, interpreter. The principle of free association is somewhat modified in connection with the interpretation of dreams. In this instance, the analyst may ask the patient to tell him whatever comes to mind in connection with this or that particular image of the dream.

The practical conditions of the treatment are also strictly regulated. A fixed schedule of fees and appointments having been agreed upon at the beginning is maintained. Any attempt on the part of the patient to deviate from the basic understanding of the analytic situation naturally becomes a subject for investigation and analysis. Changes in the basic conditions of the treatment are inadvisable and when necessary are effected by mutual consent between the patient and the analyst after the problem has been analyzed.

The technical principle behind the organization of the psychoanalytic situation is to create a set of conditions in which the functioning of the patient's mind and the thoughts and images that emerge into consciousness are as much as possible endogenously determined. The patient's thoughts and associations should come primarily from the stimulus of the persistent dynamic internal pressure of the drives as organized in unconscious fantasies. His thoughts and associations should not represent responses to external manipulation, exhortation, stimulation, or education. This is what is uniquely psychoanalytic in the therapeutic interaction. Under the conditions of the analytic situation, the influence of the inner mental forces can be more easily and clearly observed than in other more usual situations. It becomes possible for the material hitherto suppressed or repressed to be verbalized and examined. This presupposes the strictest adherence to professional principles on the part of the analyst. Everything he does must be in the interest of advancing the patient's insight through the process of analysis. Accordingly, there is no greater responsibility in the analytic situation than the strict preservation of the patient's confidentiality. Communication of any of the material of the analysis to whatever source is contrary to the spirit of the analytic situation, even when the patient believes a breach of confidentiality is in his own best interests.

Psychoanalysis involves a commitment to change through the process of critical self-examination. To maintain continuity of the analytic process, at least four sessions a week are indicated. Each session lasts at least forty-five minutes. The course of treatment runs for several years. It is clear that undertaking psychoanalytic treatment is a serious responsibility involving considerable sacrifice in time, effort, and money. These are not conditions upon which one may enter lightly.

The psychoanalytic situation has been structured in this manner with the intention of making possible the accomplishment of the goal of psychoanalytic therapy, namely, to help the patient achieve a resolution of intrapsychic conflict through understanding his conflicts and dealing with them in a more mature manner. Since the analytic situation is relatively uncontaminated by the intrusion of ordinary interpersonal relationships, the interaction of the three components of the mind—the ego, the id, and the superego—may be studied in a more objective way, making it possible to demonstrate to the patient what parts of his thoughts and behavior are determined by inner wishes, conflicts, and fantasies and what part represents a mature response to objective reality.

Mechanisms of Psychotherapy

The treatment process may be divided into four phases:

1. The opening phase
2. The development of transference
3. Working through
4. Resolution of the transference

The Opening Phase. Psychoanalytic observation begins with the very first contact the patient makes with the analyst. Everything the patient says and does is noted for possible significance and use later in the treatment. The initial set of interviews are part of the opening phase. During these interviews, the nature of the patient's difficulty is ascertained and the decision is reached whether analysis is indicated. To determine this, it is necessary for the analyst to learn as much as possible about the patient; for example, his current life situation and difficulties, what he has accomplished, how he relates to others, and the history of his family background and childhood development. Formalized history taking, following a prescribed outline, is not to be encouraged. Priorities in the subjects to be discussed should be left to the patient's intuition. Much is learned from how the patient approaches the practical task of making his problems known to the therapist and how he responds to the delineation of the analytic contract. The understanding of the analytical situation must be clearly defined from the very beginning and the respective responsibilities of both parties explicitly stated.

After a few sessions of face-to-face interviews, the second part of the opening phase begins when the patient assumes the couch. No two patients begin treatment in the same way. Some find it difficult to lie on the couch and say whatever comes to mind; others take readily to this new set of conditions. Everything the patient says and does, the position he assumes on the couch, the clothes he wears, his characteristic phrases, what he chooses to present as the opening statement of the session, whether he is on time for the appointment, are all observed as clues to unconscious mental processes.

During the opening phase, the analyst continues to learn more about the patient's history and development. He gets to understand in broad outline the nature of the patient's unconscious conflicts and he has an opportunity to study the characteristic ways by which the patient resists revealing himself or becoming aware of repudiated thoughts and feelings. Gradually the analyst is able to detect a continuous thread of themes appearing in characteristic context, following relatively uniform sequences and becoming manifest repetitively in a variety of meaningful configurations. These productions of the patient can be understood in terms of the persistent, unconscious fantasy representing wishes from childhood, dynamically active in the patient's current life in disguised and distorted ways. In the early phases, the analyst deals almost exclusively with the superficial aspects of the patient's material. He tries to demonstrate to the patient significant correlations in the material presented but he restricts himself primarily to those elements that are readily accessible to consciousness and that are not too close to the patient's basic conflicts. In ordinary cases, the initial phase of the treatment lasts from three to six months.

The Development of Transference. The next two phases of the treatment, the transference and working through, constitute the major portion of the therapeutic work and actually overlap. At a certain stage in the treatment, when it appears the patient is just about ready to relate his current difficulties to unconscious conflicts from childhood concerning wishes over some important person or persons in his life, a new and interesting phenomenon emerges. Emotionally, the person of the analyst assumes major significance in the life of the patient. The patient's perceptions of and demands upon the analyst become quite inappropriate and his response to the analyst out of keeping with reality. The relationship of the patient to the analyst becomes distorted as he tries to introduce personal instead of professional considerations into their interaction. Understanding the transference was one of Freud's greatest discoveries. He perceived that in the transference, the patient was unconsciously reenacting a latter-day version of forgotten childhood memories and repressed unconscious fantasies. *Transference,* therefore, could be understood as a form of memory in which repetition in action replaces recollection of events. It is a vulgarization of the concept of transference to think of it solely in terms of "the patient falls in love with the analyst." Transference is a much more

historical and precise phenomenon, illustrating how the forgotten past remains dynamically active in the present.

The analysis of the transference is one of the cornerstones of psychoanalytic technique. It helps the patient distinguish fantasy from reality, past from present, and it makes real to the patient the force of the persistent unconscious fantasy wishes of childhood. Analysis of the transference helps the patient understand in a very real way how he misperceives, misinterprets, and misresponds to the present in terms of the past. In place of the automatic, uncontrolled, stereotyped ways through which the patient unconsciously responds to his unconscious fantasies, the patient is now able to evaluate the unrealistic nature of his impulses and anxieties and to make appropriate decisions on a mature and realistic level. In this way, analysis helps the patient achieve a major realignment in the dynamic equilibrium between impulse and conflict. This is the kind of realignment that ultimately leads to a satisfactory resolution of the pathogenic conflict once the patient comes to understand not only the nature of the fears that motivate his defenses, but the self-punitive trends as well. For the most part, these are also unconscious.

Working Through. This phase of the treatment coincides with and continues the analysis of the transference. One or two experiences of insight into the nature of one's conflicts are not sufficient to bring about changes. The analysis of the transference has to be continued many times and in many different ways. The patient's insight into his problems by way of the transference is constantly deepened and consolidated by the process of working through, a process that consists of repetition, elaboration, and amplification. Working through acts as a kind of catalyst between analysis of transference and the overcoming of the amnesia for the crucial childhood experiences (Greenacre, 1956). Usually the experience of successful analysis of a transference phenomenon is followed by the emergence into memory of some important event or fantasy of the patient's past. Analysis of the transference facilitates recall. Recall illuminates the nature of the transference. This reciprocal interplay between understanding the transference and recollecting the past consolidates the patient's insight into his conflicts and strengthens his conviction concerning the interpretive reconstructions made in the course of his treatment.

Resolution of the Transference. The resolution of the transference comprises the termination phase of treatment. When the patient and the analyst are satisfied that the major goals of the analysis have been accomplished and the transference is well understood, a date is set for ending the treatment. Technically, the analyst's aim is to resolve the patient's unconscious neurotic attachment to him. There are a number of very striking features typical of this phase of the treatment. Most characteristic and dramatic is a sudden and intense aggravation of the very symptoms for which the patient sought treatment. It seems almost as if all the analytic work had been done in vain. Upon analysis, this interesting turn of events can be understood as a last-ditch effort on the part of the patient to convince the analyst that he is not yet ready to leave treatment and that he should be permitted to continue the relationship indefinitely. There are many motives for this unconscious attitude. In part, the patient is unwilling to surrender so gratifying and helpful a relationship. In part, it continues a continuation of some passive, dependent orientation from childhood. But most of all, it

represents a last chance endeavor to get the analyst to fulfill the very unconscious, infantile fantasy wishes that were the source of the patient's conflicts to begin with.

Another interesting thing that happens during the termination phase of treatment is the emergence of hitherto repressed memories that confirm or elaborate the reconstructions and interpretations made earlier in the treatment. It is as if the patient presents new insight or findings to the analyst as a parting gift of gratitude. Unconsciously, it often has the significance of presenting the analyst with a child, a gift of new life, as a form of thanks for the new life that analysis has made possible for the patient.

Finally, during the closing phase of treatment, the patient may reveal a hitherto concealed group of wishes amounting to a desire to be magically transformed into some omnipotent or omniscient figure, a striving he had kept secret throughout the analysis but that he had quietly hoped would be fulfilled by the time the treatment was over. It is very important during this phase to analyze all the fantasies the patient has about how things will be after the analysis is over (Schmideberg, 1938). If one fails to deal with all the problems mentioned above, the possibilities of relapse remain very high.

APPLICATIONS

Problems

What kinds of problems are suitable for treatment by psychoanalysis? Before one can begin to answer this question in any specific way, some general observations are in order. From the description of psychoanalysis as therapy, it should be clear that any potential patient must be able to fulfill certain objective as well as personal requirements. Essentially, he must be strongly motivated to overcome his difficulties by honest self-scrutiny. Because it is difficult at the beginning to predict in any definite way how long the treatment will last, the individual must be in a position to commit a considerable period in advance for the purpose of carrying the analysis through to successful termination. In addition, he must be able to accept the discipline of the conditions proposed by the psychoanalytic contract as outlined earlier in this chapter. The psychoanalytic dialogue is a very unusual form of communication, inevitably entailing frustration of transference wishes. A patient must be able to accept such frustration and to express his thoughts and feelings in words rather than action. Impulsive, willful, self-centered, and highly narcissistic individuals may not be able to accommodate themselves to such structures. People who are basically dishonest, psychopathic, and pathological liars obviously will not be equal to the task of complete and unrelenting self-revelation. Furthermore, since cooperation with the analyst in an enterprise of self-exploration requires some degree of objectivity and reality testing, functions that are severely impaired in the psychoses, psychoanalysis can rarely be used in the treatment of such conditions except under very special circumstances.

Since psychoanalysis is a time-consuming, expensive, and arduous form of treatment, it is not indicated in those conditions where the difficulties are relatively minor. Genuine suffering and pain are the most reliable allies of the analytic process. Through insight, psychoanalysis hopes to enable the patient to overcome his inner conflicts. This can be helpful only insofar as such insights can be put to constructive use in altering one's life situation. If the person's objective situation is so bad that there is nothing he can do about it, the insights of psychoanalysis will be of no avail. This can be seen for example in such cases where the analyst recognizes how the story the patient presents reflects a lifelong struggle against murderous, destructive, and self-destructive impulses, the psychological consequence of severe congenital deformity or crippling disease early in childhood. No psychological insight can compensate for the injustices of fate.

Because so much of psychoanalytic technique depends on the analysis of the transference, psychoanalysis is best suited for conditions in which transference attachments tend to be very strong. This is true in the classical psychoneurotic entities—hysteria, anxiety hysteria, obsessive-compulsive neurosis, and a variety of states characterized by anxiety. In actual practice, the symptomatology of the psychoneuroses tend to overlap. The diagnostic label attended to a particular condition usually reflects the major mechanism of defense characteristically employed to ward off anxiety. In hysteria, for example, by a process called *conversion,* the energy of a sexual wish the ego was unable to repress successfully may be transformed into alterations of body functions like paralysis, absence of sensation, abnormal sensations, and so forth. An unconscious fantasy of sucking on a penis or swallowing it may become manifest consciously in the feeling that there is an abnormal lump in the throat that cannot be swallowed—the classical globus hystericus. A symptom, it should be noted, is a compromise formation. Unconsciously, it gratifies the wish and the need for punishment at the same time.

Phobias are typical of anxiety hysteria. The phobic patient wards off anxiety by treating some external object or situation as the representative of the unconscious impulse. In one form of *agoraphobia,* the patient becomes anxious whenever she goes out on the street, the street representing the place where it is possible to realize her unconscious wishes to be a prostitute. The mechanism of defense is a double one. The internal (sexual) danger is projected onto the street, an external situation. By avoiding the external object, the patient controls an internal danger. The mechanisms of defense represent a combination of projection and avoidance.

Psychoanalysis is also applicable for different kinds of character disorders that actually represent substitutes for psychoneurotic symptoms. The anxiety evoked by unconscious conflicts may be warded off by the regular evocation of defense mechanisms that are ultimately incorporated into the structure of the character. For a person whose unconscious fantasies lead him unconsciously to misconstrue dancing as indulgence in dangerous sexual activity, it may prove much more acceptable just to avoid dancing than to experience blushing, palpitations, and sweating whenever he attempts it. The mechanisms of the inhibition are identical to those involved in the genesis of phobia. Such a person may be diagnosed as suffering from phobic character disorders. There are many forms of character disorders of this type—hysterical, obsessive, compulsive, depressive, and so on. Arlow (1972) has demonstrated how certain character traits may represent transformations from what originally had been transient perversions. In effect, such cases, which include petty liars, hoaxers, and unrealistic personalities, may be said to be suffering from character perversions.

Sexual difficulties, like premature ejaculation, and psychoneurotic depressions are ordinarily quite amenable to psycho-

analytic treatment. More generalized patterns of behavior that interfere with the patient's conscious goals for happiness and success can be traced to unconscious conflicts and can be treated psychoanalytically. Some men, for example, repeatedly fall in love with and marry the same kind of woman, although they know from previous experience that the marriage will end disastrously. Similarly, certain women seem incapable of choosing men other than those who will hurt, abuse, and humiliate them. Other people will unconsciously arrange their lives so any success is followed by an even greater failure. In these cases, their normal way of life or choice of love object or self-engineered fate is the equivalent of a psychoneurotic disorder. Such conditions can be analyzed the same way one would a neurosis.

In recent years, many of the patients seeking psychoanalytic treatment seem to be suffering from masochistic character disorders or from narcissistic neuroses. Into this latter category fall those paradoxical combinations of low self-esteem and heightened grandiosity. Mood swings, depression, tendencies toward drug dependence, compulsive strivings for recognition and success, and patterns of promiscuous sexuality are not uncommon. Such patients often complain of inner emptiness, lack of goals, hypochondriasis, and an inability to make lasting attachments or love relationships. Because of new contributions to the technical management of these problems, the prognosis of their treatment by psychoanalysis seems much better today than it did in previous years.

There are a number of conditions that may be helped by psychoanalysis under specially favorable conditions. Among these are some cases of drug addiction, perversions, borderline personalities, and, on rare occasions, psychoses. Pioneering work applying psychoanalytic principles, if not the complete technique, to the treatment of psychotics has been done by Paul Federn (1952), Frieda Fromm-Reichmann (1950), H. F. Searles (1965), and H. Rosenfeld (1954).

Evaluation

Unfortunately, there exists no adequate study evaluating the results of psychoanalytic therapy. In a general way, this is true of almost all forms of psychotherapy. There are just too many variables to be taken into account to make it possible to establish a controlled, statistically valid study of the outcome of the therapy. Several attempts have been made in this direction beginning with Otto Fenichel (1930) and including studies by Fred Feldman since 1968, H. J. Eysenck (1965), Julian Meltzoff and Melvin Kornreich (1970), R. S. Wallerstein and N. J. Smelser (1969), A. Z. Pfeffer (1963), as well as several studies by the American Psychoanalytic Association. None of the findings of these studies has proven definitive and irrefutable. By and large, the number of "cures" range from 30 to 60 per cent, depending on the studies and the criteria employed.

In any individual case in one's practice, evaluation of the outcome of treatment has to be judged in a global fashion. Comparisons have to be made between the situation at the time of beginning of treatment and the alteration in the patient's life and symptoms at the time of termination. He may have been cured of more conditions than he complained about when he first started; previously unforeseen possibilities of self-fulfillment may have been realized. On the other hand, unrecognized complicating difficulties and intercurrent events may have changed the total configuration of the pa-

tient's life. In the face of objective reality, the claims of psychoanalysis must be modest. At best, psychoanalysis tries to help the patient effect the best possible solution of his difficulties that circumstances will allow. It seeks to achieve for the patient the most stable equilibrium possible between the various forces at conflict in his mind. How well that equilibrium is sustained will also depend on how favorably life treats the patient during and after treatment. On this latter account, no one can talk with any certainty. Freud himself was quite modest about the therapeutic claims of psychoanalysis (Freud 1937). The validity of what psychoanalysis has discovered concerning human nature and the functioning of the human mind are not necessarily related to the effectiveness of psychoanalysis as treatment. Nonetheless, the fact remains that when properly applied to the appropriate condition, psychoanalysis remains the most effective mode of therapy yet devised.

Treatment

In discussing the technical conduct of a psychoanalysis, Freud compared writing about the treatment to explaining the game of chess. It is easy to formulate the rules of the game, to describe the opening phases, and to discuss what has to be done to bring the game to a close. What happens in between is subject to infinite variation. The same is true of psychoanalysis. The analytic contract, the opening phase, and the tasks of termination can be described definitively. The analysis of the transference and the process of working through consist of countless bits of analytic work. Rudolf Loewenstein (1958) approached the problem by distinguishing between tactical and strategic goals in psychoanalytic technique. *Tactical* concerns involve the analysis of the immediate presenting material in terms of some conflict, usually involving the analyst. The *strategic* goal is to elucidate the nature of the unconscious childhood fantasy and to demonstrate the many ways in which it affects the patient in his current life.

How this appears in actual practice may be demonstrated in the following illustration. The patient is a middle-aged businessman whose marriage has been marked by repeated strife and quarrels. His sexual potency has been tenuous. At times he has suffered from premature ejaculation. At the beginning of one session, he began to complain about having to return to treatment after a long holiday weekend. He said "I'm not so sure I'm glad to be back in treatment even though I didn't enjoy my visit to my parents. I feel I just have to be free." He then continued with a description of his visit home, which he said had been depressing. His mother was bossy, aggressive, manipulative, as always. He feels sorry for his father. At least in the summertime, the father can retreat to the garden and work with the flowers, but the mother watches over him like a hawk. "She has such a sharp tongue and a cruel mouth. Each time I see my father he seems to be getting smaller and smaller; pretty soon he will disappear and there will be nothing left of him. She does that to people. I always feel that she is hovering over me ready to swoop down on me. She has me intimidated just like my wife."

The patient continued, "I was furious this morning. When I came to get my car, I found that someone had parked in such a way that it was hemmed in. It took a long time and lots of work to get my car out. During the time I realized how anxious I was; the perspiration was pouring down the back of my neck.

"I feel restrained by the city. I need the open fresh air; I have to stretch my legs. I'm sorry I gave up the house I had in the country. I have to get away from this city. I really can't afford to buy another house now but at least I'll feel better if I look for one.

"If only business were better, I could maneuver more easily. I hate the feeling of being stuck in an office from nine until five. My friend Bob had the right idea—he arranged for retirement. Now he's free to come and go as he pleases. He travels, he has no boss, no board of directors to answer to. I love my work but it imposes too many restrictions on me. I can't help it, I'm ambitious. What can I do?"

At this point, the therapist called to the patient's attention the fact that throughout the material, in many different ways, the patient was describing how he feared confinement, that he had a sense of being trapped.

The patient responded, "I do get symptoms of claustrophobia from time to time. They're mild, just a slight anxiety. I begin to feel perspiration at the back of my neck and I have a sense of restlessness. The hair seems to stand up on the back of my neck. It happens when the elevator stops between floors or when a train gets stuck between stations. I begin to worry how I'll get out."

The fact that he suffered from claustrophobia was a new finding in the analysis. The analyst noted to himself that the patient felt claustrophobic about the analysis. The conditions of the analytic situation imposed by the analyst were experienced by the patient as confining. In addition, the analyst noted, again to himself, that these ideas were coupled with the idea of being threatened and controlled by his mother.

The patient continued, "You know I have the same feeling about starting an affair with Mrs. X. She wants to and I guess I want to also. Getting involved is easy. It's getting uninvolved that concerns me. How do you get out of an affair once you're in it?''

In this material, the patient associates being trapped in a confined space with being trapped in the analysis and with being trapped in an affair with a woman.

The patient continued, "I'm really chicken. It's a wonder I was ever able to have relations at all and to get married. No wonder I didn't have intercourse until I was in my twenties. My mother was always after me, 'be careful about getting involved with girls; they'll get you into trouble. They'll be after you for your money. If you have sex with them you can pick up a disease. Be careful when you go to public toilets; you can get an infection, etc., etc., etc.' She made it all sound dangerous. You can get hurt from this, you can get hurt from that. It reminds me of the time I saw two dogs having intercourse. They were stuck together and couldn't separate—the male dog was yelping and screaming in pain. I don't even know how old I was then, maybe five or six or perhaps seven, but I was definitely a child and I was frightened.''

At this point, the analyst is able to tell the patient that his fear of being trapped in an enclosed space is the conscious derivative of an unconscious fantasy in which he imagines that if he enters the woman's body with his penis, it will get stuck; he will not be able to extricate it; he may lose it. The criteria used in making this interpretation are clear: they consist of the sequential arrangement of the material, the contiguity of related themes, the repetition of the same or analogous themes, and the convergence of the different elements into one common hypothesis that encompasses all the data, namely, an unconscious fantasy of danger to the penis once it enters a woman's body. This is the tactical goal that can be achieved on the basis of this material. In this instance, it constitutes an important step toward the strategic goal, which, in this case, would consist of making the patient aware of childhood sexual strivings towards the mother, of a wish to have relations with her, and of a concomitant fear growing out of the threatening nature of her personality, and that, like a hawk, she would swoop down upon him and devour him. These interpretations would give him insight into the causes of his impotence and his stormy relations with women, particularly his wife. The material also demonstrates how a neurotic person misperceives, misinterprets, and responds inappropriately to current experience in terms of his unconscious fantasy. To this patient, having to keep a definite set of appointments with the analyst, having his car hemmed in between two other cars, being responsible to authorities, and getting stuck in elevators or in trains were all experienced as dangerous situations that evoke the symptoms of anxiety. Consciously, he experienced restrictions by rules and confinement within certain spaces. Unconsciously, he was thinking in terms of experiencing his penis inextricably trapped inside a woman's body.

This is the essence of the neurotic process—the persistent unconscious fantasies of childhood serve to create a mental set according to which the individual in a selective and idiosyncratic way interprets everything that happens to him. Therefore, neurotic conflicts do not represent conflicts with reality. They are intrapsychic conflicts (Arlow, 1963).

The material of any one analytic session is by no means always so dramatic. Yet one must be careful not to prejudge the significance and possible ramifications of any event or session no matter how trivial it may appear at first. A seemingly insignificant interaction between the patient and the analyst may lead to very important discoveries illuminating the origins and the meaning of the neurosis. For the most part, however, the major portion of the analytic work is directed toward understanding the patient's defenses and overcoming his resistances. It is not always easy to distinguish between mechanisms of defense and resistances. Typically, the *mechanisms of defense* are repetitive, stereotyped, automatic means used by the ego to ward off anxiety. A *resistance* is any one of a wide range of phenomena distracting the patient from pursuing the requirements of the analytic situation.

It may seem strange that a patient who has made so serious a commitment to understanding himself should not follow the course of action in treatment that is intended to relieve him of his symptoms. On second thought, however, this is not at all unexpected. Since the mind characteristically turns away from or tries to repress unpleasant feelings and thoughts and since the neurotic process develops when it has been unable to accomplish this end successfully, it should come as no surprise that the endeavor to both fulfill and control forbidden impulses should continue into analytic experience. Herman Nunberg (1926) showed how the patient unconsciously brings into the analysis a wish to preserve intact those very infantile strivings that caused his difficulties in the first place.

The analysis of defenses and resistances is slow, piecemeal work. Nevertheless, from it, much can be learned about how the patient's character was shaped in response to the critical events and object relations of childhood. A particularly difficult resistance to overcome during treatment comes from the use of the mecha-

nism known as *isolation*. This is the tendency for the patient to deal with his thoughts as if they were empty of feeling or unrelated to other ideas or to his behavior. A patient may begin a session, for example, by mentioning in two or three short sentences an incident that took place on his way to the session. He had passed a man on the street who suddenly, without cause or warning, extended his arm in such a way that he almost struck the patient. This reminded the patient of an incident some years earlier when he saw someone actually being hit in this very same manner. On this occasion, as in the past, the patient, not a native New Yorker, shrugged the incident off with the reassuring judgment, "Well, that's New York for you. It's a good thing he didn't have a knife." All of this was stated in an even, flat, unemotional tone.

With no transition, the patient turned to matters of closer concern to him. He described at great length and again in an even-tempered way how his boss had criticized his work in front of his colleagues. Many of the criticisms, he felt, were unjustified, but mindful of his position, he had maintained a calm, respectful demeanor throughout the meeting. Even when recounting the incident, in the session, he showed little sign of anger. When this was called to his attention, he admitted that indeed he had been angry and was surprised that he had not transmitted that feeling to the therapist. At this point, the therapist made the connection for the patient between his opening report of a near-assault on the street and the experience with his boss. Actually, the patient had been saying, "There are dangerous people abroad. If one is not careful, they may strike you, even kill you. They have murderous impulses." The incident in the street served as a convenient locus onto which the patient projected his own murderous wishes to retaliate against the boss. He dealt with these impulses in an isolated way, an intellectual judgment he made about someone else's motives.

At this stage of the treatment, he could grasp only intellectually, by inference, the intensity of his vengeful wishes. Much could be learned from the analysis of this experience beyond illustrating how the patient manages to control and to suppress his feelings. This patient was particularly vulnerable to any assault on his pride, any humiliation of his narcissism, especially if it occurred as part of a public spectacle. Later in the analysis, it was possible to demonstrate the connection between these components of the patient's character and the feelings of defeat, insignificance, and humiliation he experienced during the oedipal phase while watching his parents having intercourse in the bedroom he shared with them.

It would be impossible to catalogue all the forms that resistance can take. Some of the more usual ones may be noted here. The most direct and unequivocal form of resistance occurs when the patient finds he has nothing to say. The patient may remain silent on the couch for minutes on end. Even a trivial lateness of a few minutes may carry some hidden meaning. Often a patient may miss sessions, forget them, or oversleep. He may be tardy in paying the bill for treatment, finding very realistic explanations to account for the tardiness. Sometimes patients will talk endlessly about the trivia of day-to-day events revealing little or nothing that can be used to understand their problems. A patient may introduce a dream at the beginning of a session and make no reference to it for the rest of the analytic hour. On the other hand, the patient may fill the entire session with dreams, making it impossible to learn more than the facade of what had been recorded of the night's experience. Some patients report how they have become ardent advocates of psychoanalysis, proselytizing their friends and relatives, urging all of them to enter into treatment, at the very time when they themselves are making little effort or progress in the analytic work.

The important principle governing all manifestations of resistance is that they must be analyzed like anything else that happens in the course of analysis. What must be understood is why the patient is behaving the way he is at a particular moment. What is the motive behind his unconscious wish to break off the analytic work? What conflict is he trying to evade? Exhortation, suggestion, encouragement, prohibitions, any of a number of educational procedures that in other forms of therapy may be introduced at such a time must be carefully avoided. No matter how provocative, frustrating, or irritating the patient's behavior may be, the analyst never departs from his responsibility to make the patient understand his behavior. His attitude must remain at all times analytic.

How the analyst works can best be understood by examining three aspects of his experience while treating the patient. These are introspection, empathy, and intuition. An analyst must be capable of empathizing with his patient. *Empathy* is a form of "emotional knowing," the experiencing of another's feelings. It is a special mode of perceiving. It presupposes an ability on the analyst's part to identify with his patient and to be able to share the patient's experience affectively as well as cognitively. The empathic process is central to the psychotherapeutic relationship as it is also a basic element in all human interaction. It finds its highest social expression in the aesthetic experience of the artist and his audience as well as in religion and other group phenomena. It is based upon the dynamic effect of unconscious fantasies shared in common (Beres & Arlow, 1974). There are two distinguishing features to empathy. First, the identification with the patient is only transient. Second, the therapist preserves his separateness from the object. The analyst's empathy makes it possible for him to receive and perceive both the conscious and unconscious processes operating in the patient.

It is impossible for the analyst at any one time to keep in the foreground of his thinking all the things the patient has told him. How then does he arrive at the understanding of his patient? This is done *intuitively*. The myriads of data communicated by the patient are organized in the analyst's mind into meaningful configurations outside the scope of consciousness. What the analyst perceives of his understanding of the patient is actually the end product of a series of mental operations he has carried out unconsciously. He becomes aware of this by the process of *introspection* when the interpretation comes to his mind in the form of a free association. Not everything that comes to the analyst's mind in the course of a session is necessarily the correct interpretation. If he is working properly, it is usually some commentary on the patient's material. After introspection presents to the analyst's consciousness the result of his intuitive work, he does not necessarily impart this information to the patient immediately. He checks his idea with what he has learned from the patient and judges its validity in terms of contiguity, repetition, coherence, consistency, and convergence of theme, as outlined earlier. Intuition gives way to *cognitive elaboration*. In the long run, the validity of the interpretation is confirmed by the dynamic impact it has upon the patient's productions, that is, how it affects the

equilibrium between impulse and defense in the patient's mind.

Management

Much has been written about the analyst's emotional response to the patient. The analyst is not an unfeeling, neutral automaton as presented in caricatures of psychoanalysis. He does respond emotionally to the therapeutic interaction, but these responses he keeps to himself. He regards them as a form of affective monitoring of the patient's productions. He uses his feelings as clues to understanding the direction that the patient's thoughts are taking. If he feels angry, sexually aroused, or frustrated, he must always consider the possibility that this is precisely the mood the patient wants to generate in him. It behooves him then to uncover the patient's motive in doing so.

There is much disagreement in analytic literature about the analyst's emotional response to the patient. Sometimes this is referred to as *countertransference,* the counterpart of the patient's transference onto the analysis. These issues have been revived by Annie Reich (1960). Strictly speaking, countertransference should be reserved to those situations in which a patient and his productions evoke in the analyst conflicts relating to some unresolved childhood fantasy of his own, causing him to misperceive, misinterpret, and misrespond to the analysand in terms of his own difficulties. Some analysts see the therapist's feelings as the operation of a mechanism known as *projective identification* (Little, 1951; Tower, 1956). They interpret the analyst's feelings as identical with those the patient is experiencing and they feel it beneficial to the course of the analysis for the analyst to discuss these feelings with the patient. For some analysts, this is the principal mode of treatment. It is safe to say that most analysts in the United States do not agree with this point of view. They try to understand the significance of what they feel about the patient. They do not discuss it with the patient.

Neurotic countertransference to the patient on the part of the analyst can constitute a real problem. Ordinarily the analyst will try to analyze the problem for himself. If this is ineffective, he may seek a consultation with a colleague. If the problem persists, or if it can be demonstrated to be more pervasive than had been suspected before and to apply to other patients as well, it indicates a need for the analyst to undergo further psychoanalysis himself. When the analyst finds that he cannot control his countertransference responses, he discusses the issues honestly and frankly with the patient and arranges for transfer to another analyst.

CASE EXAMPLE

It is impossible to capture in any condensed presentation the essence of the psychoanalytic experience. The course of an analysis proceeds unevenly. Seemingly fragmented material, arduously assembled over long periods, incompletely comprehended, suddenly may be brilliantly illuminated from the work of a few dramatic sessions, when thousands of disparate threads organize themselves into a tapestry of meaning. Accordingly, any effort to describe in an overall way the course of psychoanalysis inevitably must sound oversimplified and slick. For practical purposes, only the main trends and conclusions can be described. The taxing day-to-day struggle with resistances and defenses has to be inserted into the record by one's imagination. With these warnings in mind, let us proceed to the description of a relatively uncomplicated case.

The patient, whom we will call Tom, was a junior faculty member in a prominent eastern university. At age 30 he was still unmarried, although recently he had begun to live with a woman who had studied under him when she was a graduate student. Although Tom was a popular and successful teacher, much admired and appreciated by his students, he was unable to advance professionally because he could not fulfill the requirements for the Ph.D. degree. He had passed the requisite courses and had completed his doctoral thesis except for a few notes and bibliographical references. The next step was to defend his thesis before the committee but he could not do so as long as he had not put the final touches on his thesis. This he seemed unable to do. Several years had gone by and he was afraid that all the work he had done might have been in vain.

Tom had another problem that concerned his difficulties with women. He did not seem to be able to maintain a long-term relationship with any woman. For almost a year, he had been really fond of a woman, whom we will call Anita, and at her urging, finally decided to let her live with him. That was four months ago, and since that time, he had become increasingly irritable and found himself quarreling with Anita, criticizing many of the things she did around the house. He would have liked to get her to move out but he was not quite sure how to tell her. Since she had moved in with him, his sexual performance had become much worse. Whereas previously he had suffered from premature ejaculation after entry, in the past few months, he had had difficulty getting and maintaining an erection. The only times he had been able to perform well sexually were with women he knew to be frigid.

Tom's father, a practical and industrious man, operated a small business. Through judicious and conservative investments, he was able to acquire a comfortable fortune. Although he was proud of Tom, he was unable to share his son's intellectual interests. Tom's mother, on the other hand, was a delicate, sensitive, somewhat hypochondriacal woman. As a child, she had had rheumatic fever, which had left her with a mild case of mitral-stenosis. After she was married, her doctors had advised her not to have any children. But her wish for a child overcame her doctor's admonition, and after a rather difficult labor, which left her exhausted for several months, she gave birth to Tom. When Tom was five years old, she had some kind of miscarriage. She was much concerned with Tom's development. She saw to it that he was well fed and clean. He was toilet trained by 18 months and seemed to thrive in all ways.

During the preliminary interviews, Tom stated that he was not aware of any neurotic problems he may have had in childhood. He recalled no phobias or nightmares but had been told that at the age of five he was something of a behavior problem. He had become contrary and disobedient towards his mother and had refused to let her kiss him goodnight. Once when his mother was out of the kitchen for a while, he had emptied the contents of the refrigerator on the kitchen floor. However, after a few months, he seemed to change. He reverted to the obedient child he had been before but now he became a finicky eater and remained so thereafter.

Tom was not happy about starting school. Since his mother was ill, a favorite aunt accompanied him on the first day. He was quite shy and fearful of the other children. Once he learned how to read, however, things began to change. He was clearly the best student in the class and

was well liked because he generously helped the slower students with their work. Through various activities, he soon became the most popular student in each class. He could keep his classmates amused by inventing funny stories. At lunchtime, he would readily share his sandwiches with his friends. In spite of this, he was quite fearful of the other children. He shied away from contact sports and never got involved in a fistfight. He welcomed the frequent absences from school occasioned by repeated respiratory infections. He could stay in bed, munch crackers, and eat to his heart's delight.

Tom's academic progress was not as good as his teachers and parents had expected. Being naturally gifted, it was easy for him in the lower grades to be outstanding without exerting any real effort. In high school and college, he refused to be "a greasy grind." No one was going to accuse him of putting in extra effort just to get good marks. Repeatedly, his teachers informed him and his parents that he was not working up to his potential. When he had to recite in class, his heart would pound and his face would flush even though he knew the answers to the questions posed by the teacher. On two occasions in college, on crucial examinations, he made gross blunders in interpreting the questions. Ordinarily, he should have failed, but his teachers, cognizant of his abilities, after discussing the matter with him, gave him passing grades. In the Ph.D. program, he fulfilled the requirements at a satisfactory level. It was when he had to work independently that his performance faltered.

Although he liked girls, he never seemed to get along well with them. When he was 5½ years old, he pinched the infant sister of a friend of his when no one was looking. When she began to cry, he disclaimed any knowledge of why she might be doing so. When he was 12 or 13, he recalled having a crush on a lovely girl who lived next door, but he never did anything about it. At 14 he was extremely disappointed when a girl he took to a party spent most of the evening in the company of his best friend. He never dated the girl again, but, surprisingly, his relationship with his friend remained unchanged. He felt a definite antagonism toward attractive girls thinking they were all vain and self-centered. With those girls he did date, he maintained a haughty, condescending air, teasing the girls, and from time to time, he would precipitate a rupture of the relationship through some seemingly inadvertent act that hurt the girl's feelings. He came to realize on his own that there was something malicious about his gaucherie. On several occasions, while talking to one girl, he would address her with the name of another, a slip of the tongue hardly flattering to the girl involved.

By the time Tom began his first sessions on the couch, he had broken up with Anita. At least he had told her to move out, although they remained friends. From the very beginning, he was a "good patient." He followed the rules of the analytic situation and was agreeable and deferential. He soon began to display the vast fund of knowledge he had on a great variety of subjects. In the course of some observation, I made a comment indicating some familiarity with one of the subjects Tom was discussing. This proved very upsetting to him. For a few days, he became anxious and depressed. Intellectually, he was convinced he was superior to everyone else, at least in the areas of his expertise. The only reason it was not generally acknowledged was that he did not try hard enough. He realized that he wanted me, as his analyst, to admire him, but he had not realized that behind his deferential facade, he was intensely competitive. A few days later, he reported a recurrent fantasy. He imagined what would happen if a holdup man confronted him with a gun. He would tell the villain, "My life is too important to me. Money doesn't mean anything to me—just don't hurt me," and he would passively hand over his wallet.

In the clothes closet, Tom noted a fur coat belonging to the patient who preceded him. He left the door of the waiting room open a fraction and placed his chair in a position where he could see the patient as she left the consulting room. She was an attractive woman with blonde ringlets, just the type he despised. In the sessions, he began to make disparaging comments concerning her. "How easy it is to be a woman. You just have to be attractive and everything is taken care of for you." He was certain that I was more interested in her and that I would be taken in by her self-centered complacency and smugness. It would be impossible for him to compete with her for my attention. She had the inside track. He began to realize some of the reasons for his antagonism towards such women. He felt that a woman so attractive would never pay any attention to him.

Tom began one session in a state of almost uncontrollable fury. I had begun his session seven minutes later than usual. Although this was due to my own lateness in arriving at the office, he was certain that I had done so because I was too fascinated with what my previous patient was telling me to let her go on time. He began the session by saying that while he was in the clothes closet, he had had the impulse to take the coat belonging to the previous patient and to throw it on the floor. On the way to his appointment that morning, the bus was very crowded and he had become quite anxious. People jostled him and he felt he could not breathe. He became so uncomfortable that he left the bus a few blocks earlier and walked the rest of the way to the office. He thought the city was getting too overcrowded, too many people on the relief rolls who have to be supported by hard-working citizens like himself. They were all parasites like my previous patient who probably lived luxuriously on her husband's hard-earned income.

In the ensuing weeks, he began to talk about his relationship with Anita. Her presence in his house was intrusive. She did not contribute sufficiently to the maintenance of the household. At night, after they had had intercourse, he would want to get as far away from her as possible. In fact, it would have been better if he could have told her to leave the bed completely. Several times he had a quick fantasy of choking her. In fact, he recalled a definite sense of pleasure when he saw her leaving the house. The thing that seemed to irritate him the most, however, was how careless Anita was with the food. She would take a portion of meat larger than she could eat, so much had to be thrown out. In addition, she used to leave the refrigerator door open for long periods. He would have to dispose of the milk that had gone sour. He did make the observation, "After all, I'm an only child. It never was easy for me to share." He remembered that when he was six years old, a friend of his and his sister had received a toy log cabin for Christmas. The two of them were fighting over who should occupy the house. He then remembered reading in the Bible years later how Jacob and Esau had fought with each other inside their mother's womb.

During this phase of the analysis, he began to have nightmares. The following dream is typical. The patient reported, "I was swimming in a lake, the water was dark and murky. Suddenly, I was surrounded by a school of small fish, the kind I used to raise when I was a kid. They seemed prepared to lunge at me as if to bite me. I woke up gasping for breath."

Tom learned to swim late. He was most comfortable in a pool. In an ocean, he feared being bitten by large fish or being stung by an eel. Worst of all was swimming in a lake where the reeds growing from the muddy bottom could tangle him, draw him down, and drown him. Between the ages of 8 and 12, he raised tropical fish. He was always careful to be present when the baby fish were hatched to remove them from the tank so the other fish would not eat them.

Shortly before he was five, his mother told him that he might be getting a baby sister or brother. She explained that his father had introduced something like an egg into her that had hatched and a future baby was swimming around in a special fluid inside her body. Clearly this news did not please Tom for the story goes that he pointed his ray gun at his mother's abdomen. It was during the same period that he emptied the contents of the refrigerator onto the kitchen floor. The pregnancy did not come to term. A few months later, the mother began to bleed and she was taken to the hospital. Tom saw some of the blood on the bathroom floor. From the behavior of the grownups, Tom could conclude that something terrible was happening. His mother did not come home from the hospital with a baby. What had happened was that the mother was delivered of some mass of chopped up fetal fragments; some hair and teeth had been noted among the pieces. (Apparently she had been delivered of an hyatidiform mole.) Tom was relieved that he had his mother back again and that he did not have to share her and the food with a younger sibling. But unconsciously, he imagined that he was responsible for the baby's death. He fantasied that when he was inside the mother's body, he had destroyed the potential sibling, lacerating it with his teeth. About this time, he developed an aversion to eating eggs or fish, a characteristic that persisted into his adult life. Unconsciously, he feared that these representatives of siblings whom he had destroyed within his mother's body would retaliate by destroying him from within his own body. The attractive patient in the consultation room, the grimy welfare recipients in the bus, and the sloppy Anita in his apartment all represented potential siblings he wanted to oust and destroy because they threatened to invade his territory and rob him of his mother's love and food. He feared they in turn would do to him exactly what he intended to do to them, namely, destroy them with his mouth. As he overcame these fears, he became more giving with Anita. He invited her to share his apartment again. Sexually, his potency began to improve.

His former rival, the attractive blonde with the fur coat began to intrigue him. What kind of sexual life did she lead? Through the partially open doorway of the waiting room he observed her comings and goings. Perhaps the analyst was interested in her sexually. She seemed the type to go for older men.

Before his session one day, Tom went to the bathroom and forgot to lock the door. As he was standing urinating, the blonde patient entered. Surprised and embarrassed, she withdrew in great confusion. Somehow Tom found the incident amusing and gratifying.

A short time later, he had the following dream, "I get up at night and go to the bathroom. I sit on the toilet and masturbate looking at the pictures in some porno girlie magazine. Suddenly I notice that there are two sets of large French windows. They swing open, people are passing by on what seems to be a boardwalk. I'm angry and embarrassed because they're all looking in on me. In the background I hear the sounds of a choo-choo-train going by."

Immediately, he related the dream to the experience with the previous patient. From the French windows, he could place the setting of the dream exactly. There were such windows in a room he and his parents had occupied in a rooming house at the Jersey shore where they had gone for a two week's vacation. He was four and one-half years old at the time and he was much intrigued by what was going on in the adjoining room at the rooming house. Two young women shared the room. It had a sliding door that did not close completely. Through the half-inch-wide space, little Tom tried to watch the girls getting undressed and he was especially curious when their boyfriends came to visit them over the weekend.

There had been a wreck on the Asbury Park railroad just before he and his parents had arrived at the seashore. Several people had been killed and the derailed cars had not yet been removed. He recalled for the first time that as a child he had had frequent nightmares in which he heard the huffing and puffing of a locomotive train, the volume and pitch of the noise increasing in unbearable intensity until he awoke in great anxiety. As it turned out, the room he used to occupy at home was next to his parents' bedroom and from time to time he had been aware of strange noises coming from their room.

Going to the bathroom in the dream reminded him of a number of "dirty habits" he had. After his bowels moved, he was not too meticulous about wiping himself so frequently there were stains on his underwear. His mother used to scold him about this. When he undressed at night, he would let his dirty clothes pile up on the floor for his mother to pick up in the morning. Later when he began to masturbate, he would ejaculate onto the bedsheet, leaving a stain that his mother would have to notice when she changed the bedding. He did something similar when he began to entertain girlfriends in his bedroom. In no way did he try to conceal from his parents who often were home what was going on in his bedroom and if any doubt lingered in their minds, he left unambiguous evidence in the form of a rumpled bed and a stained sheet, making clear to them exactly what had been taking place. He defended his lifelong pattern of masturbating. "To begin with," he said, "I'm completely in control. No girl can disappoint me; I've had all the satisfaction I want and I get it by myself."

Working through the themes suggested in this material was very rewarding. It was clear that the patient had witnessed his parents having intercourse during that summer vacation. His response was as complex as it was long-lasting. He felt left out, betrayed, and humiliated. In his mind, his mother became a whore who did dirty things and who preferred his father because he was more powerful and had a bigger penis, while he was so small and insignificant. In his subsequent nightmares of the sounds of the locomotive, he feared his own wishes that his parents would die during the act as the people had perished in the railroad accident. He no longer trusted his mother and this affected his attitude toward all women, especially after his sweetheart had turned her affections to his best briend when he was 12 years old. He became convinced that no woman would be interested in him

and he decided "to show them." He would grow up, become outstanding and famous, and would show that he had no use for them. He would take his vengeance by doing to his mother (and women in general) what she had done to him. He would flaunt before her the signs of his own dirty sexual activity and he would leave her and other women embarrassed, angered, and confused as he had left the blonde patient who had come into the bathroom while he was urinating. After some of these conflicts had been worked through, the blonde patient no longer seemed so haughty, and if Anita did not close the door to the refrigerator so promptly, it no longer seemed catastrophic.

Tom's interests now turned to his professional work, which for a long time he had been treating lightly. He became more demanding of his students and less deferential to the chairman of his department. In fact, he realized how often he had thought of himself being the chairman. Behind his "good guy" affability, he could see how competitive and ambitious he really was. He decided that he was being underpaid, that he needed more money, and that the thing to do was to get on with his work and earn the Ph.D. degree. Without the Ph.D., he felt like a boy. It was time to become a man.

No sooner had he begun to work on his thesis than the old inhibition returned. He blocked on using key references from important authorities in the field. He thought that I would accuse him of being a plagiarist, stealing his teacher's ideas. Guilt over stealing was not a new theme in his life. During his latency years, for a few months, in the company of a friend, he went on a stealing spree. He took some of the small change his father had left on the dresser and went to his mother's pocketbook looking for bills he knew the father had put there. From the most popular boy in his class, a born leader, he stole a fountain pen, which he hid under his shirt. From a cousin whom he admired for his strong physique and athletic ability, he stole a textbook of an advanced grade. As he put it, "I devoured the book voraciously."

From childhood on, stealing was prominent in his fantasy life. His favorite story was "Jack and the Beanstalk." "I loved to hear again and again how Jack ran off with the giant's money." His favorite movie was "The Thief of Baghdad"; the most exciting part was where the thief, Ali, goes to the mountains, climbs the great statue of the god, and steals from his forehead the largest jewel in the world, one that bestows on its owner magic, knowledge, and wealth. It reminded him of the myth of Prometheus who stole knowledge from the gods and of his own Promethean wish for omniscience. In this connection, he remembered that he had forgotten to return some books he had borrowed from the university library several years back. He recalled going with his father, at the age of four, to a turkish bath. He was awed by the gigantic size of his father's penis and wanted to reach up and touch it.

Coming a bit late for his session one day, he saw the blonde patient walking toward him on the street. He nodded to her and she acknowledged his greeting with a friendly smile. He felt he should have stopped to talk with her; perhaps he could have arranged a date that ultimately could lead to an affair. As he entered the lobby of the building, he found himself caught up in a fantasy of a violent quarrel with me because I was forbidding him to have anything to do with the patient. Going up, he thought the elevator man seemed ominously threatening. This material led to the theme that I was standing in the way

of his sexual freedom and of his achieving manhood, just as earlier in life, he had felt his father had stood in his way.

On two occasions, he lost the bill for the previous month's analysis and, depending on his memory, brought in a check for several sessions fewer than he was actually supposed to pay. He came to realize that he wanted to steal from me not just my money, but also my profession and my powers. He developed a craving for food before he came to the sessions; he was particularly fond of hot dogs and chocolate bars. For a while, he thought it would be a good idea to become an analyst himself. He could do as well, if not better. During this time, he became increasingly irritable and anxious, and the work he had undertaken to complete his Ph.D. thesis came to a complete standstill.

The anxiety that appeared during this phase of the analysis was connected to three types of dreams or fantasies. They were (1) dreams in which there was a danger of being devoured by sharks, dogs, or lions roaming in the jungle; (2) fantasies of a confrontation with a holdup man (only now Tom would often see himself fighting back); and (3) fantasies and dreams of a struggle with an adversary in an enclosed space: the lobby of my building, a tunnel, or the basement of his childhood home. He had several dreams in which he saw himself perched at the window of his basement with a gun ready to defend the house against assault by intruders.

From his associations, it became clear in time that the feared adversary who threatened to mutilate him physically represented at different times myself, his father, the chief of his department, and the man who was to serve as chairman of the oral examining board for the Ph.D. examination. An examination represented to him a bloody, competitive struggle, in which one either kills or is killed. It also had the unconscious significance of a trial where one is pronounced innocent or guilty. To pass the examination was to be permitted to enter the council of elders, to have the right to be sexual, to have a woman, and to become a father. He told Anita that until he got the Ph.D., he could not think of marrying her, but would do so as soon as he passed. Unconsciously he felt he could not become a husband or father as long as he was in analysis, which meant to him as long as his father was alive. Accordingly, successful termination of treatment had the unconscious significance of killing his father. Fear of retaliation for his murderous wishes against authority figures intensified. His impotence grew more severe; unconsciously he imagined that within the woman's vagina was the adversary who would kill or mutilate him. During this period, he recapitulated the events and fantasies of his childhood in which he competed with his father for his mother's attention. The experiences between the ages of four and five proved to be the crucial ones. They centered around the boy's hostility and envy of the father due to having slept in the same room with his parents at the Jersey coast. He recollected and reexperienced surges of tender loving feelings for his mother who risked her own life giving birth to him. He felt he has to repay her in kind. If only he could restore her heart to its original condition. As a child, he would fantasize about giving her new life in the form of a child.

After many months of working through the anxieties of these unconscious fantasies of childhood, the patient began to make progress in his work and he became potent again. He was well prepared for his Ph.D. oral exam. The day before he took the examination, confident that he would pass, while giving a talk before a large audience in a lecture hall, he had the following fantasy: his eye had fastened on the elaborate chandelier that hung from the ceiling. He imagined himself reaching up with one hand and tearing the chandelier out of its roots from the ceiling. He recalled how as a child he had been greatly impressed when he saw his father, seemingly gigantic, standing on a ladder reaching up to the ceiling to change an electric bulb. His Promethean wish was about to be fulfilled. Indeed, he did succeed.

Tom did marry Anita after he got the Ph.D. Five years after finishing the analysis, he reported that he was doing well in his work. He had been promoted and would soon be eligible for tenure. He was the proud father of a daughter and his wife was expecting a second child. Anita continued to forget to close the refrigerator door.

SUMMARY

As a system of thought and a technique for dealing with mental illness, psychoanalysis has been developing and changing over the years. What seemed at first a monolithic structure of theory is now being examined critically from many different points of view. Technical innovations and reformulations of theoretical concepts are appearing in ever-increasing numbers. In addition, the literature of psychoanalysis has expanded enormously and there are special volumes dedicated to psychoanalysis and sociology, anthropology, history of childhood, esthetics, developmental psychology, religion, and biography. Clinical investigation in the therapeutic setting according to the rules of the psychoanalytic situation remains the fundamental base of psychoanalytic knowledge and will clearly continue to be so in the future. Many alternative forms of psychotherapy appear from time to time on the horizon, draw great attention to themselves, but soon fade from the scene. Psychoanalysis has remained a steady, reliable, and growing discipline of study and treatment.

Two points have to be borne in mind about the position of psychoanalysis as therapy and a system of thought. Not all forms of mental disturbance can or should be treated by psychoanalysis. Paradoxically, the demands of psychoanalysis require the cooperation of a patient with a fairly healthy ego, well motivated to change, and capable of facing himself honestly. For properly selected patients, psychoanalysis can offer the promise of helping the individual attain the best possible solution that can be realized from overcoming inner conflicts. It does not pretend to create supermen perfectly balanced, in harmony with themselves and the universe. People who expect psychoanalytic treatment to reveal hidden talents, concealed genius, would be well advised to take other forms of treatment.

The second point to be emphasized is that the reliability of the conclusions of psychoanalytic investigation diminish the farther one gets away from the clinical base of the psychoanalytic situation. Whenever psychoanalytic knowledge and insights are applied outside the analytic situation, one must take into consideration the possibility of innumerable alternative hypotheses and influences upon the data of observation.

Because of the changing nature of the psychopathology of our time, notably the great increase in patients suffering from narcissistic, neurotic, and character disorders, from mild perversions and addictions, one can anticipate much stimulation towards new discoveries, fresh observation, original theoretical formulations, and innovative technical procedures.

ANNOTATED BIBLIOGRAPHY

For those who want to attain deeper and more immediate knowledge of psychoanalysis as theory and practice, the following books are recommended.

Freud, Sigmund. *Introductory lectures on psychoanalysis, 1915–1917.*
These lectures comprise volumes 15 and 16 of *The Complete Psychological Works of Sigmund Freud.* The books constitute a set of lectures Freud gave at the University of Vienna. His lectures are a model of lucidity, clarity, and organization. Taking a new and complicated field of knowledge, Freud develops his thesis step by step, beginning with simple, acceptable, common-sense concepts, and advancing his argument consistently until the new and the startling ideas that he was to place before his audience seem like the inevitable and logical consequences of each individual's own reflection. *The Introductory Lectures on Psychoanalysis* remains to this day the easiest and most direct approach to the understanding of psychoanalysis.

Jones, Ernest. *The life and work of Sigmund Freud.* New York: Basic Books, 1953–57.
The three-volume biography of Sigmund Freud by Ernest Jones is one of the great biographies of our time. It captures the intellectual and spiritual ambience of Freud's period in history. It is a remarkable portrayal of the personality and thoughts of a genius. In addition, this book contains an accurate and readable summary of almost all of Freud's important contributions. It traces the history and the personalities of the psychoanalytic movement to the death of Freud in 1939.

Freud, Anna. *The ego and the mechanisms of defense.* (1936) *The writings of Anna Freud.* Vol. 2. New York: International Universities Press, 1966.
Perhaps the finest and clearest writing style in psychoanalysis belongs to Anna Freud. *The Ego and the Mechanisms of Defense* is an established classic for its lucidity in portraying the theoretical implications of the structural theory and its application to problems of technique. In a relatively small volume, the author offers a definitive presentation of the

psychoanalytic concept of conflict, of the functioning of the anxiety signal and of the many ways in which the ego attempts to establish a stable homeostasis between impulse and defense. The sections on the origin of the superego on identity and of the transformations in adolescence afford the best picture of how the postoedipal child becomes an adult.

Brenner, Charles. *An elementary textbook of psychoanalysis.* New York: International Universities Press, 1973.

There is no better presentation of current psychoanalytic theory than this volume by Charles Brenner, which has become a worldwide introduction to psychoanalysis and has been translated into nine languages. It is the most comprehensive, systematic, and intelligible presentation of the subject, a worthy companion piece to Anna Freud's *The Ego and the Mechanisms of Defense.* The theoretical development flows smoothly, logically, and cautiously. In addition to the basic theory of psychoanalysis, the book describes the part played by unconscious forces in day-to-day living and surveys the remarkable contribution of psychoanalysis to human knowledge. Current trends in the field are assessed and problems still requiring exploration are examined.

Hartmann, Heinz. *Essays on ego psychology.* New York: International Universities Press, 1964.

For the advanced reader who is interested in the broadest theoretical applications of psychoanalysis to psychology, science, and sociology, there is no more authoritative exposition than this book of essays by the outstanding American psychoanalytic theoretician of the twentieth century. Hartmann discusses the concept of health, rational and irrational action, and the application of psychoanalytic concepts to social science and developmental psychology. This is not an easy set of essays to read but the meticulous student who wants to be exposed to the broadest and highest level of analytic theory will be well rewarded for his efforts.

CASE READINGS

Arlow, J. A. Communication and character: A clinical study of a man raised by deaf mute parents. *Psychoanalytic Study of the Child,* 1976, 31, 139–63.

Bornstein, Berta. The analysis of the phobic child, some problems of theory and technique in child analysis. *Psychoanalytic Study of the Child,* 1949, 4, 181–226.

Freud, S. The rat man. In S. Freud, *Three case histories.* New York: Crowell-Collier, 1963.

Winnicott, D. W. (with Alfred Flarsheim). Fragment of an analysis. In Peter L. Giovacchini, *Tactics and technique in psychoanalytic therapy.* New York: Science House, 1972, pp. 455–693.

REFERENCES

Abraham, K. The influence of oral erotism on character formation. *Selected papers of Karl Abraham, Vol. 1,* 393–496. London: Hogarth Press and the Institute of Psychoanalysis, 1924.

Alexander, F. *The medical value of psychoanalysis.* New York: Norton, 1932.

Ansbacher, H., & Ansbacher, R. (Eds.) *The individual psychology of Alfred Adler.* New York: Basic Books, 1956.

Arlow, J. A. Conflict, regression and symptom formation. *International Journal of Psychoanalysis,* 1963, 44, 12–22.

Arlow, J. A. Character perversion. In I. M. Marcus (Ed.), *Currents in psychoanalysis.* New York: International Universities Press, 1972, 20, 317–36.

Arlow, J. A., & Brenner, C. *Psychoanalytic concepts in the structural theory.* New York: International Universities Press, 1964.

Berenfeld, S. Freud's earliest theories and the school of Helmholtz. *Psychoanalytic Quarterly,* 1944, 13.

Beres, D., & Arlow, J. A. Fantasy and identification in empathy. *Psychoanalytic Quarterly,* 1974, 43, 4–25.

Bowlby, J. The nature of the child's ties to the mother. *International Journal of Psychoanalysis,* 1958, 39, 350–73.

Brenner, C. The psychoanalytic concept of aggression. *International Journal of Psychoanalysis,* 1971, 52, 137–44.

Brenner, C. *An elementary textbook of psychoanalysis.* New York: International Universities Press, 1973.

Breuer, J., & Freud, S. *Studies on hysteria. Standard edition of the complete psychological works of Freud.* Vol. 2. London: Hogarth Press, 1895.

Burton, A. (Ed.) *Encounter.* San Francisco: Jossey-Bass, 1969.

Ellis, A. *Reason and emotion in psychotherapy.* New York: Lyle Stuart, 1970.

Erikson, E. *Identity, youth and crisis.* New York: Norton, 1968.

Eysenck, H. J. The effects of psychotherapy. *International Journal of Psychiatry,* 1965, 1, 99–142.

Feldman, F. Results of psychoanalysis in clinic case assignments. *Journal of the American Psychoanalytic Association,* 1968, 16, 274–300.

Federn, P. *Ego psychology and the psychoses.* New York: Basic Books, 1952.

Fenichel, O. *Zehn Jahre Berliner psychoanalytischer Institut.* Vienna: International Psychoanalytischer Verlag, 1930.

Fenichel, O. *The psychoanalytic theory of neurosis.* New York: Norton, 1945.

Freud, A. *The ego and the mechanisms of defense.* New York: International Universities Press, 1936.

Freud, A. Observations on child development. *Psychoanalytic Study of the Child,* 1951, 6, 18–30.

*Freud, S. *The neuropsychoses of defense.* Standard Edition, Vol. 3, 45–70, 1894.

Freud, S. *Studies on hysteria.* Standard Edition, Vol. 2, 1895.

Freud, S. *The interpretation of dreams.* Standard Edition, Vol. 4, 1900.

Freud, S. *The psychopathology of everyday life.* Standard Edition, Vol. 6, 1901.

Freud, S. *Jokes and their relationship to the unconscious.* Standard Edition, Vol. 8, 1905(a).

Freud, S. *Three essays on sexuality.* Standard Edition, Vol. 7, 135–248, 1905(b).

Freud, S. *Formulations regarding the two principles of mental functioning.* Standard Edition, Vol. 12, 218–28, 1911.

Freud, S. *Totem and taboo.* Standard Edition, Vol. 13, 1–161, 1913.

Freud, S. *The history of the psychoanalytic movement.* Standard Edition, Vol. 14, 7–66, 1914(a).

Freud, S. *On narcissism, an introduction.* Standard Edition, Vol. 14, 73–104, 1914(b).

Freud, S. *Repression.* Standard Edition, Vol. 14, 143, 1915(a).

Freud, S. *The unconscious.* Standard Edition, Vol. 14, 161, 1915(b).

Freud, S. *On transformations of instinct as exemplified in anal erotism.* Standard Edition, Vol. 17, 125–34, 1917.

Freud, S. *Beyond the pleasure principle.* Standard Edition, Vol. 18, 7, 1920.

Freud, S. *Group psychology and the analysis of the ego.* Standard Edition, Vol. 18, 69–144, 1921.

Freud, S. *The ego and the id.* Standard Edition, Vol. 19, 13–68, 1923.

Freud, S. *An autobiographical study.* Standard Edition, Vol. 20, 77–176, 1925.

Freud, S. *Inhibitions, symptoms and anxiety.* Standard Edition, Vol. 20, 87–128, 1926.

Freud, S. *Analysis terminable and interminable.* Standard Edition, Vol. 23, 216–54, 1937.

Fromm, E. *The sane society.* New York: Holt, Rinehart & Winston, 1955.

Fromm-Reichmann, F. *Principles of intensive psychotherapy.* Chicago: University of Chicago Press, 1950.

Glasser, W. *Reality therapy.* New York: Julian Press, 1967.

Greenacre, P. Re-evaluation of the process of working through. *International Journal of Psychoanalysis,* 1956, 37, 439–44.

Greenacre, P. The influence of infantile trauma on genetic pattern. *Emotional Growth,* 1967, 1, 216–99.

Greenson, R. *The technique and practice of psychoanalysis.* New York: International Universities Press, 1967.

Grinstein, A. (Ed.) *The index of psychoanalytic writings.* 10 vols. issued to date. New York: International Universities Press, 1971.

Hartmann, H. *Ego psychology and the problem of adaptation.* New York: International Universities Press, 1939.

Hartmann, H., & Kris, E. The genetic approach to psychoanalysis. *Psychoanalytic Study of the Child,* 1945, 1, 11–30.

Hartmann, H.; Kris, E.; & Loewenstein, R. N. Comments on the formation of psychic structure. *Psychoanalytic Study of the Child,* 1946, 2, 11–38.

Hartmann, H.; Kris, E.; & Loewenstein, R. N. Notes on the theory of aggression. *Psychoanalytic Study of the Child,* 1949, 4, 9–36.

* All references to Freud are from the *Complete Psychological Works of Sigmund Freud,* edited by James Strachey, and published by Hogarth Press, London.

Horney, K. *New ways in psychoanalysis.* New York: Norton, 1940.

Jacobson, E. The self and the object world: Vicissitudes of their infantile cathexes and their influence on ideational and affective development. *Psychoanalytic Study of the Child,* 1954, 9, 75–127.

Jones, E. *The life and work of Sigmund Freud.* New York: Basic Books, 1953.

Jung, C. *The psychology of dementia praecox.* New York & Washington: Nervous and Mental Disease Publishing Co., 1909.

Kernberg, O. Borderline personality organization. *Journal of the American Psychoanalytic Association,* 1967, 15, 641–85.

Kernberg, O. The therapy of patients with borderline personality organization. *International Journal of Psychoanalysis,* 1968, 49, 600–19.

Klein, M. *The psychoanalysis of children.* London: Hogarth Press, The Institute of Psychoanalysis, 1932.

Kohut, H. *The analysis of the self.* Monograph Series of the *Psychoanalytic Study of the Child.* No. 4. New York: International Universities Press, 1971.

Kris, E. Preconscious mental processes. *Psychoanalytic Quarterly,* 1950, 19, 540–60.

Lewin, B. D. Sleep, the mouth and the dream screens. *Psychoanalytic Quarterly,* 1946, 15, 419–34.

Lewin, B. D. Mania and sleep. *Psychoanalytic Quarterly,* 1949, 18, 419–33.

Little, M. Countertransference and the patient's response to it. *International Journal of Psychoanalysis,* 1951, 32, 321–40.

Loewenstein, R. Remarks on some variations in psychoanalytic technique. *International Journal of Psychoanalysis,* 1958, 39, 202–10.

Lorenz, C. *King Solomon's ring.* New York: Crowell, 1952.

Mahler, M.; Pine, F.; & Bergman, A. *The psychological birth of the human infant.* New York:·Basic Books, 1975.

Meltzoff, J., & Kornreich, M. *Research in psychotherapy.* New York: Atherton Press, 1970.

Nunberg, H. The will to recovery. *International Journal of Psychoanalysis,* 1926, 7, 64–78.

Perls, F.; Hefferline, R.; & Goodman, P. *Gestalt therapy.* New York: Julian Press, 1951.

Peterfreund, E. Information systems and psychoanalysis. *Psychological Issues Monograph.* No. 25–26. New York: International Universities Press, 1971.

Pfeffer, A. Z. The meaning of the analyst after analysis: A contribution to the theory of therapeutic results. *Journal of the American Psychoanalytic Association,* 1963, 11, 229–44.

Racker, E. A contribution to the problem of countertransference. *International Journal of Psychoanalysis,* 1953, 34, 313–24.

Rangell, L. On the cacophony of human relations. *Psychoanalytic Quarterly,* 1973, 42, 325–48.

Rapaport, D. *The organization and pathology of thought.* New York: Columbia University Press, 1951.

Reich, A. Further remarks on countertransference. *International Journal of Psychoanalysis,* 1960, 41, 389–95.

Reich, A. *Psychoanalytic contributions.* New York: International Universities Press, 1973.

Rogers, C. *Client-centered therapy.* New York: Houghton Mifflin, 1951.

Rosenfeld, H. Considerations concerning the psychoanalytic approach to acute and chronic schizophrenia. *International Journal of Psychoanalysis,* 1954, 35, 135–40.

Rubinstein, B. B. Explanation and mere description: A metascientific examination of certain aspects of the psychoanalytic theory of motivation in motives and thought. Psychoanalytic essays in honor of David Rapaport. R. R. Holt (Ed.), *Psychological Issues Monograph.* Nos. 18–19, 20–79. New York: International Universities Press, 1967.

Sachs, H. *The creative unconscious.* Cambridge, Mass.: Sci-Art Publishers, 1942.

Schafer, R. *A new language of psychoanalysis.* New Haven & London: Yale University Press, 1976.

Schmideberg, M. After the analysis. *Psychoanalytic Quarterly,* 1938, 7, 122–42.

Schutz, W. C. *Joy.* New York: Grove Press, 1967.

Searles, H. F. *Collected papers on schizophrenia and related subjects.* New York: International Universities Press, 1965.

Spitz, R. The primal cavity: A contribution to the genesis of perception and its role in psychoanalytic theory. *Psychoanalytic Study of the Child,* 1955, 10, 215–40.

Sullivan, H. S. *The interpersonal theory of psychiatry.* New York: Norton, 1953.

Tinbergern, N. *The study of instinct.* London: Oxford Universities Press, 1951.

Tower, L. E. Countertransference. *Journal of the American Psychoanalytic Association,* 1956, 224, 265.

Wallerstein, R. S., & Smelser, N. J. Articulations and applications. *International Journal of Psychoanalysis,* 1969, 50, 693–710.

Weigert, E. *The courage to love.* New Haven: Yale University Press, 1970.

Winnicott, D. W. Transitional objects and transitional phenomena: A study of the first not-me possession. *International Journal of Psychoanalysis,* 1953, 34, 89–97.

Wolpe, J. *Psychotherapy by reciprocal inhibition.* Stanford, Calif.: Stanford University Press, 1958.

Zetzel, E. R. *The capacity for emotional growth: Theoretical and clinical contributions to psychoanalysis.* New York: International Universities Press, 1970.

Zilboorg, G., & Henry, George W. *A history of medical psychology.* New York: Norton, 1941.

2

Adlerian Psychotherapy

HAROLD H. MOSAK

OVERVIEW

Adlerian psychology (Individual Psychology), the personality theory and therapeutic system developed by Alfred Adler, views man holistically as a creative, responsible, "becoming" individual moving toward fictional goals within his phenomenal field. It holds that man's lifestyle is sometimes self-defeating because of inferiority feelings. The individual with "psychopathology" is discouraged rather than sick, and the therapeutic task is to encourage him, to activate his social interest, and to develop a new life-style through relationship, analysis, and action methods.

Basic Concepts

Adlerian psychology is predicated upon certain assumptions and postulates that differ in significant ways from the Freudian "womb" from which Adlerian psychology emerged. Adler throughout his lifetime credited Freud with primacy in the development of a dynamic psychology. His debt to Freud for explicating the purposefulness of symptoms and for expressing the notion that dreams were meaningful was consistently acknowledged. The influence of early childhood experiences in personality development constitutes still another point of agreement. Freud emphasized the role of psychosexual development and the Oedipus complex, and Adler focused upon the effects of the child's perceptions of his family constellation and his struggle to find a place of significance within it.

Adlerian basic assumptions can be expressed as follows:

1. All behavior occurs in a social context. Man is born into an environment with which he must engage in reciprocal relations. The oft-quoted statement by the Gestalt psychologist Kurt Lewin that "behavior is a function of person and environment" bears a striking parallel to Adler's contention that man cannot be studied in isolation (1929).

2. A corollary of the first axiom is that Individual Psychology is an interpersonal psychology. How individuals interact with the others sharing "this crust of earth" (Adler, 1958, p. 6) is paramount. Transcending interpersonal transactions is the development of the feeling of being a part of a larger social whole, the feeling of being socially embedded, the willingness to contribute in the communal life for the common weal—movements that Adler (1964c) incorporated under the heading of *Gemeinschaftsgefühl,* or social interest.

3. Adlerian psychology rejects reductionism in favor of holism. Jan Smuts (1961), who introduced the concept of *holism,* and Adler engaged in a correspondence that unfortunately has never been published. The Adlerian demotes part functions from the central investigative focus in favor of studying the whole man and how he moves through life. This renders the polarities of *conscious* and *unconscious, mind* and *body, approach* and *avoidance, ambivalence* and *conflict* meaningless except as subjective experiences of the whole man, that is, people behave *as if* the conscious mind moves in one direction while the unconscious mind moves in another. From the external observer's viewpoint all part-functions are subordinate functions of the individual's goals, his style of life.

4. *Conscious* and *unconscious* are both in the service of the individual and he uses them to further his goals. Adler (1963a) treats *unconscious* as an adjective rather than a noun, thus avoiding reifying the concept. That which is unconscious is the nonunderstood. With Otto Rank, Adler felt that man knows more than he understands. *Conflict,* defined as intrapersonal by others, is defined as a "one step forward and one step backward movement," the net effect being to maintain the individual at a point "dead center." Although he experiences himself in the throes of a conflict, unable to move, in reality he *creates* these antagonistic feelings, ideas, and values because he is unwilling to move in the direction of solving his problems (Mosak & LeFevre, 1976).

5. The understanding of the individual requires the understanding of his *cognitive organization,* the life-style. The latter concept refers to the convictions the individual develops early in life to help him organize experience, to understand it, to predict it, and to control it. *Convic-*

tions are conclusions derived from the individual's apperceptions, and they constitute a biased mode of apperception. Consequently, a *life-style* is neither right nor wrong, normal or abnormal, but merely the "spectacles" through which a person views himself in relationship to the way in which he perceives life. Subjectivity rather than so-called objective evaluation becomes the major tool for understanding the person. As Adler (1958) wrote, "We must be able to see with his eyes and listen with his ears" (p. 72).

6. Behavior may change throughout a person's lifespan in accordance with both the immediate demands of the situation and the long-range goals inherent in the life-style. The life-style remains relatively constant through life unless the convictions change through the mediation of psychotherapy. Although the definition of *psychotherapy* customarily refers to what transpires within a consulting room, a broader view of psychotherapy would include the fact that life in itself may be and is often psychotherapeutic.

7. According to the Adlerian conception, man is not pushed from behind by causes, that is, he is not determined by heredity and environment. "Both are giving only the frame and the influences which are answered by the individual in regard to his styled creative power" (Ansbacher & Ansbacher, 1956). Man moves toward a self-selected goal, which he feels will give him a place in the world, will provide him with security, and will preserve his self-esteem. Life is a dynamic striving. "The life of the human soul is not a 'being' but a 'becoming' " (Adler, 1963a, p. ix).

8. The central striving of human beings has been variously described as completion (Adler, 1958), perfection (Adler, 1964f), superiority (Adler, 1926), self-realization (Horney, 1951), self-actualiza-

tion (Goldstein, 1939), competence (White, 1957), and mastery (Adler, 1926). Adler distinguishes between such strivings in terms of the direction a striving takes. If the strivings are solely for the individual's greater glory, he considers them socially useless and, in extreme conditions, a characteristic of mental problems. On the other hand, if the strivings are for the purpose of overcoming life's problems, the individual is engaged in the striving for self-realization, in contributing to his fellowman, in making the world a better place to live.

9. Moving through life, the individual is confronted with alternatives. Since Adlerians are either nondeterminists or soft determinists, the conceptualization of a man as a creative, choosing, self-determined decision maker permits him to choose the goals he wants to pursue. He may select useful, socially contributive goals or he may devote himself to the useless side of life. He may choose to be task oriented or he may, as does the neurotic, concern himself with his own superiority, protecting himself from threats to his sense of personal worth.

10. The freedom to choose (McArthur, 1958) introduces the concepts of *value* and *meaning* into psychology, concepts that were anathema at the time (1931) that Adler wrote his *What Life Should Mean to You*. The greatest value for the Adlerian is *Gemeinschaftsgefühl*, or social interest. Although Adler contends that it is an innate feature of man, at least as potential, acceptance of this criterion is not absolutely necessary. Since man lives among his fellowmen, he possesses the capacity for coexisting and interrelating with his fellowman. Indeed, the "iron logic of social living" (Adler, 1959) demands that he do so. As a result, man is responsible for developing his social interest, and even in severe psychopathol-

ogy, total extinction of social interest does not occur. Even the psychotic retains some commonality with his more "normal" fellowman.

As Rabbi Akiva noted two millennia ago, "The greatest principle of living is to love one's neighbor as oneself." If we regard ourselves as fellow human beings with fellow feeling, we are socially contributive people interested in the common welfare and, by Adler's pragmatic definition of *normality,* mentally healthy (Dreikurs, 1969; Shoben, 1957).

If my feeling derives from my observation and conviction that life and people are hostile and I am inferior, I may divorce myself from the direct solution of life's problems and strive for personal superiority through overcompensation, through wearing a mask, through withdrawal, through attempting only safe tasks where the outcome promises to be successful, and through other devices for protecting my self-esteem. The neurotic, by virtue of his ability to choose, creates difficulty for himself by setting up a "bad me" (symptoms, "ego-alien" thoughts, "bad behavior") that prevents him from implementing his good intentions. Adler's description of the neurotic in terms of his movement was that he displayed a "hesitating attitude" toward life (1964a). Also, the neurotic was described as a "yes-but" personality (Adler, 1934); at still other times, he was described as an "If only . . ." personality (Adler, 1964a). "If only I didn't have these symptoms, I'd . . . ." The latter provided the rationale for "The Question," a device Adler used for the purposes of differential diagnosis as well as for an understanding of the individual's task avoidance.

11. Since Adlerians are concerned with process, little diagnosis is done in terms of nomenclature. Differential diagnosis between functional and organic disorder

does often present a problem. Since all behavior is purposeful, a *psychogenic* symptom will have a psychological purpose and an *organic* symptom will have a somatic purpose. An Adlerian would ask "The Question" (Adler, 1964a; Dreikurs, 1958, 1962), "If I had a magic wand or a magic pill which would eliminate your symptom immediately, what would be different in your life?" If the patient answers, "I'd go out more often socially" or "I'd write my book," the symptom would most likely be psychogenic. If the patient responds, "I wouldn't have this excruciating pain," the symptom would most likely be organic.

An internist referred a woman to an Adlerian therapist because she complained of falling sensations. He thought it was an hysterical symptom. She told the therapist that the symptoms first occurred after breaking her engagement with her fiancé. She was asked "The Question." The patient said, "If I got better, then I wouldn't have these falling sensations." The therapist then asked the internist to reexamine the patient. She was given more tests; all were negative. The physician wanted to discharge her from the hospital and re-refer her to the therapist who asked the internist to keep her in the hospital and continue the tests. Several days later, the physician telephoned, and asked, "How did you know my patient had Von Recklinghausen's disease?" The therapist not only did not know she had Von Recklinghausen's disease, he did not know what Von Recklinghausen's disease was. However, the patient was spared psychotherapy and received the medical treatment she required.

12. Life presents challenges in the form of the life tasks. Adler named three of these explicitly but referred to two others without specifically naming them (Dreikurs & Mosak, 1966). The original three tasks were those of *society, work,* and *sex.* We have already alluded to the first. However, since we exist in two sexes, we must also learn how to relate to that fact. We must define our sex roles, partly on the basis of cultural definitions and stereotypes, and train ourselves to relate to the *other,* not the *opposite,* sex. Other people, of either sex, do not represent the enemy. They are our fellows with whom we must learn to cooperate. Third, since no man can claim self-sufficiency, we are interdependent. Each of us is dependent upon the labor of other people. In turn, they are dependent upon our contribution. Work thus becomes essential for human survival. The cooperative individual assumes this role willingly. He cheerfully accepts his part in the human enterprise.

Recently a fourth (Dreikurs & Mosak, 1967) and fifth task (Mosak & Dreikurs, 1967) have been described. Although Adler alluded to the *spiritual,* he never specifically named it (Jahn & Adler, 1964). But man must deal with the problem of defining the nature of his universe, the existence and nature of God, and how one relates to these concepts he creates. Finally, man must cope with *himself.* William James (1890) made the distinction between the self as subject and the self as object, and it is as imperative, for the sake of mental health, that good relations exist between the "I" and the "me" as between the "I" and other people.

13. Since life is bigger than we are and constantly provides challenges, providing problems for us to solve, living life demands courage (Neuer, 1936). Courage is not an *ability* one either possesses or lacks. Nor is courage synonymous with bravery, like falling on a grenade to save one's buddies from injury or death. *Courage* refers to the *willingness* to engage in risk-taking behavior. Anyone is *capable* of courageous behavior provided

he is *willing*. His willingness will depend upon many variables, internal and external, such as the life-style convictions, the degree of social interest, the extent of risk as the individual appraises it, and whether the individual is task oriented or prestige oriented. Since life offers few guarantees, all living requires risk taking. It would require very little courage to live if we were perfect, omniscient, omnipotent. The question we must each answer is whether we have the courage to live despite the knowledge of our imperfection (Lazarsfeld, 1966).

The courageous man, the man with *Gemeinschaftsgefühl*, says, "Here I am!" when life challenges him, and since life is a process of overcoming, the man of courage believes with Martin Luther King, "We shall overcome!"

14. Life has no intrinsic meaning. *We* give meaning to life, each of us in his own fashion. We declare it to be meaningful, meaningless, an absurdity, a prison sentence (cf., the adolescent's justification for doing as he pleases—"I didn't ask to be born"), a vale of tears, a preparation for the next world, and so on. Dreikurs (1957, 1971) maintained that the meaning of life resided in doing for others, in contributing to social life and to social change. Victor Frankl (1963) believes the meaning of life lies in love, expressing a psychological variation of the 1950's popular song, "Nature Boy" in which the refrain went, "The greatest thing you'll ever learn is to love and be loved in return." The meaning we attribute to life will "determine" our behavior. We will behave *as if* life were really in accord with our perceptions, and, therefore, certain meanings will have greater practical utility than others. The optimist will live an optimistic life, take his chances, and not be discouraged by failure and adversity. He will be able to distinguish between failing and being a failure. The pessimist will refuse to be engaged with life, refuse to try, sabotage his efforts if he does attempt, and, through his methods of operation, endeavor to confirm his preexisting pessimistic anticipations (Krausz, 1935).

Other Systems

Students often have asked, "Do you Adlerians believe in sex too?" The question is not always asked facetiously. Freud accorded sex the status of the master motive in behavior. Adler merely categorized sex as one of several tasks the individual was required to solve. Freud employed esoteric jargon and Adler favored common-sense language. One story has it that a psychiatrist took Adler to task after a lecture, denigrating his approach with the criticism, "You're only talking common sense," to which Adler replied, "I wish more psychiatrists did." We can place other differences between these two men in columnar form.

A more extended comparison of Freud's and Adler's concepts of man may be found in articles by H. W. von Sassen (1967) and Otto Hinrichsen (1913).

Adler and the neo-Freudians. Adler once proclaimed that he was more concerned that his theories survived than that people remembered to associate his theories with his name. His wish apparently was granted. In discussing Adler's influence upon contemporary psychological theory and practice, Henri Ellenberger (1970) comments, "It would not be easy to find another author from which so much has been borrowed from all sides without acknowledgement than Adler" (p. 645). Many neo-Freudians have credited Adler with contributing to and influencing their work. In her last book, Karen Horney (1951) wrote of

Freud	Adler
1. Objective	1. Subjective
2. Physiological substratum for theory	2. A social psychology
3. Emphasized causality	3. Emphasized teleology
4. Reductionistic. The individual was divided into "parts" which were antagonistic toward each other, e.g., id-ego-superego, Eros vs. Thanatos, conscious vs. unconscious.	4. Holistic. The individual is indivisible. He is a unity and all "parts" (memory, emotions, behavior) are in the service of the whole individual.
5. The study of the individual centers about the intrapersonal, the intrapsychic.	5. Man can only be understood interpersonally, a social being moving through and interacting with his environment.
6. The establishment of intrapsychic harmony constitutes the ideal goal of psychotherapy. "Where id was, there shall ego be."	6. The expansion of the individual, self-realization, and the enhancement of social interest represent the ideal goals for the individual.
7. Man is basically "bad." Civilization attempts to domesticate him for which he pays a heavy price. Through therapy the instinctual demands may be sublimated but not eliminated.	7. Man is neither "good" nor "bad," but as a creative, choosing human being, he may choose to be "good" or "bad" or both depending upon his life-style and his appraisal of the immediate situation and its payoffs. Through the medium of therapy man can choose to actualize himself.
8. Man is a victim of both his instinctual life and of his civilization.	8. Man, as chooser, can shape both his internal and external environment. Although he is not the complete master of his fate and cannot always choose what will happen to him, he can always choose the posture he will adopt toward life's stimuli.
9. Freud's description of child development was postdictive and not based upon direct observation of children but upon the free associations of adults.	9. Children were studied directly in families, in schools and in family education centers.
10. Emphasis upon the Oedipus situation and its resolution.	10. Emphasis upon the family constellation.
11. Men are enemies. They are our competitors, and we must protect ourselves from them. Theodore Reik (1948) quotes Nestroy, "If chance brings two wolves together, . . . neither feels the least uneasy because the other is a wolf; two human beings, however, can never meet in the forest, but one must think: That fellow may be a robber" (p. 477).	11. Other men are *mitmenschen,* fellow human beings. They are our equals, our collaborators, our cooperators in life.
12. Women feel inferior because they envy men their penis. Women are inferior. "Anatomy is destiny."	12. Women feel inferior because in our cultural milieu women are undervalued. Men have privileges, rights, preferred status although in the current cultural ferment, these roles are being reevaluated.
13. Neurosis has a sexual etiology.	13. Neurosis is a failure of learning, a product of distorted perceptions.
14. Neurosis is the price we pay for civilization.	14. Neurosis is the price we pay for our lack of civilization.

"neurotic ambition," "the need for perfection," and "the category of power." "All drives for glory have in common the reaching out for greater knowledge, wisdom, virtue or powers than are given to human beings; they all aim at the *absolute,* the unlimited, the in-

finite" (pp. 34–35). Those familiar with Adler's writings on the neurotic's perfectionistic, godlike striving will immediately be struck with the similarity in viewpoint.

Horney (1951) rejected Freud's pessimism, "his disbelief in human goodness and human growth," in favor of the Adlerian view that man could grow and could "become a decent human being" and that man's potentialities "deteriorate if his relationship to others and hence to himself is, and continues to be, disturbed."

Others have also remarked upon the resemblance between the theories of Horney and Adler; the reviewer of one Horney book wrote that Karen Horney had just written a new book by Alfred Adler (Farau, 1953).

Erich Fromm's theories also express views similar to those of Adler. According to Fromm, man makes choices. The attitude of the mother in childrearing is of paramount importance. Life fosters feelings of powerlessness and anxiety. Patrick Mullahy (1955) indicates that

The only adequate solution, according to Fromm, is a relationship with man and nature, chiefly by love and productive work, which strengthens the total personality, sustains the person in his sense of uniqueness, and at the same time gives him a feeling of belonging, a sense of unity and common destiny with mankind. (pp. 251–52)

Although Harry Sullivan places greater emphasis upon developmental child psychology than does Adler, Sullivan's "man" moves through life in much the same manner as does Adler's. Thus, Sullivan (1954) speaks of the "security operations" of the individual, a direct translation of Adler's and Lene Credner's (1930) *"Sicherungen."* His "good me" and "bad me" dichotomy, in expression if not in manner of development, is essentially the same as that described by Adlerians.

So many similarities between Adler and the neo-Freudians have been noted that Gardner Murphy (1947) has concluded, "If this way of reasoning is correct, neurosis should be the general characteristic of man under industrialism, a point suspected by many Freudians and, in par-

ticular, by that branch of the Freudian school (Horney and her associates) that has learned most from Adler" (p. 569). A summary of such resemblances appears in Heinz and Rowena Ansbacher's *Individual Psychology of Alfred Adler* (1956) as well as in an article by Walter James (1947). Fritz Wittels (1939) has proposed that the neo-Freudians should more properly be called "neo-Adlerians" and a study by Heinz Ansbacher (1952) suggests that many traditional Freudians would concur.

Adler and Rogers. Although the therapies of Adler and Carl Rogers are diametrically opposed, their theories share many commonalities. Both are phenomenological, goal directed, and holistic. Each views man as self-consistent, creative, and capable of change. To illustrate, Rogers (1951) postulates the following:

1. The organism reacts as an organized whole to the phenomenal field. . . . [p. 486].
2. The best vantage point for understanding behavior is from the internal frame of reference of the individual himself [p. 494].
3. The organism reacts to the field as it is experienced and perceived. . . . [p. 484–85].
4. The organism has one basic tendency and striving—to actualize, maintain, and enhance the experiencing organism [p. 487].

Much of the early research on nondirective and client-centered therapy used as a criterion measure the discrepancy between *self-concept* and *self-ideal*. The Adlerian would describe this self-ideal congruence or discrepancy as a measure of inferiority feelings.

Adler and Ellis. Both cognitive psychologies, the two theories exhibit many points of convergence. What Adler calls "basic mistakes," Albert Ellis refers to as irrational beliefs or attitudes. Both accept the notion that emotions are actually a form of thinking, that people create or control their emotions by controlling their thinking. They agree that we are not victims of our emotions but their creators. In psychotherapy, they (1) adopt similar stances with respect to unconscious motivation, (2) confront the patient with his irrational ideas (basic mistakes or internalized sentences), (3) counterpropagandize the patient, (4) insist upon action, and (5) constantly *encourage* the patient to assume responsibility for the direction of his life in more positive channels. The last phrase seems to reflect the major disagreement between Adler and Ellis, namely, what is "positive." Ellis (1957) argues,

Where Adler writes, therefore, that "All my efforts are devoted towards increasing the social interest of the patient," the rational therapist would prefer to say, "Most of my efforts are devoted towards increasing the self-interest of the patient." He assumes that if the individual possesses rational self-interest he will, on both biological and logical grounds, almost invariably tend to have a high degree of social interest as well. (p. 43)

Adler and Other Systems. The many points of convergence and divergence between Adler and several of the existentialist thinkers have been noted by many writers (Birnbaum, 1961; Farau, 1964; Frankl, 1970). Phyllis Bottome had written in 1939 that "Adler was the first founder of an existence psychology" (p. 199). Since existential psychology is not a school but a viewpoint, it is difficult to make comparisons but the interested reader may discover for himself in an editorial by Ansbacher (1959) the lines of continuity between Adler and current existential thought.

The recognition of Adler as one of the earliest humanistic psychologists is clear.

Ellis (1970) pays homage to Adler as "one of the first humanistic psychologists" (p. 32). Abraham Maslow (1962, 1970) published five papers in Adlerian journals over a period of 35 years. As we have already observed, many of Adler's ideas have been incorporated by the humanistic psychologists with little awareness of Adler's contributions. The parameter, "The model of man as a composite of part functions" that James Bugental (1963) questions has been repudiated by Adlerians for almost half a century. Bugental proposes: "That the defining concept of man basic to the new humanistic movement in psychology is that *man is the process that supersedes the sum of his part functions.*" We may compare this proposal with that of Dreikurs (1960a), "The whole is more than a sum total of its parts; therefore, it cannot be explained by any number of qualities but only understood as an indivisible whole in motion toward a goal" (p. 194). Although Dreikurs's statement antedates Bugental's by only 3 years, the former pointed out in a previous article (1960b), "The holistic concept of man, which in theory is generally approved, is far from being understood today, and was less so in Adler's time. At that time his only support came from Gestalt psychologists. . . ." (p. 98).

HISTORY

Precursors

Adler's insistence that man cannot be studied in isolation but only in his social context was previously expressed by Aristotle who referred to man as a *zoon politikon,* a political animal (Adler, 1959). He related his description of personality types to Hippocrates's humoral theory but after 1927 made no further mention of it. Adler exhibits his affinity with the philosophy of stoicism as both Ellenberger (1970), and H. N. Simpson (1966) point out. Other commentators have noted the resemblance of Adler's writings to Kant's philosophy, especially with respect to the categorical imperative, private logic, and overcoming. Adler and Nietzsche have often been compared and much has been made of their common usage of the concept of the *will to power.* However, Adler spoke of it in terms of the normal strivings for competence and Nietzsche's references to this concept referred to what Adler would call the "useless side of life." Nietzsche stressed the *Uebermensch* (Superman) and Adler spoke of equality. Adler further stressed *social feeling,* a concept totally alien to the Nietzschian philosophy.

Throughout history, philosophers have struggled with the mind-body problem. At the dawn of the modern scientific era, the rationalistic and empirical schools of philosophy were providing explanations for the connections between mind and body. The issue lay relatively dormant within psychology and experienced a renaissance when psychologists and psychiatrists began to address themselves to the study of psychosomatic syndromes. Psychosomatic and somatopsychic hypotheses were advanced to explain how emotions could influence the production of symptoms and how bodily states might create emotional or mental illness. Adler rejected such divisions. Like Kurt Lewin (1935), he rejected categorization and dichotomies. Like Jan Smuts (1961), he was a holist; his title, *Individual Psychology,* was not meant to describe the psychology of the individual. It referred rather to Adler's holistic stance, that man could be understood only as a whole, that man was an indivisible unity. To study him atomistically was to not capture fully

the nature of man. For Adler, the question was neither "How does mind affect body?" nor "How does body affect mind?" but rather how does the individual use his body and mind in the pursuit of his goals? Although Adler's book, *Study of Organ Inferiority and Its Psychical Compensation* (1917), might seem to contradict the above statements in that Adler expresses a causalistic viewpoint, this highly original theory was formulated during the period when Adler was a member of the Freudian circle. Later he added the subjective factor,

It might be suggested, therefore, that in order to find out where a child's interest lies, we need only to ascertain which organ is defective. But things do not work out quite so simply. The child does not experience the fact of organ inferiority in the way that an external observer sees it, but as modified by his own scheme of apperception. (Adler, 1969)

Perhaps the greatest influence upon Adler was Hans Vaihinger's (1965) "philosophy of 'as if.' " According to Vaihinger, a fiction is "a mere piece of imagination" that deviates from reality but that is nevertheless utilitarian for the individual. Both the concept of the world and the concept of the self are subjective, that is, fictional, and therefore in error. *Truth* is "only the most expedient error, that is, the system of ideas which enables us to act and to deal with things most rapidly, neatly, and safely, and with the minimum of irrational elements" (Vaihinger, 1965, p. 108).

Finally, Adler's psychology has a religious tone (Adler, 1958; Jahn & Adler, 1964). His placement of social interest at the pinnacle of his value theory is in the tradition of those religions that stress men's responsibility for each other and "Love thy neighbor." Indeed, Adler (Rasey, 1956) maintained that "Individual Psychology makes good religion if you are unfortunate enough not to have another'' (p. 254).

Beginnings

Adler was born near Vienna on February 7, 1870, and died while on a lecture tour in Aberdeen, Scotland, on May 27, 1937. Graduating from the University of Vienna in 1895, Adler entered private practice as an ophthalmologist in 1898. He later switched to general practice and then to neurology. In this period, Adler gave portents of his later social orientation by writing a book on the health of tailors (1898). In this respect, he may be regarded as the progenitor of industrial medicine.

In 1902 Adler, at Freud's invitation, joined in the latter's Wednesday evening discussion circle. Biographers agree that Adler wrote two defenses of Freud's theories that may have gained him the invitation. Although textbooks frequently refer to Adler as a student of Freud, Adler was actually a colleague who had already established his own place as a physician (Ansbacher, 1962; Ellenberger, 1970; Federn, 1963; Maslow, 1962). Through the next decade, Adler had one foot in and one foot out of the Freudian circle. Although his *Study of Organ Inferiority* won Freud's unqualified endorsement, Adler's introduction of the aggression instinct in 1908 met with Freud's disapproval. Not until 1923, long after Adler had discarded instinct theory, did Freud incorporate the aggressive instinct into psychoanalysis (Sicher & Mosak, 1967) at which time Adler declared, "I enriched psychoanalysis by the aggressive drive. I gladly make them a present of it!" (Bottome, 1939, p. 63).

Adler's increasing divergence from Freud's viewpoint led to discomfort and disillusion in the Vienna Society. Adler criticized Freud's sexual stance; Freud condemned Adler's ego psychology. They disagreed on (1) the unity of the neuroses, (2) penis envy (sexual) versus the masculine protest (social), (3) the defensive role of the ego in neuroses, and (4) the role of the unconscious. Freud did not think Adler had discovered anything new but had merely reinterpreted what psychoanalysis had already said. He believed that what Adler discovered was "trivial," "methodologically deplorable and condemns his whole work to sterility" (Colby, 1951). After a series of meetings where these issues were discussed in an atmosphere of fencing, heckling, and vitriol (Brome, 1968), Adler in 1911 resigned as president of the Vienna Psychoanalytic Society. Later that year, Freud forced the choice between Adler and himself. Several members of the circle expressed their sympathy for Adler by resigning and forming the Society for Free Psychoanalytic Research, the forerunner of the *Internationale Vereinigung für Individualpsychologie*. In 1914 they published the first issue of the *Zeitschrift für Individualpsychologie*.

During the next decade, with the exception of the war period, Adler and his co-workers developed the social view of the neuroses. Their focus was primarily clinical although Adler (1914) as early as 1908 had demonstrated an interest in children and in education. In 1922 Adler initiated what was perhaps the first community-outreach program, a child-guidance center within the community. These centers were located in public schools and conducted by psychologists who served without pay. The method, for which Adler drew much criticism, was that of public family education, a method still used in Adlerian family education centers. Twenty-eight such centers existed in Vienna until 1934 when with the advent of Nazism the centers were closed. This form of center was transported to the United States by Rudolf Dreikurs and his students (Dreikurs et al., 1959). The success of these centers motivated the Vienna School authorities to invite several Adlerians to plan a school along Adlerian lines and from this invitation emerged the school described in Oskar Spiel's *Discipline without Punishment* (1962). The school emphasized encouragement, class discussions, democratic principles, the responsibility of children for themselves and for each other, educational methods that are still in use.

The social orientation of individual psychology inevitably led to interest in group methods. Adler introduced family therapy (1922). Dreikurs (1959) is credited with the first use of group psychotherapy in private practice.

Between World Wars I and II, Adlerian groups existed in 20 European countries and in the United States. In 1926 Adler was invited to the United States to lecture and demonstrate, and until 1934 when fascism took hold in Austria, he divided his time between the United States, where he was on the medical faculty of the Long Island College of Medicine, and abroad. Two of his children, Alexandra and Kurt, now practice psychiatry in New York City. With the march of Nazism, many Adlerians were forced to flee their European homelands, and after many hardships, Adlerians made the United States the center of their activities. Today Individual Psychology societies exist in the United States, England, Canada, France, Denmark, Switzerland, Germany, Austria, the Netherlands, Greece, Italy, Israel, and Australia.

Current Status

The resurgence of the Adlerian school after the dispersion from Europe was an uphill effort. Personal hardships of refugee Adlerians were compounded by the existing psychological climate in this country. The economic depression still prevailed. The Freudian school held a near monopoly both in the treatment area and with respect to appointments in medical schools. Some Adlerians defected; others became crypto-Adlerians. However, others persevered in retaining their identity and their optimism. Local societies were founded and 1952 saw the formation of the American Society of Adlerian Psychology. Several journals appeared; the two major American ones are the *Journal of Individual Psychology* and *Individual Psychologist*. The *Journal* is the successor to the *Individual Psychology Bulletin* of which Dreikurs was for many years the editor. The International Association of Individual Psychology also publishes the *Individual Psychology Newsletter,* whose editor is Paul Rom.

Training institutes that offer certificates in psychotherapy, counseling, and child guidance are found in New York, Chicago, Minneapolis, Berkeley, St. Louis, Dayton, Toledo, Ft. Wayne, Cleveland, Vancouver, and Toronto. Individual courses and programs of study are offered at many universities, such as Oregon, Arizona, West Virginia, Vermont, Governors State, Southern Illinois, De Paul, and Rhode Island College. Masters degrees based on an Adlerian curriculum are offered by Bowie State College and by the Alfred Adler Institute of Chicago. Further information concerning these offerings may be obtained from the North American Society of Adlerian Psychology, whose address is 159 N. Dearborn St., Chicago, Illinois 60601.

Although Adlerian psychology was once dismissed as moribund, superficial (i.e., an "ego psychology"), as being suitable mainly for children, it is today a viable psychology that pioneered in the holistic, phenomenological, social, teleological view of man. A value psychology, (Adler wrote *What Life Should Mean to You* in 1931), its students such as Viktor Frankl and Rollo May acknowledge their debt to Adler. Frankl (1970) who was associated with Adler from 1924 to 1927 wrote, "What he . . . achieved and accomplished was no less than a Copernican switch. . . . Beyond this, Alfred Adler may well be regarded as an existential thinker and as a fore-runner of the existential-psychiatric movement" (p. 38); May (1970) expresses his debt as follows,

. . . I appreciate Adler more and more. . . . Adler's thoughts as I learned them in studying with him in Vienna in the summers of 1932 and 1933 led me indirectly into psychology, and were very influential in the later work in this country of Sullivan and William Alanson White, etc. (p. 39)

Ego psychology has permeated other psychological viewpoints. Albert Ellis (1970, 1971) finds his rational-emotive psychology to parallel that of Adler's. The humanistic viewpoint of Abraham Maslow derives in part from Adler. In 1970 he wrote, "For me Alfred Adler becomes more and more correct year by year. As the facts come in, they give stronger and stronger support to his image of man. I should say that in one respect especially the times have not yet caught up with him. I refer to his holistic emphasis" (p. 39).

Today's Adlerian may operate as a traditional clinician. But he is still innovative. Joshua Bierer has been a pioneer in social psychiatry (1969) and a leader in the day-hospital movement (1951). Therapeutic social clubs are in operation at the Alfred Adler Mental Hygiene Clinic in New York and at St. Joseph Hospital in Chicago. Dreikurs originated multiple psychotherapy (1950) and he, Harold Mosak, and Bernard Shulman have contributed to its development (1952a; 1952b). Rudolf Dreikurs, Asya Kadis, Helene Papanek, and Bernard Shulman have made extensive contributions to group therapy. In a joint research project with the Counseling Center (Rogerian) of the University of Chicago, John Shlien, Mosak, and Dreikurs (1962) investigated the effects of time limits in therapy. Since he prefers the goal of prevention to that of healing, the Adlerian functions extensively in the area of education. Manford Sonstegard, Raymond Lowe, Bronia Grunwald, Oscar Christensen, Raymond Corsini, and Loren Grey are among those responsible for applying Adlerian principles in the school situation. Mosak (1971) has participated in a program that introduced Adlerian methods into an entire school system. All these have been students of Dreikurs, who transported the tradition from Vienna, and who himself has made the greatest contributions in this area. In the Adlerian social tradition, Adlerians may be involved in community outreach programs or dedicating their efforts to the study of subjects such as drugs, aging, delinquency, religion, and poverty.

Although many Adlerian clinicians, especially psychiatrists, are committed by virtue of their training to the disease model, the Adlerian philosophy of becoming, its preoccupation with movement, means that the contemporary Adlerian finds the growth model of personality infinitely more congenial than the sickness model. The Adlerian is not interested in curing sick individuals or a sick society. His interests lie in reeducating individuals and in reshaping society so men can live together as equals in a free society.

PERSONALITY

Theory of Personality

Adlerian psychology is a psychology of use rather than of possession. This assumption decreases the importance of the questions often raised in elementary psychology courses of: "How do heredity and environment shape the individual?" or "How much of intelligence is hereditary and how much is due to environment?" The functionalist, holistic Adlerian asks instead, "How does the individual *use* his heredity and environment?" and "How does he *use* his total resources to modify his heredity and his environment?"

Growing up in the social environment of the family, the child attempts mastery of his environment. In so doing, he learns about his strengths, abilities, deficiencies, and his place in the scheme of things. To learn, he must size up his environment. Although the child ordinarily is an excellent observer, he is often a poor evaluator and interpreter.

For Adler, the family constellation constitutes the primary social environment for the growing child whose situation is comparable to that of an immigrant in a foreign country—unable to comprehend the language and unable to be understood. Ignorant of the rules, the customs, he discovers to his dismay that he cannot find his way about the territory until he learns the appropriate language and behavior. Parents, siblings, peers, institutions, and the culture exert influences in their efforts to socialize him. Until he learns what is expected of him, he is relatively helpless, incompetent, inferior. So he observes his environment, makes evaluations, and arrives progressively at various conclusions about himself, his worth, and his environment, what it demands of him, and how he can acquire "citizenship in the new world." Through observation, exploration, trial and error, and by getting feedback from his environment, he learns what gains approval and disapproval and how he can achieve significance. Aside from his perceptions and evaluations, the child is not a passive receptor of family influences. He actively and creatively is busy modifying his environment, training his siblings, and "raising" his parents. (Listen to the mother who despairingly proclaims, "That child will be the death of me yet!") He wants to belong, to be a part of, to count. Erwin Wexberg (1929) maintains that this conative striving to belong is biological. Adler (1964b) held that it is innate as potential.

Whether this need to belong is biological or learned, every child searches for significance. He jockeys for position within his family constellation looking for a "place in the sun." One sibling becomes the "best" child, another the "worst" one. Being favored, being one of the favored sex within the family, adopting the family values, identifying or allying oneself with a parent or sibling may provide the grounds for the feeling of having a place. Handicaps, organ inferiorities, or being an orphan are other "position makers" for some children.

Of supreme importance for the child is the child's position in the family constellation. Thus, it would appear that the first child usually is a conservative, and the second is often a rebel. The baby is ordinarily either a prince or one who stands on the tips of his toes to see above his preceding siblings. If these general characteristics possess any validity, at best they exist as statistical probabilities and not as defining traits. Considering the family constellation in terms of birth order or ordinal position creates the problem of characterizing, let us say, the fifth child in the family. Although he is often encountered in the therapy situation, he never receives any attention in the literature. Birth order, per se, also ignores the sexual position of the child. The children in two-sibling families in which the possible configurations are boy-boy, girl-girl, boy-girl, and girl-boy do not possess similar characteristics based upon ordinal position alone (Shulman & Mosak, 1977).

The Adlerian prefers to study the family constellation in terms of the *psychological* position. A simple example illustrates this point of view. Take two siblings separated in age by 10 years. In birth order research, these would be treated as a first child and a second child. From the Adlerian point of view the psychological position of each child would *most likely* be that of an only child with *perhaps* the older child functioning as an additional parent figure for the younger. The italicized terms *most likely* and *perhaps* are used expressly to indicate that: (1) Adlerians do not recognize a causalistic, one-to-one relationship between family position and sibling traits; (2) whatever relationship exists can only be understood in context, that is, when one knows the family climate and the total configuration of factors in the family constellation; and (3) Adler, whenever he generalized or ventured a prediction, was fond of reminding his students, "Everything could also be quite different."

The search for significance and the consequent sibling competition reflect the values of the competitive society in which we live. We are encouraged to be first, to excel, to be popular, to be athletic, to be a "real" man, to "never say die," that "practice makes perfect," and to "dream the impossible dream." Consequently, each child must stake out for himself a piece of "territory," which includes the attributes or abilities that he hopes will give him a feeling of worth. If through his evaluations of his own potency (abilities, courage, and confidence) he is convinced that he can achieve this place through useful endeavor, he will pursue "the useful side of life." Should he feel that he cannot attain the goal of having a "place" in this fashion, he will become discouraged and engage in disturbed or disturbing behavior in his efforts to find a place. For the Adlerian the "maladjusted" child is not a "sick" child. He is a "discouraged" child. Dreikurs (1947, 1948) classifies the goals of the discouraged child into four groups—attention getting, power seeking, revenge taking, and declaring deficiency or defeat. Dreikurs is speaking of immediate rather than long-range goals. These are the goals of children's "misbehavior," not of all child behavior (Mosak & Mosak, 1975).

In the process of becoming (and Adler had used the term "becoming" in 1930 [Adler, 1963b]) an inhabitant of the new country, that is, in his transformation to becoming a socialized human being, the child forms conclusions on the basis of his subjective experiences. Since judgment and logical processes are not highly developed in the young child, many of his growing convictions contain errors or only partial "truths." Nevertheless, he accepts these conclusions about himself and others as if they were true even though they are "fictions." They are subjective evaluations, biased apperception of himself and of the world, rather than objective "reality." Thus, one can be truly inferior without feeling inferior. Conversely, one can feel inferior without being inferior.

The child creates a cognitive map, the life-style that will assist "little" him, in coping with the "big" world. As Werner Wolff (1946) has observed, the young child grows up in a world of legs—people's legs, table legs, and chair legs. A systematic review of the life-style concept being available (Ansbacher, 1967), only a brief, simplified description follows.

The convictions developed by the individual may be categorized in many ways but whatever the taxonomy, they include the individual's perception of himself in relationship to his perception of the world. The life-style includes the aspirations, the long-range goals of the individual, a "statement" of the conditions, personal or social, that are requisite for the individual's "security." The latter are also fictions and are stated in therapy as "If only . . . , then I. . . ." Mosak (1954) divided life-style convictions into four groups:

1. The *self-concept*—the convictions I have about who I am.
2. The *self-ideal* (Adler coined this phrase in 1912)—the convictions of what I should be or am obliged to be to have a place.
3. The *Weltbild* or "picture of the world"—convictions about the not-self (world, people, nature, and so on) and what the world demands of me.
4. The *ethical convictions*—the personal "right-wrong" code.

When there is a discrepancy between self and ideal-self convictions ("I am short; I should be tall") *inferiority feelings* ensue. Although an infinite variety of inferiority feelings exist, one should be mentioned that Adler discussed while he was still in the Freudian Society, which

eventuated in the rift between Adler and Freud. It assumes monumental importance in some circles today—the masculine protest. In a culture that places a premium on masculinity, some women feel inferior because they have not been accorded the prerogatives or privileges of men ("I am a woman; I should be equal to man"). But men also suffered from the masculine protest because being a man is not sufficient to provide a "place" for some men ("I am a man; but I should be a *real* man"). Since Adler believed in the equality of the sexes, he could not accept these fictions (Mosak & Schneider, 1977). As the battle for equality between the sexes is now being fought, one observes confirmation of Wexberg's prediction (1929) that "The family in its present form will surely vanish in the constantly progressing process of woman's economic emancipation" (p. 203).

Lack of congruence between convictions in the self-concept and those in the *Weltbild* ("I am weak and helpless. Life is dangerous") results also in inferiority feelings. Discrepancies between self-concept and ethical convictions ("one should always tell the truth; I lie") lead to inferiority feelings in the moral realm. Thus, the guilt feeling is merely a variant of the inferiority feeling whose several purposes are: (1) to feel important; (2) to feel superior to others who commit transgressions and do not have the decency to feel bad; (3) "to hide behind guilt feelings for things past, but [does not] attempt to create an improved present"; (4) to provide a logical excuse with which we deceive ourselves concerning our real intentions, appearing "only if one is unwilling to amend" (Dreikurs, 1950) his behavior; (5) to exempt us from punishment; and (6) to create a conflict between the "good me" and the "bad me," "between God and Satan."

These variations of inferiority feelings in and of themselves are not "abnormal." It would be difficult to quarrel with Adler's observations that to live is to *feel* inferior. It is only when the individual acts *as if* he were inferior, develops symptoms, or behaves as "sick" that we see evidences of what in the medical model would be called *pathology* and what Adlerians call *discouragement* or the *inferiority complex*. To oversimplify, the *inferiority feeling* is universal and "normal"; the *inferiority complex* reflects the discouragement of a limited segment of our society and is usually "abnormal." The former may be masked or hidden from the view of others; the latter is an open demonstration of inadequacy, default, or "sickness."

Using his "map," the individual facilitates his movement through life. It permits him to evaluate and understand experience. It enables him to predict experience and it permits him to control experience. Lawrence Frank (1939) writes in this connection,

. . . the personality process might be regarded as a sort of rubber stamp which the individual imposes upon every situation by which he gives it the configuration that he, as an individual, requires; in so doing he necessarily ignores or subordinates many aspects of the situation that for him are irrelevant and meaningless and selectively reacts to those aspects that are personally significant (p. 392).

Although the life-style is the instrument for coping with experience, it is very largely nonconscious. The life-style comprises the cognitive organization of the individual rather than the behavioral organization. As an illustration, the conviction "I require excitement" may lead to the vocational choices of actor, racing car driver, explorer, or to "acting out behavior" ("if it's illegal, immoral, or fattening, I'm for it"). Such a conviction may further lead to creating and substituting symptoms, getting into jams or exciting situations, nightclubbing or betting at the race track, sabotaging psychotherapy, livening up a party, engaging in creative acts, or discovery.

Within the same life-style, one can behave usefully or uselessly. The above distinction permits some Adlerians (Dreikurs, 1961; Nikelly, 1971a) to distinguish between *psychotherapy* and *counseling*. The former, they maintain, has as its aim the change of life-style; the latter has as its goal the change of behavior within the existing life-style.

Many people treat the understanding of the individual life-style in much the same manner that Keats recorded his poetic credo on beauty and truth,

—that is all
Ye know on earth, and all ye need to know.
(*Ode on a Grecian Urn*)

However, Adlerians postulate that man cannot be understood independently of the field in which he functions. If Adlerians accepted the "ego" (they do occasionally use it as a synonym for "self" although they do not accept the Freudian tripartite topology), they would agree with Gordon Allport (1961) with respect to the contemporaneity of the ego. To understand a person at any moment would require knowledge of his life-style (his long-range goals), the tasks that confront him, his immediate goals, and his coping behavior according to his law of movement.

Since the Adlerian literature discusses the life tasks of occupation, society, and sex so extensively, the tasks, or rather the demands of life, will not be elaborated upon here, except for some brief comments. Lewis Way (1962) points out that "The problems they pose can never be solved once and for all, but demand from the individual a continuous and creative movement toward adaptation'' (pp. 179–80). This "creative movement toward adaptation," neither in life nor in society, has as its goal the development of passively "adjusted" people, mere responders to life's problems. Rather, people can and are obliged in terms of social interest to reshape their worlds. Way uses "adaptation" as a synonym for self-fulfillment, the highest need (self-actualization) in Maslow's (1970) hierarchy of needs.

Love, as an emotion, is like other emotions, cognitively based. People are not "victims" of their emotions or passions. They create emotions to assist them in the attainment of their goals. Love is the conjunctive emotion we create when we want to move toward people.

Although the life tasks demand solution, it is possible to avoid or postpone some if one can compensate in other areas. "Even successful persons fall into neurosis because they are not more successful" (Way, 1962, p. 206). The *neurotic symptom* is an expression of "I *can't* because I'm sick"; the person's movement betrays an "I *won't* because my self-esteem might get hurt" (Krausz, 1959, p. 112). Although the neurotic individual's movements are consonant with his "private logic" (Nikelly, 1971b), he still clings to the "common sense." He knows what he should do or feel, but he "can't." Adler referred to him as the "yes-but" personality. Eric Berne (1964) has graphically described his interpersonal maneuvers in the "Why don't you—Yes, but" game. The genesis of neurosis lies in discouragement. The individual avoids and postpones or takes circuitous routes to solutions so he can "save face." Even when he expects or arranges to fail, he tries to salvage some self-esteem. A student, fearful of failing an examination,

will refrain from studying. In the event he does fail, he merely has to hold out to the world (or be self-critical) that he was lazy or neglectful but not stupid.

The *psychotic's* goal of superiority is often loftier than can be achieved by mortal man. "Individual Psychology has shown that the goal of superiority can only be fixed at such altitudes when the individual has, by losing interest in others, also lost interest in his own reason and understanding . . . common sense has become useless to him" (Adler, 1964a, pp. 128–29). In the pseudowork area, he elects himself superintendent of the mental hospital. In the pseudosocial area, the hypomanic patient resembles the cheerful extrovert and the more acutely manic patient becomes a "name dropper" and "swallows up" people (Shulman, 1962). The paranoid patient pictures people as threatening and manifests his "search for glory," to use Karen Horney's (1951) phrase, by his persecutory delusion that *they* are conspiring to do something to *me.* He is the center of the people's attention. The delusions of grandeur of the psychotic depressive patient ("I'm the *worst* sinner of all time") and of the schizophrenic who believes he is the Christ are some other "solutions" to the spiritual pseudotasks. The reifying hallucinations of talking with the Devil fall similarly in this category (Adler, 1963b, Mosak & Fletcher, 1973).

The *psychologically healthy* or *normal* individual is one who has developed his social interest, who is willing to commit himself to life and the life tasks without evasion, excuse or "sideshows" (Wolfe, 1932). He employs his energies in being a fellowman with confidence and optimism in meeting life's challenges. He has his place. He feels a sense of belonging. He is contributive. He has his self-esteem. He has the "courage to be imperfect," and possesses the serene knowledge that he can be acceptable to others, although imperfect. Above all, he rejects the faulty values his culture projects and enforces and attempts to substitute for them values more consonant with the "ironclad logic of social living." Such a person does not exist nor will any psychotherapy produce such a person. Yet this is the Adlerian ideal, and since Adler's intent was to substitute small errors for larger errors, many of these goals can be approximated in psychotherapy. Many fortunate people, trained in courage (Adler, 1928) and social interest do it for themselves without therapeutic assistance.

Variety of Concepts

The simplicity of the Adlerian vocabulary renders definition and interpretation generally unnecessary. Yet some differences of opinion and emphasis about Adlerian concepts remain unresolved. In terms of *life-style,* Adlerians disagree with respect to what it describes—behavioral or cognitive organization. *Social interest* (Bickhard & Ford, 1976) apparently is not a unitary concept but a cluster of feelings and behaviors (Ansbacher, 1968). Although social interest is often described as "innate," many Adlerians wonder what makes it "so" since it appears to be neither genetic nor constitutional. As one looks at the theories of Adler, Freud, and Jung, one is struck with the effort on the part of all three to "biologize" their theories. Perhaps it was the temper of the times. Perhaps it was because all three were physicians. Perhaps it resulted from the need to make their theories respectable during a period when psychoanalysis was held in low esteem. None of these theories would incur any great damage if "instincts," "social interest," and "racial unconscious" were treated as psycho-

logical constructs rather than as biological processes. Adler, having introduced the concept of *organ inferiority* with its consequent compensation, actually had proposed a biopsychological theory, but it must be recalled that this transpired during his "Freudian period." Later he substituted the *social inferiority feeling* for actual organ inferiority, and with the exception of one important article (Shulman & Klapman, 1968), Adlerians publish little on organ inferiority. Although people undoubtedly do compensate for organ inferiority, the latter no longer is the cornerstone of the Adlerian edifice.

Gardner Murphy (1947) takes issue with Adler's use of compensation as the only defense mechanism. Literally, Adler's writings do read that way. On the other hand, if one reads more closely, compensation becomes an umbrella to cover all of the coping mechanisms. Thus, Adler speaks of safeguards, excuses, projection, the depreciation tendency, creating distance, and identification. Although a Freudian might view these as defense mechanisms the ego employs in its warfare with the instinctual drives, the Adlerian prefers to view them as problem-solving devices the person uses to protect his self-esteem rather than as defense mechanisms. Since Adlerians do not accept the concept of *the* unconscious, such mechanisms as repression and sublimation become irrelevant in the Adlerian framework. Adlerian theory has no room for instincts, drives, libido, and other alleged movers of men.

The *Journal of Individual Psychology* refers to itself as being "devoted to a holistic, phenomenological, teleological, field-theoretical, and socially oriented approach . . . ," placing it closer to Rogers, Maslow, the existential humanists, and some of the neo-Freudians than to the one-to-one (cause-effect, stimulus-response) psychologies. Because of the emphasis on behavior (movement), Adlerian psychology and behavior-modification theory have been equated. This is an error. Adlerians, although interested in changing behavior, have as their major goal not behavior modification, but motivation modification. Dreikurs (1963b) writes, "We do not attempt primarily to change behavior patterns or remove symptoms. If a patient improves his behavior because he finds it profitable at the time, without changing his basic premises, then we do not consider that as a therapeutic success. We are trying to change goals, concepts, and notions" (p. 79).

PSYCHOTHERAPY

Theory of Psychotherapy

The past five decades have witnessed the proliferation of varieties of psychotherapy. Many hypotheses might be formulated to explain the emergence of so many schools. Such hypotheses include a consideration of the following: (1) the claims of superiority for the particular theory underlying the therapy, (2) the superiority of the types of interpretation given to patients or the absence of any interpretation, (3) the substitution of action and encounter techniques for verbal techniques, (4) the nature of the therapist-patient relationship, and (5) the superior effectiveness of the therapy. All schools have stressed their differences. Only occasionally have any proponents of schools addressed themselves to similarities. Even more rarely do we read the statement that therapy may be a single process with many variations.

All scientific schools of psychotherapy have their shares of successes and failures. A considerable number of therapies based upon nonscientific foundations probably reach equal success levels. Consequently, we may conclude that the validity of a psychodynamic theory bears no direct relationship to its therapeutic effectiveness. Like their predecessors, modern theories may also vanish from practice to appear only in the textbooks of future generations. In any event, regardless of its validity or endurance, any theory must be implemented within the context of the therapist-patient relationship. As Fred Fiedler (1950) has shown, therapeutic success is a function of the expertness of the therapist rather than of his orientation. This may help to explain the successes of modern and primitive theories.

Since the underlying psychodynamic theory is not the crucial factor in therapy, perhaps it is the special techniques that contribute to therapeutic effectiveness. This would certainly seem to have been Rogers's early position before nondirective therapy became person-centered therapy. For the early nondirective school, the creation of a warm, permissive, nonjudgmental atmosphere, reflection of feeling, and avoidance of interpretation, advice, persuasion, and suggestion were paramount in the therapeutic situation.

The Freudian assigns central importance to transference but behavior modification therapists ignore it. To many directive therapists, content and manner of interpretation are crucial. The Adlerian emphasizes interpretation of the patient's life-style and his movement.

Criteria for "getting well" correspond to the particular therapeutic emphasis. Some therapists propose depth of the therapy as being the decisive factor. For most Adlerians, depth of therapy does not constitute a major concern, if any. In this connection, therapy is neither deep nor superficial except as the patient experiences it as such. In practice we observe patients who commend us for a particular interpretation, and when we discuss it with them, we learn that they have badly garbled it. In accordance with such arbitrariness, neither interpretative framework nor content nor depth is the decisive factor in curing patients.

If neither theory nor the use of prescribed techniques is decisive, is it the transference relationship that makes cure possible? Or the egalitarian relationship? Or the warm, permissive atmosphere with the nonjudgmental therapist accepting the patient as he is? Since all of these relationships are involved in various forms of both effective and noneffective therapy, we must hypothesize either that therapeutic effectiveness is a matter of matching certain therapeutic relationships to certain patients or that all therapeutic relationships possess common factors. These factors, variations on the Christian virtues of faith, hope, and love, appear to be necessary, but not sufficient, conditions of effective therapy.

Faith. D. Rosenthal and Jerome D. Frank (1956) discuss the implications of faith in the therapeutic process. Franz Alexander and Thomas French (1946) state:

As a general rule, the patient who comes for help voluntarily has this confidence, this expectation that the therapist is both able and willing to help him, before he comes to treatment; if not, if the patient is forced into treatment, the therapist must build up this feeling of rapport before any therapeutic change can be effected. (p. 173)

Many therapeutic mechanisms may enhance the patient's faith. A simple explanation clarifies matters for some patients, a complex interpretation for others. The therapist's own faith in himself, the thera-

pist's appearance of wisdom, strength, and assurance, the therapist's willingness to listen without criticism, all may be used by the patient to strengthen his faith.

Hope. Patients seek treatment with varying degrees of hope running the gamut from complete hopelessness to hope for (and expectation of) everything, including a miracle. Because of the efficacy of the self-fulfilling prophecy, people *tend* to move in the direction of making their anticipations come true. Therefore, the therapist must keep the patient's hope elevated.

Since the Adlerian holds that the patient suffers from discouragement, a primary technique of the Adlerian therapist lies in encouragement. His expression of faith in the patient, his noncondemnation of him, and his avoidance of being overly demanding of him may give the patient hope. The patient may also derive hope from the feeling of being understood. Accordingly, the construction of therapy as a "we" experience where the patient does not feel he stands alone, where he feels security in the strength and competency of his therapist, and where he feels some symptom alleviation all may prove helpful. He may also gain hope from attempting some course of action he feared or did not know was available to him. Humor assists in the retention of hope as Lewis Way (1962) comments, "Humour such as Adler possessed in such abundance, is an invaluable asset, since, if one can occasionally joke, things cannot be so bad" (p. 267). Summarily, each therapist has faith in his methods for encouraging and sustaining hope. They are put to the most severe test in depressions and in suicide threats.

Love. In its broadest sense, the patient must feel that the therapist cares (Adler, 1963a; 1964a). The mere act of treating the patient may furnish such evidence by using techniques such as empathic listening, "working through" together, or having two therapists in multiple psychotherapy offering interest in the patient. Transfer of a patient to another therapist or from individual to group therapy may have a contrary effect unless it is "worked through."

But the therapist must avoid pitfalls such as infantilizing, oversupporting, or of becoming a victim of the patient when the patient accuses him of not caring enough. In Adlerian group therapy, the group is conceptualized as a "re-experiencing of the family constellation" (Kadis, 1956). Thus, the therapist may be accused of playing favorites, of caring too much for one or too little for another patient.

The Adlerian theory of psychotherapy rests on the notion that psychotherapy is a cooperative educational enterprise involving one or more therapists and one or more patients. The goal of therapy is to develop the patient's social interest. To accomplish this, therapy involves a changing of faulty social values (Dreikurs, 1957). The subject matter of this course in reeducation is the patient himself—his life-style and his relationship to the life tasks. Learning the "basic mistakes" in his cognitive map, he has the opportunity to decide whether he wants to continue in the old ways or move in other directions. "The consultee must under all circumstances get the conviction in relation to treatment that he is absolutely free. He can do, or not do, as he pleases" (Ansbacher & Ansbacher, 1956, p. 341). He can make the decision between self-interest and social interest. The educational process has as its goals:

1. The fostering of social interest.
2. The decrease of inferiority feelings and the overcoming of discouragement.

3. Changes in the person's life-style, i.e., his perceptions and goals (in this connection, since all apperception involves bias, the therapeutic goal, as has been mentioned, involves transforming big errors into little ones [as with automobiles, some persons need a "tune-up"; others require a "major overhaul"]).
4. Changing faulty motivation that underlies even acceptable behavior or changing values.
5. Encouraging the individual to recognize his equality among his fellowmen (Dreikurs, 1971).
6. Helping him to become a contributive human being.

Should the "student" reach these educational objectives, he will feel belonging and equal, acceptant of himself and others. He will anticipate that others can accept him as he accepts himself. He will feel that the "motive force" lies within him, that he can arrange, within life's limits, his own destiny. He will feel encouraged, optimistic, confident, courageous, secure—and asymptomatic.

Process of Psychotherapy

The process of psychotherapy, as practiced by the Adlerian, has four aims: (1) establishing and maintaining a "good" relationship; (2) uncovering the dynamics of the patient, his life-style, his goals, and how they affect his life movement; (3) interpretation culminating in insight; and (4) reorientation.

Relationship. A "good" therapeutic relationship is a friendly one between equals. Both the Adlerian therapist and the patient sit facing each other, their chairs at the same level. Many Adlerians prefer to work without a desk since distancing and separation may engender undesirable psychological sets. Having abandoned the medical model, the Adlerian looks with disfavor upon casting the doctor in the role of the actor (omnipotent, omniscient, and mysterious) and the patient in that of the acted-upon. Therapy is structured to inform the patient that a creative human being plays a role in creating one's problems, that one is responsible (not in the sense of blame) for one's actions, and that one's problems are based upon faulty perceptions, and inadequate or faulty learnings, especially of faulty values. If this is so, one can assume responsibility for change. What has not been learned can be learned. What has been learned "poorly" can be replaced by better learning. Faulty perception and values can be altered and modified. From the initiation of treatment, the patient's efforts to remain passive are discouraged. The patient has an active role in the therapy. Although he may be in the role of student, he is still an active learner responsible for contributing to his own education.

Therapy requires cooperation, which means alignment of goals. Noncoincidence of goals may not permit the therapy "to get off the ground" as, for example, when the patient denies that he needs therapy and the therapist feels that he does. The initial interview(s) must not, therefore, omit the consideration of initial goals and expectations. The patient may wish to overpower the therapist, to put him into his service, or to make the therapist powerful and responsible; and the therapist's goal must be to avoid these traps. The patient may want to relinquish his symptoms but not his underlying convictions. He may be looking for a miracle. In each case, at least a temporary agreement upon goals must be arrived at before the therapy can proceed. Way (1962) cautions,

A refusal to be caught in this way [succumbing to the patient's appeals to the therapist's vanity or bids for sympathy] gives the patient little

opportunity for developing serious resistances and transferences, and is indeed the doctor's only defence against a reversal of roles and against finding that he is being treated by the patient. The cure must always be a co-operation and never a fight. It is a hard test for the doctor's own balance and is likely to succeed only if he himself is free from neurosis. (p. 265)

Adler (1963a) offers similar warnings against role reversal.

Since the problems of resistance and transference are defined in terms of patient-therapist goal discrepancies, throughout therapy the goals will diverge and the common task will consist of realigning the goals so patient and therapist move in the same direction. The patient brings his life-style to therapy. Whatever factors influenced its creation, the life-style convictions give the patient a feeling of security. When the patient believes the therapist questions or threatens these convictions, the patient must protect himself, must resist, even when he agrees with the therapist that it may be in his self-interest (Shulman, 1964). Take away his security—what does he have left? The goals go out of alignment again. The therapist advocates, "Let go of the 'basic mistakes' " and the patient announces, "I can't" or "I won't" or "I'm scared" or "I'm not coming back" or "Let's talk about something else."

The patient, in bringing his life-style to therapy, expects from the therapist the kind of response he has trained himself from childhood to believe that people will give him. He may feel misunderstood, unfairly treated, or unloved and may anticipate that the therapist will exploit or dislike him. Often he unconsciously creates situations to invite the therapist to behave in this manner. For this reason, the therapist must be alert to what Adlerians call "scripts" and what Eric Berne (1964) calls "games" and foil the patient's expectations. A patient, for example, will declare, "Have you ever seen a patient like me before?" to establish his uniqueness and to challenge the therapist's competence to treat him. The therapist's response may just be a straightforward, but nonsarcastic, "Not since the last hour," and he may follow up with a discussion of uniqueness. Since assessment begins with the first moment of contact, the patient is generally given some interpretation, usually phrased as a guess, during the first interview. This gives the patient something to think about until the next interview. He may feel understood ("I never thought of it that way" or "I'm so relieved to learn that"). The therapist will soon find it possible to assess how the patient will respond to interpretation, to therapy, and to the therapist, and will gain some glimpse of the life-style framework. In playing the patient's game, the patient is the professional, having played it successfully since childhood (although often in self-defeating fashion), whereas the therapist is a relative amateur. The therapist does not have to *win* the game. He merely does not play it. To illustrate, only one side wins in a tug-of-war. However, if one side (the therapist) is disinterested in victories or defeats, he merely does not pick up his end of the rope. This renders the "opponent's" game ineffective and the two can proceed to play more productive, cooperative games.

The whole relationship process increases the education of the patient. For some patients it is their first experience of a good interpersonal relationship, a relationship of cooperation and mutual respect and trust. Despite occasional bad feeling, friction, the feeling of not being understood, the relationship can endure and survive. The patient learns that good and bad relationships do not merely happen; they are products of people's efforts.

He learns that poor interpersonal relationships are products of or precipitated by misperceptions, inaccurate conclusions, and unwarranted anticipations incorporated in the life-style.

Analysis. Investigation of a patient's dynamics is divided into two parts. First, the therapist wants to understand the patient's life-style and, second, his aim is directed to understanding how the life-style affects his current function with respect to the life tasks. Not all suffering stems from the patient's life-style. Many patients with adequate life-styles develop problems or symptoms in the face of intolerable or extreme situations from which they cannot extricate themselves.

Analytic investigation begins with the first moment. The way a patient enters the room, his posture, and how and where he sits (especially important in family therapy) all provide clues toward the understanding of the patient. What he says and how he says it expand the therapist's understanding, especially when he understands the patient's communication in interpersonal terms, or "scripts," rather than in descriptive terms. Thus, the Adlerian translates the descriptive statement, "I am confused" into the admonition, "Don't pin me down." "It's a habit," conveys the declaration, "And that's another thing you're not going to get me to change," as the patient attempts erroneously to convince the therapist that habits are unchangeable (Mosak & Gushurst, 1971). As therapy progresses, the therapist assesses, using processes similar to a detective except that he works toward a different goal since he is not attempting to establish culpability. He follows up clues, juxtaposes them in patterns, accepts some hypotheses, and rejects others in his efforts to understand the patient. As therapy progresses, the patient offers information one way or another, and the therapist pieces it together bit by bit like a jigsaw puzzle. Therapists vary in their interview methods.

The Life-Style Investigation. In formal assessment procedures, the patient's family constellation is explored to ascertain conditions prevailing when the child was forming his life-style convictions. We obtain glimpses of what position he found in the family and how he went about finding his place within the family, in school, and among his peers. The second portion of the assessment consists of interpreting the patient's early recollections. An *early recollection* occurs in the period before continuous memory and may be inaccurate or a complete fiction. It represents a single event ("One day I remember . . .") rather than a group of events ("We used to . . ."). Adlerians refer to the latter as a *report* rather than a recollection. Recollections are treated as a projective technique (Mosak, 1958). If one understands the early recollections, one understands the patient's "Story of My Life" (Adler, 1958), since people selectively recollect from their past incidents consonant with their life-styles. The following recollection of Adler's (1947) may serve to illustrate the consonance between his earliest recollection and his later psychological views.

One of my earliest recollections is of sitting on a bench, bandaged up on account of rickets, with my healthy elder brother sitting opposite me. He could run, jump, and move about quite effortlessly, while for me movement of any sort was a strain and an effort. Everyone went to great pains to help me, and my mother and father did all that was in their power to do. At the time of this recollection I must have been about two years old. (p. 9)

In a single recollection, Adler refers to organ inferiority, the inferiority feeling, the emphasis upon "my desire to move freely—to see all psychic manifestations

in terms of movements" (p. 10), and social feeling (Mosak & Kopp, 1973).

The summary of early recollections, the story of the patient's life, permits the derivation of the patient's "basic mistakes." The life-style can be conceived as a personal mythology. The individual will behave as if the myths were true because, for him, they are true. When the Greeks believed that Zeus lived on Olympus, they regarded it as truth and behaved as if it were true, although we have now consigned this belief to the realm of mythology. Although it was not true that Zeus existed, it is true that Olympus exists. So there are "truths" or partial "truths" in myths and there are myths we confuse with truth. The latter are *basic mistakes.*

Basic mistakes may be classified as follows:

1. Overgeneralizations. "People are hostile." "Life is dangerous."
2. False or impossible goals of "security." "One false step and you're dead." "I have to please everybody."
3. Misperceptions of life and of life's demands. Typical convictions might be "Life never gives me any breaks" and "Life is so hard."
4. Minimization or denial of one's worth. "I'm stupid" and "I'm undeserving" or "I'm *just* a housewife."
5. Faulty values. "Be first even if you have to climb over others."

Finally, the therapist is interested in what assets the patient recognizes he has. The therapist may recognize other assets in the patient but he is interested at this point in how the patient perceives his assets.

A sample life-style summary is presented. It is not intended to be a complete personality description but it does offer patient and therapist initial hypotheses as talking points for examination. Below is a typical *life-style summary*.

Summary of Family Constellation

John is the younger of two children, the only boy, who grew up fatherless after age nine. His sister was so accomplished at almost everything that, early in life, John became discouraged. Since he felt he would never become famous, he decided perhaps he could at least be notorious, and through negative traits brought himself forcefully to the attention of others. He acquired the reputation that he was pretty obnoxious and a "holy terror." He was going to do everything his way, and nobody was going to stop him. He followed the guiding lines of a strong, masculine father from whom he learned that the toughest man wins. Since notoriety came with doing the disapproved, John early became interested in and engaged in sex. This also reinforced his feelings of masculinity. Since both parents were handicapped and still "made it," John apparently decided that without any physical handicaps, the sky would be the limit for him.

Summary of Early Recollections

"I run scared in life, and even when people tell me there's nothing to be scared of, I'm still scared. Women give men a hard time. They betray men, they punish them, and they interfere with what men want to do. A real man takes no crap from anybody. But victory is hard to come by because somebody always interferes. I am not going to do what others want me to do. Others call that 'bad' and want to punish me for it but I don't see it that way. Doing what I want is merely part of being a man, and why should anyone want to interfere with my being a man?"

"Basic Mistakes"

1. He exaggerates the significance of masculinity and equates it with doing what he pleases.
2. He is not on the same wave length as women. They see his behavior as "bad"; he sees it as only "natural" for a man.
3. He is too ready to fight, many times just to preserve his sense of masculinity, and not because of the issue he is allegedly fighting over.

4. He perceives women as the enemy, even though he looks to them for comfort.
5. Victory is snatched from him at the last moment.

Assets

1. He is a driver. When he puts his mind to things, he makes them work.
2. He engages in creative problem solving.
3. He knows how to get what he wants.
4. He knows how to keep the world busy with him.
5. He knows how to ask a woman "nicely."

During the course of treatment, other forms of analysis will occur. Since the therapist views the life-style as consistent, it will express itself in all of the patient's behavior—physical behavior, language and speech, fantasy productions, dreams, and interpersonal relations, past and present. Because of this consistency, the patient may choose to express himself in any or all of these media because they all express his life-style. The therapist observes behavior, speech, and language closely during each interview. Sometimes the dialogue will center on the present, sometimes on the past, often on the future. Free association and "chit chat," except when the latter serves a therapeutic purpose, are mostly discouraged. Although dream analysis is an integral part of psychotherapy, the patient who speaks only of dreams receives gentle dissuasion (Alexandra Adler, 1943). The analysis proceeds with an examination of the interplay between life-style and the life tasks—how the life-style affects the person's function and dysfunction vis-à-vis the life tasks.

Dreams. Adler saw the dream as a problem-solving activity with a future orientation in contrast to Freud's view that it was attempting to solve an old problem. The *dream* is seen by Adlerians as a rehearsal of possible future courses of action. If we want to postpone action, we forget the dream. If we want to dissuade ourselves from some action, we frighten ourselves with a nightmare.

The dream, Adler said, was the "factory of the emotions." In it we create moods that move us toward or away from the next day's activities. Commonly, people say, "I don't know why but I woke up in a lousy mood today." The day before Adler died, he told friends, "I woke smiling . . . so I knew my dreams were good although I had forgotten them" (Bottome, 1939, p. 240). Just as early recollections reflect long-range goals, the dream experiments with possible answers to immediate problems. In accord with the view of the individual's uniqueness, Adlerians reject the theory of fixed symbolism. One cannot understand a dream without knowing the dreamer, although Adler (1936) and Erwin Wexberg (1929) do address themselves to some frequently encountered dream themes. Way (1962) admonishes,

One is reminded again of two boys, instanced by Adler [1964a, p. 150], each of whom wished to be a horse, one because he would have to bear the responsibility for his family, the other to outstrip all the others. This should be a salutary warning against making dictionary interpretations. (pp. 282–84)

The interpretation of the dream does not terminate with the analysis of the content but must include the purposive function. Dreams serve as a weathervane for treatment, bringing problems to the surface and pointing to the patient's movement. Dreikurs (1944) describes a patient who related recurrent dreams that were short and actionless, reflecting his life-style of figuring out "the best way of getting out of a problem, mostly without doing anything. . . . When his dreams started to move and become active he started to move in his life, too" (p. 226).

Reorientation. All reorientation in all therapies proceeds from persuading the patient, gently or forcefully, that change is in his best interest. The patient's present manner of living accords him "safety" but not happiness. Since neither therapy nor life offers *guarantees,* would he risk some of his "safety" for the possibility of greater happiness, self-fulfillment, or for whatever he conceptualizes his goal to be? This dilemma is not easily solved. Like Hamlet, the patient wonders whether it is better to "bear those ills we have than fly to others that we know not of."

Insight. Analytic psychotherapies frequently assign central importance to insight, upon the assumption that "basic change" cannot occur in its absence. The conviction that insight must precede behavioral change often results in extended treatment, in encouraging some patients to become "sicker" to avoid or postpone change, and in increasing their self-absorption rather than their self-awareness. Meanwhile the patient relieves himself from the responsibility of living life until he has achieved insight.

A second assumption, treasured by therapists and patients alike, distinguishes between *intellectual* and *emotional* insight (Ellis, 1963; H. Papanek, 1959), a dualism the holistic Adlerian experiences difficulty in accepting. This and other dualisms such as conscious vs. unconscious undeniably exist in the patient's subjective experience. But these antagonistic forces are creations of the patient by which he can delay action. By creating "warring forces," he awaits the outcome of the battle before meeting the life tasks. Simultaneously he can maintain a good conscience since he is the victim of conflicting forces or an emotional block. Solving one's problems is relegated to the future while the patient pursues insight. *Insight,* as the Adlerian defines it, is understanding translated into constructive action. It reflects the patient's understanding of the purposive nature of his behavior and mistaken apperceptions as well as an understanding of the role both play in his life movement. So-called intellectual insight merely reflects the patient's desire to play the game of therapy rather than the game of life. He plays the game of "yes-but" (Adler, 1964b), as Adler called it. "Yes, I know what I should do, but. . . ."

Interpretation. The Adlerian therapist facilitates insight mainly by interpretation. He interprets ordinary communications, dreams, fantasies, behavior, symptoms, the patient-therapist transactions, and the patient's interpersonal transactions. The emphasis in interpretation is upon purpose rather than upon cause, on movement rather than description, on use rather than possession. Through interpretation the therapist holds up a mirror to the patient so he can see how he copes with life.

The therapist relates past to present only to indicate the continuity of the maladaptive life-style, not to demonstrate a causal connection. He may use humor or illustrate with fables, anecdotes, and biography. Irony may prove effective but it must be handled with care. He may "spit in the patient's soup," a crude expression for exposing the patient's intentions in such a way as to make them unpalatable so he can no longer maintain his current behavior with innocence or good conscience. The therapist may offer the interpretation directly or in the form of "Could it be that . . . ?" or may invite the patient to interpret for himself. Although timing, exaggeration, understatement, and accuracy are technical concerns of the therapist, they are not too important for the Adlerian therapist be-

cause he does not view the patient as fragile.

Other Verbal Techniques. Advice is often frowned upon by therapists. Hans Strupp (1972) relates, "It has been said that Freud, following his own recommendations, never gave advice to an analysand on the couch but did not stint with the commodity from the couch to the door" (p. 40). Wexberg (1970) frowns on giving advice to a patient but the Adlerian therapist does so as did Freud, taking care, however, not to encourage dependency. In practice he may merely outline the alternatives and let his patient make the decision. This invitation develops faith in self rather than· faith in the therapist. On the other hand, he may offer direct advice, taking care to encourage the patient's self-directiveness and his willingness to stand on his own two feet.

Since the patient is considered by Adlerians as discouraged rather than sick, it is no surprise that they make extensive use of encouragement. Enhancing the patient's faith in himself, "accentuating the positive and eliminating the negative," and keeping up the patient's hope all contribute to counteracting the patient's discouragement. If he "walks and falls," he learns it is not fatal. He can pick himself up and walk again. Therapy also counteracts the patient's social values, thus altering his view of life and helping him to give meaning to it. Moralizing is avoided, although therapists must not deceive themselves into believing their system has no value orientation. The dialogue concerns "useful" and "useless," rather than "good" or "bad" behavior.

The therapist avoids rational argument and trying to "out-logic" the patient. These tactics are easily defeated by the patient who operates according to his *psy-*

chologic (private logic) rather than the rules of formal logic. Catharsis, abreaction, and confession may afford the patient relief by freeing him from carrying the burden of "unfinished business," but as has been noted (Alexander & French, 1946), these may also be a test of whether one can place trust in the therapist. If the patient experiences relief or if the therapist passes the test, the patient may increase his readiness for change.

Action Techniques. Adlerians regularly use role playing, talking to an empty chair (Shoobs, 1964), the Midas technique (Shulman, 1962), the behind-the-back technique (Corsini, 1953), and other action procedures to assist the patient in reorienting himself. The extent of use is a function of therapist preference, the therapist's training, and his readiness to experiment with the novel.

Mechanisms of Psychotherapy

The Therapist as Model. The therapist represents values the patient may attempt to imitate. The Adlerian therapist represents himself as "being for real," fallible, able to laugh at himself, caring—a model for social interest. If the therapist can possess these characteristics, perhaps the patient can, too, and many patients emulate their therapists whom they use as a referent for normality (Mosak, 1967).

Change. Having been reeducated, how does the patient change and how does he implement these changes? It is one thing to know that $2 + 2 = 4$, but if one cannot solve the problem of "How much are 2 apples and 2 apples?" the knowledge is not functional.

There comes a time in psychotherapy when analysis must be abandoned and the patient must be encouraged to act in lieu of talking and listening. Insight has to give way to decisive action.

Some of the techniques Adlerians use to cut through knots are described below. They are not panaceas nor are they used indiscriminately. The creative therapist will improvise techniques to meet the needs of the therapeutic moment, and above all, he will remember that people are more important than techniques and strategies. Losing sight of these cautions, the therapist becomes a technician who does all the "right" things but is never engaged in human encounter with another human being.

Acting "as if." A common patient refrain in treatment is "If only I could . . ." (Adler, 1963a). We often request of the patient that for the next week he act "as if." He may protest that it would only be an act and therefore phony, that underneath he would remain the same person. We show him that all acting is not phony pretense, that he is being asked to try on a role as one might try on a suit. It does not change the person wearing the suit but sometimes with a handsome suit of clothes, he may feel differently and perhaps behave differently, in which case he becomes a different person.

Task Setting. Adler (1964a) gave us the prototype for task-setting in his treatment of depressives, writing:

> To return to the indirect method of treatment: I recommend it especially in melancholia. After establishing a sympathetic relation I give suggestions for a change of conduct in two stages. In the first stage my suggestion is "Only do what is agreeable to you." The patient usually answers, "Nothing is agreeable." "Then at least," I respond, "do not exert yourself to do what is disagreeable." The patient, who has usually been exhorted to do various uncongenial things to remedy this condition, finds a rather flattering novelty in my advice, and may improve in behavior. Later I insinuate the second rule of conduct, saying

that "it is much more difficult and I do not know if you can follow it." After saying this I am silent, and look doubtfully at the patient. In this way I excite his curiosity and ensure his attention, and then proceed, "If you could follow this second rule you would be cured in fourteen days. It is—to consider from time to time how you can give another person pleasure. It would very soon enable you to sleep and would chase away all your sad thoughts. You would feel yourself to be useful and worth while."

I receive various replies to my suggestion, but every patient thinks it is too difficult to act upon. If the answer is, "How can I give pleasure to others when I have none myself?" I relieve the prospect by saying, "Then you will need four weeks." The more transparent response, "Who gives *me* pleasure?" I encounter with what is probably the strongest move in the game, by saying, "Perhaps you had better train yourself a little thus: do not actually DO anything to please anyone else, but just think out how you COULD do it!"

The tasks are relatively simple and are set at a level at which the patient can sabotage the task but he cannot fail and then scold the therapist.

The patient must understand that not the physician but life itself is inexorable. He must understand that ultimately [he will have] to transfer to practical life that which has been theoretically recognized. . . . But from the physician he hears no word of reproach or of impatience, at most an occasional kindly, harmless, ironical remark (p. 101).

A 50-year-old man who professed "genuine" intention to get married but simultaneously avoided women was instructed to seek one meaningful contact with a woman (how to do so was up to him) every day. After raising many objections, he complained, "But it's *so* hard! I'll get so tired out I won't be able to function." The therapist good-humoredly relented and informed him, "Since God rested on the seventh day, I can't ask you to do more than God. So you need carry out the task only six days a week."

One form of task setting Adler introduced is called *antisuggestion* by Wexberg (1929) and *paradoxical intention* by Frankl (1963). This method originated with Knight Dunlap (1933) and was labeled *negative practice*. The symptomatic patient unwittingly reinforces his symptoms by fighting them, by telling himself "Why did this have to happen to *me?*" He tries to divert his attention so he will not think about them and finds himself constantly thinking about them or watching himself. The insomniac keeps one eye open to observe whether the other is falling asleep, and then wonders why he cannot sleep. To halt this fight, the patient is instructed to intend and even increase that which he is fighting against.

Creating Images. Adler was fond of describing patients with a simple phrase, for example, "The beggar as king." Other Adlerians give patients similar shorthand images that confirm the adage that "one picture is worth a thousand words." Remembering this image, the patient can remind himself of his goals, and in later stages he can learn to use the image to laugh at himself. One overambitious patient, labeled "Superman," one day began to unbutton his shirt. When the therapist made inquiry, the patient laughingly replied, "So you can see my blue shirt with the big 'S' on it." Another patient, fearing sexual impotence, concurred with the therapist's observation that he had never seen an impotent dog. The patient advanced as explanation, "The dog just does what he's supposed to do without worrying about whether he'll be able to perform." The therapist suggested that at his next attempt at sexual intercourse, before he made any advances, he should smile and say inwardly, "Bow wow." The following week he informed the members of his group, "I bow-wowed."

Catching Oneself. When a patient understands his goals and wants to change, he is instructed to catch himself "with his hand in the cookie jar" as it were. The patient may catch himself in the midst of his old behavior but still feel incapable of doing anything about it at the moment. With additional practice, he learns to anticipate the situation and his behavior before their occurrence and, consequently, either to avoid or modify the situation or to change his behavioral approach. The method requires laughing at, not accusing, oneself when one catches oneself.

The Pushbutton Technique. This method, effective with people who feel they are victims of their disjunctive emotions, involves requesting the patient to close his eyes, recreate a pleasant incident from his experience, and to note the feeling that accompanies this recreation. Then he is asked to recreate an unpleasant incident of hurt, humiliation, failure, or anger and to note the accompanying feeling. Following this the patient recreates the first scene again. The lesson Adlerians try to teach the client is that he can create whatever feeling he wishes merely by deciding about what he will think. He has the button in his hands and can push it at will to create any feeling, good or bad. He is the creator, not the victim, of his emotions. To be depressed, for example, requires *choosing* to be depressed. We try to impress the patient with his power for self-determination.

The "Aha" Experience. As the patient gains awareness in treatment and increases his participation in life, he recurrently has "aha" or "eureka" experiences. "Hey, that makes sense." "Now I know how it works." "Wow, that was simpler than I thought." With this greater understanding, he generates self-confidence and optimism resulting in increased encouragement and willingness to confront life's problems with commitment, compassion, and empathy.

Posttherapy. The best part of therapy comes after therapy when the fledgling human being can leave the therapist's nest and try his wings on his own, nurturing himself, and flying like a free spirit in the universe. The patient can implement his newly acquired learnings in his own service and that of mankind. Operationally, the goal of therapy may be defined as that of making the therapist superfluous. If therapist and patient have both done their jobs well, the goal will have been achieved.

APPLICATIONS

Problems

Although Adler, like the other *Nervenärzte* ("nerve doctors") of his era, conducted one-to-one psychotherapy, his own social outlook moved him out of the consulting room and into the community. Although he never relinquished his clinical interests, he concurrently was an educator and social reformer. Joost Meerloo (1970), a Freudian, eulogizes Adler with his confession,

As a matter of fact, the whole body of psychoanalysis and psychiatry is imbued with Adler's ideas, although few want to acknowledge this fact. We are all plagiarists, though we hate to confess it. . . . The whole body of social psychiatry would have been impossible without Adler's pioneering zest. (p. 40)

Clinical. All the early pioneers in psychotherapy treated neurotics. However, psychotics were considered not amenable to psychotherapy because they could not enter into a transference relationship. The Adlerian, unencumbered by the concept of transference, treated psychotic patients regularly. Henri Ellenberger (1970) suggests that "among the great pioneers of dynamic psychiatry, Janet and Adler are the only ones who had personal clinical experience with criminals, and Adler was the only one who wrote something on the subject from his direct experience." Ernst Papanek (1971), of whom Claude Brown (1965) wrote so glowingly in his *Manchild in the Promised Land,* was director of Wiltwyck School (a reform school), and Mosak set up a group therapy program at Cook County Jail in Chicago employing paraprofessionals as therapists (O'Reilly et al., 1965). The growth model implicit in Adlerian theory has prompted Adlerians to see human problems in terms of people realizing themselves, in becoming fellow human beings. Much "treatment" then is of "normal" people with "normal" problems. A therapy that does not provide the client with a philosophy of life, whatever else it may accomplish in the way of symptom eradication or alleviation, behavior modification, or insight, is an incomplete therapy. Hence the Adlerian concerns himself with his client's problems of living and his problems of existence. Deficiency, suffering, and illness do not constitute the price of admission to Adlerian therapy. One may enter therapy to learn about oneself, to grow, to actualize oneself.

Social. Adler's interests were rather catholic. In the area of education, he believed in prevention rather than cure and founded family education centers in the community where parents and teachers could receive direct advice on childrearing. Dreikurs and his students (Dreikurs et al., 1959) have founded family education centers throughout the world. Offshoots of these centers are the hundreds of parent study groups where parents can share problems and solutions with other parents under guidance of a

paraprofessional leader (Soltz, 1967). In addition, professional therapists have used a variety of methods for teaching childrearing practices (Beecher & Beecher, 1966; Dreikurs, 1948; Dreikurs & Soltz, 1967; Allred, 1976).

Adler himself wrote on social issues and problems such as crime, war, religion, group psychology, Bolshevism, leadership, and nationalism. Among contemporary Adlerians [Angers (1960); Clark (1965, 1967a, 1967b); Elam (1969a, 1969b); Gottesfeld (1966); Hemming (1956); La Porte (1966); Lombardi (1969); and Nikelly (1971c)] the "newer" social problems of protest, race, drugs, social conditions, and the "newer" views of religion have been added to the Adlerians' previous interests.

Evaluation

Until very recently, little research has emerged from the Adlerian group. As was the case with most European clinicians, the European Adlerians were suspicious of research based upon statistical methods. A complicating factor was the *idiographic* (case method) approach upon which Adlerians relied. Statistical methods are more appropriate for *nomothetic* (group) research. Even now statisticians have not developed appropriate sophisticated methods for idiographic studies. The research methods lent themselves well to studies of "causal" factors, but the Adlerian rejected causalism, feeling that causes can only be imputed (and therefore disputed) in retrospective fashion but that they contributed little to the understanding of man.

The most-often cited studies involving Adlerian psychology were conducted by non-Adlerians. Fred Fiedler (1950) compared therapeutic relationships in psychoanalytic, nondirective, and Adlerian therapy. He found there was greater similarity between therapeutic relationships developed by experts of the three schools than between expert and less expert therapists within the same school.

A joint research study conducted by the (Rogerian) Counseling Center of the University of Chicago and the Alfred Adler Institute of Chicago examined the effects of time limits in psychotherapy (Shlien, Mosak, & Dreikurs, 1962). Patients of both groups of therapists were given 20 interviews and the groups were compared with each other and with two control groups. The investigators reported changes in self-ideal correlations. These correlations improved significantly and, according to this measure, suggest that time-limited therapy "may be said to be not only *effective,* but also twice as *efficient* as time-unlimited therapy." Follow-up of these patients in both experimental groups indicated that the gains were retained when measured one year later.

Much of the research in family constellation has also been done by non-Adlerians. Charles Miley (1969), Lucille Forer (1972) and Gardner Murphy, Lois Murphy, and Theodore Newcomb (1937) have compiled a bibliography of this literature. The results reported are contradictory probably because non-Adlerians treat birth order as a matter of ordinal position and Adlerians consider birth order in terms of psychological position (Mosak, 1972). Walter Toman (1970) recognizes this distinction in his many studies of the family constellation.

Ansbacher (1946) and Mosak (1958) have also distinguished between Freudian and Adlerian approaches to the interpretation of early recollections. Robin Gushurst (1971) provides a manual for interpreting and scoring one class of recollections. His reliability studies demonstrate that judges can interpret early recollection data with high interjudge reliability. He also conducted three validity studies to investigate the hypothesis that life goals may be identified from early recollections data, and found that he could do this with two of his three experimental groups.

Adlerian psychology would undoubtedly benefit from more research. With the shift in locus from Europe to the United States, with the accelerated growth of the Adlerian school in recent years, with the introduction of more American-trained Adlerians into academic settings, and with the development of new research strategies suitable for idiographic data, the integration of Adlerians into research activities already exhibits some signs of burgeoning.

Treatment

One can hardly identify a mode of treatment in which some Adlerian is not engaged. From a historical viewpoint the initial Adlerian modality was one-to-one psychotherapy. Many Adlerians still regard individual psychotherapy as the treatment of choice. But they did not accept some of the therapeutic conventions of the times and discounted the value of prognosis. Adlerians demonstrated willingness to undertake treatment with any who sought their services.

Dreikurs, Mosak, and Shulman (1952a, 1952b) introduced *multiple psychotherapy,* a format in which several therapists treat a single patient. It offers constant consultation between therapists, prevents the emotional attachment of a patient to a single therapist and obviates or dissolves impasses. Countertransference reactions are minimized. Flexibility in the number of therapist roles and models is increased. Patients are more impressed or reassured when two therapists independently agree.

The patient also may benefit from the experience of observing disagreement between therapists and learn that people can disagree without loss of face. With respect to the patient the advantages are as follows:

1. Multiple therapy creates an atmosphere that facilitates learning.
2. The patient can interact with two different personalities with two different approaches.
3. Therapeutic impasses are avoided by the introduction of fresh viewpoints, thus accelerating the therapy.
4. The patient may view himself more objectively, since he is both spectator and participant.
5. In the event that the therapist and patient do not "hit it off," the patient does not become a therapeutic "casualty" and is merely transferred to the second therapist.
6. The many problems related to dependency in treatment are solved more easily. These include the responsibility for the self, absence of the therapist, transference reactions, and termination.
7. Multiple therapy is an example of democratic social interaction and is thus a valuable lesson for the patient (Dreikurs, Mosak, & Shulman, 1952(b), pp. 595–96).

An additional advantage of the method lies in its use for training therapists. The supervising therapist does not rely upon the candidate therapist's report, which may be distorted through retrospective falsification. The supervisor sits in with his trainee, observes his interventions, provides him with security and support, and can comment upon the observed behavior.

Dreikurs (1959) in the mid-1920s initiated group therapy in private practice. This application was a natural evolution from the Adlerian axiom that people's problems were always social problems. Group therapy finds considerable adherents among Adlerians. Some Adlerian therapists regard group therapy as the method of choice either on practical grounds (e.g., fees, large numbers of patients to be treated, etc.) or because they believe that since human problems are primarily social problems, they are most effectively handled in the group social situation. Others use group therapy as a preface to individual therapy or to taper patients off from intensive individual psychotherapy. A number of therapists combine individual and group psychotherapy in the conviction that this combination maximizes therapeutic effect (H. Papanek, 1954, 1956). Still other therapists visualize the group as assisting in the solution of certain selected problems or with certain types of populations. Co-therapist groups are very common among Adlerians.

An offshoot of group treatment is the therapeutic social club in a mental hospital as initiated by the British Adlerian, Joshua Bierer. Similar clubs exist in New York (Mohr & Garlock, 1959) and at St. Joseph Hospital in Chicago. Although these clubs possess superficial similarities to Abraham Low's Recovery groups (Low, 1952) and to halfway houses in that all attempt to facilitate the patient's reentrance into society, the therapeutic social club emphasizes "social" rather than the "therapeutic" aspects of life, taking the "healthy" rather than the "sick" model of man. Psychodrama has been used by Adlerians, sometimes as separate therapy, sometimes in conjunction with another therapeutic modality.

Marriage counseling has figured prominently in Adlerian activities. Adlerians defied the trend of the times and preferred to treat the couple as a unit rather than as separate individuals. To "treat" merely one mate may be compared to having only half the dialogue of a play. Seeing the couple together suggests that they have a joint relationship problem rather than individual problems and invites joint effort in the solution of these problems. The counselor can observe their interaction and point out to them the nature of their interaction (Mozdzierz & Lottman, 1973; Pew & Pew, 1972). Married couples group therapy (Deutsch, 1967) and married couples study groups constitute two more settings for conducting marriage counseling.

In the early 1920s, Adler persuaded the Viennese school administration to establish child-guidance centers in the schools. The social group was the primary vehicle for treatment (Adler, 1963a; Alexandra Adler, 1951; Seidler & Zilahi, 1949). Dreikurs wrote several popular books and many articles (Dreikurs, 1948; Dreikurs & Grey, 1968; Dreikurs & Soltz, 1967) to disseminate this information to parents and teachers, and currently thousands of parents are enrolled in study groups where they obtain supplementary information on childrearing.

The preventive methods in schools as started by Adler were adopted by educators and school counselors who used them in individual classes, schools, and in one instance in an entire school system (Mosak, 1971). The methods were originally applied in the Individual Psychological Experimental School in Vienna (Birnbaum, 1935; Spiel, 1962) and have been elaborated upon in this country by many educators (Corsini, 1977; Dreikurs, 1968; Dreikurs, 1972; Dinkmeyer & Dreikurs, 1963; Dreikurs, Grunwald & Pepper, 1971; Grunwald, 1954). Human Dynamics Consultants, a division of the Alfred Adler Institute of Chicago, provides consultant and training services to schools and school systems, as well as to

hospitals, prisons, industry, the military, and other institutions.

With respect to broader social problems, Dreikurs devoted the last part of his life to the problem of interindividual and intergroup conflict resolution. Much of this work was performed in Israel and has not been reported in the literature. Kenneth Clark, a black psychologist and former president of the American Psychological Association, has devoted much of his career to studying and providing recommendations for solutions for problems of black people.

Management

The Setting. Adlerians function in every imaginable setting: the private-practice office, hospitals, day hospitals, jails, schools, and in community programs. Offices do not contain any special furnishing, but reflect either the therapist's aesthetic preferences or the condition of the institution's budget. No special equipment is used, except perhaps for special projects. Although voice recordings are a matter of individual choice, they are sometimes maintained as the patient's file. Some therapists ask their patients to listen to these recordings during or between interviews. Some voice recordings and videotape recordings have also been made for demonstration and teaching purposes. The Alfred Adler Institute of Chicago provides information concerning the availability of such recordings as well as video tapes for those who may wish to hear and observe Adlerian therapeutic interviews.

In the initial interviews, the therapist generally addresses himself to obtaining the following kinds of information (in addition to demographic information):

1. Was patient self-referred? If not, he may continue in treatment only for the

duration of his "sentence." A reluctant adolescent may punish his parents by failing to keep appointments for which he knows his parents must pay. For that matter, the patient who is sent may merely be the identified patient, so labeled by someone, usually parents. This is one reason why, when a child is referred, Adlerians prefer to see the entire family.

2. If the patient is reluctant, one must convert him into a patient if therapy is to proceed. Fourteen such "conversion techniques" appear in a therapy syllabus (Mosak & Shulman, 1963, Unit VII J).

3. What does the patient come for? Does he seek treatment to alleviate suffering? If so, suffering from what? Does he make the implicit demand that the therapist legitimize or confirm an already made decision? Does he come to get others off his back? May he think that as long as he is in therapy, he does not have to accept responsibilities or make decisions? After all, he may be designated by himself or others as "sick" or "confused."

Some new patients are "supermarket shoppers." They inform you of the number of therapists who have helped them already. Their secret goal is to be perfect. Unless such a patient's fictional goal is disclosed and he is derailed from seeking it, you may be the latest of many therapists about whom he will be telling his next therapist. Adler describes such a person as belonging to the ruling type, one who must conquer. He spends his life defeating therapists, winning Pyrrhic victories. Therapists of any orientation will recognize many such recurring types (Mosak, 1971).

4. What are the patient's expectations about treatment? A patient may check his therapist's diplomas and credentials to make sure he is not a quack. If there is no couch in the room, he worries because in the movies an analyst has a couch. Con-

trollers, persons with "verbal diarrhea," criers, and other such patients may not permit the therapist a word (and then thank him for being so helpful). Those who have read Freud and some TV viewers of psychological movies will think that free association is the order of the day.

5. What are the patient's expectations for himself? Does he expect to emerge from treatment perfect? Does he consider himself hopeless? Does he expect or demand a solution for a specific problem without any major personality alterations? Does he expect immediate cure?

6. What are the patient's goals in psychotherapy? We must distinguish between stated goals—to get well, to learn about himself, to be a better husband and father, to gain a new philosophy of life—and nonverbalized goals—to remain sick, to punish others, to defeat the therapist and sabotage therapy, to maintain good intentions without changing ("Look how hard I'm trying and the money I'm spending on therapy"). The importance of this determination cannot be overstated. The Adlerian defines resistance as that which occurs when the patient's goals and those of the therapist do not coincide. Consequently, if the therapist fails to understand his patient's goals, they may be operating at cross-purposes, and the therapeutic effort may deteriorate into a vicious circle of resistance—overcoming resistance—resistance rather than the cooperative effort for which the Adlerian therapist aims. The best technique for handling resistance is to avoid fostering it, to listen attentively and empathically to the patient, following his movement in therapy, to understand his goals and strategies, and to encourage the development of therapy as a "we" endeavor.

The patient may resist to depreciate or defeat the therapist. He must defeat the therapist because he lacks the courage to live on the useful side of life and fears that the therapist might channel him in that direction. The intensification of such escape methods may become most pronounced during the termination phase of treatment when the patient realizes he must soon face the realistic tasks of life without the therapist's support and he is not sure of his own courage to embark on an independent venture of this magnitude.

Tests. Routine physical examinations are not required by Adlerians in view of the therapy's educational orientation. Nevertheless, many patients do have physiological problems and Adlerians are trained to be sensitive to the presence of these problems. Where the therapist suspects such problems, he will make referrals for physical examination.

Adlerians are divided on the issue of psychological testing. Most Adlerians avoid nosological diagnosis, except for nontherapeutic purposes such as filling out insurance forms. Labels are static descriptions and ignore the *movement* of the individual. They describe what the individual *has,* but not how he *moves* through life.

Among the older, European-trained therapists, psychological testing was a dirty word. The older European psychological tradition included a non- or anti-testing bias (Orgler, 1965), some notable exceptions being the Rorschach, the Binet, and the Word Association Test. Apparently Adler himself, although he developed the first projective test, Early Recollections, had little use for testing. Dreikurs was distrustful of tests, his opinion of them being that they were relatively unnecessary since "the test situation indicates what is probably true. Observation permits us to determine what is true. . . ." (Dinkmeyer & Dreikurs, 1963, p. 10). Dreikurs also felt tests were un-

reliable because they could provide deceptive results and, thus, might be harmful (Dreikurs, 1968, p. 7). Dreikurs did refer patients for testing nevertheless.

Regine Seidler (1967) placed more faith in projective testing than in so-called objective tests, maintaining that the latter are actually subjective tests since "The *subjective attitude* of each and every individual toward any given test necessarily renders the test non-objective" (p. 4). Objective tests were more useful to her as measures of test-taking attitude than of what the test was purportedly measuring.

Early recollections serve as a test for Adlerians, assisting them in the life-style assessment. Younger Adlerians employ many conventional tests and some nonconventional ones for diagnostic and differential diagnostic purposes as well as in the treatment of the patient.

The Therapist. The Adlerian therapist ideally is authentically himself—a sharing, caring person. Helene and Ernst Papanek (1961) write, "the therapist participates actively. Without playing any sharply defined 'role,' he shows warmth toward and a genuine interest in the patient and encourages especially his desire for change and betterment. The relationship itself has a purpose: to help the patient help himself" (p. 117). Adler (1924) relates how he treated a mute schizophrenic patient who after three months of silence assaulted him and "I instantly decided not to defend myself. After a further attack, during which a window was smashed, I bound up his slightly bleeding wound in the friendliest way" (p. 24). Since the ideal goal in psychotherapy is to encourage the development of social interest, the therapist must be a model for social interest himself.

The Adlerian therapist remains free to have feelings and opinions and to express them. Such expression in a spontaneous way permits the patient to view therapists as human beings, discouraging any perceptions of omnipotence or perfection with which patients may invest them. If we therapists err, we err—but then the patient may learn the courage to be imperfect from this experience (Lazarsfeld, 1966). The experience may also facilitate therapy.

The therapist must not inject his evaluation of his worth into the therapy. He merely does his therapeutic job without concern for his own prestige, not reveling in his successes or becoming discouraged by his failures. Otherwise, he may bounce like a rubber ball from therapy hour to therapy hour or perhaps even within the same hour. The therapist's worth does not depend upon external factors. The center of gravity, his feeling of worth, lies within him. He accepts himself as he is and consequently can devote his full attention to *what* he is doing rather than to *how* he is doing. He is task-oriented rather than self-oriented.

The therapist reveals himself as a person. Since the therapist is authentically himself, the patient has the opportunity to appraise him as a human being. These perceptions may combine realistic judgments as well as judgments stemming from the patient's life-style. The concept of the *anonymous therapist* is foreign to Adlerian psychology. Such a role would increase social distance between therapist and patient interfering with the establishment of an egalitarian, human relationship that Adlerians regard as indispensable. The "anonymous therapist" role was created to facilitate the establishment of a transference relationship and since the Adlerian rejects the transference concept, as Freud formulated it, the maintenance of such a posture is considered irrelevant if not harmful to the relationship

the therapist wants to establish with his patient. Dreikurs (1961) deplored the prevalent attitude among therapists of not coming too close to patients because it might affect the therapeutic relationship adversely. Shulman (Wexberg, 1970, p. 88) defines the role of the therapist as that of "a helping friend." Self-revelation can only occur when the therapist feels secure himself, at home with his own feelings, at home with others, unafraid to be human and fallible, and thus unafraid of his patient's evaluations, criticism, or hostility (cf. Rogers' "congruence"). For these and other reasons, Adlerian training institutes customarily require a "didactic analysis" of their candidates.

Is the Adlerian therapist judgmental? In a sense every therapist is judgmental in that his therapy rests upon some value orientation: his belief that certain behavior is better than other behavior, that certain goals are better than other goals, that one organization of personality is superior to another form of organization. Dreikurs (1961) states, "There is always a value and moral problem involved in the cure [in all therapy]" (p. 93). On the other hand, the patient who seeks help is often a discouraged human being. To criticize him would merely reinforce his discouragement, rob him of his residual sense of personal worth, and perhaps confirm some of his life-style convictions (e.g., "People are unfair" or "I am unlovable" or "I do everything wrong"). Since two cardinal principles of the Adlerian intervention are to win the patient and to encourage him, such judgments are best avoided.

Patient Problems. If the therapist does not like the patient, it raises problems for a therapist of any persuasion (Fromm-Reichman, 1949). Some therapists merely do not accept such patients.

Still others feel they ought not to have or ought to overcome such negative feelings and accept the patient for treatment, leading to both participants "suffering." It appears difficult to possess "unconditional positive regard" for a patient you dislike. Probably Adlerians meet this situation in the same manner other therapists do.

Seduction problems are treated as any other patient problem. The secure therapist will not be frightened, panic, or succumb. If the patient's activities nevertheless prevent the therapy from continuing, the patient may be referred to another therapist, a transfer easily accomplished in multiple psychotherapy. Flattery problems are in some ways similar and have been discussed elsewhere (Berne, 1964; Mosak & Gushurst, 1971).

Suicide threats are always taken seriously (Ansbacher, 1961; 1969). Alfred Adler warned, however, that our goal is "to knock the weapon out of his hand" so the patient cannot make us vulnerable and intimidate us at will with his threats. As an example, he narrates, "A patient once asked me, smiling, 'Has anyone ever taken his life while being treated by you?' I answered him, 'Not yet, but I am prepared for this to happen at any time' " (Ansbacher & Ansbacher, 1956, pp. 338–39).

Kurt Adler (1961) postulates "an underlying rage against people" in suicide threats and that this goal of vengefulness must be uncovered. He "knocks the weapon out of the patient's hand" as follows:

Patients have tested me with the question, how I would feel, if I were to read of their suicide in the newspaper. I answer that it is possible that some reporter hungry for news would pick up such an item from a police blotter. But, the next day, the paper will already be old, and only a dog perhaps may honor their suicide notice by lifting a leg over it in some corner (p. 66).

For an extended description of problems in psychotherapy, Alexandra Adler (1943), Lazarsfeld (1952) and Oscar Pelzman (1952) discuss problems beyond the scope of this chapter.

CASE EXAMPLE

Background

The patient was a 53-year-old, Viennese-born man, in treatment almost continuously with Freudian psychoanalysts, here and abroad, since he was 17. With the advent of tranquilizers, he had transferred his allegiances to psychiatrists who treated him with a combination of drugs and psychotherapy and finally with drugs alone. When he entered Adlerian treatment, he was being maintained by his previous therapist on an opium derivative and Thorazine. He failed to tell his previous therapist of his decision to see us and also failed to inform us that he was still obtaining medication from his previous therapist.

The treatment process was atypical in the sense that the patient's "illness" hampered us from following our customary procedure. Having over the years become therapy-wise, he invested his creativity in efforts to run the therapy. Cooperative effort was virtually impossible. In conventional terms, the co-therapists, Drs. A and B, had their hands full dealing with the patient's resistances and "transference."

Problem

When the patient entered treatment, he had taken to bed and spent almost all his time there because he felt too weak to get up. His wife had to be constantly at his side or he would panic. Once she was encouraged by a friend to attend the opera alone. The patient wished her a good time, and then told her, "When you return, I shall be dead." His secretary was forced into conducting his successful business. Everyone was forced into "the emperor's service." The price he paid for this service was intense suffering in the form of depression, obsessive-compulsive behavior, phobic behavior, especially agoraphobia, divorce from the social world, somatic symptoms, and invalidism.

Treatment

The patient was seen in multiple psychotherapy by Drs. A and B, but both therapists were not present at each interview. We dispensed with the life-style assessment because the patient had other immediate goals. It seemed to us from the patient's behavior that he probably had been raised as a pampered child, and that he was using "illness" to tyrannize the world and to gain exemption from the life tasks. If these guesses were correct, we anticipated he would attempt to remain "sick," would resist giving up drugs, and would demand special attention from his therapists. As part of the treatment strategy, the therapists decided to wean him from medication, to give him no special attention, and not to be manipulated by him. Since he had undergone analysis over a period of more than three decades, the therapists thought he could probably produce a better analysis of his problems than they could. For this reason, interpretation was kept at a minimum. The treatment plan envisaged a tactical and strategic rather than interpretive approach. Some excerpts from the

early part of treatment are reproduced below:

March 8. Dr. B wanted to collect life-style information but the patient immediately complained that he wanted to terminate. Dr. C, he said, his previous therapist, had treated him differently. Therapist B was too impersonal. "You won't even give me your home phone number. You aren't impressed by my illness. Your treatment is well meaning but it won't help. Nothing helps. I'm going back to Dr. C and ask him to put me in the hospital. He gave me advice and you are so cruel by not telling me what to do."

March 19. Relatively calm. Compares B with Dr. C. Later compares B with A. Favors B over Dr. C because he respects former's strength. Favors B over A because he can succeed in ruffling latter but not former. Talk centers about his use of weakness to overpower others.

March 22. Telephones to say he must be hospitalized. Wife left him [untrue] and secretary left him [It turns out she went to lunch]. Would B come to his office to see him? B asks him to keep appointment in B's office. Patient races about office upset. "I'm sweating water and blood." When B remains calm, patient takes out bottle of Thorazine and threatens to take all. Next he climbs up on radiator, opens window (17th floor), jumps back, and says, "No, it's too high."

"You don't help me. Why can't I have an injection?" Then he informs B that B is soothing influence on him. "I wish I could spend the whole day with you." He speaks softly to patient and patient speaks quietly. Patient asks for advice about what to do this weekend. B gives antisuggestion and tells him to try to worry as much as he can. He is surprised and dismisses it as "bad advice."

March 29. B was sick on 3-26 and patient saw A. "It was useless." No longer worried about state hospital. Will now wind up as bum because he got drunk last week. His secretary gave him notice but he hopes to keep her "by taking abuse. No one treats a boss like she treats me." Got out of bed and worked last week. Went out selling but "everyone rejected me." When B indicates that he seems to be better, he insists he's deteriorating. When B inquires how, he replies paradoxically, "I beat out my competitors this week."

April 2. Has habit of sticking finger down throat and vomiting. Threatens to do so when enters office today. B tells patient about the logical consequences of his act—he will have to mop up. Patient withdraws finger. "If you would leave me alone, I'd fall asleep so fast." B leaves him alone. Patient angrily declaims, "Why do you let me sleep?"

April 9. Too weak even to telephone therapist. If wife goes on vacation, he will kill himself. How can he survive with no one to tell him to eat, to go to bed, to get up? "All I do is vomit and sleep." B suggests that he tyrannizes her as he did his mother and sister. He opens window and inquires, "Shall I jump?" B recognizes this as an attempt to intimidate rather than a serious threat and responds, "Suit yourself." Patient closes window and accuses, "You don't care, either." Asks whether he can see A next time and before receiving answer, says, "I don't want him anyway." Follows this with, "I want to go to the state hospital. Can you get me a private room?" At end of interview falls to knees and sobs, "Help me! Help me to be a human being."

April 12. Enters, falls to knees, encircles therapist's knees, whimpers, "Help me!" So depressed. If only he could end it all. B gives him Adler's suggestion to do one thing each day that would give someone pleasure. Patient admits behaving better. Stopped annoying secretary and let her go home early because of bad weather. Agitation stops.

April 15. Didn't do anything this weekend to give pleasure. However, he did play cards with wife. Took her for drive. Sex with wife for "first time in a long time." B gives encouragement and then repeats "pleasure" suggestion. He can't do it. Calm whole hour. Says his wife has told him to discontinue treatment. Upon inquiry, he says she didn't say exactly that but had said, "I leave it up to you."

April 19. Wants B to accompany him back to his office because he forgot something. Wants shorter hour this week and longer one next week. "Dr. C let me do that." When B declines, he complains, "Doctor, I don't know what to do with you anymore."

April 23. Wouldn't consider suicide. "Perhaps I have a masochistic desire to live." B suggests he must be angry with life. He responds that he wants to be an infant and have all his needs gratified. The world should be a big breast and he should be able to drink without having to suck [probably an interpretation he had received in psychoanalysis]. Yesterday he had fantasy of destroying the whole city.

This weekend he helped his wife work in the garden. He asks for suggestions for weekend. B and patient play "yes-but." B does so deliberately to point out game (cf. Berne's "Why don't you . . . Yes But" [1964]) to patient. Patient then volunteers possibility of clay modeling. B indicates this may be good choice in that patient can mold, manipulate, and "be violent."

April 29. Had birthday last week and resolved to turn over new leaf for new year but didn't. Cries, "Help me, help me." Depreciates B. "How much would you charge me to come to my summer home? I'm so sick, I vomited blood." When B tells him if he's that sick, hospitalization might be advisable, he smiles and says, "For money, you'd come out." B and patient speak of attitude toward B and attitude toward his father. Patient depreciates both, possibly because he could not dominate either.

May 1.   Didn't think he could make it today because afraid to walk on street. Didn't sleep all night. So excited, so upset [he seems calm]. Perhaps he should be put in hospital but then what will happen to his business?

Was never convinced B could help him. "We could sit here forever and all you would tell me is to get clay. Why don't you give me medicine or advice?" B points out that patient is much stronger than any medication as evidenced by number of therapists and treatments he has defeated.

He says he is out of step with world. B repeats an earlier interpretation by A that the patient wants the world to conform to him and follows with statement about his desire to be omnipotent, a desire that makes him feel weak and simultaneously compensates for his feelings of weakness. He confirms with "All Chicago should stand still so I could have a holiday. The police should stop at gunpoint anyone who wants to go to work. But I don't want to. I don't want to do anything anymore. I want a paycheck but I don't want to work." B remarks on shift from "I can't" to "I don't want to." Patient admits and says, "I don't want to get well. Should I make another appointment?" B refers decision back to him. He makes appointment.

May 6.   "I'm at the end, dying with fear [enumerates symptoms]. Since 5 this morning I'm murdering ——— and ———. Such nice people and I'm murdering them and I'm electrocuted. And my secretary and wife can't stand it anymore. Take me to a state hospital. I don't want to go. Take me. I'm getting crazy and you don't help me. Help me, *Lieber Doktor!* I went into the ladies' room twice today to get my secretary and the girls complained to the building office. I'm not above the rules. I knew I violated them. My zipper was down again [he frequently "forgets"] and I just pulled it up before you came in today." B agrees that state hospital might be appropriate if he is becoming "crazier." "Then my wife will divorce me. It's terrible. They have bars there. I won't go. I'm not that bad yet. Why, last week I went out and made a big sale!" B suggests he "practice" his fears and obsessions.

May 8.   Seen by A and B who did summary of his family constellation. It was done very tentatively because of the sparsity of information elicited.

May 13.   Complains about symptoms. He had taken his wife to the movie but "was too upset to watch it." He had helped with the raking. Returns to symptoms and begging for Thorazine. "How will I live without Thorazine?" B suggests they ought to talk about how to live. He yells, "With your quiet voice, you'll drive me crazy." B asks, "Would you like me to yell at you like your father did?" "I won't talk to you anymore."

"*Lieber Gott,* liberate me from the evil within me." Prays to everyone for help. B counters with "Have you ever solicited your own help?" Patient replies, "I have no strength. I could cry. I could shout. I don't have strength. Let me vomit."

May 15.   Demands Thorazine or he will have heart attack. B requests a future autobiography. "I don't anticipate anything" and returns to Thorazine question. B points out his real achievement in staying off Thorazine. Patient mentions price in suffering. B points out that this makes it an even greater achievement. Patient accepts idea reluctantly. B points out that they are at cross-purposes since patient wants to continue suffering but have pills; B's goal is to have him stop his suffering. "I want pills." B offers clay. "Shit with your clay."

May 20. Must have Thorazine. Has murderous and self-castrating fantasies. Tells A that he (A) doesn't know anything about medicine. Dr. C did. Why don't we let him go back to Dr. C? A leaves room with patient following. After three to four minutes he returns and complains, "You call *this* treatment?" A points out demand of patient to have own way. He is a little boy who wants to be big but doesn't think he can make it. He is a pampered tyrant and A refers to patient's favorite childhood game of lying in bed with sister and playing "Emperor and Empress."

Patient points out innate badness in himself. A points out he creates it. Patient talks of hostility and murder. A interprets look on his face as taking pride in his bad behavior. He picks up letter opener, trembles, then grasps hand with other hand but continues to tremble. A tells him that this is spurious fight between good and evil, that he can decide how he will behave.

He kneaded clay a little while this weekend.

May 22. Last weekend he mowed lawn, tried to read but "I'm nervous. I'm talking to you like a human being but I'm not really a human being." Raw throat. Fears might have throat cancer. Stopped sticking finger down throat to vomit as consequence. Discussion of previously expressed idea of "like a human being." Fantasy of riding a boat through a storm. Fantasy of A being acclaimed by crowd and patient in fantasy asks B, "Are you used to A getting all the attention?"

Complains about wife and secretary, neither of whom will any longer permit tyrannization.

June 3. Relates fantasy of being magician and performing unbelievable feats at the White House. He asked the President whether he was happily married and then produced the President's ring. Nice weekend. Made love to wife at his initiative. Grudgingly admits enjoying it.

June 10. "Ignored my wife this week." Yet he took initiative and they had sex again. Both enjoyed it but he was afraid because he read in a magazine that sex is a drain on the heart. At work secretary is angry. After she checks things, he rechecks. Pledged his God today he wouldn't do it anymore. He'll only check one time more. Outlines several plans for improving business "but I have not the strength." Wants to cut down to one interview per week because he doesn't get well and can't afford to pay. B suggests that perhaps he is improving if he wants to reduce number of interviews. Patient rejects and agrees to two interviews weekly.

June 24. Talks about fears. B tells him he will go on vacation next week. He accepts it calmly although he had previously claimed to be unendurably upset. Patient tells B that he has given up vomiting and masturbation, saying, "You have enormous influence on me." B encourages by saying patient made the decision by himself.

Sept. 4. [Patient was not seen during August because he went on a "wonderful" vacation.] He stopped all medication except for the occasional use of a mild tranquilizer his family physician prescribed. Able to read and concentrate again. He has surrendered his obsessive ruminations. He and his secretary get along without fighting although she doesn't like him. He is punctual at the office. He and wife get along well. He is more considerate of her. Both are sexually satisfied.

B and patient discuss plans for treatment. He expresses reluctance, feeling that he has gone as far as he can. After all, one psychoanalyst said that he was hopeless, recommended a lobotomy, so this was marked improvement. B agreed, telling patient that if he had considered the patient hopeless, he would not have undertaken treatment nor would he now be recommending continuation. "What kind of treatment?" B tells him that no external agent (e.g. medicine, lobotomy) will do it, that his salvation will come from within, that he can choose to live life destructively (and self-destructively) or constructively. He proposes to come weekly for four weeks and then biweekly. B does not accept the offer.

Sept. 17. Has been feeling better. Had always considered self slow reader but now reads with lightning speed. Relates dream of going down into basement where there is much cheap candy. He decides he doesn't want any.

Since yesterday his symptoms have returned. Heart palpitations.

Sept. 25. Took wife to dinner last night. Very pleasant. Business is slow and his obligations are heavy but he is working. He has to exert effort not to backslide. B schedules double interview. Patient doesn't want to see A. It will upset him. He doesn't see any sense in seeing B either but since B insists. . . . Heart palpitations disappeared after last interview. Expresses realistic concerns today

and has dropped usual frantic manner. Wants biweekly interviews. B wants weekly. Patient accepts without protest.

As therapy continued, his discussion of symptoms was superseded by discussion of realistic concerns. Resistance waned. When he entered treatment, he perceived himself as a good person who behaved badly because he was "sick." During therapy, he saw through his pretenses and settled for being "a bad guy." However, once he understood his tyranny and was able to accept it, he had the opportunity to ask himself how he preferred to live his life—usefully or uselessly. Since the therapists used the monolithic approach (Alexander & French, 1946; Mosak & Shulman, 1963), after resolving the issue of his tyranny, therapy moved on to his other "basic mistakes," one at a time. The frequency of interviews was decreased and termination was by mutual agreement.

Follow-up

Patient improved, remaining off medication. Devoting himself to his business, it prospered to the point where he could retire early. He moved to a university town where he studied archaeology, the activity he liked best in life. The relationship with his wife improved and they traveled abroad. Because of the geographical distance between them, the therapists and the patient had no further contact.

SUMMARY

Adlerian psychology as a theory of personality may be described as follows:

1. Its approach is social, teleological, phenomenological, holistic, idiographic, and humanistic.

2. Its underlying assumptions are (*a*)

the individual is unique, (*b*) the individual is self-consistent, (*c*) man is a responsible human being, (*d*) man is creative, an actor, a chooser, (*e*) man, in a soft-deterministic fashion, can direct his own destiny.

3. Its personality theory takes as its central construct the life-style, a system of subjective convictions held by the individual that contain his self-view and his world-view. From these convictions, other convictions, methods of operations, and the goals of the person are derivative. The person behaves *as if* these convictions were true and uses his life-style as a cognitive map with which he explores, comprehends, prejudges, predicts, and controls the environment (the life tasks). Since the person cannot be understood *in vacuo* but only in his social context, the interaction between the individual and his life tasks, his line of movement, is indispensable for the purpose of fully comprehending the individual.

4. "Psychopathology" and "mental illness" and similar nomenclature are reifications and perpetuate the nominal fallacy, "the tendency to confuse naming with explaining" (Beach, 1955). The "psychopathological" individual is a discouraged person. He has either never developed or lost his courage with respect to meeting the life tasks. With his pessimistic anticipations, stemming largely from his life-style, he creates "arrangements,"—evasions, excuses, sideshows, symptoms—to protect his self-esteem or he may "cop out" completely.

5. Since the person's difficulties emanate from faulty perceptions, learnings, values, and goals that have resulted in his discouragement, therapy consists of an educative or reeducative endeavor in which two equals cooperatively tackle the educational task. Many of the traditional analytic methods have been retained although they are understood, and sometimes used, differently by the Adlerian. The focus of the therapy is the encouragement of the individual, the experience of encouragement coming from many avenues in the therapy. The individual learns to have faith in self, to trust, and to love. The ultimate, *ideal* goal of psychotherapy is to release the person's social interest so he may become a fellow human being, a cooperator, a contributor to the creation of a better society, a person who feels belonging and at home in the universe. This person can be said to have actualized himself. Since therapy is learning, theoretically at least, everyone can change. On the entrance door of the Guidance Clinic for Juvenile Delinquency in Vienna was the inscription, "IT IS NEVER TOO LATE" (Kramer, 1947).

From a rather shaky start, Adlerian psychology has become a viable, flourishing system. Neglected for several decades, it has in recent years acquired respectability. Training institutes, professional societies, family-education centers, and study groups continue to proliferate. With Adlerians being trained in universities rather than solely in institutes, they are writing more and doing research. Non-Adlerians are also engaged in Adlerian research. The previously rare Adlerian dissertation has become more commonplace. Currently Adlerians in greater numbers are moving out of the clinic and into society to renew their attention to the social issues and problems Adler raised 50 years ago—poverty, war, conflict resolution, aggression, religion, and social cooperation. As Way (1962) apprises, "We shall need not only, as Adler says, more cooperative individuals, but a society better fitted to fulfil the needs of human beings" (p. 360).

Complementing the Adlerians' endeavors are individuals and groups who have borrowed so heavily from Adler, often without acknowledgment and often without awareness. Adlerian formulations are so often discovered in the writing of non-Adlerians that they have become part of what Adler might have called "the common sense." Keith Sward (1947), for example, reviewed Alexander and French's *Psychoanalytic Therapy,* writing,

—the Chicago group would seem to be Adlerian through and through. . . . The Chicago Institute for Psychoanalysis is not alone in this seeming rediscovery of Rank and Adler. Psychiatry and psychology as a whole seem to be drifting in the same direction. Adler has come to life in other vigorous circles, notably in the publications of the 'Horney' school (p. 601).

We observe glimpses of Adler in the Freudian ego-psychologists, in the neo-Freudians, in the existential systems, in the humanistic psychologies, in client-centered theory, in rational-emotive therapy, in integrity therapy, and in reality therapy. This is not an augury of the eventual disappearance of Adlerian psychology through absorption into other schools of psychology, for, as the motto of the Rockford, Illinois, Teacher Development Center, a school conducted along Adlerian lines as far as educational climate is concerned (Mosak, 1971), proclaims, "Education is like a flame . . . you can give it away without diminishing the one from whom it came (Teacher Development Center, n.d.)." As Joseph Wilder writes in his Introduction to *Essays in Individual Psychology* (Adler & Deutsch, 1959), ". . . most observations and ideas of Alfred Adler have subtly and quietly permeated modern psychological thinking to such a degree that the proper question is not whether one is Adlerian but how much of an Adlerian one is" (p. xv).

ANNOTATED BIBLIOGRAPHY

Ansbacher, Heinz L., & Ansbacher, Rowena (Eds.) *The individual psychology of Alfred Adler.* New York: Basic Books, 1956, 1958; New York: Harper Torchbooks, 1964. Paper.

An almost encyclopedic collection of Adler's writings, this volume displays both the great variety of topics that commanded his attention and the evolution of his thinking through the years. Because of the nature of the construction of this book, it is imperative that the reader read the preface.

Adler, A. *Social interest: A challenge to mankind.* (1929) New York: Capricorn Books, 1964. Paper.

This is the last exposition of Adler's thought and provides an easily read overview of Adlerian psychology.

Adler, A. *Problems of neurosis: A book of case-histories.* (1929) New York: Harper Torchbooks, 1964. Paper.

Adler presents his theory of the neurotic process and neurotic development illustrating with many case examples. H. L. Ansbacher has written an excellent introduction to the paperback edition that concisely covers the basic theory of Adlerian psychology.

Mosak, Harold, & Mosak, Birdie. *A bibliography of Adlerian psychology.* Washington, D.C.: Hemisphere Publishing Corp., 1975.

This volume contains almost 10,000 references to the literature of Adlerian psychology, is valuable to the student, and invaluable to the researcher in helping to locate Adlerian writings.

Mosak, Harold H. (Ed.) *Alfred Adler: His influence on psychology today.* Park Ridge, N.J.: Noyes Press, 1973.

Written to commemorate the centennial year of Adler's birth, this volume contains chapters by Dreikurs, Alexandra Adler, Lewis Way, Erwin Krausz, the Beechers, and others. These papers cover topics such as neurosis, black pride, Shakespeare, logical consequences, family therapy, the Oedipus myth, and sociometry.

Dreikurs, Rudolf, & Soltz, Vicki. *Children: The challenge.* New York: Duell, Sloan & Pearce, 1964.

Dreikurs and Soltz have written *the* Adlerian book on childrearing. It is the book most often studied in university training programs and parent study groups.

CASE READINGS

Adler, Alfred. *The case of Miss R: The inpretation of a life study.* New York: Greenberg, 1929.

Adler, Alfred. The case of Mrs. A.: The diagnosis of a life style. In H. L. Ansbacher & R. R. Ansbacher (Eds.), *Superiority and social interest.* Evanston, Ill.: Northwestern University Press, 1964, pp. 159–90.

Ansbacher, Heinz L. Lee Harvey Oswald: An Adlerian interpretation. *Psychoanalytic Review,* 1966, 53, 379–90.

Dreikurs, Rudolf. Case demonstrations. In R. Dreikurs, R. Lowe, M. Sonstegard, & R. J. Corsini, *Adlerian family counseling.* Eugene, Ore.: University of Oregon Press, 1959.

Mozak, Harold H. Life style assessment: A demonstration based on family constellation. *Journal of Individual Psychology,* 1972, 28, 232–47.

REFERENCES

Adler, Alexandra. Problems in psychotherapy. *American Journal of Individual Psychology,* 1943, 3, 1–5. (Also in Kurt A. Adler & Danica Deutsch [Eds.], *Essays in individual psychology.* New York: Grove Press, 1959.)

Adler, Alexandra. Alfred Adler's viewpoint in child guidance. In Ernest Harms (Ed.), *Handbook of child guidance.* New York: Child Care Publications, 1951.

Adler, Alfred. *Gesundheitsbuch für das Schneidergewerbe.* Berlin: C. Heymanns, 1898.

Adler, Alfred. Das Zärtlichkeitsbedürfnis des Kindes. In Alfred Adler & Carl Furtmüller (Eds.), *Heilen und Bilden.* München: Reinhardt, 1914.

Adler, Alfred. *Study of organ inferiority and its psychical compensation.* New York: Nervous & Mental Disease Publishing Co., 1917.

Adler, Alfred. Progress in individual psychology. *British Journal of Medical Psychology,* 1924, 4, 22–31.

Adler, Alfred. *The neurotic constitution.* (1926) Freeport, N.Y.: Books for Libraries Press, 1972.

Adler, Alfred. On teaching courage. *Survey Graphic,* 1928, 61, 241–42.

Adler, Alfred. Position in family influences life-style. *International Journal of Individual Psychology,* 1929, 3(3), 211–27.

Adler, Alfred. Individual psychology. In Carl Murchison (Ed.), *Psychologies of 1930.* Worcester, Mass.: Clark University Press, 1930.

Adler, Alfred. Lecture to the Medical Society of Individual Psychology, London. *Individual Psychology Pamphlets,* 1934, 13, 11–24.

Adler, Alfred. How I chose my career. *Individual Psychology Bulletin,* 1947, 6, 9–11. (Also in Phyllis Bottome, *Alfred Adler: A biography.* New York: Putnam, 1939.)

Adler, Alfred. *What life should mean to you.* New York: Capricorn Books, 1958.

Adler, Alfred. *Understanding human nature.* New York: Premier Books, 1959.

Adler, Alfred. *The practice and theory of individual psychology.* Paterson, N.J.: Littlefield, Adams, 1963(a).

Adler, Alfred. *The problem child.* New York: Capricorn Books, 1963(b).

Adler, Alfred. *Problems of neurosis.* New York: Harper & Row, 1964(a).

Adler, Alfred. *Social interest: A challenge to mankind.* New York: Capricorn Books, 1964(b).

Adler, Alfred. *The science of living.* New York: Doubleday Anchor Books, 1969.

Adler, Kurt A. Depression in the light of individual psychology. *Journal of Individual Psychology,* 1961, 17, 56–67. (Also in H. D. Werner [Ed.], *New understandings of human behavior.* New York: Association Press, 1970.)

Adler, Kurt A., & Deutsch, Danica. *Essays in individual psychology.* New York: Grove Press, 1959.

Alexander, Franz, & French, Thomas M. *Psychoanalytic therapy.* New York: Ronald Press, 1946.

Allport, Gordon. *Pattern and growth in personality.* New York: Holt, Rinehart & Winston, 1961.

Allred, G. H. *How to strengthen your marriage and family.* Provo, Utah: Brigham Young University Press, 1976.

Angers, William P. Clarifications toward the rapprochement between religion and psychology. *Journal of Individual Psychology,* 1960, 16, 73-76.

Ansbacher, Heinz L. Adler's place today in the psychology of memory. *Journal of Personality,* 1946, 15, 197-207. (Also in *Individual Psychology Bulletin,* 1947, 6, 32-40, and *Internationale Zeitschrift für Individualpsychologie,* 1947, 16, 97-111.)

Ansbacher, Heinz L. "Neo-Freudian" or "Neo-Adlerian?" *American Journal of Individual Psychology,* 1952, 10, 87-88. (Also in *American Psychologist,* 1953, 8, 165-66.)

Ansbacher, Heinz L. A key to existence. *Journal of Individual Psychology,* 1959, 15, 141-42.

Ansbacher, Heinz L. Suicide: Adlerian point of view. In Norman L. Farberow & Edwin S. Schneidman (Eds.), *The cry for help.* New York: McGraw-Hill, 1961.

Ansbacher, Heinz L. Was Adler a disciple of Freud? A reply. *Journal of Individual Psychology,* 1962, 18, 126-35.

Ansbacher, Heinz L. Life style: A historical and systematic review. *Journal of Individual Psychology,* 1967, 23, 191-212.

Ansbacher, Heinz L. The concept of social interest. *Journal of Individual Psychology,* 1968, 24, 131-49.

Ansbacher, Heinz L. Suicide as communication: Adler's concept and current applications. *Journal of Individual Psychology,* 1969, 25, 174-80. [Also in *Humanitas,* 1970, 6, 5-13.]

Ansbacher, Heinz L., & Ansbacher, Rowena (Eds.). *The individual psychology of Alfred Adler.* New York: Basic Books, 1956.

Beach, Frank A. The descent of instinct. *Psychological Review,* 1955, 62, 401-10.

Beecher, Willard, & Beecher, Marguerite. *Parents on the run.* New York: Agora Press, 1966.

Berne, Eric. *Games people play.* New York: Grove Press, 1964.

Bickhard, M. H., & Ford, B. L. Adler's concept of social interest. *Journal of Individual Psychology,* 1976, 32(1), 27-49.

Bierer, Joshua. *The day hospital, an experiment in social psychiatry and synthoanalytic psychotherapy.* London: H. K. Lewis, 1951.

Bierer, Joshua, & Evans, Richard I. *Innovations in social psychiatry.* London: Avenue Publishing Co., 1969.

Birnbaum, Ferdinand. The Individual-Psychological Experimental School in Vienna. *International Journal of Individual Psychology,* 1935, 1(2), 118-24.

Birnbaum, Ferdinand. Frankl's existential psychology from the viewpoint of Individual Psychology. *Journal of Individual Psychology,* 1961, 17, 162-66.

Bottome, Phyllis. *Alfred Adler, a biography.* New York: Putnam, 1939.

Brome, Vincent. *Freud and his early circle.* New York: William Morrow, 1968.

Brown, Claude. *Manchild in the promised land.* New York: Signet Books, 1965.

Bugental, James F. T. Humanistic psychology: A new breakthrough. *American Psychologist,* 1963, 18(9), 563-67.

Clark, Kenneth B. Problems of power and social change: Toward a relevant social psychology. *Journal of Social Issues,* 1965, 21(3), 4-20.

Clark, Kenneth B. *Dark ghetto.* New York: Harper Torchbooks, 1967(a).

Clark, Kenneth B. Implications of Adlerian theory for an understanding of civil rights problems and action. *Journal of Individual Psychology,* 1967(b), 23, 181-90.

Colby, Kenneth M. On the disagreement between Freud and Adler. *American Imago,* 1951, 8, 229-38.

Corsini, Raymond J. The behind-the-back technique in group psychotherapy. *Group Psychotherapy,* 1953, 6, 102-9.

Corsini, Raymond J. Individual Education. *Journal of Individual Psychology,* 1977, 33, 295-349.

Credner, Lene. Sicherungen. *Internationale Zeitschrift für Individualpsychologie,* 1930, 8(1), 87-92. (Translated as "Safeguards," *International Journal of Individual Psychology,* 1936, 2(3), 95-102.)

Deutsch, Danica. Group therapy with married couples. *Individual Psychologist,* 1967, 4(2), 56-62.

Dinkmeyer, Don, & Dreikurs, Rudolf. *Encouraging children to learn: The encouragement process.* Englewood Cliffs, N.J.: Prentice-Hall, 1963.

Dreikurs, Rudolf. The meaning of dreams. *Chicago Medical School Quarterly,* 1944, 3, 4-6, 25-26. (Also in *Psychodynamics, psychotherapy and counseling.* Chicago: Alfred Adler Institute, 1967.)

Dreikurs, Rudolf. The four goals of children's misbehavior. *Nervous Child,* 1947, 6, 3-11.

(Also in *Child guidance and education: Collected papers*. Chicago: Alfred Adler Institute, 1974.)

Dreikurs, Rudolf. *The challenge of parenthood*. New York: Duell, Sloan & Pearce, 1948.

Dreikurs, Rudolf. Techniques and dynamics of multiple psychotherapy. *Psychiatric Quarterly*, 1950, 24, 788–99. (Also in *Group psychotherapy and group approaches: Collected papers*. Chicago: Alfred Adler Institute, 1960.)

Dreikurs, Rudolf. Psychotherapy as correction of faulty social values. *Journal of Individual Psychology*, 1957, 13, 150–58. (Also in *Psychodynamics, psychotherapy and counseling*. Chicago: Alfred Adler Institute, 1967.)

Dreikurs, Rudolf. A reliable differential diagnosis of psychological or somatic disturbances. *International Record of Medicine*, 1958, 171, 238–42. (Also in *Psychodynamics, psychotherapy and counseling*. Chicago: Alfred Adler Institute, 1967.)

Dreikurs, Rudolf. Early experiments with group psychotherapy. *American Journal of Psychotherapy*, 1959, 13, 882–91.

Dreikurs, Rudolf. The current dilemma in psychotherapy. *Journal of Existential Psychiatry*, 1960, 1, 187–206(a).

Dreikurs, Rudolf. *Group psychotherapy and group approaches: Collected papers*. Chicago: Alfred Adler Institute, 1960(b).

Dreikurs, Rudolf. The Adlerian approach to therapy. In Morris I. Stein (Ed.), *Contemporary psychotherapies*. Glencoe, Ill.: The Free Press, 1961.

Dreikurs, Rudolf. Can you be sure the disease is functional? *Consultant* (Smith, Kline & French Laboratories), August, 1962.

Dreikurs, Rudolf. Psychodynamic diagnosis in psychiatry. *American Journal of Psychiatry*, 1963, 119, 1045–48. (Also in *Psychodynamics, psychotherapy and counseling*. Chicago: Alfred Adler Institute, 1967.)

Dreikurs, Rudolf. *Psychology in the classroom*. New York: Harper & Row, 1968.

Dreikurs, Rudolf. Social interest: The basis of normalcy. *The Counseling Psychologist*, 1969, 1(2), 45–48.

Dreikurs, Rudolf. *Social equality: The challenge of today*. Chicago: Henry Regnery, 1971.

Dreikurs, Rudolf. Technology of Conflict Resolution. *Journal of Individual Psychology*, 1972, 28, 203–6.

Dreikurs, Rudolf; Corsini, Raymond J.; Lowe, Raymond; & Sonstegard, Manford. *Adlerian family counseling*. Eugene, Ore.: University of Oregon Press, 1959.

Dreikurs, Rudolf, & Grey, Loren. *Logical consequences*. New York: Meredith, 1968.

Dreikurs, Rudolf; Grunwald, Bernice; & Pepper, Floy C. *Maintaining sanity in the classroom*. New York: Harper & Row, 1971.

Dreikurs, Rudolf, & Mosak, Harold H. The tasks of life I. Adler's three tasks. *Individual Psychologist*, 1966, 4(1), 18–22.

Dreikurs, Rudolf, & Mosak, Harold H. The tasks of life II. The fourth life task. *Individual Psychologist*, 1967, 4(2), 51–55.

Dreikurs, Rudolf; Shulman, Bernard H.; & Mosak, Harold H. Patient-therapist relationship in multiple psychotherapy. I. Its advantage to the therapist. *Psychiatric Quarterly*, 1952(a), 26, 219–27. (Also in *Group psychotherapy and group approaches: Collected papers*. Chicago: Alfred Adler Institute, 1960.)

Dreikurs, Rudolf; Mosak, Harold H.; & Shulman, Bernard H. Patient-therapist relationship in multiple psychotherapy. II. Its advantages for the patient. *Psychiatric Quarterly*, 1952(b), 26, 590–96. (Also in *Group psychotherapy and group approaches: Collected papers*. Chicago: Alfred Adler Institute, 1960.)

Dreikurs, Rudolf, & Soltz, Vicki. *Children: The challenge*. New York: Duell, Sloan & Pearce, 1964.

Dunlap, Knight. *Habits: Their making and unmaking*. New York: Liveright, 1933.

Elam, Harry. Cooperation between African and Afro-American, cultural highlights. *Journal of the National Medical Association*, 1969(a), 61, 30–35.

Elam, Harry. Malignant cultural deprivation, its evolution. *Pediatrics*, 1969(b), 44, 319–26.

Ellenberger, Henri F. *The discovery of the unconscious*. New York: Basic Books, 1970.

Ellis, Albert. Rational psychotherapy and Individual Psychology. *Journal of Individual Psychology*, 1957, 13, 38–44.

Ellis, Albert. Toward a more precise definition of "emotional" and "intellectual" insight. *Psychological Reports,* 1963, 13, 125–26.

Ellis, Albert. Humanism, values, rationality. *Journal of Individual Psychology,* 1970, 26, 37–38.

Ellis, Albert. Reason and emotion in the Individual Psychology of Adler. *Journal of Individual Psychology,* 1971, 27, 50–64.

Farau, Alfred. The influence of Alfred Adler on current psychology. *American Journal of Individual Psychology,* 1953, 10, 59–76.

Farau, Alfred. Individual psychology and existentialism. *Individual Psychologist,* 1964, 2(1), 1–8.

Federn, Ernst. Was Adler a disciple of Freud? A Freudian view. *Journal of Individual Psychology,* 1963, 19, 80–81.

Fiedler, Fred E. A comparison of therapeutic relationships in psychoanalytic, nondirective and Adlerian therapy. *Journal of Consulting Psychology,* 1950, 14, 436–45.

Forer, Lucille K. Bibliography of birth order literature of the 1970s. *Journal of Individual Psychology,* 1977, 33, 122–41.

Frank, Lawrence K. Projective methods for the study of personality. *Journal of Personality,* 1939, 8, 389–413.

Frankl, Viktor E. *Man's search for meaning.* New York: Washington Square Press, 1963.

Frankl, Viktor E. Fore-runner of existential psychiatry. *Journal of Individual Psychology,* 1970, 26, 38.

Fromm-Reichman, Frieda. Notes on personal and professional requirements of a psychotherapist. *Psychiatry,* 1949, 12, 361–78.

Goldstein, Kurt. *The organism.* New York: American Book Co., 1939.

Gottesfeld, Harry. Changes in feelings of powerlessness in a community action program. *Psychological Reports,* 1966, 19, 978.

Grunwald, Bernice. The application of Adlerian principles in a classroom. *American Journal of Individual Psychology,* 1954, 11, 131–41.

Gushurst, Robin S. The reliability and concurrent validity of an idiographic approach to the interpretation of early recollections. Ph.D. dissertation, University of Chicago, 1971.

Hemming, James. *Mankind against the killers.* London: Longmans, Green, 1956.

Hinrichsen, Otto. Unser Verstehen der seelischen Zusammenhänge in der Neurose und Freud's und Adler's Theorien. *Zen-*

tralblätter für Psychoanalyse, 1913, 3, 369–93.

Horney, Karen. *Neurosis and human growth.* London: Routledge & Kegan Paul, 1951.

Jahn, Ernst, & Adler, Alfred. Religion and Individual Psychology. In Heinz L. Ansbacher & Rowena Ansbacher (Eds.), *Superiority and social interest.* Evanston, Ill.: Northwestern University Press, 1964.

James, Walter T.; Karen Horney; and Erich Fromm. In relation to Alfred Adler. *Individual Psychology Bulletin,* 1947, 6, 105–16.

James, William. *Principles of psychology.* New York: Holt, 1890.

Kadis, Asya L. Re-experiencing the family constellation in group psychotherapy. *American Journal of Individual Psychology,* 1956, 12, 63–68.

Kramer, Hilde C. Preventive psychiatry. *Individual Psychology Bulletin,* 1947, 7, 12–18.

Krausz, Erwin O. The pessimistic attitude. *International Journal of Individual Psychology,* 1935, 1(3), 86–99.

Krausz, Erwin O. The commonest neurosis. In Kurt A. Adler & Danica Deutsch (Eds.), *Essays in Individual Psychology.* New York: Grove Press, 1959.

La Porte, George H. Social interest in action: A report on one attempt to implement Adler's concept. *Individual Psychologist,* 1966, 4(1), 22–26.

Lazarsfeld, Sofie. Pitfalls in psychotherapy. *American Journal of Individual Psychology,* 1952–53, 10, 20–26.

Lazarsfeld, Sofie. The courage for imperfection. *Journal of Individual Psychology,* 1966, 22, 163–65.

Lewin, Kurt. *A dynamic theory of personality.* New York: McGraw-Hill, 1935.

Lombardi, Donald M. The special language of the addict. *Pastoral Psychology,* 1969, 20, 51–52.

Low, Abraham A. *Mental health through will training.* Boston: Christopher, 1952.

Maslow, Abraham H. Was Adler a disciple of Freud? A note. *Journal of Individual Psychology,* 1962, 18, 125.

Maslow, Abraham H. Holistic emphasis. *Journal of Individual Psychology,* 1970, 26, 39.

May, Rollo. Myth and guiding fiction. *Journal of Individual Psychology,* 1970, 26, 39.

McArthur, Herbert. The necessity of choice.

Journal of Individual Psychology, 1958, 14, 153–57.

Meerloo, Joost A. M. Pervasiveness of terms and concepts. *Journal of Individual Psychology,* 1970, 26, 40.

Miley, Charles H. Birth-order research 1963–1967: Bibliography and index. *Journal of Individual Psychology,* 1969, 25, 64–70.

Mohr, Erika, & Garlock, Rose. The social club as an adjunct to therapy. In Kurt A. Adler & Danica Deutsch (Eds.), *Essays in Individual Psychology.* New York: Grove Press, 1959.

Mosak, Birdie, & Mosak, Harold H. Dreikurs' four goals: The clarification of some misconceptions. *Individual Psychologist,* 1975, 12(2), 14–16.

Mosak, Harold H. The psychological attitude in rehabilitation. *American Archives of Rehabilitation Therapy,* 1954, 2, 9–10.

Mosak, Harold H. Early recollections as a projective technique. *Journal of Projective Techniques,* 1958, 22, 302–11. (Also in Gardner Lindzey & Calvin S. Hall [Eds.], *Theories of personality: Primary sources and research.* New York: Wiley, 1965.)

Mosak, Harold H. Subjective criteria of normality. *Psychotherapy,* 1967, 4, 159–61.

Mosak, Harold H. Strategies for behavior change in schools: Consultation strategies. *The Counseling Psychologist,* 1971, 3(1), 58–62.

Mosak, Harold H. Lifestyle. In Arthur G. Nikelly (Ed.), *Techniques for behavior change.* Springfield, Ill.: C. C Thomas, 1971, 77–81.

Mosak, Harold H. Life style assessment: A demonstration based on family constellation. *Journal of Individual Psychology,* 1972, 28, 232–47.

Mosak, Harold H., & Dreikurs, Rudolf. The life tasks III. The fifth life task. *Individual Psychologist,* 1967, 5(1), 16–22.

Mosak, Harold H., & Fletcher, Samuel J. Purposes of delusions and hallucinations. *Journal of Individual Psychology,* 1973, 29, 176–81.

Mosak, Harold H., & Gushurst, Robin S. What patients say and what they mean. *American Journal of Psychotherapy,* 1971, 3, 428–36.

Mosak, Harold H., & Kopp, Richard. The early recollections of Adler, Freud, and Jung. *Journal of Individual Psychology.*

1973, 29, 157–66.

Mosak, Harold H., & LeFevre, Carol. The resolution of "intrapersonal conflict." *Journal of Individual Psychology,* 1976, 32(1), 19–26.

Mosak, Harold H., & Schneider, Seymour. Masculine protest, penis envy, women's liberation and sexual equality. *Journal of Individual Psychology,* 1973, 33, 193–201.

Mosak, Harold H., & Shulman, Bernard H. *Individual psychotherapy: A syllabus.* Chicago: Alfred Adler Institute, 1963.

Mozdzierz, G. J., & Lottman, T. J. Games married couples play: Adlerian view. *Journal of Individual Psychology,* 1973, 29(2), 182–94.

Mullahy, Patrick. *Oedipus: Myth and complex.* New York: Evergreen, 1955.

Murphy, Gardner. *Personality: A biosocial approach to origins and structure.* New York: Harper, 1947.

Murphy, Gardner; Murphy, Lois B.; & Newcomb, Theodore M. *Experimental social psychology.* Rev. ed. New York: Harper, 1937.

Neuer, Alexander. Courage and discouragement. *International Journal of Individual Psychology,* 1936, 2(2), 30–50.

Nikelly, Arthur G. Basic processes in psychotherapy. In Arthur G. Nikelly (Ed.), *Techniques for behavior change.* Springfield, Ill.: C. C Thomas, 1971(a).

Nikelly, Arthur G. Developing social feeling in psychotherapy. In Arthur G. Nikelly (Ed.), *Techniques for behavior change.* Springfield, Ill.: C. C Thomas, 1971(b).

Nikelly, Arthur G. The protesting student. In Arthur G. Nikelly (Ed.), *Techniques for behavior change.* Springfield, Ill.: C. C Thomas, 1971(c).

O'Reilly, Charles; Cizon, Francis; Flanagan, John; & Pflanczer, Steven. *Men in jail.* Chicago: Loyola University, 1965.

Orgler, Hertha. *Alfred Adler: The man and his work.* New York: Capricorn Books, 1965.

Papanek, Ernst. Delinquency. In Arthur G. Nikelly (Ed.), *Techniques for behavior change.* Springfield, Ill.: C. C Thomas, 1971, 177–83.

Papanek, Helene. Combined group and individual therapy in private practice. *American Journal of Psychotherapy,* 1954, 8, 679–86.

Papanek, Helene. Combined group and individual therapy in the light of Adlerian psychology. *International Journal of Group Psychotherapy,* 1956, 6, 136–46.

Papanek, Helene. Emotion and intellect in psychotherapy. *American Journal of Psychotherapy,* 1959, 13, 150–73.

Papanek, Helene, & Papanek, Ernst. Individual Psychology today. *American Journal of Psychotherapy,* 1961, 15, 4–26.

Pelzman, Oscar. Some problems in the use of psychotherapy. *Psychiatric Quarterly Supplement,* 1952, 26, 53–58.

Pew, Miriam L., & Pew, W. Adlerian marriage counseling. *Journal of Individual Psychology,* 1972, 28(2), 192–202.

Rasey, Marie I. Toward the end. In Clark E. Moustakas (Ed.), *The self: Explorations in personal growth.* New York: Harper, 1956.

Reik, Theodore. *Listening with the third ear.* New York: Farrar, Straus & Cudahy, 1948.

Rogers, Carl R. *Client-centered therapy.* Boston: Houghton Mifflin, 1951.

Rosenthal, D., & Frank, Jerome D. Psychotherapy and the placebo effect. *Psychological Bulletin,* 1956, 53, 294–302.

Seidler, Regine. The individual psychologist looks at testing. *Individual Psychologist,* 1967, 5(1), 3–6.

Seidler, Regine, & Zilahi, Ladislaw. The Vienna child guidance clinics. In Alfred Adler & associates, *Guiding the child.* London: Allen & Unwin, 1949, 9–27.

Shlien, John M.; Mosak, Harold H.; & Dreikurs, Rudolf. Effect of time limits: A comparison of two psychotherapies. *Journal of Counseling Psychology,* 1962, 9, 31–34.

Shoben, E. J., Jr. Toward a concept of normal personality. *American Psychologist,* 1957, 12, 183–89.

Shulman, Bernard H. A psychodramatically oriented action technique in group psychotherapy. *Group Psychotherapy,* 1960, 22, 34–39.

Shulman, Bernard H. The meaning of people to the schizophrenic and the manic-depressive. *Journal of Individual Psychology,* 1962, 18, 151–56.

Shulman, Bernard H. Psychological disturbances which interfere with the patient's cooperation. *Psychosomatics,* 1964, 5, 213–20.

Shulman, Bernard H., & Mosak, Harold H. Birth order and ordinal position. *Journal of Individual Psychology,* 1977, 33, 114–21.

Shulman, Bernard H., & Klapman, Howard. Organ inferiority and psychiatric disorders in childhood. In Ernest Harms (Ed.), *Pathogenesis of nervous and mental diseases.* New York: Libra, 1968, 49–62.

Sicher, Lydia, & Mosak, Harold H. Aggression as a secondary phenomenon. *Journal of Individual Psychology,* 1967, 23, 232–35. (Also in H. D. Werner [Ed.], *New understandings of human behavior.* New York: Association Press, 1970).

Simpson, H. N. *Stoic apologetics.* Oak Park, Ill.: Author, 1966.

Smuts, Jan C. *Holism and evolution.* New York: Viking Press, 1961.

Soltz, Vicki. *Study group leader's manual.* Chicago: Alfred Adler Institute, 1967.

Spiel, Oskar. *Discipline without punishment.* London: Faber & Faber, 1962.

Strupp, Hans H. Freudian analysis today. *Psychology Today,* 1972, 6(2), 33–40.

Sullivan, Harry S. *The psychiatric interview.* New York: Norton, 1954.

Sward, Keith. Review of Karen Horney, *Our inner conflicts. Science,* December 12, 1947, 600–601.

Toman, Walter. Never mind your horoscope, birth order rules all. *Psychology Today,* 1970, 4(7), 45–49, 68–69.

Vaihinger, Hans. *The philosophy of "as if."* London: Routledge & Kegan Paul, 1965.

Von Sassen, H. W. Adler's and Freud's concepts of man: A phenomenological comparison. *Journal of Individual Psychology,* 1967, 23, 3–10.

Way, Lewis. *Adler's place in psychology.* New York: Collier Books, 1962.

Wexberg, Erwin. *Individual Psychology.* London: Allen & Unwin, 1929.

Wexberg, Erwin. *Individual psychological treatment.* Chicago: Alfred Adler Institute, 1970.

White, Robert W. Adler and the future of ego psychology. *Journal of Individual Psychology,* 1957, 13, 112–24.

Wittels, Fritz. The neo-Adlerians. *American Journal of Sociology,* 1939, 45, 433–45.

Wolfe, W. Béran. *How to be happy though human.* London: Routledge & Kegan Paul, 1932.

Wolff, Werner. *The personality of the preschool child.* New York: Grune & Stratton, 1946.

3

Analytical Psychotherapy

YORAM KAUFMANN

OVERVIEW

Analytical psychotherapy is an attempt to create, by means of a symbolic approach, a dialectical relationship between consciousness and the unconscious. The *psyche* is seen as a self-regulating system whose functioning is purposive with an internally imposed direction toward a life of fuller awareness. In psychotherapy a dialogue ensues, via dreams, fantasies, and other unconscious products, between the conscious state of the analysand and his personal, as well as the collective, unconscious.

Basic Concepts

The last millennium in Western culture can be characterized as a period of becoming more and more rational. In the attempt to master nature and his own fate, man has tried to discard fantasies, superstitions, and flights of fancy, replacing them with a more objective vision. The resulting viewpoint made possible technology and scientific knowledge that brought much material comfort. It was inevitable that this approach, therefore, gradually would outweigh all others. Freud's contribution to civilization was to suggest that rationality and consciousness

form but one aspect of the totality of human experience, and to postulate another realm of the psyche, namely, the *unconscious.* This major assumption Jung shares with Freud. Neither of them sought to depreciate consciousness; Jung saw conscious as a terminal value to strive for; "unconsciousness is sin" (Jung, 1934). Certainly the primary effort in life and in analysis is to become more conscious, to gain more awareness. But consciousness is but a small boat on the vast sea of the unconscious. We have to face the unpleasant fact that we are not masters in our own houses, but are ruled by forces and sources of energy operating through us, rather than ruled by us. These unconscious forces Jung saw as being both destructive and creative, but dangerous if ignored and unheeded. The unconscious is not just the sum total of everything that has been repressed in the course of one's development; it also contains wellsprings of creativity and sources of guidance and meaningfulness.

Structurally, the *unconscious* and the *conscious* constitute two subsystems of the psyche. These two relativise and compensate one another; the more one-sided an attitude is in one system, the more pronounced is its opposite in the other. Thus, a young man very much steeped in religious and spiritual matters dreams: *A voice said to me, "the way to carry on for Christ is on the genitals."*

Obviously the extremely one-sided preoccupation with matters spiritual is at the expense of the instinctual aspect of life, of which fact the dreamer is here reminded in no uncertain terms. Conversely, if the instinctual side is overemphasized, the unconscious is quite likely to insist on a more spiritual attitude.

Jung postulated, in addition to the usual instincts of sex, aggression, hunger, and thirst, an instinct toward *individuation.* There exists within us, Jung believed, an autonomous force that persistently pushes us to achieve wholeness (not perfection!) much like the physiological force that guides our physical development. This force is constantly trying to launch us on a process of fulfilling our truest self, thereby finding our own wholeness and particular meaning in life. All our behavior is both consciously and unconsciously motivated. We behave partly because of reasons of which we are aware and partly because of reasons of which we are unaware. One could, therefore, explore the unconscious in the way we move, communicate, make love, and so on. One of the most fruitful ways to understand a person's unconscious is through his dreams. A dream is posited to contain a message to the dreamer's awareness from his unconscious. The message is not expressed in our everyday language, but is veiled. If the veil is lifted, the dream is said to be interpreted or translated. Analytical psychology attaches a great deal of importance to the interpretation of dreams. This process is usually the backbone of a person's analysis.

To the average modern rationalist, all this may seem ludicrous and foggy. To other civilizations, these ideas are a matter of course, an obvious aspect of life. The Naskapi Indian, for example, carries within himself, in his heart, an inner companion whom he calls the Great Man, who is immortal and toward whom an attitude of total honesty is required. He communicates with the Great Man via dreams and inner voices. Life is viewed as a deepening communication with this inner companion.

This view posits that the unconscious has an existence of its own not reducible to other modes of psychic activity such as sexuality, interpersonal relationships, or a striving for power. These play important roles in the development of the personality, but are not primary. They form only part of the warp and weft of a bigger totality. The guiding and directing quality imputed to the unconscious implies a prospective, teleological aspect. The past determines the present to a large extent, but primarily, our actions are geared with a view toward the future: we act not only because of (the past) but for the sake of (the future).

The unconscious is our storehouse of energy, the psychic sphere within which transformations and metamorphoses are made possible. One can decide to stop acting under compulsion but to no avail; no matter how resolute the decision, compulsion reappears. Take for example the case of a young man valiantly wrestling with a potential psychotic process. He has what seem to be psychotic episodes of a paranoid nature. He enters therapy with a competent therapist who helps the patient adjust to his reality. However, the patient still does not feel completely understood and still feels the threat of the psychosis. He then starts analytical therapy and it becomes clear that previous therapy had not reached his unconscious. He tells the following recurrent childhood dream:

I am standing alone on a beach facing the Pacific Ocean. The ocean has huge waves, which come rolling on and engulf me.

The clinical picture is clear: The ego is threatened by an invasion from the unconscious. A possibility of a psychotic process is indeed indicated. After several months of analysis in which close attention was given to unconscious material, the patient dreams:

I am on the beach in Acapulco with a lot of people around me having a good time. I sense turbulence in the ocean, but I know that it will not reach me; I sense very strongly the boundary between the ocean and the beach.

To *Acapulco* the patient associated the popular resort where everyone goes. The possibility of a transformation is indicated. Turbulence is still there but the patient (the dream-ego in Jungian terminology) feels more secure. Note the change from the lonely and isolated feeling of the childhood dream to this dream, which has the feeling of belonging. Later he brought in the following dream.

I am on a ship on a cruise. We are at the middle of the ocean. A plank is lowered, and we are invited to swim. The water is beautifully blue and clear. At first I am slightly anxious, but I jump in and swim, and then return safely to the ship.

The patient spontaneously added that he had always considered himself a borderline case but that he now felt he had crossed the border; he felt normal, grounded, and full of energy. Many changes were taking place in his life. He was able to finish some important tasks and had been appointed to a responsible and remunerative position.

What is the language of communication between consciousness and the unconscious? The unconscious is not directly available to consciousness. The only communication seemingly available is the *symbol.* Symbols are attempts to express something essentially unexplainable but nevertheless postulated as existing. One can have the greatest understanding of the cross as a symbol, but the cross itself, emerging in a dream, carries profound meaning to the dreamer unexplainable in rational terms. *It is a basic tenet of Jungian therapy that all products of the unconscious are symbolic* and can be taken as guiding messages. Thus, the symptoms, the neurosis itself, are not merely indications of psychic malfunctioning but show the way out of the conflict underlying them, if symbolically understood. If a man finds himself constantly attracted to mutilated women, he can infer that "his own inner woman," his feminine side, may be mutilated and crippled; that his awareness of this is needed to heal this area.

What is the source of power of the unconscious? Jung came to the conclusion that that part of the unconscious which is a direct result of each individual's particular life situation represents only a small though important part of a larger totality, which he named the *collective unconscious.* The first part is called the *personal* level of the unconscious, the second the *nonpersonal* (or transpersonal) level. What is meant here is that all human beings, from the most remote past to our present days and into the foreseeable future, share the same inherited predispositions for psychic functioning.

As an analogy, compare the libido with water and the unconscious to a flat plane. If the water were to cover that plane, there would be no differentiation in the way the water is distributed; it would also form a flat plane. If we assume, however, that the plane is covered with rocks, causing depressions and protrusions of various shapes and sizes, the water flow now is along certain *gradients*. These rocks and craters are somewhat akin to the *archetypes*. The archetypes are a priori ordering principles for potential personalities. Archetypes are out of the reach of consciousness, but over the ages, they have given rise to equivalent forms of imagery in myths, fairy tales, and works of art in many cultures. Some motifs are: transformation, death and rebirth, the hero struggle, the mother, the divine child. Archetypes exist in us as potentialities; our life circumstances (our particular culture, our family, and our environment) determine in which way and which of the archetypes are actualized. The archetype, or psychic propensity, has to be activated (or evoked) by an experiential reality, which endows it with its specific form. For instance, we all participate in the heroic struggle, but each of us experiences it differently according to talents, temperaments, and one's given environment.

The archetypes are carriers of energy; the emergence of an archetype brings forth an enormous amount of energy. Conversely, all genuine creativity is archetypal in nature (cf., Neumann, 1955). Under normal circumstances the archetypal images express contemporary motifs; modern man is not likely to dream about slaying a dragon (the archetypal imagery in Greek and Norse mythology), but rather about fighting with his mother-in-law, walking through a dark tunnel, and so on. The more archaic representations are usually activated when the life-force encounters a powerful obstruction, either through a life situation (loss of a leg, death of the beloved, a life situation that does not allow for an acceptable solution) or contrived through various methods of meditation. In both cases, a profound introversion results in a regression of the libido to more primitive levels. The archetypal realm, in its capacity as an ordering principle, provides us with a sense of meaning. If we understand all suffering as a loss of meaning, the archetype can provide the healing-power principles.

Other Systems

The Jungian point of view accords easily with other contributions to the understanding of the psyche, such as the Gestalt theory, interpersonal and Adlerian theories, and even some aspects of behavior modification, especially as far as technique is concerned. But it is most edifying to contrast it with traditional psychoanalysis. To illustrate some of the differences between the Jungian and Freudian approaches, we have chosen examples of dreams discussed in Greenson's book, *The Technique and Practice of Psychoanalysis* (1968). It is dangerous to analyze dreams of patients one does not know, but nevertheless for heuristic purposes, some conclusions may be formulated. The first dream is that of a male patient (Greenson, 1968, p. 40):

I am waiting for a red traffic light to change when I feel that someone has bumped into me from behind. I rush out in fury and find out, with relief, it was only a boy on a bicycle. There was no damage to my car.

Greenson concludes that a comparison with his father in terms of sexual ability is involved. The boy on a bicycle is interpreted as masturbation and the red light as prostitution. Greenson comes to one conclusion that the patient has a wish-fulfilling fantasy that mother doesn't want sex with father who is not very potent. As Jungians, we would take the dream more phenomenologically. The red traffic light is taken to symbolize the laws of society, some general, conventional code, a collective prohibition; the little boy is an infantile, childish force within the dreamer, something not in full control; the being bumped, uncontrolled juvenile impatience, with no harm done. The message to the dreamer by the dream in terms of an analysis of the symbols is, therefore, "You are up against the need to control your childish, infantile side, which urges you to break accepted conventions that must be respected."

A woman patient in her fourth year of analysis dreams (p. 143):

(1) *I am being photographed in the nude, lying on my back in different positions; legs closed, legs apart.* (2) *I see a man with a curved yardstick in his hand; it had writing on it which was supposed to be erotic. A red, spiny-backed little monster was biting this man with sharp, tiny teeth. The man was ringing a bell for help, but no one heard it but me and I didn't seem to care.*

Greenson feels the dream points out the dreamer's resistance to her recognition of a deep-seated hostility to a man's penis and disgust towards her own vagina. With the red monster, she associates menstrual blood, a medieval fiend out of Hieronymus Bosch. We see this dream as possibly expressing criticism of the analysis. The patient feels she is being photographed in the nude in all positions, with special interest in the area between her legs: this seems to be her experiential feeling about her analysis. Dream (2) emphasizes this point even further: the man, with whom she later associates her analyst, is judging her by bookish (writing), distorted (curved), rigid (yardstick), and erotic standards. Furthermore, the analyst himself seems to be bitten, "bugged" as it were, by something out of Hieronymus Bosch. Bosch depicted in his paintings the two instincts that the Church, in the name of Christianity, was trying to suppress: sexuality and aggression, in their various forms. If a Jungian analyst were handed this dream, he would in all probability

be asking himself whether the patient's unconscious was not picking up a sore spot of his own, namely, the analyst's repressed sexuality and/or aggression. This is not at all uncommon. We often get patients who hit us in our blind spots, and we end up treating our patients and ourselves at the same time.

If we want to be completely phenomenological and empirical, this interpretation is only a *possibility* suggested by the patient's association. The man in the dream is unknown. The patient could very well have dreamt the same dream with Dr. Greenson as the man holding the yardstick, and then we would have been more justified in our interpretation. As it is, it must be taken as a possible suggestive line of inquiry. We are on safer ground if we take this dream on a subjective level, taking the man with the yardstick as an inner man, an animus figure (see later). On that level, the dream has a paradoxical message indeed: The dreamer is excessively preoccupied with sexuality. This distorted, moralistic view of herself is in itself a result of a repression of deep-seated drive elements. Hence this interpretation would be in opposition to Greenson's formulation.

Sexuality for Jung is more than mere instinctuality; it is also creative power, a bridge between the sacred and the profane. In many religions, sexual symbolism is used to express man's complex relationship to God. It therefore partakes of a transcendental character. With the advent of Christianity, this aspect of sexuality was repressed and what remained was mere body function. Rollo May (1961) gives an example in which church spires appearing in a dream were interpreted by a Freudian as phallic symbols and by a Jungian as spirituality.

Analytical psychotherapy strongly differentiates itself from other systems in its emphasis on the purposive, prospective functioning of the psyche and the placement of the human being within a given, specific archetypal constellation, thereby allowing him to experience a sense of meaning for both his suffering and his achievement. What it objects to in other dynamic systems of psychotherapy is the exaggerated emphasis on reductive, causal thinking. One can trace human behavior to genetic antecedents, but these account for only a partial aspect of our nature; we not only react to our past, we live and relate in the present and take the future into account.

In its emphasis on the prospective and meaningful aspect of the psyche, analytical psychotherapy anticipated a lot of common ground with existential psychotherapy and logotherapy, perhaps most fundamentally in the fact that these therapies are more philosophical rather than merely biological therapies. Although one cannot deal with the data of the human psyche without theories, one can minimize the theoretical restrictions imposed upon an interpretive system. Analytical psychology considers itself to be empirical and phenomenological in that the therapist is required to lay aside his various preconceptions about human behavior and be ready to follow the vicissitudes and serpentine ways of the psyche wherever they might lead him.

HISTORY

Precursors

C. G. Jung was born in Kesswil, Switzerland, and received most of his education in Basel. In contrast to Freud, who was primarily influenced by the scientific, positivistic, and materialistic philosophy of his time, Jung grew up in a cultural tradition that constituted a reaction to the Enlightenment movement.

The hallmark of the Enlightenment was its unswerving optimism. It sought to establish reason as the prime mover, admitting the existence of emotion but seeing it as an element primarily distracting to the rational process. It was believed that by the application of the analytical method all questions ultimately could be resolved. Man was deemed able to master his imperfections by reason and force of will. The important role of aggression as a constituent of human behavior was relatively ignored. The focus was on Man, to the neglect of nature. Men were assumed to be basically the same, and individual differences were minimized.

Gradually, the Enlightenment gave way to a cultural climate that was in many ways its antithesis (Ellenberger, 1970). Reason began to be dethroned, and in contrast to the positing of a split between nature and man, the unity of the two was postulated, as well as the unity of reason and emotion. The world began to be seen as the arena for the interaction of polar oppositions, in chemistry and physiology as well as in philosophy and psychology. It followed naturally that consciousness could not be the only state extant in human beings. A hundred years after G. W. Leibnitz postulated it, the unconscious was again thrust into prominence; its manifestations were recognized as legitimate sources of inquiry, mysticism was not frowned upon, and parapsychology was earnestly studied. G. F. Creuzer published an exhaustive work on mythology and folktales, trying to understand them as symbolical productions rather than as undeveloped ways of thinking. Life was understood as a series of transformations from primordial phenomena and analogy was given a prominent place as a scientific tool. Outstanding and influential personalities of that time were the philosophers Friedrich Von Schelling, Eduard Von Hartmann, and Arthur Schopenhauer, and the physician-psychologist Carl Gustav Carus. The influence of the latter figures especially heavily in Jung's work. Not only did Carus treat the unconscious with the utmost respect, he also imputed to it a creative and healing ability (an essential element in Jungian psychology) and divided the unconscious into several parts, one of which, the "general unconscious," foreshadows Jung's concept of the collective unconscious.

Some of Jung's ideas can be traced even further back. His concept of the archetypes is adumbrated by Immanuel Kant's notion of a priori universal forms of perception as well as Plato's ideas. Kant's formulation is particularly important: We can never perceive reality as it actually is, but have to impose upon the perceptual process a set of imperatives that determine what we actually see. Jung translated the concept of philosophical imperatives into archetypes in the psychological realm.

Dream interpretation, an important part of analytic psychotherapy, was used in ancient times. Particularly famous are Joseph's interpretations of his own dream (the first "self-analysis"), the dreams of his cell mates, and, finally, those of Pharaoh. The Talmud also devotes a great deal of attention to dreams, and several dream books are known to us, notably the Egyptian, the Chaldean, and one by the Greek Artemidorus.

Beginnings

It is generally assumed that both Alfred Adler and Carl Jung began their psychoanalytic career with their association with Freud; that they started as his students,

went with him some of the way and then "deviated" from orthodox psychoanalytic theory. (The reason this version persists is probably because it agrees with the myth of the rebellious son deposing the father.) In both cases, however, the situation was quite different. Both Adler and Jung had formulated some of their major ideas before they came to know Freud. At that time, Jung was writing his medical thesis on the so-called occult phenomena (Jung, 1902). A careful reading of that initial statement of Jung's shows that it contains most of his major ideas in embryonic form.

It is ironic that Jung, later to be called vague, mystical, and abstruse, made as his next step a study bridging the gap between experimental and depth psychology. Jung was assigned by Eugen Bleuler (the head of the Burghölzli Clinic) the task of studying the association test, originally developed by Francis Galton. In this test, people are asked to respond to chosen words with the first word that comes spontaneously. Jung discovered that each person tended to respond to specific words, varying from person to person, either too quickly or too slowly, relative to an average response time for the rest of the words. From this Jung assumed that these particular words carried special meaning for that person—that the words led to some idea accompanied by affect, which Jung then called the *complex*. These complexes were usually unknown to the subject. Jung then postulated the notion that they were unconscious by virtue of repression. It seemed as if Jung had in this way adduced "proof" of the unconscious and the process of repression, both key concepts in Freud's budding theories. Moreover, it was an *empirical* confirmation, and it is important to note that all his life, Jung considered himself an empiricist, an observer of psychological data.

Not unnaturally, these discoveries resulted in a warm correspondence between Jung and Freud. The exchange of letters brought about in 1907 the meeting of Jung and Freud in Vienna. Freud was immediately captivated by Jung's tremendous energy and rich imagination. To the annoyance of his own inner circle, who felt that Jung would eventually go his own way, Freud appointed Jung the first president of the International Psychoanalytic Association.

Jung's next publication, *The Psychology of Dementia Praecox* (1907), considerably heightened his growing reputation and recognition. It was an application of psychoanalytic principles to schizophrenia, and although it contained serious misgivings about some of Freud's ideas, it was considered an important psychoanalytic contribution.

It was from a patient's report that Jung began to formulate an idea of the archetypes. One hallucination of a patient was the image of the sun as having a phallus that moved from side to side causing a wind. Jung was forcibly struck by the fact that this imagery was also used in ancient times, mentioned in sources of which this uneducated man had had no knowledge. This and similar incidents over a long period led Jung to postulate a level of primordial imagery in the unconscious common to all mankind. He called this the *collective unconscious,* and the primordial images were designated as *archetypes.* Note that Jung started out with empirical clinical data, and that theory followed. Jung thought the data were important and basic, whereas theory could be tentative and susceptible to change.

By identifying main themes in psychological material and amplifying them with parallel motifs culled from mythology, comparative religion, literature, and so

on, Jung forged a new way of looking at clinical material. He used this method first on a series of fantasies of a young woman, Miss Miller, reported by Theodore Flournoy in 1906. Out of this grew Jung's *Symbols of Transformation* (1911). This book marked a final break with Freud. Not only did it suggest a new method for a psychological approach to clinical material, it also challenged some of Freud's most basic ideas. Jung identified *libido* as general psychic energy rather than as sexual energy, thus dethroning sexuality as the all-encompassing causative element in things psychic. Disturbances in sexuality he viewed as the expression and reflection of more basic psychological conflicts—as the symptom, the outer manifestation, rather than the origin.

A word or two about Jung's style might be in order for those who attempt to read his books. In contrast to the clear, persuasive writing of Freud, Jung's manner of writing presents problems to the uninitiated. Jung writes in the way he believes the psyche functions, and sometimes tends to assume all readers are familiar with the necessary background information. Furthermore, Jung believes the psychic realities he is trying to describe never can be completely grasped by consciousness. We can understand some of their manifestations, some of their characteristics, but inherently, they are beyond our ken. We cannot, therefore, delineate them precisely, but must be content with approximations and analogies. Jung's style is mosaiclike and allusive. One illustration leads to another. If, however, one follows his train of thought carefully, a definite pattern emerges, centering around a common theme, and the seeming digressions fall into place, elucidating and elaborating the main idea. The most rewarding way to read Jung is to let oneself actively associate to the images presented; the material then comes alive and becomes meaningful. Admittedly this taxes the reader, but he may find the effort worthwhile, since it is somewhat akin to a creative process.

Current Status

The Jungian movement tended to attract introverted people primarily, who shied away from proselytizing. Jung himself was extremely reluctant to give his assent for the establishment of an institute to teach and spread his ideas. New movements tend to attract unfavorable projections, and the Jungian movement has been no exception; until about 1960, it was virtually ignored in the United States. Jung's influence, however, has been enormous, although mostly unacknowledged, and recently there has been a reawakening to his ideas. Calvin Hall and Gardner Lindzey (1962) and Ruth Munroe (1955) include remarkably favorable chapters on Jung in their respective books; some existential therapists write and speak as undergound Jungians. Three training institutes recently have been established in the United States in New York, Los Angeles, and San Francisco. The number of Jungian analysts has been steadily growing all over the world. There are important centers in Switzerland, Britain, Germany, Israel, France, and Italy. Since 1958 International Congresses have been held every two years, and several centers are publishing their own periodicals. The oldest of these is *Spring,* published by the New York Analytical Psychology Club; others are the annual *British Journal of Analytical Psychology, Psychological Perspectives* in Los Angeles, *Zeitschrift für Analytisch Psychologie und Ihre Grenzgebite* in Berlin, *La Rivista di Psicologia Analitica* in Rome, and

Quaternio in Rio de Janeiro. In most centers, the emphasis is on work with adults, but in Israel and England, a considerable contingent of analysts works with children. Group work has only recently been introduced in New York, the West Coast, and Zürich, Switzerland.

Requirements for entry into the training institutes vary from place to place. Jung's original intention was to train any mature individual with an open relationship to his unconscious; he himself trained philosophers, philologists, artists, and mathematicians, recognizing that academic education contributes very little to one's ability to function as a therapist. The training institutes, however, consider that academic standards are necessary to give proof of seriousness of purpose as well as to meet outer standards of certification. Prospective analysts are allowed a range of related fields of academic endeavor, but the final criterion of acceptance as a candidate for training comes after at least 100 hours of qualified personal analysis, recommendation of the analyst, and interviews by three analysts of the training board. At present there are about 400 qualified Jungian analysts, members of the International Association for Analytic Psychology.

PERSONALITY

Theory of Personality

Analytical psychology does not possess a detailed account of the personality equivalent to the topographic, genetic, economic, dynamic, and structural views, as does psychoanalytic theory. The psyche is viewed as composed of several subsystems, each autonomous, yet interdependent: the ego, the personal unconscious and the nonpersonal (collective) unconscious.

The Ego. The *ego* is the center of consciousness, the experiential being of the person. It is the sum total of thoughts, ideas, feelings, memories, and sensory perceptions.

The Personal Unconscious. This consists of everything that has been repressed during one's development. The *personal unconscious* is composed of elements that had once been conscious and are relatively easily available to consciousness. These elements are clustered around complexes defined as emotionally toned ideas and behavioral impulses. The complex may be thought of as having a core, which is archetypal, and therefore will lie outside the sphere of the personal unconscious; and a shell, which is the particular form it takes in a given individual. For instance, several people may have a father complex, and although by that fact they are bound to share some characteristics, the complex will take different guises with the different people.

The Nonpersonal Unconscious. This part of the unconscious includes the archetypes, which are inborn psychic predispositions to perception, emotion, and behavior. This layer of the unconscious is not directly amenable to consciousness, but can be observed indirectly through its manifestations in eternal themes in mythology, folklore and art. Some archetypes, due to their importance and frequency, have been documented more than others. For instance, Joseph Campbell (1956) has documented extensively the hero archetype. Other archetypes include rebirth, the Great Mother, the Wise Old Man, the trickster, the divine child, wholeness, God. Not all of these archetypes are actualized at all times and with the same intensity. Some of the archetypes acquire particular significance because they play an important role in the development of the personality: the persona, the shadow, the animus or anima, and the Self.

The Persona. The *persona* is the archetype of adaptation. The word originally means the actor's mask, but it is not used here in the negative sense. We need mediation between our inner psychic life and the outside world, as much as we need a skin for the same purpose for our physical being. It would be destructive if we behaved in the same way under all situations, as a teacher in front of a class, at a cocktail party, among close friends and in bed; this, indeed, is the case if we have not developed a viable persona. The persona may become rigid, as with the physician, lawyer, or minister who cannot stop being their roles even when this is uncalled for. Ideally, the persona is flexible, that is, different circumstances evoke within us different qualities and aspects that are adaptive within the given context. People often mistake this phenomenon and take it to mean that they are different people in different places. A patient brings in the following initial dream:

I am with a lot of people, who are talking to each other. I try to talk, but I can't as I have a ball of hair in my throat.

The dreamer associated the ball of hair with the phenomenon of cats licking themselves. Very often a ball of hair is indeed formed and gets stuck in their throat. To the dreamer, this act was that of preening. That is, indeed, what she does herself. She is a model, a very beautiful young lady who uses her beauty professionally. The dream tells her that her own preening is a barrier to communication with other people. She is identified with her persona and as a result totally isolated. The persona is often symbolized in dreams by masks or clothes. A person whose adaptation to reality is very faulty might find himself dreaming that he is taking his coat off only to find underneath another coat, and so on (Whitmont, 1970).

The Shadow. The *shadow* is our "other side," all that we would like not to be; it is the compensatory side to our conscious ego, as seen in the case of Dr. Jekyll and Mr. Hyde. It is all those things we would never recognize in ourselves, and what we are particularly allergic to in others. Since the shadow is unconscious, it is experienced as a *projection* onto others. Projection is the main mechanism of the psyche; everything unconscious is projected, and projection is recognized by the affectivity involved. The dynamics of projection seen this way are more encompassing than in the customary form; here, they do not necessarily involve an *erroneous* attribution of feelings or qualities to another person, but a mirror of ourselves. We might very well be correct in our perception (e.g., the other person might indeed be angry), but if it stirs strong emotions in us, that person reflects our own anger. An encounter with the shadow is the *sine qua non* of every analysis and is generally very painful. A patient who has been immobilized most of his adult life, unable to work or maintain any kind of meaningful relationship, brings the following dream.

I am walking, holding a leash in my hand, to which is attached a young man, who is very sweet and docile. All of a sudden, he turns into a ferocious beast, threatening to destroy me. I grab hold of him, and we attempt to fight, but it becomes apparent neither of us can win: the best I can do is keep him from destroying me.

Here, the dream-ego (the dreamer) is in deadly conflict with his shadow; no resolution is in sight. The dream seems to be telling the dreamer that as long as he maintains his "good" side on a leash, that is, as long as he is the "angel" his parents expect him to be, it will turn ferociously against him and he will be deadlocked.

Acceptance of the shadow is very difficult to achieve, but vitally important for adjustment. A young man who was in the throes of a very humiliating compulsion has been working for a long time on shadow aspects of himself, which he steadfastly refused to acknowledge. However, after a particularly painful experience in an encounter group, which brought home some of these aspects, he dreams:

I am on my way to find something which I know is very important. Suddenly, as I am about to turn a corner, I see a very shabbily dressed man who seems to be down in the dumps and appears very disgusting to me. He accosts me, and my first impulse is to shake him off, but all of a sudden I take pity on him and embrace him, to my own amazement.

The shadow, which very often appears in a dream as a derelict or "inferior" person, is here accepted. For this dreamer, it signaled the beginning of a conscious assimilation of his inferior side, which, in turn, made it possible for him to free himself slowly from his compulsion.

The shadow is always symbolized by figures of the same sex. As always in Jungian thought, the shadow is not all negative; if accepted and assimilated, it can become the source of creativity. In people whose conscious experience of themselves is very negative, the shadow, being a compensatory figure, will include all their positive qualities, and they will meet successful and talented men in their dreams.

The Animus and Anima. Two central elements in Chinese philosophy are the Yin and Yang. The *Yin* represents the feminine principle; it is the world of nature, creation and life, earthiness and concreteness, receptivity and yielding, the dark and containing, the collective and undifferentiated, the unconscious. The *Yang* is its opposite—the masculine principle, the driving energy, the creative and initiating, the light and hot, the penetrating, stimulating and dividing, the principle of separation and differentiation, restriction and discipline, the arousing and phallic, aggression and enthusiasm, spirit and heaven. These two principles do not oppose but complement each other. The Yin without the Yang is the status quo, inertia, and the Yang without the Yin is the enthusiastic rushing forward without the solid base of concreteness and solidity. Every element contains these two principles to varying degrees and proportions. These proportions are not unalterably fixed, they change with necessity; a given situation will require more of the Yin, and another will require more of the Yang.

This concept is much harder to grasp than that of the shadow or the persona. Rationality fails us here, but the animus-anima experience is very real nonetheless, as we will try to illustrate.

Human beings are potentially bisexual, biologically as well as psychologically. During our development one side comes to predominate over the other, the other side existing in an inferior form. Thus, males have usually the preponderance of the Yang principle in their consciousness, women the Yin. Contrasexual aspects coexist in the unconscious; thus, the male has an unconscious Yin side, the *anima;* the woman has an unconscious Yang aspect, the *animus.* Thus, on the positive side, a woman's animus is responsible for her ability to discriminate and differentiate, to judge and to act, for discipline and aggressiveness. If a positive conscious relationship cannot be maintained toward the animus, we meet the notorious animus-ridden woman, whose hallmarks are

argumentativeness, dogmatism, and behavior on the basis of prejudices and preconceived notions. Briefly, a woman's animus is her sum total of her expectations, a system of unconscious criteria with which the world is judged and experienced. The animus is symbolized by male figures appearing in a woman's dreams and fantasies, as a husband, son, father, lover, prince charming, the neighbor next door, and so on.

Conversely, for a man the anima embodies the Yin aspect. This accounts for a man's capacity for relatedness, emotionality, involvement with people and ideas, a spontaneous and unplanned approach to life and its experiences, sensuality, and instinctuality. The anima is symbolized by female figures in man's unconscious products, appearing as the beloved one, the princess, priestess, witch, prostitute, nymph. If the anima is not related to and consciously integrated, the man appears barren, abstract, and detached, as if lacking some vital element. On the other hand, an anima-possessed man is swayed by moods, depressions, and anxieties, tends to be withdrawn and detached.

The animus and anima seem to operate like autonomous personalities. We experience them, but cannot control them by mere effort of will. They are the guides to the collective unconscious, leading to the other side. Through painful encounter with them we gain some acquaintance with their mode of being, but never total control. Most of the mystery always remains. The directing and creative aspect of the anima is shown in the following dream, dreamt before the patient's starting analysis because of depression due to feelings of meaninglessness in his life:

I am standing, totally perplexed, in the midst of a Casbah-like city with serpentine and winding small streets, not knowing where to turn. Suddenly I see a young, mysterious woman whom I had never seen before, pointing the direction out with her hand. It had a very awesome quality to it.

The potentially destructive aspect of the anima can be gleaned from the following: A young man with pernicious compulsive behavior patterns that alienate and depress him, dreams:

A woman is coming after me with razor blades in her hands; she intends to kill me. I have no choice, so go after her jugular vein, killing her instead.

This man experiences women as a tremendous threat; he feels used by them, and during intercourse has fantasies of being swallowed and smothered. He is subjected to violent moods and heavy drinking. The dream shows an archetypal situation with a disastrous relationship to the anima. The dreamer will have to learn, slowly and painfully, to come to terms with his feminine side. Otherwise, the anima will be continually projected onto the women he will meet and he will have to "kill" his own capacity for emotional response. The more unaware a man is of his undeveloped, inferior anima, the more likely he is to fall victim to an infatuation with a woman who embodies this unconscious anima.

The Self. The archetype of the *Self* is an expression of man's inherent psychic predisposition to experience wholeness, centeredness, and meaning in life. The Self is our god within ourselves— although it must immediately be added that the psychological existence of such an element does not affirm or deny the metaphysical question of whether there is also a God outside of ourselves. It is the Great Man of the Naskapi Indian, the internal embodiment of ancient and timeless wisdom. We come in contact with the Self when we are faced with problems of eternal validity, with paradox, with absurd situations that admit of no rational

solutions; when we are at the end of our tether as to what to do; when we have recognized that ego adaptation is not enough and have to surrender to a higher authority, transcending the ego. At the moment of birth, ego and Self appear as one; the first half of life is devoted to their separation, requiring heroic attitudes and ego reliance. Then the process reverses itself, as the ego attitude is revealed as incomplete and insufficient, and the striving for realization of the Self begins.

The Self is the goal and the process by which this goal is achieved is called *individuation,* separating oneself from the collective and finding one's own unique way. The Self is symbolized as the Wise Old Man, the figure of Christ, Buddha, the treasure hard to attain, the jewel, and the Philosopher's stone. In patients' dreams, the analyst very often carries the projection of the Self until the patient is able to discover his own within himself.

Variety of Concepts

Sexuality. Freud equated libido with sexual energy. To Jung, libido was *psychic energy* in any manifestation, including sexual and power drives. Psychic energy operates by archetypal fields, that is, the archetype generates, as it were, an energy field. These energy configurations operate analogously to the instincts on the biological level. Thus, from an energetic point of view, the archetypes pertain to the same realm as the instincts, while being at the same time paradoxically their polar opposites, because the instincts are energy carriers on the biological level, while the archetypes are energy carriers on the spiritual level. Although this may sound unnecessarily complicated, what it amounts to is that spiritual forces, as far as the psyche is concerned, are energetically equivalent to biological instincts.

Sexuality is the biological manifestation of the union of two opposites, male and female. The union of opposites, or their reconciliation, is the life goal; we have to reconcile good and evil, active and passive, life and death, and, most importantly, the personal and the transpersonal. The last pair, which can be formulated also as the union of the ego and the Self, means experiencing the religious dimension of the psyche. This is *not* to be understood as saying that religion is nothing but sublimation of sexuality; what it *does* mean is that both sexuality and religion are expressions of the phenomenon of the reconciliation of the opposites, two realms of experience expressing different levels of the same basic reality.

The Oedipus Complex. Freud considered the Oedipal complex a central point of his theories. This refers to his observation that around the ages of three to five, boys want to possess their mother and to dispose of their father. This wish is not carried out because the boy fears castration as punishment by the father. A normal "resolution" of this state of affairs is identification with the father. Freud initially came upon this concept from his own self-analysis, later presumably finding the same mechanism in his patients, and thus he came to posit it as a universal phenomenon.

That the unconscious seems to have a mythological layer is one of the mainstays of Jungian psychology. The Oedipus story is seen as but one mythological pattern among many, all of which are potentially active in the human psyche. The Jungian approach to mythology is symbolic, whereas Freud reduced the mythologem to a literal interpretation. From our point of view, Freud seems to have missed the point about this myth.

The story can carry quite a different flavor from that imputed to it by Freud. The main theme might be that *man cannot escape his fate.* Both Oedipus and his parents try to thwart fate, with disastrous results. Countless mythologems repeat that motif, for example, Jonah refuses to obey God's command, tries to escape, and is swallowed by the whale. In the oedipal myth, Oedipus is presented with a heroic task: He must face up to the mystery of his tragic fate, the mystery of the Sphinx—to murder his father, marry his mother—and *then consciously accept the inevitable tragic guilt!* Oedipus is thus a hero who has partially failed through his unconsciousness; this "blinds" him and makes him rejoin the Furies, the angry mothers. With respect to the Freudian emphasis, it is to be noted that the incest is only incidental to the main theme. Also, the incest itself is *not* desired by Oedipus, nor is he punished for it (at most it can be said that he is punished for his *unconsciousness* of it).

In essence, therefore, the Oedipus myth is an embodiment of the gigantic, existential problem facing mankind: The price of consciousness is guilt, and this guilt needs to be accepted, a motif that first appears in the Genesis story of Paradise.

Racial Unconscious. Jung never used this term. It was introduced by his opponents and detractors to imply a racist coloration to Jung's theories. As pointed out earlier, various archetypes are inherent in all of us but only a few are evoked in each of us, the others lying dormant in the deep reaches of the psyche. Which of the archetypes are actualized depends on a variety of factors: the historical period, the cultural environment, and the particular life situation of the individual. Jung used the term *collective unconscious* for the world of the archetypes; then the term *objective psyche* was introduced as a more accurate description of the idea, and finally the concept was termed the *transpersonal unconscious,* which we consider the most apt.

Organ Inferiority. This Adlerian concept refers to the notion that most people have, or feel themselves subjectively to have, a part of the body that is inferior. This feeling of inferiority causes them to overcompensate and put much emphasis on the inferior organ. We have no quarrel with the fact that people tend to experience bodily parts as inadequate, and that this may bring about a lot of suffering leading to overcompensation; we contend, however, that the real or imagined deformity serves usually only as a hook for a projection. This projection will occur only if there exists an initial predisposition for it, that is, if there is an appropriate archetypal activation as can be seen from the fact that two people with the same deformity may react very differently to their problem. One might treat it purely as a physical handicap that must be overcome realistically and appropriately, and the other might see in it the source of all his troubles or an indication that life is against him. We would then say that in the first case, the deformity has not fallen within an activated archetype; in the second case, we see the archetype of the victim (the martyr or the Isaac Complex).

Defense Mechanism. The Jungian position generally respects *defense mechanisms* as expressions of psychic necessity; they are based upon projections of judgmental or hostile dynamics upon the other person. Projection plays a crucial part in Jungian thinking, and to a lesser extent, so does identification; but both tend to be seen not as defenses against anxiety but as processes, inevitable because of a state of primary unconsciousness.

The Pleasure Principle. Jungians do not consider pleasure to be the ultimate drive, although we do not minimize its importance. It is seen as one drive among several.

Environment and Conditioning. The analytical approach, despite what seems to be the general belief, places a great deal of importance on the effects of *environment* and *conditioning.* We stress that these two factors do not operate on a *tabula rasa,* but interact with the archetypal predispositions of the individual. The same environment will evoke different responses from different individuals. Given an archetypal constellation, conditioning can be very effective, but one cannot condition someone to a response that will run counter to his given predisposition, as has been convincingly demonstrated even in animals (Breland & Breland 1961).

Psychopathology. Analytical psychology does not view psychopathology as a disease or a deviation from a "normal" state. Symptoms are considered to be unconscious messages to the individual that something is awry with him, presenting him with a task that demands to be fulfilled. He is not allowed to go on living comfortably but is summoned, as it were, by a voice within, urgently demanding to be heard. Why some people are called and others left alone is impossible to say. The explanation can be ascribed only partially to causal aetiological factors, for very often the same traumatic conditions affect one person in one way and another in a totally different way. The symptoms themselves, viewed symbolically, frequently provide the clue to precisely that which is missing and must be developed. Our infirmities, our inferior side, provide us ultimately with the way to meaning and wholeness.

PSYCHOTHERAPY

Theory of Psychotherapy

Analytical psychotherapy does not possess a theory to speak of, except in general terms. Jung conceived therapy variously as a process of self-knowledge, a reconstruction of the personality, or even as education. He emphasized the empirical, tentative nature inherent in any therapeutic approach, objecting strenuously to any premature attempt to cast psychotherapy into a fixed structure: "Theories in psychology are the very devil. It is true that we need certain points of view for orienting and heuristic value; but they should always be regarded as mere auxiliary concepts that can be laid aside at any time" (Jung, 1954, p. 7). This is easier said than done. But Jung, for one, lived this principle as fully as possible. Nowadays, Jung is known for his revolutionary theoretical insights, but it is sometimes forgotten what a superb therapist he was as well. People who had doubts about his theoretical conceptualizations did not hesitate to consult him therapeutically. Jung as a therapist was unorthodox, doing one thing in a given case and doing the opposite in the next one, ready to modify, change, and create, constantly aware of the enormous variety in human nature; he was a pragmatist, whose motto was: "anything goes, as long as it works." Thus, when confronted in an initial interview by a woman whose main symptom was that she had not slept for several weeks, Jung sang a lullaby, putting her to sleep! In another case, faced with a woman unable to get in touch with her own inner religious function, Jung taught her the Scriptures, each session handing her an assignment and testing her the next session. In Jung's consulting room, people danced, sang, acted,

mimed, played musical instruments, painted, and modeled with clay, the procedures limited only by Jung's inventiveness and ingenuity. It is not surprising, therefore, that Jung distrusted theory, endlessly cautioning against falling prey to its rigidities and limitations. "Learn your theories as well as you can, but put them aside when you touch the miracle of the living soul" (Jung, 1954). With this caveat firmly fixed in our minds, we will attempt to delineate several general principles applicable to the therapeutic procedure, always mindful that these should be overruled when the occasion arises.

As a general rule, therapy starts with a thorough investigation of the patient's conscious state. Since the unconscious is viewed as compensatory to the conscious state, the latter has to first be established. The same dream, for example, can have quite different interpretations with differing conscious attitudes. The investigation will include the past history of the patient, various important influences in his life, his attitudes, and his values and ideas. The analyst then is able to point out inconsistencies and contradictions, peculiar reactions, and behavior patterns. Most important, the patient is thus taught the slow and difficult road to one's inner world. Confronted with unexpected questions and observations, he finds many of his tacit assumptions challenged and questioned. He starts to learn to introspect. A not unusual result of this period is a sense of tremendous confusion, following the initial sense of relief that accompanies the onset of therapy.

With most people, dreamwork is then cautiously introduced. The patient is thus launched on the awesome encounter with his unconscious. If the patient is in any way receptive to this new way, he is soon confronted with the disagreeable realization that he is not master of his own house, and that he has to contend with forces over which he has little control. To the typical, rational Western man, this is a jarring proposition. With this encounter with the workings of his unconscious side, the patient becomes acquainted with the compensatory nature of the unconscious. No sooner has a firm attitude been established in consciousness than the unconscious seems to bring out the opposite one, and the patient soon finds himself caught between pairs of opposites. This position creates tension and anxiety, but also the possibility of transformation and the resolution of the opposites by the emergence of a third entity that transcends the two poles.

An important principle is that of the quasi-intentionality of the psyche. The person's unconscious products (dreams, fantasies, artistic productions) are interpreted not only in terms of antecedent causes—although this may also apply—but primarily as pointing out the way to further development. Thus, a patient brings in the following dream:

I am in a gym, performing various exercises, with some other men. They are arranged in a line, in which they perform the exercises. I try to join the line at the head, but am rejected; I then try for the second place, and am rejected again; I try one place after the other till coming to the end of the line, and am rejected from every one of them.

At first the dreamer has difficulty associating to the dream. The analyst points out that the dream seems to involve men only. The dreamer then realizes that the men in the dream were actually boys from his all-male Catholic primary school, a place dominated by "oughts" and "shoulds." With this come unpleasant memories of the gym class, which the dreamer hated passionately. The only reason he attended was because he was

forced to; had it been left up to him, he would not have shown up at any of the classes. As an afterthought, he adds that his mother also thought "it was good for you." The imagery of the dream is direct and clear—the dreamer is being rejected from the line; he does not belong there.

Although for most people, the initial period of therapy is devoted to helping them get in touch with their inner world, for people who are overly absorbed in their introversion, the attempt is to put them in touch with the external reality. The analysis always tries to compensate for attitudes that are too one-sided.

By far the major principle of analytical therapy is for the analyst to follow scrupulously the direction and guidance of the unconscious; to abandon, as far as possible, all preconceptions and fixed ideas. For instance, it might be an analyst's clinical judgment that a patient is caught in a mother problem, but the dreams might stress a problem with the older brother. For the analyst to put aside his own judgment is a tall order, since our major way of coping with the unknown is to cling to ready-made formulas. In addition, the analyst may be presented with the necessity of not being judgmental towards lines of conduct that violate his own inner moral code. By doggedly following the wisdom of the unconscious, the patient slowly learns to accept that within himself there exists a guiding force, the Self, that points the way, painful though it might be, to a mode of being more meaningful and more whole. This force may appear in the guise of a simple "solution" to a complicated situation (e.g., a way to overcome a nagging compulsion) or it may point to a considerable complication of what seems like a simple one. It may tell the patient that there is a way out of his dilemma if he but changes his attitude, or, on the contrary, that nothing can be done about it, that he is "fated" to live with it. Dreams determine primarily the *timing* of what is being interpreted in addition to the content of the interpretation. The analyst is quite often aware of possibilities about what is going on in the patient long before the patient is. As a general rule, a Jungian analyst will refrain from introducing these interpretations unless a dream heralds the patient's readiness to assimilate them. The case management in general will be based upon the direction of the unconscious.

Psychotherapy ideally takes into consideration three modes: the fate element (which determines, for instance, what cannot be changed but has to be accepted); skill (the sum total of techniques that can be consciously formulated, taught, and communicated); and art, that intangible something (related to intuition and feeling) that weaves everything together. An exclusive emphasis on fate is likely to lead to fortune telling and card reading; a stress on mere skill entails a typical mechanical and barren approach; if the art is overplayed, we get the "wild analyst."

Process of Psychotherapy

People who have only a vague familiarity with Jung, based primarily on his more theoretical writings, tend to have a rather distorted view of Jungian therapy. They conceive of it either as an endless concatenation of symbols leading far back to antiquity or as a spinning out of esoteric fantasies. Nothing is farther from the truth. People listening in on an analytic hour are liable to hear the most mundane issues being discussed, including one's budget, relationship with one's mother-in-law or one's boss, and so on. The cardinal rule in Jungian analysis is that *the basis of any analysis is experiencing; mere intellectual understanding is insufficient.* This is not to minimize the important role of intellectual understanding, but to emphasize the importance of experiencing a psychic reality. Thus, the analyst may discourage the attempt of a patient to do away with depression; rather, the patient will be asked to stay with the depression, to let it be, accepting it as an unconscious message.

Generally speaking, the therapeutic encounter in a Jungian setting involves an active interchange between analyst and patient. As he sees fit, depending on the patient's development, the state of the transference and various other factors, the analyst will share of himself with the patient, exchanging feelings, experiences, and even dreams. In principle, the nature of the interchange is limited only by the analyst's imagination and willingness to expose himself. The mood of the hour may veer from being highly serious to humorous. The analyst may teach, suggest, cajole, give advice, reflect feelings, or give support. The main emphasis is on the conscious assimilation of the immediate experience, using as well techniques that have now become the stock in trade of Gestalt therapy and the encounter movement (breathing methods and what are now called sensitivity training activities were in use by Jungian analysts in the early twenties).

However, interpretation is the main work of the analytic process. *Interpretation* is the process of enlarging upon given data in a way that makes it possible for the patient to perceive connections, motivations, and feelings of which he has been unaware. The main thrust of the analytical process may be summarized as an attempt to make conscious as much as possible what has been unconscious; thereby a behavioral change becomes possible.

After the reality situation and the patient's phenomenological world have been established, dream interpretation is undertaken.

Dreamwork is the core of Jungian therapy. Individuals vary considerably in their capacity to remember dreams. There are some who never remember any, but they are rare in the typical patient population. The constant reinforcement of the importance attached to dreams by the analyst, the seriousness with which even the most trivial dream is treated, usually brings about a change even in those people who seem to have difficulty in remembering their dreams. We will focus here on dream interpretation, because all unconscious products (fantasies, paintings, daydreaming) are treated essentially in the same way.

Dream Interpretation. The most profitable way to look at a dream is to see it as a metaphorical drama unfolding before our eyes. In a well-conceived play, the setting is first established, physically as well as psychologically; the mood is suggested and possible conflicts are hinted at. This may be called the *exposition.* Then a *crisis* develops and the conflict is thrust to the fore. The various forces hinted at in the exposition emerge fully and we have the unfolding of the drama. Then, as a general rule, a *solution* is introduced, sometimes in the form of there being no solution, but a stalemate, or an impasse. These dynamics apply equally well to any unconscious product, such as daydreams, fantasies, fairy tales, or any other mythologem, regardless of the medium in which it is expressed; thus, psychological drawings and poems can be subjected to the same process. (*Psychological* is here emphasized to differentiate it from genuine artistic expression. The two are not mutually exclusive—often it is possible, as well as legitimate, to treat the same material

from an artistic as well as psychological point of view.)

The main difference between a classical Freudian approach to a dream and a Jungian one is based on *repression.* To Freudians a dream is the result of the emergence of repressed contents from the unconscious. As a result, it is viewed, essentially, as a distortion that must be unravelled. Thus the actual drama of the dream is referred to as the *manifest* contents of the dream, behind which there lurks the *latent* content. A Jungian views the dream phenomenologically. The drama of the dream *is* the unconscious message expressed in symbolic form, a message not necessarily repressed or hidden, but rather trying to reveal. (In all fairness, we are talking about the orthodox Freudian approach; we are quite aware that in practice many Freudians would interpret a dream along its manifest expression.)

This conceptual difference has wide practical implications about how dreams are actually interpreted. Classically, in Freudian psychoanalysis, the dreamer would be asked to "free" associate to any given symbol in the dream. Assume, for instance, that a dream in which a wheel appears is reported. The dreamer might say that the wheel reminds him of a tractor, then a tractor toy he had in childhood; a whole slew of memories pertaining to that particular period might emerge, taking the dreamer farther and farther away from the original symbol, namely, the wheel. If the dreamer is persistent in his associative process, he will ultimately reach a painful point, concerning perhaps his mother, his older brother, or perhaps a homosexual experience. Naturally these are relevant domains for psychological inquiry, but in all probability they would have little to do with that specific dream.

A Jungian, on the other hand, would

consider it of paramount importance that the specific symbol used by the unconscious is a wheel, not a tractor. The patient could have dreamt directly about the tractor, but did not. The symbol of the wheel emerged in his dream. The *association* to the tractor and that childhood period is, of course, not to be ignored. An *association* is a connection, not necessarily causal, by virtue of contiguity. Thus, the dreamer in Jungian analysis is asked to say what comes first to his mind when he thinks about, or pictures, the wheel of his dream. It could be his childhood tractor toy, his grandma's parakeet, or an ancient cart he had seen once in a movie. This is done for every symbol in the dream, for inanimate objects as well as for people. It is also done for the major occurrences in the dream. If, for instance, the dreamer is promised something in the dream, he will be asked to associate to a promise. Thus is the *associative context* of the dream established. But this is not sufficient for interpretation. The *amplifications* must be kept in mind as well. An amplification is what an object actually *is*. For example, the dreamer may associate his cousin to a lamp appearing in his dream, but essentially, a lamp is something that gives light in the darkness. Likewise, a pen might remind a dreamer of a penis (especially if he is a product of our culture), but primarily a pen is an instrument for writing. Amplification may come from yet another source. Because of the hypothesis of the archetypal nature of the unconscious, the analyst will bear in mind all possible parallels he can find (from mythology, fairy tales, literature, and so forth) to the various symbols and dramas featured in the specific dream. The more precise the equivalence, the more pertinent the amplification; amplifications that are too general can easily lead one astray.

Dreams have logic of their own. Since their language is pictorial symbolic, they state facts phenomenologically and cannot, by themselves, express connections and implications. These, as a rule, may be inferred from the sequence of the dream. Usually it may be assumed that if the dream drama includes two events that follow each other, it is implied that the second happening occurred *because* of the first. A woman dreamt that she saw a snake on the ground, that she jeered at the snake and the snake then attacked her. We may conclude that the snake attacked her *because* she jeered at it. A more appropriate attitude would have been either to flee the scene as soon as possible or try to kill it. The dream implies that the dreamer is jeering at a very powerful unconscious content that, as a result of this attitude, is threatening to annihilate her. (In this specific case, the woman had just recently overcome a serious alcoholism problem. She was supremely confident of her ability not to succumb to it any more and was recklessly playing with dangerous temptations. The snake represents the addiction potentiality, which was still lurking.)

These examples, which were chosen for their relative clarity and simplicity, might easily mislead the uninitiated to believe that dreams are easily interpreted. This is far from the case. Every therapist is chagrined to discover that there are many leads and possibilities, and ambiguity of dreams might very well allow for two completely contradictory understandings. This is why a dream *series* is of such paramount importance. A dream can be likened to a mathematical equation with many unknowns; the "solution," therefore, is at best tentative. A series of dreams supplies many more equations with the same unknowns and can be assumed to deal with the same conflict from many different angles. By finding parallels between dreams, one can often discern one's way in what might otherwise have been a jungle. Sometimes a dream is erroneously interpreted, only to be rectified by the next one; an internal checking and balancing system seems to be maintained. At our present state of knowledge, dream interpretation is a trial-and-error process. The therapist is often aware that a dream may be understood along different, even contradictory lines. Sometimes he can afford to stay with the ambiguity, but in other cases, he needs to take a risk and follow one line of interpretation rather than another, and then wait for the following dream for corroboration or disproval.

A dream can be interpreted on the objective or the subjective level. The *objective level* refers to people (or events) outside of the dreamer; for instance, if one dreams about his wife, the dream is then taken to express something about the actual relationship between husband and wife. On the other hand, the *subjective level* entails relating to all figures and activities in the dreams as pertaining to the dreamer's "inner" psyche, that is, the inner wife, friend, boss, struggle, and so on.

For example, a young man is about to get married, although he is uncertain about his feelings about his future wife. He dreams he is about to embrace her passionately when a friend rings the doorbell; his wife-to-be answers the door and stays to talk with her friend, completely ignoring her fiancé, who is left frustrated and angry. On the objective level, this dream bodes ill for the relationship, the dream implying that she is far from being really related to him. On the subjective level, however, the dream seems to be saying that the dreamer and his feminine side are not well related; that is, he has difficulty relating to people and being intimate with them. Accordingly, interpretation on the objective level would thrust the burden of the problematic relationship onto the girl's shoulders; the subjective interpretation would implicate the dreamer's own capacity for relatedness.

Sometimes a dream that has to be understood subjectively is mistakenly taken on the objective level. A patient dreams that his wife has been sleeping with an ex-boyfriend of hers. The dreamer, impulsive and given to literal interpretations, gets furious and berates his wife for infidelity, to her utter bafflement, since she has not seen this boyfriend for years; moreover, he lives thousands of miles away. The next night our patient has the same dream, but this time it is not the boyfriend who is involved but some unknown man. Obviously the first dream was suggesting that his inner wife, the anima, was having an affair with someone else, rather than actually implicating his wife.

Let us consider another example. After six months in therapy, Miriam brings in the following dream:

I am in a classroom at my alma mater with Professor P. My father is standing beside me. Professor P. is explaining how to evaluate determinants. He says that a determinant always reduces to a fraction and another number, which he does not know whether to put in the numerator or the denominator. My father says it is not important where this number is put, while I passionately insist that it is very important indeed.

Miriam has a doctoral degree in mathematics, and the dream involves mathematical symbols. To the professor she associates the first course she took with him, on the functions of a real variable. The dream, therefore, is concerned with the determination and evaluation of reality.

The professor, who is a loved and respected authority for her, explains that reality always reduces to a fraction, namely, to a situation where someone is above and someone below: That is, life is a power struggle or a battle for dominance (who is above and who under). Her father, an animus figure, claims that it should not matter. This brings to light Miriam's belief that an attempt to dominate and control is to be despised, an attitude forcibly inculcated into her by her rational, intellectual father. But the dreams bare her unconscious wish to dominate and control.

When the interpretation of the dream was offered to her, she burst into tears, and said that the previous night she and her husband had sexual intercourse, she being in the dominant position, and for the first time in her life she really enjoyed herself, an experience that frightened her so much she had blocked it completely out of her memory until the interpretation recalled it to mind. She then recalled several instances in her life when her natural ambitions and assertiveness had been rudely repressed so she was forced to adopt a passive-aggressive mode of behavior to avoid being crumbled and trodden upon by her environment.

Several comments are called for. Dream interpretation, regardless of how phenomenologically done, is still, unfortunately, a reductive procedure. The symbol is a mediator between consciousness and the unconscious, conveying much more than can be rationally expressed. When we interpret a dream we are, in effect, reducing a highly graphic and symbolic imagery to a verbal, that is, rational, statement. Something is lost in this reduction. It is incumbent, therefore, to make this statement more experiential to the dreamer. Miriam was asked to keep the imagery of the dream vividly in mind

and to be reminded of it when confronted by a situation that seemed to her to involve issues of control and dominance. In therapy she might be asked to paint the dream or to carry on a conversation with the father figure in the dream, to pursue the argument featured there. (This is referred to by Jungians as *active imagination* to underscore the fact that the person actively participates in bringing about the fantasy, as well as in its development.) Other means, appropriate to the situation, might also be employed. The dream or fantasy might be enacted in a group, with various members taking different roles generating a psychodrama.

The Heroic Attitude. The unconscious seems to require of us roughly two basic attitudes, one that derives from the Self and one that derives from the ego. The Self attitude has to do with broad life questions, having to do with a *Weltanschauung,* a philosophy of life, a religious attitude, and with fate, by which we mean the sum total of those factors governing our life over which we have no control. For instance, a woman was raised by a family in which the commandment, "Thou shalt not fail," was elevated to a religious principle. Failure was considered a sin. After several months in therapy she was awakened, three nights in a row, by a voice saying to her repeatedly "It's all right to fail! It's all right to fail!"

Mechanisms of Psychotherapy

Obviously the analytical process is not a simple one and does not lend itself to a clear explication. It is not easy to demonstrate precisely what factors are involved in a successful (or unsuccessful, for that matter) analysis. We can only try to establish tentative guidelines.

Acceptance.   This is probably the *sine qua non* of any depth therapy. During the course of the therapy, it is essential that the patient feel accepted by the therapist. This is done not so much by what the therapist actually says as it is by his genuine openness. All Jungian analysts are required to undergo a thorough analysis. They therefore experience the difference between acceptance and nonacceptance by their own analysts and get a personal understanding of its profound importance. They learn that the relationship between the analyst and the analysand is not between the "healthy" and the "sick," but between someone who has delved into his own psyche and has come out of this experience not only unscathed but enhanced, and as a result has established an ongoing dialogue with his unconscious; and someone who has not undergone this voyage. This voyage, ideally, has not inflated the analyst and caused him to feel superior, but rather has gained for him an enormous respect for the intricacy and complexity of the human psyche and, consequently, a healthy humility in the face of hidden resources and potentialities inherent in the human being he is confronting.

Of important help toward this acceptance are the symbolic approach and the prospective thrust attributed to unconscious processes. The idea of psychic lameness may need to be acknowledged, first, but then taken as a challenge to further psychic development and enrichment. One is crippled not so much because of what has happened in the past (although this is not neglected), but because one is being called from within to enlarge one's horizons, to become more of a person. The neurosis may be a "certificate of nobility" psychologically because it may reflect the presence of unused talents and capacities.

A person's neurotic symptoms may present him with an important and difficult task; this is expressed in the mythologem of Jonah, who was called upon by God to prophesy doom to Nineveh. Jonah refused, and as a result was swallowed by a whale, or, psychologically stated, he was inflicted by a neurotic or psychotic depression. The neurotic is someone trying to escape his fate; but this fate, once recognized, accepted, assimilated, and actively participated in, could lead him to a life of fuller meaning and greater wholeness—although not necessarily less suffering. Since our Western culture tends to arouse guilt over infirmities (as anthropologists point out, this is by no means a universal phenomenon), one important result of the real acceptance of the patient by the therapist is the reduction of guilt surrounding one's inadequacies. By this we mean not so much the rather superficial alleviation of guilt often attempted during the course of therapy concerning, for instance, masturbation, when the patient is assured that what he considers an inadequacy is really a common human attribute, but rather an encounter with guilt on an existential level. By relating to his inadequacy as an existential challenge, the patient learns to assume responsibility for a creative task; thus, the guilt is channeled from an inhibitive feeling into a dynamic, creative force.

Relationship to the Inner World. Western civilization, goal and achievement oriented, places a great deal of emphasis on the outside world. This is to the detriment of our other reality, the inner one, which is at least as important as the outer one. Most of the people applying for therapy have lost touch with their inner world; some of them are barely aware of its existence. One of the most profound consequences of analytical therapy is the rebridging of the gap between the outer and inner worlds. The patient is gently but persistently encouraged to pay heed to and value his inner world. The power and vicissitudes of his inner psychic life are demonstrated to him over and over, and he comes to respect it.

On the other hand, some people seem to come for therapy not because they are out of touch with their inner world but because, or so it seems, they are too much in touch with it. In fact, they seem to be flooded with unconscious fantasies. Here the analytic task is different. To establish a viable dialogue between consciousness and unconsciousness, the two have to be clearly separated from each other. The integrity of an independent conscious position needs to be established. As with human beings, real communication exists only between distinctly different positions. Being flooded is akin to an invasion, rather than to an exchange between two demarcated entities. The analysis, therefore, will have to concentrate on creating a wedge, a partition between the two systems by anchoring the patient firmly in external rational reality.

Transference. Transference is a special instance of the more general phenomenon of projection. Unconscious contents, because unconscious, are subject to projection. The subject experiences that part of his psyche of which he is not aware by attributing it to the object. In general, this object can be both human as well as inanimate. *Transference* is the sum total of all the projections that the patient endows his analyst with. Jung's attitude toward the role that the transference plays during analysis underwent drastic changes. At the beginning, he tended to agree with Freud upon the all-important function of the transference for a therapeutic cure. As Jung became more and more involved with the archetypal nature of the psyche, however, he came to minimize the role of transference as an essential element in the therapeutic process. At

this intermediate period, Jung maintained that therapy could go on comfortably without transference; that, in fact, it proceeded much more smoothly without it. It was a nuisance, he averred, and, moreover, it was a result of insufficient rapport between therapist and patient. Where this rapport has been established, he thought, there was no need for a transference. Yet ultimately Jung had to bow to the force of the clinical evidence and recognize the profound effect of the transference, as well as the therapeutic value of the analysis of the transference.

Countertransference is the analyst's projection on the patient. This phenomenon is not viewed as a hindrance to be avoided or minimized, but as a necessary concomitant, which may be fruitfully used by the therapist to guide him during the course of therapy. On a more general level, countertransference is the complementary part of the total archetype, which manifests itself in the guise of various polar opposites: guru-disciple, savior-sinner. The analyst can use his own reactions as a therapeutic tool. Those reactions provide him with information as to what is going on in the analytic process. If, for instance, the analyst perceives in himself a spontaneous urge to bully his patient, he will know the master-slave configuration is operating. In other words, he becomes aware of the contents of the activated "field."

APPLICATIONS

Problems

Since every basic human problem expresses typical human experience and reaction patterns, an understanding of archetypal dynamics may shed light on almost any problem facing mankind, from the question of aggression and war to the modern youth culture and the drug syndrome.

Jung devoted a great deal of energy to one human domain—religion. Religion is the expression of an archetypal need to endow our human existence with meaning. An understanding of the various archetypal form elements as expressed in the study of comparative religions, therefore, is crucial to a thorough understanding of how, for various peoples at different epochs, this need found its realization. Mythology in particular and folklore in general are domains in which archetypal imagery and archetypal motifs appear in practically "pure" form. Both myth and folktale are part of an essentially oral tradition that has handed these motifs down from generation to generation. That which survives such a prolonged process of erosion and distortion are the archetypal motifs in a clear and accessible form.

Art is another domain to which analytical psychology can contribute specific insights. All too often, artistic products are analyzed reductively, traced to the family constellation of the artist or to childhood traumata. Inspired art, however, is more than that. It is a personal expression of something universal and timeless, existing in each of us, the giving of a specific and personal form to an archetypal motif. It is a common hypothesis that creativity is the product of neurotic suffering—take away the neurosis and the art disappears. To this, analytic psychology takes exception. Creativity involves the ability to give realistic and visible expression to archetypal form drives without being inundated by them. An artist is different from other people in that he is burdened, as it were, with the additional energy charge of archetypal forces that press for visible manifestation. He does not create because he is neurotic, but may be neurotic because he is creative and has to contend with powerful forces within himself. A genuine artist will not be robbed of his creativity by Jungian analysis; rather he will be more adequately able to contend with his potent resources. It is only where "artistic" endeavours are used as cover-up or escape mechanisms that analysis will undo them.

Evaluation

The Jungian analyst evaluates a prospective patient's readiness for therapy along the same lines used by other clinicians: the person's emotional maturity, the kind of adjustment he has made, his level of functioning, and so forth. He will, however, place primary importance on the person's relationship with his unconscious. Using his knowledge of archetypal patterns, he will often be able to gauge the patient's stage of development and base his decisions accordingly. Some examples will illustrate.

A highly intellectualized patient who seems to have a lot of difficulty in really delving into himself and who experiences his being in analysis as a humiliating process brings, after several months, this initial dream:

I stand on the shore, under the watchful eye of the Queen and King. I am given to understand that a treasure is buried on the island facing us, and that I am to find it. I swim across to the island. On it there is a transparent wall that has to be climbed. It is covered by Venetian blinds. I peer through and see young children carrying guns. I recoil, and swim back to the mainland.

The atmosphere in the dream, the presence of the King and Queen, clearly indicate the archetypal nature of this dream (the dreamer, musically inclined, associated Wagnerian figures to the King and Queen). Because this was an initial dream, it assumes an additional importance, possibly representing the life myth of the dreamer. Here he is presented with the hero's task, to uncover the "treasure hard to attain," a motif appearing in countless myths and fairy tales. As usual, the path to the treasure is not smooth; here, besides swimming to the island without apparent difficulties, our dreamer has to overcome a wall. As he looks through it, he sees that this would entail confronting his infantile aggressive impulses, and he draws back. Prognostically, this does not augur well for the analysis and the patient's ability or willingness to see it through. The treasure, which on the archetypal level is our very essence, seems to be beyond the reach of his effort. As a matter of fact, the patient stayed in therapy for six months, then took a job in another city and stopped therapy without having touched on any deep issue in himself.

Another example is of a different kind. The patient has come to therapy in a crisis situation and has made substantial progress both in solving his current conflicts as well as in bringing about what seems a real change in his personality. He is toying with the idea of terminating and "being on his own." Now, this is a classical dilemma for the therapist who has no objective standards to determine when the analysis is to be terminated. Is the patient's wish to leave the analysis a genuinely healthy decision, or is it an urge born out of the anticipatory anxiety of delving into deeper material? In the latter case, should the therapist let the patient go, hoping he will come back at a future time when he is more secure and ready, or should he confront the patient and analyze his "resistance"? In other words, is the patient requesting an honorable discharge, or is he shirking? In the actual case, the analyst presented the patient with the two alternatives, explained that he had no way of

making the decision, and asked the patient to mull it over, bearing the alternatives in mind. The next session, the patient, not a prolific dreamer, brought the following dream:

I see a girl that I know. I want to approach her and talk to her, because I really like her, but when I half-heartedly attempt to do so, she suddenly vanishes.

To the girl he associates independence, autonomy, and self-reliance. Obviously the message of the dream is: "Your own independence, autonomy, and self-reliance still elude you." The therapist then took the stand that the patient's decision was precipitous and advised that he stay with the analysis, with which suggestion the patient concurred.

Often, when the patient's grasp of reality is more or less tenuous, the therapist is involved in a different kind of problem. Thus, a patient who has been in therapy for several months dreams:

I am standing near the ocean. It is night, and there is a full moon. Suddenly, the moon starts swinging from side to side, in bigger and bigger arcs, until it falls into the ocean. There it explodes like a hydrogen bomb with a big mushroom. The radiation made me evaporate like powder.

The dream shows a tendency toward ego disintegration. A psychotic episode is foreshadowed. Indeed, upon further inquiry the therapist learned that on the day before the dream, the patient felt he could not get up from a chair on which he had been sitting. Something was pulling him back and only the strongest effort managed to get him up. The therapist then confronted the patient with the fact that he was being threatened by a catatonic episode and both calmly discussed the alternatives involved, including hospitalization. They both finally decided to try to work at it together outside a hospital. For the next two weeks they were in close contact; it was touch and go whether the psychotic elements or the conscious ones would prevail. Fortunately, the latter won.

Treatment

Analytical psychology originally was considered applicable primarily for the person who had adjusted to the outer world very well, had accomplished what was expected of him by society, but who, entering the second half of life, found himself listless and dissatisfied. Thus, at its inception, analytical psychotherapy was an attempt to find meaning and was primarily geared for the "adjusted" middle-aged man or woman.

More than two-thirds of Jung's patients were in their second half of life. Most had paid society its due by raising a family and finding a vocation and were now confronted with the task of finding a meaning in their life. In his earlier writings, Jung stressed this division between the first "half" and the second "half" of life, maintaining that different modes of treatment were called for according to which "half" one is dealing with.

Group Psychotherapy. It is useful to recall, whenever one deals with Jung, the background against which he practiced and wrote. The beginning of the twentieth century brought in its wake a psychology that defined normalcy in terms of a collective average. Pathology was still being conceptualized in terms of deviation from a statistical norm. Jung's basic Swiss temperament rebelled against this tendency toward conformity and collectivization, and during all his lifetime, he remained steadfastly a guardian of individuality.

It is not to be wondered at, then, that Jung distrusted group therapy. To Jung, one of the most important aspects of the therapeutic process was the encounter with one's inner religion, one's sense of the divine within oneself. In a group, where so many emotions vie for attention, such an experience is harder to come by, unless the analyst is aware of this problem and takes direct actions to facilitate such experiences.

Yet there is nothing in Jung's psychotherapeutic concepts that is counterindicative of group analysis. Quite the opposite is the case; analytical concepts lend themselves admirably to the group process (Whitmont, 1964). Judiciously applied, they can turn the analytical group into a potent instrument yielding unexpected rewards.

Inherent in the group process is the enhancing of the experiential dimension. Instead of discussing the shadow abstractly in an individual hour, the shadow is lived and felt in the group. Something that may have been thrashed around for months in individual sessions becomes suddenly a gut experience in the group. Issues come to the fore that would be unlikely to arise in individual sessions. The group experience is, therefore, a complementary workshop experience to the individual analysis; each is enriched by the other.

The group experience often challenges one's relation to the mother archetype in its protecting or devouring aspect, thus reflecting one's relationship with one's personal mother. The group is also an excellent vehicle to constellate other archetypal dimensions. The transformation motif, death and rebirth, initiation, the twin brothers—all these can be evoked by various techniques as their possibilities arise spontaneously from the living situation. Psychodrama, Gestalt techniques, sensitivity training, and ritualizations may be employed. The analyst may also take a more active part in group sessions than he could allow himself in individual sessions, and the transference to the analyst is lessened considerably. This also means that the analyst can be responded to more like the human being he is rather than the archetypal role into which he is thrust in individual analysis. Often this permits negative attitudes to surface in the group, attitudes of which the analysand was too frightened to raise individually. The analyst tends to become more involved on the human dimension, which he may find more rewarding, more threatening, or more likely, both.

Family Therapy. The overemphasis on the one-to-one encounter also worked against the introduction of family therapy into the analytical armamentarium. Jungian principles, the understanding of the dynamics of shadow, animus and anima projection, of communication difficulties based upon the difference of psychological types, can serve as vital therapeutic tools. Often analytic work with only one member of a couple will lead to the dissolution of the relationship. Although this is inevitable in some cases, it is destructive and unnecessary in others. Considerations like these may make it desirable that the same analyst work with the two members individually or even treat them as a couple. Very often the archetypal situation in which the patient finds himself lends itself to more effective handling in the family constellation, and then the entire family should be treated as a unit. With very severely disturbed people, family intervention may be indicated. Above all, the analyst should be able to approach each situation with an open mind so he may be guided by the specific constellation.

Management

Jungians do not, as a rule, differ to any marked degree from other therapists working within a dynamic depth-psychological framework as far as management is concerned.

The Setting. The analyst may work in a clinic or an office, or often in his own home. No special trappings are necessary. The emphasis is on intimacy: comfortable chairs for the analyst and the analysand. The analyst may sit beside a desk, or a table, but nothing separates the analyst from the analysand, and they confront each other directly. The analyst may or may not take notes. In some cases the session takes place in a hospital. The patient is assured absolute confidentiality. Special equipment is rarely used, although in this electronic age some people express the desire to record the sessions so they can listen to them at home in leisure.

The intensity and effectiveness of the analysis is not a simple and direct function of the frequency of the sessions. One can work in depth even if one sees a patient once a month. Most analysts, however, prefer to see their patients once or twice a week, at least in the beginning. A growing number of analysts show a marked predilection for working on a once-a-week basis, increasing the number only if absolutely necessary.

Relationship. Analysts differ widely as to how they conduct the first interview. Some prefer to plunge into the thick of the problem, and others insist on a thorough anamnesis starting from earliest memories and going systematically and methodically through the various life stages and emotional development of the patient. Most analysts devote the first few sessions to a mutual evaluation of the patient and the therapist. A basic mutual liking and respect is necessary for a meaningful analysis. If the initial antagonism is too pronounced (on either side), the patient will be transferred. The analyst is aware that his initial negative reactions are projections, which may help him to work these out within himself, so his attitude and feelings toward the patient will undergo a change. However, from his own personal analysis, the analyst has gained sufficient awareness of his own blind spots and knows that even in the most thorough analysis, these cannot be completely worked through. One is never perfect, and allowances for one's weaknesses are a crucial characteristic of a good therapist. As a general rule, it is not advisable to work in a relationship with an analysand who reminds the analyst forcibly of his mother or father, and this holds true even if the parental complex was thoroughly thrashed out during the analyst's own analytical work.

The major importance of the initial sessions lies in taking stock of the unconscious reactions of analyst and analysand to each other. As we have noted before, an initial dream may throw considerable light on the mutual rapport of this particular pairing of analyst and analysand.

No routine demand for psychological testing or physical examination is usually made. Of course, it behooves the analyst to use his clinical knowledge. If the analyst is presented with a symptom, the origin of which might prove organic, he will ask for a physical checkup. In general, flexibility and an intuitive-feeling approach are the hallmarks of the good clinician.

The nature of the relationship between analyst and analysand is determined more by the nature of the two participants than by the specific school of thought to which the analyst belongs. Analysts differ in their personalities and temperaments. Some will tend to be more cerebral and aloof, others more feeling and warm; some more talkative, others more reti-cent, some more active therapeutically than others. Also, hopefully, a single analyst can alter the nature of his participation according to the specific needs of the particular person with whom he is working or the exigencies of a given situation. Broadly speaking, however, an analyst would tend to be more a listener, less active and less sharing of himself at the early stages of analysis. It is by dint of cooperating fruitfully in the analytic process that a growing intimacy and a friendship are established. As time goes on the analyst generally shares more of himself and the relationship becomes more of a peer confrontation, rather than a healer-patient one.

Patient Problems. Very little can be said regarding the kind of patient behaviors likely to cause problems to the analyst. The way in which a given analyst reacts to a specific development is more a function of his personality than it is of his theoretical persuasion. Some therapists will exclude a certain category of patients on an a priori basis, such as alcoholics, drug addicts, suicidal risks; some will refuse to work with a person if he has a gun in his possession. By these exclusions, the therapist recognizes his personal limitations. The analytical orientation as such does not preclude any given situation, and the way in which an analyst may deal with a particular kind of behavior, such as fits of crying and severe depressive episodes, is in no way theoretically predetermined. It has to do with the analyst's personality, his understanding of the situation, and his relationship with the patient.

CASE EXAMPLE

Michael is in his early twenties, the third son in a midwestern family that had four sons. He is attractive, bright and introspective, and highly sensitive to the world around him. Mood and atmosphere affect him profoundly. This sensitivity allows him to feel the implicit and unexpressed needs of other people, a quality he is able to use creatively as well as destructively in a peer group. He tends to react in an extreme and absolutist fashion, betraying an inner insecurity that comes occasionally to the surface. He can be honest with himself and with others and is deeply committed to finding his true meaning.

Michael came to therapy because of his homosexuality. Refreshingly free from the common guilt feelings aroused by societal strictures (both his and his wife's families were aware of the state of affairs), he nevertheless had failed to find satisfaction in the homosexual world. The relationships he had formed proved too flitting, uncommitted, and did not respond to a deep need. Michael expected therapy to help him form lasting and meaningful relationships in the homosexual or heterosexual world.

This was not Michael's first attempt at therapy. He had attempted to work through his problem in college, when his homosexual feelings intensified. The counselor refused to get involved with Michael's feeling and fantasy world, saying it was like a ball of yarn that was better left alone. He advised Michael to concentrate on his behavior rather than on his fantasies and attempted, as Michael experienced it, to "butch him up." As a result, he got married to a sexually shy girl, a virgin like himself. A baby girl was soon born, but the marriage rapidly deteriorated, resulting in a temporary separation. Michael came to the present therapy expecting to be told to "make a man of himself" and, in effect, to be rejected for what he was. That would have clinched his negative relationship toward the adult male world (the present analyst also being male).

The initial analytic work proceeded smoothly, contact easily established, and the first dream Michael presented was the following:

I am in the kitchen with my mother. Upstairs I can hear the sound of heavy chains clanking across the floor. Mother tells me not to worry, that father has gone insane, but that they had chained him upstairs so that he can't hurt me. She intimately places her hand over mine on the table and caresses it.

The dream seems to correspond to the actual family constellation. Michael experiences his father as weak, given to ineffectual violent rages that only emphasize his impotence. The mother stands always on the side of the children, effectively lessening any impact the father might have had. She is also seductive toward her children, especially towards Michael, her favorite. However, it would be a mistake to understand this dream as simply repeating the family psychology, the so-called oedipal character of which Michael is quite aware, for on that level the dream is adding nothing. What the dream is probably describing is the archetypal constellation of someone caught in the grips of homosexuality. The assertive capacity of the ego is under the seductive dominance of the mother archetype, the suction pull of the unconscious, of regressive fantasy, and daydreaming; hence his masculinity is chained and not trusted. The dream does not say anything about the outcome of this situation. That we are here dealing with a potentially difficult state of affairs is demonstrated in the second dream:

My father, brother, and I are pedaling out to sea in water bikes. The water is choppy and threatening. I see my father dipping my baby into the shark-infested water.

Clearly, his anima is yet in an infantile ("baby") stage; that is, his feeling side, his capacity for emotional relatedness, is still undeveloped and threatened by the dangers of the deep, the regressive urges (sharks). He will have to derive masculine strength from an inner source, hopefully as a result of the analytical relationship. Indeed, sometime later we have the third dream:

I follow Y (the analyst) in climbing a difficult terraced mountain. Y is surprised that there is a physical side to my nature, and says he enjoys my company.

Michael, who had suppressed his physical side as a result of ridicule, or lack of trust, rediscovers it in the company of his spiritual guide. Climbing the mountain can be archetypally taken as the road of individuation, the analyst representing an aspect of the Self. A further progress is made when the symbolism is more personal in the fourth dream:

Keith boasts about how many girls he has dated. Under his braggadocio I sense his insecurity, to which I respond in a fatherly way. Suddenly, we are romantically kissing. We are equals. I am transported. Mother tries to find out what has happened between Keith and me.

Keith is a high school friend Michael had not seen since that time. He had idolized Keith, seeing in him that aspect of masculinity he himself so lacked. Here, Keith is to be taken as a positive shadow figure, and the dream foresees the possibility of Michael's getting in touch with his repressed masculinity. Now that this has happened, we can expect a new attitude toward the anima, the feminine side:

Fifth dream: I am teaching my baby girl to talk.

The anima is still a baby, but the ego is developing a positive relationship to her. In the meantime, Michael had decided to reestablish his relationship with his wife, and she returned to him. Michael had also joined a group run by his analyst. The atmosphere in the sessions became more and more charged. Michael attempts to retain control over a process he feels is sweeping through him. Obviously something is afoot.

Sixth dream: I am in the group and suddenly I discover to my horror that I am dressed in a way that looks very gay. I feel ridiculous and say so to one of the girls. She is not concerned and does not take my dress as an indication of my character, just an accident. She simply rolls down the sleeves and makes minor adjustments, and the clothes look normal. A guy who is sitting behind me is dressed in a gay manner. He tries to pull me away from the girl and embraces me. His clothing is full of curved needles that jut outward, and they pierce me. I struggle and free myself. The girl's clothing is also full of pins, but they are safety pins and they are also closed.

The girl in question embodies to Michael the essence of femininity, and her acceptance of him as a man is of prime importance. The conflict depicted here is between the homosexual and heterosexual sides in Michael. The homosexual side, although potent, proves to be "prickly" and disagreeable, according to our dream. We can conclude from it that potentially Michael is able to free himself from it. It is worthwhile to note that in this dream, the dream ego (the dreamer) has made an active choice, which involved a struggle he initiated and out of which he came victorious. On the other hand, this drama still takes place in the collective (the group), that is, under the influence of the mother. The dreamer will need to reaffirm his option on his own perhaps in defiance of the mother world.

For Michael to be able actively to challenge the destructive aspect of the mother, he will have to get sustenance and support from the father world. In myths this usually takes the form of some "heavenly" intervention—Hercules is helped in his labors by Zeus, his divine father; Perseus is provided with the necessary gear (an invisible helmet and a shield) to fight the Gorgon (the Great Mother in her terrible aspect) who turns all who gaze upon her into stone. Consciously, Michael feels helpless. How will he be able to find his own masculinity when he has not had a strong father as a model? This is, indeed, difficult; Michael will have to find his father within himself, a search that will hopefully be aided by the relationship with the male analyst. In Michael's specific case, it means establishing contact with his spiritual side first, namely, broaching the religious question.

Seventh dream: The setting of this dream is a large church. In the rear Y (the analyst) is sitting behind an old wooden table reading from an ancient book. The letters are shaped like old German runes, long and narrow. But when I look close, I see that it could also be Chinese. Y is translating to a group of people, including me.

This dream had a profound effect on Michael. He was awed and puzzled by the church setting. His conflict with religion first arose when he came into puberty and started masturbating. In a characteristic absolutistic fashion, he decided that sex and religion were mutually exclusive, since the latter seemed to negate the former. He therefore discarded his religious beliefs and considered himself an atheist. Until the appearance of this dream, the religious function in him seemed to be successfully repressed. The

dream imagery, however, awakened strong positive feelings; not necessarily for the collective form of institutionalized religion, but for an individual, inner experience. The dream casts the analyst as a translator and transmitter of ancient wisdom, both of Western (the runes) and Eastern tradition. There could hardly be a better description of the analytical process from a Jungian point of view. In a further scene in the dream (not reported here), a wind, a traditional symbol of the spirit, blows through the church. The symbolism is very rich and this made the analyst decide that the analytic sessions by themselves could not support the heavy symbolic load, since the duration of the sessions is too short to permit more than a hinting at the depth and amplitude of the issues raised by this dream. Up to this point, Michael did not know of the analyst's specific theoretical orientation. The issue had never arisen, as Michael did not come to him looking specifically for a Jungian analyst. No professional terminology was ever used. With Michael's intellectual bent, the analyst had decided that overemphasis on the intellectual side would be detrimental to the course of his analysis (with another patient it might prove important to introduce an intellectual framework at the outset of the therapy). The analyst now suggested several books having to do with the symbolism of church and spirit. In this he was also guided by considerations having to do with the archetypal nature of the dream. In Norse mythology, the runes (the alphabet, knowledge, consciousness) were given as a gift to Odin when he sacrificed himself to himself on the ash tree as a symbol of transmittable culture and knowledge.

There is now a new element with which Michael must contend: the religious dimension, the spiritual side of the father archetype. The assimilation of a father figure on a more personal level will have to wait and will come only much later.

Eighth dream: I am with my father. A coarse, brutish guy appears and insults my father. I wait confidently for my father to hit him but he is afraid; he is too weak. Thereupon I hit the guy.

Here the dreamer recognizes that he has to assume masculine qualities himself, rather than look for them in vain in other people who are unable to provide them. Meanwhile, on the level of outer reality, the changes that the unconscious heralds are taking place at a very slow rate. The transformative, goal-oriented thrust to overcome the equally potent (if not more so) inertial tendency of the unconscious takes some time. Michael is very anxious to get on with it and be "quickly transformed." He then has the following dream:

Ninth dream: It is a warm summery day. I find a cocoon hanging on a vine and pick it up. The covering is a delicate green color. Its transparency allows me to see the orange wings of the butterfly inside and I realize that it is a Monarch butterfly. I cup my hands together to provide warmth for the cocoon, hoping that the warmth of my hands will help it emerge sooner. Then I realize it won't help. I must simply wait for it to emerge by itself.

The graphic beauty of this dream is breathtaking. The dreamer is knowledgeable about butterflies and knows that the Monarch, a king, is a very unusual butterfly. In the fall, the Monarchs fly from all over together, congregating and migrating thus to the South for the winter, after which they return. Butterfly is psyche in Greek and is an archetypal image for the Self, the goal of the individuation process. Michael spontaneously said that this is an initiation dream, in which he is initiated into manhood. To the Monarch he

associated his masculinity "hang up," which, initially ugly, is transformed into something beautiful that is part of the collective sense of virility. But, says the dream, the process cannot be deliberately rushed; the natural rhythms of growth have to be respected.

We realize that our presentation of Michael's case is at best an abstraction. Any attempt to communicate an alive, intense, deep relationship between two people over a few pages is impossible; only a few broad strokes out of the whole picture can be delineated. We focused on a segment as it was reflected primarily in the unconscious process; we did not dwell on the outside reality nor on the vicissitudes of the analyst-analysand relationship. We depicted the most salient dreams, omitting scores of others, not all of which were understood by far. The overall pattern is discernible more in retrospect than *in situ;* certainly, no conscious plan was followed. Finally, let us again emphasize that dreams point to possibilities, not actualities. Michael's concrete problems are far from solved. He has to emerge from his isolation and go into the world, anxious, saying, with Faust, "Yet with the flowing beard I wear,/ Both ease and grace will fail me there./ The attempt, indeed, were a futile strife;/ I never could learn the ways of life./ I feel so small before the others, and thence/ Should feel embarrassments."

SUMMARY

Analytical psychotherapy attempts to deal with the human psyche in a phenomenological-existential way using a few basic assumptions as guideposts. The psyche includes consciousness, the center of which is the ego, and the unconscious, which comprises two spheres—the personal unconscious, the sum total of everything that has been repressed during one's lifetime, and the collective unconscious or nonpersonal psyche, the general human structural archetypal psychic organism. The archetypes are instinctlike-ordering patterns of behavior, emotion, and perception. They can never be apprehended directly but are accessible to us through their effect on our behavior, feeling, or the emergence of image representations in dreams, myths, folklore, and creative art.

Jung imputed to the psyche an inherent urge toward wholeness or individuation, the state of being what one was meant to become. The psyche is assumed to function in a purposive way toward that goal, and thus operates as a self-regulating compensatory system. All unconscious products are, therefore, interpreted as messages guiding us to that goal. The emphasis is not only on the inhibiting forces of the past, but primarily on the creative potential of the present. Symptoms and pathology are not merely the end products of neurotic conflicts, but, taken symbolically, contain the way out of psychic impasse.

The psyche contains several elements that are worthy of special consideration. The Self is the archetype of centeredness. It is the agency that directs the total functioning in a holistic way. The shadow is that part of the personality at variance with the ego ideal. The anima in men and the animus in women are our countersexual parts, the experience of the "other," the guide to what we might potentially be.

Jung has left us with theoretical foundations that, although far from exhausted, are firmly established and can be successfully applied in most cases. The technical side of psychotherapy, on the other hand, has not fared as well, and there is little doubt that this is the arena where future efforts must be directed. It has

always been known, but is becoming increasingly more and more crucial, that an adequate interpretation and understanding of unconscious material, although of utmost importance, is, by itself, not enough. One is confronted more and more in one's clinical practice by instances where the dream, the fantasy, the drawing, the very nature of the problem is understood, both by the analyst as well as the analysand, and still no progress seems to be made. What we still sorely lack are effective means by which to translate the hard-won intellectual-theoretical understanding into an experiential phenomenon so a behavioral change is possible.

The verbal dimension by itself is decidedly not enough. The primitives intuited this and instituted rituals to enhance psychic phenomena. Analytical psychotherapy is also attempting to cope with this problem. To that effect, various nonverbal techniques are being incorporated into traditional practice; groups and movement, sensitivity training, and rituals are being employed so psychic facts can be experienced more deeply and hitherto unlocked doors may be thrust open.

ANNOTATED BIBLIOGRAPHY

Jung, Carl G. *Man and his symbols.* Garden City, N.Y.: Doubleday, 1964.
This is the easiest of Jung's books to understand. Jung himself wrote only the first chapter, which he completed a few months before his death. It can, therefore, be taken as a final, authoritative statement of his ideas. The other chapters are written by his followers and students, under his supervision. In contrast to some of his other, specialized writings, this book is addressed to the intelligent lay reader. In the hardcover edition, there is a wealth of pertinent illustrations. The book presents Jung's basic ideas in an easily understandable way.

Jung, Carl G. *Two essays on analytical psychology.* New York: Meridian Books, 1956.

This book, on a higher level of sophistication than *Man and His Symbols,* presents the core ideas of Jungian thought. Some issues dealt with are the structure of the personal and transpersonal unconscious; the incompleteness of Freud's and Adler's viewpoints; persona, anima and animus; and Jung's psychotherapeutic approach.

Jung, Carl G. *Modern man in search of a soul.* New York: Harcourt Brace & Co., 1933.

This is a collection of essays illustrating Jung's creative approach to psychotherapy, the role of dreams, and man's spiritual nature. It is written in a clear, engaging style, which makes for easy, enjoyable reading.

Jung, Carl G. *Memories, dreams, reflections.* Recorded and edited by Aniela Jaffé. New York: Pantheon Books, 1963.

This is the closest thing to an autobiography Jung ever wrote. It details the relationship between his inner, personal struggles and his discoveries. It is the least intellectual of his books; it is personal and warm and makes for absorbing reading.

Whitmont, Edward C. *The symbolic quest.* New York: Putnam, 1969.

This textbook presents a lucid exposition of Jung's major ideas, drawing upon clinical material for illustration. Particularly useful is the seventh chapter, which explains the way an archetypal theme is expressed in a person's life.

CASE READINGS

Adler, Gerhard. *The living symbol: A case study in the process of individuation.* New York: Pantheon Books, 1961.

A whole book devoted to an analysis of a woman suffering from claustrophobia. The material is used as a stepping stone for an examination of Jung's particular contribution to the process of analysis. Very worthwhile to gain the flavor of the experience in Jungian analysis.

Baynes, H. G. *Mythology of the soul: A research into the unconscious from schizophrenic dreams & drawings.* London: Riders & Company, 1969.

A massive book containing two case histories of people we would see today as belonging to the borderline syndrome. Written at a leisurely pace, this is a highly readable account of analytical psychotherapy in action by a very gifted teacher. One of the patients is an artist, thus providing for a case that is rare in the literature.

Rossi, E. L. *Dreams and the growth of personality: Expanding awareness in psychotherapy.* New York: Pergamon Press, 1972.

Part two of this book, pp. 23–130, contains a relatively full case history of a young woman. It is well written by a Jungian analyst who sees himself primarily as a "growth therapist."

Sullwold, Edith. Eagle eye. In Hilde Kirsch (Ed.), *The well-tended tree.* New York: Putnam, 1971, pp. 235–52.

A lovely analysis of a six-year-old Indian boy, an example of an analysis with children using a sandbox.

Lockhart, Russel A. Mary's dog is an ear mother: Listening to the voices of psychosis. *Psychological Perspectives,* Vol. VI, Los Angeles, 1975.

An example of a brief, intensive psychotherapy with a young psychotic man who was hospitalized for hallucinations.

Hillman, J. Archetypal psychology. In A. Burton (Ed.), *Operational theories of personality.* New York: Brunner/Mazel, pp. 65–98.

A case history illustration for teaching purposes.

REFERENCES

Breland, Keller, & Breland, Marian. The misbehavior of organisms. *American Psychologist,* 1961, 16, 681–84.

Campbell, Joseph. *The hero with the thousand faces.* New York: Meridian, 1956.

Campbell, Joseph. *The masks of gods.* New York: Viking Press, 1968.

Ellenberger, H. F. *The discovery of the unconscious.* New York: Basic Books, 1970.

Flourney, Theodore. Miss Frank Miller "Quelque faits d'imagination creatrice subconsciente," *Archives de psychologie,* 1906, 36–51.

Greenson, Ralph R. *The technique and practice of psychoanalysis.* New York: International Universities Press, 1968.

Hall, C., & Lindzey, G. *Theories of personality*. New York: Wiley, 1962.

Jaffé, Aniela. *From the life and work of C. G. Jung*. New York: Harper, 1971.

Jung, C. G. (1902) On the psychology and pathology of so-called occult phenomena. In *Psychiatric studies*. Collected Works. Vol. 1. Bollingen Series XX. Princeton, N.J.: Princeton University Press, 1957.

Jung, C. G. (1907) The psychology of dementia praecox. In *The psychoanalysis of mental disease*. Collected Works. Vol. 3. Bollingen Series XX. Princeton, N.J.: Princeton University Press, 1960.

Jung, C. G. (1954) *The development of personality*. Collected Works. Vol. 17. Bollingen Series XX. Princeton, N.J.: Princeton University Press, 1964.

Jung, C. G. (1911) *Symbols of transformation*. Collected Works. Vol. 5. Bollingen Series XX. Princeton, N.J.: Princeton University Press, 1967.

Jung, C. G. (1934) *The archetypes and the collective unconscious*. Collected Works. Vol. 9, Part I. Bollingen Series XX. Princeton, N.J.: Princeton University Press, 1968.

May, Rollo (Ed.) *Existential psychology*. New York: Random House, 1961.

Munroe, Ruth. *Schools of psychoanalytic thought*. New York: Holt, Rinehart & Winston, 1955.

Neumann, Erich. *The archetypal world of Henry Moore*. Bollingen Series LXI. Princeton, N.J.: Princeton University Press, 1955.

Whitmont, Edward. Group therapy and analytical psychology. *Journal of Analytical Psychology,* 1964, 9, 1, 1–21.

Whitmont, Edward. *The symbolic quest*. New York: Putnam, for the C. G. Jung Foundation for Analytic Psychology, 1970.

4

Person-Centered Therapy*

BETTY D. MEADOR and CARL R. ROGERS

OVERVIEW

Person-centered therapy is a continually developing approach to human growth and change developed originally by Carl Rogers in the 1940s. Its central hypothesis is that the growthful potential of any individual will tend to be released in a relationship in which the helping person is experiencing and communicating realness, caring, and a deeply sensitive nonjudgmental understanding. It is further unique in being process oriented, in drawing its hypotheses from the raw data of therapeutic experience, and from recorded and filmed interviews. It has been determined to test all its hypotheses through appropriate research. It has application in every field of human endeavor where the healthy psychological growth of the individual is a goal.

---

*In 1974 Rogers and his colleagues changed the name of their approach from "client-centered" to "person-centered" therapy, believing this name to describe more adequately the human values their way of working incorporates.

This chapter was written by Dr. Betty Meador, but I have read the chapter with care, made some minor changes and additions, and believe it is a good and accurate presentation of what is an increasingly pervasive point of view. I am pleased she included my account of two interviews with "a silent young man." What I am saying is that this chapter has my full endorsement.—Carl R. Rogers

Basic Concepts

The basic theory of person-centered therapy can be stated simply in the form of an "if—then" hypothesis. If certain conditions are present in the attitudes of the person designated "therapist" in a relationship, namely, congruence, positive regard, and empathic understanding, then growthful change will take place in the person designated "client." The hypothesis holds true, theoretically, in any relationship in which one person assumes the attitudes of congruence, empathy, and positive regard, and the other person perceives these attitudes.

The hypothesis rests on an underlying view of man's nature. Person-centered theory postulates man's tendency toward *self-actualization*. "This is the inherent tendency of the organism to develop all its capacities in ways which serve to maintain or enhance the organism," says Rogers (1959b, p. 196).

The forces toward self-actualization are part of man's organismic nature. In this regard, Rogers quotes Lancelot Whyte:

Crystals, plants, and animals grow without any conscious fuss, and the strangeness of our own history disappears once we assume that the same kind of natural ordering process that guides their growth, also guided the development of man and of his mind and does so still! (Whyte, 1960)

The forces of self-actualization in the infant and child bump up against conditions that significant others in his life impose upon him. These "conditions of worth" tell him he is lovable and acceptable when he behaves in accordance with the imposed standards. Some of these conditions the child eventually assimilates into his self-concept. Then, according to Rogers, "he values an experience positively or negatively solely because of these conditions of worth which he has taken over from others, not because the experience enhances or fails to enhance his organism" (1959b, p. 209).

Even though the child has imposed restrictions on his organismic urges, he continues to experience them viscerally. An incongruence develops between the organismic forces of self-actualization and his ability to translate them into awareness and action.

The question that person-centered theory has sought to answer is this: How can an individual reclaim the self-actualizing urges and acknowledge their wisdom? Broadly defined, *psychotherapy* is the "releasing of an already existing capacity in a potentially competent individual" (Rogers, 1959b, p. 221). If certain definable conditions are present, the individual gradually allows the self-actualizing capacity to overcome restrictions he has internalized in the conditions of worth. The definable conditions are that the individual perceive in the therapeutic relationship genuineness or congruence, accurate empathic understanding, and unconditional positive regard.

The three conditions are not distinct states of being from which an adept therapist intuitively selects. They are interdependent and logically related.

In the first place, the therapist must achieve a strong, accurate empathy. But such deep sensitivity to moment-to-moment "being" of another person requires that the therapist first accept, and to some degree prize, the other person. That is to say, a sufficiently strong empathy can scarcely exist without a considerable degree of unconditional positive regard. However, since neither of these conditions can possibly be meaningful in the relationship unless they are real, the therapist must be, both in these respects and in others, integrated and genuine within the therapeutic encounter. Therefore, it seems to me that genuineness or congruence is the most basic of the three conditions. (Rogers, 1959a, p. 184)

Genuineness or *congruence* is the basic ability of the therapist to read his own inner experiencing and to allow the quality of his inner experiencing to be apparent in the therapeutic relationship. That precludes his playing a role or presenting a façade. His words are consonant with his experiencing. He follows himself transparently. He follows the changing flow of his own feelings and presents himself transparently. He attempts to be fully present to his client; he is himself.

The concepts of genuineness and accurate, empathic understanding are closely related. The therapist, in the fullness of his own person, tries to immerse himself in the feeling world of his client to experience that world within himself. His understanding comes out of his own inner experiencing of his client's feelings, using his own inner processes of awareness for a referent. He actively experiences not only his client's feelings, but also his own inner responses to those feelings. Through this process he can often go beyond the words of the client to the surrounding, implicit feelings on the edge of the client's awareness.

Basic to his empathy for the client is a nonpossessive caring or acceptance of his individuality called *unconditional positive regard*. This attitude comes in part from the therapist's trust in the inner wisdom of the actualizing processes in the client, and in his belief that the client will discover for himself the resources and directions his growth will take. The therapist's caring does not take the form of advice or directions. He communicates his prizing of the client's individuality sometimes directly, often through his nonjudgmental understanding and genuine response.

Several studies have shown that client gain is significantly correlated with the attitudes of congruence, accurate empathy, and positive regard. Galatia Halkides found a positive correlation between the presence of the three attitudes and success in the clients (1958). A series of studies testing this hypothesis by Godfrey Barrett-Lennard (1959; 1962) found that clients who perceived more of the three attitudes in their therapists showed more positive gain in therapy than those who did not perceive these attitudes.

Later studies included the new theoretical dimension of person-centered therapy, the process conception of *client personality change*. The theory postulates that change takes place along a continuum, one end of which is represented by rigid, static, repetitive behavior, and the other end by behavior that changes and flows with the change and flow of inner experiencing (see Psychotherapy section). A study with hospitalized schizophrenic patients found that those patients whose therapists were high in the three attitudinal conditions show the greatest gain, especially in their schizophrenic score on the MMPI. Also, those patients who could interact in therapy at higher process levels showed greater gains than those whose behavior was relatively static and rigid (Rogers, 1967b).

In summary, individual positive change in a therapeutic relationship is precipitated when the client perceives the genuineness, empathy, and caring of his therapist. His personality change will occur in the direction of his being more and more aware of his inner experiencing, toward his allowing his inner experiencing to flow and change, and toward his behaving in congruence with his inner experiencing.

Other Systems

Rogers's attitude toward the future of the various systems of psychotherapy is stated in the following quotation in which he is speaking about research:

Its major significance, it seems to me, is that a growing body of objectively verified knowledge of psychotherapy will bring about the gradual demise of "schools" of psychotherapy including this one. As solid knowledge increases as to the conditions which facilitate therapeutic change, the nature of the therapeutic process, the conditions which block or inhibit therapy, the characteristic outcomes of therapy in terms of personality or behavioral change, there will be less and less emphasis upon dogmatic and purely theoretical formulations. Differences of opinion, different procedures in therapy, different judgments as to outcome, will be put to empirical test rather than being simply a matter of debate or argument. (Hart & Tomlinson, 1970, pp. 19–20)

The main thrust of person-centered therapy has been the empirical testing of those events that appear to facilitate growthful change in an individual. It has been the belief of those associated with person-centered therapy that the factors that precipitate growthful change are common, discoverable human events that pay no heed to the theoretical beliefs of the therapist. Characteristically, person-centered theorists have changed and expanded their theory and methods as they gained new insights from empirical testing.

It is not uncommon to find therapists of different persuasions exhibiting high levels of empathy, caring, and genuineness with their clients. The differences between person-centered therapy and other systems are frequently more apparent in the values each holds and their respective views of man than in their methodology. The general disscussion that follows considers these more basic value differences with full awareness that there is wide variation in actual practice among therapists in any given "school."

Directive Techniques. Historically those associated with person-centered therapy have stood firmly against the therapist being directive with his client, as the original name, "nondirective therapy," suggests. *Directive therapy* includes any practice that views the therapist as an expert who knows the inner workings of human beings and is able to diagnose, prescribe, and cure the individuals who come to him for help.

Central to the person-centered point of view from the beginning was the belief in the self-directing capacity of the individual. Years of experience with clients and numerous research studies have confirmed this belief and developed it to the point where today, any interference by the therapist with his client's focus on his inner experiencing process is seen as counterproductive.

The person-centered therapist conveys his reliance on the client's resources in a number of ways. Any attitude or manipulation, such as the use of esoteric language, professionalism, or diagnostic testing, is avoided. These measures are seen as removing the process of therapy from the control of the client to the therapist, transferring the locus of evaluation from the client's hands to that of the therapist, and undermining the confidence of the client in his own ability to discover his pattern for growth. Any technique such as psychodrama, Gestalt therapy techniques, and bioenergetics likewise tends to put the therapist in the role of expert and diminish the client's reliance on his own inner processes. "Psychotherapy is the releasing of an already existing capacity in a potentially competent individual, not the expert manipulation of a more or less passive personality" (Rogers, 1959b, p. 221).

Three Forces in Psychology. Rogers has identified himself with the so-called third force in psychology, that diverse group who come together under the name *humanistic psychology*. His identification with humanistic psychology is based on his advocacy of the dignity and value of the individual person in his search for growth, and on Rogers's interest in the development of a science of psychology that considers individual dignity and value as primary.

Rogers sums up the basic difference between the views of man held by psychoanalysis and by person-centered theory in this way:

I have little sympathy with the rather prevalent concept that man is basically irrational, and that his impulses, if not controlled, will lead to destruction of others and self. Man's behavior is exquisitely rational, moving with subtle and ordered complexity toward the goals his organism is endeavoring to achieve. (Rogers, 1961a, pp. 194—196)

Our defenses, he says, get in the way of our awareness of our organismic processes, which direct the individual toward positive growth. Man, when free from defensive distortion, lives in the flow of his inner experiencing, referring to the nuances of that organismic flow as guidelines for his behavior. Contrary to psychoanalytic thinking, Rogers sees the natural impulses of man, living out of his inner organismic experiencing, as constructive and conducive to health and fulfillment.

Psychoanalytic theory holds that by focusing on and understanding his past, the patient will, through the interpretations of his analyst, gain insight into his present behavior. Person-centered theory focuses on the present experiencing of the client, believing that the reestablishment of awareness of and trust in that experiencing provides the resources for growthful change.

In psychoanalysis, the analyst aims to interpret for his patient the connections between his past and his present. In person-centered therapy the therapist facilitates the client's discoveries of the meanings of his own current inner experiencing. The analyst in psychoanalysis takes the role of teacher in interpreting insights to the patient and encouraging the development of a transference relationship between the patient and himself, a relationship based on the neurosis of the patient. The therapist in person-centered therapy presents himself as honestly and transparently as he can, and attempts to establish a relationship in which he is simply the person he is, caring for and listening to another person.

In person-centered therapy, although beginnings of transference relationships occur, such relationships do not become full-blown (Rogers, 1951, p. 214). Rogers has postulated that perhaps transference relationships develop in an evaluative atmosphere where the client feels the therapist knows more about him than he knows himself, and therefore the client becomes dependent. The therapist in person-centered therapy tends to avoid any expression that could have evaluative connotations. He does not interpret meanings for the client, does not question in a probing manner, does not reassure, criticize, praise, or describe his client. Person-centered therapy has not found the transference relationship, central to psychoanalysis, a necessary part of a client's growthful change.

Differences between the person-centered point of view and behaviorism can be seen in the attitudes of each toward science and toward behavior change. Generally, *science* from a behavioristic stance is the observing, recording, and manipulation of observable phenomena. In this sense, it attempts to apply to behavior the ground rules of investigation of the physical sciences.

In this regard, the inner experiencing of persons is not subject to investigation since it is neither observable nor subject to controlled replication. Thus, a definite mind-set about what constitutes science determines what behavior can be investigated, how it can be understood, predicted, and controlled. Rogers, on the other hand, has said there may be definite limits to the extent to which the experiential can be made part of the science of psychology, but to ignore it completely and its influence on behavior is indeed tragic (Hart & Tomlinson, 1970, p. 522). For Rogers, a science of the person must try to understand human beings in all their manifestations.

For behaviorism, *behavior change* comes about through external control of stimulus and reward. For person-centered theory, behavior change evolves from within the individual. Behavior therapy's goal is symptom removal. It is not concerned with the relationship of inner experiencing to the symptom under consideration nor with the relationship between the person of the therapist and the person of the client, nor with the climate of their relationship. It seeks to eliminate the symptom as expeditiously as possible using the principles of learning theory. Obviously, this point of view is quite contrary to person-centered therapy, which believes that the "fully functioning person" relies on his inner experiencing for determining his behavior.

HISTORY

Precursors

The American Heritage Dictionary defines a *precursor* as "One that precedes and indicates or announces someone or something to come." In that sense, it is doubtful that there would be any precursors of person-centered therapy. However, to set the person-centered point of view in historical perspective, person-centered therapy could probably best be traced to some Oriental thinkers. In Martin Buber's chapter about the "Teaching of the Tao" he explains the meaning of "Wu-Wei," a reasonable translation of which is "nonaction," one of the basic Taoist virtues. He quotes Lao-Tse:

To interfere with the life of things means to harm both them and one's self. He who imposes himself has the small, manifest might; he who does not impose himself has the great secret might. . . . The perfected man does not interfere in the life of beings, he does not impose himself on them, but he helps all beings to their freedom. (Buber, 1957, pp. 54–55)

Buber continues, "Through his unity, he liberates their nature and their destiny, he releases Tao in them."

This paragraph of Lao-Tse describes very well the person that the person-centered therapist would like to become. There is also much in the Zen tradition of insisting that the individual find the answers within himself, which is in accord with the thinking voiced by Rogers, although the methods are quite different.

Skipping a number of centuries, it is probably not accidental that Rogers used a quotation from Emerson as the first statement in *Client-Centered Therapy:* "We mark with light in the memory the few interviews we have had, in the dreary years of routine and of sin, with souls that made our souls wiser; that spoke what we thought; that told us what we knew; that gave us leave to be what we inly were" (Emerson, 1838).

Rogers was influenced indirectly by John Dewey, particularly through the work of William H. Kilpatrick. Dewey's philosophy is clearly evident in books like *Freedom to Learn* (Rogers, 1969).

Another quite different influence was the work of Otto Rank. Rogers (1959b) indicated that he helped organize a three-day institute with Otto Rank and had contact with the Philadelphia group of social workers and psychiatrists whom Rank had influenced. He says Rank's thinking, ". . . helped me to crystalize some of the therapeutic methods we were groping toward."

Still later, brought to his attention by the theological students at the University of Chicago was the whole range of existentialist thinking. Martin Buber's and Soren Kierkegaard's ideas seemed most confirming of the person-centered point of view.

One can note similarities in theoretical background to Gestalt theory. Rogers's whole approach is that of field theory rather than the historical approach of Freudian psychology. It is thus based in the present, not in the past.

Probably lurking somewhere in the background is the individualism of the American frontier, the belief in self-reliance, the conviction that the individual could learn and do what was necessary for him to learn and do.

All of these influences, with the possible exception of Otto Rank, played no part in the development of person-centered therapy. Rogers learned about them later and felt confirmed by the points of view that had been expressed.

It can be said that through the centuries there have been many philosophers and some psychologists who expressed thoughts and ideas similar to those of Rogers. Yet in almost every case, his discovery of those ideas came after he had formulated his own mode of working and his own explanation of the process of therapy. For example, Samuel Tenenbaum, who wrote the definitive biography of William H. Kilpatrick, Dewey's follower, happened to be in a course with Rogers (Rogers, 1961a). It was his judgment that Kilpatrick and Dewey, too, would have been shocked by Rogers's willingness to give the student *real* freedom to make a choice. The idea that the student might reach a conclusion completely at odds with that of the instructor would doubtless have been quite unacceptable to Kilpatrick. Yet that was Rogers's conviction.

Perhaps these few paragraphs will set in some historical perspective the individuals who have in the past held similar points of view.

Beginnings

Although the growth of person-centered therapy has been shaped by many men and women who were students or colleagues of Carl Rogers, his dominance as its principal theorist and influence over more than three decades is uncontroverted. Thus, the precursors of person-centered therapy are to be found in the interaction of the man with the personal and cultural influences that surrounded him as he grew to maturity.

Rogers was born January 8, 1902, into a close-knit, midwestern, Protestant family. When he was 12, the family moved to a farm. Part of the reason for the move was that his parents believed the values of honest work and Christian principles were more likely to germinate in their children if they were away from the influences of the city. On the farm, the young man's interest in and study of scientific agriculture developed in him a lasting respect for the scientific method.

Of early influences on his thinking, Rogers mentions a number of teachers from high school through graduate school who sanctioned and encouraged his ability to be original and unique and his penchant for the scholarly. His graduate education was varied and rich as he describes in the following passage:

Having rejected the family views of religion, I became interested in a more modern religious viewpoint and spent two profitable years in Union Theological Seminary, which at that time was deeply committed to a freedom of philosophical thought which respected any honest attempt to resolve significant problems, whether this led into or away from the church. My own thinking led me in the latter direction, and I moved "across the street" to Teachers College, Columbia University. Here I was exposed to the views of John Dewey, not directly, but through William H. Kilpatrick. I also had my first introduction to clinical psychology in the warmly human and common-sense approach of Leta Hollingsworth. There followed a year of internship at the Institute for Child Guidance, then in its chaotic but dynamic first year of existence 1927-28. Here I gained much from the highly Freudian orientation of most of its psychiatric staff, which included David Levy and Lawson Lowrey. My first attempts at therapy were carried on at the Institute. Because I was still completing my doctorate at Teachers College, the sharp incompatibility of the highly speculative Freudian thinking of the Institute with the highly statistical and Thorndikean views at Teachers College was keenly felt (Rogers, 1959b, p. 186).

Thus, Rogers began his work as a therapist having been exposed both to psychoanalytic thinking through the works of Freud and his modern interpreters, Karen Horney and Harry Sullivan, and to psychology as it was developing in the United States with its emphasis on scientific method, operational definitions and the proof or disproof of hypotheses. His first position after completing his doctorate in 1931 was at the Child Study Department of a Rochester social agency. There his own ideas began to form as, from his experiences with clients, he began to sense the orderliness inherent in the experience of therapy.

About half way through his 12 years in Rochester, Rogers became acquainted with the thought of Otto Rank through social workers who had been trained in the Rankian method in Philadelphia. Rank's contention that the individual has self-directing capacities that emerge through therapy complemented Rogers's strong belief in the dignity of the individual as well as his accumulating experience with clients.

In some ways, Rank's thought strongly influenced person-centered therapy and in other ways it simply confirmed the trends already emerging. This is evident in a brief look at Rank's ideas. He delineates three factors that influence psychotherapy. The factors are the individual, the therapist, and the relationship between them. The *individual* client, Rank says, is a moving cause, containing constructive forces within, which constitute a will to health. The *therapist* guides the individual to self-understanding and self-acceptance. It is the therapist as a human being who is the remedy, not his technical skill. Of the *relationship,* Rank says the spontaneity and uniqueness of the experience of therapy lived in the present carry the patient toward health (Rank, 1936).

Seeds of Rogers's later ideas and some references to Rank and "passive therapy" appear in Rogers's first book, *The Clinical Treatment of the Problem Child,* written in 1937 and published in 1939. However, the real crystallization of the core of person-centered therapy took place between 1937 and 1941. The end of the precursor stage and the beginning of person-centered theory development coincided with Rogers's move from Rochester to Ohio State University in January, 1940. Here Rogers's new methods of psychotherapy first came into public view, and the growth of person-centered therapy into a full-blown practice and theory began.

Rogers moved to Ohio State with the intention of training graduate students in the methods implicit in his way of working with clients. He thought at the time that his writings "were essentially attempts to distill out more clearly the principles which 'all clinicians' were using" (Rogers, 1959b), a pragmatic style determined by the orderliness of the client's unfolding in the therapeutic experience. However, as he began to make his ideas explicit to graduate students, he realized his thinking was new to them and perhaps more of a new approach to psychotherapy than he had surmised. A paper presented at the Minnesota chapter of Psi Chi in December 1940, later included as chapter two of *Counseling and Psychotherapy* (Rogers, 1942), was his first attempt to develop in writing this line of thinking.

When Rogers published *Counseling and Psychotherapy* in 1942, the climate among counselors and psychotherapists was particularly receptive to a new way of working. Two major influences dominated the field of psychotherapy in the United States at the time. One was *psychoanalysis.* Although its practitioners were primarily medical doctors, nonmedical counselors and psychotherapists borrowed freely from the theories of Freud and his interpreters to explain human behavior and to derive techniques of therapy. The second influence was *directive counseling.* Basic to this technique is the view that the therapist is the expert who diagnoses his subject and on this basis selects the direction the client should take. Those theorists who emphasized diagnostic measures are included in this group. Both of these views were heavily dependent on the knowledge and skills of the therapist. The client was diagnosed, categorized, and explained with little reference to what he thought about himself. Disillusionment with these techniques inevitably occurred as counselors discovered that even though they "knew" what was wrong with a client and what he *should* do to help himself, neither this knowledge nor its communication was effective in changing his behavior.

In *Counseling and Psychotherapy,* Rogers proposed a counseling relationship whose characteristics were the warmth and responsiveness of the therapist, a permissive climate in which feelings could be freely expressed, and a freedom from all coercion or pressure. A client in such a relationship would gain understanding of himself that would "enable him to take positive steps in the light of his new orientation" (1942, p. 18). The therapist in the relationship was freed from the burden of scanning the system under which he worked to find the "right" diagnostic or interpretive category for his client at a given moment.

Originally the term *counseling* was chosen because it was a modest term, and because the word *therapy* immediately aroused a fight whenever it was used. Psychiatrists felt that therapy was their field. Consequently, the less emotion-arousing term, for both client and professional, was used. Still, *Counseling and Psychotherapy* is predominantly a technique-oriented book. Although the therapist is described as being warm, responsive, and permissive, he is not yet freed to be himself. This development was to come much later.

Rogers and his students at Ohio State had begun to make detailed analyses of counseling sessions, using for the first

time verbatim transcripts of electrically recorded interviews. In fact, the first complete published therapeutic case appeared in *Counseling and Psychotherapy*. The invention of electrical recordings facilitated the kind of scrutiny of the counseling process that Rogers's continued concern for scientific definition and hypothesis testing demanded. The purpose of *Counseling and Psychotherapy,* he stated, was to stimulate research through the presentation of numerous explicit and implicit hypotheses.

From these beginnings, Rogers's emphasis has been on understanding how and why individuals change in the process of therapy, not primarily on theory development. *Theory development* grew naturally out of the testing of hypotheses that Rogers and his colleagues and students formed from their experience with clients. The changing character of person-centered therapy is due to Rogers's consistent insistence on looking at the facts and altering methods and theory whenever experience and research so dictated.

Rogers's move to the University of Chicago in 1945, where he organized the Counseling Center, began a decade of prolific research. The publication of *Client-Centered Therapy* in 1951 introduced the name change from "nondirective counseling" to "client-centered." The change was not merely semantic. It indicated a shift in emphasis from the negative, narrower statement, "nondirective," to the positive focus on the growth-producing factors in the individual client himself. (Footnote, page 1, describes the reason for the new name change to person-centered therapy.)

Emphasis in methodology and research in this era centered on the process of personality change. The repeated reference by clients in therapy to a "self" and its changingness led to theory formulation of the self-concept, first attempted at Ohio State by V. C. Raimy (1943). Further studies of the self-concept were greatly aided by the development of the Q-sort by William Stephenson (1953). From the self-concept research came a major theoretical formulation concerning personality change. "We came to see the troubled or neurotic individual," Rogers said, "as one whose self-concept had become structured in ways incongruent with his organismic experience" (1959a, p. 192). This new understanding led to methodological changes as therapists became more conscious of making explicit the organismic experience of their clients; whereas formerly they had responded to the client's words, reflecting what they heard, now they responded to the client's implicit as well as explicit affect. This required the therapists to get behind the words of the client and into his feeling world and precipitated a new look at accurate emphatic understanding.

This decade saw the publication of *Psychotherapy and Personality Change* in 1954, a report of a number of studies of change factors in therapy. It also saw the publication of several works on the maturing theory, beginning with *Client-Centered Therapy* (1951), and continuing with "A Theory of Therapy, Personality, and Interpersonal Relationships, as Developed in the Client-Centered Framework" (Rogers, 1959b) written around 1953–54. Two further important theory papers appeared in this decade. They were "The Necessary and Sufficient Conditions of Therapeutic Personality Change" (1957) and "A Process Conception of Psychotherapy" (1958).

Rogers moved to the University of Wisconsin in 1957 and found the opportunity to test a persistent question: Would the "necessary and sufficient conditions"

and the newer process theory be applicable to hospitalized schizophrenics, as they were to the students, adults, and children who were clients at the University of Chicago Counseling Center? A five-year study sought to answer that question (Rogers, 1967b), and true to form, person-centered therapy and theory found itself incorporating changes as a result of the experience with schizophrenics. "It is already certain that the patients did a great deal to us," says one of the principal researchers, Eugene Gendlin. "I might say that our own improvement has been remarkable" (Hart & Tomlinson, 1970, p. 284).

This presentation has attempted to give the picture of person-centered therapy as a growing organism. Although Rogers has been the central figure in its development, he has had as students and colleagues many able individuals who have explored, independently, avenues of thought to which their experience and hypothesizing brought them. The characteristic close scrutiny of the actual therapeutic relationship plus the dogged refusal to be committed to any single formulation of the theory has opened those associated with person-centered therapy to the rich possibilities they have investigated. Rogers has by example and advocacy upheld the notion of science that he describes in the following passage:

It is my opinion that the type of understanding which we call science can begin anywhere, at any level of sophistication. To observe accurately, to think carefully and creatively— these activities, not the accumulation of laboratory instruments, are the beginnings of science. (Rogers, 1959b, p. 189).

Current Status

The central hypothesis of person-centered theory lends itself to application in any human relationship where either or both of the participants want genuine understanding or individual growth to unfold. The hypothesis states that if certain conditions are present in the attitude of the therapist, namely, genuineness, empathic understanding, and positive regard, then positive personality change will occur in the client (Rogers, 1957). The fleshing out of this hypothesis came with Rogers's publication of his process theory (1958) in which the orderly, sequential, positive changes an individual goes through in a therapeutic relationship were described.

Like rain off an umbrella, the influence of person-centered theory has fallen in all directions. Because the theory relies on the inner attitudes of the person designated "helper" to facilitate positive change in the "other" in a relationship, it has been embraced by professional persons in a wide variety of fields. No longer is it necessary for complex diagnostic definitions, intricate webs of theory, protocols of techniques, to be applied to situations. The person who can be real, caring, and understanding can count on being an effective facilitator of growth in a helping relationship.

As Howard Kirschenbaum of Temple University and the New School of Social Research puts it:

Carl Rogers, the founder of the client-centered approach in psychotherapy, is still one of the leading figures in the fields of humanistic psychology and education. His theories, research, and methods have revolutionized our concept of the helping relationship—in therapy, in guidance, in education, in social work, in the ministry, and in many other professions (Kirschenbaum, 1971).

To his list could be added the fields of psychiatry, industrial relations, organizational development, marriage and family counseling, speech therapy, the priesthood, and the use of nonprofessional workers in crisis centers such as "The Hot-Line"—and so on and on.

The acceptance of the fundamental hypotheses of person-centered therapy has not always been a smooth road. In the 1940s and 1950s, this was a very controversial view indeed, and debates and highly critical reviews and articles were common. Recently, however, these views, especially in the helping relationship, have become imperceptibly woven into much of current thinking in all the fields mentioned.

Rogers himself has concentrated in recent years on the application of person-centered theory and methods to enhance the growth and human relations abilities of normal individuals in a variety of settings. He has particularly explored the efficacy of the intensive small group or encounter group in facilitating individual and institutional change. Five of his books have the normal individual as the central concern: *On Becoming a Person* (1961a), *Freedom to Learn* (1969), *Carl Rogers on Encounter Groups* (1970), *On Becoming Partners: Marriage and Its Alternatives* (1972), and *Carl Rogers on Personal Power* (1977).

He began this work at Western Behavioral Sciences Institute in La Jolla, California, in 1964. In 1968 Rogers and the group of researchers who were working with him on a project for self-directed change in an educational system (Rogers, 1967a, 1969) spun off from WBSI and formed the innovative Center for Studies of the Person (CPS) in La Jolla. Rogers is currently a Resident Fellow at CSP.

As he enters these new fields, the criticisms crop up again. Here are two quotations from reviews of *Freedom to Learn,* showing how a new idea in education seems to be as polarizing as a new idea in psychotherapy. Professor R. S. Peters, an educator from the University of London, writes (Peters, 1970):

What is surprising . . . is that an author who strongly advocates openness to the experiences of others should put together a collection of papers that are meant to be of general relevance to educational problems in such a seeming state of ignorance and innocence about educational theory and practice. Freedom is fine; and so is self-directed exploration. But there are other values, both in life and in education—truth, for instance, humility, and breadth of understanding.

To show a contrast in judgment, Dr. Samuel Tenenbaum reviews the same book. Tenenbaum is a philosopher of education, the author of a definitive biography of William H. Kilpatrick, a teacher, and a therapist. Some excerpts from his review give its flavor (Tenenbaum, 1969):

Seldom does a book on education appear that so excites the imagination as to what is possible in education, so liberates the reader from viewing education in conventional ways. . . .

. . . Dr. Rogers sees the teacher as one who can release students as well as himself for growth. He, the teacher, also becomes a learner, eagerly seeking, as do his students, new meanings and insights. For Carl Rogers, education is not a mass of facts presented on examination papers, but a becoming process whose goal is ever richer and more meaningful living. In achieving these ends, the teacher is anything but an authoritarian figure, the processor of truth and wisdom, there to transmit it to students ignorant of this truth and wisdom. Each student in a good educational arrangement is given freedom to find his own truth and wisdom; and the adventure and the excitement lie in not knowing, in teacher and student finding out together. . . .

. . . In *Freedom to Learn,* one gains not only a philosophy and methodology of what is good education but also what is the good life to live.

This enormous discrepancy of judgment is similar to the judgments first made about person-centered therapy. Rogers hopes this phenomenon has the same meaning again—namely, that when vital new issues are raised in a professional field, violently opposing views are stirred up.

Person-centered theory is mature enough at this point that whatever growth or amplifications spring from its soil can do so independently of Rogers. The theory has moved, as Rogers predicted, toward a unified science of inner growth and of the conditions that facilitate it. The description of the sequential inner process that takes place as an individual undergoes positive personality change provides a basis for a common description of growth regardless of the school of psychology or the diagnosis of the client. The sequence of change in individuals needs further scrutiny, refinement, and testing as do the facilitating conditions, but the discoveries that those associated with person-centered therapy have made may lead to a unitary understanding of the process of personality change.

PERSONALITY

Theory of Personality

The development of a theory of personality has not been the primary concern of person-centered theorists:

Although a theory of personality has developed from our experience in client-centered therapy, it is quite clear to anyone closely associated with this orientation that this is not our central focus. Rather, the manner in which change comes about in the human personality has been the central core of our interest. . . . It seems to us that far more intelligent and answerable questions can be raised in regard to the *process* of personality change than in regard to the *causes* of the person's present personality characteristics (Rogers, 1959b, p. 194).

In place of a theory of therapy being a logical extension of certain beliefs about human personality, the opposite has happened. The personality theory has grown out of the clinical experience, the research, and the theory of personality *change* developed by those associated with person-centered therapy.

Because the theoretical concepts grew out of an experience of process, what has developed is a field theory, rather than a genetic theory such as Freud's. Thus, the significant forces are to be found in the immediate relationships, as in an electrical field of forces. Person-centered theory is primarily a theory of change and of therapy, that is, of the conditions that bring about change. Hence the theory of personality is primarily inferred, and the propositions "are those which are furthest from the matrix of our experience and hence are most suspect" (Rogers, 1959b, p. 222).

The Developing Infant. The person-centered personality theory begins with certain postulates concerning the human infant at birth. The world of the infant is his own experiencing. His experiencing is his only reality. Within the world of his organism, the infant has one basic motivational force: a tendency toward self-actualization.

Along with this basic motivation, the infant has the inherent ability to value positively experiences he perceives as enhancing his organism, and to value negatively those experiences that appear contrary to his actualizing tendency. This, his "organismic valuing process," serves to direct his behavior toward the goal of his own self-actualization.

The Self-Concept. As the infant grows and develops, he begins to discriminate among his experiences and to own those that are part of his own being and functioning, and to assign ownership of other experiences to other persons and things in his environment. As his awareness of his own being and functioning develops, he acquires a sense of self made up of the experiences of his own being and functioning within his environment. This is his developing *self-concept.*

The development of a self-concept is a dynamic process strongly dependent on the individual's perception of his experiences in his environment. His perception of his experiences is influenced by his need for positive regard, a universal need in human beings, pervasive and persistent (Rogers, 1959b, p. 223).

Out of the complex of experiences of satisfaction or frustration of his need for positive regard, the individual develops a sense of *self-regard,* a learned sense of self based on his perception of the regard he has received from others. This sense of self-regard becomes a pervasive construct influencing the behavior of the whole organism and has a life of its own, independent of actual experiences of regard from others. The way in which this develops is explained by the individual's introjecting conditions of worth.

Conditions of Worth. Inevitably, the child's need to retain the love of his parents gets at cross-purposes with the needs of his organism. The values he is aware of in his own organism are sometimes contrary to the values of his parents. His behavior, which springs out of his organismic needs and desires, is sometimes contrary to the behavior his parents find acceptable. When this occurs, he begins to take into his own system of self-regard the discrimination between experiences worthy of regard from significant others and those not worthy of their regard. He begins to avoid or to deny completely his organismic experiencings which he has learned are not worthy of positive regard.

These introjected conditions of worth

become a part of his self-regard system. He experiences positive self-regard when his self-experiences are in accord with experiences for which he has received positive regard; he experiences negative self-regard when his experiences are those for which he has not received positive regard. His experience of self-worth comes to depend on the conditions of worth that he has learned in his interaction with significant others in his world.

What happens to the actualizing tendency as conditions of worth develop in the self-regard system? The actualizing tendency remains the basic motivation for the individual. However, a conflict develops between his organismic needs and his self-regard needs, now containing conditions of worth. The individual, in effect, is faced with the choice between acting in accord with his organismic sense or censoring the organismic urging and acting in accord with the condition of worth he has learned. To maintain his positive self-regard, and therefore maintain his feeling of worth and feeling of self-actualization, he chooses to act in accord with the condition of worth. In other words, his need for self-regard overpowers his organismic needs. At these choice points, he may come to believe that his organismic urges are "bad" and contrary to his being a "good" person, therefore, contrary to his self-actualization. Rogers says:

Estrangement of conscious man from his directional organismic processes is not a necessary part of man's nature. Instead, it is learned, and learned to an especially high degree in Western civilization. The satisfaction or fulfillment of the actualizing tendency has become bifurcated into incompatible behavior systems. This dissociation which exists in most of us is the pattern and basis of all psychological pathology in man (Rogers, 1963, p. 24).

Fortunately, man's organismic urges do not cease upon being denied to awareness. However, their persistence poses a prob-lem for the individual. He begins to perceive his experiences selectively according to their fitting or not fitting his concept of self, now defined in part by the conditions of worth.

Experiences which are in accord with his conditions of worth are perceived and symbolized accurately in awareness. Experiences which run contrary to the conditions of worth are perceived selectively and distortedly as if in accord with the conditions of worth, or are in part or whole, denied to awareness (Rogers, 1959b, p. 226).

Whenever an individual's perception of his experience is distorted or denied, Rogers says, "a state of incongruence between self and experience, of psychological maladjustment and of vulnerability, exists to some degree" (Rogers, 1959b, p. 226).

Experiences not consistent with the individual's concept of self are conceived as a threat in that if such experiences were accurately symbolized in the individual's awareness, they would disturb the organization of his concept of self by being contrary to the conditions of worth he has incorporated. Thus, such experiences create anxiety in the person and arouse defense mechanisms that either distort or deny such experiences, thereby maintaining the individual's consistent perception of self. Because of the need to defend against accurate perception of experiences contrary to his conditions of worth, the individual develops a rigidity of perception in those areas.

Psychotherapy and Personality Change. The process of *therapy* is an intervention into the incongruence an individual has developed between his experiencing organism and his concept of self. In this relationship he may risk allowing into awareness previously distorted or denied experiences. In an atmosphere of nonjudgmental understanding, he may begin to allow previously denied organismic urges to be a part of his concept of self. Thus, in the process of therapy, ideally, the individual exchanges his conditions of worth for a trust and valuing of the wisdom of his developing organism in its entirety.

Variety of Concepts

Definitions of Constructs. In the development of person-centered theory, various systematic *constructs* have emerged, gradually acquiring sharper and more specific meaning. Also terms in common usage have gradually acquired somewhat specialized meanings in our theoretical statements.

Actualizing Tendency. An *actualizing tendency* is the inherent tendency of the organism to develop in ways that serve to maintain or enhance the organism. It involves not only the tendency to meet what Abraham Maslow (1954) terms *deficiency needs* for air, food, water, and the like, but also involves development toward the differentiation of organs and of functions, expansion in terms of growth, expansion of effectiveness through the use of tools, and expansion and enhancement through reproduction. It is development toward autonomy and away from *heteronomy,* or control by external forces.

This basic actualizing tendency is the only motive postulated in this theoretical system. The organism as a whole, and only the organism as a whole exhibits this tendency. There are no homunculi, no other sources of energy or action in the system. The self, for example, is an important construct in our theory, but the self does not *do* anything. It is only one expression of the general tendency of the organism to maintain and enhance itself.

Concepts such as *need-reduction, tension-reduction,* and *drive-reduction* are included in this concept. It also includes the seeking of pleasurable tensions, the

tendency to be creative, the tendency to learn to walk and other self-actualizing tendencies.

Tendency toward Self-Actualization. Following the development of the self-structure, actualization expresses itself also in that portion of the experience of the organism that is symbolized in the self. If the self and the total experience of the organism are relatively congruent, the actualizing tendency remains relatively unified. If self and experience are incongruent, the organism may work at cross-purposes with the subsystem of that motive, the *tendency to actualize the self.*

Experience (Noun). The term *experience* includes all that is going on within the envelope of the organism at any given moment that is potentially available to awareness. It includes events of which the individual is unaware, as well as all the phenomena in consciousness. Thus it includes the psychological aspects of hunger, even though the individual may be so fascinated by his work or play that he is completely unaware of the hunger; it includes the impact of sights and sounds and odors on the organism, even though these are not the focus of attention. It includes the influence of memory and past experience, as these are active in the moment, in restricting or broadening the meaning given to various stimuli. It also includes all in immediate awareness or consciousness. It does not include events such as neuron discharges or changes in blood sugar, because these are not directly available to awareness. *Experience* is thus a psychological, not a physiological, definition.

Experience (Verb). To *experience* means simply to receive in the organism the impact of the sensory or physiological events happening at any moment.

Often this process term is used in the phrase *to experience in awareness,* which means to symbolize in some accurate form at the conscious level the above sensory or visceral events. Since there are varying degrees of completeness in symbolization, the phrase is often *to experience more fully in awareness,* and thus indicates that it is the extension of this process toward more complete and accurate symbolization to which reference is being made.

Feeling, Experiencing a Feeling. The term *feeling* is heavily used in writings on person-centered therapy and theory. It denotes an emotionally tinged experience, together with its personal meaning. Thus it includes the emotion but also the cognitive content of the meaning of that emotion in its experiential context. It refers to the unity of emotion and cognition as they are experienced inseparably in the moment. It is perhaps best thought of as a brief theme of experience, carrying with it the emotional coloring and the perceived meaning to the individual.

Awareness, Symbolization, Consciousness. These three terms are defined as synonymous. *Awareness* is thus seen as the symbolic representation (not necessarily in verbal symbols) of some portion of our experience. This representation may have varying degrees of sharpness or vividness, from a dim awareness of something existing as ground, to a sharp awareness of something in focus as figure.

Availability to Awareness. When an experience can be symbolized freely, without defensive denial and distortion, it is *available to awareness.*

Accurate Symbolization. The *symbols* that constitute our awareness do not necessarily match, or correspond to, the "real" experience, or to "reality." Thus the psychotic is aware of electrical impulses in his body that do actually exist. It seems important to distinguish between those awarenesses that, in common-sense

terms, are real or accurate and those that are not. But how can this be conceptualized if we are trying to think rigorously?

The most adequate way of handling this predicament seems to be to take the position that all perception is transactional in nature, a construction from our past experience and a hypothesis or prognosis for the future. If the psychotic were to check the electrical currents in his body, to see whether they have the same characteristics as other electric currents, he would be checking the hypothesis implicit in his awareness. Hence when we speak of accurate symbolization in awareness, we mean that the hypotheses implicit in the awareness will be borne out if tested by acting on them.

Perceive, Perception. Perception is a hypothesis or prognosis for action that comes into being in awareness when stimuli impinge on the organism. When we *perceive* "this is a triangle," "that is a tree," "this person is my mother," it means we are making a prediction that the objects from which the stimuli are received would, if checked in other ways, exhibit properties we have come to regard, from our past experience, as being characteristic of triangles, trees, mother.

Thus we might say that *perception* and *awareness* are synonymous, perception being the narrower term, usually used when we want to emphasize the importance of the stimulus in the process, and awareness the broader term, covering symbolizations and meanings that arise from purely internal stimuli such as memory traces, visceral changes, and the like, as well as from external stimuli.

To define *perception* in this purely psychological fashion is not meant to deny that it can be defined in physiological fashion by referring to the impact of a pattern of light rays upon certain nerve cells, for example. For our purpose, however, the psychological definition seems more fruitful, and it is in this sense that the term is used in our formulations.

Subceive, Subception. R. A. Mc-Cleary and R. S. Lazarus (1949) formulated this construct of *subception* to signify discrimination without awareness. They state that "even when a subject is unable to report a visual discrimination he is still able to make a stimulus discrimination at some level below that required for conscious recognition." Thus it appears that the organism can discriminate a stimulus and its meaning for the organism without using the higher nerve centers involved in awareness. It is this capacity that, in our theory, permits the individual to discriminate an experience as threatening, without symbolization in awareness of this threat.

Self-Experience. The term *self-experience,* coined by S. Standal (1954), is defined as being any event or entity in the phenomenal field discriminated by the individual that is also discriminated as "self," "me," "I," or related thereto. In general, self-experiences are the raw material of which the organized self-concept is formed.

Self, Concept of Self, Self-Structure. These terms refer to the organized, consistent conceptual Gestalt composed of perceptions of the characteristics of the "I" or "me" and the perceptions of the relationships of the "I" or "me" to others and to various aspects of life, together with the values attached to these perceptions. It is a Gestalt available to awareness although not necessarily in awareness. It is a fluid and changing process, but at any given moment it is a specific entity that is at least partially definable in operational terms by means of a Q-sort or other instrument or measure. The term *self* or *self-concept* is more likely to be used

when we are talking of the person's view of himself, *self-structure* when we are looking at this Gestalt from an external frame of reference.

Ideal Self. The *ideal self* (or *self-ideal*) denotes the self-concept the individual would most like to possess, upon which he places the highest value for himself. In all other respects, it is defined in the same way as the self-concept.

Incongruence between Self and Experience. A discrepancy frequently develops between the self as perceived and the actual experience of the organism. Thus the individual may perceive himself as having characteristics *a, b,* and *c,* and experiencing feelings *x, y,* and *z.* An accurate symbolization of his experience would, however, indicate characteristics *c, d,* and *e,* and feelings *v, w, x.* When such a discrepancy exists, the state is one of *incongruence between self and experience.* This state is one of tension and confusion, since in some respects the individual's behavior will be regulated by the actualizing tendency, and in other respects by the self-actualizing tendency, thus producing discordant or incomprehensible behaviors. What is commonly called neurotic behavior is one example, the neurotic behavior being the product of the actualizing tendency, whereas in other respects, the individual is actualizing the self. Thus the neurotic behavior is incomprehensible to the individual himself, since it is at variance with what he consciously "wants" to do, which is to actualize a self no longer congruent with experience.

Vulnerability. The term *vulnerability* refers to the state of incongruence between self and experience, to emphasize the potentialities of this state for creating psychological disorganization. When incongruence exists, and the individual is unaware of it, he is potentially vulnerable to anxiety, threat, and disorganization. If a significant new experience demonstrates the discrepancy so clearly that it must be consciously perceived, the individual will be threatened, and his concept of self disorganized by this contradictory and unassimilable experience.

Anxiety. Phenomenologically, *anxiety* is a state of uneasiness or tension whose cause is unknown. From an external frame of reference, anxiety is a state in which the incongruence between the concept of self and the total experience of the individual is approaching symbolization in awareness. When experience is *obviously* discrepant from the self-concept, a defensive response to threat becomes increasingly difficult. Anxiety is the response of the organism to the "subception" that such discrepancy may enter awareness, thus forcing a change in the self-concept.

Threat. A *threat* exists when an experience is perceived or anticipated (subceived) as incongruent with the structure of the self. It may be regarded as an external view of the same phenomenon that, from the internal frame of reference, is anxiety.

Psychological Maladjustment. A state of *psychological maladjustment* exists when the organism denies to awareness, or distorts in awareness, significant experiences that consequently are not accurately symbolized and organized into the Gestalt of the self-structure, thus creating an incongruence between self and experience.

Defense. A *defense* is the behavioral response of the organism to threat, the goal of which is the maintenance of the current structure of the self. This goal is achieved by the perceptual distortion of the experience in awareness, to reduce the incongruity between the experience and the structure of the self, or by the denial to awareness of an experience, thus denying any threat to the self.

Distortion in Awareness, Denial to Awareness. Material significantly inconsistent with the concept of self cannot be directly and freely admitted to awareness. To explain this, the construct of *denial* or *distortion* has been developed. When an experience is dimly perceived (*subceived* is perhaps the better term) as being incongruent with the self-structure, the organism appears to react with a distortion of the meaning of the experience (making it consistent with the self) or with a denial of the existence of the experience, to preserve the self-structure from threat. It is perhaps most vividly illustrated in those occasional moments in therapy when the therapist's response, correctly heard and understood, would mean that the client would necessarily perceive openly a serious inconsistency between his self-concept and a given experience. In such a case, the client may respond, "I can hear the words you say, and I know I should understand them, but I just can't make them convey any meaning to me." Here the relationship is too good for the meaning to be distorted by rationalization, but at the same time, the meaning is too threatening to be received. Hence the organism denies meaning in the communication. Such outright denial of experience is much less common than the phenomenon of distortion. Thus if the concept of self includes the characteristic "I am a poor student," the experience of receiving a high grade can be easily distorted to make it congruent with the self by perceiving in it meanings such as, "That professor is a fool"; "It was just luck"; and so on.

Intensionality. This term is taken from general semantics. If the person is reacting or perceiving in an *intensional* fashion, he tends to see experience in absolute and unconditional terms, to overgeneralize, to be dominated by concept or belief, to fail to anchor his reactions in space and time, to confuse fact and evaluation, to rely upon abstractions rather than upon reality testing. This term covers the frequently used concept of rigidity but includes perhaps a wider variety of behaviors than are generally thought of as constituting rigidity.

Congruence, Congruence of Self and Experience. These are basic concepts that have grown out of therapeutic experience, in which the individual appears to be revising his concept of *self* to bring it into *congruence* with his *experience,* accurately symbolized. Thus he discovers that one aspect of his experience, if accurately symbolized, would be hatred for his father; another would be strong homosexual desires. He reorganizes the concept he holds of himself to include these characteristics, which would previously have been inconsistent with self.

Thus, when self-experiences are accurately symbolized, and are included in the self-concept in this accurately symbolized form, the state is congruent of self and experience. If this is true of all self-experiences, the individual would be a fully functioning person. If it is true of some specific aspect of experience, such as the individual's experience in a given relationship or in a given moment of time, we can say that the individual is to this degree in a state of congruence. Other terms generally synonymous with congruence are *integrated, whole, genuine.*

Openness to Experience. To be *open to experience* is the polar opposite of defensiveness. The term may be used in regard to some area of experience or in regard to the total experience of the organism. It signifies that every stimulus, whether originating within the organism or in the environment, is freely relayed through the nervous system without being distorted or channeled off by any defensive mechanism. There is no need of the mechanism of "subception" whereby the organism is forewarned of experiences threatening to the self. On the contrary, whether the stimulus is the impact of a configuration of form, color, or sound in the environment on the sensory nerves, or a memory trace from the past, or a visceral sensation of fear, pleasure, or disgust, it is completely available to the individual's awareness. In the hypothetical person completely open to his experience, his concept of self would be a symbolization in awareness completely congruent with his experience.

Psychological Adjustment. Optimal *psychological adjustment* exists when all experiences are similated on a symbolic level into the Gestalt of the self-structure. Optimal psychological adjustment is thus synomymous with complete congruence of self and experience or complete openness to experience. Improvement in psychological adjustment progresses toward this end point.

Extensionality. This term is taken from general semantics. If the person is reacting or perceiving in an *extensional* manner, he tends to see experience in limited, differentiated terms, to be aware of the space-time anchorage of facts, to be dominated by facts, not by concepts, to evaluate in multiple ways, to be aware of different levels of abstraction, to test his inferences and abstractions against reality.

Maturity. The individual exhibits *mature* behavior when he perceives realistically and in an extensional manner, is not defensive, accepts the responsibility of being different from others, accepts responsibility for his own behavior, evaluates experience in terms of the evidence coming from his own senses, changes his evaluation of experience only on the basis of new evidence, accepts others as unique individuals different from himself, prizes himself, and prizes others.

Conditions of Worth. The self-structure is characterized by a *condition of worth* when a self-experience or set of related self-experiences is either avoided or sought solely because the individual discriminates it as being less or more worthy of self-regard.

This important construct has been developed by Standal (1954) to take the place of "introjected value," a less exact concept used in earlier formulations. A condition of worth arises when the positive regard of a significant other is conditional, when the individual feels that in some respects he is prized and in others not. Gradually this same attitude is assimilated into his own self-regard complex, and he values an experience positively or negatively solely because of these conditions of worth he has taken over from others, not because the experience enhances or fails to enhance his organism.

This last phrase deserves special note. When the individual has experienced unconditional positive regard, a new experience is valued or not, depending on its effectiveness in maintaining or enhancing the organism. But if a value is 'introjected' from a significant other, this condition of worth is applied to an experience quite without reference to the extent to which it maintains or enhances the organism. It is an important specific instance of inaccurate symbolization, the individual valuing an experience positively or negatively, *as if* in relation to the criterion of the actualizing tendency, but not actually in relation to it. An experience may be perceived as organismically satisfying, when in fact this is not true. Thus a condition of worth, because it disturbs the valuing process, prevents the individual from functioning freely and with maximum effectiveness.

Locus of Evaluation. This term indicates the source of evidence concerning values. Thus an internal *locus of evaluation,* within the individual himself, means he is the center of the valuing process, the evidence being supplied by his own senses. When the locus of evaluation resides in others, their judgment as to the value of an object or experience becomes the criterion of value for the individual.

Organismic Valuing Process. This concept describes an ongoing process in which values are never fixed or rigid, but experiences are being accurately symbolized and continually and freshly valued in terms of the satisfactions *organismically* experienced; the organism experiences satisfaction in those stimuli or behaviors that maintain and enhance the organism and the self, both in the immediate present and in the long range. The actualizing tendency is thus the criterion.

Internal Frame of Reference. This is all of the realm of experience available to the awareness of the individual at a given moment. It includes the full range of sensations, perceptions, meanings, and memories, available to consciousness.

The *internal frame of reference* is the subjective world of the individual. Only he knows it fully. It can never be known to another except through empathic inference and then can never be perfectly known.

Empathy. The term *empathy* refers to the accurate perception of the internal frame of reference of another with the emotional components and meanings that pertain thereto, as if one were the other person, but without ever losing the "as if" condition.

External Frame of Reference. To perceive solely from one's own subjective internal frame of reference without empathizing with the observed person or object is to perceive from an *external frame of reference*. The "empty organism" school of thought in psychology is an example of this. Thus the observer says that an animal has been stimulated when the animal has been exposed to a condition that, in the observer's subjective frame of reference, is a stimulus. There is no attempt to understand empathically whether this is a stimulus in the animal's experiential field. Likewise the observer reports that the animal emits a response when a phenomenon occurs that, in the observer's subjective field, is a response.

These concepts continue to be useful in describing the process of therapy in a person-centered framework.

PSYCHOTHERAPY

Theory of Psychotherapy

Rogers makes the statement, "Therapy is of the essence of life, and is to be so understood" (1951, p. x). Person-centered therapy calls upon the whole range of the ongoing inner dynamics of the therapist and the client. The interacting of two persons out of an awareness of their individual inner responses is the dynamics of the therapeutic relationship in person-centered therapy. The focus is on the direct experiencing in the relationship:

The process is not seen as primarily having to do with the client's memory of his past, nor with his exploration of the problems he is facing, nor with the perceptions he has of himself, nor with the experiences he has been fearful of admitting into awareness. The process of therapy is, by these hypotheses, seen as being synonymous with the experiential relationship between client and therapist. Therapy consists in experiencing the self in a wide range of ways in an emotionally meaningful relationship with the therapist. The words—of either client or counselor—are seen as having minimal importance compared with the present emotional relationship which exists between the two (Rogers, 1951, p. 172).

Person-centered theory has settled on three attitudes necessary and sufficient to effect change in clients. The theory does not stress the technical skills or knowledge of the therapist. It asks him to be (a) genuine or congruent, (b) to be empathic or understanding, and (c) to be unpossessively caring or confirming. These attitudes are the catalytic agent in the person-centered therapeutic relationship. If the client perceives these attitudes and if he is uncomfortable with himself, he will engage in the process of positive personality change. This is the basic hypothesis of person-centered therapy.

Briefly, the therapist wants to convey his sincere acceptance and caring for his client. For the client to trust his caring, the client must see the therapist's realness or genuineness. These attitudes set the climate for the primary work of the therapist, his accurate, empathic understanding. A closer look at the three therapist's attitudes will demonstrate their interdependence.

Empathy. For the therapist to *understand* his client, he must focus on the client's phenomenal world. Person-centered therapists throughout the three decades of its development have continually reaffirmed this basic tenet: Understanding the world of the client *as he* (the client) *sees it* is primary in effecting therapeutic change. "This exclusive focus in therapy on the present phenomenal experience of the client is the meaning of the term 'client-centered' " (Rogers, 1959a, p. 191).

Understanding the phenomenal world of the client requires more of the therapist than merely understanding the client's words. The therapist attempts to "get into the shoes" of his client, to "get under his skin." He not only listens to the client's words, but he immerses himself in his world. His comments reflect not only what the client is saying, but also reflect the hazy area at the edge of the client's awareness. Through the therapist's communicating his understanding of the client's felt meanings, those meanings not yet conceptualized into awareness, the client broadens his understanding of himself and allows into his awareness more of his organismic experiencing. The confirmatory experience of feeling understood seems to give substance and power to the client's expanding self-concept. It is as though the client affirms, "It is o.k. to be me, even this tentative new me which is emerging." The therapist does not focus on the present experiencing of the client's world to make an interpretation or diagnosis. He believes it is the experience of feeling understood itself that effects growthful change.

Positive Regard. For the therapist genuinely to care for the client, to maintain unconditional *positive regard,* means that he will avoid any behavior that is overtly or covertly judgmental. He does not probe unnecessarily; he does not express approval or disapproval; he does not interpret. He genuinely accepts the client with all the understanding he can muster, and he completely trusts the client's resources for self-understanding and positive change. The more sincerely the therapist relies on the client to

discover himself and to follow his own processes of change, the more freely the client will do just that. The client sees, "Here is someone who repeatedly tells me in one way or another that he believes in my ability to find my way in the process of growth. Perhaps I can begin to believe in myself."

Unconditional positive regard and accurate understanding act together to provide a climate in the therapeutic relationship in which the client is gradually able to allow into his awareness and behavior those portions of his inner experiencing inconsistent with his self-concept, portions around which he has built strong defenses. As he verbalizes these formerly unallowable feelings, he receives the conformation of genuine understanding from another person and the positive acceptance of his changing, new self.

Genuineness. For the therapist to be genuine or congruent, he relies on his moment-to-moment felt experiencing in his relationship with his client. His *genuineness* permeates his attitudes of understanding and positive regard as well as guides his verbalization of his own understanding and experiencing.

In his effort to understand his client, he lets his imagination experience the experiencing his client reports. By allowing his client's experiences to be his own for a moment, he has available to himself his own visceral responses to being in the situation of the client. His understanding is not only intellectual, but also organismic, to the extent that he can "feel" what it would be like to live the experiencing of the client. Genuineness and empathy combine as he reports his felt meanings after putting himself in his client's shoes.

In the same way, positive regard is not an intellectual attitude nor a saccharine optimism toward humanity. It is a reality-based trust in the actualizing potential of the individual and is expressed in an unwillingness to interfere, direct, or evaluate the ongoing processes of another human being. Congruence in the attitude of positive regard is the therapist's insistent focus on the phenomenal world of the client, repeatedly returning to the moment-to-moment experiencing of the client as the resource for his positive change.

Congruence in the therapist's own inner self is his sensing of and reporting his own felt experiencing as he interacts in the relationship. The therapist trusts his own organismic responses in the situation and conveys those feelings of his that he intuitively believes have relevance in the relationship. His willingness and consistency in being real in the relationship provide the client a reality base he can trust and take away some of the risk of sharing himself with another.

Summary. This section has presented the three therapist attitudes that research has confirmed are necessary and sufficient in a therapeutic relationship to effect positive change in the client. It should be stressed that the basis of person-centered therapy is the "forward moving tendency of the human organism" (Rogers, 1951, p. 489). Person-centered theorists believe they have discovered the conditions for the actualization processes to free themselves of whatever strictures were holding them back. Whenever a therapist is congruent, understanding, and caring toward his client, the actualizing potential of the client will be released and the client will begin to change and grow.

Process of Psychotherapy

Rogers's manner of working has probably never been better expressed than in a section of the book reporting the research with schizophrenics (1967b, p. 401–6), entitled "A Silent Young Man." It is

reprinted here with only a few simplifying changes.

A Silent Young Man

It would surely be desirable, if it were possible, to give the reader some experience of the process of therapy as it was lived by each therapist in his interaction with his schizophrenic clients. Yet long descriptions of therapy in a variety of cases tend to be unconsciously distorted; the transcription of a whole case would be much too long for presentation (and misleading in its omission of voice qualities); and consequently some other solution must be found.

What I propose to do in this section is to present, in transcribed form, two significant and I believe crucial interviews in the therapy with James Brown (pseudonym, of course) together with my comments as therapist on this experience. This seems to be a doubly valuable approach since the two interviews presented here are available in tape recorded form to any professional worker through the Tape Library of the American Academy of Psychotherapists.[1] Thus the person who is seriously interested in the interaction in this case can read and study these two interviews and my presentation of the meanings I see in them, and can listen to the two interviews in order to judge the quality of the interaction for himself.

Let me give a few of the facts which will introduce James Brown. He was 28 years old when I first began to see him as a part of the research. A coin toss had selected him as the member of a matched pair to

[1] We are very grateful to "Mr. Brown" for his permission to make professional use of this material. The address of the Tape Library of the American Academy of Psychotherapists is 6420 City Line Avenue, Philadelphia, Pennsylvania. In their listing this is "The Case of Mr. VAC."

receive therapy. He had been hospitalized three times, the first time for a period of three months when he was 25. He had been hospitalized for a total of 19 months when I first began to see him, and for two and one-half years at the time of these interviews. He is a person of some intellectual capacity, having completed high school and taken a little college work. The hospital diagnosis was "schizophrenic reaction, simple type."

Some readers will be disappointed that I am not presenting any of the facts from his case history. A superficial reason for this is that it might be identifying of this individual. A deeper reason is that I myself, as his therapist, have never seen his case history and do not know its contents. I should like to state briefly my reasons for this.

If I were trying to select the most promising candidates for psychotherapy from a large group, then an examination of the case histories by me—or by someone else —might be helpful in making such a selection. But in this instance Brown had been selected by the impersonal criteria of our research as a person to whom a relationship was to be offered. I preferred to endeavor to relate to him as he was in the relationship, as he was as a person at this moment, not as a configuration of past historical events. It is my conviction that therapy (if it takes place at all) takes place in the immediate moment-by-moment interaction in the relationship. This is the way in which I encountered Mr. Brown, and I am asking the reader to encounter him in the same way.

At the time of these two interviews, I had been seeing Mr. Brown on a twice a week basis (with the exception of some vacation periods) for a period of 11 months. Unlike many of the clients in this research the relationship had, almost from the first, seemed to have some meaning to him. He had ground privi-

leges, so he was able to come to his appointments, and he was almost always on time, and rather rarely forgot them. The relationship between us was good. I liked him and I feel sure that he liked me. Rather early in our interviews he muttered to his ward physician that he had finally found someone who understood him. He was never articulate, and the silences were often prolonged, although when he was expressing bitterness and anger he could talk a bit more freely. He had, previous to these two interviews, worked through a number of his problems, the most important being his facing the fact that he was entirely rejected by his stepmother, relatives, and worst of all, by his father. During a few interviews preceding these two he had been even more silent than usual, and I had no clue to the meaning of this silence. As will be evident from the transcript his silences in these two interviews were monumental. I believe that a word count would show that he uttered little more than 50 words in the first of these interviews! (In the tape recording mentioned above, each of the silences has been reduced to 15 seconds, no matter what its actual length.)

In the two interviews presented here I was endeavoring to understand all that I possibly could of his feelings. I had little hesitancy in doing a good deal of empathic guessing, for I had learned that though he might not respond in any discernible way when I was right in my inferences, he would usually let me know by a negative shake of his head if I was wrong. Mostly, however, I was simply trying to be my feelings in relationship to him, and in these particular interviews my feelings I think were largely those of interest, gentleness, compassion, desire to understand, desire to share something of myself, eagerness to stand with him in his despairing experiences.

To me any further introduction would

be superfluous. I hope and believe that the interaction of the two hours speaks for itself of many convictions, operationally expressed, about psychotherapy.

The Interviews

Tuesday

T: I see there are some cigarettes here in the drawer. Hm? Yeah, it is hot out.
[Silence of 25 seconds]

T: Do you look kind of angry this morning, or is that my imagination? [Client shakes his head slightly.] Not angry, huh?
[Silence of 1 minute, 26 seconds]

T: Feel like letting me in on whatever is going on?
[Silence of 12 minutes, 52 seconds]

T: [*softly*] I kind of feel like saying that "If it would be of any help at all I'd like to come in." On the other hand if it's something you'd rather—if you just feel more like being within yourself, feeling whatever you're feeling within yourself, why that's O.K. too —I guess another thing I'm saying, really, in saying that is, "I do care. I'm not just sitting here like a stick."
[Silence of 1 minute, 11 seconds]

T: And I guess your silence is saying to me that either you don't want to or can't come out right now and that's O.K. So I won't pester you but I just want you to know, I'm here.
[Silence of 17 minutes, 41 seconds]

T: I see I'm going to have to stop in a few minutes.[2]
[Silence of 20 seconds]

T: It's hard for me to know how you've been feeling, but it looks as though part of the time maybe you'd rather I didn't know how you were feeling.

---

[2] Long experience had shown me that it was very difficult for Jim to leave. Hence I had gradually adopted the practice of letting him know, 10 or 12 minutes before the conclusion of the hour, that "our time is nearly up." This enabled us to work through the leaving process without my feeling hurried.

Anyway it looks as though part of the time it just feels very good to let down and—relax the tension. But as I say I don't really know—how you feel. It's just the way it looks to me. Have things been pretty bad lately?
[Silence of 45 seconds]

T: Maybe this morning you just wish I'd shut up—and maybe I should, but I just keep feeling I'd like to—I don't know, be in touch with you in some way.
[Silence of 2 minutes, 21 seconds]
[*Jim yawns.*]

T: Sounds discouraged or tired.
[Silence of 41 seconds]

C: No. Just lousy.

T: Everything's lousy, huh? You feel lousy?
[Silence of 39 seconds]

T: Want to come in Friday at 12 at the usual time?

C: [*Yawns and mutters something unintelligible.*]
[Silence of 48 seconds]

T: Just kind of feel sunk way down deep in these lousy, lousy feelings, hm?—Is that something like it?

C: No.

T: No?
[Silence of 20 seconds]

C: No. I just ain't no good to nobody, never was, and never will be.

T: Feeling that now, hm? That you're just no good to yourself, no good to anybody. Never will be any good to anybody. Just that you're completely worthless, huh?—Those really are lousy feelings. Just feel that you're no good at *all,* hm?

C: Yeah. [*Muttering in low, discouraged voice*] That's what this guy I went to town with just the other day told me.

T: This guy that you went to town with really told you that you were no good? Is that what you're saying? Did I get that right?

C: M-hm.

T: I guess the meaning of that if I get it right is that here's somebody that—meant something to you and what does he think of you? Why, he's told you that he thinks you're no good at all. And that just really knocks the props out from under you. [*Jim weeps quietly.*] It just brings the tears. [Silence of 20 seconds]

C: [*Rather defiantly*] I don't care though.

T: You tell yourself you don't care at all, but somehow I guess some part of you cares because some part of you weeps over it. [Silence of 19 seconds]

T: I guess some part of you just feels, "Here I am hit with another blow, as if I hadn't had enough blows like this during my life when I feel that people don't like me. Here's someone I've begun to feel attached to and now *he* doesn't like me. And I'll say I don't care. I won't let it make any difference to me—But just the same the tears run down my cheeks."

C: [*Muttering*] I guess I always knew it.

T: Hm?

C: I guess I always knew it.

T: If I'm getting that right, it is that what makes it hurt worst of all is that when he tells you you're no good, well shucks, that's what you've always felt about yourself. Is that—the meaning of what you're saying? [*Jim nods slightly, indicating agreement.*] —M-hm. So you feel as though he's just confirming what—you've already known. He's confirming what you've already felt in some way. [Silence of 23 seconds]

T: So that between his saying so and your perhaps feeling it underneath, you just feel about as no good as anybody could feel. [Silence of 2 minutes, 1 second]

T: [*Thoughtfully*] As I sort of let it soak in and try to feel what you must be feeling—It comes up sorta this way in me and I don't know—but as though here was someone you'd made a contact with, someone you'd really done things for and done things with. Somebody that had some meaning to you. Now, wow! He slaps you in the face by telling you you're just no good. And this really cuts *so* deep, you can hardly stand it. [Silence of 30 seconds]

T: I've got to call it quits for today, Jim. [Silence of 1 minute, 18 seconds]

T: It really hurts, doesn't it? [This is in response to his quiet tears.] [Silence of 26 seconds]

T: I guess if the feelings came out you'd just weep and weep and weep. [Silence of 1 minute, 3 seconds]

T: Help yourself to some Kleenex if you'd like—Can you go now? [Silence of 23 seconds]

T: I guess you really hate to, but I've got to see somebody else. [Silence of 20 seconds]

T: It's really bad, isn't it? [Silence of 22 seconds]

T: Let me ask you one question and say one thing. Do you still have that piece of paper with my phone numbers on it and instructions, and so on? [*Jim nods.*] O.K. And if things get bad, so that you feel real down, you have them call me. 'Cause that's what I'm here for, to try to be of some help when you need it. If you need it, you have them call me.[3]

---

[3] Two words of explanation are needed here. He seemed so depressed that I was concerned that he might be feeling suicidal. I wanted to be available to him if he felt desperate. Since no patient was allowed to phone without permission, I had given him a note which would permit a staff member or Jim himself to phone me *at any time* he wished to contact me, and with both my office and home phone numbers.

C: I think I'm beyond help.

T: Huh? Feel as though you're beyond help. I know. You feel just completely hopeless about yourself. I can understand that. I don't feel hopeless, but I can realize that you do.[4] Just feel as though nobody can help you and you're really beyond help.
[Silence of 2 minutes, 1 second]

T: I guess you just feel so, so down that—it's awful.
[Silence of 2 minutes]

T: I guess there's one other thing too. I, I'm going to be busy here this afternoon 'til four o'clock and maybe a little after. But if you should want to see me again this afternoon, you can drop around about four o'clock. O.K.?—Otherwise, I'll see you Friday noon. Unless I get a call from you. If you—If you're kind of concerned for fear anybody would see that you've been weeping a little, you can go out and sit for a while where you waited for me. Do just as you wish on that. Or go down and sit in the waiting room there and read magazines—I guess you'll really have to go.

C: Don't want to go back to work.

T: You don't want to go back to work, hm?

This is the end of the interview. Later in the day the therapist saw Mr. Brown on the hospital grounds. He seemed much more cheerful and said that he thought he could get a ride into town that afternoon. The next time the therapist saw Mr. Brown was three days later, on Friday. This interview follows.

Friday

T: I brought a few magazines you can take with you if you want.[5]
[Silence of 47 seconds]

T: I didn't hear from you since last time. Were you able to go to town that day?

C: Yeah. I went in with a kid driving the truck.

T: M-hm. [Voices from next office are heard in background.]
[Silence of 2 minutes]

T: Excuse me just a minute. [Goes to stop noise.]
[Silence of 2 minutes, 20 seconds]

T: I don't know why, but I realize that somehow it makes me feel good that today you don't have your hand up to your face so that I can somehow kind of see you more. I was wondering why I felt as though you were a little more here than you are sometimes and then I realized well, it's because—I don't feel as though you're hiding behind your hand, or something.
[Silence of 50 seconds]

T: And I think I sense, though I could be mistaken, I think I do sense that today just like some other days when you come in here, it's just as though you let yourself sink down into feelings that run very deep in you. Sometimes they're very bad feelings like the last time and sometimes probably they're not so bad, though they're sort of—I think I understand that somehow when you come in here it's as though you do let yourself down into those feelings. And now—

---

[4] This is an example of the greater willingness I have developed to express my own feelings of the moment, at the same time accepting the client's right to possess *his* feelings, no matter how different from mine.

[5] I had, on several occasions, given magazines and small amounts of money to Mr. Brown and loaned him books. There was no special rationale behind this. The hospital environment was impoverished for a man of Brown's sort, and I felt like giving him things which would relieve the monotony.

C: I'm gonna take off.

T: Huh?

C: I'm gonna take off.[6]

T: You're going to take off? Really run away from here? Is that what you mean? Must be some—what's the—what's the background of that? Can you tell me? Or I guess what I mean more accurately is I know you don't like the place but it must be that something special came up or something?

C: I just want to run away and die.

T: M-hm, m-hm, m-hm. It isn't even that you want to get away from here *to* something. You just want to leave here and go away and die in a corner, hm?

[Silence of 30 seconds]

T: I guess as I let that soak in I really do sense how, how deep that feeling sounds, that you—I guess the image that comes to my mind is sort of a ——a wounded animal that wants to crawl away and die. It sounds as though that's kind of the way you feel that you just want to get away from here and, and vanish. Perish. Not exist.

[Silence of 1 minute]

C: [*almost inaudibly*] All day yesterday and all morning I wished I were dead. I even prayed last night that I could die.

T: I think I caught all of that, that—for a couple of days now you've just *wished* you could be dead and you've even prayed for that—I guess that—One way this strikes me is that to live is such an awful thing to you, you just wish you could die, and not live.

[Silence of 1 minute, 12 seconds]

[6] Clearly my empathic guessing in the two previous responses was completely erroneous. This was not troublesome to me, nor, I believe, to him. There is no doubt, however, that my surprise shows.

T: So that you've been just wishing and wishing that you were not living. You wish that life would pass away from you.

[Silence of 30 seconds]

C: I wish it more'n anything else I've ever wished around here.

T: M-hm, m-hm, m-hm. I guess you've wished for lots of things but boy! It seems as though this wish to not live is deeper and stronger than anything you ever wished before.

[Silence of 1 minute, 36 seconds]

T: Can't help but wonder whether it's still true that some things this friend said to you—are those still part of the thing that makes you feel so awful?

C: In general, yes.

T: M-hm.

[Silence of 47 seconds]

T: The way I'm understanding that is that in a general way the fact that he felt you were no good has just set off a whole flood of feeling in you that makes you really wish, *wish* you weren't alive. Is that—somewhere near it?

C: I ain't no good to nobody, or I ain't no good for nothin', so what's the use of living?

T: M-hm. You feel, "I'm not any good to another living person, so—why should I go on living?"

[Silence of 21 seconds]

T: And I guess a part of that is that—here I'm kind of guessing and you can set me straight, I guess a part of that is that you felt, "I tried to *be* good for something as far as he was concerned. I really tried. And now—if I'm no good to him, if he feels I'm no good, then that proves I'm just no good to anybody." Is that, uh—anywhere near it?

C: Oh, well, other people have told me that too.

T: Yeah. M-hm. I see. So you feel if, if you go by what others—what several others have said, then, then you are *no good*. No good to anybody.
[Silence of 3 minutes, 40 seconds]

T: I don't know whether this will help or not, but I would just like to say that—I think I can understand pretty well—what it's like to feel that you're just *no damn good* to anybody, because there was a time when—I felt that way about *myself*. And I know it can be *really rough*.[7]
[Silence of 13 minutes]

T: I see we've got only a few more minutes left.
[Silence of 2 minutes, 51 seconds]

T: Shall we make it next Tuesday at eleven, the usual time?
[Silence of 1 minute, 35 seconds]

T: If you gave me any answer, I really didn't get it. Do you want to see me next Tuesday at eleven?

C: Don't know.

T: "I just don't know."
[Silence of 34 seconds]

T: Right at this point you just don't know—whether you want to say "yes" to that or not, hm?—I guess you feel so down and so—awful that you just don't know whether you can—can see that far ahead. Hm?
[Silence of 1 minute, 5 seconds]

T: I'm going to give you an appointment at that time because *I'd* sure like to see *you* then. [*Writing out appointment slip.*]
[Silence of 50 seconds]

T: And another thing I would say is that—if things continue to stay so rough for you, don't hesitate to have them call me. And if you should

decide to take off, I would very much appreciate it if you would have them call me and—so I could see you first. I wouldn't try to dissuade you. I'd just want to see you.

C: I might go today. Where, I don't know, but I don't care.

T: Just feel that your mind is made up and that you're going to leave. You're not going *to* anywhere. You're just—just going to leave, hm?
[Silence of 53 seconds]

C: [*muttering in discouraged tone*] That's why I want to go, 'cause I don't care what happens.

T: Huh?

C: That's why I want to go, 'cause I don't care what happens.

T: M-hm, m-hm. That's why you want to go, because you really don't care about yourself. You just don't care *what* happens. And I guess I'd just like to say—I care about you. And *I* care what happens.[8]
[Silence of 30 seconds] [*Jim bursts into tears and unintelligible sobs.*]

T: [*tenderly*] Somehow that just—makes all the feelings pour out.
[Silence of 35 seconds]

T: And you just weep and weep and weep. And feel so badly. [Jim continues to sob, then blows nose and breathes in great gasps.]

T: I do get some sense of how awful you feel inside—You just sob and sob. [He puts his head on desk, bursting out in great gulping, gasping sobs.]

T: I guess all the pent-up feelings you've been feeling the last few days just—just come rolling out.

---

[7] This is a most unusual kind of response for me to make. I simply felt that I wanted to share my experience with him—to let him know he was not alone.

[8] This was the spontaneous feeling which welled up in me, and which I expressed. It was certainly not planned, and I had no idea it would bring such an explosive response.

[Silence of 32 seconds, while sobbing continues]

T: There's some Kleenex there, if you'd like it—Hmmm. [*sympathetically*] You just feel kind of torn to pieces inside.
[Silence of 1 minute, 56 seconds]

C: I wish I could die. [*sobbing*]

T: You just wish you could die, don't you? M-hm. You just feel so awful, you wish you could perish.
[Therapist laid his hand gently on Jim's arm during this period. Jim showed no definite response. However, the storm subsided somewhat. Very heavy breathing.]
[Silence of 1 minute, 10 seconds]

T: You just feel so awful and so torn apart inside that, that it just makes you wish you could pass out.
[Silence of 3 minutes, 29 seconds]

T: I guess life is so tough, isn't it? You just feel you could weep and sob your heart away and wish you could die.[9]
[Heavy breathing continues.] [Silence of 6 minutes, 14 seconds]

T: I don't want to rush you, and I'll stay as long as you really need me, but I do have another appointment, that I'm already late for.

C: Yeah.
[Silence of 17 minutes]

T: Certainly been through something, haven't you?
[Silence of 1 minute, 18 seconds]

T: May I see you Tuesday?

C: [*Inaudible response.*]

T: Hm?

C: Don't know. [*almost unintelligible*]

T: "I just don't know." M-hm. You know all the things I said before, I mean very much. I want to see you

Tuesday and I want to see you before then if you want to see me. So, if you need me, don't hesitate to call me.
[Silence of 1 minute]

T: It's really rough, isn't it?
[Silence of 24 seconds]

C: Yes.

T: Sure is. [*Jim slowly gets up to go.*]
[Silence of 29 seconds]

T: Want to take that too? [*Jim takes appointment slip.*]
[Silence of 20 seconds]

T: There's a washroom right down the hall where you can wash your face.
[Jim opens door; noise and voices are heard from corridor.]
[Silence of 18 seconds] [*Jim turns back into the room.*]

C: You don't have a cigarette, do you?
[Therapist finds one.]

T: There's just one. I looked in the package but—I don't know. I haven't any idea how old it is, but it looks sort of old.

C: I'll see you. [*hardly audible*]

T: O.K. I'll be looking for you Tuesday, Jim.

Commentary

What has happened here? I am sure there will be many interpretations of this material. I would like to make it plain that what follows is my own perception of it, a perception which is perhaps biased by the fact that I was a deeply involved participant.

Here is a young man who has been a troublesome person in the institution. He has been quick to feel mistreated, quick to take offense, often involved in fights with the staff. He has, by his own account, no tender feelings, only bitter ones against others. In these two interviews he has experienced the depth of his own feelings of worthlessness, of having no excuse for

---

[9] As I have listened to the recording of this interview, I wish I had responded to the relief he must have been experiencing in letting his despair pour out, as well as to the despair itself.

living. He has been unsupported by his frequently felt feelings of anger, and has experienced only his deep, deep despair. In this situation something happens. What is it, and why does it occur?

In my estimation, I was functioning well as a therapist in this interaction. I felt a warm and spontaneous caring for him as a person, which found expression in several ways—but most deeply at the moment when he was despairing. I was continuously desirous of understanding his feelings, even though he gave very few clues. I believe that my erroneous guesses were unimportant as compared to my willingness to go with him in his feelings of worthlessness and despair when he was able to voice these. I think we were relating as two real and genuine persons. In the moments of real encounter the differences in education, in status, in degree of psychological disturbance, had no importance—we were two persons in a relationship.

In this relationship there was a moment of real, and I believe irreversible, change. Jim Brown, who sees himself as stubborn, bitter, mistreated, worthless, useless, hopeless, unloved, unlovable, *experiences* my caring. In that moment his defensive shell cracks wide open, and can never again be quite the same. When someone *cares* for him, and when he feels and experiences this caring, he becomes a softer person whose years of stored up hurt come pouring out in anguished sobs. He is not the shell of hardness and bitterness, the stranger to tenderness. He is a person hurt beyond words, and aching for the love and caring which alone can make him human. This is evident in his sobs. It is evident too in his returning to the office, partly for a cigarette, partly to say spontaneously that he will return.

In my judgment what we have here is a "moment of change" in therapy. Many

events are necessary to lead up to such a moment. Many later events will flow from it. But in this moment something is experienced openly which has never been experienced before. Once it had been experienced openly, and the emotions surrounding it flow to their natural expression, the person can never be quite the same. He can never completely deny these feelings when they recur again. He can never quite maintain the concept of self which he had before that moment. Here is an instance of the heart and essence of therapeutic change.

An Objective Look at the Process

If we look at the few client expressions in these interviews in terms of the hypotheses of this research, we can see that being deeply in therapy does not necessarily involve a ready flow of words. Let us take some of the feeling themes Brown expresses and look at them in terms of the process continuum we have conceptualized.

My feelings are lousy.
I ain't no good to nobody.
I think I'm beyond help.
I don't want to go back to work.
I just want to run away and die.
I ain't no good, so what's the use of living?
I don't care what happens.
I wish I could die.

Compare these themes with brief descriptions of the process continuum at stages 3, 4, 5, and 6 of the seven stages of the original Process Scale (first version, described in the following section).

Stage 3. "There is much description of feelings and personal meanings which are not now present." "The experiencing of situations is largely described in terms of the past." "Personal constructs are rigid but may at times be thought of as constructs."

Clearly Mr. Brown's manner of expression does not fit this stage in any respect except that his concept of himself as no good is held in rigid fashion.

Stage 4. "Feelings and personal meanings are freely described as present objects owned by the self. . . . Occasionally feelings are expressed in the present but this occurs as if against the individual's wishes." "There is an unwilling fearful recognition that one is experiencing things —a vague realization that a disturbing type of inner referent does exist." "The individual is willing to risk relating himself occasionally to others on a feeling basis."

It is evident that this matches more closely Mr. Brown's experience in these hours.

Stage 5. "In this stage we find many feelings freely expressed in the moment of their occurrence and thus experienced in the immediate present." "This tends to be a frightening and disturbing thing because it involves being in process." "There is a desire to be these feelings, to be 'the real me.' " This stage seems to catch even more the quality of the experiencing in these interviews.

Stage 6. "Feelings which have previously been denied to awareness are now experienced with immediacy and acceptance . . . not something to be denied, feared, or struggled against." "In the moments of movement which occur at this stage there is a dissolving of significant personal constructs in a vivid experiencing of a feeling which runs counter to the constructs."

While some aspects of Jim's experiencing in these interviews come close to this description, it is clear that he is not acceptant of the feelings which well up in him. It appears that ratings of the stage he has reached in these interviews would pro-

bably cluster modally around stage 5, with some elements rated 4 or 6.

Perhaps this will give the reader some feeling for both the strengths and inadequacies of our conceptualizing of the process continuum and our attempts to capture it in an objective rating scale. It is relevant to what has occurred in these interviews, yet Brown's unique expression of his feelings is certainly not fully contained in the descriptions supplied by the original Process Scale, or the further separate scales developed from it (Rogers, 1967b).

This examination of the process aspect of these interviews may help to explain something which has mystified colleagues who have listened to the interviews. They often marvel at the patience I displayed in sitting through a silence of say, 17 minutes. The major reason I was able to do so was that when Jim said something it was usually worth listening to, showed real involvement in a therapeutic process. After all, most therapists can listen to talk, even when the talk is saying very little and indicates that very little that is therapeutic is going on. I can listen to silence, when I think that the silence is likely to end with significant feelings. I should add, however, that when I ceased to be patient, or ceased to be acceptant of the silence, I felt free to express my own feelings as they were occurring in me at the moment. There are various examples of this in these interviews. I do recognize, however, that it is easier for me to be patient than it is for a number of my colleagues. I have my style, and they have theirs.

Later Events

If one expects some quick and miraculous change from such a moment of change as we saw in the Friday interview, he will be disappointed. I was, myself, somewhat surprised that in the next interview it was as though these two had never happened—Jim was inarticulate, silent, uncommunicative, and made no reference to his sobbing or to any other portion of the interviews. But over the next months the change showed. Little by little he became willing to risk himself in a positive approach to life. Yet even in this respect he would often revert to self-defeating behaviors. Several times he managed to make all the necessary arrangements for leaving the hospital to attend school. Always at the last moment he would become involved in violent altercations (completely the fault of the other person, naturally!) which caused the hospital staff to confine him and which thus destroyed all the carefully laid arrangements. Finally, however, he was able to admit that he himself was terrified of going out—afraid he couldn't make good. When I told him that this was something to decide within himself—that I would see him if he chose to stay in the hospital, and that I would continue to see him if he chose to leave— he tentatively and fearfully moved out toward the world. First he attended school, living at the hospital. Then he worked through many realistic problems regarding a suitable room, finally found a place for himself in the community, and fully moved out.

As he could permit others to care for him, he was able to care for others. He accepted friendly gestures from members of the research staff, and it meant much to him to be treated as a person by them. He moved out to make friends of his own. He found a part-time job on his own. He began to live his own life, apart from any hospital or therapy influence.

The best evidence of the change is in a letter to me, a little more than two years after these interviews. At the time I was away for an academic year. I was seeing him very infrequently at the time I left, but I made arrangements for him to see another therapist (whom he knew slightly) if at any time he wished to do so. A few months after I left, I received the following letter from him:

Hi Doc,
I suppose you thought I had died, but I'm still here.
I've often thought of you and have been wanting to write but I'll use the old excuse that I've been busy.
Things are moving along pretty fast. I'm back in school, but things have changed slightly there. Mr. B. decided to quit teaching, so everything I had planned with him fell through.

(There follow three paragraphs about the courses he is taking and his pleasure at having been given—through the rehabilitation officer—an expensive tool of his trade. He also speaks of his part-time job which is continuing. Unfortunately, this material is too identifying to quote. He continues on a more personal note):

. . . I had a wonderful summer. Probably the best in years. I sure hate to see it come to an end.
I've met lots of people and made lots of friends. I hardly saw any of the kids from school all summer, and I didn't go out to the hospital all summer. Now, when I look back, it was like going down a different road. A very enjoyable one at that.
Also I haven't seen G. S. (substitute therapist in therapist's absence) at all this summer so far. As far as I could see it was good not seeing anybody, nor having to think about hospitals, doctors, and being out there. It was more or less like being free as a bird.
In fact, Doc, I was suppose to have gone up to the university and write those tests again. Some Mrs. N. has been calling and it irritates me because *I* think I did good and all that going up there will do is spoil the effect more

or less. I don't mind seeing you, Doc. That's not the point. I still want to see you when you get back, but it is a good feeling not having to have to see anybody.

I can't really explain it, so I won't try.

I sure wish I was out there at this time. It's been down in the low 40's every night here lately and it's starting to rain a lot.

By the way, I finally went home. That was last Wednesday. I got there at noon and I could hardly wait to get back. Back to Madison, back to my room, back to my friends and civilization.

Well, Doc, I guess I've talked enough about myself and I guess about half way back, I'd have let you do all of it. Right?

All in all things couldn't be too much better for me, compared to what they have been. It sure feels good to be able to say, "To hell with it," when things bother me.

I'll write later when I have "time," Doc. Maybe I'll be mean and won't write until you do, because I did wonder how come I never heard from you before I did.

Bye for now, Doc.
Sincerely,
JIM.

In his newfound independence he has refused to see Mrs. N. and to take the follow-up tests which were so important to our research. The statistical measures at follow-up would have been definitely improved had Jim been included. But his refusal is very thought-provoking (as well as a bit amusing). Perhaps when people accept themselves as persons, they refuse to be regarded as "objects" no matter how important this is to the researcher. It is a challenging, and in some deep sense a positive, thought.

An Eight-Year Follow-up

Eight years after these interviews I received a phone call from far across the country. It opened with the familiar voice I had come to know so well: "Hi Doc, remember me?" Jim went on to tell of several efforts he had made to reach me, mistakenly thinking I was in another city.

His main message that he wanted to get across was that he was "sassy, ornery, and liberal." He is still working for the same firm, though his attitudes occasionally get him labeled as an agitator. He is still living in the same rooming house ("I'm in love with my landlady," he said, in what I *think* was a facetious remark.) He is a solid employed citizen, living a rather limited social life, but content. The fact that he wished to let me know how much our relationship had meant to him during eight long years of separation was, for me, very meaningful.

Mechanisms of Psychotherapy

Thus far, this chapter has dealt primarily with the therapist conditions or attitudes necessary for constructive change to take place in the client. These conditions form one half of the equation of psychotherapy, which is the basis of person-centered therapy. That equation has been stated by Rogers in this way: "The more the therapist is perceived by the client as being genuine, as having an empathic understanding, and an unconditional regard for him, the greater will be the degree of constructive personality change in the client" (Rogers, 1961b, p. 32).

This section will deal with the other half of the equation, namely, the "constructive personality change" that takes place in the client in a person-centered therapeutic relationship.

The interest of the researchers and theorists who worked in the development of person-centered therapy has always been the process of personality change rather than in static descriptions of personality or personality formation. It was in the search for understanding the process of change that Rogers immersed himself for a period of several months in the recordings of numerous person-centered cases judged successful by multiple criteria. He began to note a consistent pattern of change in all the cases. Personality movement was from rigidity to flow, from stasis to changingness. Rogers describes the continuum of change:

. . . it commences at one end with a rigid, static, undifferentiated, unfeeling, impersonal type of psychologic functioning. It evolves through various stages to, at the other end, a level of functioning marked by changingness, fluidity, richly differentiated reactions, by immediate experiencing of personal feelings, which are felt as deeply owned and accepted (1961b, p. 33).

Out of Rogers's study of the process of change emerged seven behavior strands within which behavior changes could be described. The strands are feelings and personal meanings, manner of experiencing, degree of incongruence, communication of self, manner in which experience is construed, relationship to problems, and manner of relating. Rogers and R. A. Rablen (1958) developed a scale to measure the stage on the process continuum at which a client was operating.

Brief and partial descriptions of each of these different stages of process are as follows:

First stage. Communication is about externals. There is an unwillingness to communicate self. Feelings and personal meanings are neither recognized as such nor owned. Constructs are extremely rigid. Close relationships are construed as dangerous.

Second stage. Feelings are sometimes *described* but as unowned past *objects* external to self. The individual is remote from his subjective experiencing. He may voice contradictory statements about himself somewhat freely on nonself topics. He may show some recognition that he has problems or conflicts but they are perceived as external to the self.

Third stage. There is much *description* of feelings and personal meanings which are not now present. These distant feelings are often

pictured as unacceptable or bad. The *experiencing* of situations is largely described as having occurred in the past or is cast in terms of the past. There is a freer flow of expression about self as an *object*. There may be communication about self as a reflected object, existing primarily in others. Personal constructs are rigid but may at times be thought of as constructs, with occasionally a questioning of their validity. There is a beginning recognition that any problems that exist are inside the individual rather than external.

Fourth stage. Feelings and personal meanings are freely described as present objects owned by the self. Feelings of an intense sort are still described as not now present. There is a dim recognition that feelings denied to awareness may break through in the present, but this is a frightening possibility. There is an unwilling, fearful recognition that one is *experiencing* things. Contradictions in experience are clearly realized and a definite concern over them is experienced. There is a beginning loosening of personal constructs. It is sometimes discovered that experience has been *construed* as having a certain meaning but this meaning is not inherent nor absolute. There is some expression of self-responsibility for problems. The individual is occasionally willing to risk relating himself to others on a feeling basis.

Fifth stage. Many feelings are freely expressed in the moment of their occurrence and are thus experienced in the immediate present. These feelings are owned or accepted. Feelings previously denied now tend to bubble through into awareness though there is fear of this occurrence. There is some recognition that experiencing with immediacy is a referent and possible guide for the individual. Contradictions are recognized as attitudes existing in different aspects of the personality as indicated by statements such as, "My mind tells me this is so but I don't seem to believe it." There is a desire to be the self-related feelings, "To be the real me." There is a questioning of the validity of many personal constructs. The person feels that he has a definite responsibility for the problems which exist in him.

Sixth stage. Feelings previously denied are now experienced both with immediacy and *acceptance*. Such feelings are not something to be denied, feared, or struggled against. This experiencing is often vivid, dramatic, and releasing for the individual. There is full acceptance now of experiencing as providing a clear and usable referent for getting at the implicit meanings of the individual's encounter with himself and with life. There is also the recognition that the self is now becoming this process of experiencing. There is no longer much awareness of the self as an object. The individual often feels somewhat "shaky" as his solid constructs are recognized as construings taking place within him. The individual risks being himself in process in the relationship to others. He takes the risk of being the flow that is himself and trusting another person to accept him as he is in this flow.

Seventh stage. The individual lives comfortably in the flowing process of his experiencing. New feelings are experienced with richness and immediacy, and this inner experiencing is a clear referent for behavior. Incongruence is minimal and temporary. The self is a confident awareness of this process of experiencing. The meaning of experiencing is held loosely and constantly checked and rechecked against further experiencing (Rogers & Rablen, 1958).

Studies using the Process Scale or its derivatives show that significant behavior variations are discernible over the course of individual or group therapy using the process variables. The initial validation studies (Tomlinson, 1962; Tomlinson & Hart, 1962; Walker et al., 1960) showed that prejudged more successful and less successful individual counseling cases, using a multiple criteria of judgment, were highly distinguishable when "blind" ratings of segments from them were made on the Process Scale. In later studies, the Process Scale has distinguished individual process movement in encounter groups (Clark & Culbert, 1965; Culbert, 1968; Meador, 1971). In all cases interjudge reliability has been satisfactory.

Examples are given below of individual movement within each strand. These ex-

amples are taken from the eight individuals in a weekend encounter group. In a study of this group, Meador (1971) found that each of the eight individuals made significant (p < .01) positive process movement during the 16 hours that the group met. That is, each individual moved from the process level at which he entered the group along the continuum toward more flexibility, toward being better able to express his feelings as they occur, toward more awareness of his inner experiencing, greater congruence, toward relating to others in the immediacy of the present.

Feelings and Personal Meanings. Change in the way a client relates to his feelings and personal meanings has to do with the degree to which he is aware of his feelings, the degree to which he owns his feelings as his, and the degree to which he can express his feelings in the moment of their occurrence. Early in the group one of the participants says:

Keith: . . . If I am going to be a member of the group, I must contribute. I don't know what, but if you're going to be part of it, you've got to contribute to the well-being of the group.
Therapist: If you knew what it was you would do it.
Keith: Yes, I would do it and sort of do it and get it over with if I had the magic formula. I guess this is what was worrying me this afternoon. I don't believe that there is a magic answer. I seem to get from you that I should try a little harder.

This is an example of someone remote from his feelings, looking outside himself for a "magic formula," a clue from others to show him how to behave in this situation. This represents behavior low on the process continuum. Gradually, Keith begins to own his feelings and to talk about them in the past tense, representative of the middle of the continuum:

Keith: There are times I am afraid, and you said yesterday "why don't you just tell everybody what you think and let it go." There are times I don't seem to be able to do that. There are other times when I can. I don't, to my knowledge, turn these on and off as a mechanism or anything like that. It happens.

Therapist: Can you get any closer at all to what it's like when you are afraid? If that clicks, I just wonder if you could just let us sink in and let us know a little more of what it seems like inside when you feel that way?

Keith: What it feels like inside when I am afraid is like your first speech in front of a large audience. Your stomach feels like a used lemon rind. It churns.

Later, Keith expresses his feelings in the moment of their occurrence in the following example,

Keith: . . . You made me a bit mad with your emptiness. I don't know whether you made me mad because maybe I am empty, or you made me mad because I don't like the idea because I don't think that it is applicable over here. . . .

Joe: Yes it is.

Keith: Well maybe, but I don't see it!

To summarize the strand of feelings and personal meanings, on the lower end of the continuum the person is remote from his feelings and disowns them. Gradually he comes to recognize that he has feelings and is able to talk about having them in the past. Later he may fearfully express his feelings as they occur, representing a higher stage on the continuum. Finally, he is able to allow his feelings to flow freely, acknowledging them and expressing them as they occur and change from moment to moment.

Manner of Experiencing. In psychotherapy the individual moves from a remoteness from his inner experiencing through the process of becoming aware of it, to a point where he uses his changing inner experiencing as a referent for behavior. For example, early in the group, Jerry says, "I would like to get an honest feeling about myself, period, and act this way in all cases." This statement indicates that he has some awareness of the changingness of his inner experience of himself, and that he would like that changingness to cease, to be more dependable, more static. Later he begins to distinguish the characteristics of his inner experiencing, although he is still holding himself at arm's length from it:

Jerry: It's an odd thing. I remember starting off thinking about this openness and I . . . I don't feel that I've been open. It's a desire to be open, and yet I seem to still be back here listening to you other people and trying to really get into it, but I . . . I can't seem to do it. Of course this empty expression to me is kind of a horrifying thought. And when you said it to Karl I immediately thought of it in relation to myself and wondered just how empty I was.

Toward the end of the group, Jerry is allowing his inner experiencing to flow and is able to move with its changingness as in this statement:

Jerry: I find weeping is good, and . . . and a cleansing thing, and if . . . uhh . . . by somebody's action in this group, like Roz . . . uhh . . . how this has a welling up of making you feel a part of the group even though it's done by an individual of the group; it seemed to make me feel a part of everybody here, and which I'll forever be indebted to you, Roz, for. And

. . . uhh . . . I had no embarrassment in coming back into the room.

Therapist: I noticed that.

Jerry: But then a wave of sadness comes over, and . . . and . . . at least I feel . . . uhh . . . which is the thing that Beth and I were discussing . . . is, well, what happens from this point on. And it's frightening, and it's . . . it's . . . uhh . . . a real dilemma. The thing that you get is that there are people that could care, and so therefore it may not be a really hopeless situation.

In this statement, Jerry mentions several aspects of his inner experiencing and translates these into meanings for his own self-understanding. This speech is representative of behavior on the upper end of the process continuum.

Personal Constructs. Another aspect of the process continuum is the way in which an individual construes his experiences. At one end of the continuum, his meanings for experiences are very rigid and seem to be placed on his experiences from the outside as though meanings were absolute truths. Beth relates her construing of male-female relationships in this way.

Beth: What amazes me is the fact that I have always felt that a man-woman relation was just sexual and that there . . . it couldn't be a love or anything beyond a superficial feeling for any other man. And it has affected me very deeply that I have moved him. But it did not occur to me to go and put my arms around him because to me this is wrong to kiss, or embrace, or love a man that I am not married to or don't feel that way towards.

Gradually the individual begins to question his personal constructs particularly as he begins to trust his inner experiencing and to find his meaning there. Later in the group, Beth is using her own feelings as referents for meaning as in this statement:

Beth: Well, I really do think that you like me now. I told you that, you know, that you weren't reaching me. I don't remember how far back it was, now, but that I wasn't digging you or reading you. You weren't, but I think you do really like me now. I feel this. So I feel we have made, at least you and I have made, contact.

Therapist: You can really believe the guy inside.

Beth: Uh-huh. Besides getting his handkerchief. I thought for a minute he was going to cuddle up, and I was going to tell him I would give it back to him, only if I could have it back again, because I want to take it home with me.

Beth can now allow the caring she feels for another man to be expressed, to value and prize her affection as she experiences it, rather than squelching her feelings in favor of a meaning she was imposing upon herself.

Communication of Self. Change can be seen in the individual over the course of psychotherapy in the way in which he talks about himself. At one end of the continuum, he is unwilling to talk about himself or talks about himself only in terms of external events. At the midpoint of the continuum, the individual talks about himself as an object he hardly seems related to. Gradually, he begins to own himself and his feelings and experiencing and to communicate himself in that way. At the beginning of the group, Carlene exemplifies the lower end of the continuum when she says, "I think that there is this need for keeping some of self to self." Slowly, she begins to communicate herself, but still speaks of herself in the third person, "You're not seeing Carlene in that, or maybe I'm not projecting Carlene, and you're questioning this."

Her movement in communicating herself is clear when she says, "I am enjoying myself here to the extent of . . . to the point where I am finding so many things out about me, and I really . . . I think that I have grown greatly since I have been here and I have found a lot of things out that I never really accepted before." Although in this statement she speaks of experiences that are not occurring at the moment, she is communicating about very recent and implicitly ongoing experiencing. Finally, Carlene exemplifies the upper end of the process continuum when, weeping, she communicates herself to another in the midst of her strong feelings about herself:

Carlene: I wanted so badly to reach out to you Jerry. . . . Uhmmm . . . I was just kind of boiling inside, and I couldn't do it. . . . And I was sitting here after Roz came over to you, and then after you left, and I wanted to go out then, and I couldn't do that either.

As Carlene came to trust the others in the group, she changed the way she talked about herself from being very remote and hidden in her communication to being open, claiming the self she was communicating.

Congruence. Another strand on which an individual changes during psychotherapy is the continuum from incongruence to congruence. *Congruence* refers to the individual's being what he feels inside, being aware of his inner experiencing and translating that into his behavior. *Incongruence* refers to his playing a role designed to cover up or hide his inner self. References to congruence often include phrases such as "taking off the mask" or "tearing down the wall." Another member of the group, Joe, speaks of his awareness of the difference between inner feelings and outward actions in these two

segments. The first is from early in the group:

Joe: Aren't we always giving off cues? And if I do not like you, Beth, I am sure that you would sense it. Just like at the cocktail party you were talking about. If I come up to you and say a few pleasant words, and then go to the other side of the room, that's one thing. But if I am really warm to you, somehow we would be tearing bricks down from this wall between us. I guess what I am trying to say is that we are really more open with people, we get these cues, more than we seem to think.

In this speech, Joe speaks of a hypothetical situation and in the inclusive "we" thus avoiding making this statement his own personal belief; he does not own the belief as an experience of his. Much later in the group, Joe expresses his experience of incongruence in a more personal way:

Therapist: We want you to say what is hard for you to say now. That was hard for you to say, "Don't forget about me," wasn't it?
Joe: Uh-huh.
Therapist: Can you finish that?
Joe: I don't want you to forget about me, and I also don't want you to remember me as just, . . . I guess I've been a nice guy because I do smile a lot. That's only a part of me. And I think, there *is* something in here, and I want you to know this guy, too.
Therapist: What is it?
Joe: I don't know. It's the guy that's inside of me. It isn't too easy to know him. I don't know . . . I can't. . . . This guy has got sweaty palms right now even though he is sitting here very calm.

Here Joe is much closer to his own experiencing and expresses his awareness of the difference between his outward behavior and his inner feelings. Becoming aware of incongruence is the intermediate step toward allowing one's inner experiencing to flow outward, shaping one's behavior. The unbroken flow between inner experiencing and outward behavior is characteristic of high-process level.

Relationship to Problems. Another strand on which individuals show movement in psychotherapy is how they talk about their *problems.* At the lower end of the continuum, the individual is either unaware of having problems or sees his problems as outside himself. As he moves on the process continuum, he begins to talk about his problems in the past, as Winnie, in this excerpt, tells how she dealt with her brother's anger: "I listened when he got mad. That was the only time that he ever expressed any hostility at all. And it was a very real moment." Movement on this strand can be seen as the individual begins to own his part in contributing to the problem, although he still speaks of problems in the past. Winnie says, "Why was I so irritated at you? What was it? Was it really the reasons that I was giving you all: and then I thought, you act like my brother. . . . Then I knew what was at the bottom of the problem, but it would take me so long to get there. But then at least I know something now that I didn't know this morning." The upper portion of the continuum is represented by behavior in which the individual has immediate access to his problems as he senses them in his experiencing. He understands that the problems are *his* and seeks the solution within himself, as in this excerpt:

Winnie: This feeling in myself has come in and has just sort of barred everything else out temporarily. It isn't that I don't feel. . . . If I stop and think about it, I feel the way about all of you that I did this morning; but this is immediate, and it is

right now, and it is a problem for me, and it is something I'm going to have to work out. I just don't know quite how.

Interpersonal Relationships. The final strand on the process continuum has to do with the way in which the individual relates to others. At the lower end of the continuum the person is very fearful of close relationships and wants to know how he should behave in the situation as Keith expressed, "If I knew what to do, I would do it and get it over with." The midpoint of the continuum is represented by behaviors in which the individual cautiously tests the relationship, frequently rationalizing why it is unsafe still to trust the relationship. Roz exemplifies this point in the following excerpt:

Roz: Well, this is how I've always been. I've formed relationships at one point, and then there's a wall there, and I think it's for the same reasons as you have said. Maybe if he sees too much of me, he'll see these things about me that I don't like and he won't like, and by his not liking it he'll just make it that much clearer to myself. . . . But I'm not satisfied with relationships that end just there.

As the individual moves toward the upper end of the continuum, he is able to express his feelings in a relationship as they occur. Roz says at the end of the group:

Roz: I love you [because] you have responded so warmly to me and you have given me love. I sort of put you up here because of that. I think when I walk away from here I know that you will be a part of me, and I'll always remember you and the experience.

A person's words are one manifestation of his inner self that we can record and analyze. His inner feelings, the nuances of his experiencing, are not directly available to us. The *process theory* is an attempt to identify inward processes through the quality or type of verbalization, the way an individual reports himself. Studies using the Process Scale have reliably correlated process movement in therapy with outcome, as well as correlating positive process movement with the presence of the three therapist conditions: genuineness, caring, and understanding. The theory is a beginning toward understanding human growth and change, and hopefully these descriptions will generate investigations into their refinement.

APPLICATIONS

Problems

The person-centered approach is theoretically applicable to any relationship where the persons want to understand each other and want to be understood; where the persons are willing to reveal themselves to some degree; and where the persons want to enhance their own growth. These characteristics are present in a wide variety of relationships, and consequently the person-centered principles are being used in more and more situations. The elements of genuineness, empathic understanding, and positive regard promote and enhance a healthy relationship regardless of the circumstances in which they are present. Because they are simple, understandable attitudes, available at least to some degree to any human being, they can be practiced by anyone and are not the exclusive acquisition of professionals through long years of training. The fact that they are simple and understandable does not mean they are easy to achieve; their acquisition is not guaranteed by professional training and in fact may take much longer than professional training.

Four categories contain most of the situations in which the person-centered principles are applied. These four are (a) counseling situations, (b) human-relations training situations, (c) small group situations, and (d) projects on institutional change. There is some overlapping of these four, but they are considered separately.

Counseling and Psychotherapy. The person-centered approach was developed as an approach to *counseling* troubled individuals, and this probably remains the most widespread application of the theory. It has been used successfully in individual counseling with all diagnostic groups: normals, neurotics, and psychotics. It is used extensively in pastoral counseling and in school counseling. It has been used in play therapy with children and in speech therapy, and in marriage and family counseling.

Human-Relations Training. Person-centered principles are used extensively in training professionals and nonprofessionals who work with people. This includes all levels of workers in the schools. It includes social workers, nurses, physicians, and aides to all these professions. It includes volunteer workers like those in the Peace Corps and VISTA and volunteers for various charitable agencies, particularly the newer agencies that do telephone counseling with troubled persons and that frequently serve persons in crisis situations. It includes training programs for leadership in many areas.

Small Groups. Another application of person-centered principles is in groups such as personal growth groups or encounter groups and in groups whose goal is tension reduction in a given situation. Sometimes the participants have their work field in common, such as groups for teachers, business executives, or ministers. Other groups are formed for married couples, families, women, or students, groups whose members have a common interest. Tension-reduction groups have been formed for labor-management disputes, black-white and other ethnic relations, student-faculty concerns, and other polarized situations. In all these groups, the emphasis is on honest communication and understanding.

Institutional Change. A fourth area in which the person-centered approach is used is in institutions seeking either orderly change or enhancement of human relations. This has included an entire school system made up of elementary schools, high schools, and a college. It has included faculties of individual schools and of an entire inner-city school system. It has included industrial plants, businesses, churches, institutions such as the YWCA/YMCA and the Boys Club. It has included government agencies at many levels.

Evaluation

This section does not pretend to be a complete review of the research on person-centered therapy. An overview of person-centered research and its influence on theory and therapy has been published. (Shlien & Zimring, 1970). A few historical highlights given here will demonstrate the interaction of the factors mentioned above in the evaluation of the personcentered approach.

Rogers in 1940 was the first to use electrical recordings of entire cases for study and training. This was before tape recordings were invented. With recordings, the person-centered group was able to make detailed studies of client change and therapist response and of the relationship between the two.

An outgrowth of recordings was the monumental study *Psychotherapy and Personality Change* (Rogers & Dymond, 1954), which reports an intensive, multifaceted look at the complete recordings plus pre-, post-, and follow-up testing of 25 clients and controls.

The satisfaction of the theory and methods with disturbed or neurotic individuals led to a five-year study with schizophrenic patients in a state mental hospital. The results are reported in *The Therapeutic Relationship with Schizophrenics* (Rogers et al., 1976b). The therapists found that in working with schizophrenics, they were forced to rely more heavily on their own experiencing in the relationship. They began to state what they were feeling during the therapy hour, and frequently their reporting seemed to precipitate movement in their clients. This has been illustrated in the earlier portion of this chapter, "A Silent Young Man." Later, research evidence confirmed that those therapists who were more able to be genuine than others had clients who made significantly more positive gain in therapy and who operated at higher process levels. This influenced person-centered therapists in general to enlarge their concept of genuineness to a more active, intuitive self-reporting.

Rogers then investigated the effect of person-centered principles in relationships with normal individuals. The vehicle for his study was the intensive small group or encounter group. Rogers sent questionnaires to over 500 persons who had participated in encounter groups under his direction. The results of his investigation are reported in *Carl Rogers on Encounter Groups* (1970). The obvious potency of the experience in an encounter group led Rogers to consider the effect such groups would have on an institution. A person-centered group carried out a three-year research study of intensive small groups on educational institutions (Rogers, 1969).

Interest in the changes institutions in our society are undergoing led this group to form in 1968 an experimental institution, Center for Studies of the Person. This is a group of some 40 members, including psychologists, sociologists, anthropologists, and journalists. They are more a psychological community than a working community. Each individual is responsible for his own income. The weekly "staff" meetings provide for exchange of ideas on the wide variety of projects members are engaged in, for personal exploration, and for touching base with the family group. One of the goals of CSP is to provide an atmosphere in which members can create and carry out the most imaginative projects possible, without the restrictions of traditional institutions.

The pattern that emerges in this description is one of natural growth. A group of researchers immerse themselves in one area of application of person-centered theory. The area is thoroughly researched, spawning new aspects of theory and method. The study reaches a natural completion, and the group moves to another area. The years of searching for explanations and understanding of the phenomena of individual therapeutic change were amply rewarded by the refinements of research discoveries. The legacy of person-centered therapy is embodied in the studies of the scores of researchers who have been associated with Rogers.

Treatment

In the earlier section on Problems, four areas of the application of person-centered theory were considered. This section describes some specific examples of ways in which the theory is translated into practical application in those four areas.

Counseling and Psychotherapy. The primary emphasis in individual therapy is the ongoing experiencing of the client. The therapist focuses on that experiencing to understand empathically the client's internal frame of reference. At the same time, he is aware of his own inner self and genuinely communicates those feelings. He seeks to maintain a balance between his understanding and caring for his client and communication of his own experiencing of the relationship, a balance that is optimally facilitative of the client's awareness of his inner self. The balance is determined by the therapist's intuitive grasp of the relationship and depends on his own creative ability to be fully present.

Personal Growth Group. The person-centered therapist's behavior in a personal growth group, is not unlike his activity in an individual setting. His attitudes toward the group members convey empathic understanding, nonpossessive caring, and genuine expression of his own ongoing feeling process. He does not "play" himself; he *is* genuinely himself, bringing all of his knowledge, experience, and his affective humanness to the relationships in the group.

The group has a wide and varied application. Participation in an intensive small group appears to facilitate therapeutic movement. In a study by Betty Meador (1971), a group of normal individuals, initially strangers, met for 16 hours over the period of a weekend. Blind ratings by independent judges found that each individual moved closer to his inner experiencing, became more able to express congruently what he was feeling, and became more real in his relationships.

The La Jolla Program: Human-Relations Training.   The La Jolla Program is a training experience for persons who lead small groups in their work. Participants come from a variety of professions, but the majority have been school counselors, ministers, priests, nuns, social workers, teachers, administrators, and psychotherapists. Three aspects of the program convey its basic character. First, there is an emphasis on the participants having first-hand experience in a variety of groups; second, the model of leadership is that the individual rely on himself as a person, not on his expertise; and, third, the 100 or more participants experience the building of a community among themselves.

The Project for Educational Innovation: Institutional Change.   The Project for Educational Innovation sought to apply person-centered principles in an educational system that was seeking positive, productive change, which included several elementary schools, a high school, and a college. A plan was designed that proposed holding intensive small groups for faculties of the individual schools, for students, for parents, for administrators, and then for mixtures of these categories (Rogers, 1967a). The plan included a research component. The hypothesis of the study was that participation in the small groups would release the creative potential of the participants and enhance their human relationships, and that results would be seen in the human relations and creativity in the classroom, in the curriculum, and in the attitudes of all groups toward the school and toward each other.

Space does not permit a more detailed description of this project and its results. It can be found in Rogers's book *Freedom to Learn* (1969) and in Morton Shaevitz and Don Barr's chapter "Encounter Groups in a Small College" (1972). The results, although complex, were generally positive. There was a loosening of the categories "student," "faculty," "administrator" and more communication among individuals in all these groups. There was more student participation in decision making at all levels and more student-centered teaching. There was more experimentation and innovation by teachers in the classroom. After the project was finished, some of the school personnel themselves obtained a grant to continue the small groups, using some of the facilitators from the research group and some from other sources. Their desire to continue having the groups was a confirmation both of the value the school personnel placed on the groups and of their willingness and ability to continue the process of change on their own.

The four situations described in this section to which the person-centered approach has been applied—individual therapy, group therapy, human-relations training, and institutional change—reflect the broadening definition of the concept *psychotherapy.* Person-centered theory holds that the process of human growth is potentially ongoing in the most withdrawn schizophrenic and in the most productive "normal" member of society. The three conditions of person-centered therapy (Rogers, 1969, p. 14) have been found to be conducive to growth in many different situations and appear to be generally applicable whether the client is an extremely troubled individual or a teacher in an elementary school. In any case, the goal of person-centered therapy is the same: the release of the self-actualizing forces in the individual.

Management

The following is a brief account of the *management* of therapy under the headings "the setting," "relationships," and "patient problems."

The Setting. Because the person-centered approach is used in a wide variety of situations, there is no one typical physical setting that would be generally applicable. The setting for a one-to-one client-therapist relationship might be a traditional office, and a group of Peace Corps Volunteers might meet in a trailer on an Indian reservation. Generally, person-centered therapists do not have specific requirements for the physical setting other than minimal needs for comfort and quiet. The setting chosen for a particular activity depends on the activity and the persons involved, whether individual or group therapy, and whether the clients are students, businessmen, women, a group of faculty, administrators, couples, and so forth.

Relationships. The relationship between client and therapist in person-centered therapy has been amply described in the preceding sections. Perhaps a word could be said about how a therapist might open an interview with a client or with a group.

In beginning an interview with an individual, the therapist speaks out of his attitude of being immediately present to the client. He might say, "This is our first hour together. I hope we can get to know each other a little bit in some meaningful way today." His emphasis in whatever he says is on the relationship and not on the "problem" of the client. Thus he immediately establishes himself as a person relating to another, not as an expert with answers.

A person-centered therapist beginning a group would speak out of the same attitude of presence to the immediate situation. His remarks come from himself, his awareness at the moment. He might say,

"We have sixteen hours to spend together. We can make of that time whatever we want. I don't know what is going to happen. I am looking forward to our interacting with one another, to our getting to know each other." In beginning a group, the therapist relies on himself, his ongoing, inner experiencing, as the resource for his participation, just as he depends on this resource throughout the group.

Patient Problems. The only patient problem discussed in this section is suicide threat. There are, perhaps, certain generalizations that can be drawn from the manner of handling such threats, which can be applied to other "patient problems."

Rogers has reported on the way in which suicide threats were handled at the Counseling Center at the University of Chicago. When a counselor reported that one of his clients threatened suicide, the counselor was asked, "Are you comfortable in your relationship with your client?" His answer might be, "Yes, but I realize that the Counseling Center will be held responsible if anything happens." Rogers would then answer, "If you are comfortable in the relationship, o.k. Deal with your client as a person. I will stand behind you if anything happens." On the other hand, if the counselor said he felt worried and uneasy, the client would be transferred to another counselor or psychiatrist.

Of the thousands of clients seen at the Chicago Counseling Center, there never was a single suicide by a client in therapy.

These guidelines can be applied to whatever "problem" a therapist is posed with in his client. If he feels comfortable in the relationship, he should treat his client as a person, not as the problem he is presenting, and the therapist should honestly react to the person with his intuitive awareness.

CASE EXAMPLE

Introduction

In 1964 Carl Rogers was filmed in a half-hour interview with a woman client for a film series, "Three Approaches to Psychotherapy" (1965). That interview contains many of the elements of person-centered therapy discussed in this chapter and is a typical example of the person-centered way of working. Since the film is available for rental or purchase (Rogers, 1965), it also gives the reader an opportunity to see and hear person-centered therapy in action.

Rogers had never seen the woman before the interview and knew his contact with her would be limited to the half hour before the cameras. In his filmed introduction to the interview, he describes the way he will· hope to be with her. He says he will, if he is fortunate, first of all, be real, try to be aware of his own inner feelings and to express them in ways that will not impose these feelings on her. Second, he hopes he will be caring of her, prizing her as an individual, accepting her. Third, he will try to understand her inner world from the inside; he will try to understand not just the surface meanings, but the meanings just below the surface. Rogers says if he is successful in holding these three attitudes, he expects certain things to happen to the client, expectations based on his experience and his research. He expects she will move from a remoteness from her inner experiencing to a more immediate awareness and expression of it; from disapproving of parts of her self to greater self-acceptance; from a fear of relating to relating to him more directly; from holding rigid, black and white constructs of reality to holding more tentative constructs; and from seeing the locus of evaluation outside herself to finding the locus of evaluation in her own inner experiencing.

The fact that the interview lasted for only one-half hour and the client was seen by the therapist only this one time emphasizes that the person-centered approach depends on the here-and-now attitudes of the therapist, attitudes as valid and constant in a brief interaction as over a long period. If the person-centered equation predicts a change in the way of being of a client, theoretically that change could be apparent even in a half-hour interview. A look at this brief interview supports the person-centered prediction.

The Interview

The interview is with a young woman, Gloria, a 30-year-old divorcee. The first portion of the interview concerns the problem Gloria presents initially, that she has not been honest with her 9-year-old daughter Pammy about the fact that she has had sexual relationships with men since her divorce. Gloria has always been honest with her children and is feeling great conflict over having lied to Pammy. She wants to know whether telling Pammy the truth about her sexual relationships will affect Pammy adversely.

At the very beginning Gloria tells Rogers, "I almost want an answer from you. I want you to tell me if it would affect her wrong if I told her the truth, or what." Later, on two occasions, she asks again for a direct answer to her question. Clearly, she wants an "authority" to tell her what to do. Rogers's responses assure her that he understands her dilemma and guide her to her own resources for answering. After each time that she asks the question and hears the response, Gloria explores her own feelings a little more deeply.

To her first request, Rogers replies, "And it's this concern about her (Pammy) and the fact that you really aren't—that this open relationship that has existed between you, now you feel it's kind of vanished?" and after Gloria's reply he says, "I sure wish I could give you the answer as to what you should tell her." "I was afraid you were going to say that," she says. Rogers replies, "Because what you really want *is* an answer."

Gloria begins to explore her relationship with Pammy and concludes that she feels real uncertainty whether or not Pammy would accept her "devilish" or "shady" side. Gloria finds she is not certain she accepts that part of herself. Again she asks Rogers for an answer: "You're just going to sit there and let me stew in it and I want more." Rogers replies, "No, I don't want to let you just stew in your feelings, but on the other hand, I also feel this is the kind of very private thing that I couldn't possibly answer for you. But I sure as anything will try to help you work toward your own answer. I don't know whether that makes any sense to you, but I mean it." Gloria says she can tell he really does mean it and again begins to explore her feelings, this time focusing more on the conflict she herself feels between her actions and her inner standards. Shortly, she again says, "I want you very much to give me a direct answer. . . ." Rogers replies:

I guess, I am sure this will sound evasive to you, but it seems to me that perhaps the person you are not being fully honest with is you, because I was very much struck by the fact that you were saying, "If I feel all right about what I have done, whether it's going to bed with a man or what, if I really feel all right about it, then I do not have any concern about what I would tell Pam or my relationship with her."

To this Gloria answers:

Right. All right. Now I hear what you are saying. Then all right, then I want to work on accepting me then. I want to work on feeling all right about it. That makes sense. Then that will come natural and then I won't have to worry about Pammy. . . .

This statement indicates that Gloria has assimilated a real insight, an understanding that the solution to her problem is in herself rather than in an authoritative opinion on how knowledge of her sex life will affect Pammy.

From this point in the interview she focuses on her inner conflict. She tells Rogers what she "wishes he would tell her" and then says she can't quite take the risk of being the way she wants to be with her children "unless an authority tells me that. . . ." Rogers says with obvious feeling, "I guess one thing that I feel very keenly is that it's an awfully risky thing to *live.* You'd be taking a chance on your relationship with her and taking a chance on letting her know who you are, really." Gloria says she wishes very strongly that she could take *more risks,* that she could act on her own feelings of rightness without always needing encouragement from others. Again she says what she'd like to do in the situation with Pammy, and then adds, "Now I feel like 'now that's solved' —and I didn't even solve a thing; but I feel relieved."

Gloria: I do feel like you have been saying to me—you are not giving me advice, but I do feel like you are saying, "You know what pattern you want to follow, Gloria, and go ahead and follow it." I sort of feel a backing up from you.

Rogers: I guess the way I sense it, you've been telling me that you know what you want to do, and yes, I do believe in backing up people in what they want to do. It's a little different slant than the way it seems to you.

Gloria's expressing the feeling, "Now that's solved—and I didn't even solve a thing but I feel relieved," exemplifies an awareness of inner experiencing, a felt meaning she has not yet put into words. She "feels relieved" as though her problem is solved. Therapeutic movement has occurred in her inner self before she understands its explicit meaning. It is interesting that she says in the same speech, "I feel a backing up from you." She *feels* the support of Rogers's empathic understanding and acceptance of her. From the person-centered point of view there is a relationship between her feeling understood and valued and her movement from seeking the locus of evaluation outside herself to depending on her own inner feeling of "rightness" for a solution to her problem.

The next portion of the interview involves Gloria's experience of her own inner valuing processes and the conflicts she sometimes feels. She explains her use of the word *utopia,* which refers to times she is able to follow her inner feelings:

When I do follow a feeling and I feel this good feeling inside of me, that's sort of utopia. That's what I mean. That's the way I like to feel whether it's a bad thing or a good thing. But I feel right about *me.*

Whether the action she takes might be thought of as "good" or "bad," if she feels right about it, that's "utopia." Rogers's response that in those moments she must feel "all in one piece" brings tears to Gloria's eyes, for those moments are all too few. In the midst of her weeping, she says:

You know what else I was just thinking? I . . . a dumb thing . . . that all of a sudden while I was talking to you, I thought, "Gee, how nice I can talk to you and I want you to approve of me and I respect you, but I miss that my father couldn't talk to me like you are." I mean, I'd

like to say, "Gee, I'd like you for my father." I don't even know why that came to me.

Rogers: You look to me like a pretty nice daughter. But you really do miss that fact that you couldn't be open with your own dad.

Gloria is now quite close to her inner experiencing, allowing her tears to flow as she thinks of her rare moments of "utopia" and then expressing a feeling that comes into awareness of positive affection for Rogers. She then explores her relationship with her father, maintaining the same closeness to her inner feelings, as she says, "You know, when I talk about it, it feels more flip. If I just sit still a minute, it feels like a great big hurt down there."

Gloria looks at and feels her deep inner hurt over her relationship to her father. She has moved significantly from seeking a solution outside herself to a problem with her children to looking inward at a painful hurt. She says she tries to soothe the hurt through relationships with fatherly men, pretending they are her father, as she is doing with Rogers.

Rogers: I don't feel that's pretending.

Gloria: Well, you're *not* really my father.

Rogers: No. I meant about the real close business.

Gloria: Well, see, I sort of feel that's pretending too, because I can't expect you to feel very close to me. You don't know me that well.

Rogers: All I can know is what I am feeling, and that is I feel close to you in this moment.

Here Rogers presents himself as he really is, offering Gloria the experience of genuine caring from another, an experience she has felt deprived of in the relationship with her real father. Shortly after this exchange, the interview ends.

Evaluation

In Rogers's filmed introduction to the interview he says he hopes to be real, caring, and understanding with his client. If he succeeds, he says, he expects Gloria will make therapeutic movement in certain explicit ways. Examples from the excerpts quoted in the previous paragraphs demonstrate the therapist's attitudes as well as the client's process.

First, Rogers hopes to be his real self, to be aware of his inner feelings and express them in ways that will not impose them on Gloria. Several examples of the therapist's genuineness occur. In Gloria's insistence on his answering her question, he maintains his belief in *her* ability to find the answer within herself. His strong inner feeling that he repeatedly expresses is that he does not have the answer for her. Still, in blocking this road, he opens another in which he just as firmly believes. He offers repeatedly to help her find the answer in herself.

The intensity of his genuineness and presence in the relationship is readily apparent from watching the film. The strength of his feelings comes through when he says, ". . . it's an awfully risky thing to *live*," or when he clearly expresses his inner self, "All I can know is what I am feeling, and that is I feel close to you in this moment." The quality of the therapist's genuineness is pervasive throughout this interview. The attitude of genuineness is not to be turned on and off, but is a state of presence and awareness of oneself that is constantly there.

Rogers expresses his caring for his client both directly and indirectly. He tells her directly, when she says she'd like him for her father, "You look to me like a pretty nice daughter." Indirectly, his attitude is one of attentiveness and acceptance of all she says. He makes himself openly available to her to facilitate her search for an answer, an offer that implies his confidence in her potential. Gloria is aware of his acceptance when she says, "I sort of feel a backing up from you." Her awareness of his caring is as necessary to her movement as his expression of the attitude.

In being understanding, Rogers says he hopes to understand not just the surface meanings but the meanings below the surface of the client's awareness. He says to Gloria, "It seems to me that perhaps the person you are not being fully honest with is you. Because I was very much struck by the fact that you were saying, 'If I feel all right about what I have done, whether it's going to bed with a man or what, if I really feel all right about it, then I do not have any concern about what I would tell Pam or my relationship with her.'" Gloria at this point becomes aware of her outward-directed search for an answer and turns to look inside herself. Rogers, in understanding her inner struggle with accepting herself, makes explicit what Gloria has been implying. Her hearing his statement precipitates a real insight for her, as though a light turns on and she understands where she must go for answers, namely, into herself. Another clear example of the therapist's understanding precipitating movement occurs as Rogers replies to Gloria's description of her "utopia" feeling. He says, "I sense that in those utopian moments, you really feel kind of whole. You feel all in one piece." Gloria becomes very tearful, lets her feelings flow, and is surprised by the warmth she feels toward Rogers and the hurt she feels in her relationship with her father. In these examples, the importance of the therapist's understanding for the client's growth becomes apparent. Still, understanding without genuineness and caring seems sterile, and the interrelatedness of the three attitudes is again clear.

The therapeutic movement the client makes follows the direction and manner that Rogers initially described. First, he says she will move from a remoteness from her feelings to an immediate awareness and expression of them. She does in fact begin the interview wanting an answer to a troubling question and does move to a point toward the end where her feelings are flowing into awareness and she is expressing them as they occur. At one point she says, concerning her wanting a father like Rogers, "I don't even know why that came to me." She is allowing her feelings to come into expression without censoring, questioning, or even knowing where they are coming from.

Rogers says she will move from disapproving of herself toward self-acceptance. At the beginning, Gloria says she is not sure she accepts her "shady" or "devilish" side. Later, she very explicitly asks to work on accepting herself and spends much of the remaining time exploring the nuances of her self-acceptance.

Another strand on which she moves is from a fear of relating to the therapist to relating more directly. Initially Gloria says, "I wish I weren't so nervous," and holds Rogers at a distance by making him in her eyes an expert, an authority. Her attitude softens to the point toward the end when she can say, "I wish I had you for a father."

Her search for an authoritative answer exemplifies another strand on which she shows therapeutic movement, her construing of reality. Initially, she believes there is a true answer that will solve her problem. She construes reality in this black and white fashion. Later, she tentatively considers relying on her own inner experiencing for solutions, as she says, "I *wish* I could take *more risks.*" Finally, she describes the utopian experience of feeling so sure of herself that whatever she does comes out of her inner experience and feels "right." This same example demonstrates the therapeutic process on the final strand Rogers mentions, that of moving from finding the locus of evaluation outside oneself to finding it in one's inner self.

The quality of this interview is like a piece of music, which begins on a thin persistent note and gradually adds dimensions and levels until the whole orchestra is playing. The intuitive interaction and response of the therapist is not unlike the interplay in a creative improvisation. Whatever wisdom science can bring to how the instruments are made and which combinations make for harmony and growth will greatly enrich the players, but may we never lose sight of the primacy of the creative human beings making the music.

There is a postscript to this brief interview. At this writing, 12 years have passed since the film was made. Once or twice each year, Gloria has written Rogers telling him of important events in her life, of times she felt lost or sad as well as fulfilled and growing. Her memory of the interview is of a warm, real, human contact, moments shared that were fulfilling. Rogers once answered a counseling student who asked what do you do if you only have a short time with a client, "If you have only thirty minutes, then give thirty minutes worth."

SUMMARY

The theoretical base of person-centered therapy is a belief in the "exquisite rationality" of human growth under optimal conditions. The actualizing tendency in man is a powerful force equipped with its own rhythm and direction.

The task of the therapist is to facilitate the client's awareness of and trust in his own actualizing processes. The primary discovery of person-centered therapy is that of the attitudes of the therapist that create the optimal climate in which the client can allow his own growth to unfold. The process of therapy is truly centered in the client whose inner experiencing dictates the pace and direction of the therapeutic relationship.

The attitude of uncompromising trust in the growth processes of individuals is as much a value system as it is a guide for therapy. As such, it is contrary to the prevailing values of the schools, the family, the church, business, and other institutions in this country. The predominant attitude in these institutions is one of cautious delimitation and an implicit skepticism of the process of human growth. One has only to imagine a family or school that might adopt an attitude of uncompromising trust in the growth process of its members in an atmosphere of genuineness, caring, and understanding to appreciate the contrast with the majority of families and schools.

It is possible that the influence of person-centered theory will be felt to a greater extent on the institutions of this country in the future, more than in the profession of psychotherapy. This is already true to some extent. The number of individuals in education and religion, for example, who are adopting person-centered principles is apparently increasing each year.

The tentative conclusion one could draw is that three decades of person-centered therapy, research, and writing offer ample statement of a rather radical value stance, one that advocates complete trust in individual growth and development

under stated conditions. As such, person-centered theory presents a compelling invitation, not only to the therapist in a client-therapist relationship, but to human clusters of all shapes, sizes, and persuasions.

ANNOTATED BIBLIOGRAPHY

Rogers, Carl R. *Client-centered therapy*. Boston: Houghton Mifflin, 1951.

In this book is the first major formulation of the person-centered point of view. It covers earlier views on the three therapist attitudes, the therapy relationship as experienced by the client, and the process of therapy itself. It indicates how person-centered therapy principles can be applied in play therapy, group therapy, administration, and teaching. There is a chapter on the training of therapists. The final chapter contains an initial formulation of the theory of therapy and personality. It is a good first reading.

Rogers, Carl R. *On becoming a person*. Boston: Houghton Mifflin, 1961.

This is Rogers's best known book. It contains much personal material, the often-reprinted chapter on the characteristics of the helping relationship, and a careful formulation of the process of therapy. It presents the philosophy behind the person-centered point of view. It faces squarely the dilemmas involved in conducting the scientific investigation of subjective phenomena. Other material includes teaching and learning and the relevance of the approach to family and group tensions. Questions are raised about the place of the individual in the world view being developed in the behavioral sciences. Readers respond especially to the highly personal character of some of the material and to the excerpts from recorded case material.

Rogers, Carl R. A theory of therapy, personality, and interpersonal relationships, as developed in the client-centered framework. In S. Koch (Ed.), *Psychology: A study of a science*, Vol. III. *Formulations of the person and the social context*. New York: McGraw-Hill, 1959, pp. 184–256.

This is not easy reading. It is a tightly woven, comprehensive statement of the conditions for and the outcomes of effective therapy, a theory of the development of personality, and a general theory of interpersonal relationships. Because it is stated in carefully defined terms, the theory as stated in this article has been the source of many research hypotheses. Also, the article contains a plea for the development of a science more suited to the study of the whole person.

Rogers, Carl R., & Dymond, Rosalind (Eds.). *Psychotherapy and personality change.* Chicago: University of Chicago Press, 1954.

This is a full report of a major research project on the outcomes of person-centered therapy. The chapters are written by many of the research staff who participated in the project. It includes the first major use of the Q Sort in measuring change in self-concept. The project involved the use of carefully selected control groups, the transcription of all interviews in all the research cases, and the assembling of large amounts of data from various personality and behavior measures. The study was outstanding in presenting data on one case of effective psychotherapy and equally complete data on a failure case. The book is regarded as a landmark in psychotherapy research.

Rogers, Carl R. *Carl Rogers on personal power: Inner strength and its revolutionary impact.* New York: Delacorte Press, 1977.

In this most recent book, the person-centered approach is presented as bringing about a quiet revolution in the helping professions, education, marriage and family relationships, and administration. It has developed beginning models for resolving intercultural tensions. One of the most widely read chapters presents a complete picture of a 16-day, intensive person-centered workshop from the planning stages to outcome. There is a case example of a quiet revolution in a day camp. There is also a chapter describing the struggles and successes of a couple involved in an open marriage. A political base for the person-centered approach is found in the actualizing tendency that provides a theoretical underpinning. An important chapter presents the emerging person as spearhead of the quiet revolution. This book more than any of the others shows the far-reaching implications of the person-centered approach.

CASE READINGS

Rogers, C. R. *Counseling and psychotherapy.* Boston: Houghton Mifflin, 1942.
A classic in the field of psychotherapy.

Rogers spends a good deal of the contents of this book in the analysis of the treatment of a college student.

Rogers, C. R. The case of Mrs. Oak. In C. R. Rogers and R. F. Dymond (Eds.), *Psychotherapy and personality change.* Chicago: University of Chicago Press, 1954. (Also found in abridged form in C. R. Rogers, *On becoming a person.* Boston: Houghton Mifflin, 1961. Also in D. Wedding & R. J. Corsini [Eds.], *Great cases in psychotherapy.* Itasca, Ill.: F. E. Peacock Publishers, 1979.)

Another classic case with more mature analysis showing how Rogers perceives therapy and his insightfulness in dealing with clients.

REFERENCES

Barrett-Lennard, Godfrey. Dimensions of perceived therapist response related to therapeutic change. Doctoral dissertation, University of Chicago, 1959.

Barrett-Lennard, Godfrey. Dimensions of therapist response as causal factors in therapeutic change. *Psychological Monographs,* 1962, 76, Whole No. 562.

Buber, Martin. *Pointing the way.* New York: Harper & Row, 1957.

Cartwright, Desmond. Annotated bibliography of research and theory construction in client-centered therapy. *Journal of Counseling Psychology,* 1957, 4, 82–100.

Clark, J. V., & Culbert, S. A. Mutually therapeutic perception and self-awareness in a T-group. *Journal of Applied Behavioral Science,* 1965, 1, 180–94.

Culbert, S. A. Trainer self-disclosure and member growth in two T-groups. *Journal of Applied Behavioral Science,* 1968, 4, 47–73.

Emerson, Ralph Waldo, "Divinity School Address," 1838.

Halkides, Galatia. An experimental study of four conditions necessary for therapeutic personality change. Doctoral dissertation, University of Chicago, 1958.

Hart, J. T., & Tomlinson, T. M. (Eds.) *New directions in client-centered therapy.* Boston: Houghton Mifflin, 1970.

Kirschenbaum, Howard. Application to the Guggenheim Foundation. Document prepared for the Guggenheim Foundation, December 1971.

McCleary, R. A., & Lazarus, R. S. Autonomic discrimination without awareness. *Journal of Personality,* 1949, 18, 171–79.

Maslow, A. H. *Motivation and personality.* New York: Harper, 1954.

Meador, Betty D. Individual process in a basic encounter group. *Journal of Counseling Psychology,* 1971, 18, 70–76.

Peters, R. S. Review of C. R. Rogers, Freedom to Learn. *Interchange,* 1970, 1, 111–14.

Raimy, V. C. The self-concept as a factor in counseling and personality organization. Doctoral dissertation, Ohio State University, 1943.

Rank, Otto. *Will therapy.* New York: Knopf, 1936.

Rogers, Carl R. *The clinical treatment of the problem child.* Boston: Houghton Mifflin, 1939.

Rogers, Carl R. *Counseling and psychotherapy.* Boston: Houghton Mifflin, 1942.

Rogers, Carl R. *Client-centered therapy.* Boston: Houghton Mifflin, 1951.

Rogers, Carl R. *Psychotherapy and personality change.* Chicago: University of Chicago Press, 1954.

Rogers, Carl R. The necessary and sufficient conditions of therapeutic personality change. *Journal of Consulting Psychology,* 1957, 21: 95–103.

Rogers, Carl R. A process conception of psychotherapy. *American Psychologist,* 1958, 13, 142–49.

Rogers, Carl R. Client-centered therapy. In Silvano Arieti (Ed.), *American handbook of psychiatry,* Vol. 3. New York: Basic Books, 1959(a). (Vol. 3, a *Supplement to the handbook,* published by Basic Books, 1966, pp. 183–200.)

Rogers, Carl R. A theory of therapy, personality, and interpersonal relationships, as developed in the client-centered framework. In S. Koch (Ed.), *Psychology: A study of a science,* Vol. III. *Formulations of the person and the social context.* New York: McGraw-Hill, 1959, pp. 184–256(b).

Rogers, Carl R. *On becoming a person.* Boston: Houghton Mifflin, 1961(a).

Rogers, Carl R. The process equation of psychotherapy. *American Journal of Psychotherapy,* January 1961(b), 15, No. 1, 27–45.

Rogers, Carl R. The actualizing tendency in relation to "motives" and to consciousness. In Marshall Jones (Ed.), *Nebraska symposium on motivation,* 1963. Lincoln, Neb.: University of Nebraska Press, 1963, pp. 1–24.

Rogers, Carl R. Client-centered therapy, Film No. 1. In Everett Shostrom (Ed.), *Three approaches to psychotherapy.* (Three 16 mm. color motion pictures.) Santa Ana, Calif.: Psychological Films, 1965.

Rogers, Carl R. A plan for self-directed change in an educational system. *Educational Leadership,* 1967(a), 24, 717–31.

Rogers, Carl R. (Ed.) *The therapeutic relationship and its impact: A study of psychotherapy with schizophrenics.* With E. T. Gendlin, D. J. Kiesler, and C. Louax. Madison, Wisc.: University of Wisconsin Press, 1967(b).

Rogers, Carl R. *Freedom to learn: A view of what education might become.* Columbus, Ohio: Charles E. Merrill, 1969.

Rogers, Carl R. *Carl Rogers on encounter groups.* New York: Harper & Row, 1970.

Rogers, Carl R. *On becoming partners: Marriage and its alternatives.* New York: Delacourte, 1972.

Rogers, Carl R. *Carl Rogers on personal power.* New York: Delacorte, 1977.

Rogers, Carl R., & Dymond, R. F. (Eds.) *Psychotherapy and personality change.* Chicago: University of Chicago Press, 1954.

Rogers, Carl R., & Rablen, R. A. A scale of process in psychotherapy. Manuscript, University of Wisconsin, 1958. (Available in mimeo form from Center of Studies of the Person, La Jolla, California.)

Shaevitz, Morton, & Barr, Don. Encounter groups in a small college. In Lawrence Solomon and Betty Berzon (Eds.), *New perspectives on encounter groups.* San Francisco: Jossey-Bass, 1972.

Shlien, John M., & Zimring, Fred M. Research directives and methods in client-centered therapy. In J. T. Hart & T. M. Tomlinson (Eds.), *New directions in client-centered therapy,* Boston: Houghton Mifflin, 1970, 33–57.

Standal, S. The need for positive regard: A contribution to client-centered theory. Doctoral dissertation, University of Chicago, 1954.

Stephenson, W. *The study of behavior: Q-technique and its methodology.* Chicago: University of Chicago Press, 1953.

Tenenbaum, Samuel. Review of *Freedom to learn. Education Leadership,* 1969, 27, 1, 97–99.

Tomlinson, T. M. Three approaches to the study of psychotherapy: process, outcome, and change. Doctoral dissertation, University of Wisconsin, 1962.

Tomlinson, T. M., & Hart, J. T., Jr. A valida-
tion study of the process scale. *Journal of
Consulting Psychology,* 1962, 26, 74–78.
Walker, A. M., Rablen, R. A., & Rogers,
C. R. Development of a scale to measure

process changes in psychotherapy. *Journal
of Clinical Psychology,* 1960, 16, 79–85.
Whyte, Lancelot. *The unconscious before
Freud.* London: Tavistock Publications,
1960.

5

Rational-Emotive Therapy

ALBERT ELLIS

OVERVIEW

Rational-emotive therapy, a theory of personality and a method of psychotherapy developed by Albert Ellis, a clinical psychologist, in the 1950s holds that when a highly charged emotional consequence (*C*) follows a significant activating event (*A*), *A* may seem to, but actually does not, cause *C*. Instead, emotional consequences are largely created by *B*—the individual's *belief system.* When an undesirable emotional consequence occurs, such as severe anxiety, this can usually be traced to the person's irrational beliefs, and when these beliefs are effectively disputed (at point *D*), by challenging them rationally, the disturbed consequences disappear and eventually cease to recur.

Basic Concepts

The main propositions of rational-emotive therapy (RET) are:

1. People are born with a potential to be rational as well as irrational. They have predispositions to be self-preserving, to think about their thinking, to be creative, to be sensuous, to be interested in their fellows, to learn by mistakes, and to actualize their potentials for life and growth. They also have propensities to be self-destructive, to be short-range hedonists, to avoid thinking things through, to procrastinate, to repeat the same mistakes, to be superstitious, to be intolerant, to be perfectionistic and grandiose, and to avoid actualizing their potentials for growth.

2. People's tendency to irrational thinking, self-damaging habituations, wishful thinking, and intolerance is frequently exacerbated by their culture and their family group. Their suggestibility (or conditionability) is greatest during their early years, and consequently they are then most influenced by family and social pressures.

3. Humans tend to perceive, think, emote, and behave simultaneously. They therefore, at one and the same time, are cognitive, conative, and motoric. They rarely act without also cognizing, since their present sensations or actions are apprehended in a network of prior experiences, memories, and conclusions. They seldom emote without thinking, since their feelings include, and are usually triggered off by, an appraisal of a given situation and its importance. They rarely act without perceiving, thinking, and emoting, since these processes provide them with reasons for acting. Just as their "normal" behavior is a function of their perceiving, thinking, emoting, and act-

ing, so, too, is their disturbed behavior similarly formed. To understand self defeating conduct, therefore, we had better understand how people perceive, think, emote, and act. To help them change their malfunctioning, it is usually desirable to use a variety of perceptual-cognitive, emotive-evocative, and behavioristic-reeducative methods in a full therapeutic armamentarium (Ellis, 1971b, 1973b, 1976a, 1977a; Ellis & Grieger, 1,977).

4. Although all the major psychotherapies employ a variety of cognitive, emotive, and desensitizing techniques, and although all (including many unscientific methods like witch doctoring and Christian Science) may help individuals who have faith and who work at applying them, they are probably not equally effective in terms of time and effort nor in terms of the elegance and long lastingness of the "solutions." Highly cognitive, active-directive, homework-assigning, and discipline-oriented therapies like RET are likely to be more effective, usually in briefer periods and with fewer sessions, than therapies that include less cognitive-active-disciplining methodologies.

5. Rational-emotive therapists do not believe a warm relationship between counselee and counselor is a necessary or a sufficient condition for effective personality change. They believe it is desirable for the therapist to accept clients but that the therapist may criticize and point out the deficiencies of their *behavior*. The RET therapist accepts the client as a fallible human being without necessarily giving *personal* warmth. He may use a variety of impersonal therapeutic methods, including didactic discussion, behavior modification, bibliotherapy, audiovisual aids, and activity-oriented homework assignments. To keep the client from becoming and remaining unduly dependent, the RET therapist often deliberately uses hardheaded methods of convincing clients that they had damned well better resort to more self-discipline.

6. The rational therapist uses role playing, assertion training, desensitization, humor, operant conditioning, suggestion, support, and a whole bag of other "tricks." As A. A. Lazarus (1971, 1976) points out in presenting his "broad spectrum" or "multimodal" behavior therapy, such wide-ranging methods are most effective in helping the client achieve a deep-seated cognitive change. RET is not really oriented toward symptom removal, except when it seems that this is the only kind of change likely to be accomplished with clients. It is rather primarily designed to induce people to examine and change some of their most basic values—particularly those values that keep them disturbance prone. If clients have a serious fear of failing on the job, the rational-emotive therapist does not merely help them to give up this particular symptom. Instead, the therapist usually tries to show them how generally to minimize their basic catastrophizing tendencies. The usual goal of RET, therefore, is not merely to eliminate clients' presenting symptoms but to help rid them of other symptoms as well and, more importantly, to modify their underlying symptom-creating propensities. There are really two basic forms of RET: (1) inelegant or general RET, which is almost synonymous with cognitive-behavior therapy; and (2) elegant RET, which includes general RET but which also emphasizes cognitive or philosophic restructuring and which strives for the most elegant kind of solution possible to emotional disturbance and is not content with palliative or low-level solutions (Ellis, 1977b). Inelegant RET tends to teach clients rational or appropriate behaviors. Elegant RET teaches them how to dispute irrational ideas and inap-

propriate behaviors and to internalize rules of logic and scientific method.

7. RET holds that virtually all serious emotional problems directly stem from magical, empirically unvalidatable thinking; and that if disturbance-creating ideas are vigorously disputed by logico-empirical thinking, as is done in the elegant form of RET, they can almost invariably be eliminated or minimized and will ultimately cease to reoccur. No matter how defective people's heredity may be, and no matter what trauma they may have experienced, the *main* reason they now overreact or underreact to obnoxious stimuli (at point *A*) is because they *now* have some dogmatic, irrational, unexamined beliefs (at point *B*). Because these beliefs are unrealistic, they will not withstand objective scrutiny. They are essentially deifications or devil-ifications of themselves or others; and when empirically checked and logically assailed, they tend to evaporate. Thus, a woman with severe emotional difficulties does not merely believe it is *undesirable* if her love partner is rejecting. She tends to believe, also, that (1) it is *awful;* (2) she *can not stand* it; (3) she *should not, must not* be rejected; (4) she will *never* be accepted by any desirable partner; (5) she is a *worthless person* because one lover has rejected her; and (6) she *deserves to be damned* for being so worthless. Such common covert hypotheses are nonsensical and devoid of empirical referents. They can be easily elicited and demolished by any scientist worth his or her salt; and the rational-emotive therapist is exactly that: an exposing and nonsense-annihilating scientist.

8. Rational-emotive psychology asserts that insights often do not lead to major personality change since, at best, they help people see that they do have emotional problems and that these problems have dynamic antecedents—presumably in the experiences that occurred during childhood. According to RET theory, this kind of insight is largely misleading. It is not the activating events (*A*) of people's life that "cause" dysfunctional emotional consequences (*C*); it is that they interpret these events unrealistically, and therefore have irrational beliefs (*B*) about them. The "real" cause of upsets, therefore, is themselves and not *what happens* to them (even though the experiences obviously have some influence over what they think and feel). In RET, insight no. 1—namely, that the person's self-defeating behavior is related to antecedent and understandable causes—is duly stressed; but clients are led to see these antecedents largely in terms of their own beliefs and not in terms of past or present activating events. Their therapist, moreover, also presses them to see and to employ two additional insights.

Insight no. 2 is the understanding that although they became emotionally disturbed (or, more accurately, *made* themselves disturbed) in the past, they are *now* upset because they *keep indoctrinating themselves* with the same kind of magical beliefs. These beliefs do not continue because they were once "conditioned" and so hold them "automatically." No! They still, here and now, *actively reinforce them,* by mixed-up thinking and foolish actions (or inactions); and it is their own present active self-propagandizations that truly keep them alive. Unless they fully admit and face their own responsibilities for the continuation of these irrational beliefs, it is unlikely they will uproot them.

Insight no. 3 is people's acknowledgment that since it is their own tendency to think crookedly that created emotional malfunctioning in the first place, and that since it is their own continuous reindoctrinations and habituations that keep this magical thinking extant in the second place, *only hard work and practice* will correct these irrational beliefs—and keep them corrected. They had better admit that insights nos. 1 and 2 are not enough! Only repeated rethinking of their irrational beliefs and repeated actions designed to undo them are likely to extinguish or minimize them. *Eternal* vigilance and counteractivity are the watchwords in this respect. Anything less than this may be beneficial; but it is likely to be only temporary and palliative.

Other Systems

RET, which is different from most other schools of psychotherapy, largely eschews free association, much gathering of material about the client's past history, and dream analysis, all of which are considered to be mostly sidetracking and thus ineffectual. RET is not concerned with the presumable sexual origins of disturbance, nor with the Oedipus complex. When transference does occur in therapy, the rational therapist is likely to attack it, showing clients that transference phenomena tend to arise from the irrational belief that they must be loved by the therapist (and others), and that they had better surrender this foolish belief. Although RET practitioners are much closer to modern neoanalytic schools, such as those of Karen Horney, Erich Fromm, Wilhelm Stekel, Harry Stack Sullivan, and Franz Alexander, than to the Freudian school, they employ considerably more persuasion, philosophical analysis, activity homework assignments, and other directive techniques than practitioners of these schools generally use.

RET overlaps significantly with Adlerian theory, but departs from the Adlerian practice of stressing early childhood memories, of making considerable use of dream material, of insisting that social interest is the heart of therapeutic effectiveness. RET is much more specific than Adler's individual psychology in disclosing, analyzing, and attacking the concrete internalized beliefs that clients keep telling themselves to create and perpetuate their disturbance; and so it is closer in this respect to general semantic theory and to philosophical analysis than it is to individual psychology.

Adler contends that the individual has basic fictional premises and goals and that he generally proceeds quite logically on the basis of these false hypotheses. RET, on the other hand, holds that the individual, when disturbed, may have both irrational premises and illogical deductions from these premises. Thus, in individual psychology, a male who has the unrealistic premise that he *should* be the king of the universe, but actually has only mediocre abilities, is shown that he is "logically" concluding that he is an utterly inferior person. But in RET this same individual, with the same irrational premise, is shown that in addition to this "logical" deduction he may also be making several other illogical conclusions: for example, (1) he should be king of the universe because he was once king of his own family; (2) his parents will be impressed by him only if he is outstandingly achieving and *therefore* he must achieve outstandingly; (3) if he cannot be king of the universe, he might as well do nothing and get nowhere in life; and (4) he deserves to suffer for not being the noble king that he *should be.*

RET has much in common with parts of the Jungian therapeutic outlook, especially in that it views clients holistically rather than only analytically; holds that the goal of therapy would better be growth and achievement of potential as well as relief of disturbed symptoms; and emphasizes individuality. In practice, however, RET deviates radically from Jungian treatment, because the Jungians are fairly psychoanalytic and are preoccupied with dreams, fantasies, symbol productions, and the mythological or archetypal contents of their clients' thinking—most of which the RET practitioner deems a waste of time, since these techniques are not too effective in showing clients what their basic philosophic assumptions are and how these can be radically challenged and changed when they are disturbance creating.

RET is in close agreement with person-centered or relationship therapy in one—and perhaps only one—way: They both emphasize what Stanley Standal and Carl Rogers call *unconditional positive regard* and what in rational-emotive psychology is called *full acceptance* or *tolerance.* Harry Bone (1968) points out that both RET and client-centered therapy have basically the same goal: helping people to refuse to condemn themselves even though they may be utterly unenthusiastic about some of their behavior. Rational therapists differ radically from the Rogerian therapist in that they actively *teach* (1) that blaming is the core of emotional disturbance; (2) that it leads to dreadful results; (3) that it is possible, although difficult, for humans to learn to avoid rating them*selves* even while continuing to rate their *performances;* and (4) that they can give up self-rating by challenging their magic-based (*must*urbatory), self-evaluating assumptions and by deliberating risking (through homework activity assignments) possible failures and rejections. The rational-emotive practitioner is more persuading, more didactic, and more information giving than the person-centered practitioner; and in these respects they are probably almost at opposite ends of the therapeutic continuum.

RET is in many respects an exis-tentialist- or phenomenologically-oriented therapy, since rational-emotive goals overlap with the usual existentialist goals of helping clients to define their own freedom, cultivate individuality, live in dialogue with others, accept their experiencing as highly important, be fully present in the immediacy of the moment, and learn to accept limits in life. Many who call themselves existentialist therapists, however, are rather anti-intellectual, prejudiced against the technology of therapy, and confusingly nondirective, while RET makes much use of incisive logical analysis, clear-cut techniques (including behavior modification procedures), and a great deal of directiveness and teaching by the therapist. It is therefore much closer, in practice, to active methods employed by existentialists like Viktor Frankl than to more passive methods used by existentialists like Rollo May.

RET has much in common with conditioning-learning therapy or behavior modification. Many behavior therapists, however, are mainly concerned with symptom removal and ignore the cognitive aspects of conditioning and deconditioning. RET is therefore much close to "broad-spectrum" or "multimodel" behavior modifiers—such as A. T. Beck, M. R. Goldfried and G. C. Davison (1976), A. A. Lazarus (1971, 1976), M. J. Mahoney (1974), and D. H. Meichenbaum (1977)—than to therapists who mainly stick to classical forms of operant conditioning or symptom desensitization. In many ways broadspectrum behavior therapy, multimodal therapy, and RET are synonymous.

HISTORY

Precursors

The philosophic origins of rational-emotive therapy (RET) go back to the

Stoic philosophers, particularly Epictetus and Marcus Aurelius. Although most early Stoic writings have been lost, their main gist has come down to us through Epictetus, who in the first century A.D. wrote in *The Enchiridion:* "Men are disturbed not by things, but by the view which they take of them." His disciple, the Roman Emperor Marcus Aurelius, notably publicized Stoicism in his famous *Meditations;* and various other philosophers, such as Spinoza and Bertrand Russell, brought its principles to the attention of the modern Western world. Shakespeare beautifully rephrased Epictetus in *Hamlet;* "There's nothing either good or bad but thinking makes it so." Several ancient Taoist and Buddhist thinkers also emphasized two main points: Human emotions are basically ideogenic in their origin; and to control or change even one's most intense feelings, one mainly would better change one's ideas. Sigmund Freud, in his first work with Josef Breuer (Freud, 1965) noted that "a great number of hysterical phenomena, probably more than we suspect today, are ideogenic." Unfortunately, in his later works he often talked about emotional processes vaguely and implied that they exist in their own right, quite divorced from thinking.

The modern psychotherapist who was the main precursor of RET was Alfred Adler. "I am convinced," he stated, "that *a person's behavior springs from his ideas*" (Adler, 1964a. Italics in original). And: "The individual . . . does not relate himself to the outside world in a predetermined manner, as is often assumed. He relates himself always according to his own interpretation of himself and of his present problem. . . . It is his attitude toward life which determines his relationship to the outside world" (Adler, 1964b). Adler (1931) put the A-B-C or S-O-R theory of human disturbance very

neatly: "No experience is a cause of success or failure. We do not suffer from the shock of our experiences—the so-called *trauma*—but we make out of them just what suits our purposes. We are *self-determined* by the meaning we give to our experiences; and there is probably something of a mistake always involved when we take particular experiences as the basis of our future life. Meanings are not determined by situations, but we determine ourselves by the meanings we give to situations." In his first book on individual psychology, Adler's motto was *omnia ex opionione suspensa sunt* (Everything depends on opinion). It would be hard to state the essential tenets of RET more succinctly and accurately.

Other important precursors of the rational-emotive approach are Paul Dubois, Jules Dejerine, and Ernest Gaukler who used persuasive forms of psychotherapy with their clients. Alexander Herzberg was one of the inventors of homework assignments. Hippolyte Bernheim, Andrew Salter, and a host of other therapists have employed hypnosis and suggestion in a highly active-directive manner. Frederick Thorne created what he once called directive therapy. Franz Alexander, Thomas French, John Dollard, Neal Miller, Wilhelm Stekel, and Lewis Wolberg all practiced forms of psychoanalytically oriented psychotherapy that actually diverged so far in practice from the mainstays of Freudian theory that they more properly can be classified in the active-directive therapy column and can in many ways be identified with RET.

In addition, a large number of individuals during the early 1950s, when RET was first being formulated, independently began to arrive at some theories and methodologies that significantly overlap with the methods subsequently outlined by Ellis (1957, 1962, 1971a). These include Eric Berne, Rogelio Diaz-Guerrera, Jerome Frank, George Kelly, Abraham Low, E. Lakin Phillips, Julian Rotter, and Joseph Wolpe.

Beginnings

After practicing classical psychoanalysis and psychoanalytically oriented psychotherapy for several years, during the late 1940s and early 1950s, Ellis discovered that no matter how much insight his clients gained, or how well they seemed to understand the events of their early childhood and to be able to connect them with their present emotional disturbances, they rarely lost their presenting symptoms, and when they did, they still retained strong tendencies to create new ones. He eventually realized this was because they were not merely indoctrinated with irrational, mistaken ideas of their own worthlessness when they were very young (as virtually all the psychoanalytic theories of personality hold), but that they actively *reindoctrinated themselves* with the original taboos, superstitions, and irrationalities they had picked up (and *invented* as well as easily learned) during their childhood.

Ellis also discovered that as he pressed his clients to surrender the few basic irrational premises that invariably seemed to underlie their disturbed symptoms, they often tended to resist giving up these ideas. This was not, as the Freudians hypothesized, because they hated the therapist, or wanted to destroy themselves, or were still resisting parent images, but because they *naturally,* one might say *normally,* tended to *must*urbate: to absolutistically demand (1) that they do well and win others' approval; (2) that people act considerately and fairly, and (3) that environmental conditions be unfrustrating and gratifying. Ellis concluded that humans are *self-talking* and

self-evaluating and *self-sustaining.* They frequently take simple preferences—such as desires for love, approval, success, and pleasure—and misleadingly define them as needs. They thereby inevitably get into difficulties usually labeled neurotic, psychopathic, or psychotic.

Ellis thus found that people are not exclusively the products of social learning but rather that their so-called pathological symptoms are the result of *bio*social learning. *Because they are human* (and not because they are reared in specific family-centered ways), they tend to have strong, irrational, empirically unvalidatable ideas; and as long as they hold on to these ideas—which nearly all of them fairly consistently do—they will tend to be what is commonly called "neurotic," "disturbed," or "mentally ill." These main irrational ideologies are not infinitely varied or hard to discover. They can be listed under a few simple headings; and once understood, they can be quickly uncovered by the rational-emotive way of classifying them.

Ellis also discovered these irrational assumptions were not effectively unblocked by most current psychotherapeutic techniques because they were so biosocially deep-rooted and so difficult for the average individual to surrender, that weak methods were unlikely to budge them. Passive, nondirective methodologies (such as reflection of feeling and free association) rarely changed them. Warmth and support often helped clients live more "happily" with unrealistic notions. Suggestion or "positive thinking" sometimes enabled them to cover up and live more "successfully" with underlying negative self-evaluations but seldom helped them get rid of these silly notions. Abreaction and catharsis frequently helped them to feel better but tended to reinforce rather than to eliminate these demands. Classic desensitizing sometimes relieved clients of anxieties and phobias but did not elegantly undermine their anxiety-arousing, phobia-creating fundamental philosophies.

What would work effectively, Ellis found in the early days of RET, to help rid a client of irrationalities was an active-directive, cognitive-emotive-behavioristic attack on major self-defeating value systems—not directed against clients but against their *unrealistic beliefs*. The essence of effective psychotherapy according to RET is full tolerance of people *as individuals* combined with a ruthless campaign against their self-defeating *ideas, traits,* and *performances*. Paraphrasing Clarence Darrow, "We respect the individual, but not his ideas."

As Ellis abandoned his previous psychoanalytic approaches, to become much more philosophical rather than psychological in his discussions of his clients' problems, and to push his clients to work actively against their major irrational premises, he found he obtained significantly better results (Ellis, 1962). Other therapists (e.g., Gullo, 1966) who began to employ RET in their own practice also found that when a difficult client, with whom various methods had been ineffectively employed, switched to rational-emotive procedures, more progress was made in a few weeks than in months or even years of the prior treatment. When RET methods were used with new clients, they frequently became significantly improved after as few as 3 to 10 sessions, even though they might have had serious disturbances of long-standing duration (Ellis & Gullo, 1972).

Current Status

The Institute for Rational Living, Inc., a nonprofit scientific and educational organization, was founded in 1959 to teach the principles of rational living. In 1968 The Institute for Rational-Emotive Therapy, a training organization chartered by the Regents of the University of the State of New York, was founded. These two institutes, with headquarters in New York City and branches in several cities in the United States and other countries, conduct activities to disseminate the rational-emotive approach, including (1) adult education courses for adults in the principles of rational living; (2) postgraduate training programs; (3) moderate cost clinics for individual or group therapy; (4) special workshops, seminars, practica, and training marathons for professionals given regularly in various parts of the world, often in conjunction with scientific meetings; and (5) the publication of books, monographs, pamphlets, and a journal, *Rational Living,* in which the latest developments in the field of cognitive-emotive therapy are published.

The Institute for Rational-Emotive Therapy, 45 East 65th Street, New York, N.Y. 10021, has a register of hundreds of psychotherapists who have received training in RET. In addition, hundreds of other therapists mainly follow RET principles, and a still greater number use some of the major aspects of RET in their work. Cognitive restructuring, employed by almost all cognitive-behavior therapists today, mainly consists of RET.

Research Studies. Many articles and books give evidence of the effectiveness of RET and related cognitive-behavior therapies with all kinds of neurotic, borderline, and psychotic individuals. Hundreds of these reports are listed in *A Comprehensive Bibliography of Materials on Rational-Emotive Therapy and Cognitive-Behavior Therapy* (Murphy and Ellis, 1979). Scores of comparative outcome studies, showing that RET seems to help various kinds of clients improve significantly more than other kinds of therapies or no-therapy control groups, have been published. Related studies also show that rationality scales derived from Ellis's (1962) 12 basic irrational ideas have acceptable validity and reliability. Outcome and rationality scale studies have been summarized and reviewed by Raymond DiGiuseppe, Norman Miller, and Larry Trexler (1977) and Ronald Murphy and Ellis (1977).

Many experiments have validated the main therapeutic hypotheses of RET. Ellis (1977b) found the vast majority of these studies support important RET contentions, for example, (1) clients tend to receive more effective help from a highly active-directive than from a more passive psychotherapeutic approach. (2) Effective therapy importantly includes the therapist's strong challenge to clients' irrational philosophies and his persuading them to adopt less self-defeating beliefs. (3) Efficient therapy includes activity-oriented homework assignments. (4) Abreaction and catharsis of dysfunctional emotions like anger may have temporary palliative effects but often prove iatrogenic in that they tend to reinforce the beliefs that people use to create these feelings; the rational disputing of these philosophies gives better and more lasting effects. (5) People largely choose to disturb themselves and can intentionally choose to surrender these disturbances. (6) Self-control has very strong cognitive, as well as behavioral, elements and effective therapy often consists of helping clients use cognitive-related self-management principles. (7) Helping clients believe they can cope with conditions of distress and stress constitute effective methods of psychotherapy. (8) A great deal of psychotherapy consists of cognitive diversion or distraction, which can be used for significant, if often inelegant, personality change. (10) Helping clients modify their beliefs helps them to make significant

changes, which are more enduring than those achieved through other methods of therapy. (11) Effective psychotherapy provides clients, in a variety of ways, with information that can help them understand how they have disturbed themselves and what they can do to make themselves less disturbed. (12) Many effective methods of cognitive therapy exist, including modeling, role playing, skill training, and problem solving.

In addition, hundreds of clinical and research papers have appeared that present empirical evidence of the validity of RET's main theories of personality. Most of the experimental studies in this area have been done by psychologists who have no stake in substantiating RET. Many of these studies are reviewed and listed by Ellis (1977b) and Murphy and Ellis (1979). These research studies substantiate the following hypotheses: (1) Human thinking and emotion do not constitute two disparate or different processes, but significantly overlap. (2) Although activating events (*A*) significantly contribute to emotional and behavioral consequences (*C*), people's beliefs (*B*) about *A* more importantly and more directly "cause" *C*. (3) The kinds of things people say to themselves, as well as the form in which they say these things, significantly affect their emotions and behavior and often lead them to feel emotionally disturbed. (4) Humans not only think and think about their thinking but also think about thinking about their thinking. Whenever they have strong feelings at *C* (consequence) after something has happened in their lives at *A* (activating events), they tend to make *C* into a new *A*—to perceive and think about their emotions (and emotional disturbances), and thereby significantly escalate, diminish, or otherwise modify these emotions and create new ones. (5) People not only think about what happens to them in words, phrases, and sentences but also do so by images, fantasies, dreams, and other kinds of pictorial representations. These nonverbal cognitions contribute significantly to their emotions and behaviors and can be used to change such behaviors. (6) Just as cognitions importantly contribute to emotions and actions, emotions also significantly contribute to or "cause" cognitions and actions; and actions contribute to or "cause" cognitions and emotions. When people change one of these three modalities of behaving they concomitantly tend to change the other two. (7) By focusing on, and cognizing about their physiological somatic processes, people can often change these dramatically. (8) Humans have strong innate as well as acquired tendencies to think, emote, and behave in certain ways, although virtually none of their behavior stems solely from instinct and practically all of it has powerful environmental and learning factors that contribute to its "causation." (9) When people expect that something will happen or expect that others will act in a certain way, they act significantly differently than when they have other kinds of expectancies. (10) When people view situations, others' reactions, and their own behavior as within their control they act significantly differently than when they view them as stemming from external sources. (11) Humans attribute motives, reasons, and causes to other people and to external events and to internal physical states; and they significantly influence their own emotions and behaviors by these attributions, even when based on false or misleading perceptions and conceptions.

Several important RET theories have not yet been adequately investigated. These include: (1) self-acceptance (not rating your "self" or "essence" but only rating your deeds and traits) leads to less emotional disturbance than self-esteem (rating yourself as "good" or "worthwhile"). (2) Giving a client RET with a good deal of warmth, approval and reassurance will tend to help this client "feel better" rather than "get better." (3) People are not so much afraid of "failure" or "rejection" as afraid of their own whining about and refusal to accept "failure" and "rejection." (4) Almost all humans with disturbed symptoms have abysmally low frustration tolerance about these symptoms; and their secondary neurotic reactions often prove much worse than their primary ones. (5) Cognitive restructuring (changing *must*urbation to desiring) is really the most important and unacknowledged element in other forms of therapy, such as psychoanalytic, abreactive, or behavioral therapy. (6) Teaching clients how to actively dispute their irrational beliefs is more effective than merely teaching them to change self-defeating to self-helping statements. (7) Various "good" or "joyful" emotions, such as pride and anger, often encourage more disturbance than health. (8) Self-penalization without self-damnation frequently is a more effective means of effecting behavior change than self-reinforcement or reward. (9) Teaching people to accept themselves with their failures rather than to avoid failing is a more elegant and enduring method of therapy than teaching them how to succeed. (10) Semantic reeducation can be an effective method of psychotherapy. (11) Teaching the logico-empirical method of science as applied to everyday problems can constitute effective therapy.

PERSONALITY

Theory of Personality

Physiological Basis of Personality. Unlike most modern systems of psychotherapy, RET emphasizes the biological

aspects of human personality. Obliquely, most other systems do this, too, since they say, at bottom, something like this: "Humans are easily influenced by their parents during early childhood and thereafter remain similarly influenced for the rest of their lives, unless some intervention, such as years of psychotherapy, occurs to enable them to give up this early ingrained influenceability and to start thinking much more independently." If what these psychotherapeutic systems implicitly contend is actually true, they have stated an "environmentalist's" position, which is really highly physiologically and genetically based, since only a *special, innately predisposed* kind of animal would be so prone to be "environmentally determined."

Rational-emotive psychology specifically acknowledges that humans are often "naturally" inclined to do *x* rather than *y,* that the family and cultural group in which they are reared unwittingly or wittingly goes along with this "natural" disposition, and that only with enormous countereffort does the individual or the culture radically change. Because, moreover, such change requires an almost incredible amount of effort, it is usually not accomplished or it is achieved through unplanned, "artificial" developments, such as technological "advances" (e.g., the Industrial Revolution).

Although RET holds that people have vast untapped resources for growth and that in many important ways are able to change their social and personal destiny, it also holds that they have exceptionally powerful innate tendencies to think irrationally and to harm themselves (Ellis, 1976). Among their biological tendencies to be self-defeating are powerful proclivities (1) to be overwhelmed, frequently, by the great difficulty of changing thinking and acting from channel A to channel B, even when the first channel brings much more unpleasant results than the second; (2) to desire greatly many patently harmful goals and things and to convince themselves that they *need,* or *must have,* what they merely *want* or *prefer;* (3) to find it most difficult to unlearn even the most inefficient habits; (4) to remain attached to many prejudices and myths learned during childhood; (5) to be overvigilant and overcautious on innumerable occasions when they could just be sanely watchful; (6) to be sorely afflicted with the "need" to prove they are superior to other humans, and that they are in some significant ways omnipotent; (7) to easily jump, when one of their views proves to be ill-founded, to an extremely opposite view that is equally foolish; (8) to resort frequently to automaticity and silly routines, when their better interests would clearly be served by conscious thinking and rethinking; (9) to keep forgetting that something is noxious, even when they have considerable evidence of its harmfulness; (10) to engage in enormous amounts of wishful thinking; (11) to find it "too hard" to sustain valuable efforts and self-disciplines and, instead, to be continually "lazy" and procrastinating; (12) to *demand* rather than to *want* others to treat them justly, and to dwell interminably on the fact that people often don't; (13) to condemn themselves instead of only assessing their poor behavior; (14) to overgeneralize about events that have occurred in the past or may occur in the future; (15) to easily become physically or psychosomatically affected when they make themselves emotionally upset.

Most of these tendencies of humans may be summarized by stating that humans are born with an exceptionally strong tendency to want and to insist that everything happens for the best in their life and to roundly condemn (1) themselves, (2) others, and (3) the world when they do not immediately get what they want. They consequently think "child-ishly" (or "humanly") all their lives and only with enormous difficulty are able to achieve and maintain "ma-ture" or realistic behavior. This is not to deny, as Abraham Maslow, Carl Rog-ers, and many leaders have pointed out, that humans have impressive self-actualizing capacities. They have; and these are strong inborn propensities, too. But, alas, they are frequently sabotaged by their inborn and acquired self-sabo-taging ways.

Social Aspects of Personality. Humans are reared in social groups and spend much of their lives trying to im-press, to live up to the expectations of, and to outdo the performances of other people. On the surface, they are "ego ori-ented," "identity seeking," or "self-centered." Even more importantly, how-ever, they usually define their "selves" as "good" or "worthwhile" when they are successfully other-directed—that is, when they believe that others accept and ap-prove of them. It is realistic and sane for people to find or fulfill "themselves" in their interpersonal relations and to have a considerable amount of what Adler calls "social interest." For, as John Donne beautifully expressed it, practically no one is an island unto himself. The healthy in-dividual *does* find it enjoyable to love and be loved by significant others and to relate reasonably well to almost everyone he or she encounters. In fact, the better one's interpersonal relations are, the happier one is likely to be.

However, what we call *emotional dis-turbance* is frequently associated with people's caring too much about what others think and stems from their be-lieving they can accept themselves only if others think well of them. When dis-turbed, they escalate their desire for others' approval, and the practical ad-

vantages that normally go with such approval, into an absolutistic, dire need to be liked; and, doing this, they can hardly avoid becoming anxious and prone to depression. Since we have our being-in-the-world, as the existentialists point out, it is quite *important* that others to some degree value us. But it is not *all*-important that they regard us very highly; and it is our tendency to exaggerate the impor-tance of others' acceptance that mainly causes our inappropriate emotions.

Emotional maturity, in other words, is a fine *balance* between caring and over-caring. If we care too much or too little about human relationships, we will tend to sabotage our own best interests (and often, as well, act antisocially). If we accept the pretty obvious reality that it is desirable, but not necessary, for us to get along fairly well with others, we will tend to be emotionally healthy.

Psychological Aspects of Personality. How, specifically, do people become psy-chologically disordered? According to RET, they usually needlessly upset them-selves as follows:

Humans have few or no *instincts,* in the classic use of this term, but have "instinc-toid" tendencies, as Abraham Maslow pointed out. They *easily* want to be loved rather than hated, to be cared for rather than neglected, and to have their desires catered to rather than frustrated. They have pronounced *individual* tastes in these respects—that is, strong or weak tenden-cies to like sugar, sports, music, or people —but they also have many common hu-man propensities. As far as disturbance-creating inclinations are concerned, they tend to be remarkably similar to practic-ally all other people.

When individuals feel upset at point *C,* after experiencing an obnoxious occur-rence at point *A,* they almost always con-vince themselves of highly inappropriate, irrational beliefs (*iB*'s) like: "I *can't stand* this Activating Event! *It is awful* that it exists! It *shouldn't* exist! I am a *worthless person* for not being able to ward it off or immediately get rid of it. And you are a louse for inflicting it on me!" This set of beliefs is irrational because (1) people *can* stand the noxious activating event, even though they may never like it. (2) It is hardly *awful,* since *awful* is an essentially undefinable term, with surplus meaning and no empirical referent. By calling the noxious activating event *awful,* the disturbed individual means (a) it is highly inconvenient; and (b) it is *more than* inconvenient, disadvantageous, and unbeneficial. But what noxious stimulus can be, in point of fact, *more than* inconvenient, disadvantageous, and unbeneficial? (3) By holding that the noxious happening in their lives *should not* exist, people really contend that they have Godly power; and that whatever they *want* not to exist *should* not. This hypothesis is, to say the least, highly unprovable! (4) By contending that they are *worthless persons* because they have not been able to ward off an unfortunate activating event, people hold that they should be able to control the universe, and that because they are not succeeding in doing what they cannot do, they are obviously worthless. They thereby posit *two* unvalidatable premises.

The basic tenet of RET is that emotional *upsets,* as distinguished from feelings of sorrow, regret, annoyance, and frustrations, are caused by irrational beliefs. These beliefs are irrational because they magically insist that something in the universe *should, ought,* or *must* be different from the way it indubitably is. Although, then, these irrational beliefs are ostensibly connected with reality (the activating events at point *A*), they are magical ideas beyond the realm of empiricism and are established by arbitrary fiat. They generally take the form of the statement, "Because I *want* something it is not only desirable or preferable that it exist, but it absolutely *should,* and it is *awful* when it really doesn't!" No such proposition, obviously, can ever be validated; and yet, oddly enough, such propositions are devoutly held, every day, by literally billions of human beings. That is how incredibly disturbance prone people are!

Once people become emotionally upset —or, rather, upset themselves!—another peculiar thing frequently occurs. Most of the time, they know they are anxious, depressed, or otherwise agitated, and also generally know that their symptoms are undesirable and (in our culture) socially disapproved. For who approves or respects highly agitated or "crazy" people? They therefore make their emotional consequence (*C*) or symptom into another activating event (*A²*) and create a secondary symptom (*C²*) about this new *A!*

Thus, if you originally start with something like "(*A*) I did poorly on my job today; (*B*) Isn't that horrible!" you will wind up with (*C*) feelings of anxiety, worthlessness, and depression. You may now start all over: (*A²*): "I feel anxious and depressed, and worthless!" (*B²*): "Isn't *that* horrible!" Now you end up with (*C²*): even greater feelings of anxiety, worthlessness, and depression. In other words, once you become anxious, you frequently make yourself anxious about *being* anxious; once you become depressed, you make yourself depressed about being depressed; and so on. You now have two consequences or symptoms for the price of one; and you often go around and around, in a vicious cycle of (1) condemning yourself for doing poorly at some task; (2) feeling guilty or depressed because of this self-condemnation; (3) condemning yourself for your feelings of guilt and depression; (4) condemning yourself for condemning yourself; (5) condemning yourself for seeing that you condemn yourself and for still not stopping condemning yourself; (6) condemning yourself for going for psychotherapeutic help and still not getting better; (7) condemning yourself for being more disturbed than other individuals; (8) concluding that you are indubitably hopelessly disturbed and that nothing can be done about it; and so on, in an endless spiral.

No matter what your original damning is about—and it hardly matters what it is about, since the activating event (A) is not really that important—you eventually tend to end up with a chain of disturbed reactions only obliquely related to the original "traumatic events" of your life. That is why the psychoanalytic psychotherapies are quite misleading—they wrongly emphasize these "traumatic events" of your life, rather than your self-condemnatory attitudes *about* these events—and that is why these therapies are virtually powerless to help you with any secondary disturbance, such as anxiety about being anxious. Most major psychotherapies also concentrate either on *A,* the activating events in the individual's life, or on *C,* the emotional consequences experienced subsequent to the occurrence of these events. But this is precisely what people wrongheadedly overfocus on, *A* and/or *C,* and rarely deeply consider *B,* the belief system, which is the vital factor in the creation of disturbance.

Even assuming, moreover, that the activating events in people's lives and the emotional consequences are important, there is not too much we can do by concentrating our therapeutic attention on these two things. The activating events belong to the past by the time we see the clients. Sometimes it was many years ago that they were criticized by their parents,

rejected by their mates, or lost a series of jobs. There is nothing that anyone can do to *change* those prior happenings.

As for clients' present feelings, the more we focus on them, the worse they are likely to feel. If we keep talking about their anxiety, getting them to reexperience this feeling, they can easily become more anxious. The most logical point to interrupt their disturbed process is to get them to focus on their anxiety-creating belief system—point *B.*

If, for example, a male client feels anxious during a therapy session and the therapist reassures him that there is nothing for him to be anxious about, he may become more anxious or may achieve a palliative "solution" to his problem by convincing himself, "I am afraid that I will act foolishly right here and now, and wouldn't that be awful! No, it really wouldn't be awful, because *this* therapist will accept me, anyway."

Or the therapist can concentrate on the activating events in the client's life, which are presumably making him anxious—by, for instance, showing him that his mother used to point out his deficiencies in making an impression on others; that he was always afraid his teachers would criticize him for reciting poorly; that he is still afraid of speaking to authority figures who might disapprove of him; and that, *therefore,* because of all his prior and present fears, in situations A^1, A^2, A^3 ... A^n, he is *now* anxious with the therapist. Whereupon the client might convince himself, "Ah! Now I see that I am generally anxious when I am faced with authority figures. No wonder I am anxious even with my own therapist!" In which case, he might feel much better and temporarily lose his anxiety.

It would be much better for the therapist to show this client that he was anxious as a child and is still anxious with various kinds of authority figures not because they are authorities or do have some power over him, but because he has always believed, and still believes, that he *must* be approved, that it is *awful* when an authority figure disapproves of him, and that he will be destroyed if he is criticized.

Whereupon the anxious client would tend to do two things: (1) He would become diverted from *A* (criticism by an authority figure) and from *C* (his feelings of anxiety) to a consideration of *B* (his irrational belief system). This diversion would help him become immediately nonanxious—for when he is focusing on "What am I telling myself (at *B*) to *make* myself anxious" he cannot too easily focus upon the self-defeating, useless thought, "Wouldn't it be terrible if I said something stupid to my therapist and if even he disapproved of me!" (2) He would begin actively to dispute (at point *D*) his anxiety-creating irrational beliefs; and not only could he then temporarily change them (by convincing himself, "It would be *unfortunate* if I said something stupid to my therapist and he disapproved of me; but it would hardly be *terrible* or *catastrophic*!"), but he would also tend to have a much weaker allegiance to these self-defeating beliefs the next time he was with an authority figure and risked criticism by this individual. So he would obtain, by the therapist's getting him to focus primarily on *B* rather than on *A* and *C,* curative and preventive, rather than palliative, results in connection with his anxiety.

This is the basic personality theory of RET: Human beings largely (although not entirely) create their own emotional consequences; they are born with a distinct proneness to do so and learn, through social conditioning, to exacerbate (rather than to minimize) that proneness; they

nonetheless have considerable ability to understand what they are foolishly believing to cause their upsetness (because they have a unique talent for thinking about their thinking) and to train themselves to change or eliminate their self-sabotaging beliefs (because they also have a unique capacity for self-discipline or self-reconditioning). If they *think* and *work* hard at understanding and contradicting their magical belief systems, they can make amazing palliative, curative, and preventive changes in their disturbance-creating tendencies; and if they are helped to zero in on their crooked thinking and inappropriate emoting and behaving by a highly active-directive, didactic, philosophic, homework-assigning therapist (who may or may not have a warm, personal relationship with them), they are much more likely to change their symptom-creating beliefs than if they mainly work with a dynamically oriented, client-centered, conventional existentialist, or classical behavior-modification-centered therapist.

Although RET is mainly a theory of personality change, it is also a personality theory in its own right (Ellis 1974, 1977c, 1978). Many of its hypotheses have been validated by scores of controlled experiments, as indicated in the *research studies* section of this chapter.

Variety of Concepts

RET largely tends to agree with the views of Sigmund Freud and Adolf Meyer that there are important biological aspects to personality disturbance; with Freud, that the pleasure principle (or short-range hedonism) tends to run most people's lives; with Karen Horney and Erich Fromm, that cultural influences as well as early family influences tend to play a significant part in bolstering people's irrational thinking; with Alfred Adler, that fictive goals tend to order and to run human lives; with Knight Dunlap and Gordon Allport, that once individuals begin to think and act in a certain manner, habituation or functional autonomy tends to take over, so they find it very difficult to think or act differently even when they want strongly to do so; with Ivan Pavlov, that although lower animals are responsively or reflexly conditioned in accordance with their primary signaling system, humans' much larger cerebral cortex provides them with a secondary signaling system through which they usually become cognitively conditioned; with Hippolyte Bernheim and Jerome Frank, that people are exceptionally prone to the influence of suggestion; with Jean Piaget, that active teaching is much more effective than passive learning; with Freud and his daughter Anna, that instead of actively and honestly condemning themselves for errors, people frequently refuse to acknowledge their mistakes and resort to all kinds of defenses and rationalizations that cover up underlying feelings of shame and self-deprecation; and with Abraham Maslow and Carl Rogers, that human beings, however disturbed they may be, have great untapped growth forces.

On the other hand, RET has serious objections to certain aspects of many popular personality theories:

1. It opposes the Freudian concept that people have clear-cut libidinous instincts, which if thwarted must lead to emotional disturbances. It also objects to the views of William Glasser and a whole host of psychological and social thinkers, who insist that all humans have needs to be approved and to succeed—and that if these are blocked, they cannot possibly accept themselves or be happy. RET, in-

stead, thinks in terms of human desires and tendencies, which only become needs when people foolishly *define* them as such.

2. RET places the Oedipus complex as a relatively minor subheading under people's major irrational belief that they absolutely have to receive the approval of their parents (and others), that they *must not* fail (at lusting or almost anything else), and that when they are disapproved and when they fail, they are totally worthless. Virtually all so-called sexual problems—such as impotence, frigidity, compulsive homosexuality, and nymphomania—are seen as resultants of people's irrational beliefs that they *utterly need* approval and success.

3. RET holds that humans' environment, particularly childhood parental environment, *reaffirms* but does not *create* strong tendencies to think irrationally and to over- or underemote. Parents and culture usually teach children *which* superstitions, taboos, and prejudices to abide by; but they do not originate their basic tendency to superstitiousness, ritualism, and bigotry.

4. RET looks skeptically at anything mystical, religious, transpersonal, or magical, when these terms are used in the strict sense. It believes that reason itself is limited, ungodlike, and unabsolute (Ellis, 1968). It holds that humans may in some ways transcend themselves or experience altered states of consciousness—for example, hypnosis—that may enhance their ability to know themselves and the world and to solve some of their problems. But it does not believe that people can transcend their humanness and become in any way more than or greater than human— that is, superhuman. They can become more adept, competent, intelligent; but they still remain *fallible* and in no way

godly. RET especially holds that minimal disturbance is correlated with the individual's surrendering all pretensions to superhumanness and with fully accepting his and the world's intrinsic limitations.

5. RET believes that no part of the human being can be reified into an entity called the unconscious, although it holds that people have many thoughts, feelings, and even acts of which they are dimly or almost completely unaware. These "unconscious" thoughts and feelings are, for the most part, slightly below the level of consciousness, are not often deeply repressed, and can usually be brought to consciousness by some brief, incisive probing. Thus, if a wife is more angry at her husband than she is aware of, and if her anger is motivated by the unconscious grandiose thought, "After all I've done for him, he *should be* having sex with me more frequently!" a rational-emotive therapist (who is aware of these unconscious feelings and thoughts of the client because RET theory indicates, when the client gives him certain evidence, that they probably exist) can usually induce her to (1) *hypothesize* that she is angry with her husband and look for some evidence with which to test that hypothesis and (2) *check* herself for grandiose thinking whenever she feels angry. In the majority of instances, without resorting to free association, dream analysis, analyzing the transference relationship, hypnosis, or other presumably "depth-centered" techniques for revealing unconscious processes, the rational-emotive practitioner can reveal these processes in short order—sometimes in a matter of minutes. He continually shows the client her unconsciously held or unawarely subscribed to attitudes, beliefs, and values and, in addition, teaches the client methods of bringing these somewhat hidden ideas to consciousness quite

rapidly and of actively disputing them, when they are inimical to her appropriately emoting and behaving, until she minimizes or eliminates them.

People often see how RET differs significantly from psychoanalysis, Rogerianism, Gestalt therapy, and orthodox behavior therapy but have difficulty seeing how it differs from more closely related schools, such as Adler's individual psychology and Glasser's reality therapy. RET agrees with almost all of Adlerian theory but has a much more hardheaded and behavior-oriented practice (Ellis, 1973b). Reality therapy appears to be similar to RET (which antedated it by almost 10 years) and, like RET, emphasizes that humans are responsible for their own feelings and actions; that they'd better not be condemned for their foolish behavior; that they have inherent tendencies toward growth and change; that they easily make themselves into short-range hedonists and had better, instead, adopt longer range hedonism; and that the psychotherapeutic process had best stick with the here-and-now instead of the past, include skill training and problem solving, show the clients alternate ways of helping themselves, be active-directive, confront and pin down elusive and resistant clients, waste virtually no time with dream analysis, and employ a good deal of humor (Ellis, 1977d, 1977f).

RET, however, has several important theoretical differences with reality therapy: (1) It does not believe that humans have a strong love *need* but only a powerful *desire,* which they self-defeatingly define as a "need" or "necessity." (2) It also holds that people *had better* accomplish things but not that they *have to;* and that they can truly accept themselves whether or not they receive recognition or success. (3) Reality therapy insists that humans have a need for an individual identity interrelated with their social identity. RET, again, sees this "need" as a strong desire and emphasizes the desirability of being oneself over the desirability of gaining "identity" or "ego" from one's social group. (4) Reality therapy stresses the immorality or irresponsibility of certain behaviors and implies that one *is* an irresponsible or bad *person* if one continues to behave immorally. RET shows people how their *acts* may be quite irresponsible but how *they* are never condemnable—no matter what! (5) Reality therapy emphasizes schools without failure and thinks children will grow up to hate themselves unless the system is arranged so they practically never fail. RET teaches children (and adults) that they can fail and fail and fail—and still accept themselves with their failures. (6) Reality therapy encourages therapists to show clients that they really care and believes this kind of therapist is necessary for client change. RET gives therapists leeway to give caring and warmth to clients if they wish to do so, but also holds that highly effective therapy can be done without such warmth, as long as therapists fully accept (but not necessarily like) their clients. In several important respects, reality therapy seems to be a more indulgent, less hardheaded, less elegant form of RET; and it largely omits the rigorous logico-empirical disputing aspects found in RET.

PSYCHOTHERAPY

Theory of Psychotherapy

According to the theory of RET, emotional disturbance occurs when individuals *demand, insist,* and *dictate,* that they must have their wishes satisfied. Thus, they *demand* that they succeed and be ap-

proved; they *insist* that others treat them fairly; and they *dictate* that the universe be more pleasant. If people's demandingness (and not their desirousness) gets them into emotional trouble, they can alleviate their pain in several inelegant and elegant ways.

Diversion. Just as a whining child can be temporarily diverted by giving him a piece of candy, so can adult demanders be transitorily sidetracked by diversion. Thus, a therapist who sees a man who is afraid of being rejected (that is, *demands* that significant others accept him) can try to arrange things so he is diverted into activities such as sports, aesthetic creation, a political cause, yoga exercises, meditation, therapizing his friends, preoccupation with the events of his childhood, and so on. While the individual is so diverted, he will hardly have the time, or inclination, to demand acceptance by others and to make himself anxious. Diversion techniques are mainly palliative, since the individual still is underlyingly a demander and as soon as he is not diverted he will probably return to his childish dictating all over again.

Satisfying Demands. If a woman's insistences are always catered to, she will tend to feel better (but not necessarily get better). To arrange this kind of "solution," a therapist can give her love and approval, provide her with pleasurable sensations (for example, put her in an encounter group where she is hugged or massaged), teach her methods of succeeding in getting her demands, or give her reassurance that she eventually, and preferably soon, will be gratified. Lots of clients will feel immensely better when given this kind of treatment; but most of them will probably have their demandingness reinforced rather than minimized by such procedures.

Magic. A boy who demands frequently

can be assuaged by magic: by, for example, his parents saying that a fairy godmother will soon satisfy these demands. Similarly, adolescent and adult demanders can be led to believe (by a therapist or someone else) that God will help them; that if they suffer enough on this earth they will indubitably go to heaven and have all their demands satisfied there; that even though they are deprived in one way (say, by being rejected), they are really a *better person* than their rejector and that therefore they can tolerate rejection; that their therapist is a kind of magician who will take away their troubles merely by their telling him or her what bothers them; that they are members of a superior group (such as the Aryan race) and that consequently they will ultimately triumph; that they are really outstanding and that everyone will finally recognize their true being and bow down to them; and so forth. These magical solutions sometimes work beautifully by getting the true believer to feel better and to give up disturbed symptoms; but they rarely work for any length of time and they frequently lead to eventual disillusionment (and sometimes suicide).

Giving up Demandingness. The most elegant solution to the problems that result from irrational demandingness is to induce the individual to become less commanding, godlike, or dictatorial. Normal children in maturing become less childish, less insistent that they must have their desires immediately gratified. This is what the rational psychotherapist tries to induce his clients to acquire: minimal demandingness and maximum tolerance. RET practitioners may, at times, use temporary therapeutic "solutions," such as diversion, satisfying the client's "needs," and even (on very rare occasions) magic. But if they do they realize that these are low-level, inelegant, palliative solutions,

mainly to be used with clients with whom there is little or no chance that they will accept a more elegant and permanent resolution of their basic demandingness. Preferably, the rational-emotive therapist strives for the highest order solution: radical minimization of *mus*turbation, perfectionism, grandiosity, and intolerance. This kind of radical solution was also attempted by religious leaders such as Buddha, Jesus, and St. Francis of Assisi; but invariably, because they refused to stay with logico-empiric methods, they strayed into irrational pathways.

In RET, the attempt to help clients minimize their dictatorial, dogmatic, absolutistic core philosophy is attempted in three main therapeutic ways: cognitive, emotive, and behavioristic.

1. *Cognitive therapy* attempts to show clients that they had better give up perfectionism if they want to lead a happier, less anxiety-ridden existence. It teaches them how to recognize their *shoulds, oughts,* and *musts;* how to separate rational (nonabsolutistic) from irrational (absolutistic) beliefs; how to use the logico-empirical method of science in relation to themselves and their own problems; and how to accept reality, even when it is pretty grim. It assumes that clients can think, can think about their thinking, and can even think about thinking about their thinking; and it consequently helps them to hone and sharpen their cognitive processes. Information-giving, explicatory, and didactic, RET is oriented toward helping people with emotional disturbances philosophize more effectively and thereby uncreate these disturbances. It not only employs a one-to-one Socratic-type dialogue between the client and the therapist; but it also, in group therapy, encourages other members of the group to discuss, explain, and reason with the ineffectually thinking client. It teaches logi-

cal and semantic precision—that a man's being rejected does not mean he will *always* be rejected, and a woman's failing does not mean she *cannot* succeed. It helps clients to keep asking themselves whether even the worst things that might happen would be really as bad as they melodramatically fantasize that they would be.

2. *Emotive-evocative therapy,* when used to help change clients' core values, employs various means of dramatizing truths and falsehoods so they can clearly distinguish between the two. Thus, the therapist may employ *role playing,* to show the clients exactly what their false ideas are and how they affect relations with others; *modeling,* to show clients how to adopt different values; *humor,* to reduce disturbance-creating ideas to absurdity; *unconditional acceptance,* to demonstrate that they are acceptable, even with their unfortunate present traits, and that they can accept themselves fully; *exhortation,* to persuade people to give up some of their crazy thinking and replace it with more efficient notions. The therapist may also direct clients, either in individual or group counseling, to take risks (for example, telling another group member what they really think of him) that will prove it is really not that risky; to reveal themselves (for example, give the details of their impotency or homosexuality), to convince themselves that others can accept them with their failings; to get in touch with their "shameful" feelings (such as hostility), so they can zero in on the exact things they are telling themselves to create these feelings. The therapist may also use pleasure-giving techniques, such as sensory awareness and being cuddled by another group member, not merely to satisfy clients' unreasonable demands for immediate gratification, but to show them they are capable of doing many pleasant

acts that they think, wrongly, they *cannot* do, and that they *can* guiltlessly seek mere pleasure for the sake of pleasure, even though others may frown upon them for so doing.

3. *Behavior therapy* is employed in RET not only to help clients change their dysfunctional symptoms and to become habituated to more effective ways of performing, but also to help change their *cognitions.* Thus their demandingness that they perform beautifully may be whittled away by the therapist's giving them assignments, such as to take risks (for example, ask a member of the other sex for a date); to deliberately fail at some task (for example, make a real attempt to speak badly in public); to imagine themselves in failing situations; to throw themselves into unusual activities that they consider especially dangerous. Clients' demandingness that others treat them fairly and the world be kind may be challenged by the therapist's inducing them to stay in poor circumstances and teach themselves, at least temporarily, to accept them; to take on hard tasks (like enrolling in college); to imagine themselves having a rough time at something and not feeling terribly upset or having to "cop out" of it; to allow themselves to do a pleasant thing, such as go to a movie or see their friends, only after they have done unpleasant but desirable tasks, such as study French or finish a report for their boss; and so on. RET often employs operant conditioning to reinforce the individual's changing behavior (e.g., smoking or overeating) or changing irrational thinking (e.g., condemning himself when he smokes or overeats).

The RET theory of psychotherapy asserts that there are many kinds of psychological treatment, and that most of them work to some degree. An efficient system of therapy includes (1) economy of time and effort, (2) rapid symptom reduction, (3) effectiveness with a large percentage of different kinds of clients, (4) depth of solution of the presenting problems, and (5) lastingness of the therapeutic results. A therapy with these elements may be labeled "elegant"—that is, approaching the ideal of psychotherapy. Clinical and experimental evidence now exists that RET works better than other psychotherapies now extant (DiGiuseppe, Miller, & Trexler, 1977; Ellis, 1977a, 1977b; Ellis & Grieger, 1977; Ellis & Harper, 1975; Smith & Glass, 1977; Lembo, 1976; Morris & Kanitz, 1975). This is because the elegance of a therapy tends to be related to the correctness of its philosophic position. Philosophically, RET more intensively combats absoluteness than any other system. Realistic and unindulgent, RET gets to the core of and ruthlessly persists at undermining the childish demandingness—the main element of serious emotional disturbance.

Process of Psychotherapy

The many roads taken in RET are aimed at one major goal: minimizing the client's central self-defeating outlook and acquiring a more realistic, tolerant philosophy of life. Since some of its methods are similar to methods used by other therapists, they are not detailed in this chapter. Most of the space here is devoted to the cognitive-persuasive aspects of RET, its most distinguishing characteristic.

Rational-emotive therapists generally do not spend a great deal of time listening to the client's history, encouraging long tales of woes, sympathetically getting in tune with emotionalizing, or carefully and incisively reflecting feelings. They may at times use all these methods; but they usually make an effort to keep them short, since they consider most long-winded monologues of this nature a form of indulgence therapy, in which the client may be helped to *feel* better but rarely aided in *getting* better. Even when these methods work, they are considered highly inefficient, sidetracking, and often unhelpful.

Similarly, the rational-emotive therapist makes little use of free association, dream analysis, interpretations of the transference relationship, explanations of the client's present symptoms in terms of his past experiences, disclosure and analysis of the so-called Oedipus complex, and other "dynamically" directed interpretations or explanations. When these are employed at all, they are briefly employed to help the client see some of his basic irrational ideas.

Thus, if a male therapist notes that a female client rebels against him, just as she previously rebelled against her father during her childhood, he will not interpret the present rebelliousness as stemming from the prior pattern, but will instead probably say something like:

It looks like you frequently hated your father because he kept forcing you to follow certain rules you considered arbitrary and because you kept convincing yourself: "My father isn't being considerate of me and he *ought* to be! I'll fix his wagon!" I think you are now telling yourself approximately the same thing about me. But your angry rebelliousness against your father was senseless because (1) he was not a *total bastard* for perpetrating a bastardly *act;* (2) there was no reason why he *ought* to have been considerate of you (although there were several reasons why *it would have been preferable* if he had been); and (3) your getting angry at him and trying to "fix his wagon" would not, probably, encourage him to act more kindly, but actually to be more cruel.

You consequently confused—as most children will—being displeased with your father's *behavior* with being "righteously" angry at *him;* and you foolishly and needlessly *made yourself* upset about his supposedly unfair treatment of you. In my case, too, you are probably doing much the same thing; you are taking the restrictions that I place on you and insisting they are *too* onerous (when in point of fact, they are only onerous); and, after assuming that I am wrong in placing them on you (which I indeed may be), you are condemning me for my supposedly wrong deeds. Moreover, you are quite possibly assuming that I am "wrong" and a "louse" for being wrong because I resemble, in some ways, your "wrong" and "lousy" father.

But this is another illogical conclusion (that if I resemble your father in *some* ways, I must resemble him in all ways) and an irrational premise (that I, like your father, am a *bad person* if I do a wrong *act*). So you are not only *inventing* a false connection between me and your father, but you are creating today, as you have done for many years now, a renewed *demand* that the world be an easy place for you and that everyone *ought to* treat you fairly. Now, how are you going to challenge your irrational premises and illogical deductions?

Rational-emotive practitioners mainly employ a fairly rapid-fire active-directive-persuasive-philosophic methodology. In most instances, they quickly pin the client down to a few basic irrational ideas. They challenge the client to validate these ideas; show that they contain extralogical premises that cannot be validated; logically analyze these ideas and make mincemeat of them; vigorously show why they cannot work and why they will almost inevitably lead to renewed disturbed symptomatology; reduce these ideas to absurdity, sometimes in a highly humorous manner; explain how they can be replaced with more rational theses; and teach the client how to think scientifically, so he can observe, logically parse, and thoroughly annihilate any subsequent irrational ideas and illogical deductions that lead to self-defeating feelings and behaviors.

Lest it be thought that this picture of what the therapist does in RET is exag-

gerated, a verbatim typescript from the recording of the first part of an initial session with a 25-year-old single woman who works as the head of a computer programmer section is presented:

T-1 [reading from the biographical information form that the clients at the Institute for Rational-Emotive Therapy in New York City fill out before their first session]: Inability to control emotions; tremendous feelings of guilt, unworthiness, insecurity; constant depression; conflict between inner and outer self; overeating; drinking; diet pills.

T-1: All right, what would you want to start on first?

C-1: I don't know. I'm petrified at the moment!

T-2: You're petrified—of what?

C-2: Of you!

T-3: No, surely not of me—perhaps of yourself!

C-3: [laughs nervously]

T-4: Because of what am I going to do to you?

C-4: Right! You are threatening me, I guess.

T-5: But how? What am I doing? Obviously, I'm not going to take a knife and stab you. Now, in what way am I threatening you?

C-5: I guess I'm afraid, perhaps, of what I'm going to find out—about *me.*

T-6: Well, so let's suppose you find out something *dreadful* about you—that you're thinking foolishly, or something. Now why would that be awful?

C-6: Because I, I guess I'm the most important thing to me at the moment.

T-7: No, I don't think that's the answer. It's, I believe, the opposite! You're really the *least* important thing to you. You are prepared to beat yourself over the head if I tell you that you're acting foolishly. If you were not a self-*blamer,* then you wouldn't care what I said. It would be important to you—but you'd just go around correcting it. But if I tell you something really negative about you, you're going to beat yourself mercilessly. Aren't you?

C-7: Yes, I generally do.

T-8: All right. So perhaps *that's* what you're really afraid of. You're not afraid of me. You're afraid of *your* own self-criticism.

C-8: [sighs] All right.

T-9: So why do you have to criticize yourself? Suppose I find you're the worst person I ever met? Let's just suppose that. All right, now *why* would you have to criticize yourself?

C-9: [pause] I'd have to. I don't know any other behavior pattern, I guess, in this point of time. I always do. I guess I think I'm just a shit.

T-10: Yeah. But that, that isn't so. If you don't know how to ski or swim, you could learn. You can also learn not to condemn yourself, no matter what you do.

C-10: I don't know.

T-11: Well, the answer is: you don't know how.

C-11: Perhaps.

T-12: I get the impression you're *saying,* "I *have* to berate myself if I do something wrong." Because isn't that where your depression comes from?

C-12: Yes, I guess so. [silence for awhile]

T-13: Now, what are you *mainly* putting yourself down for right now?

C-13: I don't seem quite able, in this point of time, to break it down very neatly. The form gave me a great deal of trouble. Because my tendency is to say *everything.* I want to change everything; I'm depressed about everything; *et cetera.*

T-14: Give me a couple of things, for example.

C-14: What I'm depressed about? I, uh, don't know that I have any purpose in life. I don't know what I—what I am. And I don't know in what direction I'm going.

T-15: Yeah. But that's—so you're saying, "I'm ignorant!" [client nods] Well, what's so awful about being ignorant? It's too bad you're ignorant. It would be nicer if you weren't—if you *had* a purpose and *knew* where you were going. But just let's suppose the worst: for the rest of your life you didn't have a purpose, and you stayed this way. Let's suppose that. Now, why would *you* be so bad?

C-15: Because everyone *should* have a purpose!

T-16: Where did you get the *should?*

C-16: 'Cause it's what I believe in. [silence for a while]

T-17: I know. But think about it for a minute. You're obviously a bright woman; now, where did that *should* come from?

C-17: I, I don't know! I'm not thinking clearly at the moment. I'm too nervous! I'm sorry.

T-18: Well, but you *can* think clearly. Are you now saying, "Oh, it's hopeless! I can't think clearly. What a shit I am for not thinking clearly!" You see: you're blaming yourself for *that.*

(From C-18 to C-26 client upsets herself about not reacting well to the session but the therapist shows her this is not overly important and calms her down.)

C-27: I can't imagine existing, uh, or that there would be any reason for existing without a purpose!

T-28: No, but the vast majority of human beings don't have much purpose.

C-28: [angrily] All right, then. I should not feel bad about it.

T-29: No, no, no! Wait a minute, now. You just *jumped.* [Laughs] You jumped from one extreme to another! You see, you said a sane sentence and an *insane* sentence. Now, if we could get you to separate the two—which you're perfectly able to do—you would solve the problem. What you really mean is: "*It would be better* if I had a purpose. Because I'd be happier." Right?

C-29: Yes.

T-30: But then you magically jump to: "Therefore I *should!*" Now do you see the difference between, "*It would be better* if I had a purpose," and "I *should, I must,* I've *got to*"?

C-30: Yes, I do.

T-31: Well, what's the difference?

C-31: [laughs] I just said that to agree with you!

T-32: Yes! See, that won't be any good. We could go on that way forever, and you'll agree with me, and I'll say, "Oh, what a great woman! She agrees with me." And then you'll go out of here just as nutty as you were before!

C-32: [laughs; this time with genuine appreciation and good humor]

T-33: You're perfectly able, as I said, to think—to stop giving up. That's what you've done most of your life; that's why you're disturbed. Because you refuse to think. And let's go over it again: (1) "It would be better if I had a purpose in life; if I weren't depressed, *et cetera, et cetera.* If I had a good, nice, enjoyable purpose." We could give reasons why it would be better. "It's fairly obvious why it would be better!" Now, why is that a magical statement, that "I *should* do what would be better"?

C-33: You mean, why do I feel that way?

T-34: No, no. It's a belief. You feel that way because you believe that way.

C-34: Yes.

T-35: If you believed you were a kangaroo, you'd be hopping around; and you'd *feel* like a kangaroo. Whatever you *believe,* you feel. Feelings come from your beliefs. Now, I'm forgetting about your feelings, because we really can't change feelings without changing beliefs. So I'm showing you: you have two beliefs—or two feelings, if you want to call them that. One, "It would be better if I had a purpose in life." Do you agree? [client nods] Now that's perfectly reasonable. That's quite true. We could prove it. Two, "Therefore, I *should* do what would be better." Now those are two different statements. They may seem the same, but they're vastly different. Now, the first one, as I said, is sane. Because we could prove it. It's related to reality. We can list the advantages of having a purpose—for almost anybody, not just for you.

C-35: [calm now, and listening intently to T's explanation]: Uh-huh.

T-36: But the second one, "therefore, I *should* do what would be better" is crazy. Now, why is it crazy?

C-36: I can't accept it as a crazy statement.

T-37: Because who said you *should?*

C-37: I don't know where it all began! Somebody said it.

T-38: I know, but I say whoever said it was screwy!

C-38: [laughs] All right.

T-39: How could the world possibly have a *should?*

C-39: Well, it does.

T-40: But it *doesn't!* You see, that's what emotional disturbance is: believing in *shoulds, oughts,* and *musts* instead of *it would be betters.* That's exactly what makes people disturbed! Suppose you said to yourself, "I wish I had a dollar in my pocket right now," and you had only ninety cents, how would you feel?

C-40: Not particularly upset.

T-41: Yes; you'd be a little disappointed. "*It would be better* to have a dollar." But now suppose you said, "I *should, I must* have a dollar in my pocket at all times," and you found you had only ninety cents. Now, how would you feel?

C-41: Then I would be terribly upset, following your line of reasoning.

T-42: But not because you had only the ninety cents.

C-42: Because I thought I *should* have a dollar.

T-43: THAT'S RIGHT! The *should.* And what's more, let's just go one step further. Suppose you said, "I must have a dollar in my pocket at all times." And you found you had a dollar and ten cents. Now how would you feel?

C-43: Superb, I guess.

T-44: No!—anxious.

C-44: [laughs] You mean I'd be guilty: "What was I doing with the extra money?"

T-45: No.

C-45: I'm sorry, I'm not following you. I—

T-46: Because you're not *thinking!* Think for a minute. Why, if you said, "I *must* have a dollar, I *should* have a dollar," and you had a dollar and ten cents, would you still be anxious? *Anybody* would be. Now why would anybody be anxious if they were saying, "I've got to have a dollar!" and they found they had a dollar and ten cents.

C-46: Because it violated their *should.* It violated their rule of what they thought was right, I guess.

T-47: Well, not at the moment. But they could easily lose twenty cents.

C-47: Oh! Well.

T-48: Yeah! They'd still be anxious. You see, because *must* means, "At *all* times I must—"

C-48: Oh, I see what you mean! All right. I see what you mean. They could easily lose some of the money and would therefore feel insecure.

T-49: Yeah. All anxiety comes from *musts.*

C-49: [long silence] Why do you create such an anxiety-ridden situation initially for someone?

T-50: I don't think I do. I see hundreds of people and you're one of the few who *makes* this so anxiety provoking for yourself. The others may do it mildly; but you're making it very anxiety provoking. Which just shows that you carry *must* into *everything,* including this situation. Most people come in here very relieved. They finally got to talk to somebody who knows how to help them, and they're very happy that I stop the horseshit, and stop asking about their childhood, and don't talk about the weather, *et cetera.* And I get *right away* to what bothers them. I tell them in five minutes. I've just explained to you the secret of all emotional disturbance. If you really followed what I said, and used it, you'd never be disturbed about practically anything for the rest of your life!

C-50: Uh-huh.

T-51: Because everytime you're disturbed, you're changing *it would be better* to a *must.* That's all disturbance is! Very very simple. Now, why should I waste your time and not explain this—and talk about irrelevant things?

C-51: Because perhaps I would have followed your explanation a little better, if I hadn't been so threatened initially.

T-52: But then, if I pat you on the head and hold back, *et cetera,* then you'll think for the rest of your life you have to be patted on the head! You're a bright woman!

C-52: All right—

T-53: That's another *should.* "He *should* pat me on the head and take it slowly—*then* a shit like me can understand! But if he goes *fast,* and makes me *think,* oh my God I'll make an error—and that is awful!" More horseshit! You don't have to believe that horseshit! You're perfectly able to follow what I say—if you stop worrying about "I *should* do perfectly well!" For that's what you're basically thinking, sitting there. Well, why *should* you do perfectly well? Suppose we had to go over it twenty times before you got it?

C-53: I don't *like* to appear stupid!

T-54: No. See. Now you're lying to yourself! Because you again said a sane thing—and then you added an insane thing. The sane thing was "I don't like to appear stupid, because *it's better* to appear bright." But then you immediately jumped over to the insane thing. "And it's *awful* if I appear stupid—"

C-54: [laughs appreciatively, almost joyously]

T-55: "—I *should* appear bright!" you see?

C-55: [with conviction] Yes.

T-56: The same crap! It's always the same crap. Now if you would look at the crap—instead of "Oh, how stupid I am! He hates me! I think I'll kill myself!" then you'd get better right away.

C-56: You've been listening! [laughs]

T-57: Listening to what?

C-57: [laughs] Those wild statements in my mind, like that, that I make.

T-58: That's right! Because I know that you have to make those statements—because I have a good *theory.* And according to my theory, people couldn't get upset *unless* they made those nutty statements to themselves.

C-58: I haven't the faintest idea why I've been so upset—

T-59: But you *do* have the faintest idea. I just told you.

C-59: All right; I know!

T-60: Why are you upset? Repeat it to me.

C-60: I'm upset because I know, I—

The role that I envisioned myself being in when I walked in here and what I [laughs, almost joyously] and what I would do and should do—

T-61: Yeah?

C-61: And therefore you forced me to violate that. And I don't like it.

T-62: "And isn't it *awful* that I didn't come out greatly! If I had violated that *beautifully,* and I gave him the *right* answers immediately, and he beamed, and said 'Boy, what a bright woman this is!' then it would have been all right."

C-62: [laughing good-humoredly] Certainly!

T-63: Horseshit! You would have been exactly as disturbed as you are now! It wouldn't have helped you a bit! In fact, you would have got nuttier! Because then you would have gone out of here with the same *philosophy* you came in here with: "That when I act well and people pat, uh, when they pat me on the head and say 'What a great woman am I!' then everything is rosy!" It's a nutty philosophy! Because even if I loved you madly, the next person you talk to is likely to hate you. So I like brown eyes and he likes blue eyes, or something. So you're then dead! Because you really think: "I've got to be *accepted!* I've got to act *intelligently!*" Well, why?

C-63: [very soberly and reflectively] True.

T-64: You see?

C-64: Yes.

T-65: Now, if you will learn that lesson, then you've had a very valuable session. Because you *don't* have to upset yourself. As I said before: if I thought you were the worst shit who ever existed, well that's my *opinion.* And I'm entitled to it. But does it make you a turd?

C-65: [reflective silence]

T-66: Does it?

C-66: No.

T-67: What makes you a turd?

C-67: Thinking that you are.

T-68: That's right! Your *belief* that you are. That's the only thing that could ever do it. And you never have to believe that. See? You control your thinking. I control *my* thinking—*my* belief about you. But you don't have to be affected by that. You *always* control what you think. And you believe you don't. So let's get back to the depression. The depression, as I said before, stems from self-castigation. That's where it comes from. Now what are you castigating yourself for?

C-68: Because I can't live up to— There's a basic conflict in what people appear to think I am and what I think I am.

T-69: Right.

C-69: And perhaps it's not fair to blame other people. Perhaps I thrust myself into a leader's role. But, anyway, my feeling right now is that all my life I've been forced to be something that I'm not, and the older I get the more difficult this *facade,* huh, this *appearance,* uh— That the veneer is coming thinner and thinner and thinner, until I just can't do it any more.

T-70: Well, but really, yeah, I'm afraid you're a little wrong. Because, oddly enough, almost the opposite is happening. You are thrust into this role. That's right: the role of something of a leader. Is that correct?

C-70: Yes.

T-71: And *they* think you're filling it.

C-71: Everyone usually does.

T-72: And it just so happens they're *right.*

C-72: But it's taking more and more out of me.

T-73: Because you're not doing something else. You see, you *are* fulfilling their expectations of you. Because, obviously,

they wouldn't think you are a leader, they'd think you were a nothing if you *were* acting like a nonleader. So you are filling their expectations. But you're not fulfilling your own idealistic and impractical expectations of leadership.

C-73: [verging on tears] No, I guess I'm not.

T-74: You see that's the issue. So therefore you *are* doing okay by them—by your job, *et cetera.* But you're not being an angel; you're not being *perfect!* And you should be, to be a real *leader.* And therefore you're a *sham!* You see? Now, if you give up those nutty expectations of yourself, and go back to their expectations, you're in no trouble at all. 'Cause obviously you're doing all right by them, and *their* expectations.

C-74: Well, I haven't been. I had to, to give up one very successful situation. And, uh, when I left they thought it was still successful. But I just could not go on—

T-75: "Because I must, I must *really* be a leader in *my* eyes, be pretty *perfect.*" You see. "If I satisfy the world, but I know I did badly, or less than I *should,* then I'm a slob! And they haven't found me out, so that makes me a *double* slob. Because I'm pretending to them to be a nonslob when I really am one!"

C-75: [laughs in agreement; then soberly] True!

T-76: But it's all your silly *expectations.* It's not *them.* And oddly enough, you are—even with your *handicap,* which is depression, self-deprecation, *et cetera*— you're doing remarkably well. Imagine what you might do *without* this nutty handicap! You see, you're satisfying them while you're spending most of your time and energy flagellating yourself. Imagine what you might do *without* the self-flagellation! Can you see that?

C-76: [stopped in her self-blaming tracks: at least temporarily convinced. Very meaningfully] Yes!

Mechanisms of Psychotherapy

From the foregoing partial protocol (which consumed about 15 minutes of the first session with the client), it can be seen that the therapist tries to do several things:

1. No matter what *feelings* the client brings out, the therapist tries to get back to her main irrational *ideas* that most probably lie behind these feelings—especially her ideas that contend that it would be *awful* if someone, including him, disliked her.

2. The therapist does not hesitate to contradict the client, using evidence from her own life and from his knowledge of people in general.

3. He usually is a step *ahead* of her—tells her, for example, that she is a self-blamer before she has said that she is. Knowing, on the basis of RET *theory,* that she has *shoulds, oughts,* and *musts* in her thinking if she is becoming anxious, depressed, and guilty, he forces her to admit these *shoulds* and then attacks them (T-16; T-17).

4. He uses the strongest philosophic approach he can think of. "Suppose," he keeps saying to her, "the *worst* thing happened and you really did do badly and others hated you, would you *still* be so bad?" (T-15). He assumes if he can convince her that *none* of her behavior, no matter how execrable, denigrates *her,* he has helped her to make a *deep* attitudinal change.

5. He is not thrown by her upsetness (C-17), is hardly sympathetic about these feelings, but *uses* them to try to prove to her that, right now, she still believes in foolish ideas and thereby upsets herself.

He does not dwell on her "transference" feelings, the way she accuses him of acting toward her. He interprets the *ideas* behind these feelings, shows her why they are self-defeating, and indicates why his acting sympathetically would probably reinforce instead of help change her demanding philosophy.

6. He is fairly stern with her, but also shows full acceptance and demonstrates confidence in her abilities by insisting that she can do better in her thinking and her behaving if she stops berating herself (T-20; T-33).

7. Instead of merely *telling* her that her ideas are irrational, he keeps trying to get her to see this for herself (T-36). He does, however, *explain* some relevant psychological processes, such as that her *feelings* come from her *thinking* (T-35; T-68).

8. He deliberately, on several occasions, uses strong language (T-18; T-50; T-53; T-56; T-63; T-65). This is done (1) to help loosen up the client; (2) to show that even though he is a professional, he is also a down-to-earth human being; (3) to give her an emotive jolt or shock, so his words may take more dramatic effect. Note that in this case the client *first* called herself a "shit" (C-9).

9. Although hardly sympathetic to her ideas, he is really quite empathic: for he is listening hard to what she is probably telling herself. In this sense, rational-emotive therapists are very empathic, since they are usually attuned to the client's unexpressed concepts (her negative ideas about herself and the world) rather than to her *superficial* feelings (her perceptions that she is doing poorly or that others are abusing her).

10. The therapist keeps *checking* the client's ostensible understanding of what he is teaching her (T-65; T-67), to make sure she truly does understand and can repeat back his message in her own words.

11. Although a meaningful dialogue obviously takes place, the therapist—as is common in early sessions of RET—does most of the talking and explaining. He gives her plenty of opportunity to express herself, but uses her responses as take-off points for further teaching. At times, he almost seems to be lecturing her. But he tries to make each "lecture" brief and trenchant and to relate it specifically to her problems and feelings. Also, at times he stops to let ideas sink in.

As can be seen from the first part of this initial RET session, the client does not receive feelings of love and warmth from the therapist. Transference and countertransference spontaneously occur, but they are quickly analyzed, the philosophies behind them revealed, and they tend to evaporate in the process. The client's deep feelings (shame, self-pity, weeping, anger) clearly exist; but the client is not given too much of a chance to revel in these feelings or to abreact strongly to them. As the therapist points out and attacks the ideologies that appear to underlie these feelings, they swiftly change and are sometimes almost miraculously transformed into other, contradictory feelings (such as humor, joy, and reflective contemplation). On the whole, because of the therapist's "coolness," philosophizing, and insistence that the client can feel otherwise than anxious and depressed, she tends to change her destructiveness into constructive feelings minutes after the session starts.

What the client does seem to experience, as the session proceeds, are: (1) full acceptance of herself, in spite of her poor behavior both during the session and in her external life; (2) renewed confidence, that she can do certain things—especially, think for herself—that at first she seems to think she cannot do; (3) a new concept, that never or rarely seems to have oc-

curred to her before, namely, that it is her own perfectionistic *shoulds* that are upsetting her and not the attitudes of others (including the therapist); (4) reality testing, in her starting to see that even though she performs inefficiently (with the therapist and with some of the people she works with), she can still recover, try again, and probably do better in the future; (5) reduction of some of her defenses, in that she can stop blaming others (such as the therapist) for her anxiety and can start to admit that she is doing something herself to cause it.

For the 15 minutes that the session chronicled above proceeds, the client is getting only *glimmerings* of these constructive thoughts and feelings. The RET intent, however, is that she will *keep* getting insights—that is, *philosophic* rather than merely *psychodynamic* insights— into her self-causation of her disturbed symptoms; that she will use these insights to change some of her most enduring and deep-seated ways of thinking about herself, about others, and about the world about her; and that she will thereby eventually become ideationally, emotionally, and behaviorly much less self-defeating. Unless she finally makes a thoroughgoing *attitudinal* (as well as symptom-reducing) change as a result of rational-emotive therapy, although helped considerably, she will still be far from the ideal RET goal of basic personality change.

APPLICATIONS

Problems

It is easier to state what kind of problems are *not* handled than the kind that *are* handled in RET. Individuals who are out of contact with reality, in a highly manic state, seriously autistic or brain injured, and in the lower ranges of mental deficiency are not normally treated. They are referred for physical treatment for custodial or institutional care, or for behavior therapy along operant conditioning lines.

Most other individuals with difficulties are treated with RET. This includes (1) clients with maladjustment, moderate anxiety, or marital problems; (2) those with sexual difficulties; (3) run-of-the-mill "neurotics"; (4) individuals with character disorders; (5) truants, juvenile delinquents, and adult criminals; (6) borderline psychotics; (7) overt psychotics, including those with delusions and hallucinations, when they are somewhat in contact with reality; (8) individuals with higher grade mental deficiency; (9) clients with psychosomatic problems.

Although innumerable kinds of individuals with varying types of problems are treated with RET, no claim is made that they are treated with equal effectiveness. As is the case with virtually all psychotherapies, the rational-emotive approach is significantly more effectual with mildly disturbed individuals or with those having a single major symptom (such as sexual inadequacy) than with seriously disordered clients (Ellis, 1962). This conforms to the prediction of RET theory that states that the tendency toward emotional upset is largely inborn, and not merely acquired, that individuals with serious aberrations are more innately predisposed to have rigid and crooked thinking than those with lesser aberrations, and that consequently they are likely to make lesser advances. Moreover, RET emphasizes hard work at changing one's thinking and at doing activity homework assignments; and it is clinically observable that many of the most dramatically symptom-ridden individuals (such as those who are severely depressed) tend to do considerably less work and more shirking (including shirk-

ing at therapy) than those with milder symptoms. Nevertheless, virtually all seasoned RET practitioners claim they get better results with a wide variety of clients than do therapists from other schools.

RET is rightly applicable for preventive purposes. Rational-emotive procedures are closely connected to the field of education and have enormous implications for emotional prophylaxis. A number of clinicians and other professionals have shown how they can prevent normal children from eventually becoming seriously upsettable. Evidence shows that when nondisturbed grade school pupils are given, along with regular elements of an academic education, a steady process of rational-emotive education, they can learn to understand themselves and others and to live more rationally and happily in this difficult world (Ellis, 1969a, 1973a; Knaus, 1974).

Evaluation

RET has directly or indirectly inspired scores of experimenters to test its major clinical and personality theories. Over 90 percent of these studies have supported its claims. Outcome studies of RET have been summarized by DiGiuseppe, Miller, and Trexler (1977) and Murphy and Ellis (1979). Experiments backing other therapeutic and personality hypotheses of RET are reviewed by Ellis (1977b).

Considering its relative newness in the field of psychotherapy, RET has made an enormous impact on both professionals and the public in recent years. In addition to the texts of Ellis and Maxie Maultsby, several other textbooks have appeared, including those by Janet Wolfe and Eileen Brand (1977), René Diekstra and Will Dassen (1976), John Lembo (1976), and Kenneth Morris and H. M. Kanitz (1975). Many rationality scales incorporating

Ellis's basic ideas have been created and validated, including those by Judith Bessai (1975), R. G. Jones (1968), and H. W. Zingle (1965). RET applications of assertion training have been included in the writings of many authorities, such as Arthur Lange and Patricia Jakubowski (1976) and Janet Wolfe (1975). Self-management texts have incorporated a great deal of RET material (Goldfried & Merbaum, 1973). RET books have been published in many different fields, including those of adolescence (Tosi, 1974); law and criminality (Church, 1975; Ellis and Gullo, 1972); religion (Hauck, 1972); executive leadership (Ellis, 1972a); children's literature (Bedford, 1974; Berger, 1971; Garcia & Pellegrini, 1974); music (Ellis, 1977d); feminism (Wolfe, 1976a, 1976b); and philosophy (Ellis, 1968).

RET has been the main content of or has been significantly incorporated into literally scores of self-help books, many of them having achieved considerable popularity. Some of the most noted of these books have been by Bill Casey, Wayne Dyer, Albert Ellis, Robert Harper, Paul Hauck, Gerald Kranzler, John Lembo, Maxie Maultsby, Jr., Rian McMullen, John Powell, Erik Thoresen, and Howard Young.

Other popular self-help books featuring RET principles have appeared in the field of marriage and the family, child management, and sex adjustment and therapy, by authors such as Daniel Blazier, Albert Ellis, Robert A. Harper, Paul Hauck, and Janet L. Wolfe.

Individual Evaluations. RET therapists may use a variety of diagnostic instruments and psychological tests, such as intelligence tests, paper and pencil personality tests, and projective techniques. Since, however, most personality tests have not been devised to show the individual's basic irrational ideas, they tend to be used rather sparingly; and at times, special tests, usually nonprojective, are given to determine what these irrational ideas are and how they change over the course of therapy. Harvey W. Zingle (1965; Zingle & Mallett, 1976) has devised a widely used test of irrational ideas, based on RET theory and practice. Zingle and his students have validated this test and reported in a series of articles and dissertations. Another paper and pencil personality test, the Personality Data Form (Ellis, 1971a), has been used in several experimental studies (Murphy & Ellis, 1979).

Treatment

RET employs virtually all forms of individual and group psychotherapy. Some of the main methods are these:

Individual Therapy. Most clients with whom RET is practiced are seen for *individual* sessions, usually on a once-a-week basis, for from 5 to 50 sessions. They generally start off their sessions by telling their most upsetting feelings or consequences (*C*) during the week. RET therapists then discover what activating events (*A*) occurred before clients felt so badly and get them to see what rational beliefs (*rB*) and what irrational beliefs (*iB*) they held in connection with the activating events. They get clients to dispute (*D*) their irrational beliefs and often give them concrete activity homework assignments to help them do this disputing. They then check up the following session, sometimes with the help of a Rational Self-Help Form or other homework report (Ellis, 1971b, 1977e; Maultsby, 1975), to see how they have tried to use the RET approach during the week; and they keep teaching clients how to dispute their irrational beliefs and keep giving them new homework assignments, until they not only start to lose their presenting symptoms but acquire a saner, more tolerant attitude toward life.

In particular, RET therapists try to show clients how (1) to rid themselves of anxiety, guilt, and depression by fully accepting themselves, as human beings, *whether or not* they succeed at important tasks and performances and *whether or not* significant people in their lives approve or love them; (2) to minimize their anger, hostility, and violence by becoming quite tolerant of other people's *being* even when they find these people's *traits* or *performances* unappetizing and unfair; and (3) to reduce their low frustration tolerance and inertia by working hard to change unpleasant reality but learning gracefully to stand it when it is truly inevitable.

Group Therapy. RET is particularly applicable to *group therapy,* because in groups, members are taught to apply RET principles to the other members of the group; so they thereby are able to help these others learn the principles better themselves and get practice (under the direct supervision of the group leader) in applying them. In group work, moreover, there is usually more opportunity for the members to be given homework assignments (some of which are to be carried out in the group itself); to get assertion training; to engage in role playing; to interact with other people; to take verbal and nonverbal risks; to learn by the experiences of others; to interact therapeutically and socially with each other in after-group sessions; to have their behavior directly observed by the therapist and other group members, instead of merely giving an after-the-fact report of it; and to engage in other group processes designed to foster active participation and radical philosophic change. The majority of RET clients are able, sooner or later, to participate in group therapy, and for many of them it is an especially good method (Ellis, 1973b).

Marathon Encounter Groups. Although RET is one of the most cognitively oriented therapies, it has been successfully modified for what Ellis (1969b) calls "A Weekend of Rational Encounter." In a *rational-emotive marathon,* the first several hours are spent in having members of the marathon group go through a series of exercises designed to get them to know each other intimately, to relate verbally and nonverbally, to bring out some of their most harrowing and "shameful" experiences, to take unusual risks, and to have intense one-to-one personal encounters. During these first hours, problem-solving is deliberately eschewed. Then, when the members of the marathon group have gotten to know each other and given up some of their defenses, many hours are spent delving into their deepest problems in the usual RET cognitive-probing manner, so most of them come to understand the philosophic sources of their emotional problems and how they can change themselves by altering these cognitions. Other verbal and nonverbal exercises to encourage encountering and intensive therapy are performed. Specific homework assignments are given to each of the marathon group members. Finally, there are closing exercises. The entire marathon lasts from 14 to 24 hours. A reunion is usually held for several hours 6 to 8 weeks later, to check on progress and on the homework assignments. In some cases, follow-up therapy is recommended. This kind of an intensive experience with RET-oriented encounter methods has proven to be an unusually enjoyable experience, as well as an effective introduction or addition to rational-emotive therapy.

Brief Therapy. RET is naturally designed for *brief therapy*. It is preferable that individuals with severe disturbances come to individual and/or group sessions for at least 6 months or 1 year, so they have an opportunity to practice what they are learning. But for individuals who are going to stay in therapy for only a short while, RET can teach them, in from 1 to 10 sessions, the A-B-C method of understanding *any* emotional problem, seeing its main philosophic source, and how to start to work to change fundamental disturbance-creating attitudes (Ellis & Abrahams, 1978).

This is particularly true for the person who has a specific problem—such as hostility toward a boss or sexual impotency—and who is not too *generally* disturbed. Such an individual can, with the help of RET, be almost completely "cured" in a few sessions. But even clients with long-standing difficulties may be significantly helped as a result of brief therapy using the rational-emotive approach. They are frequently able to keep using the principles they learned during relatively few sessions and to treat themselves, often with the help of supplementary reading of R-E materials, so they not only quickly improve but also augment their improvement as the months and years go by.

Two special devices often employed in RET with regular clients can help speed the therapeutic process and make most series of sessions relatively brief. The first of these is to tape the entire session. These recordings are then listened to, usually several times, by the clients in their own home, car, or office; so they can more incisively see their problems and the rational-emotive way of handling them. Many clients who have difficulty in hearing what goes on during the face-to-face sessions (because they are too intent on talking themselves, are easily distractable, are too anxious, and so on) are able to get more from listening to a recording of these sessions than from the original encounter with the therapist.

Second, a Rational Self Help Form or homework report (Ellis, 1977e) is frequently used with RET clients, which helps teach them how to use the method whenever assailed with any emotional problems in between therapy sessions or after therapy has ended. This form is reproduced on pages 218–220.

Marriage and Family Therapy. From its very beginnings, RET has been extensively used in marriage and family counseling (Ellis, 1957, 1977a; Ellis & Harper, 1961a; 1961b). Usually marital or love partners are seen together. RET therapists listen to their complaints about each other, then try to show that even if the complaints are justified, upsetness is not. Work is done with either or both the participants to minimize anxiety, depression, guilt, and—especially—hostility; and a kind of small-group session ensues. As they begin to learn and apply the RET principles, they usually become much less disturbed about their differences, often within a few sessions; and as they become less disturbed, they are much better able to minimize their incompatibilities and to maximize their compatibilities. Sometimes, of course, they decide that they would be better off separated or divorced; but usually they decide to work at their individual and collective problems, to tackle some of their basic disturbances, and to achieve a happier marital arrangement. They are frequently taught contracting, compromising, communication, and other relating skills. The therapist is concerned with each of them as individuals who can be helped emotionally, whether or not they decide to stay together. But the more they work at helping themselves, the better their relationships tend to become.

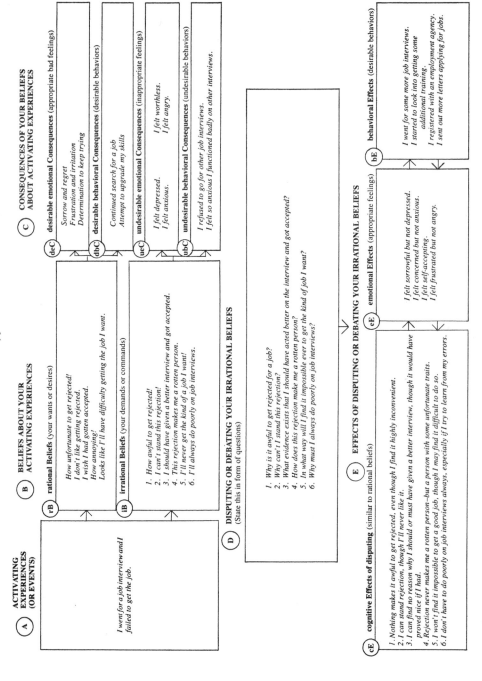

RATIONAL SELF HELP FORM

Institute for Rational-Emotive Therapy   45 East 65th Street, New York 10021

INSTRUCTIONS: Please fill out the **ueC** section (undesirable emotional Consequences) and the **ubC** section (undesirable behavioral Consequences) **first.**
Then fill out all the A-B-C-D-E's. PLEASE PRINT LEGIBLY. BE BRIEF!

(A) **ACTIVATING EXPERIENCES (OR EVENTS)**

(B) **BELIEFS ABOUT YOUR ACTIVATING EXPERIENCES**

(rB) rational Beliefs (your wants or desires)

(iB) irrational Beliefs (your demands or commands)

(C) **CONSEQUENCES OF YOUR BELIEFS ABOUT ACTIVATING EXPERIENCES**

(deC) desirable emotional Consequences (appropriate bad feelings)

(dbC) desirable behavioral Consequences (desirable behaviors)

(ueC) undesirable emotional Consequences (inappropriate feelings)

(ubC) undesirable behavioral Consequences (undesirable behaviors)

(D) **DISPUTING OR DEBATING YOUR IRRATIONAL BELIEFS** (State this in the form of questions)

(E) **EFFECTS OF DISPUTING OR DEBATING YOUR IRRATIONAL BELIEFS**

(cE) cognitive Effects of disputing (similar to rational beliefs)

(eE) emotional Effects (appropriate feelings)

(bE) behavioral Effects (desirable behaviors)

1. FOLLOW-UP. What new GOALS would I now like to work on? ....

....

....

....

What specific ACTIONS would I now like to take?..

....

....

2. How soon after feeling or noting your undesirable emotional CONSEQUENCES (ueC's) or your undesirable behavorial CONSEQUENCES (ubC's) of your irrational BELIEFS (iB's) did you look for these iB's and DISPUTE them?.................

....

....

How vigorously did you dispute them? ....

....

If you didn't dispute them, why did you not do so?...

....

3. Specific HOMEWORK ASSIGNMENT(S) given you by your therapist, your group or yourself: ....

....

....

4. What did you actually do to carry out the assignment(s)? ....

....

5. How many times have you actually worked at your homework assignments during the past week?..........................

....

6. How many times have you actually worked at DISPUTING your irrational BELIEFS during the past week?...............

....

7. Things you would now like to discuss with your therapist or group ....

....

....

In family therapy, the rational-emotive practitioner sometimes sees all the members of the same family together; or he may see the children in one session and the parents in another; or he may see them all individually. Some joint sessions are usually held, to see what the interactions among family members actually are; but there is no fetishistic sticking *only* to joint sessions. Whether together or separately, parents are frequently shown how to accept their children and to stop condemning *them,* no matter how execrable their *behavior* may be; and children are similarly shown that they can accept their parents and their siblings even when their traits and deeds are highly disappointing. The general rational-emotive principles of tolerance for oneself and for others are repeatedly taught; and as these are imbibed and applied, family relationships tend to become remarkably improved. As is common in RET procedures, bibliotherapy supplements counseling, and the family participants often find they can significantly help themselves by reading RET materials like *A New Guide to Rational Living* (Ellis & Harper, 1975), *A Rational Counseling Primer* (Young, 1974), *How to Live with and without Anger* (Ellis, 1977a), *How to Live with a "Neurotic"* (Ellis, 1957), *A Guide to Successful Marriage* (Ellis & Harper, 1971b), *The Art and Science of Love* (Ellis, 1969c), *How to Raise an Emotionally Healthy, Happy Child* (Ellis, Wolfe, & Moseley, 1972), and *The Rational Management of Children* (Hauck, 1967).

Management. The *setting* of rational-emotive sessions is much like that for other types of therapy. Most individual sessions take place in an office, but there may well be no desk between the therapist and the client, and RET therapists tend to be informally dressed and use down-to-earth language. Because they presumably have relatively few ego hangups and because they do not care too much what others, including clients, think of them, they tend to be more open, authentic, and less "professional" than the average therapist. The main special equipment used is a cassette tape recorder, with the client being encouraged to bring his own cassette, to make a recording of the session, and to take it home for replaying.

Relationships between client and therapist are somewhat different in RET than in many other forms of therapy. Rational-emotive therapists are highly active; give their own views without hesitations; usually answer direct questions about their personal life; do a good deal of the speaking, particularly during early sessions; and are quite energetic and often directive in group therapy. At the same time, they may engage in considerable explaining, interpreting, and "lecturing"; may be objective, "cool," and hardly warm or friendly to most clients; and may easily work with clients they personally do not like, since they are much more interested in helping them with their emotional problems than relating personally to them. Because they tend to have complete tolerance for all individuals, no matter how execrable their behavior, RET therapists are often seen as "warm" and "caring" by clients, even though they may have relatively little personal interest in them.

Resistance is usually handled by showing clients that they resist changing their outlook and behavior because they would like a magical easy solution rather than to work at changing themselves. Resistance is not usually interpreted in relation to their particular feelings about the therapist. If a female client tries to seduce a male therapist, this is not usually explained in terms of "transference" but in terms of (a) her dire needs for love; (b) her normal attraction for a helpful person; and (c) the natural sex urges of two people who have intimate mental-emotional contact. If the therapist is attracted to the client, he usually admits his attraction, but explains why it is unethical for him to have sex relations with her.

Client Problems. No matter what the presenting problem, the therapist does not become overinterested in *it,* nor does he devote too much time and energy to trying to induce the client to fully *express* it or the emotions surrounding it. Rather, he almost always tries to get the client to see and to tackle the basic ideas or philosophies that underlie it. This is notably shown in the course of the workshops and seminars for executives. In the course of these workshops, the participating executives constantly bring up business, management, organizational, personal, and other problems. But they are shown that whatever these specific problems are, they invariably have a problem about the problem; and it is *this* (emotional or philosophic) problem that the rational-emotive method zeroes in on and helps the individual quickly and effectively solve. Then he or she usually has little difficulty in solving the original, objective problem (Ellis, 1972b).

The one main exception to this rule are individuals who are so inhibited or defensive that they do not permit themselves to feel, and who therefore may not even be aware of some of their underlying problems. Thus, the successful businessman, who only comes for psychological help because his wife insists they have a poor relationship, and who claims that nothing really bothers him other than his wife's complaints, may have to be jolted out of his complacency by direct confrontation by the rational-emotive therapist or group, and may be able to see that he really has a problem mainly by such powerful confrontation. RET marathon group therapy may be particularly helpful for such an individual, and may so shake him up that he finally expresses underlying anxieties and resentments and begins to feel that he truly has problems he can work on.

Extreme emotionalism in the course of RET sessions—such as crying, psychotic behavior, and violent expressions of suicidal or homicidal intent—are naturally difficult to handle. But the therapist is bolstered in handling them by his own presumably rational philosophy of life and of therapy, which includes these ideas: (1) Client outbursts make things difficult, but they are hardly *awful, terrible,* or *catastrophic.* It is merely too bad that they occur. (2) Behind each outburst is some concrete, irrational idea. Now, what is this idea? How can it be forcefully brought to the client's attention and what can be done to help him change it? (3) No therapist can possibly help every client all the time. If this particular client cannot be helped and has to be referred elsewhere or lost to therapy, that is unfortunate. But it does not mean that the therapist is a failure with a capital F, and that he cannot go on to help others.

Profound depressions are usually handled by the rational-emotive therapist by showing the clients, as quickly, directly, and vigorously as possible, that they are probably causing their depression by (1) blaming themselves for what they have done or not done; (2) castigating themselves for being depressed and inert; and (3) bemoaning their fate because of the hassles and harshness of environmental conditions. This self-condemnation is not only revealed but energetically attacked; and, in the meantime, the therapist may give clients reassurance and support, may refer them for supplementary medical treatment, may speak to their relatives or friends to enlist their aid, and may recommend temporary withdrawal from some involved activities. Through an immediate and direct assailing of clients' extreme self-deprecation and self-pity, the therapist is often able significantly to help deeply depressed and suicidal people in a short period.

The most difficult clients are usually the chronic avoiders or shirkers, who keep looking for magical solutions. These individuals are forthrightly shown that no such magic exists; that if they do not want to work hard to get better, it is their privilege to keep suffering; that they are entitled to goof, are not *terrible persons* for goofing, but that they could live much more enjoyably if they worked at helping themselves; and that to help them get going a form of people-involved therapy, such as group therapy, is frequently a method of choice. Results with these kinds of individuals are still relatively poor in RET (and virtually all other kinds of therapies); but persistence and vigor on the part of the therapist often finally overcome this kind of resistance.

CASE EXAMPLE

This section is relatively brief, since it concerns the case of the 25-year-old computer programmer, part of whose initial session was given earlier in this chapter. Other case material on this client follows.

Background

Sara R. came from an orthodox Jewish family. Her mother died in childbirth, when she was two years of age, and she was raised by a loving, but strict and somewhat remote, father and tyrannical paternal grandmother. She did well in school, but had few friends up to and including college. Although fairly attractive, she was always ashamed of her body, did little dating, and occupied herself mainly with her work. At the age of 25,

she was head of a section in a data processing firm. She was highly sexed, masturbated several times a week; but only had intercourse with a male once, when she was too drunk to know what she was doing. She had been overeating and overdrinking steadily, since her college days. She had three years of fairly classical psychoanalysis, thought her analyst was "a very kind and helpful man," but got little or no help from the process. She was quite disillusioned about therapy, as a result of this experience, and only came to see the present therapist because the president of her company, who liked her a great deal, told her that he would no longer put up with her constant drinking and insisted that she come to see the writer.

Treatment

Rational-emotive treatment continued for 6 sessions, along the same lines as indicated in the verbatim transcript included previously in this chapter, followed by 24 weeks of RET group therapy and 1 weekend of rational encounter.

Cognitively, the client was repeatedly shown that her central problem was that she devoutly believed she *had to be* almost perfect and that she *must not* be criticized in any major way by significant others. She was persistently taught, instead, to refrain from rating her *self* but only to measure her *performances;* to see that she could never be, except by arbitrary definition, a worm or a shit, even if she never rid herself of her overeating, her compulsive drinking, and her other foolish symptoms; to see that it was highly desirable but not necessary that she relate intimately to a man and to win the approval of her peers and her bosses at work; and first to accept herself *with* her hostility and then to give up her childish *demands* on others that led her to be so hostile to them. Although she was an arrant believer in the "fact" that she and others *should* be extremely efficient and follow strict disciplinary rules, and although she time and again resisted the therapist's and the group members' assaults against her moralistic *shoulds,* she was finally induced to replace them, in her vocabulary as well as in her internalized beliefs, with *it would be betters.* She claimed to have completely overthrown her original religious orthodoxy; but she was shown that she had merely replaced it with an inordinate demand for certainty in her personal life and in world affairs; and she was finally induced to give this up, too.

Emotively, Sara was fully accepted by the therapist *as a person,* even though he ruthlessly assailed many of her *ideas* and sometimes humorously reduced them to absurdity. She was assertively confronted by some of the group members, who took her to task for condemning other members of the group for their stupidities and for their shirking; and she was helped to relate to these people in spite of their inadequacies. The therapist and some of the others in her group and in the marathon weekend of rational encounter in which she participated used vigorous, down-to-earth language with her, which she first got "shook up" about but which she later began to use to some extent herself. When she went on a drinking bout for a few weeks and felt utterly depressed and hopeless, two of the group members brought out their own previous difficulties with alcohol and drugs and showed how they had managed to get through that almost impossible period of their lives; another member gave her steady support through many phone calls and visits. At times, when she clammed up or sulked, the therapist and other group members forced her to open up and voice her real feelings; then they went after these defenses, with RET analyses, and showed her what foolish ideas (especially the idea that she had

to be terribly hurt if others rejected her) lay behind them and how these could be uprooted. During the marathon, she was able, for the first time in her life, to let herself be really touched emotionally by a male who, up to that time, was a perfect stranger to her; and this showed her that she could afford to let down her long-held barriers to intimacy and to let herself love.

Behavioristically, Sara was given homework assignments of talking to attractive males in public places and thereby overcame her fears of being rejected. She was shown how to stay on a long-term diet (which she had never done before) by only allowing herself rewarding experiences (such as listening to classical music) when she had first kept to her diet for a certain number of hours. Through the use of role playing with the therapist and other group members she was given training in being assertive with people at work and in her social life, without being hostile.

Resolution

Concomitant with her individual and group therapy, and probably as a result of the combination of cognitive, emotive, and behavioristic approaches, Sara progressed in several ways she (and the group members) thought were important: (1) She stopped drinking completely, lost 25 pounds, and appeared to be maintaining both her sobriety and her weight loss. (2) She became considerably less condemnatory of both herself and others and began to make some close freinds. (3) She had satisfactory sex relations with three different males and began to go steadily with the second one of the three. (4) She only rarely made herself guilty or depressed, accepted herself with her failings, and began to focus much more on enjoying than on rating herself.

Follow-up. Sara had RET individual

and group sessions for six months—occasional follow-up sessions for the next year. She married her steady boyfriend about a year after she had originally begun treatment, having two premarital counseling sessions with him following their engagement. Two and one-half years after the close of therapy, she and her husband visited one of the regular Friday night workshops given by the therapist at the Institute for Rational Living in New York City and they reported that everything was going well in their marriage, at her job, and in their social life. Her husband seemed particularly appreciative of the use she was making of RET principles, and noted that "she still works hard at what she learned with you and the group and, frankly, I think that she keeps improving, because of this work, all the time." She smilingly and enthusiastically agreed.

SUMMARY

Rational-emotive therapy (RET) is a comprehensive system of personality change that includes a large variety of cognitive, emotive, and behavior therapy methods. It is not merely an eclectically or pragmatically oriented form of psychological treatment but is based on a clearcut theory of emotional health and disturbance: The many techniques it employs are used in the light of that theory. Its major hypotheses also relate to childrearing, education, social and political affairs, and for the extension of people's intellectual-emotional frontiers and the abetting of their unique potential for growth. Rational-emotive psychology is hardheaded, empirically oriented, rational, and nonmagical. It fosters the use of reason, science, and technology in the straightforward interest of man and woman. It is humanistic, existentialist, and hedonistic; it makes growth and hap-

piness the relevant core of a person's intrapersonal and interpersonal life.

RET theory holds that people are biologically and culturally predisposed to choose, to create, to relate, and to enjoy, but that they are also just as strongly predisposed to conform, to be suggestible, to hate, and arbitrarily to block their enjoying. Although they have remarkable capacities to observe, to reason, and imaginatively to enhance their experiencing and to transcend some of their own essential limitations, they also have an incredible facile and easy propensity to ignore reality, to misuse reason, and rigidly and intolerantly to invent gods and demons that frequently sabotage their health and happiness. In the course of their refusals to accept reality, their continual *must*urbation, and their absorption in deifying and devilifying themselves and others, they almost always wind up with fairly severe manifestations of what is called "emotional disturbance."

More specifically, when noxious stimuli occur in peoples' lives at point A (the activating event), they usually observe these events fairly objectively and conclude, at point rB (their rational belief), that this event is unfortunate, inconvenient, and disadvantageous, and that they wish it would change for the better or disappear, and they appropriately feel, at point C (the consequence), sad, regretful, frustrated, or annoyed. These appropriate feelings usually help them to try to do something about the noxious activating event, so they feel a new consequence, namely, neutrality or joy. Their inborn and acquired hedonistic orientation thereby encourages them to have, in regard to noxious or unpleasant activating events (or activating experiences), thoughts ("I don't like this; let's see what I can do to change it") and feelings (sorrow and annoyance) that enable them to reorder their environment and to live more enjoyably.

Very often, however, when similar noxious activating events occur in people's lives, they observe these events intolerantly and grandiosely and conclude, at point *iB* (their irrational beliefs), that they are awful, horrible, and catastrophic; that they *must* not exist; and that they absolutely cannot stand them. They then inappropriately feel the consequence, at point *C,* of worthlessness, guilt, anxiety, depression, rage, and inertia. Their inappropriate feelings usually interfere with their doing something constructive about the noxious activating events, and they tend to condemn themselves for their unconstructiveness and to experience more feelings of shame, inferiority, and hopelessness. Their inborn and acquired person downing, antihumanistic, god-and-devil-inventing philosophy encourages them to have, in regard to noxious or unpleasant activating events, foolish thoughts ("How awful this is and I am! There's nothing I can do about it!") and inappropriate feelings (hatred of themselves, of others, and of the world) that drive them to whine and rant and to live less enjoyably.

RET is a cognitive-emotive-behavioristic method of psychotherapy uniquely designed to enable the individual to observe, to understand, and persistently to attack his irrational, grandiose, perfectionistic *shoulds, oughts,* and *musts.* It employs the logico-empirical method of science to encourage people to surrender magic, absolutes, gods, and devils; to acknowledge that nothing is sacred or all-important (although many things are quite important) and nothing is "awful" or "terrible" (although many things are exceptionally unpleasant and inconvenient); and to gradually teach themselves and to practice the philosophy of desiring rather than demanding and of working at changing what they can change and gracefully lumping what they cannot.

In conclusion, rational-emotive therapy is a method of personality change that quickly and efficiently helps people resist their tendencies to be conforming, suggestible, and unenjoying. It actively and didactically, as well as emotively and behaviorally, shows people how to abet and enhance one side of their humanness while simultaneously changing and living more happily with (and not repressing or squelching) another side of their humanity. It is thus realistic and practical, as well as idealistic and future oriented. It helps individuals more fully to actualize, experience, and enjoy the here and now; but it also espouses long-range hedonism, which includes planning for their own (and others') future. It is what its name implies: rational *and* emotive, realistic *and* visionary, empirical *and* humanistic. As, in all their complexity, are humans.

ANNOTATED BIBLIOGRAPHY

Ellis, Albert. *How to live with a "neurotic."* New York: Crown Publishers, 1957. (Revised edition, 1975.)
The first book published on RET showing how almost anyone can use it to cope with and to help disturbed individuals at home or on the job. Also the first psychology book using a new linguistic device called E-prime language, or "semantic therapy," which eliminates the use of any form of the verb "to be," allowing no implication that human behavior remains fixed or unalterable.

Ellis, Albert. *Reason and emotion in psychotherapy.* New York: Lyle Stuart, 1962. Paperback edition, New York: Citadel, 1977.
The first book presenting RET in textbook form, mainly written for therapists and clinicians but also widely used by people who want to help themselves overcome their emotional problems.

Ellis, Albert. *Growth through reason: Verbatim cases in rational-emotive therapy.* Palo Alto, Calif: Science and Behavior Books; and Hollywood: Wilshire Books, 1971.
Verbatim dialogues between rational-emotive therapists and their clients, with Dr. Ellis stopping the tape, so to speak, at frequent in-

tervals to explain what is happening—what techniques of RET the therapist is using and what growth is taking place. Two of Dr. Ellis's therapy dialogues are included, as well as those by other therapists using RET: Drs. Ben N. Ard, Jr., H. Jon Geis, John M. Gullo, Paul A. Hauck, and Maxie C. Maultsby, Jr.

Ellis, Albert. *Humanistic psychotherapy: The rational-emotive approach.* New York: Julian Press and McGraw-Hill Paperbacks, 1973.

Presents, for the public and the profession, an up-to-date version of RET that emphasizes both its humanistic and its active-directive aspects. Places humans squarely in the center of the universe and shows how they have full responsibility for choosing to make or not make themselves emotionally disturbed.

Ellis, Albert, & Grieger, Russell. *Rational-emotive therapy: Handbook of theory and practice.* New York: Springer, 1977.

A sourcebook of some of the most salient and classic writings on RET, with sections on the theoretical and conceptional foundations of RET, the dynamics of emotional disturbance, primary techniques and basic process of rational-emotive therapy, and RET with children.

Ellis, Albert, & Harper, Robert A. *A new guide to rational living.* Englewood Cliffs, N.J.: Prentice-Hall; and Hollywood: Wilshire Books, 1975.

A completely revised and rewritten version of the RET self-help classic. One of the most widely read self-help books ever published and the one most often recommended by cognitive-behavior therapists to their clients. A succinct, straightforward approach to RET based on self-questioning and homework.

CASE READINGS

Ellis, Albert. A twenty-three-year-old woman, guilty about not following her parents' rules. In A. Ellis, *Growth through reason: Verbatim cases in rational-emotive therapy.* Palo Alto, Calif.: Science and Behavior Books; and Hollywood: Wilshire Books, 1971, pp. 223–86.

Ellis presents a verbatim protocol of the first, second, and fourth sessions with a woman who comes for help because she is quite self-punishing, impulsive and compulsive, afraid of males, has no goals in life, and is guilty about her relations with her parents.

The therapist quickly zeroes in on her main problems and shows her that she need not feel guilty about doing what she wants to do in life, even if her parents keep upsetting themselves about her beliefs and actions.

Maultsby, Maxie C., Jr. A relapsed client with severe phobic reactions. In A. Ellis, *Growth through reason: Verbatim cases in rational-emotive therapy.* Palo Alto, Calif.: Science and Behavior Books; and Hollywood: Wilshire Books, 1971, pp. 179–222.

Maultsby presents a verbatim first session and parts of subsequent sessions with a 24-year-old undergraduate student who had been previously hospitalized for a psychotic episode, who had 30 sessions of traditional psychotherapy, who reported significant improvement in most of his problems after 50 sessions of group rational-emotive therapy, but a year later reported that his gains were being whittled away, that he was becoming afraid of having a concussion and a consequent major loss of his intelligence, that he again felt stupid in his school work, and that he blamed many of his personal failings on an automobile accident. Maultsby deals with this relapsed client in an active-directive manner and in relatively few additional sessions helps him get to the point where he no longer feels disturbed.

Ellis, Albert. Verbatim psychotherapy session with a procrastinator. In A. Ellis & W. J. Knaus, *Overcoming procrastination.* New York: Institute for Rational Living, 1977, pp. 152–67.

Ellis presents a single verbatim session with a procrastinator who was failing to finish her doctoral thesis in sociology. He deals with her problems in a direct, no-nonsense manner typical of rational-emotive therapy; and as a result of a single session, she later reports she finished her thesis although she had previously been procrastinating on it for a number of years.

REFERENCES

Adler, A. *What life should mean to you.* New York: Blue Ribbon Books, 1931.

Adler, A. *Superiority and social interest.* Ed. by H. L. Ansbacher & R. R. Ansbacher. Evanston, Ill.: Northwestern University Press, 1964(a).

Adler, A. *Social interest: A challenge to mankind.* New York: Capricorn Books, 1964(b).

Beck, A. T. Cognitive Therapy and the emotional disorders. New York: International Universities Press, 1976.

Bedford, S. *Instant replay.* New York: Institute for Rational Living, 1974.

Berger, T. *I have feelings.* New York: 1971.

Bessai, J. *A factorial assessment of irrational beliefs.* M. A. Thesis, Cleveland State University, 1975.

Bone, H. Two proposed alternatives to psychoanalytic interpreting. In E. Hammer (Ed.), *The use of interpretation in treatment.* New York: Grune and Stratton, 1968, pp. 169-96.

Church, V. A. *Behavior, law and remedies.* Dubuque, Ia.: Kendall/Hunt, 1975.

Diekstra, R. F. W., & Dassen, W. F. M. *Rationele Therapie.* Amsterdam: Swets and Zeitlinger, 1976.

DiGiuseppe, R.; Miller, N.; & Trexler, L. A review of rational-emotive psychotherapy outcome studies. *Counseling Psychologist,* 1977.

Ellis, A. *How to live with a "neurotic."* New York: Crown Publishers, 1957. Rev. ed., 1975.

Ellis, A. *Reason and emotion in psychotherapy.* New York: Lyle Stuart, and Citadel Press, 1962.

Ellis, A. *Is objectivism a religion?* New York: Lyle Stuart, 1968.

Ellis, A. Teaching emotional education in the classroom. *School Health Review,* November 1969(a), 10-13.

Ellis, A. A weekend of rational encounter. In A. Burton (Ed.), *Encounter.* San Francisco: Jossey-Bass, 1969(b), pp. 112-27.

Ellis, A. *The art and science of love.* Rev. ed. New York: Lyle Stuart and Bantam Books, 1969(c).

Ellis, A. *Personality data form.* New York: Institute for Rational Living, 1971(a).

Ellis, A. *Growth through reason.* Palo Alto, Calif.: Science and Behavior Books; and Hollywood: Wilshire Books, 1971(b).

Ellis, A. *Executive leadership: A rational approach.* New York: Institute for Rational Living, 1972(a).

Ellis, A. *The sensuous person.* New York: Lyle Stuart and New Library, 1972(b).

Ellis, A. Emotional education with groups of normal school children. In M. M. Ohlsen (Ed.), *Counseling children in groups.* New York: Holt, Rinehart & Winston, 1973(a). (Reprinted: New York: Institute for Rational Living, 1973.)

Ellis, A. *Humanistic psychotherapy: The rational-emotive approach.* New York: Julian Press and McGraw-Hill Paperbacks, 1973(b).

Ellis, A Rational-emotive theory. In A. Burton (Ed.), *Operational theories of personality.* New York: Brunner/Mazel, 1974, pp. 308-44.

Ellis, A. *Sex and the liberated man.* New York: Lyle Stuart, 1976(a).

Ellis, A. The biological basis of human irrationality. *Journal of Individual Psychology,* 1976(b), 32, 145-68.

Ellis, A. *How to live with—and without— anger.* New York: Readers' Digest Press, 1977(a).

Ellis, A. Rational-emotive therapy: Research data that supports the clinical and personality hypotheses of RET and other modes of cognitive-behavior therapy. *Counseling Psychologist,* 1977(b), 7(1), 2-42.

Ellis, A. RET as a personality theory, therapy approach, and philosophy of life. In J. L. Wolfe & E. Brand (Eds.), *Twenty years of rational therapy.* New York: Institute for Rational Living, 1977(c).

Ellis, A. *A garland of rational songs.* New York: Institute for Rational Living, 1977(d).

Ellis, A. *Rational self help form.* New York: Institute for Rational Living, 1977(e).

Ellis, A. *Fun as psychotherapy.* Cassette recording. New York: Institute for Rational Living, 1977(f).

Ellis, A. Toward a theory of personality. In R. J. Corsini (Ed.), *Readings in current personality theory.* Itasca, Ill.: F. E. Peacock Publishers, 1978.

Ellis, A., & Abrahms, E. *Brief psychotherapy in medical and health practice.* New York: Springer, 1978.

Ellis, A., & Grieger, R. *Handbook of rational-emotive therapy.* New York: Springer, 1977.

Ellis, A., & Gullo, J. M. *Murder and assassination.* New York: Lyle Stuart, 1972.

Ellis, A., & Harper, R. A. *A guide to rational living.* Englewood Cliffs, N.J.: Prentice-Hall, 1961(a). (Paperback edition, Hollywood: Wilshire Books, 1971.)

Ellis, A., & Harper, R. A. *Creative marriage.* New York: Lyle Stuart, Inc., 1961(b). (Paperback edition, under the title, *A guide to successful marriage.* Hollywood: Wilshire Books, 1971.)

Ellis, A., & Harper, R. A. *A new guide to ra-*

tional living. Englewood Cliffs, N.J.: Prentice-Hall; and Hollywood: Wilshire Books, 1975.

Ellis, A.; Wolfe, J. L.; & Moseley, S. *How to raise an emotionally healthy, happy child.* Hollywood: Wilshire Books, 1972.

Freud, S. *Standard edition of the complete psychological works of Sigmund Freud.* London: Hogarth, 1965.

Garcia, E., & Pellegrini, N. *Homer the homely hound dog.* New York: Institute for Rational Living, 1974.

Goldfried, M. R., & Davison, G. C. *Clinical behavior therapy.* New York: Holt, Rinehart & Winston, 1976.

Goldfried, M. R., & Merbaum, M. (Eds.) *Behavior change through self-control.* New York: Holt, Rinehart & Winston, 1973.

Gullo, J. M. Counseling hospitalized patients. *Rational Living,* 1966, 1(2), 11–15.

Hauck, P. A. *The rational management of children.* Roslyn Heights, N.Y.: Libra Publishers, 1967.

Hauck, P. A. *Reason in pastoral counseling.* Philadelphia: Westminster Press, 1972.

Jones, R. G. *A factored measure of Ellis' irrational belief system with personality and maladjustment correlates.* Ph.D. dissertation, Texas Technological College, 1968.

Knaus, W. *Rational emotive education.* New York: Institute for Rational Living, 1974.

Lange, A., & Jakubowski, P. *Responsible assertion training.* Champaign, Ill.: Research Press, 1976.

Lazarus, A. A. *Behavior therapy and beyond.* New York: McGraw-Hill, 1971.

Lazarus, A. A. *Multimodal therapy.* New York: Springer, 1976.

Lembo, J. *The counseling process: A rational behavioral approach.* Roslyn Heights, N.Y.: Libra Publishers, 1976.

Mahoney, J. J. *Cognition and behavior modification.* Cambridge, Mass.: Ballinger, 1974.

Maultsby, M. C., Jr. *Help yourself to happiness.* New York: Institute for Rational Living, 1975.

Meichenbaum, D. H. *Cognitive behavior therapy.* New York: Plenum, 1977.

Morris, K. T., & Kanitz, H. M. *Rational-emotive therapy.* Boston: Houghton Mifflin, 1975.

Murphy, R., & Ellis, A. *A comprehensive bibliography of materials on rational-emotive therapy and cognitive-behavior therapy.* New York: Institute for Rational Living, 1979.

Smith, M. L., & Glass, G. V. Meta analysis of psychotherapy outcome studies. *American Psychologist,* 1977, 32, 752–60.

Tosi, D. J. *Youth: Toward personal growth, a rational-emotive approach.* Columbus, Ohio: Charles E. Merrill, 1974.

Wolfe, J. L. Short term effects of modeling/behavior rehearsal, modeling/behavior rehearsal plus rational therapy, and placebo. Ph.D. dissertation, New York University, 1975.

Wolfe, J. L. *How to be sexually assertive.* New York: Institute for Rational Living, 1976(a).

Wolfe, J. L. *Rational-emotive therapy as an effective feminist therapy.* 1976(b), 1 (1) 2–7. Reprinted: New York: Institute for Rational Living, 1976(b).

Wolfe, J., & Brand, E. (Eds.) *Twenty years of rational therapy: Proceedings from the First National Conference on Rational Therapy.* New York: Institute for Rational Living, 1977.

Young, H. S. *A rational counseling primer.* New York: Institute for Rational Living, 1974.

Zingle, H. W. *Therapy approach to counseling underachievers.* Ph.D. dissertation, University of Alberta, 1965.

Zingle, H. W., & Mallett, M. *A bibliography of R-E-T materials, articles and theses from the University of Alberta.* Edmonton, Canada: University of Alberta, 1976.

6

Behavioral Psychotherapy

DIANNE L. CHAMBLESS and ALAN J. GOLDSTEIN

OVERVIEW

Behavioral psychotherapy consists of two related systems of treatment: (a) *behavior therapy,* based on the work of Joseph Wolpe, and (b) *behavior modification,* based on the work of B. F. Skinner. The first system follows a classical conditioning model, and the second is derived from operant conditioning.

In both systems, problematical behaviors (affective, cognitive, or motoric) are seen as responses to stimuli, internal and external, and psychological distress is viewed as the result of ineffective or maladaptive learning. Behavioral treatment is based on implementing experimentally derived laws of learning so desirable behaviors replace less functional ones.

Basic Concepts

A basic assumption of behavioral approaches to therapy is that people have become what they are through learning processes, or more correctly through the interaction of the environment with their genetic endowment. Problems, therefore, are generally learned and can be unlearned; deficits occur when there has been inadequate learning, and these deficits can be corrected through provision of the necessary learning experiences. Naturally, physical conditions resulting from inherited or acquired disorders impose certain restrictions, for example, a severely retarded person cannot learn calculus. Faced with an individual with a maladaptive learning history, the psychotherapist's task is to collaborate with the client in a program designed to generate corrective learning experiences.

Possibly because of the diverse populations they treat, different learning theory therapists focus on varied aspects of clients' problems. In *behavior therapy,* originated largely by Wolpe (1958), the emphasis is on reducing anxiety that is presumed to underlie most "neurotic" behavior. Behaviorists of this school rely heavily on a Pavlovian model and assume anxiety has been classically conditioned to harmless stimuli. As a result a number of treatment techniques have been developed by behavior therapists for deconditioning autonomic nervous system responses to key stimuli in the client's environment.

Behavior modification evolved from Skinner's work on operant conditioning (1938), which emphasized changing the frequency of overt behaviors. Skinner (1953) viewed most emotional problems as reactions to overcontrolling, punitive environments. Fear is conditioned to situations for which one has been punished, and subsequently even thoughts about these situations elicit anxiety, guilt, and shame. Depression results when there is no escape from noxious stimuli, when one feels helpless. Anger springs from blocked or ineffective revolt against the controlling or punitive agent. Under such conditions, according to operant theory, maladaptive habits will develop through reinforcement by escape from these aversive feelings.

Skinner also notes that sometimes problems occur from a lack of control; however, control can be learned. Much of the work in behavior modification has been in adding controls and teaching new presumably desirable behaviors that have not been already learned.

There is a lot of overlap between behavior therapy and behavior modification, the differences being primarily in the emphasis placed on respondent or operant behavior, respectively. The most comprehensive therapeutic approach combines techniques from both schools. Many clients need not only relearning but also new learning, since anxiety has often blocked them from learning more effective responses.

A distorted view of the practice of behavior therapy-behavior modification has resulted from a literal interpretation of H. J. Eysenck's statement, ". . . There is no neurosis underlying the symptom, but merely the symptom itself. Get rid of the symptom (skeletal and autonomic) and you have eliminated the neurosis" (Eysenck & Rachman, 1965, p. 10). This statement highlights differences with other theories of psychotherapy, particularly psychoanalytic therapy, but, taken out of context, it results in an overly simplistic view of behavioral treatment. In fact, behaviorists do not assume the "symptom" or presenting complaint is the entire prob-

lem. Occasionally this is so, but more frequently it is part of a larger problem as yet undefined by the client. Most human problems are comprised of numerous components—thoughts, feelings, and actions including interactions with other people. No one of these components is the "real" problem or causes the real problem. Rather, they are all part of the problem that needs correction.

The range of application of behavioral methods is enormous. The "client" may be a single individual, a class, or an entire community. Problems treated may be as narrow as "ineffective study habits," as broad as an "inadequate personality," or as fundamental as the "inability to feed oneself." Behavior therapists-modifiers may be school counselors, psychotherapists in psychiatric clinics and private practice, nurses and hospital aides, or community consultants. The amount of involvement with the client may be as little as one contact by letter or as much as a 24-hour-a-day program for life (with permanently institutionalized populations). In a controversial novel, *Walden Two* (1948), Skinner advocated application of behavioral principles to all activities of a community including work and child care. A. E. Kazdin (1977) has reviewed the mixed results of several communities that have attempted to implement this fantasy.

As knowledge of behavioral technology has spread, so has public concern about its use. Much of the outcry seems based on the failure to discriminate the methodology of behaviorism from some of the distasteful ways it has been used. The laws of learning are value-free but may be implemented toward goals perceived as good by some and evil by others. This has been particularly the case with behavior modification because of the populations with which it has commonly been employed.

Children, prisoners, retardates, and inmates of mental institutions live under restricted conditions, and some civil libertarians fear that behavior modification techniques will limit what little freedom and control these individuals still have. In some cases, basic rights were denied to institutionalized clients. Such reprehensible actions have been curbed by the judicial system. However, wide publicity about these particular programs has resulted in the erroneous equation of behaviorism with "Clockwork Orange" conceptualizations (Burgess, 1963).

Although guidelines must be set to avoid future abuses, it is important to remember that institutional control was not invented by behaviorists. Hospital inmates have always been rewarded with weekend passes for "sane" behavior, children given good grades for "attentiveness," and prisoners awarded parole for "good behavior." The application of behavioral principles has not resulted in the exertion of more control over institutionalized clients, but rather in clearer contingencies for such rewards and punishments. In traditional systems, inmates are sometimes punished when they fail to meet a particular criterion of acceptable behavior, even when that criterion requires responses they are incapable of making. In proper behavioral programs the staff helps the clients attain mutually desired target goals through operant principles.

Another frequently heard criticism is that behavior modification has been used in a repressive manner to further the ends of "the system." This has been the case all too often; however, these are the actions of particular individuals. Conformity is not an inherent goal of behaviorism. Although classroom token economies probably overemphasize "good behavior," academic achievement and creativity can also be increased through reward. Although students have often been the target of change programs, pupils have also been taught to modify their teachers' behavior (Gray, Graubard, & Rosenberg, 1974)! Skinner (1953) has suggested that a major function of psychotherapy should be teaching clients to generate self-controlling stimuli. It is toward this end that behavior therapists and cognitive behavior modifiers commonly work with their clients.

Very close to the issue of control is the furor raised by a basic tenet of philosophical behaviorism—*determinism*. Every behavior is considered to be completely determined by antecedent factors, leaving no room for cherished philosophical notions such as *free will*. Skinner in particular has been the target of much animosity around this issue. In defense he compares his critics to the outraged contemporaries of Copernicus, who dared to suggest the earth was not the center of the universe (1953). One can employ the therapeutic techniques generated by behaviorism without having to concur that determinism is a principle of "reality" (none of us will ever know what reality is); determinism may be viewed simply as a useful concept for approaching and dealing with human problems.

Other Systems

Behavior therapists frequently take concepts from other models and translate them into behavioral terms and incorporate them into a broad learning-theory system. To deny their origins, however, would be to ignore the important contributions of training in other therapeutic systems. No system of therapy is all right and others all wrong; rather, some systems are better for some clients and some therapists than others. Each therapist should find a conceptual system that allows most satisfactory work with client populations. The therapist who adopts a learning-theory approach will find certain advantages to the system.

Validation. Behavioral psychotherapy emphasizes empirical validation—a point largely ignored by other approaches with the notable exception of Carl Rogers' person-centered therapy. Establishing observable goals and evaluating progress toward those goals is an important aspect of behavior therapy-modification. When improvement is not obtained with one technique, the behavioral therapist ordinarily shifts to a new approach. In dogmatic systems, the patient who has not improved is presumed to need more of the same treatment. In behavioral psychotherapy, it is usually clear to client and counselor when termination is appropriate, since goals have been clearly defined. Consequently there is less chance of therapy becoming an interminable process.

Change Process. After months or years of verbal psychotherapy, clients sometimes remark, "Okay, now I understand what I'm doing and why but how do I go about changing it?" At that point, the therapist may reflect, "You're feeling pretty frustrated at not knowing how to change and you wish I could tell you how," and then interpret the increased frustration as a result of unmet dependency needs. In most cases such responses are not particularly helpful. Once it is clear what change the client wants to make, behavioral techniques seem effective in bringing about changes. Some clients, left to their own devices to find a way to change, are able to do so. Nevertheless, experimental psychologists demonstrated years ago that trial and error behavior is not the most efficient way to learn. Much time and money can be saved when the therapist has specific ways of helping the client learn new behaviors or unlearn maladaptive ones, rather than just waiting for the client to stumble on a good approach. Thus the desired changes are likely to occur more quickly through behavioral treatment than with other therapies.

The behavior therapist is not a passive partner just waiting for change to occur. The therapist is free to be much more active than in other therapies and will usually make direct suggestions. Clients do not appreciate being told what to do before they have clarified what they want. Once goals have been set, they generally want help in attaining these goals and usually expect "helpers" to provide guidance. The coherent set of principles provided by learning theory aids the therapist in selecting ways to break down desired changes into manageable steps. Therapeutic interventions flow logically from the functional analysis of the problem.

Blame-Free Therapy. Behavior therapy-modification does not depend on a disease model. Diagnosis and labeling are used only to attain direct implications for treatment. Problems and assets are assumed to result from learning; consequently clients in behavior therapy are not viewed as sick but as having difficulties. The therapist or counselor generally functions more like a consultant or a teacher than a "doctor." Therapy is seen as a collaborative process to be explained to the client every step of the way. There is no need for mystery, and nothing is "done to" a client. Since it is the counselor's task to reduce the desired goal to digestible chunks of learning, a client who cannot master a particular step is not blamed for resisting, or saying "I can't" instead of "I won't." Statements about resistance are basically pejorative and are excuses for a therapist who has not reduced a client's anxiety sufficiently to make new learning possible or who has failed to control an important variable. This is not to say that behaviorists do not encounter clients they are unable to help; they do, but this indicates inadequate methods, not inadequate clients.

Some traditional psychotherapies, particularly psychoanalytically oriented therapy, have been especially destructive to women. Female clients have learned to blame themselves for inadequacies in a system where anatomical facts are presumed to have inevitable consequences. Although sexism exists among behaviorists, it would be totally inconsistent with learning theory to assume that, for instance, a woman is "masochistic" because her anatomy or her environment shaped her that way. The behavioral approach logically leads to attempting to reverse those learning contingencies, rather than urging acceptance of her lot as a second-class citizen. Clients usually respond to a learning-theory analysis of their problems with a great sense of relief on finding they are not seen as sick or weak; they appreciate the positive orientation toward changing the problematic situation rather than dwelling on it.

Present and Future Orientation. Many clients seeking counseling for particular complaints find themselves spending a great deal of time in what seems to them a useless practice—talking about their childhoods. Delving into the past can be fascinating for introspectively inclined people but most clients are more interested in symptom relief, the sooner the better. Many people have given up on getting assistance for their problems because they were unable to convince their therapists that they needed help on what was concerning them in the present rather than delving into the past. The emphasis in behavioral psychotherapy is on chang-

ing behavior specifically related to the presenting problem of the client. An important trend in behavior modification is teaching the client general strategies that can be applied not only to the current problem but also to difficulties that may crop up in the future, thereby training the client to become his or her counselor.

HISTORY

Precursors

The history of conditioning, the underpinnings of behavior therapy, begins with Ivan Sechenov (1829–1905), the father of Russian physiology. About 1863 he described the functions of the brain in terms of a reflex arc that had three components: sensory input, process, and efferent outflow. All behavior, Sechenov stated, consisted of responses to stimulations, with interactions of excitations and inhibitions operating at the central part of the reflex arc. Using this model, Pavlov (1849–1936) embarked on a series of classical experiments wherein salivary responses in dogs were conditioned to various stimuli. In these experiments, he demonstrated many of the phenomena later extended to all types of learning.

In America the dominant force in behaviorism was Edward Thorndike (1913), who proposed the "law of effect" as the major factor in learning. The law stated that bonds between stimuli and responses were "stamped in" by reward and weakened by punishment. Responses carried over to new situations to the degree that these new situations resembled the original set of stimuli. Thorndike's theory was an ancestor of Skinner's operant conditioning theory. In 1927 Bekhterev and Pavlov were translated into English with considerable impact on American psychology. Different theories competed with Thorndike's, and concepts were derived to explain complex behavior in behavioral terms. The rivalry among learning theorists like E. R. Guthrie (1935), C. L. Hull (1943), E. C. Tolman (1932), and B. F. Skinner (1938) led not only to heated debate but also to controlled experiments designed to test hypotheses derived from the various theories.

Beginnings

It is difficult to pinpoint the earliest contributors to behavior therapy-modification, for there were many isolated investigations that were never pursued. One of the most noteworthy was the induction of a phobia by John B. Watson and Rosalie Rayner (1920) in a child known as "little Albert." Albert, who had demonstrated no fear when presented with white furry objects, received a number of trials of aversive conditioning to the sight of a white rat that was paired with a loud noise. Albert subsequently showed fear in the presence not only of a white rat but also of other white furry objects such as cotton and rabbits. The experimenters outlined four different procedures they intended to try to remove Albert's fear, all of which are now useful behavioral techniques. Unfortunately Albert left the hospital before they could do so. It should go without saying that such an unethical experiment would not be replicated today. Four years later, Mary Cover Jones (1924) demonstrated the efficacy of one of the procedures suggested by Watson and Rayner with a rabbit phobic child. Three-year-old Peter M. had a rabbit brought slowly closer to him while he was eating, and by the end of the experiment he could cheerfully pet the animal—a successful procedure that presaged Wolpe's development of systematic desensitization (1958).

The history of aversion therapy shows more continuity. N. Kantorovich (1929) is most often credited with the first clinical use of this approach. Using a counterconditioning model, he treated 20 alcoholic patients by giving them alcohol along with "a strong electrodermal stimulus." A stable reflex took place that was marked by "withdrawal of the hands and body, and mimeo-somatic responses of repugnance," in the presence of alcohol. He reported that most clients refrained from the use of alcohol after treatment. L. W. Max (1935) reported the treatment of a homosexual fetish by the administration of strong shocks in the presence of the fetishistic stimulus. He noted that the effect of three months of treatment was cumulative and that an important variable was the intensity of shock (low-intensity shock was found to be ineffective). Throughout the 1950s, studies were reported in which chemical-aversive stimuli (*emetics*) were used to produce nausea contiguous with alcohol or fetishistic stimuli (reviewed by Rachman & Teasdale, 1969). The results of these early techniques have been improved upon by closer attention to effective procedures as established in the laboratory. Joseph R. Cautela's innovation of the use of imaginal noxious stimuli (1967) has made aversive techniques more acceptable to practitioners and clients.

John Dollard and N. E. Miller (1950) broke important ground for behavior therapists-modifiers by restating psychoanalytic theory and practice in learning-theory terminology. This paved the way for the application of scientific principles and experimental data to the behavior of therapists and clients, a thread picked up by Wolpe (1958) and Skinner (1953), the pioneers of modern behavioral treatment.

Skinner's followers, most notably O. R. Lindsley (1956) and C. B. Ferster

(1961), demonstrated that behavior could be altered through operant conditioning. Teodoro Ayllon and his colleagues (e.g., Ayllon & Michael, 1959) established the therapeutic potential of these techniques with psychotic inpatients, and in 1965 Ayllon and N. H. Azrin published their landmark work using a token economy with chronic schizophrenics. This model has since been productively followed in many different settings with diverse populations (Kazdin, 1977).

Focusing on neurotic behaviors, Wolpe (1958) experimented with using feeding and gradual approach to teach "experimentally neurotic" cats to enter feared situations. Wolpe reasoned that the eating response inhibited the low amounts of anxiety generated by small steps toward the feared stimulus. Extrapolating from this work to humans, he taught clients with fears to relax in an attempt to use relaxation to inhibit the anxiety they might experience in approaching their feared stimuli (either in imagination or in reality). The result was systematic desensitization, a highly effective treatment for phobias. Further influences on the evolution of behavior therapy were books by H. J. Eysenck (1960) and L. P. Ullman and Leonard Krasner (1965), which brought together diverse applications of behavioral techniques within a unified conceptual framework.

Current Status

In the years since the appearance of Wolpe's pioneering book (1958), publications in the area of behavior therapy have increased in geometric proportions. There were only scattered, periodic reports of the use of behavior therapy in the early 1960s, but by 1970 publications such as the *Journal of Abnormal Psychology* and *The British Journal of Psychiatry*

were devoting a considerable percentage of space to articles on behavior therapy. A number of journals now exist for the publication of articles exclusively behavioral in scope including *Behaviour Research and Therapy, The Journal of Experimental Analysis of Behavior, Behavior Therapy,* the *Journal of Behavior Therapy and Experimental Psychiatry, Cognitive Therapy and Research, Behavior Modification, Biofeedback and Stress Reduction,* and the *Journal of Applied Behavioral Analysis.*

The quality of articles has shown considerable refinement over time. Most early items were case reports and theoretical articles; now experimental papers predominate. Professional associations concerned with behavioral therapies have been established and have growing memberships. The most prominent of these is the *Association for Advancement of Behavior Therapy* (AABT), which holds an annual convention.

In formal training in psychotherapy, the trend toward behavioral models has been overwhelming. In 1960 there were probably no departments of psychology or psychiatry in which behavior therapy was even tangentially included. By 1970 hardly any department involved in graduate training in clinical psychology was without at least some percentage of clinical training devoted to behavioral methods and theory, and some psychology departments had become almost exclusively behavioral in orientation. AABT maintains a list of behaviorally oriented internship placements for clinical psychology students.

The parallel development in psychiatry has not been as rapid, but largely psychoanalytically oriented residency programs may now include some behavioral training, as is the case at the medical schools of Temple University and the University of

Pennsylvania. The Behavior Therapy Unit at Temple Medical School offers postdoctoral and postresidency training in behavioral psychotherapy. The new field of behavioral medicine is growing in departments of psychiatry such as those at the University of Pennsylvania and Thomas Jefferson University where problems that are both psychological and physical such as obesity, alcoholism, and psychosomatic illnesses are studied and treated with behavioral interventions, including biofeedback (see Katz & Zlutnick, 1975).

After the appearance of Wolpe's 1958 book, research in behavioral treatment gained rapid momentum. Initially all well-controlled studies relied on nonclinical populations (e.g., Paul, 1966), and although these continue to be the majority, studies using clinical populations are more common (e.g., Drabman & Spitalnik, 1973). An additional trend is the emphasis on investigating the treatment of homogeneous problems to determine what method is most effective for which problem.

At this time, research in processes is in the early stages and presents a confusing picture. The techniques of *systematic desensitization* and *flooding* have been extensively researched, and research on the active components of other techniques is expanding. Fueled by contradictory findings, arguments continue among the proponents of different theoretical models. There is less information about the client's impact on the treatment process and on therapist variables. *What are the characteristics of clients for whom currently available treatments fail? Why does a client cooperate with treatment and improve with one therapist after refusing the same intervention from other therapists?* Clearly there is much work left to be done, and in the foreseeable future doc-

toral students need not worry about a lack of dissertation topics.

PERSONALITY

Theory of Personality

On the whole, little attention has been devoted to the development of a behavioral model of personality theory. One notable exception is Eysenck's work on defining personality factors through factor analysis of quantifiable traits such as compulsiveness, sociability, responsiveness, depression, and rigidity (Eysenck, 1967; Eysenck & Eysenck, 1969). He has derived second-order concepts of introversion-extroversion (E) and neuroticism (N). He suggests that neuroticism denotes a predisposition to neurotic behavior but is not identical with it, so someone who is high on neuroticism but who has not encountered stresses in life may not necessarily engage in neurotic behavior.

Both N and E are based on psychological structures that can be specified; neurotic and extroverted behaviors are the outcome of an interaction between experience and individual reactions mediated by these structures. According to Eysenck's theory (1967), individual differences in the thresholds to stimulation of the visceral brain are responsible for differences in neuroticism-emotionality, and high N scorers have a more labile, more easily aroused autonomic system, with a tendency for arousal to die down less readily. Individual differences in E are mediated by differential thresholds to stimulation of the ascending reticular activating system, in that introverts are characterized by a higher state of cortical arousal and extroverts by a lower stage of cortical arousal. These states of high or low arousal mediate excitatory and inhibitory states, leading to high excitatory-low inhibitory states in introverts, and low excitatory-high inhibitory states in extroverts. (Note that the terms *inhibition* and *excitation* here refer to states of the cortex; if the cortex is in a state of excitation arousal, it inhibits the activities of the lower centers, thus producing inhibited behavior; a state of inhibition in the cortex frees the lower centers from cortical control, thus leading to uninhibited behavior.) (Alcohol *depresses* cortical activity, but *disinhibits* behavior.) (Eysenck & Beech, 1971, p. 559)

In a preliminary way, Skinner (1953) has sketched the fashion in which a behaviorist might view personality variables. In his system, the *self* represents a functionally unified system of responses, and one's awareness of that self (*self-knowledge*) is a description of one's own behavior. This concept leaves open the possibility that any one person might exhibit a number of selves. Moods and dispositions are construed as second-order probabilities, that is, the probability that a given circumstance will raise the probability of a given response. For example, saying that a man has a "fiery" disposition is saying that it is very likely if someone steps in front of him in line, he will turn red, shout, start swinging his fists, and so on. Skinner finds that when other theorists speak of traits, they are referring to what he sees as differences in processes or differences in the independent variables to which people have been exposed. Thus, the assumption of high intelligence is abstracted from the observation that someone learns quickly (a process discrimination).

An important independent variable affecting "personality" is a history of excessive punishment that reinforces people for certain maladaptive operants. A shy person thus can be understood as one who emits avoidance behavior ("shy" away from people) based on previous punishing experiences for nonavoidant behavior (such as being "friendly").

Behavioral terminology becomes admittedly laborious, and in their private moments, behaviorists tend to use "personality" labels as a kind of shorthand. What is the advantage to this more laborious fashion of talking about specific characteristics? The advantage in using Skinner's precise language is that one avoids reifying a descriptive adjective. In viewing a trait as ongoing behavior, one sees the possibility for change and frequently such behavioral descriptions suggest treatment intervention. Meeting a person who has stopped smoking, one might think: "What self-control!" Another person who is still puffing away is likely to be told, "You need more self-control!" This leads nowhere, for self-control is not a thing; it is a process, a series of learnable behaviors. Thus the smoker wastes time despairing over lack of self-control when he could be asking the nonsmoker to specify how she controls herself. In recent years, considerable attention has been given to clarifying and teaching self-control behaviors to clients in behavior therapy-modification.

It is likely that as cognitive behavioral approaches mature there will be a behavioral theory of personality. The interest in cognitive processes is focusing attention on consistencies in an individual's response despite changes in the external environment. Such consistencies are viewed as "rules" or "general coping strategies" and differ from "traits" in an important fashion. Cognitive behavioral workers put considerable emphasis on staying close to an empirical level. Consequently they are unlikely to indulge in abstract, unverifiable descriptions of human behavior.

Variety of Concepts

Behaviorists assume that people develop those consistencies known as "personality" through maturation and through the "laws of learning." These core concepts are briefly reviewed here as familiarity with them is assumed in this chapter. For a more thorough review, see Albert Bandura (1969) or F. H. Kanfer and J. S. Phillips (1970).

Classical Conditioning. In *classical conditioning,* learning is demonstrated by the acquisition of a conditioned response. A stimulus that already elicits a response, an *unconditioned stimulus,* is presented in close temporal contiguity with a *neutral stimulus,* which ordinarily either elicits no response, or a different response. With repetitive pairings of the neutral stimulus and the unconditioned stimulus, the neutral stimulus develops the capacity to elicit a response similar to the one elicited by the unconditioned stimulus and at this point the originally neutral stimulus is called a *conditioned stimulus.* When a response to the conditioned stimulus appears, it is called the *conditioned response.* With humans the most important classically conditioned responses are emotional. For example, a child who is punished for masturbating may develop a conditioned anxiety about sexual self-stimulation that may persist into adulthood.

Higher organisms do not have to experience an unconditioned stimulus directly (reviewed by Bandura, 1969). Observational learning, in which one watches someone else being conditioned, is quite effective; actually, autonomic arousal in an observer may be even greater than that of the direct subject (a case of overempathy!). Consequently, many childhood fears are learned when children see others actually being hurt or merely appearing frightened.

Operant Conditioning. In *operant conditioning,* the probability that a response (the *operant*) will be emitted by the organism is increased when the response is followed by a rewarding stimulus—known as *positive reinforcement.* *Negative reinforcement* (not to be confused with punishment) occurs when the operant is reinforced by its capacity to terminate an aversive stimulus. School children are positively reinforced for doing better academically if high scores lead to extra recess time. If a child sits down promptly in her seat to stop a teacher's shouting, "Sit down and behave," the probability of sitting down quickly is increased by negative reinforcement. Another child, however, may find that aversive attention is better than being ignored and may consequently increase time out of his seat. In this case, a presumably negative stimulus (teacher's shouting) acts as a positive reinforcer (*reward*) of the behavior his teacher is trying to extinguish.

Desired responses are greatly facilitated by shaping when the desired responses are not those the subject generally makes. In *shaping,* one reinforces increasingly closer approximations to the goal. For example, in training a mute child to talk, the teacher may first reward the child for (a) watching the teacher's lips, then (b) for making any sound in imitation of the teacher, then (c) for forming sounds similar to the word uttered by the teacher, and so on, until only correct imitations are rewarded.

In a punishment procedure, the aversive stimulus is presented after the target operant occurs, to decrease its occurrence. Although this punishment tactic is an all-time favorite of parents and teachers, the results of punishment are quite inconsistent. Combined with positive reinforcement for more adaptive responses, at times punishment is useful, but it should not be the treatment of choice in attempting to change behavior.

Reinforcement contingencies affect the probability that behaviors will occur once they are learned. Observing the reinforcers received by others may be sufficient to alter the rate of a behavior, but conditioned behavior will extinguish if it does not eventually result in reinforcement. A number of factors mitigate the effects of external reinforcement. *Perceived reinforcement* may be more important than actual reinforcement. Thus a child accustomed to getting all A's may perceive a B in science as nonreinforcing and give up on science. Another child, used to earning C's may feel elated at getting a B and work harder than ever in science class. Another powerful factor is *self-reinforcement,* which may override the control of immediate external contingencies. One's tendency to self-reinforce or self-punish, and the rates at which one does so, are probably established through observation of the self-reward practices of important models.

Stimulus Control. In operant conditioning, an organism's behaviors usually fall under the control of *discriminative stimuli* that indicate the probability of a particular type of reinforcement under different circumstances. A misbehaving child may be a demon in one class and well-behaved in another. When this is the case, it is likely that the teachers serve as discriminative stimuli. One teacher may pay attention when the boy is "bad," and another may ignore such behavior and praise him for working constructively. After being paired with a type of reinforcement consistently, discriminative stimuli frequently become conditioned

stimuli for an affective response. For example, we may find that we feel good at seeing someone with whom we have had rewarding interactions.

People serve as discriminative stimuli for one another's actions. In social situations, observing others' behavior provides clues in determining which responses are likely to be reinforced. Once the observer acts, the behavior then functions as a discriminative stimulus and/or conditioned stimulus for the next responses of those he or she was originally watching. As a result, social interactions are an extremely complex interplay of reciprocal cueing and reinforcement.

Extinction. After a conditioned response is established, it is, except under special circumstances, likely to be *extinguished* through repetitive presentations of the conditioned stimulus without the unconditioned stimulus or through repetitive performances without reinforcement. Like acquisition, extinction may be accomplished vicariously.

When a positively reinforced response is being extinguished, a burst of emotional behavior common to punishment procedures may occur. Consequently, the extinction procedure may not seem to be working at first, but if it is continued the response will generally extinguish. For example, a child protesting bedtime may cry even louder when her parents stop rushing to her side. However, if the parents can hold out, the child will stop crying. If they crumble, she will learn that loud crying is the ticket to success.

Generalization. When a response has been conditioned to a particular conditioned stimulus, stimuli similar to the conditioned stimulus also have the power to evoke the conditioned response. This phenomenon is referred to as *stimulus generalization.* The response varies in strength, depending upon the similarities of the generalized stimulus to the conditioned stimulus. As the stimulus becomes less similar, the strength of the response becomes weaker. The phenomenon of generalization, like the others discussed here, has been demonstrated in all modes of learning, including conditioned emotional responses, motor learning, and verbal learning.

An example of semantic generalization is furnished by J. I. Lacey and R. L. Smith's (1954) experiment in which only the word *cow* was followed by electric shock when presented in a list of words. Heart-rate monitoring showed that, after conditioning, other rural words in the list—such as *plow, corn,* and *tractor*—also elicited the conditioned response, but nonrural words did not.

An experiment by C. E. Noble (1950) demonstrated that the visual presentation of a nonsense syllable followed by shock resulted in generalization to the subvocal thought of the word. Stimuli conditioned to an unpleasant or painful unconditioned stimulus are avoided. Thus, experiments such as Noble's give an operational definition of the concept of *repression* and allow for the study of its parameters.

When an extinction procedure is applied to a generalized stimulus, extinction occurs more rapidly than extinction to the conditioned stimulus. The farther out the stimulus is on the generalization gradient—that is, the more dissimilar it is to the conditioned stimulus—the more rapidly extinction occurs. If, after extinguishing the response to a generalized stimulus, the experimenter again presents the original conditioned stimulus, he finds that the conditioned response has been weakened. This phenomenon, called *generalization of extinction,* is of considerable importance in understanding clinical techniques used in the extinction of neurotic behavior.

Counterconditioning. Extinction occurs in classical conditioning when the unconditioned stimulus is withheld. The elimination of the conditioned response can be further facilitated if, in addition to withholding the unconditioned stimulus, the experimenter presents another unconditioned stimulus in its place. When that elicits an unconditioned response incompatible with the conditioned response, *counterconditioning* is said to occur. Similarly, in operant conditioning, extinction is hastened if the experimenter not only withholds reward for the undesired behavior but also provides reinforcement for other, incompatible behaviors.

Mediational variables. Learning theory is becoming increasingly complex. Although it was simpler to remain outside the "black box," accuracy in predicting human behavior can be increased by including cognitive factors. Human beings can be given *information* about reinforcement contingencies that will alter the rate or magnitude of their responses. If their experience does not validate this information, however, their behavior will change to fit the true contingencies. (There are limits to the impact of information, particularly when the original conditioning occurred under conditions of very high arousal.)

Another important variable in learning is *attention* to proper cues. Rewards may affect acquisition rate by increasing one's incentive to attend to tasks. Fatigue or high anxiety may interfere by disrupting the subject's focus on task-relevant stimuli. *Retention* is particularly important in observational learning. Even if the subject carefully attends to the task and is motivated to perform, later performance is only possible to the degree that the information has been properly stored. Rehearsal and systematic verbal encoding are most helpful here, and anything that interferes with the encoding process, such as distraction by new stimuli, will affect performance capacity. Coaching subjects in effective coding strategies will enhance retention.

PSYCHOTHERAPY

Theory of Psychotherapy

Psychotherapy is a corrective learning process. Although the content may be highly charged, changes still occur in the fashion described by the laws of learning. Behavioral treatment is based on the assumption that all behavior occurs in response to stimulation, external or internal. Thoughts, actions, and feelings are elicited by unconditioned or conditioned stimuli. The first task of the behavioral psychotherapist is to delineate the probable S-R connections for the client. This crucial portion of the therapy is called the functional or behavioral analysis.

During this analysis, the counselor attempts to determine under what circumstances maladaptive responses occur. Since relearning experiences will center around the problem areas delineated during the analysis, errors made at this diagnostic stage usually lead to ineffective treatment. Through this analysis, both therapist and client arrive at an understanding of the problem and, usually, how it developed. Such "insight" is powerful; it reduces the anxiety that stems from feeling possessed by irrational forces. Nevertheless, to change, the client usually needs more than insight. Clients often say about previous therapy something like, "My therapist convinced me I don't go out alone because of my irrational unconscious desire to be raped, but I'm still afraid. What can I do about it?" Behaviorists assert that the "something more" required is reconditioning.

Obviously, the process of behavior therapy is not straightforward reconditioning. A therapist cannot impose conditioning or relearning since the most potent technique is useless without the client's cooperation. Therapeutic techniques must be embedded in the context of a "working relationship" between a therapist and a client who are pursuing a common goal. If this is not the case, then, in the majority of cases, therapy will be ineffective. With a cooperative relationship established, the stage is set for therapy, but such a relationship alone is not sufficient for maximally effective therapy. It has been argued that the success claimed by analytically oriented therapists and the success demonstrated by Rogerian therapy rest upon variants of relationship. Learning theorists view relationship therapy as an extinction process in which clients reexperience disturbing events in a safe setting. This occurs when such experiences are discussed with an understanding and accepting therapist; however, a more systematic relearning experience is more powerful. Even experts in analytic therapy emphasize the necessity of the client's actually engaging in new responses in the environment if therapy is to be effective (e.g. Fenichel, 1945).

Frequently clients suffer needlessly because of inaccurate beliefs, for example, "If I have anxiety attacks, I must be losing my mind," or "If I masturbate, I won't be able to have good sex with a partner." When this is the case, it is crucial that the therapist correct these misconceptions, for it is fruitless to attempt to have a client do things he believes are dangerous. Generally, unless misconceptions are of recent origin, correcting them is comforting but leaves residual fear or guilt. The client may now say, "Okay, I know that learning to have an orgasm through masturbation will help me be able to have one with my husband, but I still feel awful when I masturbate.'' Thus although correcting erroneous beliefs is an important preparatory step in therapy, affective responses and overt behavior may well require separate attention and reconditioning. The form of that relearning experience varies with the presenting problem and the characteristics of a particular client.

Process of Psychotherapy

Establishing a Working Relationship. In interactional psychotherapy of any kind, a positive working relationship is a prerequisite for psychotherapeutic change. The therapist can create an atmosphere of trust by communicating (a) that she or he understands and accepts the client without judgment; (b) that the two of them will be working together toward the client's goals; and (c) that she or he has the expertise to guide the client's progress toward those goals.

A common error of neophyte behavior therapists is to try to employ change techniques before a good relationship is sufficiently established. This ruptures any forming rapport and gives the client the impression that she or he has not been fully understood and accepted as a unique person. If, however, the therapist spends the early sessions really listening to the client's feelings and concerns, obtaining a clear picture of what is concerning the client, therapy will proceed much more smoothly. Although behaviorists are often portrayed as cold and mechanical, a study of recordings of therapy sessions yields a different picture. When measured on variables used in the study of client-centered therapy, behavior therapists showed high warmth and positive regard for their clients (equal to other psychotherapists in the study) and higher em-

pathy and self-congruence than the other therapists (Sloane et al., 1975). In addition, behavior therapists were rated as having greater depth of interpersonal contact with their clients. This close relationship provides a source of motivation for the difficult tasks the client will face in treatment.

Making a Functional Analysis. The analysis is begun by taking a detailed history of the presenting complaint, its course, and particularly, its interaction with current relationships. This may be followed by a history of childhood family relationships, of performance in school and work, and of sexual and social development. Throughout this analytic process, the therapist has many opportunities to communicate compassionate understanding of the difficulties the client has experienced. The client is encouraged to shift from self-blame to self-acceptance; the therapist may assert that given this learning history, it is impossible for the client to be any other way.

In taking a history, the therapist may uncover the antecedent stimuli to current maladaptive behavior. This allows the therapist to point out the orderliness in the client's behavior, how it has been learned, and also to describe how therapy will proceed as a process of relearning. The outcome is an agreement on the goals of therapy. At the end of the functional analysis, the therapist proposes a treatment plan for reaching the selected goals and explains the rationale for the plan in detail. This provides the client with an idea of his role in treatment; this knowledge facilitates positive outcome and reduces the dropout rate in therapy (Orne & Wender, 1968).

In making the behavioral analysis, it is extremely important to get specific, concrete details about the situations in which the presenting problem arises and to determine whether the client has alternative behaviors, and, if so, whether he is blocked from using them through anxiety. Answers to these questions will determine the treatment strategy.

For example, if the client is unable to be assertive or is inhibited in the expression of warm feelings, it must be determined whether he does not know how to express himself, is inhibited by fears, or both. If he does not have the skills, the therapist may teach them by *modeling* (showing the patient) and having the client practice these skills through role playing. If, on the other hand, the client already has the response potential but is inhibited by fear, he may benefit from desensitization procedure. In interpersonal situations, role playing is usually effective in reducing anxiety sufficiently for the client to express himself in actual life situations.

If the client has specific fears unrelated to social interactions, such as claustrophobia, systematic desensitization may be in order. However, a fear such as claustrophobia may be a generalized response of minor importance. For example, a client requested treatment for claustrophobia, but questioning revealed that she was feeling trapped in her marriage and that this feeling preceded the onset of claustrophobia, and to a lesser extent, fears such as being detained under hair dryers and waiting in lines. It was further noted that she felt trapped in her marriage because she was unable to express her needs to her husband and often felt taken advantage of. This led to resentment and a desire to "get out." She felt unable to do so, as she believed she was incapable of taking care of herself. Fears of enclosed places, lines, and beauty parlors were not treated directly; instead she was trained and encouraged in being assertive. When she was able to stand up for herself, the claustrophobia disappeared.

It is a rare case indeed that does not have anxiety at its core. Nevertheless, anxiety is not always so apparent. Psychosomatic complaints often are connected to anxiety in less obvious ways. For example, a client complaining of intestinal distress reported she had undergone surgery several weeks before and that the surgeon had insisted she seek psychotherapy to prevent a recurrence of the somatic problem. She was not aware of any psychological problems and flatly stated that her "stomach" was her only problem. A thorough behavioral analysis based on her own account revealed no psychological difficulty, but her husband stated she never displayed any negative emotional expression whatsoever and that she was constantly being imposed upon. The client was asked to keep a diary in which she recorded each occasion she. felt intestinal distress and to note all the surrounding circumstances including events of the hours preceding painful sensations. A pattern emerged over several weeks. She consistently experienced intestinal pain soon after doing something for another that was inconvenient or when someone, usually her husband, was angry or seemed annoyed with her. When questioned why she did not refuse inconvenient requests or stand up to her husband, she saw clearly that being assertive would make her anxious.

The behavior therapist may base the functional analysis on interviews with the client and important people in the client's life or on information gained by having the client keep a journal. Questionnaire data are often useful. Interpersonal problems may be more clearly defined if the therapist and client role play interactions with which the client reports difficulty. When the therapist has a particularly difficult time making the analysis, observing the client in the situation where the problem occurs may lead to a wealth of information. Obviously there are times when this would be impossible or in poor taste, but direct observation is used much less frequently than it should be.

The therapist takes an active, directive role in formulating the behavioral analysis as well as in the therapy process. Sloane et al. report that behavior therapists were found to exercise more control over the content of the sessions than other therapists, to talk longer, and to give more information. Contrary to hypotheses derived from Rogerian therapy, this did not result in clients perceiving behavior therapists as less warm and empathic or as more authoritarian and critical (Sloane et al., 1975). Throughout the therapy process, the behavior therapist must balance the need to seek information and instigate change with the client's immediate needs to ventilate and get support. Too much emphasis on either need may obstruct progress.

The following verbatim segment from a first interview with a 45-year-old man illustrates the process of gathering data and beginning the functional analysis. The text has been edited for the sake of conciseness.

Mr. X: Actually it is sort of hard to answer: "What is the problem?" I guess what I should have is a definite problem that can be attacked but unfortunately it is just more general.

Dr. G: Can you give me an idea about the things that are disturbing you?

Mr. X: What it is, is that it is exactly the same in my entire life, it hasn't changed any but as I am getting older I think it gets kind of worse. I have often thought that if I had some other job, if I was something

other than a painter I wouldn't have been alone so much and maybe all this does help. But I am a painter and I like to be a painter.

Dr. G: Do you teach or have some other activities which put you in touch with people?

Mr. X: Well, you see I did teach and then it just seemed too silly to go on, I had so much to do.

Dr. G: Oh, I see.

Mr. X: I guess I should do something else but I don't. I don't help myself very much in the areas that I could.

Dr. G: Well, perhaps you can give some idea of the kind of situations that you find yourself in which are uncomfortable for you.

Mr. X: Well, I think that what it is, is that I am just afraid, just generally. I get panicky just at the wrong time. For instance, one time at the YMCA they were having sort of an obstacle course to test your reactions. I had very good reactions but it was sort of a jumping through this and that and I just sort of couldn't do it at all if people were watching.

Dr. G: The fact that there were people watching you made you feel more nervous than you would have otherwise.

Mr. X: Yeah, that is it entirely. Alone I could have done it easily.

Dr. G: When you are in the company of people, particularly, you find yourself. . . .

*   *   *   *   *

Mr. X: I went to psychoanalysis and I just could not relax. I couldn't say what came into my mind first thing and I just couldn't relax. I told him that I am far too conscious of myself and everything I say I am editing and I am thinking one jump ahead. Probably alone I could but I just couldn't perform in front of him.

Dr. G: O.K. All of the kinds of things that you have mentioned thus far have to do with being observed or evaluated perhaps in some way. That is, in the analysis, and in the reaction-time test you took.

Mr. X: There are times when I feel tenser and one thing that is odd is when I go to bed I feel very good. That is when I feel the best. I don't know whether it is because the day is over and that takes care of it.

Dr. G: That seems like a very reasonable explanation. There are things that occur during the day which trigger your . . .

Mr. X: But they oughtn't to be, if there is *anybody* who shouldn't be anxious on earth it would be me.

Dr. G: Why do you say that?

Mr. X: Well I have a . . . I guess what I should say from an outsider's point of view is that I haven't really got any great responsibilities and everything is going very well with my painting.

Dr. G: I see, well O.K. When someone experiences tenseness and anxiety the thing that is often elusive but very important is, what is it that this response has been learned to? That is, it doesn't happen in a vacuum.

Mr. X: There is something else as I say again where I could help myself more. I have got a lot of paintings, portraits, I have a lot to do if I would just do them and get them over with but they sort of pile up. That gets me very nervous.

Dr. G: O.K. So then one of the things that you respond to with nervousness is a kind of responsibility about work in the sense that you are not doing it quickly enough or intently enough and you become uneasy even though you know you are producing at a reasonable rate. Is that a reasonable statement in your mind?

Mr. X: Yeah, It is more, the thing is, I paint very fast and I do have successes more than I have failures. When I have a failure I just sort of collapse and think—well I had better give up painting.

Dr. G: What constitutes a failure?

Mr. X: Well it would be a portrait that just doesn't click. Like last summer I was working on two portraits the whole summer long and it was just crazy to put in all that time when I could have done ten others. I would have liked to just call up the people and say "I'm sorry I can't paint you." But it was somebody who could help me a lot so I went on with the thing and got it done. Even then as each day the thing didn't turn out if I had just begun again and every day had just done it and gotten it over with.

Dr. G: This is your own judgment that comes into play? Not someone else evaluating you?

Mr. X: No. Actually, it is all my own judgment because when the committee for this portrait came to look at it, I didn't really want them to see it, but they approved it. But I didn't like it.

Dr. G: So it is not really what other people think of you but rather your own judgment.

Mr. X: Well, the thing is that I have learned that when I like it they like it and when I don't like it they don't like it even though they might say they like it. A lot of people say that they like things and they don't.

Dr. G: So then often it does depend on their evaluation?

Mr. X: Yes, I would say that I am overly concerned with people's opinions.

Dr. G: O.K. So when people are not approving or are critical you find yourself becoming tense?

Mr. X: Yes. I mean, when people praise me it goes in one ear and out the other. And yet when they say something critical I pay attention to it.

Dr. G: And it bothers you?

Mr. X: Yes.

Dr. G: Even if you feel it is not justified?

Mr. X: Well the thing is that I am a person who unfortunately sees both sides of everything.

Dr. G: So if someone is critical you are prone to accept . . .

Mr. X: I think maybe they are right.

Dr. G: Is there any difference in terms of their prestige?

Mr. X: Oh yes.

Dr. G: How does that go?

Mr. X: Well, I am very impressed with people's positions in life. There are certain people who just look critical to me, they can get me very nervous and then my talking can go back to where it was when I was ten. I am just completely clobbered and I sit there just thinking: "This is crazy." But it doesn't help.

Dr. G: You don't have much conscious control over it, it is an automatic response to these people as a result of the kind of experiences you have had. You respond with nervousness to the person who has prestige, as you see it.

Mr. X: Well . . . , not exactly that because . . . no, it isn't the prestige because I have done portraits of people who are very prominent and they don't get me nervous.

Dr. G: All right, then there are some particular characteristics about some people; I wonder what they might be? Can you think of perhaps one or two of them, of people who might make you very uncomfortable when you are in their presence?

Mr. X: I guess it would be somebody who would have no compassion or sympathy.

Dr. G: How do you determine this? What sort of things do they do or say that . . . what is it about their behavior that you observe?

Mr. X: I am not sure that I could . . . It would just be a person who would have the attitude "Come, come, let's get going with this. Let's not tarry."

Dr. G: Someone who tends to be impatient?

Mr. X: Yes. I think so. Well I guess maybe it is just somebody who I feel is a critical person. I guess that would be it. A lot of people even though they are very prominent are not critical people. Even some people, there is one man I am painting now, who tries to pretend he is ferocious but he doesn't come across that way.

Dr. G: So he doesn't make you uncomfortable.

Mr. X: It would just be somebody who would be more bossy and who I feel is critical and I am not going to come over too well, I am not going to pass.

Dr. G: You are not going to please.

Mr. X: And yet I don't know why I feel that because it isn't as if I don't please people. I have been working long enough.

Dr. G: I think some of the confusion you are experiencing is that you are trying to put this into a rational context when in fact these kinds of feelings are not at all rational in that they are not appropriate to the reality of the situation. They are logical in the sense that they tend to be consistent—certain events or people will trigger it.

Mr. X: I am consistent in everything that I do; very consistent.

Dr. G: In terms of things that make you uncomfortable?

Mr. X: Yes. Another thing that makes me very uncomfortable is getting anywhere on time. I think it really doesn't make any difference if I am a little late or something but I think again it is that I don't want anybody to be mad at me so I make sure that I get there on time.

Dr. G: I see. Well then, one sort of consistency begins to occur and that is feeling that people may not approve of something you do makes you feel uncomfortable.

Mr. X: Yes, very definitely. I like to drink and yet I can go out to a party and yet have sort of no desire to have a drink and yet when I am home I want a drink. I think that is odd.

Dr. G: That too can be that if you have a drink you may lose some of your inhibitions which you carry into the party and then you will be negatively evaluated in some way. People will see you in a different way which might be critical.

Mr. X: Well, it is. I do know that sometimes if I just have a certain amount to drink my talking can get very bad. (Patient talks with a slight stutter.) I don't know what happens, I just get a little too relaxed, I guess. But I don't sort of feel the urge to have one drink even, yet at home I get a definite feeling that I would like to have a drink.

Dr. G: I see. Well, you are very careful in the presence of other people. Very much aware of how they are seeing you.

Mr. X: Yes, I think absolutely to an abnormal degree. I do lots of portraits of children. I do children better and I get on very well with children. I think the way I get on with children is the way I should get on with everybody.

Dr. G: So there is a difference in terms of reaction to people depending on certain characteristics; one, their age; two, their propensity to be critical; and three, the amount of prestige that they may have so that perhaps the person you are most uncomfortable with is someone who has a very high position in life, tends to be very critical and is perhaps older than yourself. Would you say that?

Mr. X: Yes. . . . The thing is, let's say, if I am going to paint somebody and if they are coming to me to be painted it is

not as if I am begging them for a chance, they are coming to me.

Dr. G: Well, you are still in a position of having to please.

Mr. X: Yes.

Dr. G: O.K. I think I have a pretty good idea now about the kind of interpersonal interactions that probably trigger the anxiety and make you feel uncomfortable. In pursuing this so precisely I may have closed out other things that you want to talk about that are of importance to you so let me open that up as a possibility.

The client went on in this first interview to relate a fear of cancer and heart disease. Hypochondriacal concerns are common in inexpressive, inhibited people. It could be seen that there was a core anxiety around criticism, even though at this point in therapy this was not clear to the client. This information was elicited by the therapist's pursuing each complaint in concrete, specific terms rather than accepting the client's rather vague generalizations.

Once the therapist has established a tentative functional analysis, it is explained to the client by using everyday examples how maladaptive responses are learned and can be unlearned. Therapist and client then form a contract, implicit or explicit, to begin corrective learning experiences. These may be systematically provided through a number of specific behavioral techniques although undeniably a certain amount of change also occurs through the relationship with the therapist and the heightened self-awareness created by self-examination.

Corrective Learning Techniques. Only some of the most common techniques can be described here. The interested reader may find more detail in the books listed in the annotated bibliography section of this chapter.

Systematic Desensitization. Wolpe (1958) describes a technique through which anxiety may be reduced by counter-conditioning, through relaxation. Graded anxiety-producing stimuli are repetitively paired with a state of relaxation until the connection between those stimuli and the response of anxiety is eliminated. Using the information obtained from the client, clusters of anxiety-producing stimuli are isolated and arranged in hierarchal order. For example, if it has been determined that the client has anxiety to criticism, it is possible to arrange criticism situations from most disturbing to least disturbing. For a particular client, Mr. A, such a hierarchal arrangement is presented in order from most disturbing to least disturbing.

1. Mr. A's father telling him he is no good
2. College professor telling Mr. A his paper is not satisfactory
3. A good friend telling Mr. A his hair is too long
4. A casual acquaintance visiting Mr. A when his apartment is messy
5. Being watched while participating in sports
6. A store clerk seeming annoyed when Mr. A is browsing

Each of these situations may be influenced in terms of its power to elicit anxiety by introducing variations in the characteristics of the other person; the older and more authoritarian, the more distressing. Each situation requires several sub-hierarchies taking into account these variables. Variations in scenes with the father, for example, were presented with differing degrees of expression of criticism.

As a prerequisite to relaxation training, the client is told how relaxation will be used in desensitization, and how it might conceivably be useful day to day, as she or he will be aware of indicants of tension much earlier and will now have a way of reversing the process. In addition, one can learn to relax only selected parts of the body so that relaxation can be used in tense situations. For example, if waiting to deliver a report in a conference should prove to be anxiety provoking, one can relax just his arms.

The relaxation technique most frequently used is a shortened form of that described by Jacobson (1938), although any other facilitating technique may be used. Suggesting thoughts of previously relaxing situations, such as lying on a beach, is frequently employed. The essential requirement is that the client reach a stage of subjective quiescence, a feeling of calmness and well-being, for this is the state to be paired with the potentially anxiety-producing scenes.

After being introduced to relaxation, the client is asked to practice on his or her own between sessions, 20 to 30 minutes a day in a quiet place when chances of being interrupted are minimal. At the next session the client is usually able to relax quickly the muscles already covered; he or she is then taken through additional parts of the body with particular emphasis on the facial muscles. When this is accomplished, desensitization may begin.

Since the technique relies upon imagined situations, it is far more versatile than *in vivo* procedures. Obviously, abstract and interpersonal situations included in the example hierarchy are not possible to arrange *in vivo,* so that controlled exposure to objective stimuli is limited to a small percentage of fear-producing objects. Fortunately, experiences in imagination transfer very well to the objective world. Mr. A, having successfully imagined a clerk's displeasure without anxiety finds that such a situation in reality no longer bothers him. A popular misconception is that this technique is applicable only to phobias. On the contrary, it has been shown to be quite effective in a large variety of anxiety-producing situations (Wolpe, 1973) including interpersonal ones. Instructions to the relaxed patient and mode of scene presentation are presented in detail by Wolpe (1973).

If the client is unable to employ visual imagery, *in vivo* desensitization may be used when the fear-provoking stimuli are accessible under controlled conditions. Indeed, *in vivo* exposure is generally more effective and, when possible, should be used. Animals or small objects may be actually brought closer and closer while the client relaxes; such problems as claustrophobia may be approached incrementally. Behavior therapists have driven clients to bridges, used closets, kept a pigeon in the office, used slides and movies, taken clients onto roofs, and asked secretaries and colleagues to play roles for the sake of *in vivo* desensitization. In short, the behavior therapist-modifier needs to be inventive and free from the archaic notion that therapy only takes place while seated in an office.

Flooding. In the technique of *flooding,* fear-evoking stimuli are presented in imagination or *in vivo* with the therapist adding fresh anxiety-provoking cues as the client reports less anxiety. The session is terminated when the client responds with considerably less anxiety than at the beginning of the session. Flooding frequently requires sessions of from one to two hours in length, since brief periods may be ineffective or even harmful. The first report of the use of this technique was by N. Malleson (1959). Subsequently T. G. Stampfl and D. J. Levis (1967) described a technique called *implosive therapy,* which was analogous to a laboratory extinction paradigm. Implosive therapy differs from flooding techniques in that it includes the use of psychodynamic themes such as Oedipal complex material, the inclusion of which has since been shown to be unnecessary (e.g. Marks, Boulougouris, & Marset, 1971) and even to result in less effective treatment than flooding (Marshall et al., 1977).

Flooding usually proceeds more quickly than desensitization and obviates the need for relaxation training. It is, therefore, particularly useful for clients whose fears of loss of control preclude relaxing, if relaxing is perceived as threatening. *In vivo* flooding is faster and more effective than flooding in imagination (reviewed by Marks, 1972) and should be used whenever fear-inducing stimuli can be produced in reality.

The flooding technique requires that the therapist get as much information as possible concerning situations that trigger inappropriate anxiety. In a case of agoraphobia, a client reports that going out of the house leads to anxiety, and that the anxiety is worse in public conveyances, elevators, and crowds. She fears that she may faint and that people will then stare at her and think she is crazy. She fears she might be sent to an asylum and that no one will take care of her children, and so on. The client is asked to close her eyes and to imagine as vividly as possible what will be described without reflecting on it or evaluating its appropriateness. The therapist begins describing an anxiety-evoking situation in vivid detail starting with the client's preparing to go out alone. The flooding therapist is guided by the client's reactions: the more anxiety, the more appropriate the narrative. Modifications are made on the basis of new clues given by the client's reactions or statement. The same theme is repeated if it continues to arouse anxiety; it will be repeated as frequently as possible over as many sessions as necessary. Criteria for continuing are reports that anxiety is decreasing between sessions and that the client is instead entering formerly avoided situations. Flooding is obviously an arduous procedure for both client and therapist, requiring many throat lozenges for the therapist unused to speaking continuously for hours. When effective, the changes are so immediate and dramatic that both participants feel amply rewarded for their exertions.

For *in vivo* flooding, the therapist and client enter the most anxiety-provoking situation the client is willing to tolerate, and they remain until the client feels more comfortable. Pursuing the example of an agoraphobic client, the session might be spent in a crowded department store or on a bus. The therapist persuades the client to remain even though she is anxious and helps her realize that her anxiety will be reduced if she does not run away. Once the client is less anxious, she is asked to repeat the same step on her own. This approach greatly hastens the recovery of clients too fearful to carry out homework assignments alone.

Assertive Training. This intervention is frequently used to modify maladaptive interpersonal behavior, which may play a role in a wide variety of disorders. *Assertive training* is a combination of interventions for teaching clients to act on the assumption that they have the right to be themselves and to express their thoughts and feelings as long as they respect the rights and dignity of others. Assertiveness differs from aggression in that it includes expression of not only anger or irritation, but also warm and loving feelings. Perhaps *appropriate expression training* more accurately conveys the meaning (Goldstein, 1976)—*appropriate* in the sense that the expression should accurately convey the person's feelings to pro-

duce the most positive of possible results; *expression* in that one is taught ways of conveying how one truly feels.

The therapist evaluates the need for training in appropriate expression, primarily through listening to clients' descriptions of their interactions with others and through inquiries about particular types of relationships. To determine what areas of interpersonal relating need improvement, the therapist asks for specific, detailed accounts of interactions leading to feelings such as guilt or inferiority. A number of inventories for exploring the client's ability to be assertive in various situations are now available (e.g., Gambrill & Richey, 1975; Rathus, 1973).

Some people may handle almost all interactions inadequately. They tend to be overpolite, apologetic, avoid any confrontation, allow others to take advantage of them, and at the same time, they harbor feelings of resentment, anger, or fear of others, or suffer psychosomatic disorders or depression. An extroverted person who lacks the ability to assert himself appropriately will tend to be aggressive and insensitive, riding roughshod over others. More commonly, a generally adequate person may have difficulty in specific situations, such as interactions with parents or with superiors at work. Usually such specific difficulties are readily seen as a problem by the client who probably has sufficient expressive responses in his repertoire, but which are blocked in the specific situations by anxiety. The more generally unassertive person usually.has no awareness of the relationship of this inadequate behavior to unpleasant feelings and somatic complaints, and there may be accompanying rationalizations such as "not wanting to be pushy," or "the meek shall inherit the earth." Such people often believe that others ought to be less assertive or that others should be able to guess their needs. In these cases, clients need to learn the relationship between their symptoms and low self-esteem and their lack of appropriate behavior. In treatment, small assignments with a high probability of successful outcome should be given first, and a great deal of interaction with the therapist must take place in preparation for the "real event."

When it has been agreed that appropriate expression training is in order, the therapist usually asks the client to keep a diary of interactions and to keep a score of situations handled well and those handled badly, the criterion being how she or he feels during and after the interactions. These interactions are gone over in detail in the therapy hour. When an interaction has been problematical, the therapist gets information about what each person said and may suggest alternative modes of verbal behavior. Often the client will be too anxious in the actual situation to respond appropriately. In this case, the therapist may role play the situation with the client, first modeling by taking the client's role and then allowing the client to repeat the "performance" until he or she is able to respond in a way that leaves him feeling good. During role play, the client is usually anxious, just as if the situation were real. This anxious state decreases steadily as the client repeats the role-playing performances over and over again.

In addition, many clients find books on assertiveness to be helpful, such as those by R. E. Alberti and M. L. Emmons (1970) and S. A. Bower and G. H. Bower (1976). In recent years, interest in assertiveness training has grown enormously, sparked in part by the recognition that sex-role stereotyping has led to a common lack of assertiveness in women. Assertiveness-training groups for women have

become a fad, and a spate of popular books of uneven quality has appeared. A common deficit in these new offerings is insufficient emphasis on the difficulties both men and women experience in intimate communication (c.f. Goldstein, 1976). Readers interested in learning more about teaching assertiveness will find *Responsible Assertive Behavior: Cognitive-Behavioral Procedures for Trainers* (Lange & Jakubowski, 1976) to be an excellent starting point.

Aversive Techniques. The most controversial of behavioral techniques makes use of punishing (aversive) stimuli such as emetics, electric shock, or unpleasant imagery. When reporting on behavior therapy, the popular press emphasizes such techniques and often gives the impression that punishment is the behaviorist's major tool. On the contrary, punishment is used quite infrequently by behavior modifiers even though many clients initially ask for help via punishment in curbing unwanted behavior. To begin with, no behavior should be punished if no alternative behavior is available. For example, if a client complains of sexually deviant behavior, the first therapeutic intervention is usually directed toward reducing any inhibitions about normal sexual contact. This may be accomplished by a combination of desensitization procedures and training in appropriate expression. Generally the unwanted urges decrease when anxieties about "normal" sex, that is, sex with a consenting partner, diminish.

Such an approach is dictated not only by the moral imperative to employ the least unpleasant method when there is a choice but also by the experimentally demonstrated futility of eliminating behavior through punishment when no alternative modes of satisfaction are available. Opening up alternatives is important in most cases in which punishment might otherwise be used. Alcoholics and other drug abusers, exhibitionists, compulsive eaters, and those who engage in other stereotyped, compulsive behaviors almost always present a picture of poor interpersonal relationships and a deficit of behavior that results in social rewards. To ignore this aspect in favor of using punishment as a treatment technique is to insure the failure of treatment and perhaps to run the risk of making the client worse. Occasionally someone presents a problem not accompanied by social inhibitions or behavioral deficits; or, having successfully treated the interpersonal problems, the therapist finds that the undesirable behavior persists. Aversive treatment may then be appropriate. If properly applied, punishment tends to work rapidly and with a moderate probability of success.

There is seldom any justification for using aversive stimuli such as electric shock, since unpleasant images have much the same impact. In covert sensitization (Cautela, 1967), the client imagines unpleasant consequences in conjunction with the unwanted behavior; this results in diminished interest in the formerly desirable stimuli. For example a man bothered by cross-sex dressing urges (*transvestism*) may be asked to imagine feeling nauseated as he reaches for women's clothing, then vomiting all over the clothing. As he throws away the stinking clothes and tells himself he will not cross-dress any more, he imagines himself feeling much better or considerably relieved. As the covert sensitization progresses, the client imagines himself feeling nauseated even at the thought of cross-dressing, and so on. Thus aversion conditioning can be changed into a self-control procedure.

Token Economy.   The *token economy* is perhaps the most widely used and the most demonstrably efficacious behavioral treatment (Kazdin, 1977). Pioneered by Teodoro Ayllon and N. H. Azrin (1965) with chronic psychotic inpatients, this approach has been used with school students, alcoholics and addicts, juvenile delinquents, adult offenders, retardates, and even entire communities. A token economy allows the application of operant shaping and reinforcement to individuals or groups in a standardized fashion by nonprofessional personnel. Particular behaviors considered more desirable or useful than those currently emitted are chosen for reinforcement through the administration of tokens (such as poker chips), which may then be exchanged for concrete items or for privileges. Target behaviors chosen may be completing work assignments by inpatients, completing a number of math problems by a student, or reducing the amount of litter in a campsite by campers. Tokens in these cases might be exchangeable for a movie, extra recess time, or money.

Tokens provide concrete feedback for the client about the level of performance and do so more powerfully than other reinforcers such as praise (Kazdin, 1977). Over time, responses can be shaped so higher levels of performance or higher quality performance is required for further token reinforcement. Reinforcement principles may be applied in myriad fashions limited only by the creativity of the behavior modifier in finding effective reinforcers and ways of applying them. A cheap and ingenious reinforcer that has been implemented with young children is allowing a period of running around the classroom to reinforce a previous period of quiet work.

In a comprehensive review of token economies, A. E. Kazdin (1977) notes that the greatest problem with this approach is the transfer and maintenance of learned responses, since desired behaviors are likely to extinguish if the program is stopped. He suggests selecting behaviors likely to be naturally reinforced by the environment, extending programs to the settings to which transfer is desired, or bringing environmental stimuli into the training sessions. These and other suggestions basically reflect the need to apply more carefully the laboratory principles such as intermittent reinforcement and fading to the clinical setting. The other major reason for the breakdown of successes wrought by token programs is staff failure to continue reinforcement procedures. Although teachers or psychiatric aides may be pleased with the changes, if they are not monitored occasionally and taught to self-monitor, they, just like the clients, are likely to revert to the prior, less effective methods. Moral: even the reinforcers need reinforcement!

Cognitive Behavior-Modification Techniques. Perhaps the greatest shift in the field of behavior therapy in the 1970s has been that toward the role of cognition in human distress (e.g., Mahoney, 1974). Following the observations of cognitive therapists such as A. T. Beck (1967) and Albert Ellis (1962), cognitive behavior therapists have accepted the notion that changing thoughts will often change feelings and behavior. The emphasis in therapy is generally on self-statements that lead to anxiety or depression, such as "If I fail this test, my whole life will be ruined." Cognitive behavior therapists like M. R. Goldfried (e.g., Goldfried & Goldfried, 1975) and D. H. Meichenbaum (1975) have systematized their interventions according to experimental data and learning principles.

Clients are first given an overview of the rationale for changing their self-

verbalizations and asked to monitor these self-statements to analyze their particular maladaptive internal comments. Once clients have been convinced their self-statements are instrumental in creating the negative feelings for which they sought treatment, active cognitive restructuring can begin. Instructions are given to use feelings of anxiety as cues to stop and think about what self-statements are being made. Clients are to substitute immediately a more rational self-statement and may be asked, in addition, to use muscle relaxation to further negate the unpleasant feelings. Opportunities to practice restructuring are created in the office through the use of stressful films, imagination of a graded series of anxiety-provoking situations, or group role playing. Graded procedures have the advantage of allowing clients to build up the strength of the new more adaptive habit before facing very difficult situations where they might get overwhelmed. This approach is particularly helpful for clients with social anxiety.

Another technique stemming from the cognitive behavioral approach is instruction in social-personal problem-solving strategies (Goldfried & Goldfried, 1975). This is particularly useful with clients who complain of chronic indecisiveness. Clients are given a general orientation to the procedure emphasizing that one can learn to cope with problems. The second phase focuses on concretely defining the problem before moving into a brainstorming session during which alternatives are to be generated in a nonevaluative atmosphere. Only after a number of alternatives have been listed is the client allowed critically to examine and determine the utility of each possibility. When each alternative has been weighted, the client then selects one to implement for a test period. If the strategy appears to work, it can be further refined; if results are unsatisfactory, the client can select a different alternative from the original list or generate more alternatives on the basis of new information gained during the verification process.

Some of these approaches are easily carried out in group settings and may be theme oriented such as coping with test anxiety or deciding on a major for undergraduate students. The emphasis, however, is on learning general skills that have a broad range of applicability. The expectation is that clients treated in this way are learning principles so they can become their own therapists when faced with new anxieties or new choice points.

Mechanisms of Psychotherapy

Behaviorists maintain a rather constant skepticism about the mechanism responsible for change in behavior. "Explanations" are viewed as hypotheses. Some behaviorists maintain that knowing the "why" would be interesting, but find it of secondary importance to finding out scientifically *if* it works; and if so with what people, and what behaviors, in the hands of what therapist, and with what combinations of all these variables the highest predictability of successful outcome can be assured. However, others have pursued a better understanding of mechanisms with the hope that such understanding will lead to a sharpening of techniques and a further increase in predictability of outcome. These two approaches supplement one another.

Systematic Desensitization. Currently the most accepted explanation for the success of systematic desensitization in reducing fears is based on a Guthrian (Guthrie, 1935) counterconditioning model (Kazdin & Wilcoxin, 1976). This view holds that pairing the anxiety-

evoking stimulus with any response other than anxiety reduces the amount of fear associated with that stimulus. Others have advanced the notion that counterconditioning is not necessary as long as no negative consequences are associated with the presentation of the anxiety-provoking stimulus (Marks, 1978). This view is supported by findings (reviewed by Kazdin & Wilcoxin, 1976) that neither relaxation nor a hierarchical arrangement of stimuli is necessary for the success of systematic desensitization. Despite the popularity of the counterconditioning paradigm, A. E. Kazdin and L. A. Wilcoxin (1976) concluded that systematic desensitization may work because it generates high expectancy for change in clients. Thus despite considerable research, agreement is lacking on the effective mechanism(s) underlying systematic desensitization, although few would dispute that it works.

Flooding. Most researchers have accepted an extinction paradigm as the basic mechanism for flooding. There is some variation in beliefs about what constitutes the necessary stimuli to be extinguished. There is little experimental validation for claims by T. G. Stampfl and D. J. Levis (1967) that "dynamic" cues such as anal or Oedipal material need to be included and that high levels of anxiety must be elicited and extinguished for beneficial results (reviewed by Marks, 1978). Although flooding is usually a package of modeling, response prevention (blocking avoidance or escape responses including rituals), and prolonged exposure to the feared stimuli, Marks argues that prolonged exposure is the essential ingredient. Studies of changes in the anxiety response within and across sessions generally show a steady pattern of diminished anxiety as measured by subjective report and psychophysiological measures such as heartbeat (Foa & Chambless, 1978; Marks, 1978). Perhaps during prolonged exposure, clients develop coping mechanisms or change their attitudes toward the phobic object. Although these changes may occur, it is unlikely that they account for all the alterations, as different components of the anxiety response commonly change at different times during flooding, with overt behavioral and physiological measures changing faster than subjective reports of anxious feelings.

Assertive Training. Few process studies are available, and none has been conducted with abnormal populations. With students being trained to increase their ability to refuse requests assertively, R. M. McFall and his colleagues (McFall & Lillesand, 1971; McFall & Twentyman, 1973) found behavior rehearsal to be the most important component. Overt and covert rehearsal were equally effective, and coaching (giving general principles to follow) added significantly to the students' improvement. Modeling, however, did not add anything to behavior rehearsal and coaching.

Token Economy. In operant psychology research, control groups are rarely used. Instead the effectiveness of a procedure is usually demonstrated by the *A-B-A design*. The procedure *(A)* is introduced and the performance variables are measured before the procedure is withdrawn *(B)* and the variables are measured again. Procedure *A* is then reintroduced. Differences on the performance variables during periods *A* and *B* give the experimenter a measure of the impact of *A*. Subjects thus serve as their own controls. Such experiments indicate that contingent token reinforcement is responsible for the behavior changes in question (Kazdin, 1977).

The original work by Ayllon and Azrin 1965) provides a good illustration of this.

Hospitalized patients verbalized that they were working for such nonspecific reasons as personal satisfaction, but they stopped working if tokens were given noncontingently, that is, regardless of job performance. When tokens were given only for work on nonpreferred jobs, they ceased working on preferred jobs and worked on nonpreferred ones.

Aversion Therapy. I. M. Marks (1976) reviewed recent data on aversion therapy and could not find conclusive evidence that aversion procedures set up a conditioned anxiety response to previously attractive stimuli. He noted that successful aversion therapy generally results in a neutral response to the deviant stimuli, not a negative one. It does seem that an aversive rather than neutral stimulus is important in outcome; however, backward conditioning (which should be ineffective) works as well as forward conditioning.

APPLICATIONS

Problems

Behavior therapy has been developed specifically for the treatment of unadaptive behavior; it requires cooperation of the recipient, must be tailored to the unique behavior patterns of each client, and must follow her or his specific desires. The use of behavior therapy with psychotic patients was never a goal of its originators although some advocates of implosion therapy have claimed it benefits schizophrenics. Once psychotic symptoms are in remission or controlled by medication, the use of some behavior therapy techniques, particularly assertion training, may be indicated. The client's intelligence level does not seem to be highly correlated with successful behavior therapy treatment; nonetheless, the office practice of behavior therapy generally requires that the client be capable of carrying out instructions between sessions.

Behavior-modification procedures are applicable to a wide range of clients including those not able to participate in their own treatment planning. Psychosis and retardation cannot be cured by operant techniques; however, people with these problems can be aided in making a better adjustment through the proper use of reinforcement principles. The behavior modifier is stymied, however, when circumstances or ethical considerations do not permit sufficient control over stimuli and reinforcers to effect desired changes.

Behavioral treatments, like all psychotherapies, work best with motivated clients. It is the therapist's responsibility, when working with an "unmotivated" client, to try to rearrange the contingencies that maintain the undesired behavior. There are times when the therapist cannot do so and will fail. This happens, for instance, when a client dislikes working and receives a pension because he is too "sick" to work.

Since, in general, behaviorally oriented therapists are active and directive, they usually have difficulty with clients whose strong needs for interpersonal control make them resistant to instruction. This is not an insurmountable problem and can be circumvented by a skilled therapist. The therapy in such cases, however, may well be prolonged.

Behaviorists, like all other therapists, encounter a number of clients of marginal adjustment who require long-term supportive therapy. In such cases, a stable relationship with a caring person seems more beneficial than any given intervention. Their overall adjustment is unlikely to be affected by a brief behavioral regime; yet within the context of supportive therapy, behavioral interventions,

most commonly assertion training, may be helpful. One can view such clients' problems in the context of their learning histories and conceptualize their therapy process as a slow shaping procedure—in a sense, a reparenting experience.

Two studies have examined characteristics of clients for whom a particular treatment is most effective. A. O. DiLoreto (1971) compared the effects of systematic desensitization, client-centered therapy, and rational-emotive therapy on interpersonal anxiety in college students. RET and systematic desensitization were found to be equally effective with introverts, and client-centered therapy and desensitization were equally effective with extroverts. Thus, systematic desensitization was the most broadly effective therapy with both types of clients. Working with psychiatric clients with "mixed neuroses," R. B. Sloane et al. (1975) found behavior therapy to be effective with a broader range of clients than psychoanalytically oriented therapy, which tended to work best with intelligent, highly verbal clients. Such studies tend to debunk the myth that behavioral treatment is appropriate for only a limited population.

Evaluation

Formally or informally, behavioral therapists usually assess the severity of the client's target problems at the end of the provisional behavioral analysis and again at the end of treatment. Follow-up information is highly desirable but is not always obtained in clinical practice. The target problems are those the therapist and client contract to change, usually including the presenting complaint. The specificity with which these problems are defined in behavioral treatment lends itself to more reliable assessment than the diffuse changes described in case reports of other therapeutic systems. Commonly, the client will complete questionnaires before and after treatment that should reflect changes made in therapy. Improvement rates of 90 percent cited by Wolpe (1958) with a group of "mixed neurotics" and of 62 percent by A. A. Lazarus with a group of "severe neurotics" (1963). Although such figures are encouraging, the goal of behavioral treatment is demonstrable improvement on controlled trials. To support the arguments of behaviorists, this improvement should be faster and/or greater than that obtained with conventional therapies. In their efforts to meet this challenge, behaviorists have conducted hundreds of studies. A small sample of the experimental results on each of the techniques discussed in the Psychotherapy section follows.

Systematic Desensitization. In a 1969 review article, G. L. Paul lists 20 controlled analogue studies in which there is overwhelming superiority of systematic desensitization therapy over no treatment, insight-oriented psychotherapy, or pseudotreatment. The most impressive study in design sophistication is reported by Paul (1966). Public-speaking fear in college students was treated by either systematic desensitization or insight-oriented psychotherapy. A pseudotherapy group, no-treatment group, and no-contact group were included as controls. Treatment was conducted by five experienced, dynamically oriented therapists trained in systematic desensitization for the study. Systematic desensitization was shown to be decidedly superior to both insight-oriented and pseudotherapy treatments, which yielded equivalent results but were in turn superior to no treatment controls.

Studies of desensitization using a clinical population are rare, partly due to the difficulty of obtaining subjects. People with specific phobias are rarely so handicapped as to seek treatment. In a series of studies at the Maudsley Hospital in London, researchers determined that desensitization was not particularly effective for agoraphobics (Gelder & Marks, 1966; Gelder et al., 1967; Marks, Boulougouris, & Marset, 1971; Marks, Gelder, & Edwards, 1968); such clients suffer panic attacks and fear leaving home and being in public places. Specific phobics (clients afraid of small animals, water, heights, etc.), on the other hand, improved more rapidly or to a greater degree with systematic desensitization than with individual psychotherapy, group psychotherapy, or hypnotic suggestions. Differences in outcome for the two kinds of phobias may result from desensitization's minimal impact on panic attacks, the core problem in agoraphobia (Goldstein & Chambless, 1978).

Flooding. Studies of flooding in fantasy have reported mixed results largely due, it seems, to differences in procedure. In reviewing the available literature in 1972, Marks concluded that most studies found flooding to be effective with college students' phobias if (1) scenes were presented by a live therapist rather than a tape recorder, and (2) scenes of long duration were used (as mandated by originators of the flooding paradigm). A typical study is that by Marshall et al. (1977). In this experiment therapists gave snake-phobic college students three imaginal flooding sessions of 40 minutes each. These students did significantly better at posttest on a behavioral approach task and on subjective ratings of anxiety when compared with students who received no treatment or to students given a placebo treatment.

After the disappointing results of desensitization studies with agoraphobics emerged, the results of the study by Marks, Boulougouris, and Marset (1971) generated considerable excitement. When the clients received six sessions of flooding, both specific phobics and agoraphobics improved significantly. Many studies have now replicated this finding (reviewed by Goldstein & Chambless, 1978). In a series of systematic studies, the Maudsley group found that *in vivo* flooding, particularly long sessions, was even more effective than flooding in fantasy (reviewed by Marks, 1978). This finding has been replicated at other centers as well, and flooding *in vivo* is now considered the treatment of choice for agoraphobia. Before the Maudsley experiments, the subjectively derived evaluation of systematic desensitization was that it was an adequate treatment for agoraphobia, since some patients improved markedly. Failures were deemed to be the result of inadequate behavioral analysis, and / or the therapist's inexperience (Lazarus, 1966). Consequently, these changes are an important illustration of the evolution of behavioral techniques as shaped by research findings.

Assertive Training. Research in assertion training is in the beginning stages. The best controlled studies are by McFall and his colleagues (McFall & Lillesand, 1971; McFall & Marston, 1970; McFall & Twentyman, 1973). Their studies have relied on college student volunteers and have dealt only with the ability to be assertive in refusing requests. Using only two to four sessions of behavior rehearsal, sometimes with coaching and modeling added, significant improvement in refusal behavior was found when experimental subjects were compared with students who got a placebo treatment. Assertiveness was measured through the use of inventories and behavioral role-playing situations.

J. P. Galassi, M.P. Kostka, and M. D. Galassi (1975) followed up students who

had previously participated in an assertiveness-training group or a control procedure. After one year they found the subjects who had attended the eight, 1½-hour group sessions were still out-performing the control group on inventories and behavioral assessment tasks. They were thus able to demonstrate the sustained effects of a broad and extensive training experience. Such findings are collaborated by M. B. Kincaid (1978), who offered seven sessions of group-assertiveness training to mostly nonstudent women who sought such a group. Although her study suffers from impressionistic and uncontrolled observations, it is one of the few studies in which the subjects were not college student volunteers.

D. C. Rimm et al. (1974) treated overly aggressive male college students with group assertiveness - training or with a nondirective counseling group intended as a placebo. The men who participated in the assertion-training group did better at posttest on objective measures of assertiveness (as opposed to aggression) in role-play situations. In addition they were rated as more comfortable during the role play by independent assessors and overall rated themselves as less angry and less "uptight" than the placebo subjects. Although the generalizability of this study is limited by the small number of subjects, the findings are similar to those of an unpublished pilot study by Rimm, Keyson, and Hunziker (1971) cited in the Rimm et al. (1974) paper. These reports are intriguing, and it is refreshing to change the exclusive focus on underassertive women.

Token Economy. There is more evidence to support the impact of token economies than for almost any other behavioral intervention (Kazdin, 1977). Its effectiveness has been demonstrated with a wide variety of groups including "normal" adults and children, juvenile delinquents, mentally retarded persons, and psychiatric patients in inpatient and day-care facilities. Changes effected have included increased self-care and maintenance activities, increased job attendance and performance, increased positive social interactions and decreased antisocial behavior, and increased study time and academic performance. Application of token reinforcement and/or response cost (loss of tokens) almost always results in the desired changes in a majority of clients when controlled conditions apply. Transfer of training to other settings is more difficult to effect, although some studies document evidence of generalization, such as a lower frequency of reinstitutionalization for clients who have participated in token programs.

Not all clients respond to a token program. Occasionally this is due to a lack of effective backup reinforcers. At other times, the client's behavior of concern occurs infrequently, for example, violent acts. In these cases, group token contingencies have weakened impact, and individualized programs designed to supplement the overall program may lead to better outcome. To date, too little attention has been given to determining the characteristics of clients who do not respond. Consequently, directions that might be fruitfully pursued remain undefined.

Aversion Techniques. Based on early attempts, it appeared that behavior therapy-modification had nothing more to offer in the treatment of homosexuality than other modes of treatment. Twenty-five percent of clients showed heterosexual adjustment after treatment. Motivated male clients who had some history of previous attraction to women fared better than others. Designing their procedures on the basis of laboratory find-

ings, M. P. Feldman and M. J. MacCulloch (1971) obtained impressive results; 66 percent of their aversion-treated clients reported heterosexual adjustment at follow-up but only 20 percent of the verbal psychotherapy clients did so. By dividing their population according to a history of some prior attraction to women, they found their procedure successful only for clients who had experienced at least one occasion of pleasurable heterosexual encounter.

There is now little reason to use emetic drugs or electrical shock, for covert sensitization has been found to be effective in reducing urges to engage in undesired sexual behavior (Barlow et al., 1972; Barlow, Leitenberg, & Argras, 1969). For example, E. J. Callahan and Harold Leitenberg (1973) studied the comparative effectiveness of covert sensitization and electrical aversion therapy with sexual deviates using single-case designs. Both techniques were effective in reducing erections to the deviant stimuli, but covert sensitization seemed to work better on reducing unwanted subjective feelings of arousal. Only one study (Bancroft, 1970) has systematically evaluated the effects of systematic desensitization to heterosexual anxiety with male homosexual clients. J. Bancroft found that these clients reported a significantly more positive attitude toward heterosexuality at posttest and follow-up; they also showed more arousal to female slides.

The track record of aversion therapy with other problems such as obesity (reviewed by Stunkard & Mahoney, 1976), alcoholism (reviewed by Nathan, 1976) and smoking (reviewed by Flaxman, 1976) is not impressive. These are difficult problems to treat, and it is unlikely that any one technique will result in successful outcome. Aversive techniques will probably prove helpful when combined with other approaches in a multifaceted treatment program.

Cognitive Behavioral Techniques. Outcome research in cognitive behavior therapy-modification is just beginning, as the techniques themselves are rather recently devised. Several studies have examined the effects of this treatment on people suffering from depression with positive results. F. G. Taylor and W. L. Marshall (1977) offered six sessions of therapy to depressed college students. Some got a behavioral treatment designed to increase reinforcing activities and to decrease behaviors that led to depression, for example, lack of assertiveness. Others focused on recognizing and changing distressing self-statements, and a third treatment group received a combination of both therapies. All three active treatments led to improvement on self-reported depression as compared to a waiting-list control group. In addition, the cognitive behavioral group was found to fare better than the groups getting only cognitive or only behavioral treatment. B. F. Shaw (1977) obtained similar findings with a quasi-clinical population. A. J. Rush et al. (1977) compared the use of antidepressant medication and Beck's cognitive behavior therapy with depressed psychiatric patients. The cognitive behavior group not only improved more on self-ratings and psychiatrists' ratings but also fewer of them had reentered treatment by follow-up. Rush et al. noted that these findings are impressive because verbal psychotherapy is generally found to be less effective than drugs with such clients. In two studies, cognitive behavior techniques have been used with anxiety-related problems and found superior to standard systematic desensitization (Meichenbaum, 1972) and to biofeedback (Holyrod, Andrasik, & Westbrook, 1977).

Cognitive behavior modification-therapy despite its youth is quickly taking its place beside such venerables as systematic desensitization as an empirically effective approach. With a new journal dedicated to this approach *(Cognitive Therapy and Research),* one can be assured that researchers will be well motivated to continue this line of inquiry.

Summary. For the first time in the history of psychotherapy, empiricism rather than theoretical assumption is shaping therapeutic strategy. The way in which therapy is done is evolving as a result of experimental evaluation, with neophytes being taught to do therapy based on experimental results.

Treatment

Behavior modification, although initially devised for single case studies, is perhaps more commonly applied to groups: classes of students, living units of juvenile delinquents, even whole college dormitories. As long as methods for monitoring and effecting consequences can be devised, the number of people subject to modification efforts is limitless. Indeed, one can readily see the need for global modification programs in areas like population expansion and energy resources.

Behavior therapy, on the other hand, has remained predominantly a one-to-one type of treatment. As behavior-therapy techniques have become more widely accepted, however, the use of homogeneous problem groups has grown, particularly at college counseling centers. The most popular type of group is the assertiveness-training group, but other types include preorgasmic women's groups, test-anxiety groups, and social-skills training groups.

Given a large enough number of clients with a similar problem, an ingenious counselor can structure a group approach to treat that problem. Besides assertiveness training, techniques that have been adapted for group use include systematic desensitization, flooding, cognitive restructuring, and modeling. A theoretical basis for extension of behavioral therapy into less structured groups is presented by Goldstein and Wolpe (1971) who advocate heterogeneous groups on the grounds that unique possibilities are created for behavioral analysis and therapeutic intervention.

Behavioral counseling has been effectively extended to the family arena by pioneers like G. R. Patterson (e.g. Patterson & Reid, 1970) and R. B. Stuart (1969); however, too little use is being made of this approach. On the other hand, it is fairly common to include some contact with the spouse in primarily individual therapy. This may take the form of a separate session with the spouse or conjoint sessions, which can provide the therapist with valuable first-hand observation of patterns of interaction.

Management

Setting. Usually behavior therapy is conducted like traditional psychotherapies in 50-minute weekly office sessions. Instead of the analyst's couch, the telltale sign of the behaviorist is a recliner in which relaxation is practiced (and in which the therapist can collapse after a difficult session). Adherence to this mold is probably more for the therapist's benefit than for the client's, since *in vivo* work is generally superior to working in imagination or talking about the problem. This frequently requires the therapist to mobilize and go wherever the client has difficulty—elevators, expressways, gro-

cery stores, restrooms, airplanes, and so on. Some extremely fearful clients are seen in their homes or treated by telephone. Since prolonged exposure is superior to short exposure, sessions frequently last over an hour in *in vivo* exposure and may be conducted daily for a period of weeks.

On the other hand, sometimes once a week is too much. This is almost always the case toward the end of therapy, but even early in treatment, after the behavioral analysis is made, a client who is diligent at homework may need sessions less frequently. When homework practice is necessary and the opportunity for such practice is infrequent, sessions may be spaced at two- to three-week intervals. In programs where the counselor serves primarily to monitor a client's planned regime, for example, weight-reduction programs, 15- to 30-minute sessions two or three times a week are more satisfactory than the traditional 50-minute hour. "Therapy" may take place in a schoolroom, a hospital ward, the client's home, a housing project, and so on. "Sessions" may last for the rest of the client's life, as in institutions for the profoundly retarded, or one session may be the only face-to-face contact with follow-up conducted by telephone.

Clients frequently learn of behavior therapy-modification through the popular press or may be referred by former clients. Less frequently, probably because of misconceptions, clients are referred by physicians and other therapists. The rules of confidentiality are adhered to; the behaviorist as much as the most dedicated "humanistic" therapist is concerned with guarding the individual trust of the person in therapy. Fees are generally based on a per hour charge, but occasionally there is a fixed fee for participation in a time-limited program.

There is a great variability in the extent to which behavioral therapists suggest the use of medication and hospitalization. Hospitalization may be necessary for extremely depressed or violent clients and for clients who require constant supervision to prevent their engaging in compulsive behavior, for example, rituals, drug use.

Use of Ancillary Personnel. Behavior modifiers have long trained teachers, nurses, psychiatric aides, parents, paraprofessional workers, and so on to carry out the operant programs. In fact, this is probably the primary fashion in which such treatment is delivered. In Great Britain, behavior therapists have turned most of the actual treatment of obsessive-compulsive and phobic clients over to specially trained nurse therapists whose results are equal to those of psychologists and psychiatrists (Marks et al., 1975). Since behaviorists can clearly specify desired interventions, there is no need to rely on highly trained and therefore expensive personnel. Although this practice is more common in clinic settings, some private practitioners have begun to incorporate this approach as a way to lower treatment costs, which would be otherwise prohibitive. An additional benefit is that the use of ancillary personnel expands the number of clients who can be effectively treated, an important point for centers with long waiting lists.

CASE EXAMPLE

Initial Visit

When the client came in for treatment, she was disheveled and walked at a shuffling pace. Wringing her hands and crying, she complained of the way her husband treated her, yet claimed his behavior to be her fault. Although she had been chronically depressed and anxious for several years, this was her first visit to a psychotherapist. She was thirty years old, a homemaker, and had three young children.

Upon exploring the reasons for her agitation, the therapist learned that she felt inadequate and indecisive as a mother and unloved as a wife. She described her husband as critical and emotionally unsupportive. When she was pregnant with their third child, he told her that he really did not like her and suggested an abortion, since he was thinking of a separation. In addition, she got upset when others were annoyed with her and she became distressed and felt rejected when her husband was as much as five minutes late in returning home.

In this first interview, the therapist encouraged the client to talk about her unhappiness and her concerns, which she had been unable to share with anyone. Talking provided her with some support and temporary relief and also served to form an emotional bond on which to base the working relationship.

People who report they are always depressed or anxious are frequently unaware of their variations in mood and, consequently, of the stimuli to which they are responding; the therapist therefore asked her to keep a record of any upsetting events. He also gave her a Fear Survey Schedule to complete and bring back at the next visit.

Second Interview

The client was again constantly tearful and appeared extremely depressed. She had kept records indicating some of her problem areas. She had noted becoming very upset at a movie but had not specified what had bothered her. With the therapist's probing, she recalled that the scene that disturbed her showed people drinking. On following this clue, the therapist learned that she avoided bars and disliked her husband's having an occasional drink. She was unaware of what disturbed her about drinking.

Her second observation was that she was unhappy about her husband's tendency to withdraw emotionally during affect-laden discussions. At such times, she wanted him to hold her. This augmented the information from the first interview about their relationship. Third, she found she became agitated whenever her children quarreled, particularly if one child teased another. She related this to having been teased by other children as a child. These feelings made it difficult to perceive herself as a competent mother, another general complaint from the first session. Sudden noises were also recorded to be anxiety-provoking, but since this is a general feature of chronic anxiety, it was not particularly informative.

Finally, she ruminated about a dentist's appointment her husband had missed. She had made the appointment for him and feared the dentist would see her as unreliable and be critical of her.

Therapist and client went over items of the Fear Survey Schedule together. In general, her responses confirmed the picture of a woman overreactive to criticism, disagreement, anger, and rejection. A second theme that emerged was anxiety about sickness and death. This information had not been previously volunteered, but the client now mentioned that she became highly anxious when her children were sick, particularly if one had a respiratory disorder. She did not know why she felt this way, but this fear contributed to her uneasiness about being a mother.

The rest of the second session was used to begin taking a life history. She reported an intense attachment to her father, who gave her a great deal of warmth and support. At the same time, she was exquisitely sensitive to his criticisms. Her father's drinking was a source of great concern to her, as she feared he would not get home safely. At this point, the therapist hypothesized a connection between her anxiety and her present discomfort about drinking. Another connection was established when she related that her father taught her to avoid annoying anyone; his creed was "Keep a low profile" and "Don't cause a fuss" (by showing emotionality). On asking her about her current ability to express herself, the therapist found she was so inhibited that she would cross streets to avoid greeting people she knew casually. This provided an opening for the beginning of appropriate expression training. Working in a hierarchal fashion, the therapist asked her as homework to greet anyone she knew slightly during the next week.

Third Session

The theme of anxiety about criticism was further explored. As the client agreed this was a problem area, treatment by systematic desensitization was suggested and explained. With the therapist's help, she hierarchically arranged a list of people whose criticism bothered her. Her husband was at the top, followed by a neighbor, and then her mother-in-law. Relaxation training was started, and the client was requested to practice daily. A review of the prior week's assertiveness homework (greeting acquaintances) followed with the client reporting that, to her surprise and pleasure, people were friendly rather than rejecting when she approached them. Since her list of distressing moments indicated most problems occurred with her husband, assertiveness training was now focused on the interactions with him. Keeping with the hierarchal approach, she and the therapist role played appropriate ways of dealing with her husband by starting with rather trivial matters, such as who got the car that day. A typical simulated exchange was as follows:

Wife: I need the car to take the children to the doctor today, but I see you have to use it to go to a meeting. I can take the children to their appointment, then pick you up, and you can drop me at home on your way to the meeting.

Husband: Look, you just get to the doctor some other way. My work comes first, and I need the car.

Wife: I know your work is important; that's why I've offered to go out of my way to bring you the car. It's just as important to me to get the children to the doctor, and I really do have to have the car.

First the therapist played the client, then she took over her role, and he played the husband until she could stand up for herself with minimal anxiety.

Fourth-Sixth Sessions

The client reported she was handling her husband more assertively and was feeling good about the grudging admiration she was earning from him. This was contrary to her catastrophic expectations that he would beat her or leave her. She looked less depressed and seemed to have more energy. Assertiveness training was now expanded to more threatening areas. She realized she was dissatisfied with the deterioration of their sex life. Her husband had become very perfunctory about

love making. As a result she had turned off, neither initiating sex nor pleasurably anticipating it. After discussion and role play, she stated she was ready to tell her husband of her dissatisfaction and to let him know what she needed.

Desensitization was begun on two themes—criticism and her husband's coming home late. Progress on the latter was made rapidly. When she could comfortably imagine his arriving 45 minutes late, she found she no longer became anxious or felt rejected. At the same time, her perceptions of other events she had seen as rejection were changing; such attitude changes frequently occur when anxiety is lessened. She began to see that some of her husband's criticalness stemmed from his feeling pressured and unsupported. As she felt stronger, she felt more capable of being supportive. On the criticism theme, desensitization progressed by having her imagine being rebuked about a decision by progressively more threatening people, until she could imagine being criticized by her husband without her suffering anxiety. The less anxiety she had about the possibility of being criticized, the less indecisive she felt. Thus it seemed that anxiety had been interfering with her ability to make choices.

Seventh Session

The client's husband was beginning to feel insecure with her new strength, a common reaction of one partner when another changes rapidly. As his wife changed, he became more aware of his own anxieties. Since his schedule and the therapist's made sessions for couples difficult, the therapist suggested brief, supportive therapy with another counselor. He accepted this suggestion and found his sessions quite helpful.

Eighth Session

Desensitization to criticism and disapproval continued, including scenes in which she was faulted for her abilities as a housekeeper. She was now able to respond assertively when her husband was overcritical and, in addition, had let him know she wanted prolonged sex play before intercourse and lengthier intercourse before he ejaculated. Behavior rehearsal of assertive responses to criticism continued with the client mastering situations much more quickly. She appeared much less depressed. She walked more quickly, was dressed more neatly, and did not cry during the session.

Ninth Session

Often during the process of desensitization or flooding, the client will become aware of important material related to his problem but forgotten or unnoticed until that point. Apparently extinction of lower level fears allows material to surface that was previously too threatening even to think about. That was the case with this client who reported thinking during the prior week of her father's death from emphysema five years ago. He had been very ill for 1½ years before his death, and this period was terribly unhappy for her. While she spoke of this, she seemed to enter a state of deep mourning and appeared more deeply depressed than before. The therapist encouraged her to share her feelings of loss, then to make connections between this event and her current anxiety about respiratory disorders and other illness in family members.

Tenth-Twelfth Sessions

The client related her continued improvement in becoming more expressive and less concerned about criticism. She was enjoying contact with people and with her husband who now appreciated her assertiveness. They were both happy about the change in their sexual relationship, and the client was once again orgasmic.

Desensitization was extended to include stimuli having to do with her father's illness and death, as well as memories of his being drunk. She was bothered by vivid images of these times, which still greatly upset her. These images were set off by anything that reminded her of those events, for example, hospitals, ambulances, and people slurring their words as if drunk. These were so anxiety-provoking that desensitization was begun simply with the word *father*. She progressed through imagining people drunk in movies, then in real life, before imagining her father drunk. In another hierarchy, she imagined scenes related to her father's illness until she could imagine her children being ill with no anxiety.

At this point, she no longer required behavior rehearsal to help her become more assertive with her husband. The difficulties she continued to have could be resolved with discussion and coaching.

Thirteenth-Fourteenth Sessions

The client no longer showed signs of depression and in fact was quite ebullient in describing all the good things that were happening. She had been calm despite one child having a cold, and she was increasingly happy about the pleasure she was getting from sex. She was also feeling more empathic of her husband's insecurities and need for reassurance.

Desensitization to scenes connected with her father's death continued, including watching him as he was placed in an ambulance—the most painful memory for her. Since she was nearing completion of the hierarchy and doing very well, the therapist suggested she begin to consider termination.

Fifteenth Session

The client began the session by complaining that all her problems were back; yet there was no depressed air about her. With further exploration, it was apparent that she was reacting to the idea of terminating therapy. Such reactions are common. The session was spent discussing her feelings about separation from the therapist. He assured her she would be free to return for further therapy or for occasional booster sessions. She seemed comfortable with the idea of termination by the end of the hour.

Sixteenth-Eighteenth Sessions

The client was again feeling very good. The remaining time in therapy was spent finishing desensitization to stimuli concerning her father's death. At one year follow-up, she stated she was enjoying life, felt fully functional, and had experienced no recurrence of depression.

Unfortunately, in the space alloted for this case example, one cannot begin to demonstrate the complexities of weaving the behavioral techniques in with the ongoing process of therapy. This skeletal account may seem lifeless when compared to the dynamic changes that actually took place. The reader is encouraged to read lengthier case studies for a more balanced view of the sensitive interplay of relationship variables, timing, and behavioral interventions (see Eysenck, 1976; Goldfried & Davison, 1976; Goldstein & Foa, in press).

SUMMARY

In this chapter, behavioral psychotherapy (behavior therapy and behavior modification) has been described as a set of empirically derived procedures employed in the context of a positive, working relationship between therapist and client. These procedures stem from a unified learning-theory framework that provides a conceptual system from which therapeutic interventions logically follow.

The conceptual system promotes the integration of research with clinical practice, so clinical experience provides new questions for basic and applied research, and research findings alter clinical interventions. As governmental agencies and insurance companies take increasing financial responsibility for psychotherapy services, it is likely that approaches that can demonstrate their effectiveness, like behavioral psychotherapy, will come to the fore.

Prevention of chronic emotional problems through early identification and intervention is an important social frontier. This is being met by using behavioral methods to correct learning deficits in crucial areas like social functioning before maladaptive patterns rigidify. In addition, there is a shift toward community-based programs in which psychologists attempt to modify the environment as well as the so-called patient, so fewer clients will require institutionalization. The experience behavior modifiers have gained with system-wide programs should be valuable in these developments.

Overall in psychotherapy there seems to be a trend toward an integration of therapeutic systems. Behavioral principles are being absorbed by practitioners of other systems, and behaviorists are systematically addressing phenomena formerly viewed as "intrapsychic" and are paying more attention to relationship variables in therapy. This should be a positive development, as there is little to be gained from dogmatism and much to learn from concentration on the development of effective treatments, whatever their origin.

ANNOTATED BIBLIOGRAPHY

Bandura, A. *Principles of behavior modification.* New York: Holt, Rinehart & Winston, 1969, 677 pages.
This volume is unmatched in providing a theoretical framework for behavioral interventions. Although the research review is necessarily dated, it is valuable. Bandura does a superb job of integrating basic and applied research on cognition and behavior with theoretical concepts.

Gambrill, E. *Behavior modification: Handbook of assessment, intervention, and evaluation.* San Francisco: Jossey-Bass, 1977, 1231 pages.
This mammoth work is an up-to-date review of behavioral research and therapy techniques including cognitive behavioral approaches. Gambrill is admirably unbiased in her presentation, which is consistently guided by empirical findings. The overall flavor of the book is operant, and it will thus provide the reader with a different perspective than the other recommended readings.

Goldfried, M. R., & Davison, G. C. *Clinical behavior therapy.* New York: Holt, Rinehart & Winston, 1976, 301 pages.
The title of this book is quite accurate. The authors set out to provide a description of their clinical practice of behavior therapy, as opposed to the more rigorous and more limited picture presented in journals. They have succeeded admirably.

Goldstein, A. J., & Foa, E. B. (Eds.) *Handbook of behavioral interventions.* New York: Wiley, in press.
This book is highly clinical, including large amounts of verbatim transcripts from therapy sessions. The chapter authors demonstrate how and what they do in therapy rather than abstractly recount what they think they do.

Kanfer, F. H., & Goldstein, A. P. (Eds.) *Helping people change.* New York: Pergamon Press, 1975, 536 pages.

This book covers topics such as operant methods, cognitive change methods, self-control techniques and relationship-enhancement. Many of the chapter authors are the leaders in the field in their particular topic. The emphasis in this excellent volume is on how these techniques are used clinically rather than the presentation of a scholarly review. Information on the research supporting the efficacy of these techniques is also included.

CASE READINGS

Goldfried, M. R., & Davison, G. C. *Clinical behavior therapy.* New York: Holt, Rinehart & Winston, 1976. (Extended case illustration, pp. 245-65.)
Goldfried and Davison describe the progress of therapy with a 35-year-old depressed woman. The client's anxiety, depression, and poor self-image were treated with a variety of techniques, including anxiety-management training, assertive training, problem solving, and thought stopping. The importance of relationship variables is exemplified.

Lobitz, W. C.; Lo Piccolo, J.; Lobitz, G. K.; & Brockway, J. A closer look at simplistic behavior therapy for sexual dysfunction: Two case studies. In H. J. Eysenck (Ed.), *Case studies in behaviour therapy.* London: Routledge & Kegan Paul, 1976, pp. 237-71.
Illustration of the therapeutic process with two couples for whom marital and personality problems impeded progress.

Meyer, V.; Sharpe, R.; & Chesser, E. Behavioral analysis and treatment of a complex case. In H. J. Eysenck (Ed.), *Case studies in behaviour therapy.* London: Routledge & Kegan Paul, 1976, pp. 149-72.
The treatment of a woman complaining of agoraphobic and obsessive-compulsive symptoms. The authors discuss reasons for the success of this treatment when prior behavior therapy had failed.

Wolf, M.; Risley, T.; & Mees, H. Application of operant conditioning to the behaviour problems of an autistic child. *Behaviour Research and Therapy,* 1964, 1, 305-12.
The authors describe the treatment of a three-year-old boy by operant techniques such as shaping, time-out, extinction, and reinforcement. Goals accomplished were dimin-

ished destructive behavior and temper tantrums, and increased appropriate verbalization.

Wolpe, J. *Theme and variations: A behavior therapy casebook.* New York: Pergamon Press, 1976.

Wolpe reports the treatment of a middle-aged professor suffering from hypertension and gastrointestinal pains. Systematic desensitization and assertive training are employed.

REFERENCES

Alberti, R. E., & Emmons, M. A. *Your perfect right: A guide to assertive behavior.* San Luis Obispo, Calif.: Impact Press, 1970.

Ayllon, T., & Azrin, N. H. The measurement and reinforcement of behavior of psychotics. *Journal of the Experimental Analysis of Behavior,* 1965, 8, 357-83.

Ayllon, T., & Michael, J. The psychiatric nurse as a behavioral engineer. *Journal of Experimental Analysis of Behavior,* 1959, 2, 323-34.

Bancroft, J. A comparative study of aversion and desensitization in the treatment of homosexuality. In L. E. Burns & J. L. Worsley (Eds.), *Behavior therapy in the 1970s.* Bristol: Wright & Sons, 1970.

Bandura, A. *Principles of behavior modification.* New York: Holt, Rinehart & Winston, 1969.

Barlow, D. H.; Agras, W. S.; Leitenberg, H.; Callahan, E. J.; & Moore, R. C. The contribution of therapeutic instruction to covert sensitization. *Behaviour Research and Therapy,* 1972, 10, 411-15.

Barlow, D. H.; Leitenberg, H.; & Agras, W. S. Experimental control of sexual deviation through manipulation of the noxious scene in covert sensitization. *Journal of Abnormal Psychology,* 1969, 74, 596-601.

Beck, A. T. *Depression: Clinical, experimental, and theoretical aspects.* New York: Harper & Row, 1967.

Bower, S. A., & Bower, G. H. *Asserting yourself.* Reading, Mass.: Addison Wesley, 1976.

Burgess, A. *Clockwork Orange.* New York: Norton, 1963.

Callahan, E. J., & Leitenberg, H. Aversion therapy for sexual deviation: Contingent shock and covert sensitization. *Journal of Abnormal Psychology,* 1973, 81, 60-73.

Cautela, J. R. Covert sensitization. *Psychological Record,* 1967, 20, 459-68.

DiLoreto, A. O. *Comparative psychotherapy: An experimental analysis.* Chicago: Aldine-Atherton, 1971.

Dollard, J., & Miller, N. E. *Personality and psychotherapy.* New York: McGraw-Hill, 1950.

Drabman, R., & Spitalnik, R. Social isolation as a punishment procedure: A controlled study. *Journal of Experimental Child Psychology,* 1973, 16, 236-49.

Ellis, A. *Reason and emotion in psychotherapy.* New York: Lyle Stuart, 1962.

Eysenck, H. J. (Ed.) *Behaviour therapy and the neuroses.* New York: Pergamon Press, 1960.

Eysenck, H. J. *The biological basis of personality.* Springfield, Ill.: C. C Thomas, 1967.

Eysenck, H. J. (Ed.) *Case studies in behaviour therapy.* London: Routledge & Kegan Paul, 1976.

Eysenck, H. J., & Beech, H. R. Counter-conditioning and related methods. In A. E. Bergin & S. L. Garfield (Eds.), *Handbook of psychotherapy and behavior change: An empirical analysis.* New York: Wiley, 1971.

Eysenck, H. J., & Eysenck, S. B. G. *The structure and measurement of personality.* San Diego, Calif.: Knapp, 1969.

Eysenck, H. J., & Rachman, S. *The causes and cures of neurosis.* San Diego, Calif.: Knapp, 1965.

Feldman, M. P., & MacCulloch, M. J. *Homosexual behavior: Therapy and assessment.* Oxford: Pergamon Press, 1971.

Fenichel, O. *The psychoanalytic theory of neurosis.* New York: Norton, 1945.

Ferster, C. B. Positive reinforcement and behavioral deficits of autistic children. *Child Development,* 1961, 32, 437-56.

Flaxman, J. Quitting smoking. In W. E. Craighead, A. E. Kazdin, & M. J. Mahoney (Eds.), *Behavior modification.* Boston: Houghton Mifflin, 1976.

Foa, E. B., & Chambless, D. L. Habituation of subjective anxiety during flooding in imagination. *Behaviour Research and Therapy,* 1978.

Galassi, J. P.; Kostka, M. P.; & Galassi, M. D. Assertive training: A one year follow-up. *Journal of Counseling Psychology,* 1975, 22, 451-52.

Gambrill, E. D., & Richey, C. A. An assertion inventory for use in assessment and research. *Behavior Therapy,* 1975, 6, 550-61.

Gelder, M. G., & Marks, I. M. Severe agoraphobia: A controlled prospective trial of behaviour therapy. *British Journal of Psychiatry,* 1966, 112, 309-19.

Gelder, M. G.; Marks, I. M.; Wolff, H. H.; & Clarke, M. Desensitization and psychotherapy in the treatment of phobic states: A controlled inquiry. *British Journal of Psychiatry,* 1967, 113, 53-73.

Goldfried, M. R., & Davison, G. C. *Clinical behavior therapy.* New York: Holt, Rinehart & Winston, 1976.

Goldfried, M. R., & Goldfreid, A. P. Cognitive change methods. In F. H. Kanfer & A. P. Goldstein (Eds.), *Helping people change.* New York: Pergamon Press, 1975.

Goldstein, A. J. Appropriate expression training: Humanistic behavior therapy. In A. Wandersman, P. J. Poppen, & D. F. Ricks (Eds.), *Humanism and behaviorism: Dialogue and growth.* New York: Pergamon, 1976.

Goldstein, A. J., & Chambless, D. L. A reanalysis of agoraphobia. *Behavior Therapy,* 1978, 9, 47-59.

Goldstein, A. J., & Foa, E. B. (Eds.) *Handbook of behavioral interventions.* New York: Wiley, in press.

Goldstein, A. J., & Wolpe, J. Behavior therapy in groups. In H. Kaplan & B. J. Sadock (Eds.), *Comprehensive group psychotherapy.* Baltimore: Williams & Wilkins, 1971.

Gray, F.; Graubard, P. S.; & Rosenberg, H. Little brother is changing you. *Psychology Today,* 1974, 7, 42-46.

Guthrie, E. R. *The psychology of learning.* New York: Harper, 1935.

Holyrod, K. A.; Andrasik, F.; & Westbrook, T. Cognitive control of tension headache. *Cognitive Therapy and Research,* 1977, 1, 121-33.

Hull, C. L. *Principles of behavior.* New York: Appleton-Century-Crofts, 1943.

Jones, M. C. The elimination of children's fears. *Journal of Experimental Psychology,* 1924, 7, 382-90.

Kanfer, F. H., & Phillips, J. S. *Learning foundations of behavior therapy.* New York: Wiley, 1970.

Kantorovich, N. Novoye refleksologii nervnoy i fiziologii sistemy [An attempt of associative-reflex therapy in alcoholism], 1929, 3, 436-47. (*Psychological Abstracts,* 1930, 4, 493.)

Katz, R. C., & Zlutnick, S. (Eds.) *Behavior therapy and health care.* New York: Pergamon Press, 1975.

Kazdin, A. E. *The token economy.* New York: Plenum, 1977.

Kazdin, A. E., & Wilcoxin, L. A. Systematic desensitization and non-specific treatment effects: A methodological evaluation. *Psychological Bulletin,* 1976, 83, 729-58.

Kincaid, M. B. Assertiveness training from the participants' perspective. *Journal of Professional Psychology,* 1978, 9, 153-60.

Lacey, J. I., & Smith, R. L. Conditioning and generalization of unconscious anxiety. *Science,* 1954, 120, 1045.

Lange, A. J., & Jakubowski, P. *Responsible assertive behavior: Cognitive behavioral procedures for trainers.* Champaign, Ill.: Research Press, 1976.

Lazarus, A. The results of behavior therapy in 126 cases of severe neurosis. *Behaviour Research and Therapy,* 1963, 1, 69-79.

Lazarus, A. A. Broad-spectrum behavior therapy and the treatment of agoraphobia. *Behaviour Research and Therapy,* 1966, 4, 95-97.

Lindsley, O. R. Operant conditioning methods applied to research in chronic schizophrenia. *Psychiatric Research Reports,* 1956, 5, 118-53.

Mahoney, M. J. *Cognition and behavior modification.* Cambridge, Mass.: Ballinger, 1974.

Malleson, N. Panic and phobia: A possible method of treatment. *Lancet,* 1959, 1, 225-27.

Marks, I. M. Flooding (implosion) and allied treatments. In W. S. Agras (Ed.), *Behavior modification.* New York: Little, Brown, 1972.

Marks, I. M. Management of sexual disorders. In H. Leitenberg (Ed.), *Handbook of behavior modification and behavior therapy.* Englewood Cliffs, N.J.: Prentice-Hall, 1976.

Marks, I. Behavioral psychotherapy of adult neurosis. In S. Garfield & A. E. Bergin (Eds.), *Handbook of psychotherapy and behavior change* (2nd ed.) New York: Wiley, 1978.

Marks, I.; Boulougouris, J.; & Marset, P. Flooding *vs* desensitization in the treatment of phobic patients: A crossover study. *Brit-*

ish Journal of Psychiatry, 1971, 119, 353–75.

Marks, I. M.; Gelder, M. G.; & Edwards, G. Hypnosis and desensitization for phobias: A controlled prospective trial. *British Journal of Psychiatry,* 1968, 114, 1263–74.

Marks, I. M.; Hallam, R. S.; Philpott, R.; & Connolly, J. C. Nurse therapists in behavioral psychotherapy. *British Medical Journal,* 1975, 3, 144–48.

Marshall, W. L.; Gauthier, J.; Christie, M. M.; Currie, D. W.; & Gordon, A. Flooding therapy: Effectiveness, stimulus characteristics and the value of brief *in vivo* exposure. *Behaviour Research and Therapy,* 1977, 15, 79–87.

Max, L. W. Breaking up a homosexual fixation by the conditioned reaction technique: A case study. *Psychological Bulletin,* 1935, 32, 734.

McFall, R. M., & Lillesand, D. B. Behavior rehearsal with modeling and coaching in assertion training. *Journal of Abnormal Psychology,* 1971, 77, 313–23.

McFall, R. M., & Marston, A. R. An experimental investigation of behavior rehearsal in assertive training. *Journal of Abnormal Psychology,* 1970, 76, 295–303.

McFall, R. M., & Twentyman, C. T. Four experiments on the relative contributions of rehearsal, modeling, and coaching to assertion training. *Journal of Abnormal Psychology,* 1973, 81, 199–218.

Meichenbaum, D. H. Cognitive modification of test anxious college students. *Journal of Consulting and Clinical Psychology,* 1972, 39, 370–80.

Meichenbaum, D. Self-instructional methods. In F. H. Kanfer & A. P. Goldstein (Eds.), *Helping people change.* New York: Pergamon Press, 1975.

Nathan, P. E. Alcoholism. In H. Leitenberg (Ed.), *Handbook of behavior modification and behavior therapy.* Englewood Cliffs, N.J.: Prentice-Hall, 1976.

Noble, C. E. Conditioned generalization of the galvanic skin response to a subvocal stimulus. *Journal of Experimental Psychology,* 1950, 40, 15–25.

Orne, M. T., & Wender, P. H. Anticipatory socialization for psychotherapy: Method and rationale. *American Journal of Psychiatry,* 1968, 124, 1202–12.

Patterson, G. R., & Reid, J. B. Reciprocity and coercion: Two facets of social systems.

In C. Neuringer & J. L. Michael (Eds.), *Behavior modification in clinical psychology.* New York: Appleton-Century-Crofts, 1970.

Paul, G. L. *Insight vs. desensitization in psychotherapy: An experiment in anxiety reduction.* Stanford, Calif.: Stanford University Press, 1966.

Rachman, S. J., & Teasdale, J. *Aversion therapy and behavior disorders: An analysis.* London: Routledge & Kegan Paul, 1969.

Rathus, S. A. A 30-item schedule for assessing assertive behavior. *Behavior Therapy,* 1973, 4, 398–406.

Rimm, D. C.; Hill, G. A.; Brown, N. N.; & Stuart, J. E. Group assertive training in the treatment of inappropriate anger expression. *Psychological Reports,* 1974, 34, 791–98.

Rush, A. J.; Beck, A. T.; Kovacs, M.; & Hollon, S. Comparative efficacy of cognitive therapy and pharmacotherapy in the treatment of depressed outpatients. *Cognitive Therapy and Research,* 1977, 1, 17–37.

Shaw, B. F. Comparison of cognitive therapy and behavior therapy in the treatment of depression. *Journal of Consulting and Clinical Psychology,* 1977, 45, 543–51.

Skinner, B. F. *The behavior of organisms.* New York: Appleton-Century-Crofts, 1938.

Skinner, B. F. *Walden Two.* New York: Macmillan, 1948.

Skinner, B. F. *Science and human behavior.* New York: Macmillan, 1953.

Sloane, R. B.; Staples, F. R.; Cristol, A. H.; Yorkston, N. J.; & Whipple, K. *Psychotherapy versus behavior therapy.* Cambridge, Mass.: Harvard University Press, 1975.

Stampfl, T. G., & Levis, D. J. Essentials of implosive therapy: A learning-theory-based psychodynamic behavioral therapy. *Journal of Abnormal Psychology,* 1967, 72, 496–503.

Stuart, R. B. Operant interpersonal treatment for marital discord. *Journal of Consulting and Clinical Psychology,* 1969, 33, 675–82.

Stunkard, A. J., & Mahoney, M. J. Behavioral treatment of the eating disorders. In H. Leitenberg (Ed.), *Handbook of behavior modification and behavior therapy.* Englewood Cliffs, N.J.: Prentice-Hall, 1976.

Taylor, F. G., & Marshall, W. L. Experimental analysis of a cognitive-behavioral therapy for depression. *Cognitive Therapy and Research,* 1977, 1, 59–72.

Thorndike, E. L. *The psychology of learning.* New York: Teachers College, 1913.

Tolman, E. C. *Purposive behavior in animals and men.* New York: Appleton-Century-Crofts, 1932.

Ullmann, L. P., & Krasner, L. (Eds.) *Case studies in behavior modification.* New York: Holt, Rinehart & Winston, 1965.

Watson, J. B., & Rayner, R. Conditioned emotional reaction. *Journal of Experimental Psychology,* 1920, 3 (1), 1-14.

Wolpe, J. *Psychotherapy by reciprocal inhibition.* Stanford, Calif.: Stanford University Press, 1958.

Wolpe, J. *The practice of behavior therapy.* New York: Pergamon Press, 1973.

7

Gestalt Therapy

JAMES S. SIMKIN

OVERVIEW

Gestalt therapy is a noninterpretative, ahistoric, existentially based system of psychotherapy originally founded by Frederick (Fritz) S. Perls (1893–1970) in which awareness is the primary focus in the here-and-now. Most interactions between the Gestalt therapist and patients are dealt with in an I-Thou manner, rather than assigning or assuming transference or countertransference meaning.

By concentrating on what is going on (the *process*) rather than what could or should be going on (the *content*), the patient is encouraged to take responsibility for what he is doing. Being in contact with the potential nourishment or toxicity of behavior enables assimilation or rejection of that behavior. Choice and growth are thus enhanced through organismic self-regulation.

The focus in Gestalt therapy is on immediate present awareness of one's experience. Cognitive explanations or interpretations of "causes" or "purposes" are rejected.

Basic Concepts

Psychotherapy involves the interaction of at least two people—the therapist and the patient-client—in the individual approach. It can extend to an interactive process among several people in dealing with couples, families, and groups.

Self-referred psychotherapy consumers usually consist of people who are suffering and seeking relief from anxiety, guilt, phobias, disordered thinking, interpersonal difficulties, and so on. Others who may wind up in the psychotherapist's office have been referred by parents, relatives, spouses, physicians, teachers, counselors, probation officers, judges, and so forth.

Psychotherapy providers are usually mental health specialists specially trained to help emotionally troubled people cope with, adjust to, or overcome their problems. The majority of psychotherapy providers come from the three major mental health disciplines: clinical psychology, psychiatry, and clinical or psychiatric social work.

Many psychotherapists adopt the view that man is not capable of coping with the complexities of modern life. Thus, as a result of the human being's lack of equipment to live naturally and spontaneously in a complex society, it is necessary either to teach him new interpersonal skills and/ or to teach him to suppress his natural inclinations to be able to survive and live amicably in our highly complicated, civilized culture.

Gestalt therapists believe, along with adherents of other psychotherapeutic schools and their adherents, that man is born with the innate capacity to cope with life but is taught by significant others (usually parents) that he is inherently "bad" or "selfish" or "unfair," and that he introjects these attitudes toward self that lead to his lack of self-acceptance and reinforce his basic self-distrust.

Fritz Perls (1948, p. 73) saw man as a "biological event." He believed that personality reintegration could be successful only if every human activity was regarded as a biological process. Joen Fagan, however, includes Perls among those theorists who emphasize self as opposed to personality development. She says,

The self theorists concentrate on the internal and integrative functions of personality, and motivation is directed toward maintaining the integrity of the organism and toward growth and development of its unique capacities. Sickness is related to losing touch with one's own being as manifested by distortions in perception (awareness), consciousness and self-expression. For healing to occur, the individual must regain awareness of his uniqueness and find ways of expressing this. (Fagan, 1974, p. 7)

Awareness. The primary therapeutic tool in Gestalt therapy is *awareness,* which may be defined as being in touch with one's own existence. Awareness is the ability to focus on what exists (what is actual) in the now. Patients in Gestalt therapy are often asked to report what they are aware of at the moment. This subjective awareness, whether thoughts, or sensory-motor impressions, or feelings, *are* the patient's immediate subjective reality. One of the first crucial lessons learned by the patient is that what he is aware of is what exists for him. There is no right or wrong reality. What is, is.

Perls suggested the concept of "universal awareness as a useful hypothesis that runs counter to . . . treat(ing) ourselves as things. We *are* awareness rather than *have* awareness. Awareness, consciousness, or excitement are similar experiences. With the hypothesis of universal awareness we open up to considering ourselves in a living way rather than in the aboutisms of having a mind, ego, superego and so forth" (Perls, 1975, p. 69).

Contact and Support. To make good contact with one's world, it is necessary to risk reaching out and discovering one's own contact boundaries through the experience of what is "me" and "not me." Erving Polster and Miriam Polster describe *contact* as:

the lifeblood of growth, the means of changing oneself and one's experience of the world. Change is an inescapable product of contact because appropriating the assimilable or rejecting the unassimilable novelty will inevitably lead to change." Or, contact may be thought of as "the awareness of, and behavior toward the assimilable novelties; and the rejection of the unassimilable novelty. What is pervasive, always the same, or indifferent, is not an object of contact." (Perls, F. S. et al., 1951 in Polster & Polster, 1973, p. 101)

For adequate contact, it is necessary to have adequate *support.* Much of the work in Gestalt therapy deals with the development of appropriate support for desired contactfulness. Support systems may include breathing, the undercarriage of one's body, knowledge, interest, concern for others, and so on.

For example, to support the expression of whatever emerging excitement accompanies either interpersonal or intrapsychic contact, it is necessary for a person to have an adequate support of oxygen. Thus, if a person begins to feel angry, to support and express this anger, he will need to breathe deeply. Cutting off one's breath can result in altering the feeling of emerging anger into anxiety. Or, "in walking and standing it is important to note whether the person is using his legs as a foundation upon which he can rest confidently, using it as a base for posture or movement. Some people's legs seem spindly and promise poor support. Others keep their knees locked as if support comes only from rigidity. Still others have legs which flop about and offer only minimal support" (Polster & Polster, 1973, p. 165).

I and Thou. In Gestalt therapy, the interaction between therapist and patient is stressed. The assumption is made that the way in which the patient deals with his world is reenacted in the way he deals with the therapist. Rosenblatt writes: "I want to assist you, individuals, persons, to become whole, to integrate (from *integer*) your lives. To do this, I need assistance from you, from the individual himself. You become my teacher and I become your student, to learn who you are, how you live your life. We become partners in an open-ended, free-wheeling venture to get to know each other, to assist each other" (Rosenblatt, 1975, p. 3). Erving Polster describes the relationship between therapist and patient "as participants in a two-way encounter, not in the separation previously enunciated by special dispensations to the therapist . . . the verity of each actual experience can be taken seriously for its own sake" (Polster, 1968, pp. 7–8).

Polster (1968) considers Gestalt therapy as a contemporary psychotherapy because it integrates a variety of recent theoretical changes in the field; it addresses itself to current social needs; makes use of language in a way that allows for description of process, appreciation of function, and awareness of self; allows each therapist to develop a personal style and a ranging repertoire of procedures and incorporates the integrative principles of encounter, awareness, and experiment.

Other Systems

G. M. Yontef compares Gestalt therapy with several other systems. He notes that,

the theoretical distinction between Gestalt Therapy, behavior modification and psychoanalysis is clear. In behavior modification, the patient's behavior is directly changed by the therapist's manipulation of environmental stimuli. In psychoanalytic theory, behavior is caused by unconscious motivation, which becomes manifest in the transference relationship. By analyzing the transference the repression is lifted, the unconscious becomes conscious. In Gestalt Therapy the patient learns to fully use his internal and external sense so he can be self-responsible and self-supportive. Gestalt Therapy helps the patient regain the key to this state, the awareness of the process of awareness. Behavior modification conditions [by] using stimulus control, psychoanalysis cures by talking about and discovering the cause of mental illness (The Problem), and Gestalt Therapy brings self-realization through Here-and-Now experiments in directed awareness. (Yontef, 1971, pp. 33–34)

Yontef continues on to describe the uniqueness of Gestalt therapy as compared to more recent models of psychotherapy as offered by Carl Rogers (post 1960), George Bach, Eric Berne, Will Schutz, Virginia Satir, Viktor Frankl, William Glasser, Albert Ellis, and others. Some of these differences include a genuine regard for holism and multidimensionality. "Gestalt Therapy views the entire biopsychosocial field, including organism/environment, as important. Gestalt Therapy actively uses physiological, sociological, cognitive, motivational variables. No relevant dimension is excluded in the basic theory" (Yontef, 1971, pp. 33–34).

Emphasis in Gestalt therapy is on the awareness of process rather than on content, paying attention to the obvious rather than looking for underlying or hidden meanings. Assuming responsibility for one's own behavior, thoughts, fantasies, and so on rather than assigning blame on one's parents, past experience, society, and so forth is an integral part of the therapy.

When a patient is asked to report his experience in the now, the therapist will point out that "talking about" what occurred five minutes ago, last night, or 20 years ago is "remembering," using the now to "talk about" what was remembered. In Gestalt therapy emphasis on the *now* literally means teaching the patient how to get into and stay in the awareness continuum. Laura Perls states:

the aim of Gestalt Therapy is the *awareness continuum,* the freely ongoing gestalt formation where what is of greatest concern and interest to the organism, the relationship, the group or society becomes Gestalt, comes into the foreground where it can be fully experienced and coped with (acknowledged, worked thru, sorted out, changed, disposed of, etc.) so that then it can melt into the background (be forgotten or assimilated and integrated) and leave the foreground free for the next relevant Gestalt. (L. Perls, 1973, p. 2)

She emphasizes the underlying existential phenomenological philosophical dictum in Gestalt therapy that whatever exists is here and now. Actual experience of any present situation does not need to be explained or interpreted; it can be directly contacted, felt, and described.

Experimentation is used in Gestalt therapy to teach patients how to discriminate which behavior satisfies needs. Yontef (1971) notes that the experimental focus in Gestalt therapy is influenced both by Oriental religions and by phenomenological theory. It is the patient rather than the therapist who decides goals. In Gestalt therapy, the process of discovery through

experimentation *is* the end point rather than the discovery itself.

From the above, the reader can begin to see significant differences between the aims and approaches of Gestalt therapy in comparison to behavior modification, psychoanalysis, and other therapeutic schools that emphasize insight and reconditioning.

More specifically, S. A. Appelbaum deals with some of the major differences in the two systems in regard to interpretation. He says,

In Gestalt Therapy the patient quickly learns to make the discrimination between ideas and ideation, between well-worn obsessional pathways and new thoughts, between a statement of experience and a statement of a statement. The Gestalt goal of pursuing experience and not explanations, based on the belief that insight which emerges as the gestalt emerges is more potent than insight given by the therapist, does help the patient and the therapist draw and maintain these important distinctions. (Appelbaum, 1976, p. 757)

Concerning resistance, Appelbaum goes on to state:

Psychoanalysts usually make resistance the figure without self-consciously attending to the ground of the open, "working" state of consciousness as such; Gestalt therapists make the working state of consciousness the figure, with what are in effect resistant states of mind and consciousness unlabeled and undesignated as such, though very much attended to. They agree on the nature of resistance, however. The Gestalt emphasis on helping the patient discover "the mechanism by which he alienates part of his self-processes and thereby avoids awareness of himself and environment" is a serviceable definition of resistance. (Yontef, 1969, in Appelbaum, 1976, p. 763)

Although James Simkin, who sees himself as a Gestalt therapist, has been described by a Jungian analyst as practicing analytical psychotherapy (incidentally, he has also been told by hypnotists that he practices hypnosis, by behavior therapists that he practices behavior therapy, etc.!), he finds much to disagree with in the Jungian system. The concept of a collective unconscious, although useful to certain extremist political groups, burdens and unnecessarily narrows freedom of choice on the part of the client-patient. The symbology of that system is fanciful and Procrustean for those therapists who take symbology seriously. There are just too many straightjackets in analytical psychology for a creative psychotherapist, *despite* Jungians having supported and fostered much creativity through some of their dream work.

Gestalt therapists who emphasize the facilitating of the client's growth potential would find themselves extremely uncomfortable with Ellis's "disputing" the client's "irrational beliefs." Observing Ellis working with Gloria in the Shostrom film (1965) in which he cajoles, disputes, pushes, sells, persuades, and so on, leaves the impression that Ellis attempts to embarrass or shame the person he is working with into giving up their beliefs. A better, and perhaps more descriptive term of Ellis's therapy would be shaming-argumentative therapy, a term coined by Simkin.

Other therapies such as reality therapy, which "know" what is real and unreal or what is good or bad for the client or that push the client toward making a decision, and the like, are all treatment methods in which the therapist has the onus of interpreting and defending the culture rather than facilitating the growth of the person he is working with.

Perls was very impressed with J. L. Moreno's psychodrama and, having come from a theatrical background himself, incorporated many psychodramatic techniques into Gestalt therapy. On several public occasions, Perls acknowledged his gratitude to Moreno in this regard. However, he used only his psychodramatic techniques, not his sociometric theory.

Over the past decade, many persons claim they practice "TA and Gestalt." By this they mean they have combined transactional analysis and Gestalt therapy. Usually these people use the TA theory and *some* Gestalt therapy techniques. Unfortunately, unless in the hands of a very gifted clinician, this combination can result in poor psychotherapy. This writer, for example, once witnessed what he evaluated as good therapeutic work only to see it interrupted before completion. To make matters worse, the interruption was used to diagram on a blackboard the psychotherapeutic transactions in TA terminology. The rationale for this bizarre behavior was stated to be that the client could *increase* his awareness by conceptualizing the process!

Good therapeutic work from this writer's perspective allows the client to integrate new behavior organismically through awareness rather than interrupting the organismic assimilative process by focusing on cognitive explanatory intellectualizations. Mixing what is essentially a cognitive-rational approach (TA) with what is essentially an experiential-existential approach (Gestalt therapy) is like trying to amalgamate water and oil—they simply do not mix well unless you keep shaking them continuously. The moment you stop, they begin to separate.

HISTORY

Precursors

Any history of Gestalt therapy would necessarily need to focus primarily on the professional development of Fritz Perls, its principal founder.

One of the centers of intellectual ferment in Europe in the mid-1920s following World War I was Frankfurt-am-Main where Perls was exposed to some of the leading Gestalt psychologists of that era as well as existential philosophers and psychoanalysts. After acquiring the M.D. degree, Perls had gone to Frankfurt-am-Main in 1926 as an assistant to Kurt Goldstein at Goldstein's Institute for Brain Damaged Soldiers. Here he was exposed to Professors Goldstein and Adhémar Gelb and he met his future wife, Laura, the following year. Laura Posner (Perls), a psychology student at the time she met Perls, received the D.Sc. degree from the University of Frankfurt in 1932. She was knowledgeable in the field of general psychology and more specifically the emerging impactfulness of Gestalt psychology. Her influence on Perls was generally known and has led many people to consider her the co-founder of Gestalt therapy.

Another important figure in Perls's intellectual development was the philosopher Sigmund Friedlander. From Friedlander's philosophy Perls incorporated the concepts of differential thinking and creative indifference, which are spelled out in Perls's first book, *Ego, Hunger and Aggression* (1947).

Gerald Kogan (1976) traces two major influences on Perls's development. He considers the impact of Laura Perls from 1927 through the early 1950s, Karen Horney and Wilhelm Reich from 1924 to 1936, and Kurt Goldstein, Adhémar Gelb, and other Gestalt psychologists from 1926 on as his primary European influences. Secondary European influences, according to Kogan, included J. C. Smuts, Sigmund Friedlander, and I. A. Richard. Smuts was the prime minister of South Africa when Perls moved there with his family (having first escaped from Nazi Germany and then Nazi-occupied Holland). Before becoming prime minister,

Smuts had written a major book on holism and evolution that, in effect, examined the broader ecological world from a Gestalt perspective. Another secondary European influence was the previously mentioned Friedlander and Richards (1924–25) who wrote on the *Meaning of Meaning*[1] and Alfred Korzybski, the semanticist. Perls was also influenced appreciably by Wilhelm Reich who was Perls's analyst in the early 1930s and "who first directed my [Perls] attention to a most important aspect of psychosomatic medicine—to the function of the motoric system as an armour" (Perls, 1947, p. 5).

Beginnings

The manuscript for *Ego, Hunger and Aggression* was written in 1941–42. In its first publication in South Africa in 1946, it was subtitled *A Revision of Freud's Theory and Method.* The subtitle of the book when it appeared in 1966 was changed to *The Beginning of Gestalt Therapy.* The actual term *Gestalt therapy* was first used as the title of a book written by Fritz Perls, Ralph Hefferline, and Paul Goodman in 1950 and published in 1951.

Shortly after the publication of this book, the New York Institute for Gestalt Therapy was organized. The institute was headquartered in the apartment of Fritz and Laura Perls in New York City. The living room of this apartment was used for seminars, workshops, and groups, and both Fritz and Laura Perls had private offices on the second floor. Among those who studied with Perls at that time were Paul Goodman, Isadore From, Elliott Shapiro, Leo Chalfen, Iris

---

[1] In Perls's first book, *Ego, Hunger and Aggression,* there is a reference to Korzybski's *Science and Sanity,* which Perls had become aware of only after having written his manuscript.

Sanguilano, James Simkin, and Kenneth A. Fischer.

During the fall of 1952, the New York Institute for Gestalt Therapy announced a series of workshops in psychotherapy that included Principles and Techniques of Gestalt Therapy, Practicum for Gestalt Therapy, The Classroom as a Laboratory for Psychotherapy, the Pathology of Speech and Writing, and Speech Analysis as a Tool of Therapy and the Problem of Psychosomatic Medicine. Fritz Perls led the first workshop, Laura Posner Perls the second, Elliott Shapiro the third, Paul Goodman the fourth, and Paul Weisz the fifth. These workshops plus intensive courses for therapists not residing in New York City continued through 1954. The brochure describing the 1953 winter session included workshops on Principles, Techniques, Films, Psychology of Sex, Emotional Resistances, Emotional Reeducation and Psychotherapy, the Emotions of the Teacher in Emotional Reeducation, Aspects of the Psychotherapeutic Process, and Predicting Changes during Psychotherapy with Psychological Tests. Instructors for these workshops included the same faculty as in the fall of 1952 with the addition of Leo Chalfen who was offering the Predicting Changes course. Before the American Psychological Association meetings, which were held in New York City in 1954, a special intensive workshop limited to 15 qualified psychologists was given over a three-day period. During the previous year, intensive workshops had been scheduled in Cleveland, Ohio, and Miami. A similar workshop had been scheduled in Los Angeles during the Easter holiday period in 1954. By 1955 the study group that began in 1953 in Cleveland had progressed sufficiently to form a Gestalt Institute of Cleveland, which was incorporated in 1963 as a nonprofit educational organization.

Perls moved to the West Coast in 1960 at which time Simkin arranged a Gestalt therapy workshop for him. Perls, Walter Kempler, and James Simkin offered the first Gestalt therapy training workshops at the Esalen Institute during the summer of 1964. These training workshops continued under the leadership of Perls and Simkin through 1968. After Perls moved to Cowichan, Canada, Simkin along with Irma Shepherd, Robert W. Resnick, Robert L. Martin, Jack Downing, and John Enright continued to offer Gestalt therapy training through 1970.

Current Status

Gestalt therapy training has continued in New York City since the early 1950s. The primary institute (two new institutes were recently formed) is located in Laura Perls's residence in New York City. A San Francisco Gestalt Therapy Institute was organized in the late 1960s by Jack Downing, Cynthia (Werthman) Sheldon, and others. The organizing members had been in therapy and training with Perls in the San Francisco and Big Sur areas. This institute is currently located in San Francisco. The Gestalt Therapy Institute of Los Angeles was organized in 1969 by three of Simkin's trainees: Robert W. Resnick, Robert L. Martin, and Eric H. Marcus. There are currently two institutes in the San Diego area: the Gestalt Institute of San Diego, primarily organized by Tom Munson, located in La Jolla, California; and the Gestalt Training Center-San Diego, La Jolla, California, organized in 1973 by Erving and Miriam Polster.[2] Simkin has been offering training in Gestalt therapy since January 1972 at Big Sur, California.

[2] Erving Polster was one of the original organizers of the Cleveland Institute and its director of training for fifteen years.

Since the early 1970s Gestalt therapy institutes have been springing up all over the United States (e.g., Chicago, Boston, New Haven, Dallas, Miami, Hawaii, and so on) as well as in Europe and other continents. According to the most recent Gestalt therapy directory, there are now some 53 institutes and the list grows almost daily. There are no established standards for institutes, trainers, and trainees. Each institute has established its own criteria for training, membership, selection, and so on. Attempts in the recent past to organize a nationwide conference for establishing standards for trainers have not been successful. It is incumbent on Gestalt therapy consumers to evaluate the educational, clinical, and training background of people calling themselves "Gestalt therapists."

The following are examples of the criteria used in selection of Gestalt therapy trainees at established institutes:

1. At the Gestalt Therapy Institute of Los Angeles ". . . open to psychotherapists who are licensed or license-eligible in the State of California as well as some other professionals whose work involves them in working with people. Only psychotherapists are eligible for the advanced training program."
2. At the Gestalt Training Center-San Diego ". . . is a training center for those professionals who want to amplify their understanding of Gestalt method and their skills in the application of its principles."
3. The Three-Year Post Graduate Training Program at the Gestalt Institute of Cleveland is offered to:

a. Qualified mental-health professionals holding a terminal degree in their respective fields. It is expected that the major emphasis for these people will be on the extension of their psychotherapeutic skills.

b. Human-service professionals, not engaged in the practice of psychotherapy, for whose activities in the community and its institutions the training program would prove relevant and stimulating.

c. Graduate-level students preparing for professional careers in a mental-health discipline in the behavioral sciences, or in an area of human-service work in which our methods would be a relevant extension to basic professional competence. It is a general policy that preference in selection is given to students who have completed at least one year of graduate training in a university setting.

PERSONALITY

Theory of Personality

Perls in outlining a theory of personality raised the question of what the relationship is of the world and the self. "What makes us interested in the world? How come I cannot function, cannot live, just as a kind of autistic organism, completely self-contained? A living organism is an organism which consists of thousands and thousands of processes that require interchange with other media outside the boundary of the organism" (Perls, 1969, p. 14). He indicated that the ego boundary had to be negotiated because there is something outside that is needed. "There is food outside: I want food; I want to make it *like* mine, like *me*. So, I have to like this food. If I don't like it, if it is un-like me, I wouldn't touch it" (pp. 14–15).

The process of getting something through the ego boundary is called *contact*. Making contact requires the expending of energies. This expending of energies and taking in food to produce energy is called *metabolism*. "Both the metabolism of the exchange of our organism with the environment, and the metabolism within our organism is going on continually, day and night" (p. 15). There are also strict laws that govern metabolism. Perls gives a hypothetical example in which he walks through a hot desert and loses 8 ounces of fluid. The awareness of loss of fluid comes through the phenomenon we label "thirst." When the organism is in a state of depletion (minus 8 ounces of fluid) what happens is that:

suddenly in this undifferentiated general world something emerges as a gestalt, as a foreground, namely, let's say, a well with water, or a pump, or anything that would have plus 8 ounces. This minus 8 ounces of our organism and the plus 8 ounces in the world can balance each other. The very moment this 8 ounces goes into the system, we get a + water which brings balance. We come to rest as the situation is finished, the gestalt is closed. The urge that drives us to do something, to walk so and so many miles to get to that place, has fulfilled its purpose. (p. 15)

According to Perls, as soon as a situation is closed, we are open to the next unfinished situation. He saw life as basically "practically nothing but an infinite number of unfinished situations—incomplete Gestalts. No sooner have we finished one situation when another comes up" (p. 15).

As one of the three types of existential therapies,[3] Perls sees Gestalt therapy as having its support in its own formation "because the Gestalt formation, the emergence of the needs, is a primary biological phenomenon" (Perls, 1976, p. 33). This differs from the other types of existential therapy that borrow their support from conceptual rather than phenomenological bases, for example Sartre's dependence on socialism, Heidegger's on language, or Binswanger's on psychoanalysis.

Theoretical Models. The theoretical model of the psychodynamic schools of personality—chiefly the Freudian school—envisions the personality like an onion consisting of layers. Each time a layer is peeled away, there is still another layer until one finally comes to the core. (Incidentally, in the process of "analysis" of the onion, one may have very little or nothing left by the time one comes to the core!). Simkin envisions personality more like a rubber ball that has only a thick outer layer and is empty inside. The ball floats or swims in an environment so at any given moment only a portion is exposed while the rest is submerged in the water. Thus, rather than inventing an unconscious or preconscious to account for behavior we are unaware of, Simkin suggests that unaware behavior is the result of the organism not being in touch with its external environment due to its being mostly submerged in its own background (internal environment) or fantasies (Simkin, 1976, pp. 17–18).

Perls, originally trained as a Freudian, conceptualized personality as being multilayered. The most external layer he labeled the *cliché layer.* Very little genuine self is invested in manufacturing polite sentences such as "How are you?" "Have a nice day," or asking others questions about themselves or their family without any real interest. Below this surface layer is a second layer that may be called the *role-playing layer.* Originally in learning these roles there was quite a bit of self invested. However, at present the role playing is usually automatized and serves as a masking of a genuine self. These learned roles can be that of a father or mother, professor or student, son or daughter, and the like. Beneath the role-playing layer Perls described the *impasse layer.* This is experienced as a feeling of emptiness or no-thingness in the Zen sense. For many people the subjective experience of

---

[3] *Logotherapy* (Viktor Frankl), *Daseinanalyse* (Ludwig Binswanger), *Gestalt Therapy* (F. S. Perls).

being without clichés or roles is extremely frightening. The fourth layer is the *implosive-explosive layer.* At this level, the person is closely aware of emotions that are either expressed or imploded. The fifth layer is the *genuine personality* stripped of all of the learned (usually phony) ways of being in the world.

In expanding his personality theory, Perls claims that "from the survival point of view, the most urgent situation becomes the controller, the director, and takes over" (Perls, 1976, p. 33). He cites an example when in an emergency, say the sudden outbreak of a fire, the fire emerges as foreground. If one ran from the fire and depleted his supply of oxygen, one would stop to breathe because breathing would now take precedence over running. From this example, he proceeds to what he calls:

The most important, interesting phenomenon in all pathology: self-regulation versus external regulation. The anarchy which is usually feared by the controllers is not an anarchy which is without meaning. On the contrary, it means the organism is left alone to take care of itself, without being meddled with from outside. And I believe that this is the great thing to understand: *That awareness per se—by and of itself—can be curative.* Because with full awareness you become aware of this organismic self-regulation, you can let the organism take over without interfering, without interrupting; we can rely on the wisdom of the organism. And the contrast to this is the whole pathology of self-manipulation, environmental control, and so on, that interferes with this subtle organismic self-control. (Perls, 1976, p. 33)

Perls considered the difference between *self*-actualizing and self-*image* actualizing as very important. Although some people have a self, most people have a void as a result of protecting themselves in self-imposed roles. Basically the protection of image has the implication that you have no right to exist in the world as you

are. "There is only one thing that should control: the *situation.* If you understand the situation you are in and let the situation you are in control your actions, then you learn to cope with life" (Perls, 1976, p. 35). Perls explicates the above example of driving a car. Instead of a preplanned program, "I want to drive 65 miles per hour," a person cognizant of the situation will drive a different speed at night or differently when in traffic or still differently when tired, and so on.

Being in the World. Perls divided people into three broad categories of being in the world. He classified some people as *shouldistic* people. A shouldistic person lives primarily on the basis of imposed rules and regulations. Behavior is matched against a yardstick of an imaginary ideal of how one should or shouldn't be in the world. This type of person is forever evaluating or grading himself against a so-called ideal or standard.

Another way of being in the world Perls labeled as *aboutistic.* In this group, one finds the intellectuals, thinkers rather than doers, people who are invested in either the past or the future. Thus, an aboutistic person will be centered in either the past or the future rather than in the *now.* They talk about, think about, reminisce about, predict the future, recall the past, and are rarely in the present.

The third classification used by Perls, he labeled *isistic.* These would be people whose orientation is existential and who accept themselves as they are, see the world as it is, and expend relatively little energy in attempting to reform themselves or others.

Variety of Concepts

Organismic Self-Regulation. Gestalt therapy theory is based, in large part, on the principle of *homeostasis.* All healthy organisms have an inherent drive toward growth and need satisfaction. If there has been no interference with this basic need, the self-regulatory person will trust his own nature and identify with becoming himself rather than striving toward becoming someone who he is not.

The base of the healthy individual's identifications is his own organism, and not a rigid exclusive set of "shoulds" and "shouldn'ts" which he attempts to live up to by conscious self-manipulations at the expense of alienating large portions of himself. Living consumes energy, and the individual must transform energy from his environment into energy of his organism to continue to grow. The process of growth is assimilation: the transformation of what is not self to what is self. Healthy functioning relies on the continued potential availability of all of the organism to become involved in this contact with its environment for the effective satisfaction of its predominant need. (Carmer & Rouzer, 1974, p. 21)

Figure-Background Formation. Gestalt psychology theory supporting organismic self-regulation is based on the principles of figure-background formation. Once a configuration is formed that has the qualities of a good Gestalt, the organismic need that has been foreground is met and a balance or state of satiation or no-need is achieved.

When a need is met, the Gestalt it organized becomes complete and it no longer exerts an influence—the organism is free to form new gestalten. When this gestalt formation and destruction are blocked or rigidified at any stage, when needs are not recognized and expressed, the flexible harmony and flow of the organism/environment field is disturbed. Unmet needs form incomplete gestalten that clamor for attention and, therefore, interfere with the formation of new gestalten. (Yontef, 1971, p. 3)

As Perls (1948) puts it, "The most important fact about the figure-background formation is that if a need is genuinely satisfied, the situation is changed" (Perls, 1948, pp. 51–52).

Polarities. If organismic self-regulation is interfered with, a number of splits may result. These polarities (lack of integration) are often the primary focus of the therapy. Perhaps the best known and most frequently encountered split in our time is the topdog versus underdog polarity. During the process of socialization, many children are *mis*educated and forced to introject (swallow whole) ideals and behavior that do not suit them. This results in an enforced morality rather than an organismically compatible morality. As a result, the person frequently feels guilty when he behaves in accordance with his wants as opposed to his shoulds.

To counteract the dictates of the topdog, a person will develop an underdog to placate his shoulds. The underdog makes promises, New Year's resolutions, and the like, and is a built-in sabotage mechanism. In some people, an enormous amount of energy is invested in maintaining the topdog-underdog split, the resolution of which would require a recognition of one's own suitable morality as opposed to an introjected one.

Another split is deliberate concentration versus spontaneous concentration. Again, as in the topdog-underdog split, one part of the organism is experienced as a sabotaging resister that attempts to avoid distractions. "When one forces oneself to attend to what does not of itself draw one's interest, excitement accumulates not toward this 'chosen' object of attention, but in the struggle over the 'distraction' which might really fire one's interest" (Perls, Hefferline, and Goodman, 1951, p. 55).

Lack of genuine integration can also create splits such as body-mind, self-external world, infantile-mature, biological-cultural, unconscious-conscious, and so on. These splits or polarities do not exist in reality, as such, but are conceptualized and rigidly maintained as if they existed.

Aggression and Responsibility. All personality theories include some description of a basic life energy or force. For Bergson this was *élan vital;* Freud called this life force *libido,* and for Perls the basic energy underlying personality is *dental aggression.* Perls believed the way in which the personality grew was through biting off an appropriate-sized piece (be this food or ideas or relationships, etc.) and by chewing (considering), discovering whether that which was bitten off was nourishing or toxic. If nourishing, through chewing and swallowing, the organism is able to assimilate and make it part of oneself. If toxic (unpalatable), the organism is able to spit it out (reject). This requires a person to be willing to discriminate and to trust his taste and judgment.

Each person, according to Gestalt therapy theory, is responsible (response—*able*) for one's own decisions. The healthy person accepts this responsibility with enthusiasm and excitement. In neurotic disturbances, some individuals confuse responsibility with obligation and, rather than responding freely to a situation, burden or obligate themselves. In such instances, one's own wants and needs are ignored and one responds to shoulds instead.

PSYCHOTHERAPY

Theory of Psychotherapy

Perls believed that the ultimate goal of psychotherapy was the achievement of "that amount of integration which facilitates its own development" (Perls, 1948, pp. 572–731). An example of this kind of facilitation is the analogy of a small hole

cut into an accumulation of snow. Once the draining process begins, the base that began as a small hole enlarges by itself. He believed that every child first required the gratification of its immediate needs and then facilitation of development of its inherent potentialities. Unfortunately, children are usually shaped to meet the approval of parents and society, which involves the crippling of some inherent attitudes and artificial development of others. As a result, the spontaneous personality is superseded by a deliberate one. To facilitate self-actualization, patients in Gestalt therapy are taught unitary thinking—to start with the obvious: that existence is actuality. It is awareness. Unitary thinking does not recognize past, present, or future; it only recognizes processes. Walter Kempler sees psychotherapy "as a process created for the purpose of influencing symptomatic psychological processes. In Gestalt Therapy all symptoms are seen as signals of a distressed process; i.e., a process that is not evolving suitably according to one of the points or participants in that process" (Kempler, 1973, p. 267).

Another way of viewing both Perls's and Kempler's theoretical consideration of psychotherapy is to consider that all psychotherapeutic interactions are processes embedded in a context involving therapist, patient(s), and their milieu. At any given moment, what may be perceived as figure could be the therapist's posture, the patient's voice quality, the amount of natural or artificial light in the consulting room, the wailing fire engine outside of the office, the texture of the rug, and so on.

For successful psychotherapy to take place, Perls believed it was necessary for the patient to achieve *integration.* For him integration required identification with *all* vital functions—not only with *some* of the patient's ideas, emotions, and actions. Any rejection of one's own ideas, emotions, or actions resulted in alienation and the reowning of these allowed for the wholeness of personality as opposed to the gaps or holes that existed before. The task, then, in the therapy is to have the person become aware of his previously alienated parts and taste them, consider them, and assimilate them if they are palatable (ego-syntonic), or reject them if they prove to be unpalatable (ego-alien). Simkin has used the simile of a cake in encouraging patients to reown the parts of themselves that they have considered noxious or otherwise unacceptable; just as the oil, or flour, or baking powder, and so forth by themselves can be distasteful—as a part of the whole cake they are indispensable to insure its success (Simkin, 1968).

Process of Psychotherapy

The following excerpt is an example of how one workshop started.[4] Following a short introduction, a suggested exercise involved each of the participants and very quickly one of the participants asked to work.

Jim: Good evening. I'd like to start with a few sentences about contract and then suggest an exercise. I believe that there are no "shoulds" in Gestalt therapy. What you do is what you do. What I do is what I do. I do have a preference. I prefer that you be straight with me. *Please* remember, this is a preference, not a should. If you feel that you *should* honor my preference, then that's *your* should! When I ask you, "Where are you?" and

the like, my preference is that you tell me—or tell me that you're not willing to tell me. Then our transaction is straight. Any time that you want to know where I am, please ask me. I will either tell you, or tell you I am unwilling to tell you—so that our transaction will be straight.

Now for the exercise. Please look around the room and select someone you don't know or don't know well—whom you would like to know or know better . . . O.K.? Now here are the rules. You may do anything you like to "know" the other person better, except talk! John?

John: The lady with the brown sweater.

Jim: Marilyn, are you willing to be "known" by John?

Marilyn: Yes.

Jim: Elaine, please select a partner.

Elaine: That man—I believe he said his name was Bert.

Jim: Are you willing, Bert?

Bert: My pleasure!

Jim: Nancy?

Nancy: I would like to know Agnes better.

Agnes: That's fine with me.

Jonathan: Well, that leaves me to Phil.

Jim: Yes, unless you're willing to include me.

Jonathan: No thanks. I'd rather get to know Phil! (group laughter).

The group broke into dyads, and for several minutes, the person who had asked to know the other was the aggressor, "exploring" the other with his sensory modalities (touch, taste, smell, etc.) lifting, pulling, dancing with, and so on. Then the partners in the dyad were asked to switch and the "aggressor" became the "aggressee" as the exercise was repeated.

Jim: O.K., I'm interested in knowing more about your experience. If you have made any discoveries about *yourself* and

---

[4] The clinical examples in this section are taken from Simkin's (1975) chapter, Gestalt psychotherapy, in Bannister's *Issues and Approaches in the Psychological Therapies.*

are willing to share, please tell the rest of us what you found out.

Bert: I discovered that I felt awkward and uncomfortable when Elaine was the aggressor!

Elaine: I sensed your discomfort and found myself concerned with what you thought of me.

Bert: I would like to work on my always having to be "masculine"—my avoidance of my passivity.

Jim: When?

Bert: Now! [At this point Bert leaves his chair in the circle and sits in the empty chair across from the therapist.] I feel anxious. My heart is pounding and my hands feel sweaty, and I'm aware of all of the others in the room.

Jim: Is there anything you would like to say to the others?

For the next 15 to 20 minutes Bert worked in the "hot seat." When he finished, the therapist turned his focus (awareness) back to the group.

Selection, Composition, Frequency. Patients selected for inclusion in Gestalt therapy groups need to be screened to determine their willingness and ability to work within the Gestalt therapy framework. Ordinarily this screening is done through individual interviews in which the therapist assesses through the therapeutic encounter rather than through psychodiagnostic evaluations the patient's willingness to work.

Gestalt therapists usually experience maximal involvement with heterogeneous groups. Thus groups will be composed of males and females, young and old, with a wide range of occupations, a variety of presenting problems, and so on. One such typical group had an actor, a student, two housewives, a physicist, an X-ray technician, an attorney, a nurse, a drama coach, a psychologist, and a painter. The age range for this group was from the early twenties to the late fifties. There was an equal number of men and women in this group.

Ordinarily Gestalt therapists reserve the right to bring new people into groups, with group participants allowed to veto additional members during the initial session of that new member.

Workshop Style. A good deal of the work done in Gestalt therapy is conducted in workshops, which are scheduled for a finite period, some for as little as one day. Others are weekend workshops ranging from 10 to 20 or more hours and still others are more extended, ranging from a week through several months in duration. A typical weekend workshop membership consists of one Gestalt therapist and 12 to 16 people. Given longer periods (ranging from one week up to a month or longer) as many as 20 people can be seen by one therapist. Usually if the group is larger than 16 participants, co-therapists are used.

Since workshops have a finite life and there are just so many hours available to the participants, usually there is high motivation on the part of most participants to get into the "hot seat," that is, to be the focus of attention and to "work."[5] Sometimes, rules are established so no one can work a second time till every other participant has had an opportunity to work once. At other times, no such rules are set. Thus depending on a person's willingness, audacity, and drive, some people may get intense therapeutic attention several times during a workshop.

Use of the Hot Seat and Other Techniques. Abraham Levitsky and James Simkin (1972) have described in some de-

---

[5] In Gestalt therapy jargon, *work* means to be the primary focus of the therapist's attention.

tail the use of the "hot seat" and other techniques in Gestalt therapy. Many therapists follow Perls's lead in the use of the "hot seat" technique and will explain this to the group at the outset somewhat as follows:

According to this method, an individual expresses to the therapist his interest in dealing with a particular problem. The focus is then on the extended interaction between patient and group leader (I and Thou).

As therapist and patient work together, occasions arise in which the patient is asked to carry out some particular exercise, for example, "Could you repeat what you just said, but this time with your legs uncrossed?" or "Could you look directly at me and say this?" The attitude with which these exercises are carried out is an important element. The patient is gradually educated and encouraged to undertake these exercises in the spirit of experiment. One cannot really know the outcome beforehand even though a specific hunch is being tested. The spirit of experiment is taken seriously and the question raised "What did you discover?" The discovery is the most potent form of learning. (Levitsky & Simkin, 1972, p. 140)

Mechanisms of Psychotherapy

Although some people claim they are interested in changing their behavior, most people seeking psychotherapy mainly want relief from discomfort. People who are motivated to seek out psychotherapy usually come with some complaint that may be some generalized malaise: anxiety, depression, disordered thinking, and the like; or specific discomforts like headache, stiff necks, sore backs, knotted stomachs, and so on. The specific discomfort that originally brought the patient to consult a physician and for which no organic condition could be found results in a referral to a psychotherapist. Those with specific complaints usually expect that relief from the discom-

fort will result from the therapist doing the work rather than through their own efforts.

A. R. Beisser postulates what he calls the *paradoxical theory of change.* He states that:

. . . *change occurs when one becomes what he is, not when he tries to become what he is not.* Change does not take place through a coercive attempt by the individual or by another person to change him, but it does take place if one takes the time and effort to be what he is. Change does not take place by "trying," coercion, or persuasion, or by insight, interpretation, or any other such means. Rather, change can occur when the patient abandons, at least for the moment, what he would like to become and attempts to be what he is. The premise is that one must stand in one place in order to have firm footing to move and that it is difficult or impossible to move without that footing.

The person seeking change by coming to therapy is in conflict with at least two warring intrapsychic factions. He is constantly moving between what he "should be" and what he thinks he "is," never fully identifying with either. The Gestalt therapist asks the person to invest himself fully in his roles, one at a time. Whichever role he begins with, the patient soon shifts to another. The Gestalt therapist asks simply that he be what he is at the moment. (Beisser, 1970, pp 77–78)

The analytic therapist, by contrast, uses devices such as dreams, free associations, transference, and interpretation to achieve insight that, in turn, may lead to change. The behaviorist therapist rewards or punishes behavior to modify it. The Gestalt therapist believes in encouraging the patient to enter and become whatever he is experiencing at the moment. He believes with Proust, "To heal a suffering one must experience it to the full."

The Gestalt therapist further believes the natural state of man is as a single, whole being—not fragmented into two or more opposing parts. In the natural state, there is constant change based on the dynamic transaction between self and the environment. Consequently, Gestalt therapy theory sees man as an individual, an indivisible entity, a holistic unity, rather than as a fragmented composite. The human person is in a constant state of change to maintain his integrity. Or, in a simple and accurate manner, we represent a truly humanistic psychology.

APPLICATIONS

Problems

Irma Shepherd discusses some of the limitations and cautions in the Gestalt approach. She considers below the kinds of patients who are most suitable for working within the Gestalt therapy framework:

In general, Gestalt therapy is most effective with overly socialized, restrained, constricted individuals—often described as neurotic, phobic, perfectionistic, ineffective, depressed, etc.—whose functioning is limited or inconsistent, primarily due to their internal restrictions, and whose enjoyment of living is minimal. Most efforts of Gestalt therapy have therefore been directed toward persons with these characteristics.

Work with less organized, more severely disturbed or psychotic individuals is more problematic and requires caution, sensitivity, and patience. Such work should not be undertaken where long-term commitment to the patient is not feasible. The patient needs considerable support from the therapist and beginning faith in his own self-healing process before he can undertake to experience in depth and intensity the overwhelming pain, hurt, rage, and despair underlying most psychotic processes. (Shepherd, 1970, pp. 234–35)

A good rule of thumb is that Gestalt therapy can be the treatment of choice for those people with whom the Gestalt therapist has had the most experience and feels the most competent and comfortable. Thus, with the exception of individuals who lack impulse control, who are given to acting out, or who are grossly sociopathic or psychopathic, adolescent populations, neurotic populations, children, adults, men or women, borderline states, and so on are all possible populations amenable to being worked with in the Gestalt therapy framework.

In the aforementioned Joen Fagan and I. L. Shepherd book (1970), W. Kempler describes working with families, Janet Lederman works with behavior problem children, Simkin works with a passive patient, Fagan works with a woman with expressive difficulties, R. C. Cohn works with a child with recurrent stomach aches, and crisis intervention is described by V. F. O'Connell. Other examples include J. E. Barnwell's (1968) work with ghetto adults in a poverty program and J. E. Enright's (1975) Gestalt therapy in interactive groups.

In keeping with the aforementioned rule of thumb, Gestalt therapy has been successfully employed in the treatment of a wide range of "psychosomatic" disorders including migraine, ulcerative colitis, and spastic necks and backs. Gestalt therapists have successfully worked with couples, with individuals having difficulties coping with authority figures, and with a wide range of intrapsychic conflicts not the least of which has included topdog-underdog struggles.

Evaluation

As a group, Gestalt therapists are singularly unimpressed with formal psychodiagnostic evaluation specifically and research methodology in general. Most Gestalt therapists would argue that their approach *is* experimental: that each session is seen as an existential encounter in which both the therapist and the patient engage in calculated risk taking (experiments) involving a willingness to explore heretofore unknown or forbidden territories. This is not to say that "acting-out" is encouraged. Rather, with a firm grounding in personality theory, psychopathology, theories and application of psychotherapy, and so on, as well as adequate clinical experience and the establishment of a trust relationship, the participants in the therapeutic encounter are encouraged by the therapist to experiment with new behavior and then cognitively-emotionally share what the experience was like. It is important to emphasize that because of the impactfulness of Gestalt therapy and the ease with which strong, frequently buried affective reactions can be reached, it is necessary to have first established what Simkin calls "safety islands" to which both the therapist and patient can comfortably return. It is also imperative for the therapist to stay with the patient until he or she is ready to return to these "safety islands."

As an example of the above, after an especially strong emotionally laden experience, the Gestalt therapist asks the patient whether he can see him or (if in group) can see members of the group. The patient will be encouraged to make visual or tactile or other contact with the therapist or with one or more group members and report what his experience in making contact is like. Another "safety" technique to reassure all concerned is to have the patient shuttle back and forth between making contact in the now with the therapist or group members and with the emotionally laden unfinished situation that the patient was experiencing, until all of the affect has been discharged and the unfinished situation worked through.

Simkin has been interested in assessing the effectiveness of Gestalt therapy in workshops as contrasted with weekly therapy. During the years 1970 and 1971 he developed some clinical impressions in the form of feedback from people coming to residential workshops, and compared the feedback of these patients with feedback that was obtained from patients who were seen in a more traditional manner the previous two years. Seventy-five percent of the patients who attended the residential workshops reported that they received what they came for or more. This claim was made by 66% of those who were in weekly therapy. The percentage of patients who claimed they received no help, or got worse, was approximately equal for those coming to the residential workshops and those coming for weekly therapy (14 percent). The remainder in both the traditional and the workshop style were people who claimed they "got something" from the experience. (It is interesting to note that patients that had either the individual or group work on a "spaced" basis and the workshop on a "massed" basis favor the massed basis by a ratio of about 9–1). Feedback data have been obtained from over 200 people who have attended both workshops and traditional therapy.

Simkin also experimented with training in Gestalt Therapy and has data on the results of an experiment massing close to 300 hours of training into a three-month period. What was attempted was to provide an intensive training experience for five therapists in a residential setting. The number of hours available was comparable to (or more than) the number of hours of training in the more formal institutes. Personality inventories, peer group ratings, the A.B. Therapist Scale, clinical impressions of the trainees and other measurements were utilized. Evidence supports the possibility of successfully massing training in a three-month period. A follow-up study, in which the five therapists returned for a week, seven months after their training, indicated that the *direction* of change (shown during the three month period) continued. In addition the quality of their work in dealing with patients showed a consistent positive increase as reflected by both patient's and supervisor's rating of their work. (Simkin, 1976, pp 27–28)

Treatment

From its beginnings, Gestalt therapy has been used with individuals displaying a wide variety of emotional problems ranging from neuroses through psychotic states. Again, almost from the beginning, Gestalt therapy has also been applied to the problems of individuals and groups where psychopathology was not the dominant or even a relevant feature.

Some of the earliest workshops (1952 on) in Gestalt therapy were offered to diverse specific groups such as educators, dentists, actors, and physicians. The purpose of these workshops was to augment the professional skills of the participants through the experiential learning and application of Gestalt therapy.

Inasmuch as Gestalt therapy reflects the personality and specific experimental attitudes of the therapist, it is not surprising that one of the earliest Gestalt therapy students (Iris Sangiulano) experimented with multiple therapists for an individual patient (Mullan & Sangiulano, 1958).

Individual Application. Although Gestalt therapy has acquired a reputation of being primarily applicable to groups, it has been used right from its inception, and it still is extensively used with individuals. As noted in the previous section on Problems, in Fagan and Shepherd's book (1970), there are several examples of such individual therapy: Simkin's (1970), *Mary: A session with a passive patient*; Fagan's (1970), *Anne: Gestalt techniques with a woman with expressive difficulties*; Close's (1970), *Gross exaggeration with a schizophrenic patient*; and Cohn's (1970), *A child with a stomachache: Fusion of psychoanalytic concepts and Gestalt techniques.*

Group Psychotherapy. One of the earliest applications of Gestalt therapy was in group therapy. Laura Perls conducted her training groups as therapy groups from the very beginning as did several other trainers in the New York, Cleveland, and West Coast areas. Fritz Perls considered individual therapy as ob-

solete in the early 1960s, and wrote a paper in which he said, "Lately, however, I have eliminated individual sessions altogether except for emergency cases. As a matter of fact, I have come to consider that all individual therapy is obsolete and should be replaced by workshops in Gestalt Therapy. In my workshops I now integrate individual and group work" (Perls, 1967, p. 306).

Some of the critics of Gestalt therapy have described the Gestalt therapist's style of group work as doing individual therapy in a group setting. To a large extent this criticism is valid since many Gestalt therapists do not emphasize or deal with the group dynamics, nor do they strive for the development of group cohesiveness.[6] Other Gestalt therapists, such as Laura Perls, Daniel Rosenblatt, and the Polsters, for example, have been and are concerned with the group interactive processes and focus as much or more on these as on the individual in the group who states: "I want to work."

Other Treatment Modalities. The application of Gestalt therapy to working with families has been most extensively elaborated by Walter Kempler, the author of the chapter on Gestalt therapy in the first edition of this text (Kempler, 1973, pp. 251-86). The most complete description of Kempler's work appears in his *Principles of Gestalt Family Therapy* (1974).

Another application of Gestalt therapy has been through the medium of art. The most notable exponent of this approach is Janie Rhyne. A distillation of her work has appeared in her book, *The Gestalt Art Experience* (1973).

Gestalt therapy has also been used in

---

[6] For a discussion of the Cleveland Institute's emphasis on Gestalt group process, see "Principles of Gestalt Group Process." (Zinker, 1977. Pp. 161 ff.)

short-term crisis intervention (O'Connell, 1970); as an adjunct treatment for visual problems (Rosanes-Berret, 1970), for awareness training of mental-health professionals (Enright, 1970), with behavior problem children (Lederman, 1970), with staff training for a day-care center (Ennis and Mitchell, 1970), with *Teaching Creativity to Teachers and Others* (Brown, 1970), with a dying person (Zinker and Fink, 1966), and with organization development (Herman, 1972).

Management

In the writer's private practice, the office consisted of a suite with a waiting room and an exit hall. One door opened from the waiting room into the consultation room and another door led to the exit hall, which opened into the main corridor of the office building in which the suite was located. Upon entering the waiting room, the patient pressed a button that lit a light in the waiting room and the consultation room. This light could be turned off from inside the consultation room, letting the patient know that his presence was acknowledged. Toward the end of the 1960s when an associate entered the practice, a larger suite designed along similar lines with two entrance doors to a larger and smaller consultation room leading from the waiting room was leased. Again each of the consultation rooms had separate exit doors into an exit hall, which led back into the building's main corridor. With two therapists there were two buttons with name plates and lights above each name similar to the system used when there was one consultation room. Furniture in the offices was comfortable and unpretentious. Several chairs were equipped with legs that had rollers, so patients and therapist could move about the office easily. The floor was carpeted and

the suite soundproofed. One wall of the office was lined with books and journals.

Initial appointments were usually arranged over the telephone and handled directly by the therapist or his associates. Referrals were from a number of sources: other Gestalt therapists, physicians, former patients, and other psychotherapists.

Record Keeping. Initially all interviews were audiotaped on slow-speed, reel-to-reel, audio tape recorders. Later initial interviews and selected other interviews were videotaped and process notes kept on other interviews. During the initial interview, fees were established based on the patient's income, obligations, and size of family. A chart was available showing three fee schedules based on the above three criteria. Patients selected their own fees and agreement was made that fees would be increased or decreased with changing income, size of family, and other obligations. Although these three fee schedules periodically increased over a 13-year span, increases were never passed on to patients already in therapy. Patients could elect to pay by the session or be billed monthly. All audiotaping, record keeping, and process notes were done by the therapist. Monthly billing was done by the therapist's wife from records kept by him.

During the 13 years that this writer had offices in Beverly Hills, the offices were always located in a medical building and close contact was maintained with medically trained colleagues should emergency situations arise requiring hospitalization.

During the two years before moving to Big Sur, the practice changed appreciably with the addition of two more associates. For the four Gestalt therapist associates, two two-room suites were required, each containing a large consultation room suitable for groups. Referrals were handled through the rotation of each associate covering telephone inquiries one week a month. Weekly meetings were held to assign cases on the basis of suitability and scheduling availability. All cases assigned to associates were supervised either individually or in group supervisory consultations.

Initial Therapy Session. During the initial contact, patients were told that three preliminary sessions would be required to assess their suitability for working with the particular psychotherapist in a Gestalt therapy framework. At the end of the three sessions, or sometimes sooner, a decision was reached about continuing or the psychotherapeutic process. Some of the considerations involved in the evaluation process included deciding on individual and/or group therapy; estimating the capacity on the part of the therapist to establish a trusting, caring relationship; and letting the patient decide on an adequate sample basis if he found both the therapist and the therapy suitable for him. If either the therapist or the patient decided to discontinue because of interpersonal conflicts and/or an inability to deal with the specific psychopathology, referrals to other psychotherapists were offered before termination.

CASE EXAMPLE

Peg was originally seen in a Gestalt training workshop where she worked on the grief and anger she felt toward her husband who had committed suicide. His death left her with the full responsibility of raising their children and beginning a career outside the home to support herself and her family. She was in her late 30s at that time.

With considerable courage and initiative, Peg had organized a crisis clinic sponsored by a prominent service organization in the large Southern California city in which she resided. She was one of eleven people who participated in making a Gestalt Therapy Training Film with Simkin (1969). The following is excerpted from the film, *In The Now:*

Peg: I have a . . . recurring dream. I'm standing on the ground, up Camp Pendleton. There's an open, rolling countryside. Wide dirt roads criss-crossing all over it. A series of hills and valleys and hills and valleys. And I'm standing by the side of one of these dirt tracks. And off to my right I see a tank, like in the army—marine tanks with the big tracks . . . and there's a series of them and they're all closed tight and they're rumbling over these hills and valleys in a line, all closed up. And I'm standing beside this road and I'm holding a platter of Tollhouse cookies. And they're hot cookies. And they are just on the platter—I'm just standing there, and I see these tanks coming by one at a time. And as the tanks come past, I stand there and I watch the tanks. And as I look to my right I see one—and there's a pair of shiny black shoes, running along between the treads of the tank as it comes over the hill. And just as it gets in front of me . . . the man bends down and the tank goes on, and he comes over toward me and it's my best friend's husband. And I always wake up. I always stop my dream . . . there. The first time I thought it was a funny dream . . . and I laughed. It doesn't seem so funny anymore.

Jim: True. What are you doing?

Peg: Trying to stop my teeth from chattering.

Jim: What's your objection?

Peg: I don't like the feeling of anxiety and fear I have now.

Jim: What do you imagine?

Peg: Ridicule.

Jim: Okay. Start ridiculing.

Peg: Peg, you're ridiculous. You're fat . . . you're lazy. You're just comic. You're pretending to be grown up and you're not. Everybody looking knows that you're a kid inside, masquerading as a thirty-nine-year-old woman and . . . it's a ridiculous disguise. You haven't any business being thirty-nine. A ridiculous age. You're comic. You have a job you don't have the remotest idea how to do. You're making all kinds of grandiose plans that you haven't brains enough to carry through and people are going to be laughing at you.

Jim: Okay, now please look around and note how people are laughing at you.

Peg: I'm scared to. [Looks around, slowly] They appear to be taking me quite seriously.

Jim: So who is laughing at you?

Peg: I guess . . . only my fantasy . . . my . . .

Jim: Who creates your fantasy?

Peg: I do.

Jim: So who's laughing at you?

Peg: Yeah. That's so. I . . . I'm really laughing at what's not funny. I'm not so damned incompetent. [Pause]

Jim: Where are you at this moment?

Peg: In the kitchen. I'm a better yeast baker than I am a cookie baker. That's where I want to be. I want to be in the kitchen. I want to be playing Harriet Housewife again.

Jim: Yeah . . . you don't want to be out in the battlefield.

Peg: I'm not very well suited for that.

Jim: So?

Peg: So I blew half the insurance money and I can't quit.

Jim: You can't be Harriet Housewife . . .

Peg: I am part of the time. I'm sick of pretending to be competent at something I'm mediocre at . . . I'm average. Adequate, but not outstanding . . .

Jim: What are you really good at?

Peg: I'm good with people. I'm not judgmental. I'm good at keeping house. I'm a good seamstress, good baker, I . . .

Jim: Maybe you'll make somebody a good wife.

Peg: I did.

Jim: Maybe you'll make somebody a good wife again.

Peg: I don't know.

Jim: So say that sentence. "I don't know if I'll ever make somebody a good wife again."

Peg: I don't know if I'll ever make someone a good wife again.

Jim: Say that to every man here.

Peg: I don't know if I'll make someone a good wife again. I don't know if I'll make someone a good wife again. I don't know if I'll make someone a good wife again. I don't know if I'll make someone a good wife again. I don't know if I'll make someone a good wife again.

Jim: What do you experience?

Peg: Surprise. Boy . . . I assumed I would never make anybody a good wife again.

Jim: Right.

Peg: Who'd want the cookies? They're a drug on the market. The markets are glutted with cookies.

Jim: Yeah. How about good wholesome bread?

Peg: That's harder to get. I'm all right, Jim.

Jim: I know. You didn't sound too convincing to me.

Peg: But I know too.

Jim: Do you know that?

Peg: Here and now . . . I feel more like bread than cookies. Something to be. [Pause—begins to smile]

Jim: What do you experience right now?

Peg: Satisfaction. Pleasure. I feel good. I feel done.

Although Peg's "ticket of admission" was a dream, what became foreground was her anxiety and fantasies of being ridiculed. The dream served as a vehicle for starting and, as is frequently the case, the work led to a most unpredictable outcome.

At the weekend workshop during which the training film was made, Peg met a man to whom she was attracted and who, in turn, was attracted to her. They began to date and within a few months they married.

A second sample of Gestalt therapy follows, selectively excerpted from a book to illustrate some techniques (Simkin, 1976, pp. 103–18). The following is a condensed transcript of a two-hour workshop in a TV studio with six volunteers at Bradley University, Peoria, Illinois, May 1971 (Simkin, 1976, pp.103–18). The morning session included a lecture-demonstration and film showing.

Jim S: I'd like to start with saying where I am and what I'm experiencing at this moment. This seems very artificial to me, all of these lights and the cameras and the people around. I feel breathless and burdened by the technical material, the equipment, etc., and I'm much more interested in getting away from the lights and the cameras and getting more in touch with you. [Inquires as to the names of participants of the group and introduces himself.]

I am assuming that all of you were in the audience this morning, that you saw the film and the demonstration; and my preference would be to work with you as you feel ready to work. I'll reiterate our contract, or agreement. In Gestalt therapy the essence of the contract is to say where you are, what you are experiencing at any given moment; and, if you can, to stay in the continuum of awareness, to report where you are focusing, what you are aware of.

We have a couple of empty chairs and sometimes if it becomes appropriate for you to work with a part of yourself, or another person, I'll ask you to imagine that that part of you or the other person is in the empty chair and to work "as if." I'm willing to work with you on anything—a dream, an interpersonal problem, an intrapsychic conflict, whatever.

I'd like to start first with having you say who you are and if you have any programs or expectations.

Jim 2: Right now I'm a little tense, not particularly because of the technical equipment because I'm kind of used to that. I kind of feel a little strange about being in a situation with you. This morning I was pretty upset because I didn't agree with a lot of the things you were talking about, and I felt pretty hostile to you. Now I more or less accept you as another person.

Jim S: I'm paying attention to your foot now. I'm wondering if you could give your foot a voice.

Jim 2: My foot a voice? You mean how is my foot feeling? What's it going to say?

Jim S: Just keep doing that, and see if you have something to say, as your foot.

Jim 2: I don't understand.

Jim S: As you were telling me about feeling hostile this morning, you began to kick and I'm imagining that you still have some kick coming.

Jim 2: Uh, yeah. I guess maybe I do have some kick left, but I really don't get the feeling that that's appropriate.

Mary: My heart was really racing. It still is. I feel very hot . . . no life . . . hot, sweating off anxiety. I found you this morning surprisingly kind and gentle, much more so than I had experienced you in the films that I'd seen. I felt that I could have been either one of those other two women you spoke of.

Jim S: Would you be willing to say what you are experiencing at this moment?

Mary: Well, my whole body is throbbing. I feel my whole . . . well, it's just pulsing. I'm just pulsing.

Jim S: That excites me. I like your pulsing.

Mary: That pleases me.

Jim S: I hope this is in color. You look very colorful now.

Mary: I feel colorful. I feel alive. I felt alive this morning.

Lavonne: Right now I'm feeling very tense.

Jim S: Who are you talking to, Lavonne?

Lavonne: I was just thinking about this morning. I was feeling very hostile. I still think I am somewhat hostile.

Jim S: I am aware that you are avoiding looking at me.

Lavonne: Yes, because I feel that you are very arrogant.

Jim S: That's true.

Lavonne: And as if I might get into a struggle with you.

Jim S: You might.

Lavonne: So the avoidance of eye contact is sort of a putoff of the struggle. I have some things that I'd like to work on. I don't know whether they can be resolved.

Jim S: Would you be willing to tell me what your objections are to my arrogance?

Lavonne: Well, it's not very comforting. If I have a problem and I talk to you about it and you're arrogant, then that only makes me arrogant.

Jim S: You respond in kind is what you are saying. Your experience is you respond that way.

Lavonne: Yes. Right on. Then at this university I feel that I must be arrogant and I must be defensive at all times. Because I'm black, people react to me in different ways . . . different people . . . and I feel that I have to be on my toes most of the time.

Jim S: [looks at her toes]: I was checking.

Lavonne: Well, I am on my toes now.

Mary: I want to work on my feelings for my older son and the struggle that I have with him—only, I suspect it is really a struggle I'm having with myself.

Jim S: Can you say this to him? Give him a name and say this to him.

Mary: All right. His name is Paul.

Jim S: Put Paul here [empty chair] and say this to Paul.

Mary: Paul, we have a lot of friction. Every time you go out of the drive on your own, independent, I hate you for it. But . . .

Jim S: Just a moment. Say the same sentence to Mary. Mary, each time you go out the drive, independent, I hate you for it.

Mary: That fits. Mary, each time you go out the drive, independent, I hate you for it, because you are not being a good mother.

Jim S: I don't know about your because.

Mary: No. That's my rationale. That's the same I do to myself doing yoga.

Jim S: You sound identified with Paul.

Mary: I am. I know this. I envy his freedom, even from the time he was a little kid and went to the woods. I envied his ability to go to the woods.

Jim S: Tell Paul.

Mary: Paul, even when you were a little boy and you would go for all day Saturday, and not tell me where you were going but just go, I envied you for it. I envied you very much, and I felt hurt because I couldn't do it too.

Jim S: You couldn't, or you wouldn't?

Mary: I would not do it. I wanted to, but I would not do it.

Jim S: Yeah. For me to have somebody around that keeps reminding me of what I can do and don't really pisses me off.

Mary: This is what I do to myself. I keep reminding myself of what I can do and won't do. And then I don't do anything. I'm at a standstill. Firmly planted.

Jim S: I'd like you to get in touch with your spitefulness. Put your spitefulness out here and talk to Mary's saboteur.

Mary: You idiot! You've got the time to do your work. You also have the energy to do your work . . . which you dissipate. You get involved in umpteen dozen things so you will have an excuse not to do your work, or to do anything else that . . . [Pause] You just spend time making yourself miserable and complicating your life.

Jim S: What's going on here? [Points to Mary's hand]

Mary: Yes. Tight-fisted . . . won't do.

Jim S: Are you tight-fisted?

Mary: Yes, I think I am.

Jim S: O.K. Can you get in touch with the other part of you—your generous self?

Mary: I don't really know my generous self very well.

Jim S: Be your tight-fisted self just saying, "Generous self, I have no contact with you, I don't know you, etc."

Mary: Generous self, I don't know very much of you. I think you try every now and then when you give presents to people instead of giving yourself. You withhold an awful lot that you could give.

Jim S: What just happened?

Mary: I rehearsed. I just wasn't talking to my generous self. I was talking to . . . you, primarily. I was withholding part.

Jim S: I have difficulty imagining you as a withholding person. You came on in the beginning as very vibrant and alive . . . to me, very giving.

Mary: I don't know whether I really am giving or not.

Jim S: Say that again please.

Mary: I don't know whether I really am giving or not. Sometimes I feel like I do give and what I give is not accepted as a gift. And sometimes I want to give and I can't. And I feel sometimes I have given too much and I shouldn't have.

Jim S: Yeah. This is what I'm beginning to sense. Some hurt. You look like you've been hurt—in the past. That you've been vulnerable and somehow hurt in the process.

Mary: To some degree I'm hurting.

Jim S: To me you look like you're hurting now, especially around your eyes.

Mary: I know that, and I don't want to do that . . . I don't want to show that.

Jim S: O.K. Would you be willing to block?

Mary: [covering her eyes]: When I do that, I can't see you.

Jim S: That's true.

Mary: When I do that, I can't see anyone.

Jim S: Very true. When I block my hurt, no one exists for me. This is my choice.

Mary: I made it my choice too.

Jim S: I am enjoying looking at you. To me you are very generous at this moment.

Mary: You are very generous to me. I feel that you are. I hear you respond to me and I feel that I'm responding to you.

Jim S: This is what I'm experiencing with you. Responding. My style—I call it follow-the-leader. Wherever you want to go, I am willing to go with you, usually. And I enjoy very much going with you.

Mary: I'm glad. That makes me happy.

Jim S: I'm curious if you can come

back to Paul for a moment now. Encounter him and explore what happens.

Mary: Paul, I want to be warm to you, and I want to be generous to you, and I think I might hurt you by being so. You're six feet tall now and sometimes I very much want to come up to you and just give you a kiss good night or just put my arms around you and I can't do it anymore.

Jim S: You can't?

Mary: I won't. I won't, because, uh . . . I've been shoved away.

Jim S: You've been hurt.

Mary: Yeah, I've been hurt. Paul, I think it's your own business if you want to shove me away, but that doesn't stop me from being hurt.

Jim S: I like what, I believe, Nietzsche once said to the sun, "It's none of your business that you shine at me."

Mary: I keep hoping that, Paul, when you're 25 or if you go to the Army or whatever . . . that I can kiss you goodby. [pause] I'll try to remember what Nietzsche said to the sun.

Jim S: O.K. I enjoyed working with you.

Mary: Thank you.

SUMMARY

Fritz Perls prophesied a little over two decades ago that Gestalt therapy would come into its own during the 1960s and become a significant force in psychotherapy during the 1970s. His prophecy has been more than fulfilled.

At the time Simkin began training in Gestalt therapy in 1952, there were perhaps a dozen people seriously involved in the movement. Currently there are scores of training institutes, hundreds of psychotherapists who have been trained in Gestalt therapy, and many hundreds of nontrained or poorly trained persons who

call themselves "Gestaltists." Thousands of people have been exposed to experiencing Gestalt therapy—many with quite favorable results—others with questionable or poor outcomes.

Because of the unwillingness on the part of Gestalt therapists to set rigid standards for the selection and training of psychotherapists there is a wide range of criteria for the selection and training of Gestalt therapists. Some people having experienced a weekend here or a weeklong there consider themselves amply equipped to replicate the techniques they saw employed—as if *that* were Gestalt therapy. Other psychotherapists spend months and years in training as Gestalt therapists and have an enormous respect for the simplicity and infinite innovativeness and creativity that Gestalt therapy requires and engenders.

Despite the fact that Gestalt therapy attracts some people who are looking for shortcuts, it also has attracted a substantial number of solid, experienced clinicians who have found in Gestalt therapy not only a powerful psychotherapy but also a viable life philosophy.

Those looking for quick solutions and shortcuts will go on to greener pastures. Gestalt therapy will take its place along with other substantive psychotherapies in the next several decades. It will continue to attract creative, experimentally oriented psychotherapists for many years to come.

To summarize, a quote from Levitsky and Simkin (1972) seems appropriate:

The methods and techniques of Gestalt therapy flow from a number of general principles. Gestalt therapy is a broad and very ambitious approach not only to the problems of psychotherapy but to the problem of existence. Inasmuch as Gestalt therapy contains a philosophy of growth, of healthy human functioning, it is essentially a philosophy of being.

The phenomenon of self-awareness and the recognition of one's finiteness lead to the experience of existential anxiety, an unavoidable part of existence. The Gestalt therapist, therefore, is not concerned with curing the patient of anxiety. The aim is rather to help him accept anxiety as part of the very nature of things.

If we were to choose one key idea to stand as a symbol for the Gestalt approach, it might well be the concept of authenticity, the quest for authenticity.

If we regard therapy and the therapist in the pitiless light of authenticity, it becomes apparent that the therapist cannot teach what he does not know.

A therapist with some experience really knows within himself that he is communicating to his patient his (the therapist's) own fears as well as his courage, his defensiveness as well as his openness, his confusion as well as his clarity. The therapist's awareness, acceptance, and sharing of these truths can be a highly persuasive demonstration of his own authenticity. Obviously such a position is not acquired overnight. It is to be learned and relearned ever more deeply not only throughout one's career but throughout one's entire life.

ANNOTATED BIBLIOGRAPHY

Fagan, J., & Shepherd, I. L. (Eds.) *Gestalt therapy now.* Palo Alto, Calif.: Science and Behavior Books, 1970. (Also, New York: Harper & Row, Harper Colophon Books [Paperback], 1971.)
This collection of articles on the theory, techniques, and applications of Gestalt therapy is the best single collection incorporating original articles by F. S. Perls, Laura Perls, Erving Polster, Walter Kempler, James Simkin, I. L. Shepherd, Abraham Levitsky, and other leading Gestalt therapists. Each section has an introduction by the authors and the appendix has an up-to-date bibliography of books, articles, tape recordings, and films that were available in 1970 when the book was first published.

Simkin, J. S. *Gestalt therapy mini-lectures.* Millbrae, Calif.: Celestial Arts, 1976.

This book consists of a first section containing an introductory chapter covering Gestalt therapy in groups that was primarily prepared for a textbook dealing with group psychotherapy and group counseling. The second section—*Theoretical and Practical Issues*—consists of short minilectures concerning a range of topics that cover most of the concepts and constructs popular in Gestalt therapy. The third section deals with techniques. Section four is an extensive example of working with a dream in Gestalt therapy and the fifth section—*Clinical Work*—is a condensed transcript of a two-hour workshop at a midwestern university in the early 1970s. A total of 41 references are included.

Polster, E., & Polster, M. *Gestalt therapy integrated: Contours of theory and practice.* New York: Brunner/Mazel, 1973.
The Polsters have written a scholarly, penetrating book that is described by Milton Berger in the Introduction as timely and reflecting a humanistic viewpoint. The book covers topics such as The Now Ethos; Figure and Ground; Resistance; Contact-Boundary, Contact Functions and Contact Episodes; Awareness; Experiment; and a description of working with a variety of groups in a section labeled Beyond One to One.

Hatcher, C., & Himmelstein, P. (Eds.) *The handbook of Gestalt therapy.* New York: Jason Aronson, 1976.
This is a collection of articles in Gestalt therapy. Some appear in this volume for the first time. Others have appeared in other sources. Although this volume is marred by a number of typographical errors and several poor selections, it contains the most up-to-date bibliography in existence (chapter 32) and several outstanding contributions such as Appelbaum's, "A Psychoanalyst Looks at Gestalt Therapy"; Gerald Kogan's, "The Genesis of Gestalt Therapy"; and Miriam Polster's, "Women In Therapy: A Gestalt Therapist's View."

Perls, F. S. *In and out of the garbage pail.* Moab, Utah: Real People Press, 1969 (Bantam, 1971).
This is Fritz Perls's autobiography, written over a period of three months in 1969, about one year before he died. It has a wide-ranging, free-floating style that includes poetry and prose, tragedy and humor, seriousness and lightness, and a host of other polarities that

characterized the primary founder of Gestalt therapy. For those individuals never having had the opportunity to meet him in person, this book is the next best thing.

Perls, F. S. *Gestalt therapy verbatim.* Moab, Utah: Real People Press, 1969.

It is in this book that the world-famous Gestalt therapy prayer appears:

I do my thing, and you do your thing.
I am not in this world to live up to your expectations
And you are not in this world to live up to mine.
You are you and I am I,
And if by chance we find each other, it's beautiful.
If not, it can't be helped. (1969, p. 4)

The first section, called "talk" (about 65 pages), deals primarily with the theory of Gestalt therapy, in a seminar style, with interspersed questions from participants. The bulk of the book is specific verbatim transcripts of Perls' Gestalt therapy work with people who attended a weekend, dreamwork seminar and excerpts of audiotapes of a four-week, intensive workshop.

CASE READINGS

Perls, F. S. Jane's three dreams. In *Gestalt therapy verbatim.* Moab, Utah: Real People Press, 1969, pp. 251-72.

Three dreams, labelled Jane I, Jane II, and Jane III, are presented verbatim. In the section called Jane III, Jane continues to work on an unfinished part of the dream she had worked on in Jane II.

Perls, L. P. Two instances of Gestalt therapy. *Case reports in clinical psychology,* Kings County Hospital, Brooklyn, N.Y., 1956. (Also found in P. D. Pursglove [Ed.], *Recognitions in Gestalt therapy.* New York: Funk & Wagnalls, 1968, pp. 42-63.)

Laura Perls presents the case of Claudia, a 25-year-old black woman who comes from a lower middle-class West Indian background, and the case of Walter, a 47-year-old Central European Jewish refugee.

Simkin, J. S. *Individual Gestalt therapy.* A.A.P. tape library (31, 50 minutes), Orlando, Florida, 1957.

The eleventh hour with a 34-year-old actor. Emphasis is on the present, nonverbal communications leading to production of genetic material. The use of fantasy dialogue is also illustrated in this piece of work.

Simkin, J. S. The use of dreams in Gestalt therapy. In C. J. Sager & H. S. Kaplan (Eds.), *Progress in group and family therapy.* New York: Brunner/Mazel, 1972, pp. 95-104.

A verbatim transcript of a patient working on a dream concerning his youngest daughter. He tells this dream in a group workshop in which he has worked with several of the group's members before.

Fagan, J. Three sessions with Iris. *The Counseling Psychologist,* 1974, pp. 42-59. (Also in C. Hatcher & P. Himmelstein [Eds.], *The handbook of Gestalt therapy.* New York: Jason Aronson, 1976, pp. 673-721.)

Dr. Fagan describes her work with Iris as "being an example of good, hard, routine work with a resistant patient in individual therapy in a heavily Gestalt style" (1976, p. 674). The patient was a volunteer for a doctoral dissertation and had agreed to be videotaped and had had no previous experience with Gestalt therapy.

REFERENCES

Appelbaum, S. A. A psychoanalyst looks at Gestalt therapy. In C. Hatcher & P. Himmelstein (Eds.), *The handbook of Gestalt therapy.* New York: Jason Aronson, 1976, pp. 753-78.

Bannister, D. (Ed.) *Issues and approaches in the psychological therapies.* London: Wiley, 1975.

Barnwell, J. E. Gestalt methods and techniques in a poverty program. In Simkin, J. S. (Ed.), *Festschrift for Fritz Perls.* Los Angeles: 1968.

Beisser, A. R. The paradoxical theory of change. In J. Fagan & I. L. Shepherd (Eds.), *Gestalt therapy now.* Palo Alto, Calif.: Science and Behavior Books, 1970.

Brown, G. I. Teaching creativity to teachers and others. *Journal of Teacher Education,* 1970, 21, 210-16.

Carmer, J. C., & Rouzer, D. L. Healthy functioning from the Gestalt perspective. *The Counseling Psychologist,* 1974, 4, 20-23.

Close, H. T. Gross exaggeration with a schizophrenic patient. In J. Fagan & I. L. Shepherd (Eds.), *Gestalt therapy now.* Palo Alto, Calif.: Science and Behavior Books, 1970, pp. 194-96.

Cohn, R. C. A child with a stomachache: Fusion of psychoanalytic concepts and Gestalt techniques. In J. Fagan & I. L. Shepherd (Eds.), *Gestalt therapy now.* Palo Alto, Calif.: Science and Behavior Books, 1970, pp. 197-203.

Ennis, K., & Mitchell, S. Staff training for a day care center. In J. Fagan & I. L. Shepherd (Eds.), *Gestalt therapy now.* Palo Alto, Calif.: Science and Behavior Books, 1970, pp. 295-300.

Enright, J. B. Awareness training in the mental health professions. In J. Fagan & I. L. Shepherd (Eds.), *Gestalt therapy now.* Palo Alto, Calif.: Science and Behavior Books, 1970, pp. 263-73.

Enright, J. B. Gestalt therapy in interactive groups. In F. D. Stephenson (Ed.), *Gestalt therapy primer: Introductory readings in Gestalt therapy.* Springfield, Ill.: C. C Thomas, 1975, pp. 127-41.

Fagan, J. Gestalt techniques with a woman with expressive difficulties. In J. Fagan & I. L. Shepherd (Eds.), *Gestalt therapy now.* Palo Alto, Calif.: Science and Behavior Books, 1970, pp. 169-93.

Fagan, J. Personality theory and psychotherapy. *The Counseling Psychologist,* 1974, 4, 4-7.

Fagan, J., & Shepherd, I. L. (Eds.). *Gestalt therapy now.* Palo Alto, Calif.: Science and Behavior Books, 1970.

Herman, S. N. The Gestalt orientation to organizational development. In *Contemporary organization development.* Bethel, Maine: National Institute of Applied Behavioral Science, 1972, pp. 69-89.

Kempler, W. Gestalt therapy. In R. J. Corsini (Ed.), *Current psychotherapies.* Itasca, Ill.: F. E. Peacock Publishers, 1973.

Kempler, W. *Principles of Gestalt family therapy.* Costa Mesa, Calif.: Kempler Institute, 1974.

Kogan, G. The genesis of Gestalt therapy. In C. Hatcher & P. Himmelstein (Eds.), *The handbook of Gestalt therapy.* New York: Jason Aronson, 1976, 235-57.

Lederman, J. Anger and the rocking chair. In J. Fagan & I. L. Shepherd (Eds.), *Gestalt therapy now.* Palo Alto, Calif.: Science and Behavior Books, 1970, pp. 285-94.

Levitsky, A., & Simkin, J. S. Gestalt therapy. In L. N. Solomon & B. Berzon (Eds.), *New perspectives on encounter groups.* San Francisco: Jossey-Bass, 1972, pp. 245-54.

Mullan, J., & Sangiulano, I. A. Interpretation as existence in analysis. *Psychoanalysis and psychoanalytic review,* 1958, 45, 52-64.

O'Connell, V. F. Crisis psychotherapy: Person, dialogue, and the organismic approach. In J. Fagan & I. L. Shepherd (Eds.), *Gestalt therapy now.* Palo Alto, Calif.: Science and Behavior Books, 1970, pp. 243-56.

Perls, F. S. *Ego, hunger and aggression.* London: Allen & Unwin, 1947 (San Francisco: Orbit Graphic Arts, 1966).

Perls, F. S. Theory and technique of personality integration. *American Journal of Psychotherapy,* 1948, 2, 565-86.

Perls, F. S. Group vs. individual therapy. *ETC,* 1967, 24, 306-12.

Perls, F. S. *Gestalt therapy verbatim.* Moab, Utah: Real People Press, 1969.

Perls, F. Resolution. In J. O. Stevens (Ed.), *Gestalt is.* Moab, Utah: Real People Press, 1975, pp. 69-73.

Perls, F. S. Gestalt therapy verbatim: Introduction. In C. Hatcher & P. Himmelstein (Eds.), *The handbook of Gestalt therapy.* New York: Jason Aronson, 1976, pp. 21-79.

Perls, F.; Hefferline, R. F.; & Goodman, P. *Gestalt therapy.* New York: Julian Press, 1951.

Perls, L. Some aspects of Gestalt therapy. Manuscript presented at Annual Meeting of Orthopsychiatric Association, 1973.

Polster, E. A. A contemporary psychotherapy. In P. D. Pursglove (Ed.), *Recognitions in Gestalt therapy.* New York: Funk & Wagnalls, 1968, pp. 3-19.

Polster, E., & Polster, M. *Gestalt therapy integrated.* New York: Brunner/Mazel, 1973.

Rhyne, J. *The Gestalt art experience.* Monterey, Calif.: Brooks/Cole, 1973.

Rosanes-Berret, M. B. Gestalt therapy as an adjunct treatment for some visual problems. In J. Fagan & I. L. Shepherd (Eds.), *Gestalt therapy now.* Palo Alto, Calif.: Science and Behavior Books, 1970, pp. 257-62.

Rosenblatt, D. *Opening doors. What happens in Gestalt therapy.* New York: Harper & Row, 1975.

Shepherd, I. L. Limitations and cautions in the Gestalt approach. In J. Fagan & I. L. Shepherd (Eds.), *Gestalt therapy now.* Palo Alto, Calif.: Science and Behavior Books, 1970, pp. 234-38.

Shostrom, E. (Ed.) *Three approaches to psy-*

chotherapy: Rogers, Perls, Ellis. Orange, Calif.: Psychological Films, Inc., 1965.

Simkin, J. S. (Ed.) *Festschrift for Fritz Perls.* Los Angeles: Author, 1968.

Simkin, J. S. *In the now.* A training film. Beverly Hills, Calif.: 1969.

Simkin, J. S. Mary: A session with a passive patient. In J. Fagan & I. L. Shepherd (Eds.), *Gestalt therapy now.* Palo Alto, Calif.: Science and Behavior Books, 1970, pp. 162–68.

Simkin, J. S. *Gestalt therapy mini-lectures.* Millbrae, Calif.: Celestial Arts, 1976.

Yontef, G. M. *A review of the practice of Gestalt therapy.* Los Angeles: Trident Shop, California State University, 1971.

Zinker, J. C. *Creative process in Gestalt therapy.* New York: Brunner/Mazel, 1977.

Zinker, J. C., & Fink, S. L. The possibility for psychological growth in a dying person. *Journal of General Psychology,* 1966, 74, 185–89.

8

Reality Therapy

WILLIAM GLASSER AND LEONARD M. ZUNIN

OVERVIEW

Reality therapy is a series of theoretical principles developed by Dr. William Glasser, a psychiatrist, in the 1950s. It is applicable to individuals with behavioral and emotional problems as well as any individual or group seeking either to gain a success identity for themselves and/or to help others toward this same goal. Focusing on the present and on behavior, the therapist guides the individual to enable him to see himself accurately, to face reality, to fulfill his own needs, without harming himself or others. The crux of the theory is personal responsibility for one's own behavior, which is equated with mental health.

Basic Concepts

The first step in changing behavior is to find out what the behavior is we are trying to correct. We must face reality and admit that we cannot rewrite a person's history. No matter how cruel and unusual are the circumstances that led to a person's behavior, we must make it clear to him that past events are not to be used as an excuse for behaving in an irresponsible manner. No matter what "happened" to him in

the past, he must take full responsibility for what he does *now*.

Until an individual accepts the fact that he is responsible for what he does, there can be no treatment. It is not up to therapists to advance explanations for irresponsibility. Individual responsibility is the goal of treatment and unhappiness is the result and not the cause of irresponsibility.

Reality therapy is based upon the premise that there is a single, basic psychological need that all people possess from birth to death: the need for an identity, the need to feel that each of us is somehow separate and distinct from every other living being on the face of this earth and that no other person thinks, looks, acts, and talks exactly as we do. This need is universal and transcends all cultures. Its significance is evidenced, for example, in religious teachings of both primitive and civilized societies. Every organized religion appears to deal with the basic question of what happens to a person's identity after death.

Identity has been defined as "a stream with many fibers that runs through all the days of your life and ties them together in a unique strand called 'I.' " Further, it is not sufficient only to realize that one is a distinct identity; in addition one must have meaning associated with one's identity for full mental health. That is, one must also see oneself as having either a success identity or a failure identity, based upon one's relationship with others.

Reality therapy differs from other therapeutic endeavors, such as psychoanalysis, the strict behavioral therapies like operant conditioning, and from some of the newer therapeutic fads, in that reality therapy is applicable not only to the problems of people who are irresponsible and incompetent, but also because it can be applied equally well to daily living. It is not a therapy exclusively for the "mentally ill," incompetent, disturbed, or emotionally upset; it is a system of ideas that can help anyone learn to gain a successful identity and to help others do so. Reality therapy is readily understandable and it may be applied by anyone who understands these principles without prolonged, specific training other than the application of effort, sensitivity, and common sense.

That the principles of reality therapy are easily understood, that they may be applied by anyone—parents with children, ministers with their congregations, husbands and wives with each other, employers with their employees, salesmen with their prospects—in no way makes this theory less valid or its associated therapy less professional. The value of the therapy is not diminished simply because a system of ideas is understandable and usable by the majority of individuals. The reality therapist brings to problem situations a special ability, rather a wider variety of abilities, to become involved, a basic ingredient of reality therapy. He has more understanding how to make successful plans and more experience guiding people to examine their plans and their

behavior. He confronts them with the irresponsibility of their behavior and leads them toward commitments, while not accepting excuses they may attempt to make. Of significance: what the therapist attempts to do should be clearly understandable to the patient and to everyone involved.

Once successful involvement has been established, the principles of reality therapy evolve into a system or a way of life that helps a person become successful in almost all of his endeavors. If he is not successful, we try at least to understand where he lacks success and try, even if success seems impossible, to search in one direction after another to understand that options in life are never really closed. There are innumerable options in society to find success one way or another. Transference, as described in other therapeutic approaches, not only occurs in the therapeutic experience but also occurs in the experiences, on a regular basis, of everyday life.

We all make certain assumptions and have certain distorted impressions about other individuals. These distorted impressions are based upon our experiences from other sources and with other people. For example, when we meet someone for the first time, we may like or dislike him for reasons unknown or unclear to us. It may be that he reminds us of a past friend or acquaintance or relative or loved one, because each new person triggers old associations. Rather than attempt to enhance this phenomenon and then analyze it, the reality therapist attempts to decrease the distortion. The reality therapist presents himself as himself and, in fact, as therapy progresses, attempts to shatter distortions the patient may have. He may question them but never reinforce them. If the patient relates to the reality therapist as saying, "You remind me of my father," the reality therapist may say, "I am not your father, but I would be interested in knowing what you see as similar in us." Rather than reinforcing the development of transference phenomenon and then analyzing the so-called transference, the reality therapist attempts in every way possible to present himself as a genuine, concerned, real person, helping the patient face reality, understand reality, and accept reality.

Other Systems

Reality therapy differs from conventional therapy in six major aspects:

1. Reality therapy rejects the orthodox concept of mental illness in the various categories by which it is described—paranoic, schizophrenic, manic, and so forth. We believe most forms of mental disturbance are best described as irresponsibility; and, regardless of behavior symptoms, the proper solution is to show the patient the unreality and self-defeating nature of his behavior. The reality therapist helps the patient discover behavior that will satisfy and/or help him fulfill his basic psychological needs without hurting himself or other people. Reality therapy, of course, acknowledges that a tiny fraction of so-called mental disturbances are caused by biochemical disorders or brain damage.

2. Conventional theory of psychotherapy generally places great emphasis on examining the patient's past experience. It is believed that once the patient understands the root causes of his behavior, he will change. Reality therapy disagrees with this point of view and is not particularly interested in the patient's past behavior. If it had been successful, the person would not be in need of therapy. The en-

tire focus in reality therapy is on the present and the future.

3. Conventional psychiatry places great emphasis on the theory of *transference,* which states that the patient can be induced to transfer to his therapist attitudes, feelings, and ideas he held or still holds toward important and significant people in his past. The therapist then attempts to make the patient aware of his transference and, through this insight, enable him to change his behavior. The reality therapist feels that significantly constructive benefit is achieved by relating to the therapist as himself and not as a transference figure. Most patients live with enough misconceptions and distortions of reality and do not need to have these misconceptions enhanced in a therapeutic situation.

4. Conventional psychotherapy such as that done by Freudians and Jungians believes that if a patient is to change, he must gain insight into his unconscious mind. Unconscious conflict is considered more important in many cases than conscious problems. Thus the emphasis on dreams, transference, and free association. The reality therapist does not permit patients to use unconscious motivations as an excuse for misbehavior. The emphasis is upon what the patient is doing, particularly his present attempts to succeed or what he intends to do. It is our contention that insight does not of itself produce change, although it may be intellectually interesting.

5. Orthodox psychiatry generally avoids specific value judgments. It also avoids dealing with the issue of right and wrong, of good and bad, of correct and incorrect. Deviant behavior is considered a product of mental illness, and the patient is often felt not morally responsible because he is considered helpless to do

anything about it. The basic premise of reality therapy is almost the exact opposite. The patient's problem is seen as the result of his inability to comprehend and apply values and moral principles in his daily life. The patient is confronted with the fact that he is responsible for his own behavior. The reality therapist believes that no basic change can occur in therapy or in life unless and until an individual acknowledges that he is responsible for his behavior.

6. Conventional therapy does not generally include teaching people to behave in a better manner by setting up specific plans and helping people to make commitments to follow through with these plans. Conventional therapy generally assumes that once patients understand themselves and the unconscious sources and roots of their problems, they will spontaneously learn better behavior themselves. This notion is explicitly stated in Carl Rogers's person-centered theory. Reality therapy, on the other hand, seeks to teach patients better ways of behaving that will enable them to fulfill their basic psychological needs.

An increasing number of individuals have been expressing ideas, aspects of which are identical to or closely aligned with William Glasser's ideas.

Dr. O. Hobart Mowrer broke with theories of behavior that pictured man as a helpless victim of heredity or environment. He has developed a new method known as *integrity therapy* for treating emotional problems. His philosophy is almost the opposite of Freudian theory. Mowrer states that instead of mental problems resulting from the individual's attempts to live up to a naturally high moral code, they occur when man does not live up to his own moral convictions. Mowrer has stated that "the problem pre-

sented by psychopathology is one that is best conceptualized, not as illness, but rather as a kind of ignorance and moral failure and the strategy of choice of preventing and correcting these conditions is manifestly educational and ethical" (Mowrer, 1961).

Dr. Willard H. Mainord seems to agree with reality therapy concepts in many important respects. First, he is dissatisfied with orthodox therapy, especially psychoanalysis, as are Thomas Szasz, Albert Ellis, and many others. Second, he believes the mentally disturbed are not sick in the medical sense, but are irresponsible. Third, he believes the therapist must help the patient to discover that irresponsibility does not pay and responsibility does. Fourth, he thinks a good society is one where virtue is rewarded. "If the patient," says Dr. Mainord, "is held responsible for productivity and for accurate communication, the 'crazy' behavior will have no payoff value and will disappear sometimes dramatically" (Mainord, 1973).

"The Third Force" psychology of Abraham Maslow (1954), the late distinguished psychologist, is closely aligned to reality therapy. Maslow believed most individuals have a capacity for creativeness, spontaneity, caring for others, curiosity, continual growth, the ability to love and be loved, and all other characteristics found in self-actualized people. A person who is behaving badly is reacting to the deprivation of his basic needs. If his behavior improves, he begins to develop his true potential and move toward greater health and normalcy as a human. Maslow believed one of the great errors of the behavioral scientist, the psychiatrist, and the psychologist is the belief that right and wrong behavior have no scientific basis. Maslow, like Glasser, thought that in the final analysis, irresponsibility was just as damaging to the individual as to his society.

The psychiatrist Alan Wheelis (1970) in his book *The Desert* states that:

much of our suffering is just so obscure . . . frigidity, social anxiety, isolation, boredom, dissatisfaction with life—in all such states we may see no correlation between the inner feeling and the way we live, yet no such feeling can be independent of behavior; and if only we find connections we may begin to see how a change in the way we live will make for a change in the way we feel.

HISTORY

Precursors

Reality therapy is one of the newest of man's formal attempts to explain mankind, to set rules for behavior, and to map out how one person can help another achieve happiness and success. At the same time, paradoxically, it represents one of the oldest sets of maxims referring to human conduct. It consists essentially of eight homilies, none of them startling or new, such as "Focus on the present and not the past"; "Make no excuses"; and "Make a commitment." Even the combination is not startlingly new. Undoubtedly, all of the elements of our theory are contained in one way or another in many of man's well-developed philosophies or religions. It is, perhaps to damn our system in some peoples' eyes, nothing but common sense—but this, as Voltaire reminds us, is quite uncommon.

Our most direct spiritual ancestor was Dr. Paul DuBois, a Swiss physician who developed "Medical Moralizing." Quoting from Lewis Wolberg (1954):

Dubois . . . held conversations with his patients and taught them a philosophy of life whereby they substituted in their minds

thoughts of health for their customary preoccupations with . . . disease . . . he insisted that the physician treat the patient as a friend, not merely as an interesting case. . . . The physician must be sincere in his conviction that the patient would get well.

In reading DuBois's major book (DuBois, 1909), we are struck with the similarity to ours of the approach he pioneered of commonsense discussions based on a sense of equality mixed with feelings of humanity. Although we cannot go along with his major theoretical points, DuBois nevertheless represents a breakthrough in terms of relating to patients. This attitude of friendly counselor, basing his discussions on common sense, was picked up by others, notably Jules Déjèrine (Déjèrine & Gaukler, 1913), and in this country by that redoubtable innovator of group psychotherapy, Dr. Joseph H. Pratt (1916), who followed in Déjèrine's footsteps.

For reasons we can hardly determine, this commonsense point of view was swept aside, crushed to obliteration by the steamroller of Sigmund Freud, whose pansexual views and mythologies dominated the psychiatric scene from the end of World War I to the middle 1940s. However, in the shadow of this colossus, a number of other more modest men continued in what we may call the DuBois tradition. Perhaps Alfred Adler may be considered DuBois's greatest proponent. Although we have no knowledge that Adler knew of DuBois's teaching, it would seem incredible that he did not. Another great psychiatrist, possibly America's greatest homegrown psychotherapist, founder of the so-called psychobiological school, Adolf Meyer also urged an empiric commonsense point of view. Abraham Low who argued for a low-cost, commonsense psychotherapy, the founder of *Recovery, Incorporated,* a mission to the mentally ill, also belongs to this tradition.

At the time that William Glasser began to formulate his theories, which eventually formalized into reality therapy, he had heard vaguely of some of these people, but had not read any of their works—and consequently was not directly influenced by them. As we will see in the next section, even those who did directly influence him probably were not too aware of these other men who worked or had worked more or less in the same tradition or philosophy as reality therapy. What we have here is a kind of cultural parallelism, and it would be interesting to speculate why in the first half of the twentieth century people such as Sigmund Freud and Carl Jung with their complex mythologies, so far removed from common sense, flourished, while others who worked on a low-key basis were essentially neglected. It may be, as Edwin Boring (1950) has postulated, that there exists a *Zeitgeist* (spirit of the times), and that when an idea is enunciated, if the world is not ready for it, the idea dies. It may well be that there now is a change in the tide of conceptualization, and the emergence of other systems, also of the commonsense nature (such as Albert Ellis's rational-emotive therapy, Harold Greenwald's direct decision therapy, and O. Hobart Mowrer's integrity therapy), and the reemergence of Alfred Adler's individual psychology seems evidence that man is becoming more rational, less mystic, more scientific, and more willing to trust his own judgment rather than having a need for mystics and mystical transpersonal conceptualizations and other nonsense.

Although reality therapy has many points of similarity with other systems, especially Adler's individual psychology, and although it is in the tradition of common sense as exemplified by Paul Du-Bois's work, it nevertheless represents an independent creation and has a unique structure of its own that makes it a complete system, different essentially from any other, even though a brother or a first cousin of some other schools of thought.

Our major position is that we are seeking the truth—we are seeking economy and efficiency—we are seeking completeness—as are many others, but in our judgment no other system so clearly relates to the wisdom of the ages or the sayings of the ancients as this newest of current systems of psychotherapy. Reality therapy represents, as the name indicates, the simplest, most complete, most sensible, and most rational of all therapies centering on reality, eschewing all rationalizations, excuses, explanations, and distortions, and is simply pure good sense and logic artfully applied.

Beginnings

Reality therapy, as a systematic treatment approach, was first developed about 1956 by Dr. William Glasser during his residency in psychiatry at the University of California at Los Angeles. His supervisor, Dr. G. L. Harrington, had moved to California after a decade at the Menninger Foundation. The two men were drawn together by doubts about traditional psychotherapy. The seeds of Dr. Harrington's ideas had been planted by Helmuth Kaiser, who had started clinical practice as a traditional psychoanalyst. Dr. Kaiser, a psychologist, was in private practice as a psychoanalyst in Germany from 1930 to 1933. Because of political events, Kaiser moved to Spain in 1934, then to France, and finally, in 1939, to Israel where he remained for approximately 10 years. During his residency in Israel, Kaiser began to write about the changes that had occurred in his thinking regarding psychoanalysis. In 1949 Kaiser was appointed training analyst at the Menninger Foundation. His ideas were radical by the standards of that day, and his departure from the rigid rules of classical analysis was shown in his supervision of Dr. Harrington. For example, through the efforts of Kaiser, Harrington, while in traction after an accident, was encouraged to continue seeing his patients in his hospital room.

Kaiser loved to write in dialogue and one of his most beautiful articles is called "Emergency (Seven Dialogues Reflecting the Essence of Psychotherapy in an Extreme Adventure)" (Kaiser, 1962), which appeared several months after Kaiser's death. The prologue to the seven scenes, written in dialogue and without psychiatric explanation or didactic pontification, states:

Just as the normal function of an organ or an organism is frequently illuminated by pathologic events, so the views of a therapist on the essential nature of his daily work may become unusually lucid when they are applied to an extreme and unusual case which is theoretically possible but has never occurred in real life.

The following seven dialogues sketch such an unusual case. The views of the therapist in the story are my views. They are not easy to present or to transmit, not because they imply a complicated theory, but because they are simple where one expects the elaborate. Where they are expressed in abstract terms, as a textbook would do, the reader is likely to miss their meaning, as if he had to decipher a melody from the grooves of a gramophone disc.

The sequence of scenes contained, in condensation, interaction betweeen the therapist and his patient. However, I do not intend to prove, but only to show.

In the ensuing dialogues, Kaiser dramatized the plight of a woman who sought the help of a psychiatrist, and during their interview, it became apparent that she had come for help for her husband. The woman explained that her husband also was a psychiatrist but that he was resistant to seeking help. The psychiatrist she consulted with handled the matter in the traditional manner, demonstrating his interest and concern but also explaining his inability to help the woman's husband if he would not come for help. However, the woman suggested that the psychiatrist become her husband's patient, and, without her husband's knowledge, treat him. That is, the psychiatrist (her husband) who thought he was the therapist would indeed be the patient; and the psychiatrist who was labeled the patient would actually function as the therapist. The psychiatrist stated, in surprise,

"You suggest that I, a psychiatrist, call a colleague of mine, another psychiatrist, and ask him for his professional help, ask him to take me into treatment for some real or invented troubles of mine, while, in reality, I am hired by his wife to treat him? Do you realize what this means?" The woman proudly responded, "I know what it means! It means doing the only thing which could probably save him!"

Helmuth Kaiser in this story illustrated the nucleus and the germ that grew into the treatment approach of reality therapy. He demonstrated in the interviews between the two men the essentiality of meaningful, genuine communication. He illustrated the unimportance of specific labeling of "patient and therapist," of "counselor and counselee," or of "client and doctor" for an effective therapeutic interchange to occur. He indicated that therapy could be practiced in any situation between two human beings. He also, and perhaps inadvertently, illustrated that a basic assumption for therapy is that the therapist be healthier than the patient and that, if he is not, he must at least be healthier in the area of the patient's illness.

In the interest of putting reality therapy in broad context, much the same notion of the nature of the true role of therapist and patient was being formulated at the same time by George A. Kelly (1955). But at the time of Glasser's formulation, he was not aware of Kelly's work.

In 1962 Dr. Harrington was placed in charge of a ward of the Veterans Administration Neuropsychiatric Hospital in West Los Angeles. At the time that Dr. Harrington and Dr. Glasser introduced the nuclear concepts of reality therapy, Building 206 housed the most chaotic, chronic, fixed psychotic patients in the hospital. Care was essentially custodial. The average discharge rate was about two patients a year. There appeared to be an unspoken contract between the staff and the patients, in which the patients agreed to stay "peacefully psychotic." Harrington began to shatter this contract when he took over the ward. Stepping down at his own request from an administrative position, he returned to what was for him the more enjoyable and congenial post of clinical ward physician. The impact of the new program soon began to show on the ward. Increasing numbers of patients began to be discharged. With Harrington's and Glasser's approach, in the unit where 210 patients averaged 17 years of confinement, 45 went home the first year, 85 the second, 90 the third.

During this same period, Dr. William Glasser was getting comparably successful results at the Ventura School for Girls. Dr. Glasser, a graduate of Western Reserve Medical School in 1953, had taken his psychiatric training at the Veterans Administration and the University of California, both in Los Angeles. In 1956 he became consulting psychiatrist to the Ventura School for Girls, a state institution for the treatment of seriously delinquent, adolescent, and teen-aged girls. He

had recently published his first book, *Mental Health or Mental Illness?* (Glasser, 1961), which laid the basic foundation and the refinement of the techniques and principles of reality therapy. The successful results at the Ventura School for Girls brought about a radical change in staff attitude. The girls began to enjoy the program of this correctional institution and expressed feelings of interest and enthusiasm. The staff's initial resistance to change and innovation rapidly disappeared as they also became involved in the meaningful and rewarding business of helping others. Out of these experiences, the theory and concepts of reality therapy continued to evolve. Glasser used the term *reality therapy* for the first time in April 1964, in a formal manuscript entitled "Reality Therapy, a Realistic Approach to the Young Offender" (Glasser, 1964). The following year *Reality Therapy* (Glasser, 1965), dedicated to Dr. Harrington, was published. In 1966 Glasser began consulting in the California school systems, spending much time with a saturation program in the Watts-area elementary schools, and he introduced modifications of the basic principles of reality therapy. The ramifications and the applications of reality therapy reaped positive benefits. Glasser compiled these ideas into the book *Schools without Failure* (Glasser, 1969).

In 1965, at the Ventura School for Girls, Dr. Glasser's ideas were used by Dr. Leonard Zunin, a psychiatrist who had studied under Dr. Allen Enlow, another protégé of Helmuth Kaiser. Later he worked with Dr. Harrington and first became associated with Glasser while they both were consultants at the Ventura School for Girls in 1965. He used the principles of reality therapy in developing specific programs for the drug abusers at the Ventura School. Later, as assistant chief of neuropsychiatry at Camp Pendleton Naval Hospital, he applied reality therapy principles in developing a group program for Vietnam war widows, entitled "Operation Second Life." Dr. Zunin reassociated with Dr. Glasser in 1969 when he joined the newly formed Institute for Reality Therapy as its first director, with Dr. Glasser as founder and president. Zunin's interest in the initial phase of therapeutic involvement culminated in his book *Contact: The First Four Minutes* (Zunin 1972).

Current Status

The Institute for Reality Therapy presents training courses for selected professionals, such as physicians, psychologists, the clergy, social workers, probation officers, police officers, nurses, lawyers, judges, and teachers. Courses and programs are offered on a regular and continuing basis, including repeated introductory courses of study, as well as intermediate and advanced courses. Lectures of general interest to both the professional and lay community are offered from time to time by the staff at the Institute in the Southern California area and in other parts of the United States and Canada.

Special interest seminars and workshops are presented periodically through the institute. The sessions use the special skills of the institute staff, which includes psychiatrists, psychologists, and social workers, in diverse areas such as small- and large-group interaction, family and marital problems, juvenile and adolescent problems, drug abuse, grief, and many other related areas. College credits are arranged with several local colleges.

Consultation services using the concepts of reality therapy are available to courts, probation, police and welfare departments, entire communities, and private and public schools interested in a unified approach. Teams of consultants provide a broad base for teaching the application of reality therapy in a variety of settings.

Following the publication of Glasser's book *Schools without Failure,* written specifically for application of reality therapy techniques in the school system, the Educator Training Center, a special division of the Institute for Reality Therapy, was established. This center, also in the Los Angeles area, was assisted in its development by a grant from the Stone Foundation.

In 1970 the William Glasser-LaVerne College Center was established at LaVerne College in Southern California for the purpose of providing teachers with an off-campus opportunity to gain graduate and in-service credits while working within their own schools to provide an exciting educational environment for children.

Programs through the Educator Training Center, as is also the case through the Institute for Reality Therapy, the parent organization, are offered not only in Southern California but also throughout the United States and Canada. Opportunities are provided for school districts to plan staff in-service training programs with the Educator Training Center staff.

The Educator Training Center (ETC) was created by Dr. Glasser to research ideas and to develop methods for combating school failure. As a result of three years of work, its staff of professional educators has developed a series of programs that include a practical in-service program that any elementary school can use to eliminate failure—to become a "school without failure." The program, called SWF (Schools Without Failure) seminars, carries graduate credit for the teachers who are enrolled and is carried on outside of school hours, at each of the participating schools in a specific district.

The purposes of the SWF Seminars are:

1. To provide opportunities for principals and teachers to develop a positive, personal philosophy of education so they may develop their own school without failure.
2. To provide ways of building constructive communication within the school and between the school and the community.
3. To provide a process for developing classroom skills and procedures needed by teachers and principals to implement a success-oriented curriculum.
4. To provide the background for building a school environment in which the staff and the students may deal realistically with their problems through the resources at hand.

Objectives of SWF Seminars are to provide each school involved with an opportunity to learn:

1. How to develop a success-oriented philosophy
2. How to motivate students to personal involvement
3. How to develop respective communication with students through class meetings
4. How to help students develop responsible behavior
5. How to make the curriculum relevant for today's students
6. How to remove failure from the curriculum
7. What exciting opportunities exist for teachers to improve their school
8. How to work effectively with other members of the staff
9. How to eliminate discipline as a major problem of the school
10. Effective techniques for involving

parents and the community in the work of the school

The Educator Training Center is also in keeping with Glasser's increasing interest in preventing delinquency before it occurs. He believes that education is the key to sound human functioning. In *Schools without Failure,* he states, "we will never succeed in patching people up; we must get them responsibly involved from early childhood in an educational system in which they can succeed enough to function successfully in our society." Glasser objects to the deterministic point of view and does not accept the rationalization of failure commonly accepted today, that young people are products of a social situation that precludes success. He feels that blaming their failure upon their homes, their communities, their culture, their background, their race, or their poverty is a dead end for two reasons: (1) It removes personal responsibility for failure; and (2) it does not recognize that success is potentially open to all young people.

PERSONALITY

Theory of Personality

Reality therapy views *identity* as the single, basic requirement of all mankind, which transcends all cultures and exists from birth to death. Although identity can be viewed from several different viewpoints, it is most useful to regard identity from a therapeutic vantage point, as *success identity* versus *failure identity.*

Each individual develops an identity image. He feels he is relatively successful or unsuccessful. We are not referring to success as measured in titles or labels or finances, but rather in terms of the individual's own self-image. This may or may not conform to the image others have of him. It is indeed possible for an individual to regard himself as basically a failure in life when others around him regard him as an outstanding success.

Formation of a failure identity seems to occur most often at age five or six, coincidental with the age at which the child enters school. Before that time, most children view themselves as successful. It is about this age that we find the individual developing the social skills, verbal skills, intellect, and thinking ability that enable him to begin to define himself in terms of being a successful or unsuccessful person. As the months and the years progress, the individual who regards himself as successful appears to associate with other successful people, and the individual who sees himself as a failure associates with others who have failure identity. The two groups become increasingly detached and divergent. For example, it is indeed rare for a person with a success identity to have, as a close and personal friend, someone who is a known criminal, felon, heroin addict, and so forth. Gradually the incongruity and the disparity between the two groups is widened. There results a kind of commonality of individuals with success identity and failure identity. Focusing on those with failure identity, since reality therapy is concerned with them, we find that commonality for these individuals in this category is loneliness.

In our Western culture these individuals all appear to experience an extreme degree of loneliness. Lonely people clearly have difficulties in helping other lonely people, except to provide transient solace. At the same time, individuals with a success identity continue to compete, usually in a constructive manner, and reinforce one another's successes. Failures have difficulty, on a regular basis, in facing the real world and find it uncomfortable, anxiety

evoking, disparaging, and depressing to compete.

In reviewing those individuals who seem to have a success identity, it appears they have two traits that are consistent and ever present. First, they know that somewhere out there in the world, there is at least one other person who loves them for what they are. Also they love at least one other person in the world around them. Second, individuals with a success identity have the knowledge and understanding that most of the time they are worthwhile human beings and, at least one, and hopefully more than one, other individual also feels they are worthwhile. In reality therapy, we see *worth* and *love* as two very different elements. Consider, for example, the extreme case of the "spoiled" child. One may fantasize that a child, if showered with "pure love," whose parents' "goal" was never to frustrate or stress or strain this child in any way, and when he was faced with a task or difficulty always had his parents to perform this task for him, this child always relieved of responsibility would develop into an individual who would feel loved but would not experience worth. Worth comes through accomplishing tasks and achieving success in the accomplishment of those tasks. On the other hand, not infrequent is the depression of a man of seemingly broad business success who knows he is worthwhile to others. He is aware that many people view him as a successful, worthwhile human being. This man, however, may be experiencing an absence of love in his life, because he cannot point to one person and say "there is at least that one individual that I truly love and who truly loves me." This lack of believing that he is loved for himself rather than admired for his success explains his depression, which may seem paradoxical to those who do not understand the difference between worth and love.

The identity we develop comes from our involvement with others as well as our involvement with ourselves. Our identity develops from recalling objects of one's love and gratification because that which we love and have loved tends to be associated with and psychologically incorporated into ourselves; what we admire, we tend to exemplify; what we dislike, we tend to reject. We also discover our identity by observing those causes or concerns with which we are involved. That to which we devote our energy and our time is a reflection of what and who we are. We discover an identity of ourselves during crises. In a moment of panic or threat of self-exposure or embarrassment, we behave often in ways impossible for us to predict. By reflecting back on our behavior during these moments we further clarify and understand who we are.

Others also play an important role in helping us to clarify and understand our identity. What others reflect back to us, if we are willing to give our eyes and ears the freedom to see and hear, is a most meaningful mirror of one's identity. This is what occurs in psychotherapy and in friendships. Our beliefs and value systems, our religion or lack of religion, and our philosophy further clarify our identity. We also see ourselves in relation to the living conditions, climate, and economic and social status of others.

Finally, our physical image in relation to others, including our physical structure, our grooming, and our clothes, help us to see ourselves in relation to others and to clarify our own identity.

Those individuals who appear to develop a failure identity and have difficulty and feel a sense of discomfort in a real world handle this sense of discomfort in two general ways. They may either deny reality or ignore it. What is called *mental illness* is actually the various ways in which an individual denies reality. Mental illness may manifest itself in a wide variety of behaviors. In reality therapy, we do not feel that specific diagnostic terms are helpful or useful in providing an effective method of change for the mentally ill. The person who is mentally ill has distorted the real world in his own fantasy to make himself feel more comfortable. He denies reality to protect himself from facing the feeling of being meaningless and insignificant in the world around him. For example, both the grandiose delusion and the persecutory delusion of the so-called schizophrenic provide support or solace for him. Is there any difference between the individual who believes the FBI, the CIA, the president, and all the political leaders are following him and the individual who thinks he is Jesus or Napoleon or God or the governor or the president? Both individuals change the world in their own minds and in their own fantasy to assist them in feeling important, meaningful, and significant.

Those individuals who ignore reality are people we believe are aware of the real world and choose, rather than to deny and change reality in their own mind, to simply ignore it. These individuals are referred to as delinquents, criminals, "sociopaths," "personality disorders," and so on. They are basically the antisocial individuals who choose to break the rules and regulations of society on a regular basis, thereby ignoring reality.

Variety of Concepts

In contrast to other theoretical psychotherapeutic frameworks, which discuss a variety of instincts and drives, reality therapy asserts that each human being has the single most important basic social need for identity. This need is intrinsic and inherited within each individual and transmitted from generation to generation. It is a need for an individual identity interrelated with one's social identity. A person's identity defines him in relation to others. This need for involvement is an integral part of the organism and is the primary intrinsic driving force governing all behavior. Although early parental influence is exceedingly important and crucial, other areas such as peer relationships and, specifically, involvement in school potentially wield a tremendously unrecognized magnitude of influence on the evolving identity of the child. Ordinarily, one thinks the need for love or acceptance will be fulfilled in the home rather than in the school or outside institutions. However, teachers are overwhelmed with children who need affection, and who are struggling with their own identity and self-concept. Children's needs for success identity come from all sides and especially from significant adults as evidenced from Albert Bandura's research (1973). Ordinarily, outside the family group, teachers represent the most significant adults in the lives of children. Glasser believes that helping to fulfill the needs for love and worth is unequivocally one of the functions of school, and unless this is recognized, individual failure identity can unknowingly be reinforced. In his book *Schools Without Failure* (1969), he discussed how the school can and should get involved to help children fulfill their need for love and worth. In the context of school, love can best be thought of as social responsibility. When children do not learn to be responsible for each other, to care for each other, and to help each other, not only for the sake of others but for their own sake, love becomes a weak and limited concept. Glasser believes that the schools have not adequately faced the

problem of failure caused by loneliness. Cultural and environmental influences have a profound effect upon shaping the identity of the child, which begins to formulate in each individual as a success or a failure identity by the age of five or six.

Individual autonomy is directly related to maturity. This is the ability to let go and relinquish environmental supports and substitute individual internal psychological support, the ability of an individual to psychologically stand on his own two feet. This, of course, does not mean not to be involved, not to give, not to love, and so forth. It means for the individual to take responsibility for who he is and what he wants in life and to develop responsible plans to fulfill his needs and his goals.

We believe all individuals have goals and that these goals can be developed in a hierarchy of levels of aspiration. In a rather philosophical sense, it is literally impossible not to have a goal in life, even if the goal is not to have a goal.

In reality therapy, individuals are assisted in understanding, defining, and clarifying their life goals, both immediate and long-term. In fact, this is one of the first steps in our form of psychotherapy. The individual is also assisted in clarifying the ways in which he hampers his progress toward his goals and he is assisted in understanding alternatives. With the phase of compromise, planning, and modification of behavior, resultant change in behavior begins to occur.

The concept of *alternatives* is dealt with directly in therapy. Often people with emotional problems see very few, if any, alternative avenues of approach, and part of the function of the therapist is to assist the patient in understanding that alternatives are usually available. Even a man facing a firing squad has some limited alternatives. He might pray, curse, collapse, spit, hold his breath, scream, try to escape to the best of his ability, face the firing squad with equanimity, bite his lip, stick out his tongue, and so on. These alternatives are limited since the apparently inevitable fact is that the person will be shot regardless of what he will do. However, they are not as limiting as they might seem even in this restricted example, because by various shifts in behavior, in rare instances, individuals have been known to have executions stayed. The alternatives, of course, in life's situations go far beyond the alternatives of a man facing a firing squad. In reality therapy, a person may first be asked to list all the possible alternatives to a situation without any initial judgment of the values or practicalities of these alternatives. When one eliminates judgment of alternatives, he can have an open mind in listing them. Interestingly, when alternatives become apparent in a nonjudgmental way, the individual is often amused by how ridiculous are some of the alternatives he might choose. Nonetheless, this step of listing all alternatives possible helps each person to understand that alternatives are unlimited. After this concept is integrated into the thinking of a person facing a difficult situation, the therapist can assist the person in placing various value judgments on the most reasonable possible alternatives and ferreting out the most likely and effective alternatives. From this more limited list of alternatives, the individual then can begin to weigh and select his eventual choice.

The unconscious, as has been defined by other systems, for example, by the psychoanalytic approach, we believe has little evidence to support its validity. The evidence for the existence of an unconscious is shaky, including hypnosis, dreams, the psychopathology of everyday life—slips of the tongue, and so forth. We believe this is not adequate evidence for the existence of a well-defined unconsciousness. Certainly it is apparent that each individual has various levels of memory recollection, and however scientifically significant it may be to understand these various levels of memory, they are not germane to the psychotherapeutic process and not helpful in helping people to change current behavior. Not that an accurate concept of the unconscious is irrelevant or unimportant, but just that it is, in our opinion, not related to doing clinical therapy. Furthermore, it is our opinion that individuals forget not only traumatic and unfortunate incidents that happen to them in the past but also forget positive, meaningful, and character-building experiences. Far too little attention has been placed on understanding this latter notion.

The concept of *individual uniqueness* has been discussed earlier in this chapter and is essential to motivation. To understand that each individual believes and knows he is unique in the world is directly related to his success versus failure identity.

We believe each individual has a health or growth force. Basically people want to be content and enjoy a success identity, to show responsible behavior and to have meaningful interpersonal relationships. Suffering does not disappear without a change in identity, which amounts to a change in what one is and how one thinks, feels, and behaves. Identity change follows change in behavior. *To a great extent, we are what we do, and if we want to change what we are, we must begin by changing what we do and undertake new ways of behaving.* We do believe that certain homeostatic mechanisms cause the individual to protest and resist change in behavior, since existing behavior for better or for worse represents to some limited extent security as well as in some cases entrenched and conditioned modes of behaving. The effort to change, which may be considerable, only comes from motivation through involvement with meaningful others—thus the importance of the therapeutic involvement in reality therapy. Further, fixed change usually occurs only if action is maintained over a significant period.

Learning is an integral concept of reality therapy. Learning occurs in all activities of life and is one of the mainstays of the psychotherapeutic process. A wide variety of learning concepts and basic learning theory is incorporated into the general framework of the theoretical as well as the clinical base of reality therapy. A special kind of learning occurs through the involvement in the psychotherapeutic situation. *We are what we do, and to a great extent, we are what we learn to do, and identity becomes the integration of all learned and unlearned behavior.*

A variety of previously established concepts in use by other psychotherapeutic systems is not relevant to reality therapy. These concepts among others include the Oedipus complex, racial unconsciousness, organ inferiority, libido, fictive goals, private logic, and collective unconsciousness. Again, it is not our intent to state that these concepts are in error although they may very well be, or that they are not important, but only that they are not necessary in the practice of psychotherapy.

PSYCHOTHERAPY

Theory of Psychotherapy

The principles of reality therapy are meant to be used flexibly in context with the needs of the patient. In working with individuals, this general theoretical framework should provide helpful guidelines in directing specific techniques. Basic to reality therapy is the concept of *involvement*. For purposes of psychotherapy, *involvement* and *motivation* can be considered synonymous. The first three principles of reality therapy are ways in which the therapist becomes responsibly involved with the person he is trying to help.

Principle I: Personal. In reality therapy, the therapist communicates that he cares. Aloofness and cool detachment are not considered helpful. Warmth, understanding, and concern are the cornerstones of effective treatment. For this reason, the use of personal pronouns such as "I, you, we" by both the therapist and the patient is encouraged because they facilitate involvement.

Being *personal* in reality therapy means the therapist is willing, if appropriate, to discuss his own experiences. He is willing to have his values challenged and he is willing to admit that he is far from perfect. Rather than attempting to enhance transference, the reality therapist presents himself as a genuine person interested in the individual with whom he is working. Being personal in reality therapy means caring, following through, working hard to achieve the goals of the therapy—that is, real changes in behavior in terms of mutual goals.

Being personal means conveying your belief that people have the ability to be happier and do better, that they are capable of functioning in a more responsible, more effective, and more self-fulfilling manner. If the therapist does not believe this about the patient, he does the patient a disservice by continuing in a treatment situation.

If the patient does not feel accepted by the therapist, his chances of benefiting are markedly decreased. The purpose of becoming personal in reality therapy is to help people become involved with someone who can help them understand that there is more to life than focusing on misery or symptoms or irresponsible behavior. However, it is an important part of the caring relationship to define the limits of involvement. It is not possible for a therapist to become deeply involved with everyone who comes for help. He becomes involved only within the context of the office. The therapist has to be honest about this. He cannot promise what he cannot follow through. In the early part of therapy, anything is open for discussion. If the individual talks about a subject other than his problems, this is not seen as a resistance but rather as worthwhile. Focusing on misery tends to reduce the value of therapy and increases rather than decreases the person's involvement with his own misery. Many people who enter into therapy with a reality therapist are often surprised when they find themselves talking about a wide variety of subjects. They may say, "Well, I feel better and I function better but I wonder if I ought to be talking about such things instead of my deep and serious problems." The therapist reassures the patient that these conversations *are* worthwhile and that, in discussing such things, they are closer to solving problems than if they talked about problems exclusively. This is difficult for some patients to understand, especially those who have had experience in other kinds of therapy where they talked about their incompetencies continually.

The therapist and the person needing help become warmly involved but entanglement must be avoided. The therapist must define the situation so the patient understands exactly what the relationship is, where it is, and where it is going. This reality delineation is readily accepted by patients. To keep the relationship within the bounds of reality is the therapist's responsibility but it takes experience to do this properly. This is one of the major tests not only of the successful therapist but also the successful parent, clergyman, teacher, doctor, employer, and so forth.

Principle II: Focus on Present Behavior rather than Feelings. No one can gain a successful identity without being aware of his *present behavior.* When a person believes, as has wrongly been postulated by some psychotherapeutic movements, that feelings are more important than behavior, he will have difficulty achieving a success identity. We contend there is a basic fallacy in the notion "When I feel better, I do more." Feelings and behavior are interrelated and mutually reinforcing. This is a circular phenomenon. When people feel better, indeed they do more constructive things; and when they do more, they feel better; and when they feel better, they do more; and so on. When we complete work, we do feel better; but also, when we feel better, we do more work. The fallacy lies in the notion that it is easier to make ourselves feel better than to stimulate ourselves to action and thereby feel better. Feeling and doing are intimately related, and it is our experience that it is far easier to affect this cycle at the "doing" rather than the "feeling" point. What this means is: we cannot order ourselves to *feel* better but we can always order ourselves to *do* better; and so *doing better* makes us *feel better.*

Reality therapy rests on the premise that human beings have only limited control over feeling and thinking. This is exemplified by simple experiments such as trying not to think of the color red for three minutes or our inability to feel good simply because we want to do so. If control over thoughts and emotions were possible, we should pass laws requiring all individuals to feel good at all times. Although this is not recognized by some individuals in the field of mental health, it has been understood by those in the legislative field. There is not a single law governing thinking or feeling. Reality therapy is based upon the premise that, since individuals can more easily control their behavior than their thinking and feeling, it is on behavior that we as therapists must concentrate. Although it is not usually possible to change feelings significantly, without first making some kind of change in behavior, we are not suggesting that feelings are unimportant; they are of utmost importance. If people behave toward each other in a competent, responsible way, then eventually, if not immediately, there are good feelings tied to this relationship. Good feelings are an index of a good relationship.

If a patient states, "I feel miserable and depressed," rather than replying, "Tell me more about it" or "How long have you felt this way?" the reality therapist responds by saying, "What are you doing that makes you feel depressed?" This statement does not deny feelings or that feelings are unimportant, but rather that the therapist relates feelings to behavior. We accept as fact that patients feel badly and, in fact, that's probably why they came to the therapist in the first place. But when asked what they are doing to make themselves depressed, patients usually are amazed. When they begin to relate what they have done over the last few days, it often becomes apparent that any person would be depressed were he doing the same thing. We find that patients begin to regard themselves and their symptoms in a different light when confronted with the normalcy of their depressive feelings. Patients take a totally different view of themselves and their symp-

toms when told (if applicable) that the therapist would be much more concerned about them if they were doing what they are doing and did not experience depression or loneliness. This principle pinpoints behavior and not feelings as the problem. The therapist might even ask the patient why he is not more depressed. This difficult question is a provocative one for most individuals seeking help. When they begin to outline the various things that assist them from becoming even further depressed, we begin to understand their islands of strength and can then assist them in becoming aware of their own assets.

Patients never say to us, "Tell me what to feel." They only say, "Tell me what to do." So in reality therapy, the second main principle of focusing on behavior is to get the patients to become aware of what they actually do. Unless one becomes aware of one's behavior, there is no hope of learning how to behave more competently, thereby gaining the successful identity that naturally makes one feel better. Immediately then, in the first phases of reality therapy, interwoven with our warm and understanding attitude, we continually ask the patient what he is doing.

This second principle is poignantly illustrated in the intimate love relationships. Unless those in love do things together, have fun, and enjoy each other, the feelings of love and warmth and closeness begin to fade. Only by sharing meaningful behavior can a relationship live and grow.

Feelings are tied to everything a person does; and by exploring and directing what he does, we help him toward better behavior—and thus better feelings. We never deny feelings, but we do not give emphasis to them; rather, we say, "Now that

I understand how you're feeling, let's examine what you're doing. What are you doing now? Let's take a look at that.''

Principle III: Focus on the Present. In reality therapy, we deal with what is going on currently in the person's life based upon the conviction that the past is fixed and cannot be changed. All that can be changed is the immediate present and the future.

Similar to our position on feelings, we do the same with the past. Although the prime focus in reality therapy is the *present,* when the past is discussed it is always related to current behavior. For example, if a person describes a crisis experience that occurred several years ago, the therapist will ask how that event is related to his present behavior.

Traditional psychotherapeutic approaches often emphasize the traumatic encounters an individual faced. In reality therapy, when we do discuss the past, we keep the following in mind: (1) It is useful to discuss character-building experiences in the individual's past and to relate them to current behavior and current attempts to succeed. (2) If we discuss past events, we usually attempt to discuss constructive alternatives he might have taken at the time. (3) If we discuss difficulties the individual encountered as a result of his behavior, rather than focusing on why he "got into so much difficulty," we focus on why he did not get into even more difficulty!

Case histories in the traditional format are notorious and tragic misrepresentations. Professionals in the field of mental-health counseling are trained to concentrate on the failures, shortcomings, traumas, and problems with which the person has had to cope. The amount of time in a typical case history spent on the assessment of a person's strengths and positive attributes is sadly minimal. Therapists are not trained to look for strengths but rather to look for failures. Ask people in an audience of therapists to introduce themselves and to "say a few words about yourself." They will speak up readily, talking about their positions, their labels, and their positive successes. But if asked to give a thumbnail sketch of one of the patients with whom they are working, they would probably outline a list of life failures and traumas, such as: "I have in mind a 17-year-old promiscuous girl whose father was an alcoholic and whose mother was highly irresponsible and often beat the child until she was 10 at which time she ran away from home and was arrested for stealing. She failed the 7th grade in school and then hitchhiked across country." The example shows graphically how differently we view success and failure.

Our patients and clients know this is the kind of information their charts contain, and it does not take a great deal of perception or sensitivity on our part to be aware of how they believe we view them. What a different picture we would have of patients if we devoted at least 50 percent of the space of a case history to an assessment of the person's successes and personality strengths.

Principle IV: Value Judgment. In reality therapy, we believe each individual must judge his own behavior and evaluate what he is doing to contribute to his own failure before he can be assisted. Once a person's behavior is clarified, perhaps for the first time in his life, he can begin to look at his own behavior critically and judge whether it is constructive. Reality therapy asks that each person make a *value judgment* about whether his behavior is responsible, and thereby good for him and those with whom he is meaningfully involved. If what he is doing is hurting himself or hurting others—and he is the one to make this judgment—his behavior is irresponsible and should be changed. No one really changes his behavior, unless he first understands what he is doing.

No one does anything unless he is convinced at that time that "this is the best thing for me now." Even people with failure identity behave, in all ways, to confirm this identity, thinking: "this is the best I can do, I can't do any better." In reality therapy, we get the patient to evaluate his behavior and we do not allow him the luxury of saying, "Well, it's all I can do; I know it's bad for me, but I'll do it anyway." Once we get his behavior on the table, we insist that he evaluate it. He's got to look at it, he's got to decide, "Is what I'm doing really helping me?" This is also what occurs in any constructive parent-child relationship or in a worthwhile marital relationship. The therapist's responsibility, however, is not to tell someone else how to live his life but rather to guide him in directions that will provide him with happiness without hurting others or himself.

The value of behavior has to be decided, not in the limited context of the person alone, but in the broader context of himself and those around him important to him. The reality therapist should not shrink from moral judgments when confronted by the patient, but his main task is to see that the patient faces the morality of his behavior. We believe it is irresponsible for a therapist to excuse misbehavior, that is, behavior the patient has judged is wrong. We believe each individual should do the best he can, not only for himself but also for others. It has been our experience that better behavior reaps the maximum constructive and fulfilling gain for the individual. It is our premise

that emotional health depends on a willingness to work within the framework of society. We are not saying that individuals should accept society uncritically, but rather, if they want to change it or establish a new morality, they first have to take responsibility for their own behavior.

The therapist does not make value judgments for the patient for this would relieve him of the responsibility for his behavior. But the therapist guides the patient to an evaluation of his own behavior.

Principle V: Planning. Much of the meaningful work of therapy is the process by which we help the individual make specific *plans* to change failure behavior to success behavior. This is true not only of the therapist but also of parents, ministers, teachers, employers, and so on.

It is not possible for every helping person to have experienced every situation, but a person with more satisfactory life experiences is better able to help others make plans. Therefore, the reality therapist may refer the patient to an expert in a specific area with which the patient is concerned. Part of the skill of any good planner is the ability to recognize his own limitations and to guide those he is trying to help to the proper sources for valid information.

A crucial concept in therapy, as well as in all aspects of life, is that once a good plan is made, it must be carried out. A significant portion of the therapeutic involvement encompasses making realistic plans within the limits of the motivation and abilities of the patient. The reality therapist must keep in mind that it is better to err by formulating plans that are simple than to make complex plans with a high risk of ending in failure. Since the people we are trying to help already have as part of their own self-concept a failure identity, it follows that they will likely gain a success identity through successes and not through failures. Therefore, if a student who has never studied develops a plan with the therapist that he is now going to study 2 hours, five nights a week, this plan is probably not as good as one that might establish that the patient will study 10 minutes a night on Monday, Wednesday, and Friday. It would be far better if this student, on returning, would report that he studied 10 minutes Monday night, 10 minutes Wednesday night, and on Friday night, instead of studying 10 minutes, he became so involved with his studies that when he looked at the clock 12 minutes had passed. The patient is thus a step closer to achieving success identity than if he had to tell the therapist that he studied for 2 hours every night, except Wednesday night, when he began watching TV after the first hour. Successes breed successes, and failures breed gloom and defeatism. Ernest Hemingway, when asked "Do you ever anticipate failure?" said, "If you anticipate failure, you'll have it."

It is extremely important to put the plan in writing, perhaps in the form of a contract. The differential weight attached to the written versus the spoken word was long ago discovered by the legal profession. The reality therapist finds written contracts an exceedingly useful tool. It is our frequent experience that plans not explicitly put into writing can be easily forgotten or misremembered.

The reality therapist does not leave out the details of the planning, but works directly and closely with the patient. For example, if a patient is going to seek a job during the week, the reality therapist will usually not leave it at that. He may ask the patient what day of the week, what time of the day? He may discuss what the patient is going to wear, what the patient anticipates the personnel employer might

ask, and how the patient will respond. He concerns himself with details.

The reality therapist does not see plans as being absolute. Plans are seen as one way of demonstrating multiple alternatives in life. There is usually a whole variety of plans to solve any problem and, if one's plan does not work, there is no harm in making other plans until an option is arrived at that will appear feasible. To be locked in on one's plan is the same as being involved with one's self and locked into one's misery.

Along with making plans in accordance with value judgments, there is the need for flexibility, for understanding that if a plan does not work, one should reevaluate it and try again along a different path.

Principle VI: Commitment. Commitment is a keystone of reality therapy. It is only from making and following through with plans that we gain a sense of self-worth and maturity. After an individual has made a value judgment about a portion of his behavior, has then been assisted in developing a plan to change that behavior in accordance with his value judgment, the next step is to assist him to make a commitment to carry out the plan. Making a plan only becomes meaningful if the individual makes a decision to carry it out. Organizations, whether business, professional, or helping such as Alcoholics Anonymous have, by long experience, become aware that commitments in front of others assume more binding and meaningful proportions.

In assisting an individual to make a commitment to follow through with his plan, reality therapy differs from other therapeutic approaches that stress the emphasis of having individuals make a commitment to themselves, rather than to others. Typically the patient might say to a nonreality therapist, "If you want me to do this, I'll do it for you." A traditional therapeutic response might be, "If you want to do it, don't do it for me; do it for yourself." It is our experience in reality therapy that to ask people to make commitments for themselves is often too much to ask. This is the end stage rather than the first stage. Therefore, if a patient says to the therapist, "I'll do it for you," the reality therapist, in the early and intermediate stages of therapy, will respond favorably and positively. A primary characteristic of individuals who have failure identities is that they have a strong unwillingness to commit themselves.

Most commitments in the world are from one human being to another. People do make meaningful commitments to God, to inanimate objects, or to animals, but in general, a commitment is a vow that a person makes to other people. Even if the commitment is made to oneself, it is, indirectly, primarily associated with that person's relationship with other human beings. A person may make a commitment to himself to shine his shoes daily, not because he enjoys shining his shoes but because he thinks that doing so will win him acceptance from others in society.

It is not in making commitments to others that people get into difficulty, but rather, some people begin to be overcommitted to themselves. The reality therapist assists in making sensible commitments. Success is only success in relation to others. Without others, it is impossible to establish a successful identity. Therefore, once an individual begins to make commitments to others, he gains a more successful identity. As reality changes, so commitments must change. A commitment made one day may not be viable on another day. It is our job as therapists to evaluate and reevaluate continually the reality of the society in which our patients live.

Principle VII: No Excuses. Therapists would be foolish to assume that all commitments that a patient makes will be achieved, that all plans will be successful. Plans fail sometimes but the reality therapist makes it clear to the patient that *excuses* are unacceptable. When the patient explains that a particular plan failed, it has been our experience that little therapeutic gain occurs from exploring whether the plan failed for a valid reason. For example, if a student decided he would study for 15 minutes on a particular evening as part of a plan, and then explains that he studied for 10 minutes when his house caught fire, or that he became interested in a TV football game, an exploration of either situation is not helpful. The reality therapist does not concern himself with why the plan failed but rather that the plan did fail and it is now the therapist's job to make a new plan or modify the old one. Far more benefit is gained from working with the patient on redeveloping the plan than in discussing the reasons for the plan's failure. The new plan may be the same as the old plan, with the addition that each time the house burns down, studying will be terminated for that evening. Reality therapists do not continually say, "Why did it go wrong? Why did you fail?" We are not detectives; we are relating as human beings and not as lie detectors—we believe people know why things go wrong. Things go wrong; things fail ordinarily when individuals do not do what they said they were going to do. Of course, the circumstances may have become more difficult than anticipated, but the patients' responsibility certainly did not decrease because of more difficult circumstances—it increased.

The therapist should not depreciate the patient for failing or blame him. We just say, "Are you going to fulfill your commitment or not? If you say you are, when?'' Or we say, "The plan didn't work. Let's make a new one together.''

It is absolutely necessary to the principles of reality therapy not to accept excuses. If the patient wants to make excuses, the therapist might say, "I'm not asking you why things went wrong. I'm asking when you are going to do what you said you were going to do?" To belabor the whys of a plan's failure is to reinforce failure identity. Our job is to change the patient to a success identity either by a recommitment to the old plan or by formulating a new one.

The real discipline of doing reality therapy is the ability not to accept excuses, not to probe for fault, not to be a detective by trying to find out "why," and not to depreciate or demean the patient for failure, but rather to assume that a commitment, according to a reasonable plan, is always possible.

Principle VIII: Eliminate Punishment. As important as not accepting excuses—and a very difficult thing for most people to do who are imbued with standard morality—is to *eliminate punishment* when a person fails.

Punishment as a way of changing behavior works poorly on those individuals with a failure identity. Although the essential goal of punishment is to get people to change their behavior, throughout history punishment has been an ineffectual social tool. Any kind of negative, depreciating statements by a therapist becomes punishment.

Therefore, it is important that therapists do not punish patients with critical statements such as "I knew you would not do it," or "see, you've done it again." In making such statements, the therapist punishes the patient and thereby reconfirms his failure identity.

Punishment is quite different from the natural consequences of behavior following contractual planning. For example, if a parent makes a commitment to a child that he is going to allow the child certain privileges and if the child accepts certain responsibilities and fails in those responsibilities, the parent is no longer obligated to keep the commitment. If the parent says, "You can use the family car on Saturday nights providing you wash it once a week," and the child does not wash the car, the parent has every right to refuse the use of the car. This is not punishment. This is a logical consequence similar to what Rudolf Dreikurs (1958) suggested as a major procedure in training young children for responsible family living. Punishment for failures of plans not only reinforces failure identity but also harms the therapeutic relationship.

To the extent that the reality therapist eliminates punishment and does not accept excuses for failure, helping the patient substitute reasonable value judgments and make plans in accordance with those value judgments, helping him to make a commitment to follow through with his plans, he is truly assisting individuals to gain a success identity.

Process to Psychotherapy

The reality therapist by overall general therapeutic standards can certainly be called verbally active. Viktor Frankl, the founder of logotherapy, when asked by one of his psychoanalytic colleagues to define *Logotherapy* in one sentence, reportedly asked his colleague first to define the essence of *psychoanalysis* in one sentence. The answer given to Frankl was "during psychoanalysis, the patient must lie down on a couch and tell you things that sometimes are very disagreeable to tell." Whereupon Frankl retorted, "Now, in Logotherapy the patient may remain sitting erect, but he must hear things that sometimes are very disagreeable to hear." Using this same model, we might define the essence of *reality therapy* as: "in reality therapy the patient and the therapist both sit erect facing each other and the patient and the therapist hear things that are both very agreeable and very disagreeable." This is meant facetiously and certainly not meant as a true capsule version of reality therapy. Nonetheless, there is a conversational exchange between therapist and patient that encompasses both disagreeable as well as agreeable facets. However, the focus is on the individual's strengths, attributes, and potentials as related to his behavior and his experiences, particularly his current attempts to succeed in life.

Setting limits is an important part of the function of the reality therapist. The therapist assists the patient in understanding not only the limits of the therapeutic situation, although there may be an intense personal involvement, but also the limits as well as the nonlimits that life places upon the individual. For example, if a patient asks, "Can I call you after hours?" the reality therapist would, of course, respond with, "I certainly hope you would call if there is an urgent situation in which I can be of help." However, we believe that the therapist might also say, "I hope you would call if you have a significant success." Most patients are astounded and surprised when a therapist suggests he might be interested in good news as well as problems via telephone. However, the concept of emphasizing the positive is constantly in the reality therapist's mind. The contractual arrangement as discussed in the planning stage under the section Theory of Psychotherapy is a type of limit setting, since the plan may include the limits of the therapeutic involvement, and since, on occasion, it has been found helpful to set a specific time limit or duration for psycho-

therapy. At the end of this period, therapy is stopped at least for a time. Some people are able to work more effectively, more positively, when they know therapy will consist of a specific number of visits. This is particularly helpful in the area of marriage or family counseling.

A reality therapist focuses frequently on "pinning down the patient." This is also brought out in the planning phase of behavioral goals. Unfortunately, this is an area where many therapists of a variety of approaches do not follow through. For example, if a teen-age girl who has never sought a job before says to the therapist, "Next week I am going to look for my first job," a reality therapist would not say, "Good, let me know how it works out," but rather he might respond with a series of very precise questions such as:

Therapist: What day next week?
Girl: I don't know. I thought Monday or Tuesday.
Therapist: Which day. Monday or Tuesday?
Girl: Well, I guess Tuesday.
Therapist: You guess or will it be Tuesday?
Girl: Tuesday.
Therapist: What time Tuesday?
Girl: Well sometime in the morning.
Therapist: What time in the morning?
Girl: Oh, well, 9:30.
Therapist: Fine, that is a good time to begin looking for a job. What do you plan to wear?
Girl: Well I never thought it would make a difference. What do you think I should wear?
Therapist: [Discusses several alternatives to grooming and dress relative to job hunting] How are you going to look up what jobs to apply for?
Girl: I thought I would look in the morning paper in the classified section.
Therapist: [The therapist might discuss

the pros and cons of also looking in the Sunday paper as the girl may not be aware of the larger classified section on that day of the week. The therapist might even go through the classified section with her.]

The therapist might terminate the "pinning down" phase of dealing with the girl by saying, "What are you going to do if you are called in for an interview?" If the girl has difficulties and becomes uncomfortable explaining that she did not know it was a possibility, the therapist and the girl might even do some role playing with the therapist taking the position of a potential employer. Finally, the therapist might say to the girl, "What will you do if the first two or three or four job interviews are unsuccessful?" The therapist would never say, "How would you feel?" That would be a totally fruitless question. Of course, the girl would feel badly, she might feel depressed. The therapist, by asking "how would you feel?" is certainly not assisting the girl to deal with the potential failure in trying to obtain a position. Rather, the therapist might say, "If you are unsuccessful on the first day, what are your plans or what will you do?" That is a matter they can both deal with, by planning ahead. In general, the more specific the questions and the more a therapist "pins down" the patient with respect to the details of anticipated change in behavior, the more he is increasing the chances for the patient's successful handling of the situation.

Constructive arguing or intelligent heated discussions in some situations may be an integral part of the psychotherapeutic process. If the therapist asks the patient what the patient believes about something, and the patient answers and then asks the therapist his beliefs and disagrees with him, we do not believe there is always a hidden meaning behind the disagreement. Rather, the disagree-

ment can be on a responsible and intellectual level. In fact, discussions of this sort can lend a great deal of support to the patient's self-concept as an individual who has something to offer, something of value to say and defend.

Humor is, and should be, a regular part of the whole therapeutic process. The ability to laugh freely is an integral part of a well-balanced self-concept and approach to life. In fact, the ability to laugh at one's own follies, one's own mistakes, and one's own accidental errors is one of the highest forms of a mentally healthy self-concept. When people become burdened and overwhelmed with emotional problems, it appears that this ability to laugh at themselves is the first facet of humorous expression that disappears. They may still retain the ability to laugh at others. Laughing and humor are related to joy and happiness. We are not suggesting this is all that joy and happiness are, but it is a part of a healthy life and a positive self-image.

Confrontations are used frequently, particularly when "no excuses" is the stance the therapist takes. This can be, and often is, one of the hardest positions for the therapist to assume. That is, to say to the individual who has failed, "You said you would do it, when will you do it?" For the therapist not to accept excuses or rambling explanations for failure is essential to eventual follow-through of plans. Confrontation with irresponsible behavior is part of the job of doing therapy.

Verbal shock therapy can be used effectively in some therapeutic situations. It is not frequently used in the context of practicing reality therapy but does have a special place when timing, as well as degree of involvement, are taken into consideration. For example, a patient may say, "What do you think is wrong with me?" and the therapist might respond by saying, "I think you are crazy." After a pause and some reflections from the patient about that, the therapist should go on to explain that the word *crazy* as he meant it can be defined as someone who is acting in an irresponsible way, trying to fulfill his needs by hurting either himself or others.

Harrington was once asked by a patient, who was rambling on, why he (Harrington) was looking out of the window while the patient was talking, and Harrington retorted, "Anything is more interesting right now than what you are saying." This facetious kind of verbal shock confrontation or insult does have merit and value when used correctly and when the therapist has an understanding of the situation and of the patient. One is reminded of the definition that a gentleman never hurts anyone's feelings unintentionally!

Analysis of dreams is not part of the reality therapist's function. We believe there is virtually no evidence to indicate that analysis of dreams has any therapeutic value. That does not mean it does not have relevance or significance. The relating of dreams can even be used as a defense to avoid discussing one's current behavior. However, on occasion if a patient insists on relating a dream, most reality therapists would listen if the act of listening was felt to be meaningful to the patient.

Generally, however, we try to get involved with the patient in his real life. What he does, what he plans: we want to get him to evaluate this with us and remake plans and then carry them out. Ours is not a therapy where we do much speculation or listen to fantasy. It is real and when the patient begins to understand how real it is, he becomes rapidly more responsible.

Mechanisms of Psychotherapy

What happens beneath the surface in the psychotherapeutic process is difficult to say, and whatever it is, it probably varies from patient to patient. However, in the context of reality therapy, the therapist should have some specific goals in mind regarding his expectations from the patient. These goals are more in terms of concepts and values of individual responsibility and meaning rather than of behavioral goals that are the goals the patient establishes for himself.

There is a strong focus on helping the individual understand and accept himself as he is—that is, as he is as a human being, with his own internal limitations and abilities, rather than how he is behaviorally. Although certainly, things may determine or be related to each other, reality therapy does not rest on a deterministic philosophy but rather on an understanding that man is ultimately self-determining. What he becomes, within the limits of his own inherited endowment and the environment, is what he has made out of himself. Every man has the potential for being responsible or irresponsible, and which way he behaves depends upon *decisions* rather than *conditions*.

Criteria for success in psychotherapy for the most part depends on the goal or goals the patient has established for himself with the assistance of his therapist. Certainly the ability to express feelings of mature and responsible love, the ability to give and take, the ability to be aware of feelings of anger and resentment as well as feelings of tenderness and love in himself and others, in addition to many other factors, are important in the effective functioning of an individual. However, there are no rigid criteria for termination of psychotherapy except, in a general way, responsible behavior, and, in a secondary way, fulfillment of the goals established.

Early in therapy, the individual should become aware that the therapist is interested in him as a person and that the therapist believes the patient can do better or be happier than he is at that time and that the therapist accepts him as a total person, but does not necessarily accept all of his specific behaviors. Also, in the initial phase of therapy the patient should become aware that the therapist is dealing with what is going on in the present and focusing on behavior and relating feelings to behavior.

In therapy, self-awareness is viewed in terms of increasing the patient's focus of concern with the present rather than the past or the distant future, and to gain an ability to avoid rehashing the past and criticizing and demeaning himself for mistakes made or anticipated. What can happen is that if this does not occur, the patient will spend all his time either going backward or forward and there is no time left to enjoy the present. Hopefully, the individual can learn within himself to understand and expand his attributes, his strengths, and his potentials—to put himself and the things and people around him in the positive and to make and follow through with plans independently.

If the patient can act in increasingly responsible ways, resolve crises and adjustment problems through accepting that he is responsible for himself and his behavior and that he can fulfill his needs without hurting himself or other people, he is no longer in need of therapy. The reality therapist does assume a great deal of overt responsibility for the conduct of therapy, and it is our experience that this approach, rather than weakening the patient's self-confidence, strengthens his self-confidence and increases his feelings of adequacy. These effects are enhanced by deep and serious interest in the patient and by direct focus and concentration on specific major behavioral issues. With the patient attempting to understand and clarify within his own thinking the nature and alternatives of the issues he faces in life and a variety of ways they can best be resolved, an important phase begins for the patient, as he begins to apply the techniques he learns in therapy to his daily life. It is the involvement with the therapist that makes this possible. Involvement, therefore, is the basic mechanism upon which reality therapy is based.

APPLICATIONS

Problems

Reality therapy has not been applied to global problems such as those of war and overpopulation. If its theory and its procedures are correct for individuals taken singly, it is probably correct for individuals en masse, whether the collection of people is as small as a family or as large as a nation. However, reality therapy principles have been applied to a specific global problem and, with a great deal of success, that of education. Glasser believes the main obstacle in successful education is our present educational philosophy, a philosophy of noninvolvement, nonrelevance, and limited emphasis on thinking. Education, he believes, must move toward the opposite philosophy—involvement, relevance, and thinking—or we will not solve the overwhelming problems of children who fail in school. *Schools without Failure* (Glasser, 1969) presents suggestions for making involvement, relevance, thinking, realities in a school system.

Further, reality therapy has not been applied to common and important problems such as pollution or social problems of prejudice and race relations. We see no reason why reality therapy principles would not work in dealing with those national or global problems noted above. An area where reality therapy has been used extensively with great success is the treatment of delinquency and the resultant unemployment, which is intimately related to a problem of failure.

Specific individual problems such as problems of anxiety, maladjustment, marital conflicts, perversions, and psychoses have all been treated successfully by the application of reality therapy.

Specific unusual problems such as those of autism and severe mental retardation cannot be treated effectively with the use of reality therapy since the treatment program is essentially through the spoken word or, in unusual cases, by the written word between patient and therapist. In such cases, most probably, operant conditioning techniques are the method of choice.

Finally, from the standpoint of broad global context, we believe reality therapy is most applicable to the problems people face in Western civilization. It was developed in the United States, geared for the values and overall philosophy of our way of life, and it probably has limitations in cultures and societies with significantly different value-system foundations.

Reality therapy has been applied successfully to group therapy with military widows (Zunin & Barr, 1969). The participating widows were considered to be normal, healthy persons experiencing a significant life crisis. The group was designed to assist the women in handling the crises more effectively. Outpatient meetings were held on a once-weekly basis. The major focus of the group meetings was on the "here and now" and on gaining an increased understanding of one's individual potentials. Although the past was not ignored, the emphasis was on helping each participant to understand better her own attributes, strengths, and abilities.

Using the principles of reality therapy, an opportunity was provided for a group of people sharing a common life tragedy to exchange constructive ideas, thoughts, and experiences that helped them deal with their lives in a more effective and satisfactory manner. Of prime importance, the orientation and image of this group was viewed in the framework of health and normalcy, rather than a group therapy for the resolution of deep-rooted conflicts, characterological weaknesses, or neurotic frailties. No attempt was made to curtail or suppress the normal mourning reactions.

As the initial, and often incapacitating, shock reaction wanes following the loss of a spouse, it is frequently replaced by depression, self-recrimination, outwardly directed anger, and feelings of guilt, self-pity, hopelessness, and helplessness. During this phase of reorganization, the women were assisted in a constructive social and psychological readjustment of their lives.

This pilot program demonstrated quite clearly that individuals in various stages of a similar life-crisis situation can receive considerable assistance using reality therapy in a group-method approach.

In summary, we believe these techniques are applicable to a wide variety of problems because the essence of reality therapy is problem solving. When people face problems individually or in a group as large as a nation, these ideas should apply.

Evaluation

In reality therapy, we do not deal with individual diagnoses. In fact, it is our strong feeling that individual diagnoses do a great disservice to those individuals already burdened with emotional problems and adjustment difficulties. With the exception of a few specific diagnoses, such as phenylketonuria for which known biochemical or biological deficiencies exist and are causatives in the illness, specific diagnostic labels are useless. To argue whether a neurosis and psychosis are different or whether a neurosis is lesser than a psychosis is to argue about an irrelevant subject. Consider the misfortune of being labeled a schizophrenic. The label can be worse than the disease as far as incapacitating one in the course of life's activities. Perhaps at some point in the future, psychiatry and all the mental-health professions will have advanced to a degree that specific labeling of various types of problems will be accurate and effective. At this point, our reliance on labels misleads us, misinforms us, and is nonutilitarian. It is not an accurate shorthand in which to convey problems from one mental-health professional to another. Rather the label often creates great distortions because of varying definitions and understandings about what the label means.

Evaluations of effectiveness of treatment are generally not considered to be meaningful. We have not advanced to a sufficient degree of sophistication to be able to measure items such as happiness, fulfillment, and creativity in society, let alone in an individual. The aim and purpose of all approaches of psychotherapy have been to change attitudes, emotions, and behavior in the hope that the sufferer will experience less distress and function more effectively and responsibly. What distinguishes reality therapy from other therapies in the context of evaluation is mainly the variety of methods evolved for obtaining the above-noted goals.

There have been no long-term significant studies on the effectiveness of reality therapy in outpatients. At the Ventura School for Girls, some changes in statistics indicated that the institution of reality therapy in the program significantly reduced the recidivism rate.

Reality therapy has unequivocally been demonstrated as an effective tool in reducing disciplinary problems, increasing school performance, and enhancing teacher involvement with each other, with students, and with the school system. A detailed study substantiating this was conducted by John English (1970) and presented at the 21st Annual Conference of the California Association of School Psychologists and Psychometrists.

The principal purpose of a study by Richard Hawes (1971) was to assess the effects of a Schools Without Failure program on the black child's belief in self-responsibility versus powerlessness, self-concept, and classroom behavior. This was in consonance with one of the Reality Therapy Schools Without Failure Program's major objectives, that is, to encourage individual responsibility in children and thereby affect their classroom behavior and enhance their self-concept. Three hundred and forty black pupils from the third and sixth grades of these two schools made up the sample for the study, which was conducted over a period of 16 weeks.

Analysis of results indicated that the experimental school program did significantly affect the belief in internal locus of control for success and failures of the third- and sixth-grade black pupils included in the study. The third- and sixth-grade pupils attending the experimental school showed significant increases in:

1. Behavior toward tasks assumed to be appropriate to the school setting
2. Behavior in which processing and seeking information were salient and apparent
3. Behavior primarily motivated by the satisfaction derived from interacting with other people through a given activity or task
4. The number of teacher and child interactions
5. The number of child-initiated interactions
6. Decrease in behavior characterized by compliance

The experimental school's third graders significantly increased their behavior motivated primarily by the sense of competence mastery and achievement derived from a given task or classroom activity. Sixth-grade pupils from the control school showed a moderately significant decrease of compliant behavior.

Treatment

Reality therapy evolved in its initial phase in dealing with three different categories of problems: in Glasser's work with delinquent teen-age girls; second, from his work with private outpatients with a variety of problems; and third, and almost simultaneously, it was correlated with the work that G. L. Harrington was doing with severely psychotic individuals at the Veterans Administration Hospital. Its practical value and utilitarian function in the application of these concepts was rapidly found relevant to all three areas.

In Harrington's application of reality therapy in institutionalized psychotic patients, he found two additional modifica-

tions that enhanced his work with the patients. First was the initiation of a three-phase program within the single unit where he worked. That is, patients moved from phase I where they were essentially given custodial care to phase III when they were ready to seek outside employment and living situations. The system was geared so within the general milieu was a built-in motivation to progress from phase I to phase III and progression was based upon reduction of "crazy" talk and "crazy" behavior as well as increasing demonstration of responsible behavior and relevant conversation. This phase division has been used effectively by several other institutions practicing reality therapy, among them the William Roper Hull Progressive Education Center in Calgary, Alberta, Canada, whose director is Brian Sharpe. This home and school for delinquent and disturbed boys and girls is run entirely on the principles of reality therapy and has four phases as developed by Mr. Sharpe. He has found the principles of reality therapy useful as Harrington did and is also able to enhance appropriate placement of staff according to their backgrounds, interests, and abilities in dealing with individuals in the specific phases.

One aspect of dealing with the so-called psychotic patient is that spearheaded by Harrington, when he did not allow the patient to talk "crazy." This technique has been used by all others practicing reality therapy with similar success. Patients are told "I am not interested in hearing your crazy behavior, your delusions, and your hallucinations, but rather I am interested in what you want out of life, in your attempts to succeed in the world and in the healthy you." "If you want to talk crazy, talk to someone else." Most reality therapists have, therefore, not heard a delusion or hallucination expressed since they have been practicing reality therapy. It has been long since known that in a situation where two individuals are meaningfully involved, each has strong desires to please the other. If one is involved with a "psychotic" individual having hallucinations and delusions, an interest in hallucinations and delusions on the part of the therapist reinforces the patient's desirability to have them. When no interest or a negative interest is demonstrated, reality therapists find that hallucinations, delusions, and psychotic expressions begin to deminish rapidly. This is analogous to a therapist in the first visit asking a patient if he has any dreams. If the patient says, "I do, but I never remember them," and the therapist continues to ask that question at each consecutive visit, usually at the end of five or six visits, the patient is enthusiastically and regularly remembering and reporting his dreams. In a meaningful and involved psychotherapeutic relationship, if the therapist asks often enough, he may get just what he wants, and if he wants psychotic behavior, and keeps asking about it, chances are, he will get it.

Group psychotherapy is used regularly applying the principles of reality therapy by most individuals. The principles can easily and effectively be incorporated into the group process and the group is a very powerful instrument by which to implement commitments and plan making. Consider, for example, an individual involved in a group situation making a commitment and then a plan, writing the plan down and having each individual in the group read the plan and sign his or her name. The initial leverage to keep the commitment comes from involvement with meaningful others, which is reinforced when the individual is involved in a group setting. If he is involved with the group members and wants to retain this involvement, the motivation to keep the commitment is greatly enhanced every time he looks at the paper describing one of his plans, signed by the group's members. Co-therapists are used regularly and found to be a useful adjunct in reality therapy groups.

Marriage therapy or conjoint marital counseling is often practiced by reality therapists. We view this as a time-limited series of visits usually from 5 to 15. At the end of that period, if the couple has not made significant progress, a total reevaluation of the situation is in order or possibly a respite of several weeks or months in the continuation of therapy, after which another reevaluation would follow.

Initially in marriage counseling, it is important for the therapist to clarify the couple's goals by asking questions such as, "Are you here even though you have already made the decision to end the marriage, but want to be able to say 'we have tried everything'?" or "Are you here because you want to evaluate the pros and cons of continuing in this marriage?" or "Have you made the decision that you definitely want to preserve the marriage but are having difficulties that you have been unable to resolve effectively and want professional help?" If the patients and therapist are not first aware which of these reasons each of the partners has come to therapy for, he may be dealing with a couple who essentially want a divorce but do not say so while the therapist is actively seeking to improve the relationship. In marriage counseling, we recommend the therapist be quite active, asking a variety of questions in trying to understand the overall pattern of the marriage and of the interrelationship.

Specific sexual counseling has been incorporated into the practice of reality therapy by some therapists with great success. Those using sexual counseling have developed some modifications of the Masters and Johnson (1970) program.

In marriage counseling, a variety of questions that would reorient the couple in refocusing their attentions on one another can be extremely useful, for example: (1) questions that help them define their similarities and differences in taste and interests; (2) understanding how they go about seeking friends as a couple; and (3) understanding how much there usually is to know about each other and how much of their "knowledge" is actually based upon assumption.

Familiarity is not intimacy. Just as many children even as they grow to adults know their parents only as "parents" and not as "people," the same is true frequently when a spouse is asked questions regarding the values and philosophies of their marriage partner. If a married couple wanted to bring in their family album, the reality therapist might feel this would be extremely helpful in terms of both understanding their relationship and growth together from a positive viewpoint.

In reality therapy, ancillary individuals are often asked to come into the office for a visit. They may be a friend, a spouse, a teacher, a child, or anyone else significant in the patient's life. This is done to help the therapist understand the patient and help the patient understand himself or herself through the eyes of people he respects. These ancillary people are brought in not for the reality therapist to help them deal with their problems, but really so the therapist can ask them to help him to understand the patient better. It is our strong recommendation that except in very highly unusual situations, these ancillary individuals in the person's life should always be seen in the session together with the patient.

Reality therapy is a verbal therapy; it requires conversation and as such has some limitations. For example, it cannot be used by individuals who cannot talk. There have been several cases of people who were unable to speak and wrote their comments on a paper with a successful therapeutic conclusion; however, it requires an exchange of communication either by the spoken word or in unusual cases by the written word. Therefore, limitations include its inability to apply to autistic nonverbal children and to severely mentally retarded individuals who cannot communicate adequately either verbally or through the written word. Reality therapy has been used with moderately mentally retarded individuals.

As mentioned in previous sections of this chapter, there has been strong use of reality therapy principles with appropriate modifications in the school system and, as such, this use represents an important phase in the application of reality therapy to prevent mental illness. Reality therapy has been used in a significant way in race relations to the extent that it was developed in the black community, Watts, California, and also incorporated with success in schools facing problems with race relations. Multiple-family therapy has been used by at least one reality therapist to a limited degree with no difficulty in successfully applying these same principles.

In industry, reality therapy has been used to deal with organizational problems as well as to improve the individuals' organizational effectiveness. Intensive two- or three-day group programs using reality therapy restricted to executives of specific firms, such as banks, have been found to be relevant and effective for improving organizational and individual functioning.

Management

The reality therapist's goal during the first interview and perhaps the first several interviews is to establish an involvement with the patient that includes discussing his present attempts to succeed and his present behavior, and also, to help the individual see that he is responsible for his own behavior.

We believe that no real therapeutic progress occurs unless and until an involvement between therapist and patient is established, as motivation and involvement are directly related. It is usually futile to attempt to direct patients in making plans and commitments to plans that would change their behavior unless there is a strong involvement. The commitment is as strong as the involvement. Further, until an individual acknowledges, accepts, and understands his responsibility for his own behavior, no truly constructive plan to change that behavior and hence therapeutic progress can occur.

Therapist and patient are seated comfortably in chairs positioned so the individuals can look at one another.

No specific fee is recommended. Fees vary. Therapists from a variety of disciplines including psychiatry, psychology, and psychiatric social work practice reality therapy, and the average fees in these fields vary from city to city. Fees and plans for payment should be discussed openly, early in therapy.

Most reality therapists see their patients once weekly. We find it is rarely necessary to see a patient twice weekly but this may be done for a short time. Most reality therapists believe the duration of sessions should be flexible, but because of the practicality of maintaining schedules, most therapists see patients for 45 minutes to 1 hour per visit depending upon their *modus operandi.*

We do not believe any real significance should be attached to matching the patient and therapist. Certainly some personalities relate better to one another. However, of prime importance is the be-

lief by the therapist that the patient can do better and/or be happier than he is right now. The therapist must also be willing to become meaningfully and responsibly involved with that patient.

Psychotropic medications are used conservatively by psychiatrists who practice reality therapy. In the case of institutionalized criminal offenders, we find, by long experience, that psychotropic medication tends to remove responsibility for behavior and justify irresponsible behavior; therefore, use of psychotropic medications is avoided in such cases.

We do not believe interpretive confrontation, insight, nondirective interviews, and techniques such as free association are therapeutically constructive. The use of prolonged silence by the therapist when the patient is also silent is not considered useful or worthwhile as a therapeutic technique. Dream analysis is not used either.

Specifically, the reality therapist focuses on behavior and on establishing a personal, involved relationship in a responsible manner, and deals with the present, particularly the present attempts to succeed in the world. The reality therapist does not spend time acting as a "detective." If a patient states, for example, "I am a liar; I lie all the time and you can never believe anything I say," it would not be surprising for a reality therapist to say, "I believe you; I don't want to waste our time together by trying to determine if what you are telling me is the truth. I am interested in helping you and working with you; you can believe me and I expect to believe you." We often find that with hostile patients, it is helpful not to confront the patient with his hostility initially but rather to deal directly with the content of what he is saying. (This same technique is found useful in responding to hostile questions at lectures.)

The so-called *flight into health* is a frequently discussed concept in the therapeutic circles and seems to be variously defined but primarily indicates the unanticipated, rapid, positive recovery made by a patient after a short period of therapy. This is often doubted by the therapists and probably relates to a fear of "false recovery" and a probable return to previous irresponsible behavior. In reality therapy, this is something we generally do not find to be true and we accept any constructive, responsible changes in an individual as progress. Perhaps the single most useful and important test in ascertaining the depth and sincerity of a change to increasingly constructive behavior is a willingness to do something meaningful in an involved way for other people, in addition to doing something for oneself. In an institution, this is particularly a good test for an individual who is seemingly doing exceedingly well, yet may be acting in this manner as a so-called facade to "get out earlier." Of course, maintenance of this behavior even if it is initially started as a facade usually results in positive reinforcement and hence a desire to continue to change. However, the additional desire to do something for another individual, another peer in the institution, is seen as strong indication of the depth, the degree, and the quality of the change in behavior.

CASE EXAMPLE

This is the case history of a woman, age 30, dissatisfied with her husband, and in love with a much older man she wants to have an affair with. She has a strong dislike for her mother and contempt for her weak father. She has two children and has trouble managing them. She is ambitious, but does not know what she wants to do in life and thinks she can become an interior decorator. She has never had a sexual affair out of marriage, and she has not had a climax after her marriage but several with her husband before marriage. She has a compulsion to carry a particular coin in her purse; otherwise she feels her children will die. She admits she is a poor housekeeper, has a poor memory, and is disorganized.

During the initial visits the therapist concentrated on creating a meaningful therapeutic involvement. This was done in part by being personal, warm, friendly, and concerned about her difficult current life situation. Initial emphasis was placed on exploring this woman's strengths, potentials, and attributes. An exploration of her current life was made with particular attention to the activities she enjoyed. These were activities with her husband, family, friends, children, hobbies, and so forth. This discussion not only served to enhance the therapeutic involvement but also provided the woman with an enhanced self-esteem and an increased understanding of her strong qualities and reinforced the fact that she had something to offer herself and others at this point in life. It was important to the therapist that he not allow her to paint a picture of herself as only disorganized, lonely, desperate, and dissatisfied.

An intensive inquiry into her current activities in a detailed fashion was made during the initial phase of therapy. This included a detailed understanding of her interaction with her husband when they are together and their behavior toward each other, her interaction with her friends and her children, and her behavior regarding participation in organizations, religion, school, and so forth.

As therapy progressed, she was assisted directly in understanding that there were many alternatives available to her and that these alternatives would be explored and discussed. Individuals in situations like this often, as a result of their inner conflicts, have an inability to see alternatives, thinking there is "really no choice." Her suffering certainly indicated serious inner conflict and certainly each side of the conflict was a result of many factors. Her suffering, the therapist surmised, would not disappear without a change in her behavior. She was assisted in understanding that her attitude, thinking, and personality would follow, and not precede, a change in behavior. She was assisted in understanding that, to a large extent, we are what we do and if we want to change what we are, we must begin by changing what we do and undertake new directions of behavior.

The full responsibility of her marriage, of her disorganizations in the home and her ambivalence about having an affair, was clearly placed on her as the responsible person. She was repeatedly confronted with her alternatives and guided toward assuming responsibility for decisions. At the same time, her ambitions were mobilized and she was assisted and directed in exploring her interests in a meaningful and constructive manner, particularly her interest in interior decorating. In fact, the possibility of going into interior decorating was focused on a good deal in the therapeutic situation including areas such as the curriculum involved, the opportunities for her as an interior decorator, the study course, the advantages and disadvantages of pursuing that field of endeavor, and so on. Discussion of past history or childhood residual feelings for her mother and father were gently discouraged. Her present relationship with her mother and father was explored with an attempt to understand her current relationship with them and perhaps to improve it. Discussion of feelings of hopelessness, depression, or loneliness were continually converted into questions regarding her behavioral activities, attitudes, and modes of interaction.

As therapy progressed, this woman was assisted in making specific value judgments about all aspects of her behavior. "Is what you are doing in this particular situation getting you what you want—if not let's talk about what you can do to change this situation to enable you to get what would be more satisfying to you." The making of plans to alter her specific behavior took a relatively long period and the therapist thought it was desirable to write out with the patient during the therapy sessions some of the plans, or to have the patient write as they were talking. The woman was guided in making specific value judgments, which not only took into consideration her feelings, for example, about having an affair, but legal, sociological, moral, and humane issues as well.

In the area of her unsatisfactory sexual relationship with her husband, the therapist initially explored their current sexual behavior and attitudes by first trying to assess her knowledge and sophistication about a sexual relationship. Not much attempt was made to explore her compulsion to carry the particular coin in her purse except to say it was indeed irrational behavior and that perhaps she was actually giving the responsibility for the well-being of her children to the coin, rather than acknowledging it as her own. However, no attempt was made to provide repeated insights and explore the psychodynamics of the coin compulsion.

If the involvement is strong enough at a time when the patient persists in talking about this, the therapist might even say, "I am not going to talk to you about crazy and irrational behavior, but only about healthy behavior and your current attempts to succeed and to help yourself in life.'' It might be noted here that when the patient established a success identity, the irrational need for the coin was resolved.

After the patient made value judgments about specific aspects of her behavior and was assisted in plan making to pursue interior decorating, to improve sexual behavior, and to enhance the relationship with her husband, she was then faced with making a commitment to follow through with the plan. As explained in the outline of reality therapy, if the plans failed at any point, rather than exploring the reasons for failure, or the excuses for failure, the therapist in a nonjudgmental but a warm and caring way proceeded to make a new plan with the patient rather than focus on why the old plans failed.

During the course of therapy, in this particular situation, it was important for the therapist to see the husband at least once. This visit was to be held conjointly with the patient unless either of them preferred that the husband be seen alone. The therapist said he would see the husband alone if he wished, but he made it clear to both parties, that he (the therapist) would prefer to see them together. To see the husband alone, he explained, would mean the therapist could not really use the information gleaned from that interview in the therapeutic situation with the wife. Great benefit is derived from seeing the husband, which would give an added dimension of understanding of the patient, provide an opportunity for the therapist to test the reliability of the patient's reporting, and give the husband an opportunity not only to ask questions of the therapist, or of the patient in front of the therapist, but also to

understand fully that some of the struggles at least that the patient was dealing with in therapy had to do with the marital situation. It might be that after seeing the husband, the desirability of a period of several visits of conjoint marital therapy would be explored, but this would depend upon the progress of therapy, the attitude of the husband, and the nature of the first conjoint visit. After this explanation, the patient stated she preferred to have a conjoint meeting with the therapist, and this did take place.

It had been noted in the case history that the patient had a poor memory. Had the therapist thought there was any indication that this memory was a result of physical or organic problems, a full medical and neurological workup would have been recommended.

This patient was seen on a once-weekly basis and sat as all patients in reality therapy do, on a chair, facing the therapist.

During the course of the therapy, the therapist repeatedly emphasized that he was interested in dealing with the present, particularly with her present attempts to succeed and to deal with her problems in a mature and effective manner. With this woman, it was necessary for the therapist to assure her that he would stay with her until the problems she came for were resolved. Any resort by the patient to "I can't" in discussing situations was appropriately converted to "you mean you won't or you don't want to—let's explore the pros and cons." Until this woman realized she was responsible for her own behavior and that she was not in an irreconcilable or irreversible situation, no therapeutic progress occurred. She finally realized and acknowledged that, in fact, she was responsible for her behavior, whether in relation to her husband, her children, her possible lover, or the coin in her purse. Thus, the patient was assisted in understanding her capacity for more worthwhile behavior within her immediate surroundings. Her ultimate choice to change those surroundings and her decision to change her behavior and her subsequent maintenance of her decisions were the therapy.

SUMMARY

The first important step in correcting behavior is to find out what one is trying to correct. If we want to face reality, we must admit that we cannot rewrite a person's history, no matter how much we understand the unfortunate circumstances that led to his behavior. There is nothing this information can do for us or for him except to reinforce the concept that, indeed, he has a reason to act the way he does and to excuse this transgression on the ground that he is "sick." No matter what happened to him in the past, he still has the responsibility for what he does now.

Until an individual accepts the fact that he is responsible for what he does, there can be no treatment in our field. It is not up to us to advance explanations for irresponsibility, but rather to recognize that individual responsibility must be the goal of treatment, and that unhappiness is the result and not the cause of irresponsibility.

The single basic need that all people in all cultures possess from birth to death is the need for an identity, the belief that we are someone in distinction to others. The two basic need pathways are those of love and self-worth. For a person to feel he is a success in the world, he must believe that at least one other person loves him, and that he also loves another person. He

must believe that at least one person "out there" thinks he is a worthwhile human being, and he, himself, must also think it. If a person cannot develop an identity through these two pathways, he attempts to do so through two other identity pathways, delinquency and withdrawal, or "mental illness." These pathways do lead to an identity, but a failure identity. One outstanding feature of all individuals with a failure identity is that they are lonely.

In working with an individual, we believe that unless he and the therapist are involved, he is not motivated; that in therapy and counseling, motivation and involvement, in a general way, can be considered synonymous.

Following the concepts of reality therapy, there are eight principles: (1) The relationship must be personal. (2) We must focus on behavior rather than emotions, because only behavior can be changed. (3) We must focus on the present, on what the individual is doing now, and his present attempts to succeed. (4) We must have the individual make a value judgment about what he is now doing that is contributing to his failure. (5) The individual is assisted in developing a plan to alter his behavior and plan a better course. (6) He must choose a better way and commit himself to his choice. It is from commitment that individuals develop maturity. (7) When an individual has made a commitment to change his behavior, no excuse is accepted for not following through. The therapist, in a nonjudgmental manner, assists the individual in developing a new plan rather than focusing on the reasons the old ones failed. (8) The therapist eliminates punishment, which always reinforces failure identity, and instead invokes discipline.

Through accepting responsibility for their own behavior, and acting maturely to change their behavior constructively, individuals find they are no longer lonely; symptoms begin to resolve; and they are more likely to gain maturity, respect, love, and that most important success identity.

ANNOTATED BIBLIOGRAPHY

Glasser, William. *Mental health or mental illness.* New York: Harper & Row, 1961.

In this, Dr. Glasser's first book, he describes in clear language how we function. He uses small, easily understood diagrams to show how neurotic, psychotic, and other behavior-disordered persons differ from people who function adequately. This is an excellent book for those beginning the study of psychology.

Glasser, William. *Reality therapy.* New York: Harper & Row, 1965.

In this book, Dr. Glasser describes his concept of therapy. He postulates that because of loneliness and inadequacy, most people refuse to take the responsibility to fulfill their basic needs, which he claims are love and worth. He describes how the reality therapist gets personally involved with his client, and from this warm, friendly relationship, he teaches the client that he is responsible for what he does and how to do it more responsibly. This book is a significant step in the change from psychoanalytic therapy to a therapy of personal involvement, with the emphasis on present behavior and the gaining of responsibility.

Glasser, William. *Schools without failure.* New York: Harper & Row, 1969.

In this book, Dr. Glasser applies the concepts of reality therapy to the schools. He shows how school failure causes a child to become discouraged, give up, and then begin irresponsible behavior. He describes many school practices that promote a sense of failure in the student and shows how these may be corrected through more teacher involvement, less failure, less rote instruction, more thinking, and more relevance.

Glasser, William. *The identity society.* New York: Harper & Row, 1972.

Here Glasser documents a shift in motivation that took place in the Western world shortly after World War II. Following the lead of Marshall McCluhan, he describes how people, rich and poor, shifted from goals such as security to roles such as personal identity and fulfillment. This shift has caused people to be much more demanding of what they want from life. He then discusses this motivation shift as it affects childrearing, the family, marriage, and corrections. Throughout he shows how reality therapy works most effectively with this motivational shift.

Glasser, William. *Positive addiction.* New York: Harper & Row, 1976.

In this book, Dr. Glasser sets forth the thesis that addiction can be positive or strengthening as well as negative and weakening. He describes a variety of positive addictions such as running and meditation, explains how they are achieved, and sets forth a theory of how they may be strengthening. This is a true self-help book, because through positive addiction, anyone by himself or herself can grow stronger.

CASE READING

Glasser, William. The case of Aaron. In William Glasser, *Reality Therapy,* New York: Harper & Row, 1965. Pp. 135–140.

This is one of the earlier cases reported by Glasser of an eleven-year-old boy, the therapist's first child patient. A highly obnoxious person, Aaron had been treated very permissively by prior therapists, and Glasser tried without success using the same tactics. Finding no success in this procedure, Glasser shifted suddenly to being assertive and even aggressive, something new for this spoiled child. A firm logical approach worked wonders. Part of the interest in this case is that at the time that Glasser reported his results he had not as yet formulated his reality approach, and this incident shows the growth of Glasser as a therapist and as a theorist.

REFERENCES

Bandura, Albert. *Aggression: A social learning analysis.* Englewood Cliffs, New Jersey: Prentice-Hall, 1973.

Boring, Edwin. *A history of experimental psychology.* New York: Appleton-Century-Crofts, 1950.

Déjèrine, Jules, & Gaukler, Ernst. *Psychoneurosis and psychotherapy.* Philadelphia: Lippincott, 1913.

Dreikurs, Rudolf. *The challenge of parenthood.* New York: Duell, Sloane, & Pearce, 1958.

DuBois, Paul, *The psychic treatment of mental disorders.* New York: Funk & Wagnalls, 1909.

English, J. The effects of reality therapy on elementary age children. Paper for the California Association of School Psychologists and Psychometrists, Los Angeles, California, March 1970.

Glasser, William. *Mental health or mental illness?* New York: Harper & Row, 1961.

Glasser, William. Reality therapy, a realistic approach to the young offender. *Journal of Crime & Delinquency,* April 1964, 135–44.

Glasser, William. *Reality therapy.* New York: Harper & Row, 1965.

Glasser, William. *Schools without failure.* New York: Harper & Row, 1969.

Hawes, Richard M. Reality therapy in the classroom. *Dissertation Abstracts International,* University of the Pacific, November 5, 1971, Vol. XXXII.

Kaiser, Helmuth. Emergency (Seven dialogues reflecting the essence of psychotherapy in an extreme adventure). *American Journal of Psychiatry,* 1962, 2, 97–117.

Kelly, George A. *The psychology of personal constructs.* New York: Norton, 1955.

Mainord, Willard A. Therapy 52. In Ratibor-Ray Jurjevich (Ed.), *Direct psychotherapies.* Coral Gables, Fla.: University of Miami Press, 1973, pp. 129–64.

Maslow, Abraham H. *Motivation and personality.* New York: Harper & Row, 1954.

Masters, William H., & Johnson, Virginia. *Human sexual inadequacy.* Boston: Little, Brown, 1970.

Mowrer, O. Hobart. *The crisis in psychiatry and religion.* New York: Van Nostrand, 1961.

Pratt, J. H. The home sanitarium treatment of consumption. *Johns Hopkins Hospital Bulletin.* 1906, *17,* 140–44.

Wheelis, Alan. *The desert.* New York: Basic Books, 1970.

Wolberg, Lewis R. *The technique of psychotherapy.* New York: Grune & Stratton, 1954.

Zunin, Leonard M., & Barr, Norman I. Therapy program aids servicemen's widows. *U.S. Medicine,* 1969, 6, 37–41.

Zunin, Leonard M. (with Natalie Zunin). *Contact: The first four minutes.* Los Angeles: Nash Publishing, 1972.

9

Experiential Psychotherapy[1]

EUGENE T. GENDLIN

OVERVIEW

Existential psychotherapy holds that one can change oneself in present living. One's past does not have to determine how one lives. People are not machines that work by mathematical necessity. Anxiety is not sickness but avoided possibilities of living. *Experiential* psychotherapy works with felt concreteness. This is not primarily emotion, words, or muscle movements, but a *felt sense* of the complexity of situations and difficulties.

Basic Concepts

Four basic concepts of experiential psychotherapy are: (1) experiential felt sense, (2) differentiation, (3) carrying forward, and (4) interaction.

Experiential Felt Sense. By being outwardly and inwardly quiet, one can *sense* one's whole situation at that moment. At first there may be a blank, but in a minute or less, one can feel one's body from the inside. One can sense tension, ease, joy of living, or sadness. But there are not only

---

[1] Experiential Psychotherapy is the name for the writer's own approach, which has roots in existentialism. This chapter discusses existential psychotherapy in general and experiential psychotherapy in particular.

such general sensations. One can also find a specific, highly complex sense of any particular problem or situation. This *felt sense* is not just emotion. It is not just being sad or glad. Rather, such a felt sense contains thousands of different aspects, all of them felt together. There are no words to say all that is in a felt sense. It includes the whole past leading up to the situation, all of one's experiences with it, everything one perceives about it, and much more.

Observation and research (see later) show that psychotherapy is effective only when people work directly with the felt sense of any problem. If they do not, they work only with thoughts or with already familiar emotions, without being in touch with the gigantic amount of information that is right there in the felt sense.

If one attends directly inward, trying to sense how the *whole* problem feels, a felt sense of it forms. It is much more and different from one's usual thoughts and familiar emotions. The felt sense is the body's knowledge of the problem. It is how the body is living the problem.

At first one should try to get a word or a phrase that fits the felt sense as a whole. Does it feel jumpy? Scary? Icky? Constricted? Or how does it feel? When a word or phrase fits, one can feel the rightness of it in one's body. The word or phrase provides a "handle" that helps one hold on to a felt sense for a minute or two.

If one continues to pay attention to a felt sense, *new* thoughts and *new* emotions emerge from it. The body does this on its own. The body moves a step. One can feel the felt sense ease, shift, release, and along with this shift, the new words and feelings emerge. One can directly sense oneself changing physically. Unless that happens, there has not really been any change. Thinking alone does not change one very much. By feeling the same old emotions over and over, one cannot change very much either. Therapeutic change is a bodily shifting, and when it occurs, there is no doubt about its having happened.

Differentiation. At first a felt sense is one whole. Soon it turns out to have many different facets. Sorting out some of these facets is called *differentiating*. One can never get them all, nor is that necessary. The body totals them and gives one the focal points.

The thousands of facets that are in a felt sense are not already separated. Human experiencing is not made up of already cut units like a bag of marbles. Experiencing is always a whole like a living animal, not like a bag of marbles. Therefore the specific thoughts and feelings one differentiates are not in the felt sense literally like they are when they emerge. A human being is a living activity, not a bag of thoughts, feelings, images, or *contents* of any kind.

The differentiated contents are made freshly now. The spirit, attitude, and circumstances in which one focuses inwardly have a great deal to do with what contents emerge. Of course, they are made *from* the whole of one's living including the past. But how what comes is shaped depends also on the present process.

Most theories assume that a human being is made up of certain units: ego and superego, mythological figures, anxiety bonds, drives, and so on. Existentialists and the experiential philosophy deny this. Such contents are already differentiated. It is an error to imagine already differentiated contents as if they were lying there, waiting, before one differentiates. Experiencing is capable of being differentiated so units or contents emerge, but it is never itself these contents. Experiencing as a living process is always more and different than any such contents.

Experiencing also does not stand still. It is liv*ing,* act*ing.* By living differently right now, inwardly and outwardly, one can change.

Therefore differentia*ting* itself has to be understood as an activity. By letting a felt sense form and become differentiated, one can feel a bodily change taking place. This change is called *carrying forward.*

Carrying forward. The right words for a felt sense have a physically felt effect. One can feel one's body easing slightly; a kind of inward nodding occurs. The body feels just a slight bit better because the words fit. There is a greater physical release when the felt sense becomes differentiated and new thoughts and feelings emerge. Again one can physically sense they are right.

Many thoughts may come in one's mind that lack that physical effect. These do *not* carry the bodily sense forward. Most people have accusing voices in their heads that make insulting or critical comments. One thinks, "Oh, I know what the trouble is. I'm just lazy. I could pull myself together but I won't do it." After such thoughts, the felt sense of the problem may be lost. One has nothing except the bad feeling made by the accusations.

One has to get the felt sense back again by ignoring all such voices and words that do not carry forward the felt sense. One must ask again, "What does the *whole* problem feel like, *to me?*"

Other thoughts that fail to carry forward come as well. After all, no human being has a problem without knowing quite a lot about it. All that old knowledge floats through one's head. Usually such old knowledge, however true, is useless. It makes no physical release. It does not carry the body forward.

Ignoring all those thoughts, and returning always to the felt sense, one waits.

It takes a minute or two until a thought or feeling emerges along with a physically felt effect in the felt sense. One can feel the body being carried forward. There is that physical easing, that felt release, and it is made by the emerging thought or feeling. There is not any doubt that *this* set of words or *this* specific feeling is right, at least for the moment.

It is important to know that what carries forward is right only for the moment. In a minute or two, another step of carrying forward will occur, and what one then thinks or feels might be very different. Therefore even if one does not like what just came, one receives it, welcomes it. It is a step. One is changing. One's body is being carried forward. Soon there will be another step. No major problem is solved in one step.

Carrying forward shows that what we are is not defined in a fixed way. One can experience this existentialist assertion directly when several steps of carrying forward occur, one after the other. *What* the problem seemed to be changes. *What* one found directly inside changes. Contents are made and remade in ongoing living; they are not just in us, fixed.

Without air one cannot go on breathing, without food one cannot go on eating; hence air and food carry these physical processes forward. Similarly, something from the interpersonal environment may be needed to carry one's living process forward. Similarly, speaking the right words to someone, and even to oneself, can carry one's bodily living of some situation forward.

Carrying forward is always a change. It is just that change which is implicit or prefigured in how the body is, just now, and how bodily living is stopped just now, or narrowed or blocked.

When a felt sense is carried forward, what is done or said is that which was missing and which needed release. Therefore to say exactly what one feels is also a changing of what one feels. One seems merely to be saying it, but a few moments later, one also feels in new ways.

The steps of a therapeutic process cannot be determined either by the therapist or by the patient. No prior logical decision can lead it. A perfectly right interpretation may be confusing at one point and helpful at a later point. What comes now is what must come now, what is next for the organism. By carrying forward what is implicit now, a different next step is able to come up later.

Some set of words, or some course of action, can carry forward. For example, one might find just what to do in some puzzling situation. The action can give that energy-releasing, physically felt shift of the whole felt sense. Events and other peoples' responses can also carry one forward.

Carrying forward is very different from giving in to some emotion. Carrying forward is a movement of the felt sense, and a felt sense is always wholistic. For example, if one is angry at someone, blowing up may feel good but it does not necessarily carry forward the *whole* sense of the situation. Even to get that whole sense, one must be silent for a minute or two so it can form inside. The felt sense of the whole is different from the emotion of anger. The felt sense is broader, more complex; it includes everything that is involved in this situation. When one finds a course of action that fits and releases that whole sense, only then is it carrying forward. This is what existentialists call *authentic*. Of course, there are situations in which blowing up does carry one's whole sense forward, but one must get in touch with a felt sense to know whether this is so in a given situation. That is very different from giving in to a strong familiar emotion.

It may seem puzzling that words, actions, events, and other peoples' responses can carry one's body forward and change it. There is an inherent connection between how one's body is sensed inwardly and what happens outside. This is called *interaction*.

Interaction. Any living creature *is* an ongoing interaction with its environment. Its body cannot go on living even for moments without inhaling and exhaling, exchanging energy and matter with its environment. One cannot take a living body out of its interaction with its environment and have it remain alive. Interaction is not *only* physical, it is *always* physical. When an animal is startled by something happening outside, its heart pounds and there are chemical changes inside its body. Humans are like that, too, although the external events that affect their bodies can be more complex. *We live our interpersonal, intellectual, and spiritual situations within our bodies. They are bodily interactions.*

The reader can sense physical tensions of difficulty whenever some part of this chapter is hard to grasp. Similarly, the excitement, if any, that this theory can engender will include a physical process.

The body is no mere machine. It physically lives all the complexity one can know, and more. The physical body is much more than physiology knows. It is our complex interaction of living. Therefore any problem or difficulty is also a physical constriction. Any step of solution is also a physical release.

Furthermore, the body "knows" what next step is needed. It knows that exhaling is needed when one holds one's breath. It knows food is needed when one is hungry. It requires no value judgment to decide what one needs when it is hot—one needs it to be cooler. Of course, the body's next step (for instance, needing it to be cooler) does not yet determine exactly what to do (open the window, take off one's sweater, or some other action). But the body also has in it all one has ever experienced of all circumstances (including all about windows and sweaters and all one ever experienced with the people present). The body can total together all the considerations and enable one to sense what next step will carry forward that felt sense of the whole.

Other Systems

Other therapeutic systems fall into two types. The first is the *content* type. These systems purport to say what human experience and pathology are and what contents are in a person. The systems say little about what a therapist *does*. These older theories are very valuable if used experientially to carry forward what a person concretely feels and lives. If used experientially, one would not accept any one theory; one would use all of them. They give us essential concepts and insights. Carrying forward can often occur more quickly and powerfully with these concepts. They are valuable and should be learned. But if these concepts are not used experientially, they are likely to be traps. They can set one's mind and practice in a narrow way, obstructing one's sense of the other person's fresh, actual experiencing. Such systems are the psychoanalytic, the Jungian, transactional analysis—any system that insists on certain supposedly basic contents and deals with people only through these. These systems can also be called single-theory systems.

The second type of other systems is the *single-technique* type. These systems hold that all one needs is one procedure. Among these are the person-centered, Gestalt, operant, rational-emotive, and many other therapies, each featuring just one basic procedure. These procedures may range from not very effective "techniques" such as arguing to highly powerful ones, some of which any therapist should certainly adopt.

Both types suffer from the claim to exclusiveness. One must work out one's problems by talking of infantile sexual conflicts or one does not fit psychoanalysis. One must get better with the featured technique alone, or one is a hopeless case.

These techniques can be employed effectively or ineffectively. The theories themselves do not specify how. They only say what—either what the patient should come up with or what the therapist should do. Eighty years of experience with psychotherapy have shown that one can belong to any theoretical orientation and have success or failure. Therefore the orientation is not what makes one effective. What is basic is how one uses the techniques of any orientation. In the works of Freud, there is little detail on just how to practice. Most of what Freud wrote concerns what patients experienced and why. Freud used free association and interpretation.

Highly vague statements are made about the "timing" of interpretations, but this is supposedly something intuitive that cannot be defined. *Working through* is a general phrase naming the whole process of therapeutic working; again it is something supposedly not definable. Freud said it is the most important aspect of psychoanalysis, but he did not say how to do it better. Transference is the basic tool of psychoanalysis, but how a therapist "handles" or "overcomes" it is not stated.

Similarly, Jung's works are full of valuable insights and contain a good theory of human life, but when one seeks to be instructed how to conduct therapy, very little is said. Jung specifies that the patient should negotiate with the constellated figures and should be "active" in daydreams, not much more than that.

These older systems were almost exclusively concerned with patient content, and not with therapist procedure. In contrast, the newer orientations offer little theory and center on procedures, usually one technique. One is asked to believe that this single technique is universally effective and all that is needed.

These exclusive techniques are too few, too exclusively held, one against the other. They work only some of the time. When? *When is there a therapeutic effect?* It is when the patient not only says and knows, but when there is also a directly felt experiential shift. That happens usually only if the patient works directly with a felt sense.

Throwing out all other theories would sacrifice many essential concepts. Instead, one can change how such theory is used. These theories are very valuable, but only if one always returns to life and the theory is constantly exceeded, transcended. When one succeeds in articulating words that feel right, such moments are powerful. They are a further living, often involving tears and strongly sharpened feelings. But moments later, how one articulates oneself may alter what one said earlier. The later moments may be possible only with words quite different from a different theoretical frame of reference. Therefore one should accept no content theory as giving one a picture of humans or of a given person. Rather, there must be a constant interplay between the person and the concepts. Similarly, no one set of right actions can be specified for humans, but the relation between experiencing and authentic right action can be characterized. This relation is "carrying forward."

The experiential method thus *cuts across* all theories of psychotherapy and explains why all have successes and failures. It depends on the relationship to experiencing, which may or may not have been maintained step by step.

One must reject both the translation of people into concepts and the subjection of people to a universal mechanical "technique."

Other systems also tend to render people as pure bodies *or* pure psyches. Both of these approaches can be effective, although bodily felt experiencing is not directly reached by either of them. The pure body approaches and the pure psyche approaches both know that the other side is lacking and needed. But the richness of bodily felt experiencing is missed even if one combines body and psyche, once the two are thought of separately. Felt meaning is neither muscles nor emotions, nor both together. It is the bodily felt sense of one's living in one's situations. The body systems and the psyche systems hit upon this only indirectly, because they fail to lead patients to attend directly in the right manner to the right dimensions of body life.

Yoga and Wilhelm Reich's (1949) systems work directly with the body, with muscles, movements, and postures. Such work does lead to improvements in psyche and ways of living. Both Yoga and Reich stress that while working with the body, certain psychological processes are necessary. Yoga stresses meditation. Reich urges one to "work through" the psychological and interpersonal feelings that arise when one releases certain muscles and works with one's body. Systems that work with the body directly want to consider body and psyche as one and want to work not only with muscles but also with feelings.

From the other side, insight therapies all stress that the working-through process must be more than words and thought. Intellectualization alone produces little change. Difficulties must be relived, not merely discussed or figured out (and, of course, relived differently from when they were lived originally). There has to be some kind of feeling-work, not mere think-work. However, these older systems could not say very much about how to get that to happen or even just what it is. Clearly, however, just thinking is not enough; a physically felt and lived process is needed.

Both sides are getting at something in the middle! Neither just muscles nor just thoughts really make up the crucial psychotherapeutic process. That is bodily experiencing—not just the muscle of the body, not just thoughts, but the physically felt sense of the complexity, the differentiable concreteness. The experiential system works with that concrete sensing that is physically felt and also contains implicit cognitive, perceptual, and situational complexity.

HISTORY

Precursors

Søren Kirkegaard, Wilhelm Dilthey, Edmund Husserl, Martin Heidegger, Martin Buber, Jean-Paul Sartre, and Maurice Merleau-Ponty are the major philosophers of existentialism.

Kirkegaard (*1813-55*). Kirkegaard (1974) said that if a person, while anxious, could stand the anxiety and keep from identifying with some role or definition, that person would find the true nature of what it is to be human. This is never identical with anything that can be said, or any definition, situation, or role.

Dilthey (*1833-1911*). Dilthey (1961) revolted against the view of humans in the mathematical natural sciences. He held that the life process is highly organized, and that logic is only a few patterns derived from the life process. Science cannot claim to explain and reduce life to these few thin patterns.

Husserl (*1859-1938*). Husserl (1950) rejected the notion that experience consists of sounds and colors (pure sense perceptions). If one examines experience as it is had, one hears a door slamming or sees a person or a tree, not just color and shape. It is only a theory that experience consists of bits of sound and color. What we say should not be mere theory. It should emerge directly from experience. This way of basing thought Husserl called *phenomenology*. Existentialism is phenomenological; it seeks to articulate experience as actually had, rather than inventing some theoretical scheme.

Heidegger (*1889-1976*). Heidegger (1960, 1967) begins his philosophy by showing that a human being is a "being-in-the-world." People are always already "thrown" into certain situations before they begin to reflect upon themselves. But situations and facts exist only in terms of one's living and striving. A wall is a barrier to someone who wants to cross it, but it is a protection to someone who wants a defense. By itself the wall is not a situation. It is not a fact. Facts are facts only in terms of someone who "projects a future." Some person imagines some possibility that is not yet present and wants to

bring this about. Or the person may be concerned to avoid the imagined possibility. Either way, human action is in terms of possibilities that do not yet exist. One can, of course, project countless abstract possibilities, but one can project one's own "authentic" possibilities only by sensing how one is already living in one's situations.

Heidegger says that any feeling always already includes an implicit understanding of how and why we are in each situation. Such a feeling or sense of the situation is not "stuff inside" but a sense of how one is being in the world. If one is willing to take on how one is already being, one can project new and further possibilities authentically. This means the possibilities will arise directly from oneself, from one's own being in the world. But such possibilities are not determined by logic or physical necessity. They do not follow necessarily but are spontaneous creations. Provided one begins with one's actual being in the situation as it already is, there is a radical openness about what is possible.

Buber (*1878-1965*). Martin Buber (1948) emphasized the concrete relationship process, as contrasted with knowing-about. This might be conveyed best by one of his examples:

When I was eleven . . . I used to . . . steal into the stable and gently stroke the neck of my darling, a broad dapple-grey horse. . . . I must say that what I experienced in touch with the animal was the Other, the immense otherness of the Other . . . which let me draw near and touch it. . . . I felt the life beneath my hand, it was as though the element of vitality itself bordered on my skin, something that was not I, . . . palpably the other. . . . The horse . . . very gently raised its massive head, ears flicking, then snorted quietly, as a conspirator gives a signal meant to be recognizable only by his fellow-conspirator. But once . . . it struck me about the stroking, what fun it gave me, and suddenly I became conscious of my hand

... something had changed. ... The next day when I stroked my friend's head, he did not raise his head.

Sartre (b. 1905). Sartre (1956) called the life process, which is not reducible to logical definitions, "existence." He contrasted *existence* with *essence*, the classical philosophic word that means "definition." "Existence precedes essence," an existentialist slogan, means that humans make definitions, and therefore can never be ultimately captured in them. No one is just a professor or a waiter or a homosexual or just anything that can be defined. To define is to hold static, to make a thing of human living. One can live as though one were a professor, doing only what fits that role, but this involves holding up the role and straining to hold it up. This holding up and straining is the human living that always exceeds any role. Thus not changing, as much as changing, is a life process that is more than definitions.

Existentialist philosophers are difficult to read and easily misunderstood. The word *existence* easily becomes a paradoxical abstraction; it also is always what it is not; it exceeds what one can say; it can become vague unless one remembers that it is not something one thinks, but what one is and lives.

Sartre, in his novel *Nausea* and in his philosophy (1956), calls existence "nausea." Persons who do not like themselves feel their own sense of themselves as a kind of sick feel. Sartre likes to present things negatively, to convey them strongly. He says he does not mean nausea as from spoiled meat, but the concrete sense of being alive. One feels one's existing, and this is basic to "authenticity" and "authentic relating" (Heidegger, 1960, ch. V; Sartre, 1956, p. 338).

The present author formulates existentialism in a new way. Without this "experiential" emphasis, existentialism seems negative; it tells that one cannot define humans, that one cannot hold them static, that one cannot reduce them to mathematical necessity, but existentialism does not say how to apply these negatives. Their positive use rests on direct access to one's living process beyond words and definitions. This access is through "felt sense," but that expression is here used in a highly specific way (quite different from "emotion") as defined in the section Basic Concepts.

Merleau-Ponty (1908-61). Merleau-Ponty (1962) held that the living body has the characteristics the earlier philosophers attributed to existence. The body is conceived not only in the way physiologists conceive it, but Merleau-Ponty considers our bodily concreteness as our existence. "We are in the world through our body."

Beginnings

As a therapeutic method, experiential psychotherapy must cite Carl Whitaker, John Warkentin, and Thomas Malone as precursors, as well as Otto Rank, Jesse Taft, Frederick Allen, and Carl Rogers.

Rank held that:

As long as one makes the feeling experience as such, in which the whole individuality is revealed, the sole object of the explanation and understanding, one finds one's self on sure ground, and also, in my opinion, insures the only therapeutic value, that is, to allow the patient to understand himself in an immediate experience which, as I strive for it in the therapeutic process, permits living and understanding to become one. (Rank, 1950, p. 26)

Jesse Taft (1953) and Frederick Allen (1942) emphasized the interaction process between patient and therapist. They sought to work with each problem not as a discussion about it, but as the way in which the patient manifested that problem in the very interaction with the therapist right there and then.

Carl Rogers (see chapter 4, this volume) sought to respond to the client's momentary "feeling"—a word, however, that was never made quite clear. Rogers would not only carefully repeat the crux of each of the client's messages—an essential of all good communication that should always be practiced—but would also emphasize the feeling aspect of the communication. Rogers discovered if one does respond to feelings that there is movement. The next thing that comes to the person is not necessarily what follows logically from what was last said. Rather, it follows from the feeling of what was said. Experiential philosophy would say of this that exactly attending to what one just now is changes or moves that. Steps come from the felt edge.

Carl A. Whitaker and Thomas P. Malone (1953) wanted their therapeutic method to move beyond mere verbal discussion and conceptual insight. Using their own spontaneous fantasies as well as genuine emotional reactions toward the patient, their method made for a very rich, impactful, personal interaction.

Ludwig Binswanger (1962) developed *Daseinsanalyse,* which can be translated as *existential analysis,* or the analysis of one's human condition. The word *analysis* here often means not a therapeutic process, but a theoretical analysis.

Medard Boss (1963) carried existential analysis further and articulated specific interpersonal patterns of malfunction.

Rollo May (1967; May, Angel, & Ellenberger, 1958) is the founder of existential psychotherapy in America. He emphasized direct responsibility for one's own life. May courageously reasserted the human person's independence in the face of pseudodeterminist factors that seem to compel one to draw back and avoid life. For May anxiety appears in two roles. Its valuable role is to open possibilities of living differently by facing what makes one anxious. Its painful and despaired role is to avoid these possibilities and attempt to live narrowly and resignedly. In the latter case, the anxiety is the mark of untimely deadness, of a too-narrow existence. The term *existential neurosis* characterizes many more people in our time than Freud's "classical" neurotic patterns. May developed a therapy in which the main focus is on the unmet challenges of life. He did not make it fully clear just how one moves from avoiding to meeting these challenges, although some of the way is marked by the "valuable" rather than "sick" role assigned to anxiety. May holds that there is a positive life-enhancing "daemon" in a person that one must trust.

Viktor Frankl (1965) reached America in translation somewhat later. His "logotherapy" (the word *logos* roughly means "meaning") is concerned with an inherent need for meaning and values in a human life. Having personally suffered and survived the concentration camps and the loss of his family, his conviction that humans can affirm life in spite of suffering and the loss of everything and everyone deserves respect. Existentialism's call for freedom despite circumstance often seems applicable only to fortunate people. Frankl disproves that and is able to aid the patient to find meaning and value.

Experiential philosophy (Gendlin, 1962, 1969a, 1973) is concerned with various relations between symbols and experiencing. Words, thoughts, and other symbols (also actions) can carry experiencing forward or fail to do so, and in various ways. There is a new kind of logic.

The existentialists do not say how one recognizes when some thought or action is authentic and when it is not. Yet just this is their central principle. One application of E. T. Gendlin's philosophy makes it possible to define an authentic "carrying forward" in an observable way. Among other results, research measurement of carrying forward during therapy became possible (Gendlin et al., 1968).

The experiential method lets one use the power that symbolizing gives, and yet returns again to the experiential "felt meaning" one wishes to articulate. One does not remain inarticulate but neither does one get caught in conceptual boxes. One can keep whatever conceptualizing showed, and yet return to an experiential sense that is capable of further steps that do not necessarily follow logically from the conceptualization.

Gendlin's theory of personality change (1964) applies the philosophy (Gendlin, 1962) to psychotherapy.

Current Status

Experiential psychotherapy today includes therapists who think in experiential terms, as well as some who employ only one older theory but do so in an experiential way. Many therapists in the older groups hyphenate their orientation name, for example, "Jungian-Experiential." Not the vocabulary but the way it is used unites experiential therapists. A therapist is "experiential" if the emphasis is on the lived and felt steps of change in the patient. Words are only tools for getting such steps. Any theory might help to find the words and interactions that fit and make a change. Any theoretical words are instantly discarded, at least for the moment, if they fail to carry forward (Friedman, 1976; Mullan & Sanguillano, 1964).

How would a therapist employ a theory during therapy in an old-fashioned, non-experiential way? There are certain pitfalls such a therapist can fall into.

For example, therapist O, practicing within an older theory, figures out the patient in terms of that theory. Certain conclusions follow from the theory. The therapist tells the patient these conclusions. The patient denies them. They argue. Time is lost. The patient wants to bring up and explore certain other feelings, but the therapist claims to know what these feelings mean. The patient does not explore these feelings freshly. Instead, the therapist convinces the patient that the theoretical interpretation is right. The patient goes home and tries to make the interpretation fit. The patient finds much turmoil inside. The interpretation does not fit but much is stirred up anyway. The therapist, next time, cannot hear what was stirred up. The patient's feelings are subtle and personal, and the therapist is too convinced to listen with the kind of step-by-step care that would be needed to differentiate them. The patient also is not very able at being in touch with these as yet unclear edges. Neither patient nor therapist gets in touch with what is really there, and they do not carry it forward. Therapy of this sort is sometimes hurtful, sometimes an interesting discussion between two people, one of whom (the therapist) cannot listen very well.

In contrast, therapist E, practicing experientially, using many theories but none of them fixedly, has a comment and expresses it. The patient denies it. The therapist instantly says something like, "Never mind, what I said couldn't have been just right. Sense inwardly to see what you *do* find there." There is a silence for a while. The patient then says what formed there, inwardly, just then. Now the therapist finds a quite different theory providing words to help articulate what the patient just found. Or perhaps no theory but simple common words will carry forward. The therapist helps the patient hold on to, and differentiate, what is directly sensed just now. As a result, further changes and shifts occur in the patient. Quite often different words will help articulate these further changes. In this way, the patient gets the benefit of all the therapist's knowledge without getting trapped in any one view.

PERSONALITY

Theory of Personality

Experiential theory holds that body and psyche are one system, developing in interaction with other people. Human infants are born with the brain-half which functions in speech larger than the other half. Body structure at birth implies that a language will be learned. What language is learned depends on the group the child is born into. Similarly, the infant will have some kind of sexual development but which of the great variety of patterns will develop depends upon the culture. Yet, these cultural patterns are *bodily* developments.

Because a human life process is a cultural process, it atrophies if there is not social responsibility and social action. Humans inherently have ethical, communal, social dimensions. The specific content or code of action is not specified, but must be devised by each person in an actual historical context. Ethics is not an imposition of values on people. Rather values are implicit in any experiencing and include social dimensions. Human living is inherently with others, not only in its origins, but also in the significance and scope of one's developing into a unique person. Even the hermit "away from" others is a meaningful figure to the people he left and to those who bring him food. His mediations and significance are in-

terhuman and are for him a human life of world significance and an example for others. No one can really "drop out of society"; to drop out is a message to others and a social act.

The person is simultaneously bodily, social, and psychological in every moment and bit of experiencing. Physiology, sociology, and psychology are different "levels of analysis," but it has been a mistake to keep them separated.

For example, schizophrenia has been found to be associated with certain chemical differences in the body, but there is also a higher incidence of schizophrenia in poor neighborhoods, and there are also distinct family factors that occur more frequently in the childhoods of schizophrenics. This is a puzzle to those who want only one or another of these three levels of explanation. But any person is always bodily, and social, and psychological. To study the person apart from the community, to conceive of "personality" as purely internal machinery, is an error.

Early studies of the drug LSD found that it creates paranoid psychoses. Scientists studied the drug by isolating the subject in a small, whitewashed room and observing the subject through a peephole. Under these conditions, the drug regularly produced paranoid psychoses. Why then did many other people report different effects? It was because under different conditions the same drug produces different results. With music and friends, the drug is different. Same drug, same human body—why not the same results? Because the human body is also a "being-with." The body is not only the structure physiologists study but also a functioning process, a living-in in an interhuman context. Chemotherapy drugs also appear to produce different results when given to someone functioning in a world of people, work, and love from what they produce when given to patients isolated in a hospital.

Having shown personality to have physiological and interpersonal components, "neurosis" can now be discussed as both social and as involving a narrowing of the bodily experiencing process.

Rollo May (1967; May, Angel, & Ellenberger, 1958) in the 1950s found much "existential neurosis" in people, that is, an inability to sense oneself and life from one's own inside and with zest in living. *Existential neurosis* is the inability to "own" one's life and conduct, to be "autonomous" (May, Angel, & Ellenberger, 1958) and "authentic," to have direct access to an inner basis and source of actions and choices. From this lack of autonomy, a sense of emptiness, worthlessness, despair, and anxiety results. There is a grayness, a pervasive disappointment with life, and a loss of meaning. Loss of meaning results not from merely looking at what is happening, but from a failure to live further.

T. Hora also views *neurosis* this way:

Existential anxiety drives man to seek manifold modes of protection and avenues of escape. Such defensive strivings lead to inauthentic modes of existence and disorganization of the personality, that is, mental disorders of various kinds and degrees. Defensive strivings cripple man's existence by robbing him of his freedom and creative spontaneity. Seeking to escape from the dread of losing his life, man lives in dread of losing his defenses. He clings to them rigidly and becomes increasingly immobilized by them. Finally, that which he clings to, clings to him. (Hora, 1962)

Ronald Laing (1967) views *conformity* as a pressure against feeling real social concern for others, a pressure to ignore experience. People deny most of what goes on inside. In many family systems, this social repression of inward experience holds members within a system of roles unreal for them all.

Psychological maladjustment is not the classical neurosis, nor any "bad content" inside, but the loss of touch with one's inward experiencing.

Experiential theory does not yield a classification of neuroses or a catalog of pathological experiences. Not *what* is experienced, but *how* one proceeds from it determines whether anything is optimally human or a malady. What *is* a malady is living by the values of others, without being in touch with one's own flow of life.

Some degree of this failure to carry forward can be found in anyone. One need only ask in what situations one becomes tense, engages in certain repetitious scenarios, or behaves in ways one does not understand and deplores. In any such instances, one is not living and sensing the unique richness of the specific situation. Rather one is repeating a thin outline, a "frozen whole" that is the same in all instances and is not modified by each new situation (Gendlin, 1964).

What one has experienced in the past should aid one to experience the next event, but not because the next event is like the past. Rather, the past is reshaped as it functions implicitly in new experience. One experiences the new experience, not the old. But in neurosis, the same old structure is experienced, not what is going on now.

If neurosis can be considered a being out of touch with one's potentially rich, ongoing experiential flow, psychosis is an even more radical narrowing of this flow. Experiments with drugs and isolation chambers have shown that a psychosis can be induced in nearly anyone. How the drugs do this is not yet known, but if one is with people in a close and trusting relationship, the effect of a drug is likely not to be a psychosis. Similarly, in the sensory-deprivation experiments in which almost all sensory input is cut off, one is isolated. How is one to understand this connection between isolation and induced psychosis?

It is a basic concept of experiential theory that experiencing is an interactional process with the environment. In isolation there is less interaction and therefore less experiencing. But experiencing is also the interpretive mass, the sense one has of what is going on, and the sense that interprets words and events. In isolation one therefore loses some of the capacity to interpret what words and events mean. Along with this is lost one's sense of self and sense of ownership of one's own body. A narrowed ongoing interactive flow of experiencing therefore involves depersonalization and inability to interpret.

With narrowed experiencing, any bit of event has maximized results. In psychosis, hypnosis, dreams, and drug states, any event, sound, or view is therefore amplified. In normal functioning, such a bit would be part of much other ongoing interaction with the external environment. So much would not be determined by just one bit of event.

What is termed *psychosis* is a narrowed manner of experiencing, not pathological contents inside a person. Contents are being *newly* and differently made in such states; they are not things inside that come out.

No doubt a "cure" for psychosis will involve bodily factors, much as drugs can bring it about now. But a "cure" will also involve social and psychological factors. The interpersonal isolation into which some people are driven, or into which they retire, almost certainly has much to do with psychosis. Some as yet unknown drug might conceivably reverse the bodily

condition made by isolation, but then there would still need to be different people and life circumstances so the person would not become narrowed and isolated again.

Personality is not so much *what* one is (the content nouns) as *how* (the process verbs) one carries oneself forward in living, feeling, responding, and relating. The quest to "find out what I am" begins to change and carry further what one is. Personality is not stuff inside. Well functioning is a "zig-zag" (Gendlin, 1967) between outward and inward attention so one's outward speech and action can carry forward the inwardly sensed whole.

Variety of Concepts

The Freudian and similar views want to make personality into a system of distinct factors. Since one is only aware of a few such factors at any one time, all the others must be placed in a mysterious realm of which the person is not conscious. This realm is said to contain clearly formed thoughts and contents of consciousness such as ideas and wishes. But these contents are clear not to the person, but rather to some second person within the person. Sartre (1956) has given a good critique of the absurdity of the person inside the person, that "censor" who must be conscious of everything to be able to decide what the person should not be conscious of. Such a theory makes two conscious people out of one.

The contrary view that there is no unconscious at all is too simple. The observations that led to the theory of the unconscious must be accounted for. This can be done best if a living person is not viewed as so many contents, ideas, wishes, needs, but instead as a complex experiencing process. If the complexity is viewed as *uncompleted* and as *implicit* in feeling, there need not be another level on which thousands of different aspects are perfectly clear to some person inside the person.

Experiential theory holds that the unconscious is the body. Many aspects of unconscious processes, only some of which can be differentiated at one time, function implicitly in bodily experiencing (see "Basic Concepts"). They shape any given bit of speech or behavior. When people differentiate one of the many aspects that shaped a bit of speech or behavior, the aspect is then *in retrospect* said to have been "unconscious."

Many theories assign to family and childhood a determining role in the development of personality and psychopathology. Existential therapists would not agree that a person *must* be as upbringing has made the person, since further living can be a remaking of the person. The responsibility for how one is cannot be put upon the past. What does determine our "determinism" is our present yielding to our fears of other people, our present avoidance of places and circumstances in which we would change, our present refusal to accord our inner feelings attention and respect.

Experiential psychotherapists do find childhood events entering into therapy. One lives the present *with one's past.* But the effect of the past is not that of mechanical forces. Rather, one must live it forward, and thereby it also changes. One lives present events with the whole maze of implicit facets. An event is, to an extent, the person's past; yet the event now also changes how that past is with us. Therefore the person's past and childhood are involved, implicitly, in the experiencing of the present event. Patients in psychotherapy usually find that *both* their childhood *and* their present living are involved in a given situation. Both must be reworked insofar as they are implicit in the experiential process now.

One can say that one needs to work only with the present, but this can very definitely include crying now about what happened long ago, or having compassion now with oneself for having gone through what happened long ago. One experiences the present with one's past. Both are changed if there is growth. It may sound odd that the past is changed in the present, but it is, insofar as the past functions now.

Existentialists consider *anxiety* not the cause but the symptom of poor living. Anxiety is not what stops one, but exactly the opposite. It indicates an opening for radical change.

Existentialists similarly view *guilt* not as a cause of neurosis, something sick one ought not to have, but as the person's sense of missed life challenges and avoided encounterings of others. Guilt marks missed opportunities, violated sensitivities that need to be part of holistic valuing and carrying forward. (See "Basic Concepts.")

Existentialism emphasizes the awareness that one will die. The life one now clutches so anxiously will be lost anyway. Once this fact is truly met and accepted, there is a freedom for doing something with life between now and its end. Again, this is not so much a theoretical statement as a freer way of living. While one experiences that one's *death* will come, one is unlikely to be inhibited by anything petty. One lives beyond the everyday concerns and stoppages.

PSYCHOTHERAPY

Theory of Psychotherapy

The theory of psychotherapy is discussed under two headings: (1) the *planes of therapeutic work,* and (2) the *manner of process.*

Planes of Therapeutic Work. Therapy can occur on a number of *planes:* One can work with the body, with the situation, with interpersonal relationships and feelings, and with felt sense. There are these four planes because human beings have these four kinds of "environment." Human living is an interaction process. It is interaction with all four of these environments.

There is a *physical* environment that includes the physical surroundings, air, water, food, and also the body itself. The body is the environment for the cells and tissues within the body. Therapeutic change can therefore take place on the bodily plane as one works with diet, breathing, muscles, as in Yoga and Reich's (1949) system.

Humans also have a *behavioral* environment. The structure of situations, where one works, when one gets up and goes to sleep, have a lot to do with how one lives. Changing the order in which one does one's tasks, for example, can make a lot of difference. Getting out of the house, finding places to go and new people to meet, may sometimes make more change than therapy on other planes. Behavior modification therapies work on this plane.

Humans have their main living in interaction with *other persons,* and human feelings and emotions are all about that. Feelings may seem things inside, but when they are articulated, they turn out to be toward other people, past or current. An individual's personality largely consists of patterns of relating and feelings toward others. Therefore most therapies work on this plane, with the patient's emotions and ways of relating to the therapist and to others.

There is also a fourth plane, which is new to most people. It is the plane on which a felt sense can form *if one attends there.* It requires some practice to find

this new "space" or "environment." One can sense the body from the inside and that creates a new plane. At first one may sense only some vague tension or ease "there." A felt sense of any problem or concern can then form there.

The felt sense is a totaling by the body of all relevant considerations from all three of the other planes. But the advantage of the felt sense is that it gives us all these considerations in one whole. In it the aspects of the other three planes are not already cut up. When one of the other three planes is considered by itself, its contents are already formed, cut up into this and that, food or water, this muscle, this place and time and task, these people and these emotions. In contrast, a felt sense will lead to quite new aspects of the other three planes, because the felt sense includes them in an implicit way, rather than as cut up contents.

One can work with one of the other planes in relation to a felt sense. One need only let a felt sense form quite often, between steps on one of the other planes. Therefore when an experiential therapist works on the other planes, this is not simply "eclecticism," the mere sticking together of divergent methods. The experiential therapist uses the other planes differently and systematically, because they are each put in relation to a felt sense, from which one then returns to the other plane with new discriminations.

Existentialism puts the emphasis on the making of contents from what is at first directly lived but not yet defined. In experiential focusing, one can move from anything defined on the other three planes to where a felt sense can form. When it does, one can move from it to new definable aspects on the other planes.

Therapists of other orientations do sometimes succeed in obtaining broad personality change even though they work on only one of these planes. This is possible because there is, after all, only one organism. Hence if one works on one plane, the body's living on the other plane can also change. But we do not yet understand just when they all change, and when not.

It is more effective to work on all four planes. With some individuals, there can be considerable movement on all of them. Some individuals will long be stopped on one of these planes; yet they experience immediate change when they work on a new plane. It is really only the current groupings of theories and therapists that divide these planes. In the person they co-exist. There is therefore no reason why one should opt to work on only one of them. Unless major satisfying life changes are achieved on the given plane, one is well advised to work also on the other planes.

The Manner of Process. What kind of living is going on matters more than what is being said. If the manner of the living process, just now, is the same as usual, the result will not be change, even if the words are all about being different.

Consider this report from an experiential therapist:

In the first interview, right at the start, the client said, "It's always very important to me, in any situation, if I'm going to be the active one, or the other person. You have to tell me, right now before we start. Are you going to be active, or am I?" Usually, as a therapist, I don't answer questions like that. But he was very insistent and I almost told him that, of course, he had to be the active one here. But instead, I said, "You're feeling an urgent need to get this started, and you are pushing on me to declare myself." From there he could further explore his feeling and we could also confront each other, each standing his ground.

In this example, if the therapist had said, "You will be the active one," *the manner of process* between them would

have been the opposite of the words. In telling the client how things are going to be here, the therapist would have been active, the client passive.

Instead, the therapist was aware that the client was being quite active, in demanding an answer, while of course letting himself in for falling into the passive role by asking the therapist to decide. The therapist emphasized the active aspect of the moment, the client's demanding and pushing on him.

The therapist might have said, "You are giving me a chance to decide and make you passive." Had the therapist pointed out, in this critical way, that the patient was asking him to decide, the patient would have been passive, getting caught, being seen before he could see himself.

The example is illuminating because of the neat contradiction between the words and the manner of experiencing that was possible here. But it is not a matter of phrasing this or that response. The whole therapy would not have been spoiled, whatever answer the therapist made here. What matters is the overall manner of experiencing during most of the interviews.

In the above example, the manner of the process was either active or passive for the client. Other differences in manner might be welcoming or rejecting, expansive or constricting, outreaching or withdrawing, and many other qualities. The manner of the process determines the contents that will form and the outcome.

Here is another example:

One client complained of a persistent feeling of tension in his chest. The therapist said, "Let yourself feel everything that goes with that tension, all of its meaning and feeling quality." (This was an invitation to the client to let a felt sense form.) Several times the client tried but failed to let himself get closer to it. "I hate it," he said, in explanation of why it was difficult for him to feel all that went with the tension. The therapist said,

"You have to approach it in a friendly way. Welcome it in so we can ask what all goes with it." This time the method succeeded and the client sat silently for about a minute. When he spoke again, he said, "It's funny, but when I welcome it, I feel it dissolving."

It seems mysterious. Why should *it* dissolve just when he was welcoming it in? But *it,* the content, was made by a process. The process that made the tension content was his nonwelcoming, self-condemning attitude toward most of his own feelings and his harsh manner of process with himself and others. When he altered *the manner of process,* the content was also instantly different.

One client once said: "I want to be someone I could look up to." He imagined himself different, but his manner of imagining was still one of staying as he was and looking up to this new self as if it were someone else. He was not changing his usual manner of process.

Another client had dreamt that he was given a beautiful, elegant, and energetic horse. He wanted very much to climb on this horse, as the dream ended. In his therapy hour, he tried over and over to imagine himself on the horse, but instead always found himself looking at the horse. The therapist said, "Let's both stand up." When they were standing, the therapist asked the client to *be* the horse. "Imagine that you are on stage, this is a children's play, you are in the costume of a great big horse. Let your body move, now, as if you were." Only then did the manner of his process assume the energetic and forward-moving quality the image of the horse had indicated.

Most people's effort to change themselves is carried on in such a way that the very effort only duplicates the problem. The above examples all illustrate this. It is quite natural. After all, who is making the effort? It is the given person. In what way

will the effort be made? Probably in the usual way in which that person approaches things. But what is the person trying to change? That very way. Most of our efforts to change ourselves fail because although we may think all sorts of new ideas, the manner of the process is still the old one. Therefore its results will be the same old contents, even if the words and thoughts are of something new.

Effective therapy requires some way to institute a new manner of process. This is possible if another human being responds in new ways and thereby makes the ongoing interaction different from what one usually experiences.

In focusing, too, there is a different manner of process. By welcoming and accepting whatever comes, one lives openly, expansively, actively, gently, courageously. The *manner* of the focusing process makes for some minutes of living that change one from one's usual self-critical, rejecting, constricted, avoidant, over-controlled ways. Focusing instructions achieve this indirectly. If one tells people to be accepting, they usually condemn themselves for being so condemning. If one tells them to relax, they become more tense from the frustration of being unable to relax. If one tells them to stop trying to control every feeling, they try to control their tendency to control things. This is no help. The same manner of process continues.

Focusing instructions, instead of telling people to do something that only invites their same manner once again, tells them something totally different they can do. They are asked to pay attention and wait, in such a way that a felt sense can form. It will form, if one waits, sensing down inside. The body will do it. One lives in the body's own manner, rather than in the usual ways. But the body's manner of living during the formation of a felt sense is all those good ways people would have argued are impossible for them.

The changed manner of process continues as one allows the felt sense to become differentiated. One receives and accepts, with some kind of interest, whatever comes up. At first, what comes may seem quite unlovely, but soon it will change. Why? Because the manner of the process is already different.

Psychotherapy is based on the assumption that if one talks about, and becomes aware of, one's unlovely aspects, these will change. The ordinary person wonders why this would be so. One would expect only more trouble from so much attention to undesired aspects. Psychotherapists know that if one examines these, they change. But there has not been a good explanation why they do. Indeed, sometimes they do not change! They change only if the *manner* of the process of examining and becoming aware is new and changed. The eventual outcome of a process is like the manner of that process.

There are differences in manner of process both inwardly and in the interaction between two people. A constricting, threatening argument in which neither person has the ease and safety to listen to the other rarely leads to good results. The contents that will come up are generated by the living process now! If one senses the present manner of process to be negative, there is not much use in expecting good contents.

On the other hand, if one can remain and respond peaceably, both to one's own reactions, whatever they are, and to the other person's, if one can give the other person room for whatever comes up, however unlovely, then what will eventually come up will be helpful. This is so even if the content of this moment is undesirable, threatening, disappointing, and even if intellectually one can see no solution.

In society one is usually taught to respond in kind. If there is no trace of ease or caring in the other person, one is not expected to respond with ease or caring. But this is a very reactive and unoriginal way of living. It means that if the manner of process is poor, one must leave it that way and engage in it that way. On the contrary, one can originate a different manner of process. It is not always easy, but it is much better to strive for that than to struggle with the contents while the manner of process is negative.

In psychotherapy, too, it is more important how a therapist responds than just what the words or theory are. If the patient is made to be passive, lectured, given insights that surprise and do not fit, interrupt the patient's own inward development—that manner of process will determine the outcome of therapy much more strongly than the usefulness of this or that insight. People usually pay attention to *content,* to *what* is being said. It is valuable to sense the manner of process that is going on in oneself and in the other person. If the kind of living going on is not good, expansive, acceptant, one must work on changing that. If it is, no matter how bad the content sounds, it will improve.

When the content changes, one looks backward and thinks the good content must always have been there. When the manner of process is poor and there is no change, one blames the bad contents in the person. Both are false. Contents are not in there as such. A vastly complex mesh of not separate facets is there. What emerges as defined content depends on the manner of process.

There are a number of ways to work with the experiencing of a person.

Experiential Focusing. Focusing

FOCUSING MANUAL

. . . .

This is going to be just to yourself. What I will ask you to do will be silent, just to yourself. Take a moment just to relax . . . . 5 seconds. All right—now, just to yourself, inside you, I would like you to pay attention to a very special part of you . . . .
Pay attention *to that part where* you usually feel sad glad or scared. 5 seconds. Pay attention to that area in you and see how you are now.
See what comes to you when you ask yourself, "How am I now?" "How do I feel?" "What is the main thing for me right now?"
Let it come, in whatever way it comes to you, and see how it is.

. . . .
30 seconds or less

. . . .
If, among the things that you have just thought of, there was a major personal problem which felt important, continue with it. Otherwise, select a meaningful personal problem to think about. Make sure you have chosen some personal problem of real importance in your life. Choose the thing which seems most meaningful to you.

. . . .
10 seconds

. . . .
1. Of course, there are many parts to that one thing you are thinking about—too many to *think* of each one alone. But, you can *feel* all of these things together. Pay attention there where you usually feel things, and in there you can get a sense of what *all of the problem* feels like. Let yourself feel *all of that.*

. . . .
30 seconds or less
. . . .

2. As you pay attention to the whole feeling of it you may find that one special feeling comes up Let yourself pay attention to that one feeling.

. . . .
1 minute

. . . .
3. Keep following one feeling. Don't let it be *jus* words or pictures—wait and let words or picture come from the feeling.

. . . .
1 minute

. . . .
4. If this one feeling changes, or moves, let it d that. Whatever it does, follow the feeling and pa attention to it.

. . . .
1 minute

. . . .
5. Now, take what is fresh, or new, in the feel of i *now* . . . . . . and go very easy.
Just as you feel it, try to find some new word or pictures to capture what your present feeling is all about. There doesn't have to be anything that you didn't know before. New words are best but old words might fit just as well. As long as you now find words or pictures to say what i fresh to you now.

. . . .
1 minute

. . . .
6. If the words or pictures that you now have make some fresh difference, see what that is. Let the words or pictures change until they feel just right in capturing your feelings.

. . . .
1 minute

. . . .
Now I will give you a little while to use in any way you want to, and then we will stop.

Figure 9.1

means attending to a felt sense. The client cannot do that if there are no silences. Therefore if silences do not occur naturally, the therapist asks the client to remain quiet inwardly as well as outwardly. If instead the client continues to speak, the therapist first responds to what is said and then asks again for silent focusing.

Gendlin (1969b; Gendlin et al., 1968) has developed focusing instructions with silent periods between. Sometimes they are not given all at once but more in-

formally, one at a time during psychotherapy.

Focusing is like asking the felt-sense questions. One leaves the questions unanswered until something comes directly from the felt sense. (See Figure 9.1.) In focusing one accepts whatever comes in all its *uniqueness.* Most people miss their own uniqueness. They label and categorize themselves and others. For example, people frequently call certain ways of theirs "lazy." They call some of their feelings "self-pity." If one examines these commonly used labels, one can see they are purely external viewpoints. From inside there is no such thing as "lazy," only an experiential complexity of why one does not want to do something. "Self-pity" is only an external assessment. The phrase implies there is no validity in how one feels. In therapy people must credit their unique reactions, perceptions, and ways of living their situations, and they must differentiate felt sense to find these.

Sometimes a person says, "I am afraid there is nothing inside me." This is said when a person has long lived without attending inwardly, without experiencing to find anything valid or valuable there. Of course, this very fear and these hesitations and the sense of nothing being there are themselves the experiencing of that moment. One asks: "What does this 'empty' feel like?" or "What is the whole feeling that goes with being scared there is nothing inside me?"

The therapist accords validity to the client's unique feelings and the client's implicit sensing of any situation. This sense may change but just now it is what is here, and there is a validity in it.

The client is responsible for evaluation. The client's own demand for change guides the therapy. But how is one to know what is one's own demand for change, as distinct from the expectations of others and society? Only in a person's felt sense can there be an *own direction*.

In a felt sense, there is not only malaise or pain or construction; one also senses the expansion that would come from living more freely. This type of therapy does not lead the patient to "adjust to society," but instead seeks to carry forward the incipient implicit direction the person can sense. Usually the person has given up this own sense of direction because of various pressures and fears. But even if the person freely seeks such an *owned* direction, it may not be there immediately. A wholistic felt sense must first be allowed to form. Then a direction of fuller, free living and owned values will be implicit in it. Letting a felt sense form, and differentiating it, is *focusing*.

Relational Encounter. How would an experiential therapist work with the relationship? The therapist attends to the ongoing living of both people.

1. The therapist attends not only to the client's words but to how they are said and how the client is living in this moment. This means observing the person's face, body, voice, gestures, and taking the person in much more broadly than verbally. One must also ask oneself: What is the client doing or trying to do in saying this? How is the client approaching the problem? How is the client relating to the therapist? Can therapist and client work on what they are doing together?

2. Therapists must also confront their own feelings, reactions, fears, embarrassments, stuck points, angers, impatiences—whatever is felt, and must sense whether and how these are related to the present interaction with the client. Sometimes the therapist should directly express any of these, knowing that whatever is felt by one party in an interaction is also in some sense relevant to the other. It may not as yet be clear just how it is relevant. There is often a willingness to "risk oneself." However vulnerable such expressions may make the therapist, only an open interaction can broaden living—the attenuation or stoppage of which is the essence of psychological ills. If the client's interaction (which is to say the client's experiencing) is to move past its stoppages, the therapist—who is the person just now being lived with—must allow the interaction to be open and to be carried forward. If the therapist stops interactions, or lets

them remain stopped, how can the client find this situation one in which experiencing moves beyond stoppages?

The therapist may find what to respond to either by attending sensitively to the client's momentary living or to the therapist's own. Of course, the assumption is that the therapist wants to help. Within this positive commitment the direct encountering of moments that involve anger, boredom, and so forth will help. Just expressing negative feelings at people does not help, when not in such a broader context of positively felt aims.

Seemingly threatening or negative aspects of interaction are not the only ones that are openly encountered and allowed their implicit steps of interaction. The same is true of positive feeling, rushes of care and admiration, warmth and liking. These are too frequently avoided or attenuated by social habit. The therapist would openly express not some topic heading ("I feel bored with you" or "I feel some real warmth for you"), but more of the texture of intricacies one always finds in any actual experience, something perhaps about one's hesitancy in expressing it, or just how it does and does not apply.

Truthfulness is vital in an existential encounter. The client cannot live with some imagined therapist who is not here, only with the one who is. Whatever the ways it might be nice for the therapist to be, these must be discarded if the therapist in fact cannot be that way. What the therapist is may not be wise or good or the best that can be imagined, but what counts is whether the therapist is willing to be lived with. One can only live with how the therapist actually is—which certainly can include wishing that one felt otherwise, but must include how one actually feels, and has just reacted. Fortunately therapy depends on the openness and honesty that

makes the interacting possible. It does not depend on goodness and wisdom.

Experiential therapists do not use the word *technique,* because it sounds mechanical, as if the technique does the therapy. Techniques used mechanically are usually ineffective and confusing. Not the technique but the kind of living occurring will be effective. If the person is made the passive object of some kind of manipulation, that will be more determinative of the result than the technique. Any technique can be used experientially, if both persons' authentic experiencing is made the basis of how it is used.

For example, focusing instructions may seem to be a technique. They should be given informally. One should listen to the person's reactions in between. During the silence, it is good for the person giving the instructions to focus as well. It makes for a good climate. Most other techniques can also be used in this open, responsive way.

Mechanisms of Psychotherapy

The word *mechanisms* does not fit people any more than *technique.* There are not mechanisms because the person is not mechanical. Mechanism of therapy usually means exactly what makes the change. Existentialists say that what a person is, is made by the living the person does. Hence a person changes only through more and different living. This is seemingly circular: How does the person come to live differently? The answer is: by living differently. Earlier it was shown that the *manner of process* determines the content.

The question of change is answered if one recognizes that the psychotherapy process itself is the further living that makes the person different. The *mechanisms* of psychotherapy are the ways in which, because of the therapist, the patient's living is immediately different. One person can make an authentic encounter for both, even when the other would not have done that. One person living expressively one side of an interaction, differentiating one side of it, also openly differentiates the other person's living. Both people are, after all, living one and the same interaction process with each other. What one person is open about does not go on only in that person. It goes on with the other and in the other as well. Being honest about oneself in an interaction also opens up for the other whatever is happening.

Of course, what the therapist does and says will not be the only way to articulate the interaction with the client. The client will soon join in and articulate it openly from the other side. However, even if there is no overt communication (as with mute patients during schizophrenia), an authentic process of interaction can nevertheless be made for both with only one person talking (Gendlin, 1967).

A chief responsibility of the therapist is to engender concrete interaction and to share openly one side of it. There are always many implicit aspects of any moment's interaction that can be carried forward. The other chief responsibility is to respond to, and stay in touch with, the client's experiencing as far as the client can articulate it. The client's articulations do not cancel out the therapist's, but neither are they made doubtful by ·differences between them. Each stands on its own. One person's open articulation of experiencing with another person also articulates the other person's experiencing.

This "mechanism" of change can be seen at work both in therapy interaction and in focusing. During focusing, one's manner of experiencing is already different, before the content changes. For example, although one may not be able to

live courageously and openly in the world, one does live in that manner when one allows the coming of all feelings. Although one may not know how to change some narrowness or stoppage, in the very letting come and letting be, one is, just then, living beyond one's usual narrow way. Because one lives in a new manner during the first step of focusing, a little later a second step, a felt shift, and new feelings emerge.

The exact mechanism of change is a bit of living in a new manner. Changed contents result.

APPLICATIONS

Problems

The experiential approach can anchor any concepts by attending to one's felt sense. For example, religious vocabulary, if not used experientially, can replace or constrict experientially sensed meaning. Instead, religious vocabulary can articulate experienced spiritual significances. By the experiential method, one can articulate specific aspects of felt experiencing in the cosmic context. Any vocabulary can be grounded, by giving each concept a relation to specific experienced aspects.

There is also a method of political freedom implied in the experiential method. It leads to a different *kind* of social movement that pays maximal attention to *how* people are in it, rather than just its conceptualized program. Not that purposes and program are unimportant, but they can only be realized from how people are together. The reverse order does not work. Idealistic programs and purposes have often had oppressive results. As was shown earlier, contents are made from process. What kind of contents result depends upon the manner of process they come from. This is also true of social movements. A process that involves treating anyone as a mere tool cannot generate humanly freeing results, whatever the desired aims. The process must be freeing to those involved, or it cannot free others.

The social change now needed cannot come from merely inventing new social roles and patterns. There must be change in how people are together and interact with each other. Politics cannot continue to be conducted in formal, unexpressive, impersonal ways.

People in traditional societies felt identified and supported by their social roles. Nowadays, in urban settings, people have lost any such identification with roles. Instead of supporting the individual and giving identity, roles and routines have to be "held up" artificially. One behaves as "one" is supposed to, in each setting, under each "hat." Only when one comes home does one expect to be sustained. The resulting weight thrown on marriages has had a disintegrating effect on family life. The current generation is slowly moving beyond empty role patterns and beyond the silent acceptance of emptiness and despair. There is an increasing emphasis on authentic relationships and open expression and articulation of one's experiencing.

To make this more possible people need to know that articulating one's experiencing begins with feelings that are at first vague. People need to make such exploration safe for each other. They need to welcome the first vague and stumbling steps from each other and in themselves. People need to know that in a series of such steps, the contents change. When one knows this, one can welcome what one hears from a close other person, even when it does not sound at all hopeful.

Such a process of fresh experiential encountering must become a central feature of any new social roles. The first question

is not whether women do this and men that, or whether staff members have this role and directors that role. All this is changing, to be sure. But the crucial question is whether the people are freed to engage in experiential articulation with each other. Only in that way can they devise forms and patterns that express their living and carry it forward. The understanding that this kind of interaction will occur is the fundamental change in roles. Until now, whatever the roles called for, they excluded such a process. With it people can create and recreate uniquely differentiated roles to fit them.

The existential ethic can sound as if it advocates violating promises and loyalties in the name of being "new" each day. Existential ethics does emphasize that one is not bound helplessly to some code, that we must each day reaffirm the values we go by.

Experiential philosophy emphasizes differentiation and articulation. What may at first seem like an "open and shut" situation with few alternatives comes to have many new possibilities, if a person articulates the wholistic felt sense of the situation. Thus, if some past promise does not feel right today, simply violating the promise will also fail to carry the whole felt sense forward. A new way must be found by differentiating the felt sense of all that is involved. Probably one will also need an interaction with the person to whom the promise was made. That person can articulate in just what exact respects something like fulfilling the promise is needed. In such an interaction, and from such differentiated specifics, a new way can be found.

Evaluations

Focusing has been studied in the context of business (Iberg, 1978), creative writing (Bonime, 1977), problem-solving (Zimring, 1974; Kantor, 1976), spirituality (Campbell & McMahon, 1976–77).

The fact that focusing is a bodily process is shown by EEG correlates of a moment of carrying forward (Don, 1977–78). A study on aging also shows the physical aspect. J. E. Gorney (1967) found that high experiencing scale ratings applied to data from a decade ago from an old-age-home population predicted those who were still alive ten years later. In another sense, the bodily aspect of focusing is shown by work on focusing and dance (Alperson, 1974) and healing (Olsen, 1978).

Focusing can use imagery instead of words (Olsen, 1974; Gendlin, 1970; Prouty, 1977; Askins, 1977). In dreams high experiencing level is associated with high psychological differentiation as measured on Witkin's Draw-A-Person test (Hendricks & Cartwright, in press). Medard Boss (1958) has written about dreams (Gendlin, 1977).

Focusing can be used in groups (Hendricks, 1978) and with children (Rainsford, 1977). Focusing can be successfully taught (Van den Bos, 1973; Platt, 1971; McMullin, 1972; Gendlin, 1978).

Experiential psychotherapy is applicable to all psychological problems. This can be seen from the types of cases discussed in the literature ranging from value problems of well-functioning people to the treatment of so-called schizophrenics (Siirala, 1964; Gendlin, 1972; Brunswick, 1975; Hinterkopf, 1975, 1977), borderline patients (Gray, 1976) and retardates (Prouty, 1976).

Diagnostic categories are more likely to mislead than to help. Some therapists try to treat patients differently according to the diagnostic classification. But no valid different ways of treatment are established for the different categories. Each therapist invents different modes of treatment to go with the different categories. From an experiential point of view, such variations in treatment are highly artificial. For reasons undiscoverable by the patient, the therapist behaves in certain odd ways. Diagnostics get in the way of responding humanly to human beings.

Terms such as *psychotic* and *neurotic* classify conditions rather than types of people. The basic therapy process is the same, but one can specify certain details for people while they are in certain conditions. For example, if someone is fighting hallucinations, it is well to explain that attention to feelings is very different from letting hallucinations come. People during psychosis commonly try to shut out every kind of experiencing, if they can, to avoid hallucinations and other very unpleasant experiences. The therapist might explain: "How you *feel* is, for instance, how you feel now, with me, a little nervous about talking to me, maybe? A feeling is like that." People who experienced psychosis and were given focusing instructions with such an explanation have later reported it was a great relief to let themselves have feelings again. They had held themselves totally tight out of fear of hallucinations.

When can a therapy be called successful? Is it enough if the patient feels better? One would evaluate it as a success only if there are also large changes that enhance the patient's actual living. Although hard to measure, such changes should be perfectly obvious.

Existentialists are often hostile to measurement and research. They oppose the kinds of variables and quantifications usually employed in research. But it is quite possible to form new variables directly from experiencing and this makes for more significant research. Any facet of experiencing can be defined observably because humans are not just subjective, not just inward. Experiencing is interaction, hence anything experienced has observable aspects.

For example, with the Experiencing Scale (Klein et al., 1970), one can predict successful and failure outcomes in therapy. In a series of studies (Gendlin et al., 1968), it was found that therapy will eventually be successful if during the interviews the client attends to as yet unclear directly felt experiencing. If what occurs in therapy is mostly talking, thinking, explaining, reporting, discussions of the relationship or any other topic, without experiential focusing, no progress is made and failure occurs.

Treatment

The existential emphasis on personal encountering between therapist and client implies a pattern of service very different from that of a "doctor" "treating" a patient. Buber (1961), in a dialogue with Rogers, stated that any effort to "treat" a person reduced that person to an object, rather than a real other.

The medical model is inappropriate to the existential emphasis on making oneself real in one's living situations with others. How can the medical model be overcome? One solution is the creation of "networks" in which people serve *each other*. An instance of such a pattern is discussed here because it is a most hopeful pattern for the future.

Changes is the name given to a group of approximately 60 people including some clinical students and a few professionals. They meet once a week, and every evening some of them cover a telephone. A telephone number has been publicized, and Changes has been advertised as "helping with problems, finding places to stay, jobs, or people." It is clear that the em-

phasis of Changes is not purely psychological.

When someone calls, immediate contact and response is provided. (Training in listening, focusing, and other methods is provided to all.) The caller is invited to the informal group covering the telephone and to the larger meeting on Sundays.

People coming to Changes need not specify whether they come for help or to help others. Everyone will eventually do both, whatever the initial reason for coming. No one is made to be an object of the work of others. Very upset and "psychotic" people are "carried" by the group, and they often are helpful with others even while still quite upset.

No one who comes depends on just one person; a "team" forms to help with any problem. Thereby the person has a choice. Someone with whom working really seems to help can be chosen for closer work. When something becomes burdensome to one member, others can take over.

A high degree of existential community develops between some of the people. People are in the network not only to serve others, but also to serve themselves. At times no new member comes, only the old members—but these of course consist largely of people who came for help a short while ago and are still "being helped," only that distinction drops out.

When a group is to discuss someone, that person is present. It is more difficult to express one's troubles with a person present, but it is also more authentic and growth producing for everyone. If the person is attacked or criticized, there is an understanding in Changes that someone else will insure that the attacked person's side is fully heard and validated. This makes it possible for people to be more authentic. The degree of authenticity varies, of course, as everyone must struggle for it, but there is a powerful group push in that direction and a discovery that to achieve community feeling requires authentic process.

A number of therapists including this author give training, taking some persons from this community into therapy, and sending private-paying patients to Changes, where they can much sooner change their life situations, meet new people, leave home, and make many other essential life moves.

For example, one team working with an upset woman called upon many other people. People came to stay with her, to sleep there, to help for a little while. The team formulated the following rules for working with her.

1. You can talk about *both* everyday stuff *and* heavy stuff; you can be social or tell about what you're doing, or anything.

2. Reassure her that she is wanted—that you're glad she's here, at those times when her paranoid trip comes on or before you leave.

3. Be absolutely straight and honest about whatever you're feeling at the moment. She is very sensitive and easy to talk to and it's important to be honest with her.

4. If you or she are leaving, anchor her on when she is to come back, or when she'll see you again, for instance: "So you'll be here again tomorrow at six."

5. Her feelings are contagious; you may feel reverberations in you afterwards. So if you feel things like she has, that's what we've all experienced. It helps to talk to someone afterwards.

Management

In experiential therapy the office setting consists of chairs, the lawn, the floor of a hospital room, someone's house—wherever two people can sit and see each other. The office does not include a couch. The infantilization of the couch is usually rejected by experiential therapists. The patient should live in the best, most active, and awake manner. To be passive, whether by lying down or by drugs, hypnosis, or lack of sleep may help engender *content,* but the fully active *manner* of process is necessary for positive change.

A tape recorder may be used, but the patient is told that it can be turned off whenever requested. Confidentiality is practiced absolutely.

Sometimes other participants are brought into the therapy interview. These might be spouses or friends the patient brings, or they might be consultants. A sensitive third person listening and commenting can be a powerful aid.

For example, here is a report from one therapist.

Bob was a private patient I had sent to the Changes group. Bob once brought Les, a Changes member, to the session. I knew Les but thought the client (Bob) had brought Les as a way of distancing from me. The last session had been stormy. Bob had demanded something I needed not to give. Bob intimated that the therapy was over. Having long invested much in Bob, I felt abruptly and ill treated, as if my own needs could have no place at all with Bob. Certainly this was not a very attractive or therapistlike feeling, and I felt more comfortable responding to Bob's very understandable feelings than expressing my own. I responded to Bob's feeling, both in the session and in a subsequent phone call up to the point when Bob hung up the telephone. Bob and I began the session by exchanging our feelings. I said I was angry. The session proceeded for some 10 minutes, when Les interrupted to say to me, "I haven't yet heard *you* say more about being angry." I stopped and realized that, indeed, I had again been taking the more comfortable road of pursuing Bob's side of the issue. I then turned to Les: "Let me tell it *to you,* and Bob can listen," I said.

In a difficult interaction between two people, it often helps if a third person will listen and respond first to just one person for some time, and then just to the other for a while. In this way, the people in the relationship each get a chance to sit quietly and listen. The other person can go through many steps with the third party, steps that could not be made within the troubled interaction. When these steps emerge, they change the sense of the trouble not only for the person speaking, but also in the person who is only listening.

This explains the therapist's next comment:

What Bob could say after my many authentic steps was much more deeply from himself than he could have done at each step. The subsequent process led Bob into his own most intolerable point of being turned down and experiencing a kind of leaving his body, which was long the crux of his repeated psychotic periods. Valuable steps followed him.

It may not be logically clear how his process arrived there, when it had not done so earlier, but it makes "experiential sense." My intensity and visibility enabled partly by Les allowed him to feel beyond where he had been stuck with me.

The above instance brings home something of the informality and existential reality of this type of setting and management of therapy. Honesty is a chief tool of experiential encountering. Not only some one emotion or fact, but steps into the finer texture of the therapist's feelings must be expressed. To do so, the therapist needs to attend to the flow of as yet inarticulate feelings within, and to speak from that.

Hospitals and other professional settings do not usually have people better able to deal with psychological problems than, say, a community of average people. Specific training can be given to all as in Changes. Unfortunately, most of the training of professionals concerns medicine, statistics, animal psychology, theol-

ogy, agency policy, and so on. The accredited, trained M.D. or Ph.D. may be less able to help people than the person who has lived the same years out in the world under difficult circumstances. Experientially authentic listening and relating are as rare among professionals as among others. Professional psychiatry and clinical psychology often consist of the less sensitive and less experienced trying to cure the more sensitive and more experienced of their life troubles. Quite often it does not work well. Therefore, the structure of professional authority must be recognized for what it is, a structure of socially assigned responsibility—a hierarchy of roles, not a hierarchy of competences. There is no use in sending a difficult person to a hospital unless what is wanted is an incarceration procedure to protect someone's life. It is usually no use saying that someone will help the person there. The hospital may be needed, for not everyone can bear to remain outside. It should be used with the person's express agreement, or only when life is surely threatened. If used, the person should be visited there and assured that contact will be kept.

Often people want to send someone to the hospital because they, not the upset person, can no longer bear the strain. A community is the only effective answer, for then there are others not yet worn out. But if everyone is tired, the person should be allowed to leave the community freely. After all, the person came to the therapist or the community freely. A false sense of responsibility leads people to interfere with someone's freedom and ability to move on to others in the world.

CASE EXAMPLE

Joe is a 32-year-old man who came to the Changes community, knows most of the people, and worked most closely with Jane.

Joe was sent to Changes by a minister who described him as recently released from a state hospital, now driving back and forth between this city and another city for two days, unable to stop and with no place to go. The minister found him a place to stay, and a string of people from the Changes community invited him to their homes or arranged to take him to places they were going during the day.

Within two weeks, people grew tired of Joe. He seemed able only to make "canned jokes" or talk about how much he hated drugs. He seemed unable to make normal conversation.

Jane, a clinical student, was one among others trying to think through the problem Joe posed. People seemed to respond to Joe only politely, and no one was trying for more personal contact. Jane set up specific times, twice a week, just for that. As she puts it: ". . . to listen, see him, let him know he's being felt about by another person. Honesty was the basis of the relationship for both of us." When she did that, she found that: "He's a detailed and complex person with a deep moral sense. In his worst times of psychological chaos and violence, I could feel him caring for me, telling me how important my travelling with him was, even when I was afraid."

Now far from giving nothing to respond to, Joe began talking of some of his nearly unspeakable experiences, some of them in prison. In his present struggle, Joe was hearing voices saying things to him so intolerable that it made him want either to die or kill someone. It was a frightening time.

The second set of problems about Joe was different from the first. How could Joe be helped with his immense tension?

What about being scared for him? "The therapist" and her consultant agreed she would use relaxation (hypnosis induction). She had learned hypnosis but it was agreed not to use suggestion of any kind, only relaxation.

She remembers the day: "He came—no sleep for two nights—very tense, couldn't sit still, couldn't help himself get off the 'freak out.' The tension was getting worse and worse, spiraling. I took a deep breath and did heavy relaxation to help him down into livable space." When the time of about half an hour was over, Joe movingly told her he was amazed he could have trusted her to do that, and that it had been a time of feeling good, the first in a long while. The use of many methods on an experiential base is shown by this use of relaxation in the context of forming an experientially authentic relationship.

Changes sometimes refers people to a drug program. The psychiatrist prescribed prolyxin for Joe, which was helpful.

Joe at first could not focus experientially, but in bits and pieces an inward truth came about that he had not experienced before. Jane describes herself as "listening, validating his experience, showing myself, *staying with.*"

In one session, he talked of his guilt for having abandoned a political identity. The therapist respected—as she really felt—Joe's values and his attempt to live with integrity and interpret his incredibly difficult past with similar integrity.

Throughout, the therapist said what she thought and felt without any censoring process and, characteristically for her, with no time between her feeling and her blurting it out.

Joe, more suspicious and untrusting than most people, could not help but know that he experienced her as she really was and felt, despite often spoken amazement at his being able to trust anyone, at his being able to be open and vulnerable with anyone.

A job was found for Joe as a janitor and he kept the job throughout the next period.

One time he could almost not bear up under the voices. That day Joe decided he had to go to a hospital. The therapist said she would arrange it and did. Admission for him was arranged in the relatively best available public hospital in the city. When the therapist saw Joe, she said that *she* did not think he should go, and she hoped he would wait. (It is in such a relationship as this one that one can trust a person to call or come if things get too awful.) The therapist describes this period: "Saw him every day and held on to the other end of the phone sometimes at night, hoping my presence would help hold down some reality in the falling-apart world." The crisis passed.

Among a group of friends, with a job, and in an ongoing authentic relationship, it may well have been the drug that turned the tide; yet drugs had not done much for him when he was in the hospital. Drugs have different effects in the context of different life processes (see "Personality"). He had left the hospital in bad condition after taking the same drug for a long time.

Within a few more months, Joe was working, found a woman to live with, and an apartment on which he worked elaborately. He entered a college on public assistance.

A characteristic session with Joe continued to include the therapist's struggle to get him to stop, attend, feel, and give enough peace and time to that to enable him to sense a step from there. There was still a tendency to go too fast for that.

The sessions became less frequent and Joe was seen only in the large weekly meetings or socially.

Joe was coming more and more out of his silence and isolation. Now he became a fascinating conversationalist. His personal rendition of well-known pieces of literature had the colorfulness such renditions have when done by someone who loves the piece. In hearing him like that, one day, it was suggested that Joe ought to teach! This brought out that Joe actually had an ambition to teach in the official school system. He explained it would be the ultimate overcoming of the entire society that had always been so against him. "I'm teaching your kids in your school . . ." he would be saying to them all. The warmth, poetry, and love in his talk was clear. It was not vengeance but an answer to all the negativities in his past life.

At times now, there were still therapeutic sessions, but Joe was not, so to speak, "in therapy." These now rare sessions were not about recurrences of anything, but new phases. In one he worked through the rupture of his relationship with the woman.

At "follow up," three years later, the therapist attended Joe's graduation from college with honors. His current problems do not prevent him from functioning.

The therapist writes insistently, in true existential fashion, that she was not a therapist:

Some real deep bond of friendship developed between us; we went together through so many places, many of which stretched the limits of ordinary intelligible experience, and have no words. That makes for a special caring and knowing each other. The word "therapy" cannot be used. It makes him seem in the one-down position and that doesn't fit. I respect his experience and wonder often if I would have the strength, intelligence, and courage he did, if the world had dealt me such experiences to integrate and move beyond.

This attitude very well expresses what Buber meant by opposing the very idea of psychotherapy as reducing the existential reality of the other.

SUMMARY

In existential psychotherapy the person is considered to be "existence" beyond definitions and conceptual patterns. One changes by existing differently. There is an emphasis on "authenticity," making life and choices one's own. Anxiety points to avoided possibilities of living. Authentic relating to others is stressed.

In experiential psychotherapy these points become more specific. A person works directly with the felt process of experiencing. Beyond one's definitions, concepts, and familiar feelings, a felt sense can form. This is a wholistic sense of all that is involved in some problem or situation. It is how one is living in that situation, and it contains much more information than one can think or perceive separately. Such a felt sense becomes differentiated into new thoughts, feelings, perceptions, and courses of action. These were implicit in the felt sense but not yet fully formed. When right words or actions are found, one senses a bodily release, a direct experience of concretely changing. Such words or actions carry forward one's experiencing process. A problem usually involves many steps of carrying forward before it is resolved. What one differentiates at first will change in further steps. Knowing this, one can receive and welcome each step more easily, whether what emerges seems desirable or not. One has a sense of the wholistic freeing and rightness of the eventual resolution. Experiencing is interaction. Therefore a felt sense is not something subjective and inside, but one's sense of how one is living in the world with others, and all the past involved in that, as well as a not fully formed future direction.

Because human experiencing is interaction, when a therapist interacts more openly, honestly, and expressively with a client, the client's experiencing thereby occurs more openly, honestly, and in a more carried further way. Although the two people articulate their mutual interaction differently, and the interpretation from each side is valid, there is really only one interaction process. Either person can therefore change the manner of experiencing they are both living together.

People are not made up of "contents," or already cut pieces. They are living processes. What we think of as the contents inside us (thoughts, feelings, traits, patterns) are actually made by, and from, the experiential process. If that process is going on in a new manner, the contents one finds inside will also be new. The results of psychotherapy will be like the manner of experiencing the client lives in the therapy hours. If people are made passive, lectured, given insights they cannot grasp from inside, the contents they find inside themselves will be like that manner of living—passivity, helplessness, incapacities, and fears of unknown feelings.

The experiential psychotherapist asks the client to attend inwardly and to see what wholistic body sense of the problem forms there. The client then lets words form to name that felt sense. Specific new feelings and perceptions soon emerge from the felt sense. Whatever client or therapist says is checked against the felt sense, to see if there is a distinct bodily release, a "felt shift." When people change, they can feel themselves changing in a concrete bodily way.

This process differs from discussions and inferences, and from strong but familiar emotions. Research with the EXP Scale has also shown that those patients are later found successful who during the interviews often refer to a bodily felt sense that is not as yet clear to them.

Experiential psychotherapy can employ any theory, vocabulary, and procedure but these are not simply taken over "eclectically." Rather, other theories and procedures are used in relation to the person's felt sense and discarded if there is no carrying forward. If something the therapist says or does succeeds in carrying forward, the therapist does not necessarily remain with the initial idea, but helps pursue the unique and often surprising steps that emerge from the felt sense.

The person is bodily, social, and individual. These are not separate in the person. *Bodily* means not mere muscle sensations but the sense of one's body from the inside. This always turns out to include personal and situational meanings. What one is as a self cannot be separated from how one lives in situations with other people. A felt sense includes physical, social, and individual aspects before they have been separated.

The "medical model" of an authoritative doctor working on a passive patient does not fit psychotherapy. There is a more mutual interaction of two expressive people. Ideally, as in the community network called Changes, people are all trained in specific ways to help each other. All teachable interpersonal skills, focusing, and differentiating one's felt sense can come to be part of society generally, available to everyone. This would also change the rigidity of social roles so people can newly and uniquely differentiate the roles to fit themselves and carry their living forward.

ANNOTATED BIBLIOGRAPHY

Heidegger, Martin. *Being and time,* translated by Macquarrie and Robinson. New York: Harper & Row, 1962.
In *Being and Time,* Heidegger presents a fundamental philosophy. There are no things or facts as such. Mathematical, chemical, social, or any other facts are made in interaction with humans. We must go behind what appears as a fact, behind the sciences and the situations in our living, to see our own involvement in how the facts were made in the first place.

Humans do not exist in space and time; rather we generate space and time. Space is "over there" from someone's "here." We duck to avoid being hit by something coming at us, which is not yet here, and thus generate the space between. More fundamental, time is generated in human living by all our ways of being concerned about what has not happened yet, what we desire or seek to avoid.

Ordinary objects, too, from this viewpoint, reveal contexts of human "care." A hammer, for instance, involves the things to be made and held together with nails and the whole carpentry workshop and the people who will use the things and the activities in which these things will function. A hammer is not simply a thing sitting before us to observe. We could not see all this if we only looked at it. Human care and living are thus basic to time, space, and objects.

Humans have no fixed nature, not even like that of a hammer. Humans are rather the generating of contexts and cannot be understood as mere things or products. Therefore humans are anxious because what we are is never settled. What we are never *is* anything. We are not even the possibilities we project; we are the projecting. In envisioning the time of one's inevitable death, one can become free from everyday ways of being lost in cares, free to be authentic in the creativity of one's human openness and in the responsibility for choosing what one does.

Four basic aspects of human nature are mood, understanding, interpretation, and language. These are "equally basic," which means all four always have *already* participated in any human experience. Even a mood we ignore is implicitly our situations and how we live them and the other people involved in them. Human situations are always structured by linguistic distinctions, and this, too, is implicit in the mood. One must choose to be "what one already is and has to be," revealed in one's mood, and it is the understanding implicit in the mood which reveals that. Thereby, then, what seemed fixed is opened to the inherent human creativity of new possibilities.

Rank, Otto. *Will therapy*. New York: Knopf, 1950.

In *Will Therapy,* Rank makes "the feeling of experience . . . the central factor in the therapeutic task" (p. 5). Rank denies that one must go back to understand the past. A person's whole reaction pattern is always here in the present experience. Repression is overcome by working with "the immediate emotional denial (by) making . . . the connection with the reality of the moment. This convinces the patient, as it were, against his will-to-illness, that he can live in the present, if only he will, if only he dares to will, without getting guilt feelings" (p. 40).

Everyone has a basic duality: fear of life and fear of death. Neurosis is a "self-restriction of the life function in the interest of protecting from death (fear avoidance)" (p. 149). In the neurotic, the latter is too strong. There is a battle between the positive will to live and the negative will to avoid and restrict. The neurotic must learn to will and to overcome the guilt feelings this may entail. The negative will must be defeated not only inwardly; the patient must also "kill the destructive ego in the therapist. The patient must remain victor if he is to feel himself healed, that is, capable of living, and the danger of the therapist lies in the fact that he himself instinctively wants to be victorious" (p. 179). Therefore the therapist must not take over and direct, or fight against, the patient's negative will. The patient would then have to lose the struggle with the therapist, or else the patient would be left with the negative side. If permitted, on the other hand, the patient will usually assign to the therapist that part of the ego that is most disturbing and will fight against the therapist in that role. In doing so, the patient changes. The patient "defends himself against having the therapist want to change him, and with right, but he alters himself continually," if the therapist temporarily accepts the ego role assigned to him.

Rank interprets only what the patient can experience in the moment and eliminates all other interpretation.

In the end phase, the patient puts reality into the place of the therapist—a reality that changes with every experience. The patient becomes equal to that reality "by inner differentiation" (p. 183).

CASE READINGS

Binswanger, L. The case of Ellen West. In Rollo May; Ernst Angel; & Henri Ellenberger (Eds.), *Existence.* New York: Basic Books, 1958.

Boss, Medard. A patient who taught the author to see and think differently. In M. Boss, *Psychoanalysis and daseinanalysis.* New York: Basic Books, 1963.

Holt, Herbert. The case of father M. A segment of an existential analysis. *Journal of Existentialism,* 1966, 6, 469-495. Also in Wedding, D., & Corsini, R. J. (Eds.) *Great cases in psychotherapy.* Itasca, Ill.: F. E. Peacock Publishers, 1979.

Jacobi, Y. A case of homosexuality. *Journal of Analytical Psychology,* 1969, 14, 48-64.

REFERENCES

Allen, F. H. *Psychotherapy with children.* New York: Norton, 1942.

Alperson, E. Carrying experiencing forward through authentic body movement. *Psychotherapy, T.R.P.,* 1974(a), 77(3), 211-14.

Askins, M. *Hemispheric lateralization and image focusing.* Ph.D. dissertation, California School of Professional Psychology, 1977.

Binswanger, L. *Grundformen und Erkennis-nis Menschlichen Daseins.* Munich: Rinehardt, 1962.

Bonime, F. Creative writing course. The New School of Social Research, New York, 1977.

Boss, M. *The analysis of dreams,* translated by A. J. Pomerans. New York: Philosophical Library, 1958.

Boss, M. *Psychoanalysis and daseinsanalysis,* translated by L. B. Lefebre. New York: Basic Books, 1963.

Brunswick, L. K., & Hinterkopf, E. Cultivating positive empathic self-responding. *Voices: The air and science of psychotherapy,* 1975, 11, 62-65.

Buber, M. *Between man and man.* New York: Macmillan, 1948, p. 23.

Buber, M., & Rogers, C. R. Transcription of dialogue held April 18, 1957. In C. R. Rogers, *On becoming a person.* New York: Houghton-Mifflin, 1961, p. 57.

Campbell, P., & McMahon, E. *Cosmic congruence.* New York: Sheed & Ward, in

press. (Report to the Members of the Institute for Research in Spirituality, 1976–77,
Milwaukee, Wisconsin.)

Dilthey, W. *Gesammette Schriften.* Vol. 10.
Stuttgart: Teubner, 1961.

Don, N. S. The transformation of conscious
experience and its EEG correlates. *Journal
of Altered States of Consciousness,*
1977–78, 3(2), 147–68.

Frankl, V. *The doctor and the soul.* New
York: Knopf, 1965.

Friedman, N. From the experiential in therapy
to experiential psychotherapy: A history.
Psychotherapy, T. R. P., 1976, 13(3),
326–43.

Gendlin, E. T. Initiating psychotherapy with
"unmotivated" patients. *Psychiatric Quarterly,* 1961.

Gendlin, E. T. *Experiencing and the creation
of meaning.* New York: Free Press of Glencoe, 1962.

Gendlin, E. T. A theory of personality
change. In P. Worchel & D. Byrne (Eds.),
Personality change. New York: Wiley,
1964.

Gendlin, E. T. Neurosis and human nature in
the experiential method of thought and
therapy. *Humanitas,* 1967, 3(2).

Gendlin, E. T. Experiential explication and
truth. In F. R. Molina (Ed.), *The sources of
existentialism as philosophy.* Englewood
Cliffs, N.J.: Prentice-Hall, 1969(a).

Gendlin, E. T. Focusing. *Psychotherapy,
T. R. P.,* 1969(b), 6(1).

Gendlin, E. T. Therapeutic procedures with
schizophrenic patients. In M. Hammer
(Ed.), *The theory and practice of psychotherapy with specific disorders.* Springfield:
C. C Thomas, 1972.

Gendlin, E. T. Experiential phenomenology.
In M. Natanson (Ed.), *Phenomenology and
the social sciences.* Evanston: Northwestern
University Press, 1973.

Gendlin, E. T. Phenomenological concept vs.
phenomenological method: A critique of
Medard Boss on dreams. *Soundings,* 1977,
40(3).

Gendlin, E. T. Focusing teaching tapes. Lone
Rock, Wisc.: Lone Rock Media, 1978.
(Tape)

Gendlin, E. T.; Beebe, J.; Cassens, J.; Klein,
M.; & Oberlander, M. Focusing ability is
psychotherapy, personality and creativity.
In J. M. Schlien (Ed.), *Research in*

psychotherapy. Vol. 3. Washington, D.C.:
American Psychological Association, 1968.

Gendlin, E. T., & Olsen, L. The use of imagery in experiential focusing. *Psychotherapy, T. R.P.,* 1970, 7(4).

Gorney, J. E. *Experiencing among the aged.*
Ph.D. dissertation, University of Chicago,
1967. (In Gorney, J. E. & Tobin, S. S., *Experiencing among the aged.* Paper presented
at Twentieth Annual Scientific Meeting of
the Gerontological Society, 1967.)

Gray, J. P. The influence of experiential
focusing on state anxiety and problem-
solving ability in "borderline" patients.
Ph.D. dissertation, California School of
Professional Psychology, 1976.

Heidegger, M. *Sein und Zeit.* Tübingen: Max
Niemeyer, 1960.

Heidegger, M. *What is a thing?* (with an
analysis by E. T. Gendlin). Chicago: Regnery, 1967.

Hendricks, M. The focusing group. In T.
Brouillette (Ed.), *The changes book.* Unpublished manuals, Changes, Chicago:
1978.

Hendricks, M., & Cartwright, R. Experiencing in dreams: An individual difference
variable. *Psychotherapy, T.R.P.,* in press.

Hinterkopf, E. Beneficial therapeutic skills
successfully taught to mental patients.
Evaluation, 1977, 4, 63.

Hinterkopf, E., & Brunswick, L. K. Teaching
therapeutic skills to mental patients. *Psychotherapy, T.R.P.,* 1975, 12, 8–12.

Hora, T. Psychotherapy, existence and re-
ligion. In H. M. Ruitenbeck (Ed.),
Psychoanalysis and existential philosophy.
New York: Dutton, 1962.

Husserl, E. *Ideen Zu Einer Reinen
phanomenologie und phanomenologischen
philosophie.* Haag: Martinus Nijhoff, 1950.

Iberg, J. R. The effects of focusing on job interview behavior. Ph.D. dissertation, University of Chicago, 1978.

Kantor, S., & Zimring, F. M. The effects of
focusing on a problem. *Psychotherapy,
T.R.P.,* 1976, 13(3).

Kierkegaard, S. [*The concept of dread*], translated by W. Lowrie. Princeton: Princeton
University Press, 1974.

Klein, M. H.; Mathieu, P. L.; Kiesler, D. J.;
& Gendlin, E. T. *The experiencing scale
manual.* Madison, Wisc.: University of
Wisconsin Press, 1970.

Laing, R. D. *Politics of experience.* New York: Pantheon Books, 1967.

McMullin, R. Effects of counselor focusing on client self-experiencing under low attitudinal conditions. *Journal of Counseling Psychology,* 1972, 19(4).

May, R.; Angel, E.; & Ellenberger, H. F. (Eds.) *Existence.* New York: Basic Books, 1958.

May, R.; Angel, E.; & Ellenberger, F. (Eds.) *Existence.* New York: Basic Books, 1958.

Merleau-Ponty, M. *Phenomenology of perception.* New York: Humanities Press, 1962.

Mullan, H., & Sanguillano, I. *The therapist's contribution to the treatment process.* Springfield, Ill.: C. C Thomas, 1964.

Olsen, L. The therapeutic use of visual imagery in experiental focusing. Ph.D. dissertation, University of Chicago, 1975.

Olsen, L. *Focusing and self-healing.* Los Angeles: Continuum Tape Montage, 1978. (Cassette Tape)

Platt, A. B. The utilization of hypnosis to teach focusing ability. Ph.D. dissertation, University of Chicago, 1971.

Prouty, G. Pre-therapy: A method of treating pre-expressive psychotic and retarded patients. *Psychotherapy, T.R.P.,* 1976, 13(3), 290–94.

Prouty, G. Protosymbolic method: A phenomenological treatment of schizophrenic hallucinations. *Journal of Mental Imagery,* 1977, 1(2), 339–42.

Rainsford, B. *Knowing me, knowing you.* Chicago: Coronet Instructional Media, 1977. (Film)

Rank, O. *Will therapy.* New York: Knopf, 1950.

Reich, W. *Character-analysis.* New York: Farrar, Straus & Giroux, 1949.

Sartre, J. P. *Being and nothingness.* New York: Philosophical Library, 1956.

Siiralla, M. Schizophrenia: A human situation. *American Journal of Psychoanalysis,* 1964, 23(1).

Taft, J. *Dynamics of therapy in a controlled relationship.* New York: Macmillan, 1953.

Van den Bos, G. R. An investigation of several methods of teaching experiential focusing. Ph.D. dissertation, University of Detroit, 1973.

Whitaker, C., & Malone, T. B. *The roots of psychotherapy.* New York: McGraw-Hill, 1953.

Zimring, F. M., & Balcombe, J. K. Cognitive operations in two measures of handling emotionally relevant material. *Psychotherapy, T.R.P.,* 1974, 11(3).

10

Transactional Analysis

JOHN M. DUSAY AND
KATHERINE MULHOLLAND DUSAY

OVERVIEW

Transactional analysis (TA), as originated by Dr. Eric Berne in the 1950s, is a complete theory of personality; TA also uses a wide variety of related treatment techniques specifically designed to meet the needs and goals of clients. TA adheres to the presence of three active, dynamic, and observable ego states labeled the Parent, the Adult, and the Child, each of which exists and operates in any individual. Each person has a basic innate need for *strokes* (recognition) and will design a *life script* (plan) formed during childhood, based upon early beliefs about oneself and others. These existential beliefs are reinforced by the person engaging in repetitive, stereotyped *games* (unstraight social interactions) with others. The dynamic representation of any individual's psychological energy forces (Critical Parent, Nurturing Parent, Adult, Free Child, and Adapted Child) may be graphically portrayed on the person's *egogram* (a bar graph of one's personality portrait). One's egogram energy balance will remain "fixed" unless one actively decides to change one's behavior. An effective TA therapist is a highly trained, potent catalyst, who facilitates change and growth in clients.

Basic Concepts

TA therapists share certain challenges and basic questions with all other psychotherapists: Why are people the way they are? What are the basic human commonalities? How and why do individuals differ from one another? Why do they develop and retain negative patterns of thinking, feeling, and behaving even when doing so hurts them? Why do people resist changing, even when a therapist offers them a vehicle for change? TA offers both the answers and the effective directions to such questions through its theoretical concepts and its systematic approach. TA's simple vocabulary (Berne, 1964; Harris, 1969; James & Jongeward, 1971) is intentionally designed to enable clients to demystify the esoteric jargon of traditional therapies. Some basic terms used in TA are: *ego states,* which consist of Parent, Adult, and Child; *transactions; games; strokes; scripts;* and *egograms.* An important TA attitude will be noted throughout this work: Concepts are not only expressed verbally, but also have accompanying symbols—circles, arrows, triangles, and bar graphs, which increase clarity and understanding, as well as represent a commitment by the therapist to explain his viewpoint. The therapist and client both share these mutual "tools" and simple vocabularies; and while this tends to eliminate some of the therapist's magic, the client is facilitated to "own" his appropriate share of responsibility for treatment.

Ego States. When Eric Berne discovered his client was sometimes thinking, feeling, and behaving like a child and at other times like a rational adult, he differentiated between two distinct ego states: the Child and the Adult. The *Child* ego state within each of us is sometimes creative, intuitive, and emotional; at other times, rebellious or conforming. Originally Berne labeled the Child ego state the *archaeopsyche,* which connoted the developmentally archaic, regressive ego state (Berne, 1961). The *Adult* ego state, which is the realistic, logical part of us, he termed the *neopsyche,* which referred to computing and data processing. Each ego state has its own observable mannerisms, special repertoire of words, thoughts, emotions, body postures, gestures, voice tones, and expressions. The Child ego state behaves, sounds, and "comes on" like an actual child, regardless of the person's biological age. The Adult ego state resembles a computer in that it takes in, stores, retrieves, and processes information about oneself and the environment. The Adult deals exclusively with facts and logical data in a nonemotional way.

Soon, another basic aspect of human behavior became evident—the *Parent* or *exteropsyche,* which is both an introjection from and an identification with one's actual biological parents. The Parent ego state expresses one's value systems, morals, and beliefs. These attitudes may take the form of promoting growth in others as well as being critical and controlling. The Parent may portray traits and mannerisms of one's actual mother, father, and

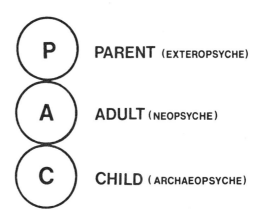

EGO STATE DIAGRAM

Figure 10.1

occasionally other parenting figures. The Parent in a person may be judgmental and opinionated, as well as nurturing and protective. One's Parent ego state is frequently familial and cultural in origin in that it is often passed down from parents to their children, who in turn pass it down to their children. (The three ego states are capitalized as Parent, Adult, and Child to distinguish them from the biological entities of parents, adults, and children.)

The completed tripartite system of one's personality structure is symbolized by three connected, distinct circles to represent that they are unique, separate, and independent entities. Each ego state functions independently from the others and has separate boundaries, wherein it contains specific properties (see Figure 10.1). The three ego states are dynamic; they are unlike Freud's personality structure of id, ego, and superego, which are hypothetical concepts and not observable phenomena.

Transactions. Social action begins when two (or more) people get together. Psychologically speaking, two people in a room means there are actually six structured ego states (three and three) present and these ego states may transact and communicate with one another. A transaction is a unit of human communication. *Transactions* are defined as a stimulus and a related response between two persons' ego states; the word *transaction* is preferred over the more general term *communication* for clarity and precision. There are two basic levels of transactions: the *social level,* which is overt or manifest, and the *psychological level,* which is covert or latent. These two levels of transactions are visually symbolized by arrows: the socially stated, overt transaction is represented by a solid-line arrow, and the psychologically stated, covert transaction is symbolized by a dotted-line arrow.

Games. When these two levels (psychological and social) are actively operating at the same time, a game is usually taking place. A *game* is defined as an orderly series of ulterior transactions (with both an overt and a covert level), which results in "payoffs" with specific bad feelings for both game players. The overt series of transactions is straightforward and in this particular example is an Adult-to-Adult transaction: The boss asks his secretary, "What time is it?" She answers, "3 o'clock." However, his covert nonverbal message (represented by the dotted lines of his Parent to her Child) is, "You're always late." Her hidden nonverbal response (dotted lines of her Child to his Parent) is, "You're always criticizing me." Even though neither the boss nor his secretary express these hidden sentiments out loud, each is fully aware of the hidden messages and each will receive a personal payoff of bad feelings. The boss is playing his part in the game colloquially known as *Now I Got You, You SOB* (NIGYYSOB), and he feels angry and powerful; his secretary is playing *Kick Me* (*KM*) and feels bad and picked on (see Figure 10.2). People transact in certain stereotyped ways that are predictable and unique for each person and these are called games; each of the players ends up with "bad feelings" called *rackets*. After several repeated episodes of these games

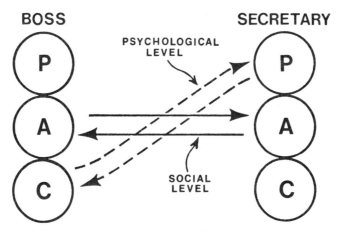

A GAME DIAGRAM

Figure 10.2

with themselves and perhaps with other players, the secretary will entitle herself to a "free" depression while the boss will entitle himself to a "free" rampage and rage.

Strokes. The basic motivation for any human social interaction is based on one's ongoing needs for *strokes* (human recognition). When straightforward strokes are not available, that is, "I like you," people will employ ulterior methods and use games to receive strokes. Although positive strokes feel better than negative strokes, negative strokes áre better than *no* strokes at all! Specific patterns of giving and receiving strokes are learned, and they are unique to each family. The ways that people give and get strokes serve to shape each individual's personality. During one's infancy and early childhood, "strokes" are hopefully given and received by actual touching, holding, and cuddling. This touching is necessary for

the healthy survival of any newborn human infant (Spitz, 1945). Somewhere between the ages two and four, the stroking tends to become less physical and more verbal, although actual physical stroking remains important throughout life from infancy to old age. Stroking can be positive (caring and approving) or negative (damaging and disapproving). Because strokes are essential to each person's survival, negative strokes are sought if positive strokes are not available.

Script. Through one's early interactions with parents and others, a pattern of stroking develops, which may be either supportive or attacking (Berne, 1972). From this stroking pattern, the child at some point early in life makes a basic existential decision about himself, essentially that he is either OK as a person or not OK. This basic decision is then reinforced by continuing messages, both verbal and nonverbal, the person receives

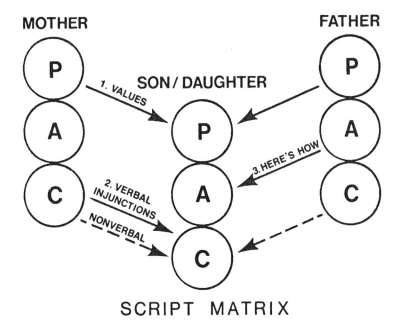

SCRIPT MATRIX

Figure 10.3

throughout life. The developing child not only makes these crucial decisions about himself, but also develops a viewpoint about what other people are like. The child decides either that other people are OK and to be trusted or that they are not OK (Berne, 1964; Harris, 1969). This process of deciding about both oneself and others becomes one's basic belief system.

Through the script matrix (Steiner, 1971), we can note the Parent ego states of both mother and father supply (1) their *values,* morals, opinions, and prejudices to the developing Parent ego state of their child. The Child ego states of both mother and father provide (2) the *injunctions* or the negative messages to the Child ego state of their child. On the basis of these early verbal (solid line) and nonverbal (dotted line) messages (which are frequently incongruent and incompatible), the Child ego state of the young child will *decide* what life will be like. The Adult ego states of usually the opposite-sex parent of the child usually provide (3) the "Here's How" message of how to make it through life (see Figure 10.3).

One's script or life course is based upon one's early existential decisions; scripts incorporate specific elements from myths, fairy tales, and theatrical dramas in that they include a wide variety of characters, along with the elements of suspense, surprise, triumph, tragedy, anger, scare, joy, and other emotions. One's life script may be either winning or losing, hamartic (tragic) or banal; and each script includes specific roles. Some people approach life as heroes and heroines (K. Dusay, 1975), and others operate as villains, rescuers, persecutors, victims (Karpman, 1968), or perhaps as innocent bystanders. After the child incorporates early messages from his parents, his script develops into a strong belief system, so when the client arrives at the psychotherapist's office some twenty,

thirty, or more years later, his basic life script is both apparent and staunchly defended.

Egogram.   Although TA's structure of personality is symbolized by the three circles of ego states, the function and amount of energy placed within these ego states is symbolized by the *egogram* (J. Dusay, 1972). The circles illustrate which ego states are involved in the transactions, and the egogram exemplifies, in bar graph form, *how much* energy exists in the five functional ego states of any person. The Parent is divided into its functional aspects of both Critical Parent (CP) and Nurturing Parent (NP); the Adult (A) is not divided as it is unemotional and functions solely as a computer; and the Child is divided into its Free Child (FC) functions, which are natural and uninhibited, and its Adapted Child (AC) functions, which are compliant or rebellious. These basic psychological energies are present in each person in varying amounts.

Because each person has a distinct and unique personality, these five psychological forces are aligned in different amounts and balances in each individual. An egogram is constructed on a five-position bar graph that represents CP, NP, A, FC, and AC; the higher columns signify the greater amounts of time and energy expended in these ego states, and the smaller columns portray lesser degrees of time and energy. The egogram operates with a constancy hypothesis in that when one raises the time and energy in an ego state, another ego state will lose energy. This is a simple illustration of the growth model. A person's egogram will remain fixed and not change unless the person actively decides to change the energy balances in his ego states (see Figure 10.4). The *Critical Parent* is the part of one's personality that criticizes or finds fault; the CP is also assertive, directing, limiting,

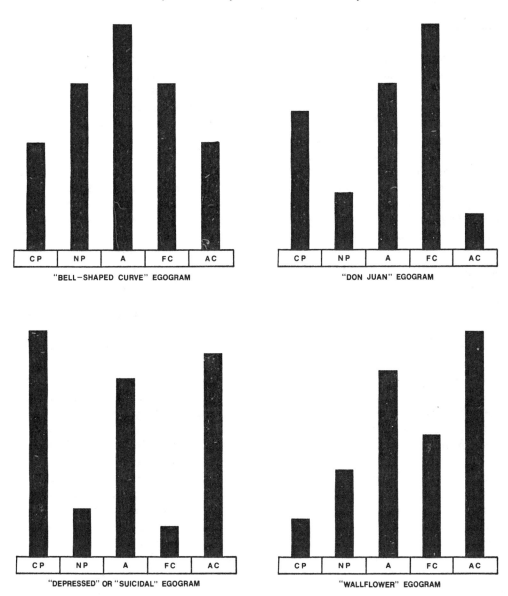

EXAMPLES OF EGOGRAMS

Figure 10.4

makes rules, enforces one's value system, and stands up for one's rights. (Too much CP is dictatorial.) The *Nurturing Parent* in a person is empathetic and promotes growth. (Too much NP is smothering.) The *Adult's* function is clear, rational thinking. The Adult is factual, precise, accurate, nonemotional, and nonjudgmental. (Too much Adult is boring.) The *Free Child* is spontaneous, curious, playful, fun, free, eager, and intuitive. (Too much FC is seen as out-of-control.) The *Adapted Child* is conforming, compromising, adapting, easy to get along with, and compliant. The Adapted Child may also manifest itself as a pseudorebel that does the opposite of everything that is expected. (A person with too much AC will manifest behavior in a myriad of ways; some of the most common ways are being guilty, depressed, or robotlike, or throwing temper tantrums reminiscent of small children.)

Since each person has a psychological energy portrait (or egogram) of his personality, the complexities and changes of the human personality can be described through this system. There are neither "good" nor "bad" egograms per se; yet certain generalizations may be formed about certain egogram balances. A *bell-shaped egogram* implies that the personality has a well-balanced energy system with psychological energy fairly evenly distributed. A *Don Juan* will have a high Free Child (interested in fun and sexual trysts), a high Critical Parent (knows how to tell the women to get lost), a low Nurturing Parent (does not care about their feelings), a medium high Adult (he logically knows how to find women), and a low Adapted Child (feels little guilt and will not compromise). A *Wallflower* by contrast is highest in Adapted Child (she is worried about what others will think about her), low in Free Child (is seldom playful or fun); her

Critical Parent is low in that she will seldom assert herself or stand up for her rights. A depressed or suicidal person will be quite low on Nurturing Parent (both to oneself and others), and also low on Free Child (feels little zest for life and happiness).

Other Systems

TA differs from other systems of personality in that explanations about human behavior are viewed on the basis of Parent, Adult, and Child ego states. Human behavior that is not explained in terms of these dynamic ego states is not TA, although statements from other fields may sound similar to TA statements. Freud once remarked that it is one thing to flirt with an idea and another thing to be married to it. The transactional analyst is married to the concept of ego states.

A major difference between psychoanalysis and TA is that TA does not rely upon a theory of the unconscious. Although Berne himself never denied this theory, he and his followers find that the concept of a dynamic unconscious is unnecessary for the practice of TA. A basic difference between TA and Freudian theory is that while the Freudian structure of the id, ego, and superego are *hypothetical* constructs, the Parent, Adult, and Child ego states are *observable* phenomena. Ego-state recognition and the alignment of these states on an egogram enable one to predict future behavior as well as make inferences of past history. A further difference is in methods of treatment. In classical psychoanalytical approaches, the therapist may attempt to remain anonymous or may welcome transferences. The TA therapist does not remain anonymous and will point out his or her transactions and, when applicable, his own game participations.

Myths, folk tales, and the occurrence of

universal symbols are important to both the TA therapists as well as to Jungian analysts. TA practitioners, however, emphasize the *direct* transactions that are passed down between the parents and their children, as well as other direct transactional influences such as the replaying of myths on television, radio, literature, movies, and other mass media. Jungian analysts adhere to a mystical transmission that occurs by way of archetypes or through the collective unconscious.

A TA practitioner will agree with Carl Rogers's person-centered approach in that one's growth potential may be released by a reality-based, nonjudgmental therapist. In addition to reflecting and validating the client's statements, the TA therapist will frequently stop, interrupt, confront, and point out inconsistencies to the client. Consequently, the TA therapist will be more overtly active than a Rogerian therapist.

Alfred Adler's individual psychology is compatible with TA, especially in script theory (Adler, 1963). Adler said, "If I know the goal of a person, I know in a general way what will happen . . . psychic phenomenon . . . can only be grasped and understood if regarded as a preparation for some goal . . . an attempt at a planned final compensation and a (secret) life plan." Berne (1972) said, "The only exceptions which a script analyst would take to these (Adler's) statements are (1) that the life plan is not unconscious; (2) that the person is by no means solely responsible for it; and (3) that the goal and the manner of reaching it (the actual transactions, word for word), can be predicted much more precisely than even Adler claimed" (p. 59).

TA differs from Albert Ellis's rational-emotive therapy (RET) in that the TA therapist places the burden of explanation and interpretation mainly upon the client rather than the therapist. In TA the client is provided specific tools for growth, yet is ultimately encouraged to make his own explanations and interpretations. As compared to RET, TA has more recently placed less emphasis on rational explanations; rather, TA emphasizes that a client should directly replay early emotions and feelings rather than talk about emotions, and then go through a redecision process (Goulding, 1974).

Both TA and behavior modification have as their goals the observable and manifest changes in the clients' behavior. Where these two systems differ is in the TA focus on the redecision process. TA emphasizes that when a person is young, he reacts to environmental stresses, receives injunctions, and then makes basic decisions about himself and others. These early decisions became manifest in here-and-now thinking, feeling, and behaving. TA analysts encourage clients to trace these stereotyped, learned, not-OK experiences back to their prototype, earlier childhood origins. When this episode is reestablished, the client is then encouraged to maintain a self-conversation between the scripted Child part and a positive "growth" ego state that is represented on his egogram. Although Skinner's behavior modification theory views a person more as a helpless victim who reacts to external stimuli, TA, by contrast, sees each person as autonomous, responsible, and able to restructure his behavior by making *new* decisions about self and life.

Many TA therapists incorporate versions of Gestalt techniques that were practiced by Fritz Perls (1969). Although TA emphasizes a person's intellectual cognition (which was discounted by Perls), TA also supports a client's emotional expressions (which was favored by Perls). TA's use of cognitive models is evident in its clearly stated theory of personality; by comparison, Perls left little in the way of a clear record or system for his later theories and techniques. The major difference between TA and Gestalt is TA's use of a therapeutic treatment contract (see Psychotherapy section). TA therapists and their clients use specific, oral, measurable goals by which both the therapist and the client are mutually involved and directed.

Although TA compatibly shares the basic focus on personal responsibility for one's own behavior with reality therapy, as developed by William Glasser, the TA therapist places greater importance on history and antecedent behavior. Although working in the present, and considering that the future is important in TA, the TA therapist views present behavior patterns that lead to problems as *rackets*—repetitive behavior with corresponding emotions—originating in early script messages. The reality therapist says, "We must face reality and admit that we cannot rewrite history"; the TA therapist begins with the here-and-now expression of "bad" feelings and encourages the client to trace these back to the early decisive moments and redecide.

As far as actual living in the world is concerned, TA shares with experiential psychotherapy and existential analysis a high esteem for personal qualities of honesty, integrity, autonomy, and authenticity—and the most important social manifestation of intimacy. However, TA places importance on personality structure and views the problem of "self" to be a balance of ego state structure and function. The internal dialogue between Parent, Adult, Child, and the social expression of criticism, nurturing, logic, creativity, and adaptation (compliance or rebellion) have a stereotyped habitual pattern in those who lack autonomy. Pathology exists and follows rules, and recognizing what is, is a step in the direction of autonomy, and freedom from old habits.

Similarities exist between encounter and TA in that both are practiced in groups, workshops, and marathons. Many techniques used by encounter leaders are also used by TA therapists; however, TA therapists use specific techniques tailor-made for each individual to raise low energies in an individual's deficient ego states. No particular type of encounter maneuver is thought by the TA analyst to be appropriate for everyone. Rather, each technique is geared and designed for each individual's unique personality egogram. Pillow pounding, rage, and anger expressions are beneficial only for those people who have a poorly developed Critical Parent; they are *not* indicated for those who already have too much anger! Likewise, exercises in expressing feelings are necessary only for those who have too much Adult and have limited their emotional and social responses; these techniques are not as beneficial for those who are already uninhibited and open with their feelings.

A comparison of TA with eclectic systems is difficult since each eclectic psychotherapist will operate idiosyncratically. TA therapists use their mutual, firm, solid, consistent theory; this foundation is liberating for both the therapist and the client. Therapists who call themselves eclectic may or may not use certain ideas in common with TA. Eclectics frequently mix bits and pieces from other theoretical approaches; they may also jump back and forth from one framework to another in theory, and thereby confuse structures, function, behavior, phenomenology, history, and social systems with one another. This resembles mixing apples with oranges; and frequently, a clear path or a defined strategy may be missing.

HISTORY

TA was evolved by Eric Berne in the mid-1950s, at a time in history when psychoanalysis was the primary psychotherapy; communication theory was being applied to emotional problems; and group therapy was emerging as an important modality. The literature and impact of these three influences were especially important to the development of TA.

Precursors

Ego-State Precursors. Wilder Penfield's research (1952) at McGill Medical School, where Berne was a medical student, deserves special mention. Penfield reported that the memories of epileptics are retained and replayed in their natural form.

The subject feels again the emotions which the situation originally produced in him, and he is aware of the same interpretation, true or false, which he himself gave to the experience in the first place. This evoked recollection is not the exact photographic reproduction of past scenes and events. It is a reproduction of what the patient saw and heard and felt and understood (p. 178).

Penfield's remarkable neurosurgical experiments further demonstrated that different ego states (Penfield did not use the term *ego state*) are reexperienced under direct electrical stimulation of the brain and that one experiences a complete revival in the present of both the experience and the memories along with the corresponding feelings of a past situation (Penfield & Roberts, 1959). Berne, a psychiatrist, was especially interested in ego psychology, which was then an important topic in the New York Psychoanalytic Institute circles because of the influence of Heinz Hartmann, Ernst Kris, and others. Berne was impressed with the apparent intact structure of the past states of the ego.

Pharmacological studies of the early work with LSD-25 by Chandler and Hartman (1960) describe the reactivation of the archaic states, and they discuss the employing of two simultaneous states: one oriented to current external and psychological reality; and the other reliving (not merely recalling) scenes dating back to the first year of life. These scenes are accompanied with vivid color, detail, and a feeling of actual experience with all of the original intensity.

Paul Federn (1952), Berne's personal analyst, first expressed in the psychiatric field what Penfield and the drug experimenters later proved: The complete states of the ego are permanently retained and may be reactivated. Federn used the term *ego state* and this met resistance from those more accustomed to thinking in orthodox conceptual terms, rather than shift to a phenomenological approach. Eduardo Weiss (1950), Federn's exponent, described ego states as one's actually experienced reality, with the complete contents that one relived from a past period. Weiss reiterated what Penfield proved: The ego states of former age levels are maintained in a potential existence within the personality, and they may be evoked under special conditions: hypnosis, dreams, and psychosis.

Before Berne's elucidation of the structure of the three basic ego states, both ego psychologists described, and anatomists and pharmacologists, proved the general existence of intact ego states.

Games and Transactions Precursors. Although many general communication theorists such as Alfred Korzybski and Norbert Wiener were studied by Berne and other early TA theorists, the application of the communication-system theory to the psychological issues by Gregory Bateson and Jurgen Ruesch (1951) and their Palo Alto associates in the Bay Area of San Francisco where TA was concomitantly developing became a direct influence. Bateson (Bateson et al., 1956) espoused the double-bind theory of schizophrenia, a communication model that essentially postulates there are two different and incompatible levels of communication between a schizophrenogenic mother and her child. As each level is incompatible with the other, the dependent child has no easy escape except for psychosis. Berne independently specified these two types of levels (overt and covert), and from this he developed rules for games (the corresponding game for a double bind is *Corner*).

Years before, Karl Abraham (1948) had described various character types, and he related these personality characteristics and behaviors to specific fixations that occurred at various stages of psychosexual development. He labeled these according to specific orifices: oral, anal, urethral, and genital; he described their patterns of interaction with other people. Berne later compared Abraham's analyses of character types with specific game patterns: Oral types play *Do Me Something;* anal types play *Schlemiel* or *Now I Got You, You SOB;* urethral types play *Kick Me;* and genital types may play *Rapo.* Berne was quite impressed by Abraham's work, and he presented a panel entitled "Character Types and Game Analysis" at the American Psychiatric Association meeting in 1969.

René Spitz's important work (1945) emphasized the importance of both the quantity and quality of early mother to child transactions; this research is frequently quoted by TA writers and became the inspiration for the term *strokes* (see page 377).

Script Precursors. The notion of *scripts* is not a new one; many allusions in classical and modern literature are made to the fact that the world is a stage and all the people on it are players. Joseph Campbell (1949), the mythologist, takes the view that human lives follow the similar patterns of myths; his works are influential to TA script theorists; Berne once remarked that *The Hero with a Thousand Faces* is the best textbook for script analysts. Much of Campbell's thinking is based on Jung's and Freud's ideas. Jung's notion of *archetypes* (which correspond to Berne's "magic figure" in a script) and the *persona* (the style in which a script is played) were useful to Berne, who, although he admired Jung's focus of attention on myths and fairy tales, found that mystical discussions were difficult to understand and relate to real people without elaborate training. Freud directly related many aspects of human living to a single drama: Oedipus. Berne, who was a serious student of psychoanalysis for three decades, initially accepted and later rejected the notion that each patient is an Oedipus who exhibits the same reactions and drama within his head. Instead, Berne viewed Oedipus as a single possibility of the many that may take place in a patient's life.

Adler (1963) was interested in an individual's goal, which he likened to a secret life plan. Goals, types of scripts, and therapeutic contracts became an important influence to Berne.

Action and Energy Precursors. Abraham Maslow (self-actualization), Will Schutz (encounter), Fritz Perls (Gestalt transfer of energy), and other growth therapists had a profound precursory effect upon the present practice of TA. More direct theoretical applications have been employed by his followers after

Berne's death in 1970. Berne occasionally went to Esalen Institute, the influential growth center on the Big Sur Coast of California, and met with Fritz Perls (Gestalt), Will Schutz (encounter), Virginia Satir (family dynamics), Michael Murphy (human growth), and others involved in the human-potential movement. Robert Goulding, John Dusay, and other TA teachers conducted Esalen workshops; and importantly, Berne's followers became directly exposed to profound growth psychologies that appeared simultaneously with TA's development in northern California. Indeed, many encounter, marathon, and Gestalt leaders embraced TA's theories, as they would enrich TA with their human experiential techniques.

Beginnings

Like many psychiatric innovators, Eric Berne was formally trained in classical psychoanalysis. However, in the mid-1950s, he amiably parted from the psychoanalytical school of thought in favor of employing more rapidly effective techniques to cure patients. TA's history until Berne's death in 1970 is the history of his theory and techniques (J. Dusay, 1975). Berne began doing group therapy when he was an army major in World War II; following his discharge, he began unique experiments on the nature of intuition; he published six articles on intuition between 1949 and 1962 summarized by J. Dusay, (1971), and published posthumously in 1977 (Berne, 1949, 1977). The intuition articles reflect the evolution of TA, and they trace Berne becoming the leader of an innovative approach.

The singularly most important discovery to TA was the dynamic nature of three distinct ego states, which occurred in 1955 when Berne worked in a group with Belle, a 40-year-old disturbed housewife who was discharged from a state hospital, and behaved in two distinct ways toward the men in her life:

Belle would subtly mock and jeer at men whom she considered weak and tease and torment those men whom she felt were strong. She was continually intrigued and confused as to whether the therapist was weak or strong, and she confessed her fantasy that she could see the conformation of his genitals and then attempted to determine if his penis were flabby or erect. She remembered doing the same with her father. Her husband reminded her of a strong man implacable as stone, whose tremendous erections frightened her. . . . She became . . . nauseated when her husband had an erection and could not bear to fantasize about it. . . . She became . . . indisposed when her husband told her a graphic joke about an erection. . . . She could intellectually discuss the vagina but could not bear thinking of it as actually pictured, "a raw, red slimy gash." The image terrified her and she desperately avoided it. . . . Smells also played a significant part in this type of imagery with her (Berne, 1955, pp. 634–58).

Berne called these images Belle experienced *primal images.* They gave rise to the primal judgments she made about men in her life: "This man is flaccid," and "This man is virile." Berne observed these same types of primal judgments occurring in everyday life: "He's an asshole (prick, stinker, jerk, pushover, fart, bleeding heart)." Primal judgments were also seen to be zonal and connected to oral, gastrointestinal, anal, genital, and excretory functions, and that people relate to others according to their primal images and judgments. Berne noted that the "bleeding heart" and the "jerk" were prone to find each other.

The first phase of TA began with Berne's discovery and delineation of ego states (J. Dusay, 1977a), which are a coherent system of thinking, feeling, and behaving. Berne elucidated his discovery of ego states:

An 8-year old boy vacationing at a dude ranch in his cowboy suit helped the hired man unsaddle a horse. When they were finished, the hired man said, "Thanks, Cowpoke." The "assistant" replied, "I'm not really a cowpoke. I'm just a little boy." The patient went on to remark, "That's just the way I feel. Sometimes I feel that I'm not really a lawyer. I'm just a little boy."

This story illustrates the separation of two ways of feeling, thinking, and behaving in this particular patient; everything that was said was heard by two different people, one an adult lawyer and the other an inner little boy. This particular patient was in treatment for a compulsive gambling habit. Sometimes he used a rational, logical gambling system, which was occasionally successful, but more often he governed his behavior with superstitious and little-boy ways of explaining his losses. . . . It became apparent that there were two types of arithmetic employed (Berne, 1957, p. 611).

Both systems were conscious, deliberate, visible, and active parts of the patient's ego system.

Berne emphasized that the archaic intuitive faculty of the Child could be cultivated by the therapist. Dynamically, intuition works best when the Child predominates, the Adult monitors, and the Parent reduces its influence. To Berne, creativity was the Child knowing and the Adult confirming.

TA moved into its second phase (1958–65) with Berne's attention to the *transaction,* which is a stimulus from one person's ego state and the corresponding response from another person's ego state. Berne's interest in communications theory enabled him to recognize that there were often two different types of messages emanating from one source. For instance, a radio would emit a meaningful message, "It's raining in California," and another

simultaneous type of communication would be pops, whirrs, and radio static. With these two types of communication in mind, Berne observed what happens when people get together, and he formulated a specific, concise definition of communication, along with the corresponding three rules (see p. 393). By observing both the overt and covert levels of transacting individuals, Berne began to classify games.

Human behavior that involves two levels of communication, with predictable, stereotyped, and destructive actions that are motivated by hidden desires and lead to specific *payoffs* (bad feelings), were labeled games. The first game Berne analyzed was *Why Don't You . . . ? Yes, But . . . ,* which occurred during one of his therapy groups:

Patient S: I wish we could fix the leak in our roof.
Respondent 1: Why don't you ask your husband to do it?
Patient S: That's a good idea, but he has to work this weekend.
Respondent 2: Why don't you do it yourself?
Patient S: I would but I don't have any tools.
Respondent 3: Why don't you get some tools?
Patient S: Yes, but we overspent our budget this month.
Respondent 4: Why don't you . . . ?
Patient S: Yes, but . . . yes, but . . .

On the overt social level, Patient S provides an Adult stimulus by requesting help for her specific problem; the respondents reciprocate with straightforward Adult advice. On her covert psychological level, she is transacting on a Child-Parent level and secretly implying, "Just you try to suggest something I haven't already thought of, hee-hee." The group members try and try with the result that they become frustrated and S maintains a triumphant, coy smile on her face.

An entire classification of psychological games has been elucidated (Berne, 1964) in *Games People Play*. People are inclined to have a specific repertoire of favorite games they play; they base their entire social relationships upon finding suitable partners to play the corresponding opposite roles. Berne and members of the original San Francisco TA seminar were pursuing the question, "Why do different people play the same games over and over?" Freud's repetition compulsion (which specifically related to the death instinct) was an appealing, yet obscure, notion that did not satisfactorily answer this question. Because plausible explanations were sought, TA historically moved into its third phase (1960–70), which resulted in script theory. A *script* is "a life plan based on a decision made in childhood, reinforced by the parents, justified by subsequent events, and culminating in a chosen alternative" (Berne, 1972). The direct script message transmissions from parents to their children became symbolized by Claude Steiner (1971) with the script matrix (see Figure 10.3).

As TA theorists began to delve into folk and fairy tales, they found various lifestyles were based on specific characters with whom patients and their relatives identified. These could be traced back to ancient myths, with their victims, persecutors and rescuers (Karpman, 1968), and the more popular heroines and heroes who starred in popular folk tales, dramas, movies, novels, and television shows (K. Dusay, 1976). One's script became written and fixed in the Child (p. 39) and reinforced through fantasies, dreams, and, later, "reality."

Berne was a prolific writer who published 64 articles and 8 books. He originated the TA Bulletin, which later emerged as a quarterly, *Transactional Analysis Journal*. Berne was at the height of his creativity, insight, and power when he died of a coronary infarction in the summer of 1970.

Current Status

Since Berne's death, a fourth phase of TA has emerged: energy transfers, distribution, and action. The *egogram* (J. Dusay, 1972) symbolizes the amount of time and energy any person exudes in one's ego states. The energy system of an egogram remains constant, unless a person actively changes his balance and relationship to one another through direct energy transfers (raising weak, underused ego states). Since 1970 TA practitioners have developed many suitable techniques for raising energy levels in the various ego states.

The clinical use of TA will relate to one of the four phases of TA's development: (1) ego states, (2) transactions and games, (3) script analysis and redecision, and (4) egogram energy shift.

The San Francisco TA Seminar was formerly called the San Francisco Social Psychiatry Seminar (founded by Berne in 1958) and today is known as the Eric Berne Seminar of San Francisco. This is the world's longest ongoing weekly seminar for group therapy. From the original 8 members who met in Berne's office in the 1950s, the *International Transactional Analysis Association* (ITAA) presently includes over 10,000 members in the United States and throughout the world. The ITAA is experiencing rapid growth in Europe, Japan, South America, and India.

Berne maintained that trying to "look" professional was not as important as curing patients. He willingly taught his system to all interested persons in the helping professions. With the ITAA, an advanced, rigorous training program is available for members to train formally for a period of two to five years to attain clinical competency and certification as TA therapists and teachers. Two distinct lines of advance training have evolved and presently exist: advanced clinical training (for mental-health professionals) and special fields training (for teachers and business-oriented persons).

In 1971 the Editorial Board of the *Transactional Analysis Journal* instituted the Eric Berne Memorial Scientific Awards for outstanding contributions to TA theory and practice. Each year, TA persons are nominated who have devised original and applicable concepts to Berne's goal of "curing patients faster"; the winner is chosen by the advanced members' votes of the ITAA. In 1971 Claude Steiner (1971) received the award for his development of the *Script Matrix;* in 1972 Stephen Karpman (1968) received the second award for the *Drama Triangle;* in 1973 John Dusay (1972) received the third award for his development of the *Egogram and the Constancy Hypothesis;* in 1974 Jacqui and Aaron Schiff (1969, 1971) jointly received the award for their development of the *Reparenting Techniques and Passivity Confrontation* they employ in their residential treatment centers for schizophrenics; in 1975 Robert and Mary Goulding (1976) won the award for *Childhood Decisions and Redecisions;* in 1976 Patricia Crossman (1966) won it for recognizing the importance of *Permission, Protection and Potency;* and in 1977 Taibi Kahler (1975) received it for the *Miniscript.* The Eric Berne Scientific Award winners' theories are viewed as part of TA theory and practices.

PERSONALITY

Theory of Personality

The basic motivating factor for all human social behavior is one's lifelong need for human recognition, which TA therapists term *strokes.* Strokes may be either physical (a hug) or verbal ("you're nice"). René Spitz (1945), a child psychoanalyst, studied the mortality rate of infants in two types of orphanages in England; he found that the extent to which the children were physically stroked and handled had a profound effect upon their survival.

TA analysts maintain that continual strokes are necessary throughout one's life; a lack of strokes has a deleterious and long-lasting effect, both physically and emotionally. Strokes may be positive or negative.

Habitual criminals with high recidivism rates illustrate that negatives strokes are better than no strokes at all. The primate studies of Harry Harlow (1958) demonstrate that isolated baby monkeys reared either without mother monkeys or those "fed" by surrogate wire monkeys become emotionally disturbed and exhibit abnormal behaviors. Sensory-deprivation experiments with normal adults at Harvard (Vernon, 1961) illustrate that both cognitive and motor functioning will rapidly deteriorate and deficits will persist for days, even after the persons go back into a normal environment. Illusions and hallucinations can be produced by a temporary lack of sensory stimuli. More than 700 TA articles and descriptions of strokes have appeared in scientific journals and related literature since 1957 (Blair & McGahey, 1974, 1975).

Human children growing up begin to look for ways to get both verbal and symbolic strokes from others when physical strokes are not forthcoming. Although spoken words may become the major sources of strokes for people in later life, it is doubtful whether words alone can ever completely replace actual physical touching.

As specific stroking patterns develop, they may be more clearly understood by attention to both the structural and functional analyses of ego states, transactions, psychological games, and scripts.

Structural Analysis. *Ego states* are defined as a consistent pattern of feeling and experiences directly related to a corresponding consistent pattern of behavior. A distinct tripartite system of Parent, Adult, and Child, which are separate entities, has been described and is the subject of structural analysis proper. Although most of the salient features of ego states have been presented in the History section, it is important to reemphasize that ego states are a phenomenological system based upon here-and-now observable data, in contrast to psychoanalytic concepts that primarily emphasize developmental stages and view pathology as resulting from fixations in development.

One's ego states are not related to one's chronological age, except developmentally during early childhood when one's Adult and Parent are not yet fully developed. A teenager may have a staunch moral and value system (P); an 8-year-old boy may look to the right and left for oncoming cars before crossing the street (A); a 65-year-old chairman of the board will gleefully chase his young, sexy secretary around the conference table (C).

Certain pathologies in personalities can be structurally understood with the three ego states (see Figures 10.5, 10.6, and 10.7). Figure 10.5 illustrates a normal personality structure, whereby each ego state has a distinct and separate boundary. Figure 10.6 is the structure of a delusion. In this instance, there is a Child-Adult delusion in that the separating boundaries have broken down. The Child's fantasies and dreams are inappropriately mixed in

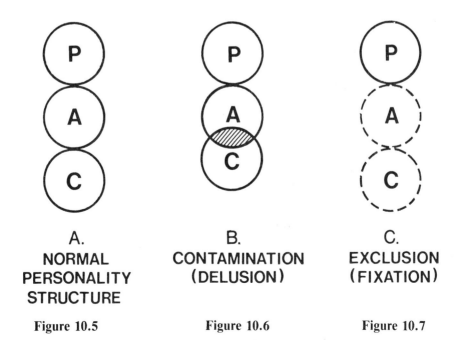

A.
NORMAL
PERSONALITY
STRUCTURE

B.
CONTAMINATION
(DELUSION)

C.
EXCLUSION
(FIXATION)

Figure 10.5   **Figure 10.6**   **Figure 10.7**

with Adult reality and logic testing. This person might say, "The TV is giving me special instructions." His Adult is accurate that there is a TV transmitting information. The Child ego has regarded itself as the center of the TV's attention, thereby causing a break in the boundaries between the Adult and the Child. Figure 10.7 illustrates the structure of an exclusion. The Parent is represented by a heavy, dark, solid circle; the Adult and the Child have only dotted lines. This strong boundary insures that the Parent is in charge, and the Adult and Child are excluded. A fundamentalist country preacher who obsesses himself with finding sins is operating from an excluding Parent ego state.

The Functional Aspects of Personality. The structural description of ego states with their circles and boundaries indicates the "what and where" of the personality; the concept of "how much energy" of the five ego state forces (Critical Parent-CP; Nurturing Parent-NP; Adult-A; Free Child-FC; and Adapted Child-AC) is answered by the functional approach of the egogram.

Any group of trained ego-state observers can readily identify these five basic forces within people, and each will construct similar egograms of the same person. They will consensually agree on the personality-force balance, or imbalance, as depicted on the subject's egogram. These same egograms can be drawn accurately week after week by different trained observers. The ego states will line up differently on each person's egogram, and they correspond directly to the

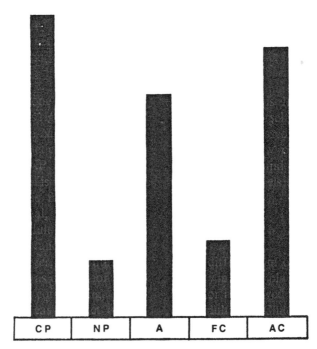

SELF DESTRUCTIVE EGOGRAM

Figure 10.8

specific complaints and problems these people express. An egogram with an excessively high CP, a high A, a high AC, a low NP, and a low FC is characteristically associated with a person who is self-destructive (see Figure 10.8). Other consistent findings reveal that when a very high AC is combined with a very low NP, the common complaint will be of loneliness and lack of friends (see Figure 10.9). A certain type of obesity, colloquially labeled "Big Mama," is correlated with a very high NP, a high AC, a low CP, and a very low FC. This Big Mama egogram is common among overweight persons in the helping professions: social workers, nurses, dieticians, and those who live with demanding spouses and children who seem to require an abundance of nurturing and strokes. These persons spend most of their energies giving to others and unfortunately get very little back for their FC in the way of strokes. People who are too low in CP get taken advantage of and pushed around. Persons who are quite low in NP are lonely, depressed, and ungiving; those low in A have difficulty concentrating and problem solving; those low in FC have lost their creativity, intuition, and the zest of life. Persons who are low in AC do not compromise, conform, and are difficult to get along with.

A person's egogram reflects the type of person one is, the probable types of problems, and the strengths and weaknesses within one's personality. The egogram also provides a personal map for growth and change. Although there is no ideal egogram, people experience difficulties when one ego state is extremely low and

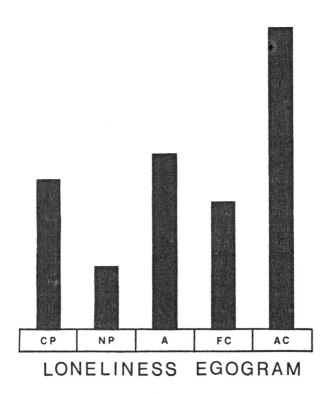

| CP | NP | A | FC | AC |

LONELINESS EGOGRAM

Figure 10.9

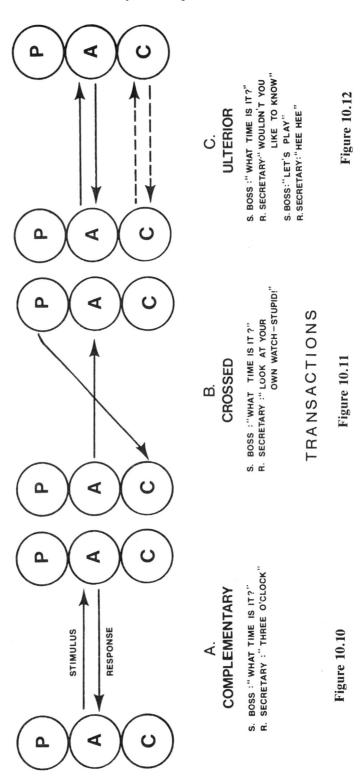

C.
ULTERIOR

S. BOSS :"WHAT TIME IS IT ?"
R. SECRETARY:" WOULDN'T YOU
                         LIKE TO KNOW"
S. BOSS:" LET'S PLAY"
R. SECRETARY:" HEE HEE "

Figure 10.12

B.
CROSSED

S. BOSS :"WHAT TIME IS IT ?"
R. SECRETARY :" LOOK AT YOUR
          OWN WATCH—STUPID!"

Figure 10.11

TRANSACTIONS

A.
COMPLEMENTARY

S. BOSS :" WHAT TIME IS IT ?"
R. SECRETARY :" THREE O'CLOCK "

STIMULUS

RESPONSE

Figure 10.10

another is disportionately high. Relative to that, a harmonious egogram becomes a matter of balance in the relationship between the ego states. A creative artist needs a high FC; a successful district attorney needs a high CP; an accountant needs a strong A; a diplomat needs lots of AC; and a therapist needs a well-developed NP.

Transactions and the Three Rules of Communication. TA focuses keen attention upon how different individuals tend to communicate with one another. A *transaction* is defined as a stimulus and a related response between various ego states of two or more people, and, graphically, they are symbolized by arrows. The two primary types of transactions are the *social* overt and easily observed level, represented by a solid arrow; and the *psychological* covert, body-language level, represented by a dotted arrow.

The three specific types of transactions, with their three corresponding rules of communication, have been delineated (see Figures 10.10, 10.11, 10.12). In Figure 10.10, entitled Complementary Transaction, the arrows are parallel. The boss (A) asks the secretary (A), "What time is it?" He gets a complementary straightforward, overt response (A to A), "It's 3 o'clock." The first rule of communication involves a complementary transaction: *Whenever the arrows are parallel, communication can proceed indefinitely.* Communication does not have to be A-A; it can be P-P, C-C, P-C, C-P, C-A, A-P, P-A, or the reverse. In Figure 10.11 there is a crossed transaction and the arrows are crossed. The boss asks (A-A), "What time is it?" and the secretary angrily answers (P-C), "Look at your own watch!" This crossed transaction effectively stops the communication about "time" between them. Therefore, the corresponding second rule of communication

is: *whenever the arrows cross, communication on the specific subject ceases immediately.* This second rule of communication clarifies the phenomena of *transference* as described in psychoanalytic literature. The therapist says, "You seem to be late for your Friday appointment" (A-A), and the client reports, "You're always criticizing me for being late—just like my father" (C-P). A *countertransference* is when a therapist crosses a complementary transaction; that is, the client says, "How long do you think my treatment will be?" (A-A). The therapist replies, "You shouldn't ask questions like that" (P-C). Figure 10.12 illustrates an ulterior transaction with dual levels (the social and the psychological) occurring simultaneously. The boss again asks the secretary the time (A-A social level and C-C hidden psychological level). She gives him the time (A-A social level and C-C playful psychological level). A dual-level transaction with an ulterior message is necessary for a psychological game. This leads to the third rule of communication: *Behavior cannot be predicted by attention to the social level alone; the psychological message is the key to predicting behavior and understanding the meaning.* The first game ever discovered (p. 386), WHY DON'T YOU . . . YES, BUT . . . , is one in which the client enticed the group to "try" to help her solve her problem. After continuing to try, they became frustrated and finally gave up, while the client coyly smiled and triumphantly exulted that no one could solve her problem (ha-ha). Analyzing and identifying the ulterior transactions are necessary to understanding psychological games.

Psychological Games. A *game* is played between two or more people, and each game has certain traits in common. The players transact on an *open* (overt)

$$C + G = R \dashrightarrow S \dashrightarrow X \dashrightarrow P$$

GAME FORMULA

Figure 10.13

level, and at the same time transmit a *hidden* agenda (covert level). Consider Fanny the secretary, who complained that she was unable to hold a job, having been fired twenty times in ten years. She stated she wanted a solid, long-term working relationship with an employer (she also wanted a long-term, social relationship in her life). Her therapist agreed with her goal and contracted to work with her to achieve it (see treatment contracts under Psychotherapy). During their initial interview, Fanny started by criticizing the therapist's necktie; then she began to rearrange her chair and the rest of the office furniture; and finally, she "accidentally" knocked over the therapist's favorite lamp. As Fanny was apologizing and bending over to reposition the lamp, she placed the distinctive target of her posterior near the therapist's foot, which he instantly considered kicking. Suddenly, with an intuitive laugh, he checked his anger and his foot. Fanny turned to face him with a knowing look, and she, too, began to laugh as they both became aware that she was playing a physical version of her favorite *Kick Me* game (see Figure 10.2).

On the obvious social level (solid lines), Fanny said to the therapist (A-A), "Please help me with my problem." The therapist responded (A-A), "Your problem seems psychological. Let's work it out." On the surface, their conversation sounded A-A; however, on the hidden psychological level (broken lines), Fanny's C was inviting the therapist's P to kick her as she insulted his clothing, rear-

ranged his furniture, and knocked over his favorite lamp. This same pattern of interaction, occurring in the therapist's office, directly corresponded with her past history of repeated rejections and was reflected in her chief complaint. In Fanny's case, an unknowing therapist may have actually responded by playing her game, by kicking her out of treatment as an inappropriate candidate for psychotherapy, and by thinking, "Some patients just mess up the office and don't get any better, no matter what you do." Fanny's payoff could have been, "Why do rejections always happen to me?"

A TA analyst understands a personality by first observing the "here-and-now" transactional sequences between himself and the client. Games conform to a general yet specific game formula (Figure 10.13): $C + G = R \rightarrow S \rightarrow X \rightarrow P$. The initial Con (C) is the "bait" in which the client (Fanny) transacts on an ulterior level from her C to the therapist's P. On the surface, her transaction looks like a straightforward request for help; yet underneath, she is secretly asking for a rejection as she "hooks" the therapist's feeling of omnipotence, which is seen as the Gimmick (G). His response (R) is initially accepting and forgiving, as he continues to overlook her critique of his necktie and her rearrangement of his furniture. Fanny continued to annoy him; yet the therapist remained composed until the final Switch (S) of feelings. The therapist and client both felt a Cross-up (X), which quickly led to the final Payoff (P) for both. Had the therapist not stopped the game, his Payoff would have entitled him to feel angry at his ungrateful client; and Fanny's Payoff would have entitled her to another desired rejection as well as a potential banishment. Certain symptoms and syndromes of psychopathology can be understood by analyzing the final payoffs of games. By playing their favorite games, people will repetitively collect payoff *trading stamps,* which are those specific treasured feelings about themselves and others; Fanny received "black and blue" trading stamps each time she was kicked out and fired. After she collected enough stamps, she would entitle herself to a "free depression" and perhaps end up in the hospital. Although some psychotherapists will observe the precipitating event, the TA analyst will look at the entire system of events for each interactional pattern. These continuing repetitive patterns of payoffs and their corresponding negative feelings are seen as *racket feelings.* These are the common feelings that persons have chosen to use, since a young age, whenever they are in stressful situations. Persons will commonly choose racket feelings of being sad, scared, or angry. A racket feeling is the same feeling used over and over, regardless of whether it is appropriate. Game sequences and rackets are important to the therapist in understanding a client's present behavior and personality, as well as being indicators for probable future behavior. A person who commits suicide has a long history of collecting rejections and playing self-negating games. Therefore, by correctly diagnosing and interrupting games, rather than unknowingly entering into them, the therapist can thwart a client's entire payoff system.

Berne referred to the first-, the second-, and the third-degree states of games (1964). A *first-degree game* is considered socially acceptable in that no one gets

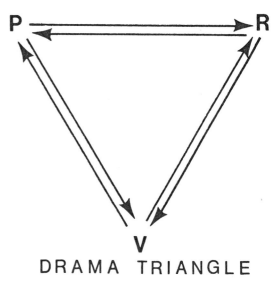

DRAMA TRIANGLE

Figure 10.14

physically hurt, although one may be admonished or yelled at. A *second-degree game* is more serious, in that there is frequently a punch in the nose or face slap. A *third-degree game* is deadly serious and may be "played for keeps." The payoffs are frequently ostracism, a messy divorce, a trip to the court room, or to the morgue. Game switches are characteristically sudden, abrupt, and dramatic—particularly in second- and third-degree games.

Game players operate from three distinct roles—the victim, the persecutor, and the rescuer—and they make switches between these roles. The role switches are illustrated on a drama triangle (Karpman, 1968). Each role is interchangeable and persons frequently switch back and forth during the course of the game (see Figure 10.14). Fanny entered treatment as a *victim,* complaining of being fired and of having a miserable childhood. The unwitting therapist commenced as a *rescuer.* Fanny then switched into a *persecutor* by criticizing the therapist's necktie, rearranging his furniture, and knocking over his lamp, while the therapist became a victim of her persecutions. Quickly, he switched into a persecutor as his anger mounted, while Fanny quickly switched back into her familiar victim role and positioned her bottom by his foot. Role switches occur quickly and dramatically; they have been the backbone of drama and theater throughout the centuries. Role switches occur throughout mythology, fairy tales, all successful literature, and even in everyday TV soap operas (K. Dusay, 1976).

Authentic behavior is differentiated from game behavior, although it may have some similarities. The client enters the therapist's office, and straightforwardly says, "Help, I need some support." The therapist offers support, and the client says, "Thank you," smiles, and leaves. No dramatic switch has occurred; this exchange remains a straightforward simple set of complementary transactions.

Scripts. The important question for understanding personality is: why do different individuals choose specific games? The answer is found by analyzing the crucial transactions between parents and their children during the early development years; this system is illustrated on a script matrix (Steiner, 1971; Fig. 10.3). Fanny was given a typical Standard Success Story (SSS) by her parents: "Go to college, make money, get married, and have children." These *values* (Arrow 1) were introjected from the P ego states of her parents to her developing P ego state. Fanny accepted her parents' values and eventually made them her own. The *injunctions* (Arrow 2) are usually unspoken and delivered as a "curse" from a parent's C to the child's C (technically the Adapted Child—not the autonomous Free Child). Injunctions are usually delivered from the parent of the opposite sex and they are frequently sym-

bolized by a dotted line, in that they are seldom discussed or stated out loud. Fanny's father had difficulty in being close and intimate, and he would insinuate "get lost" messages. Because he nonverbally ignored her with his scowl and frowns, Fanny began to decide she was not a worthwhile person and could not make it ("don't be" and "don't make it"). The *values* from her father ("be a success") directly contradicted his injunctions ("don't be" and "don't make it"). Confronted with the dilemma of these incongruent messages, Fanny looked to her mother for an answer of how to get along in a family like this. As a child, Fanny noted that her mother pestered and irritated her father for attention—her *technique* (Arrow 3). After her father mentally and physically assaulted her mother, she would sulk into her separate bedroom. Fanny's mother thus "showed" Fanny specific techniques how to be a pest and get rejected, the *here's how* (Arrow 3), which was her personal version of the *Kick Me* game. Values, injunctions, and techniques comprise the elements of one's script. The values are also called the *counterscript* or *counterinjunction*. When Fanny was not getting "kicked," she was being a success-oriented, well-behaved person.

Scripts have been both written and theorized about by TA analysts throughout the last decade. Berne's views about script formation are found in *What Do You Say After You Say Hello?* (1972). Berne classified specific types of scripts: an *over and over* script corresponds to the myth of Sisyphus; an *always* script relates to persons who perpetually suffer; an *until* script insures that the individual will be unhappy until a significant event happens; a *never* script forbids happiness and love; an *after* script requires that the person complete many things first, and then enjoy himself after; *open-ended* scripts insure that persons will lose their vitality and enthusiasm as they drift into old age. To Berne the five requirements of a script are (1) directives from parents, (2) a corresponding personality development, (3) a confirming childhood decision about oneself and life, (4) a penchant for either success or failure, and (5) a convincing way of behaving.

Berne viewed how the contents of one's script and their corresponding myths and fairy tales would occur in the therapist's office. As was Berne's style, he would begin with the presenting problem, and then he would take it back into the past. A client wearing a bright red, hooded cape came into his office complaining that her wolfish boyfriend had just jilted her, and she sighed, "Why does this always happen to me? Wolves seem to prey on me." Not surprisingly, her favorite fairy tale was Little Red Riding Hood, frequently told to her by her mother when she went to bed at night. The Child part of her mother would emphasize that wolves prey on helpless victims. Berne traced the genesis of this human script back to the tale of Europa who was kidnapped by Zeus disguised as a bull. Berne's impression was that the mythologies in the fairy tales show up in modern living. Steiner's book *Scripts People Live* (1972) has distinguished between the banal scripts and the *hamartic* (tragic) scripts. K. Dusay (1975) has made an analysis of the recurrence of fairy tales and myths in the therapist's office by analyzing the scripts and egograms of classical heroes and heroines throughout history.

Variety of Concepts

Varieties within the TA Family. Although all TA therapists work with the psychology of ego states, there are diver-gencies and different focuses, depending upon the various types of problems encountered.

Robert and Mary Goulding work mainly with therapists and mental health professionals in a marathon or retreat setting. Jacqui and Aaron Schiff work basically with a schizophrenic population who are either unable or unwilling to be responsible for themselves at the onset of treatment. Claude Steiner works with counter-culture radicals, students, and alternate life-style individuals. Martin Groeder set up the Aescalapian program in prison systems. Dru Scott, Dorothy Jongeward, Muriel James, and others problem-solve in nonclinical settings with business and industry. The uses and ramifications of TA continue to be widespread and diverse, as the refinement in personality theory inevitably develops.

Decision-Redecision Methods. Robert and Mary Goulding are the co-directors of the Western Institute for Group and Family Therapy and they provided an important redecision model used by many TA therapists, especially in the treatment of nonpsychotic individuals. They emphasize early childhood decisions wherein a young child decides to be an "OK" or "not-OK" person, based upon the injunctions he received. The Gouldings have identified and classified the types of childhood decisions that result from injunctions such as "don't be you," "don't think," "don't feel," "don't be a child," "don't grow up," and "don't be." Because one's basic life decision had survival value in early childhood, the individual develops racket feelings that are the same habitual, stereotyped, emotional responses to each situation. Early decisions and racket feelings are carried throughout life, and a client will protect them in therapy through impasses (Goulding & Goulding, 1976).

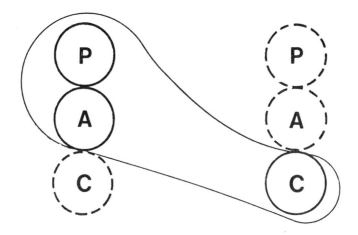

SYMBIOSIS
Figure 10.15

In redecision work, a milieu for change is created, the individual reexperiences decision moments and then chooses to redecide about himself by self-confrontation.

Reparenting. The Cathexis approach to TA (or Schiff family method) was founded by Jacqui Lee Schiff. Both her theoretical model and treatment is focused upon seriously disturbed persons who have generally been diagnosed as schizophrenic. Although the common end point of therapy is autonomy, initially the client is passive, dependent, and accepts no responsibility for his behavior. Four passivity behaviors have been identified by Jacqui and Aaron Schiff (1971): (1) doing nothing; (2) overadaptation; (3) agitation; and (4) incapacitation or violence. These behaviors are attempts to reestablish or maintain a symbiotic relationship (see Figure 10.15).

In a *symbiotic* relationship, a mother and her child become intimately linked in a mutually dependent way, and they behave as a *single* individual; usually the mother functions as the operating Parent and Adult, and her offspring maintains only the Child ego state. In other words, two persons are operating as one complete individual in a symbiotic relationship. Symbiosis is normal during early infancy; later it is seen as pathological. A discount is an internal mechanism whereby a person will deny oneself and others as responsible or capable. Jacqui and Aaron Schiff have identified the four principal discounts that maintain a symbiosis and "entitle" the person to remain passive. One can discount: (1) the existence of a problem ("The fire in the house is not a problem"); (2) the significance of the problem ("Well, the house is on fire but it isn't important"); (3) the solution to the problem ("Well, the house is on fire, but there's nothing that can be done about it"); and (4) discounting oneself and others ("Yes, the house is on fire, and it possibly could be changed, but I cannot do anything about it and neither can you"). By employing these discounts, a person effectively removes his responsibility to solve problems. *Grandiosity* is another mechanism defined by the Schiffs that involves either a maximized or minimized exaggeration about a person, problem, or event, in which a person entitles himself to stay the same and thus justify the symbiosis ("I am too scared to think"). The Schiffs employ unique, and frequently controversial, treatment methods (Schiff et al., 1975).

TA and Variations from Other Theories. Comparisons among TA and some other important therapies were made in the Overview section. TA theory is based upon the "here-and-now" social interactions, and does not adhere to a theory of the dynamic unconscious. The "unconscious" mind is not focused upon by TA analysis; instead, actual stroking patterns are. One's drives are viewed as being script determined and programmed by early parental messages, rather than being seen as drives and instincts. Transference and countertransference phenomena are seen as two specific types of transactions. *Homeostasis* is considered from an energy system on the egogram. *Resistances* to one's growth and change in psychotherapy are viewed functionally as a stronger ego state force holding down a lower force. A highly critical individual (high CP, low FC, and low NP) was being seen in a TA group because he had few friends. His case illustrates the principles of resistance. When the TA therapist asked the group members to take off their shoes and sit on the floor, this "true grit" person stood up, banged his fist, and roared, "I won't take off my shoes—that's stupid! I came here to get friends—not to take off my shoes!" His resistance was seen as protecting the homeostasis of his personality (his CP holding down his FC).

Rebellion to a TA analyst is a type of conformity to a script injunction and is seen as a pseudorebellion. Taking exotic pills is following an early message of "You're crazy." Authentic rebellion is breaking away from the script.

A final note to consider when comparing conceptual variations among different psychotherapies was made by Eric Berne (1963) when he noted that a great fallacy, to either affirm or negate a particular argument, is to employ different viewpoints. Any finding may be described functionally, structurally, phenomenologically, clinically, chemically, molecularly, and so on. Many times theorists will mix up these systems and will thus negate a finding that is described in one modality by using a frame of reference from another mode, which gives an end result of mixing apples and oranges.

PSYCHOTHERAPY

Theory of Psychotherapy

Transactional analysts focus upon three primary areas for psychotherapy: egogram balances, game interruptions, and script redecisions. A client's change in one area will facilitate a corresponding change in his other areas. *Balance* is a key word in personality change; and although a TA therapist does not expect clients to be *homogenized* (all with the same egogram), efforts are made to insure that no one ego-state force is gravely underenergized. One's awareness of specific games one plays will lead to a position of choice for interrupting these stereotyped, habitual patterns. A game-free individual is frequently rewarded both with interpersonal and social intimacy, which is not possible through game playing. A person's script redecision will facilitate the individual in living an autonomous life, which is free from the influences of parental injunctions.

Although a TA therapist becomes a catalyzer of change, there is a basic underlying TA assumption that the client alone is responsible for his life, choices, and basic survival in the unique family environment. A person's negative existential life decisions (I'm not OK, or you're not OK) about himself and others do not need to be dragged around throughout life like a bag of dirty laundry. Instead, people have the ability to review their negative childhood decisions and thereby change their minds, personalities, and life-styles. Unfortunately, many people give up their recognition of personal power and actively deny and defend their lack of responsibility.

A few TA approaches have unique views concerning the individual's responsibility. Steiner's "radical" therapy focuses upon oppressive social institutions, and he emphasizes positive social action in addition to personal psychotherapy. The Schiff family techniques are designed for psychotic clients who may initially regress to a dependent child state and are then reparented and reraised with new OK messages. Eventually these clients establish a personal responsibility for their lives.

Process of Psychotherapy

To facilitate a client's personal responsibility, a TA therapist will use a simple, common vocabulary; will enter into a contractual treatment goal; and will then use specific techniques designed to enhance each individual's own power and responsibility. These three areas are generally used by all TA therapists and are seen and heard in TA treatment settings.

Simple Language. The simple vocabulary of TA, ego states (Parent, Adult, and Child), games (colloquially expressed, for example, Now I Got You, You SOB), scripts, and strokes are easily

learned and have also been successfully taught to mentally retarded people who can understand these concepts. Family members (parents and their children) are on an equal vocabulary footing, and even well-educated professionals are encouraged to talk straight and not hide behind big words and complex jargon. The time and energy a client spends in treatment is directed toward getting better—not in defining and redefining.

Unfortunately, naive critics of TA sometimes focus exclusively upon the colloquial words they have heard about so they can quickly discount the scientific profundity of the theory. A popular joke in TA circles concerns a TA therapist who sat next to an astronomer on an airplane flight. The astronomer asked what he did for a living and the TA therapist replied that he did TA. The astronomer then exclaimed, "Oh, I know all about that—'I'm OK, You're OK!'" The TA therapist politely smiled, then asked, "What do you do for a living?" and the response was "I'm an astronomer." The TA therapist smiled, and quipped back, "Oh, I know all about that—'Twinkle, Twinkle, Little Star!'"

Contractual Therapy. A key question in contractual therapy is, "How will both you and I know when you get what you came for?" This poignant statement immediately clarifies the underlying attitude that the client and therapist are mutual allies and will work to accomplish a mutual goal. Throughout the therapy contract, each will initiate a process of defining their mutual responsibilities in achieving the goal; the therapist will not enter in a passive spectator position and the client will not sit back waiting for the therapist to perform a miracle (seen as the game of *Do Me Something*). A TA treatment contract has the four major components of a legal contract:

1. *Mutual assent:* A simply stated contract *goal* between the Adult ego states of both the therapist and the client is made; both persons become Adult ego state allies. "I will have sex again," from an impotent man; "I will hold a job for at least one year," from an habitually fired person; "I will not kill myself accidentally, or on purpose," from a suicidal person, are all examples of contracts. Contracts are also stated by specific egogram changes, "I'll be satisfied when the group constructs my egogram with my Free Child to be greater than my Adapted Child." Therapy contracts are frequently reviewed, updated, and changed. Mini or weekly contracts may also lead to a more profound change—"I will speak to three people this week"—as a step toward a long goal of having an intimate social relationship.

Initial difficulties in making contracts may take the form of games that a TA therapist will need to be aware of. A client may take two hours off from work and risk being fired, or he may pay a substantial fee to the therapist and continue to say that he does not know what he wants to change about himself. A TA therapist may then ask, "What does your Parent say you *should* get out of treatment? What *fantasies* does your Child have? What will your Adult decide to be a worthwhile goal?" Unless a therapist and client have mutual assent about a common goal, the therapist may become a nontherapeutic, rescuing, advice giver, and not a catalytic mutual ally of the client.

2. *Competency:* The TA therapist will agree to provide only those services he can *competently* deliver in the area of his expertise. The therapist will also actively confront the client's misperceptions and fantasies about the assumed "magical" powers of the therapist. A competent therapist would not contract with a 55-year-old man to become the world's champion 100-yard-dash runner. However, the therapist may contract with him to exercise and become healthy. A client also needs to be competent in achieving his goals of the contract. If the client is still legally or financially dependent upon parents, they need to be included in the treatment contract. Occasionally social agencies and legal guardians need be a part of a treatment-contract planning session. Therapists will attest to this when working with families that quickly pull the client out of therapy when he begins to change.

3. *Legal object:* The contract must have a *legal* aim or objective. "Provide me with mind altering drugs, Doctor, so I can become more aware of myself," is not a legal contract. "I want to graduate from college with a B-average," may be an acceptable contract.

4. *Consideration:* Usually the *consideration* is the therapist's fee in the form of money the client agrees to pay. The therapist will provide his expertise and the therapeutic time. TA therapists who treat clients either in social agencies or under circumstances where the client is not expected personally to pay for therapy will encourage the client to offer a type of consideration, perhaps in the form of a service, a painting, a poem, or some other produce which represents the client's commitment to therapy.

Specific Techniques to Enhance Personal Responsibility. People who experience themselves as powerless to change continue to reinforce this position by habitually broadcasting their plight. The TA therapist will confront this observation to create an awareness of self-power in the individual. When a client says, "I *can't* think," the TA therapist will confront with, "I *won't* think!"

When a client says, *"She makes* me feel bad,"* the therapist will correct with, *"I choose to feel* bad—in response to her." Persons who continually say, "You know," and other cliches, are confronted and shown why others do not take them seriously. *Gallows humor* is inappropriate smiling, laughing, and inviting others to laugh at one's tragic situation. A client with a serious drinking problem who says, "I just had one little drink . . . hee-hee," is confronted that drinking himself to death is not funny. J. McNeel (1975) has elaborated specific, commonly used TA techniques and attitudes that clients use to rob themselves of power, based on observations of a three-day TA treatment marathon led by Robert and Mary Goulding (see Applications section). Blackboards are commonplace in TA groups so clients can visually represent their explanations in clear ways to commit their ideas. Chalk is frequently handed to clients who play the game of *Stupid,* to provide them with permission to problem-solve. TA emphasizes symbols and simple diagrams so both the therapist and the client can clearly delineate their ideas.

Although TA therapists use simple vocabularies, treatment contracts, and specific pertinent techniques to restore the client's power, the types of therapy may differ widely. Originally, Berne designed TA as an adjunct to psychoanalysis, to be practiced in small groups with seven or eight clients that meet for two hours weekly. Now people are seen individually, in families, as couples, in marathons, in inpatient and outpatient wards, in prisons, and in business and industry settings. Each modality has certain advantages and disadvantages (see Applications section). What can be typically seen and heard by TA practitioners varies widely beyond the above general processes, depending upon the type of problems, the treatment set-

tings, and the styles of the therapists. Therapists are encouraged to use their personal attributes and not fit into a TA mold. Some common processes are discussed below, and although attention to games, scripts, and ego-state structure and function does not follow a particular order in treatment, the descriptions provide the historical development of these processes.

Game Analysis by Confrontation. During the initial interview, the therapist observes the usual social amenities, like saying "Hello," and neither uses gimmicks to increase stress, nor leans over backward to provide comfort. The business of establishing a treatment contract, deciding on whether the therapist and client are able to work together, and choosing a proper treatment setting (individual, group, family, etc.) are the usual topics.

Because games are habitual, stereotyped patterns of transacting, they will usually begin to manifest in the initial interview and the therapist is keenly interested in picking up game clues, such as a person telling a sad history of failure and then subtly smiling. This tips off the therapist that two levels of transactions are occurring, and as soon as the therapist is aware of a game occurring, the decision to intervene is made (see Applications, pages 409–418, for a description of intervention).

In addition to observing the client's dual levels of transacting, the communication pattern between therapist and client is also observed. Eric Berne called himself a "martian" in therapy and indeed called all TAers "martians." This implied that the therapist transcended the setting and observed how he and the client transacted with each other; that is, "When the therapist offers a suggestion the client says, 'Yes . . . but . . . ,' and the therapist looks disgruntled." The therapist therefore observes the process and himself as well as observing the client; this is reminiscent of Theodore Reik's "Listening with the Third Ear" and Harry Stack Sullivan's observing the interpersonal processes.

More important than the therapist's knowing what is happening is the awareness of the client and *interruption* of the patterns. Groups are often useful because of the increased transactional possibilities, and other clients may pick up blind spots of the therapist. Verbal interruptions are extremely important for counteracting games; that is, the therapist quickly says, "But . . . ," just before the client says it himself; or when a young female *Rapo* player is complaining that men are just interested in her body, as her skirt slips slowly up her thighs, the therapist acknowledges the seductive moves, and says, "I think I know why!"

In addition to verbal interruption, the therapist may actually stand up and ask the client to do likewise; they then both stand back and comment on what is going on between the two of them; like Berne's "martian" observers, they have an Adult to Adult ego-state conversation. Occasionally an empty chair is offered and the client is asked to sit in it and describe the ongoing interaction.

Game Interruption by Psychodrama. When a client enters into a game with either the therapist or another group member, or even when the client talks about a game he played with someone outside of the group ("My wife and I had another *Uproar*"), the TA therapist may structure a psychodrama. The client becomes the director and is asked to stand up (a client-empowering technique) and then choose two people in the group to play his and his wife's roles in the game in the identical ways they play "Uproar."

The therapist encourages the client-director to think, direct, and plot out the important game moves that will lead to the usual conclusion or the negative payoff feelings that both players received. The client-director may actually reexperience his own feelings while directing the psychodrama which will provide clarity and even release of affect. By using this type of psychodrama, the client is able to step outside of his own game system; in this way he can view, think, and direct his own part in the game. This client-director role is seen as the "martian" position in that the client can be an interested observer, rather than a habitual participant in his own behavior. Through these maneuvers, the client will gain a new awareness and experiment with corrective procedures.

Script Treatment. An individual will gain social control by an intact, aware Adult; yet many individuals need also to direct their energies into reversing their basic life scripts.

Fanny, the woman who was repeatedly fired from her jobs, was able to catch herself and stop playing *Kick Me* when she used her Adult. She also decided to continue her therapy to make a script change. Fanny remembered being kicked out of many groups while she was growing up: the Brownies' summer camp, various grade school classes, high school classes, a social club, her college sorority, and finally being fired from each job she held. Her earliest memories included banishment and punishments for her behavior by her impatient parents. She developed negative stroking patterns that became the foundation of her script. Her early injunctions were "Get lost, you bother me." After receiving a bombardment of these injunctions, Fanny decided to live her life getting put down and kicked as this was how she got "strokes" and survived in her family. Through therapy and script redecisions, Fanny was able to change her script and stop her negative patterns.

Script Reversal. Berne devised the original script-change technique in the 1960s; he believed in a mutual, trusting relationship between the client and the therapist, which would facilitate the client receiving a potent *counterinjunction* (the opposite of what mother or father said to the client), thereby removing the negative influences. Berne, after attaining a suicidal client's trust, would state decisively, *"Do not kill yourself."* Many suicidal clients responded to him that *no one* ever said that to them before.

Eric Berne, Claude Steiner, Stephen Karpman, Patricia Crossman, John Dusay, and other participants of the early San Francisco seminars considered the script injunction to be like an electrode, which is lodged in the Child. The term *electrode* is appropriate because scripted individuals habitually and automatically react in predictable, destructive manners under a wide variety of circumstances. Therefore, Berne's powerfully potent, curative, counterscript message, delivered at the proper time, enabled persons to revise their scripts.

Reparenting. Another form of script intervention is the *reparenting* technique discovered and developed by Jacqui Schiff and others. Reparenting was developed for applications of TA theories to severely disturbed and psychotic patients. Severely disturbed individuals have a natural tendency to regress and relive early childhood experiences. Reparenting is done in a therapeutic, residential treatment center, and the clients are rereared by positive parenting. This treatment may take many years and there is a direct, active commitment by the therapist who performs the functions of the new par-

ents; although reparenting is viewed as controversial, it has been found to be effective in work with "untreatable" schizophrenics (Schiff, 1970, 1975).

Redecision. A popular and effective technique to bring about script change is *redecision therapy* in a TA framework using Gestalt techniques, formulated by Fritz Perls. By the use of double chairs, Perls had the client separate the negative and the positive parts of himself to oppose them against one another. Robert and Mary Goulding took this further by combining Perl's techniques and Berne's theories to create an environment for a client's growth and change (Goulding, 1972, 1974). They are chiefly credited for the development of redecision work. Berne once said that anything that has been learned can be unlearned. This is also valid for redecision, and a detailed description is included in the Applications Section (pages 409–418).

Ego-State Oppositions. Persons can change their weaknesses into their

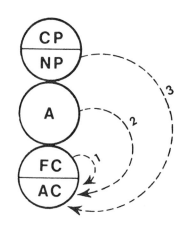

EGO STATE OPPOSITION

Figure 10.16

strengths and redecide about their life scripts by transferring their ego-state energies to lesser used ego states (J. Dusay, 1972). (See Figure 10.16.)

Script decisions commonly take three general forms: (1) "I'm sad," a person who has decided he is not OK in relation to others; (2) "I'm mad," a person who decided to be OK at the expense that other people are considered to be not OK; and (3) "I'm scared," a person who has decided he is not OK and neither are the other people. Individuals coming into treatment will, during times of stress, revert into their habitual stereotyped patterns of thinking, feeling, and behaving. A person who has decided to be not OK will look, think, feel, and behave depressed. The same will occur with a person who has decided to be scared or one who has decided to become mad. A trained TA therapist will watch for these habitual script patterns to occur and then will move into an ego-state opposition process and employ the techniques described by John Dusay in his *TA Treatment-Training Manual* (1978). The process goes this way:

1. The client is encouraged to enhance the here-and-now expression of the "racket" feelings. The therapist may recognize telltale signs and symptoms of the client's racket behavior, such as tense muscles, and will instruct the client to become temporarily more tense. This facilitates the client's reexperiencing of negative feelings that he can move from the here-and-now back to earlier decisive moments of childhood.

2. The individual is asked via a regressive technique, such as hypnosis or guided fantasy, to close his eyes and trace the same feeling back to the earliest recollection. Breuer and Freud (1893/1962) termed these early feelings *hyper-esthetic memories.*

3. When a person has gone back to an early moment of making a script decision, the therapist encourages the client to *oppose* that decision with another growth ego state. For instance, depressed persons will oppose their scripted Adapted Child ego states with their underused Free Child states by being directed to switch between them using empty double chairs (Arrow 1). A "mad" person who is frequently paranoid will be encouraged to oppose the Adapted Child with the Adult to distinguish clearly which persons are friends and which are not (Arrow 2). A scared person will be encouraged to oppose that part with the Nurturing Parent for reassurance (Arrow 3). This process hastens the transfer of psychological energy and begins the road toward a script redecision. The client, not the therapist, uses and summons his own psychological strengths to oppose these stubbornly held viewpoints of himself.

4. Resistances commonly arise when the client slips out of the "curative" ego state and back into the "stuck" scripted state. An adroit TA therapist will quickly confront this behavior so the resistant person will not reinforce the stuck pathology.

There are several advantages to doing script redecision work in a group setting. Other members are inspired and can reflect on their own situation; the therapist is aided as other members confront resistances; other group members can correct blind spots that occasionally occur in one-to-one therapy; and the client himself or herself is both congratulated and happily stroked for positive work.

When redecision work is not successful, the usual reason occurs when the client is opposing the negative, adapted self with a non-growth force. Sometimes the growth force (nurturing, logic, or creativity) is overwhelmed by the strength (stubborn-

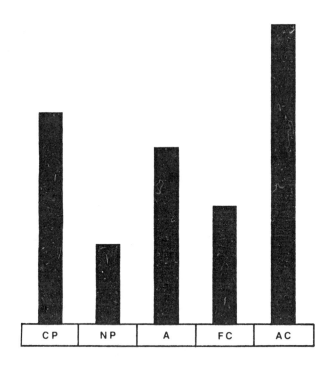

FANNY'S EGOGRAM
Figure 10.17

ness) of the scripted part. This is where attention to transfer of energy seen on the egogram is important.

Egogram Transfer of Energy. When one shifts energies from an overused ego state to a low-power ego state, the experience is exhilarating and becomes self-reinforcing. Fanny usually behaved as a "naughty little pest" intent on provoking negative responses from others. The initial scripting she accepted dictated that this behavior was her most profitable method of getting strokes. Her *Kick Me* game behavior was functionally part of her Adapted Child ego state, and it was this part of her personality that overwhelmed other people (See Figure 10.17).

The delightful and creative side of Fanny's Child ego state, her Free Child,

was barely functioning as she experienced little fun, creativity, or sexual enjoyment. It was as if her annoying "pesty" part, the Adapted Child, had most of the power and drained it away from the fresh and creative side. Her Adult was solid; she was bright and a good thinker. However, she seldom had any spare energy to help or console others, and this was reflected in her relatively low-functioning Nurturing Parent. Fanny copied her father's temper and judgmental nature when she criticized and found fault with others. This was reflected in the high amount of energy in her Critical Parent.

For Fanny functionally to approach the world in a different and more constructive way, a shift is necessary (Figure 10.17). Her Free Child and her Nurturing Parent need enhancement and greater energy investment, and this is one of the reasons the group-therapy milieu may be superior to individual psychotherapy. In a group, there are exercises that can be repeated and practiced with others to raise a low-energy ego state; for example, nurturing can be developed by hugging, or the exercise of giving authentic positive comments to other people can be practiced. She at first resisted doing this, but she started out slowly and persisted until she raised and became conditioned in her low ego states. After nurturing others, she was better able to nurture herself. John Dusay colloquially refers to this as *mental jogging*. Many encounter-group techniques are useful in raising low-energy ego states in people. Free Child, important for Fanny, is elicited by humor. Creativity exercises are encouraged in the group-therapy setting, such as looking for nonverbal clues.

Of course, each person has different ego-state imbalances and needs to raise, energize, and strengthen the lower, weaker ego states. Briefly, those who are low in the Critical Parent aspect are encouraged to use assertiveness techniques; those low in Nurturing Parent will need to participate in empathy and caring-for-others techniques; persons low in Adult are given thinking exercises; those who do not have enough Free Child are invited to be spontaneous and participate in creative, intuitive activities; and those who are low in Adapted Child are encouraged to practice the art of compromise and getting-along-with-others exercises. An important concern in shifting psychological energies is that individuals practice *raising what is low for them* and that they do not take what is a useful technique for others and indiscriminately apply it to themselves.

To facilitate a script redecision, a client

is encouraged to go back in time to an early feeling and decisive moment; he is then directed to oppose a well-established ego-state force, which becomes a major problem for the client in that his personality is already low in the very force that is needed to bring about a cure. For example, Fanny was depressed, and to overcome depression, she needed to oppose and raise her Free Child in relation to her Adapted Child. Her greatest problem was that her Free Child was low and her Adapted Child was high (see Figure 10.17). It took many weeks of Free Child raising techniques for her to be able to confront her own Adapted Child self to a significant degree. A person's weak ego states need strengthening as they are the very personality forces needed to make a redecision and change the balance of one's egogram. Lonely persons, chronically anxious people, and those with severe dependency needs who fear abandonment are people who need to nurture themselves and others; however, the Nurturing Parent is the lowest force on their egograms. By analyzing someone's egogram, one can predict the curative oppositional force for that particular individual. (See p. 378 for a more complete definition of the five functional ego states.) Likewise, a low Adult force is prevalent for distrustful paranoid problems (a low Nurturing Parent and a low Adult are evident in severe examples). Suicidal, depressed, and lethargic persons manifest a low Free Child.

A growth-oriented opposing force needs to be sufficiently developed to reverse a lifelong (early childhood decision) pattern that shows up in one's "here-and-now" manifestation of personality.

Various settings provide an effective milieu for change. These retreats come in various forms such as Esalen Institute on the Big Sur Coast, the Western Institute for Group and Family Therapy in Watsonville, and other therapeutic centers where persons may reside for several weeks and months in a strong Nurturing Parent, Adult, and Free Child atmosphere to undergo personal, lasting changes. TA groups provide a similar safe atmosphere where both growth and change are stroked and reinforced.

In summary, the major ways that people change are through their own efforts by stopping games, redeciding scripts, and redistributing the energy balances on their egograms.

Mechanisms of Psychotherapy

Many clients enter treatment because they are in pain, meaning they receive their strokes in negative self-destructive ways. A few persons are in an immediate crisis situation. Some enter because they are bored or lonely, receiving strokes in stereotyped, repetitive ways or just not receiving enough strokes. Some people are so unaware of their own social difficulties that others bring them to treatment. Some persons enter either out of curiosity or for a growth experience; many trainees pursue this course. Whatever leads a client to a therapist's door, if change is to occur, there will be a difference in stroke receiving.

Thinking, feeling, and behaving are important in change, and are all included in the basic definitions of ego states. TA is an ego psychology.

Mechanisms underlying the psychotherapy triad of game interruption, script redecision, and ego-state energy shift cause the difference. A game is a habit, with a stereotyped social set of behavior, thinking (from Parent or Child ego state) that justifies the behavior; for example, "I'm just a loser," he says, as he belts

down another drink. Even the accompanying affect is habitual. When asked, "Have you ever felt this way before?" the answer is usually, "Always." The mechanism of game interruption is the bringing to awareness the client's involvement with different ego states and establishing the Adult as the executive. With the Adult in control and monitoring, usually brought about by the therapeutic operation (sometimes by the receiving of information alone), the client can choose. Berne said that treatment was at a terminal phase when choice was available (1966, p. 245): "At this juncture, transactional analysis has completed its task with or without interpretation in the area under consideration. TA does not try to 'make the patient better' but to bring him into a position where he can exercise an Adult option to get better." The therapist is, in an existential sense at least, indifferent as to which choice the patient makes. All he can do is make it possible for the patient to choose. There is, however, no use in trying to conceal from the patient the fact that the therapist is biased by his own prejudices in favor of health and sanity.

When games are successfully interrupted, the client has social control. Although clients may substitute other games, equally destructive, they also have an excellent chance of developing positive new ways of relating.

The underlying mechanism of script redecision is usually accomplished concomitantly with game therapy, by overcoming early childhood decisions and by applying an opposing force against the stubbornly held decision. A chief reason for using a psychoregressive technique is to lay bare the earlier moments before the client added years of justification (by game playing) and reinforced his script decision. Although the TA therapist may use double chairs to separate ego states and allow for their external replay, the same forces are occurring in the client's head. Although one's feelings and affect are primary in script redecision work, they are usually followed by one's Adult, cognitive confirmation and discussion.

The mechanism of ego-state energy shift is mainly behavioral. It is necessary to build up weak areas on an egogram to oppose the adapted script-bearing part. Most TA groups use humor and encourage the airing of hunches and intuition to develop the Free Child. Nurturing behavior such as touching, hugging, and giving authentic positive strokes is encouraged; and away from the treatment setting, the client prescribes corrective nurturing behavior for himself, for example, taking an orphan to the zoo, and so on.

Just when a person actually strengthens a weaker ego-state force is difficult to ascertain, but an analogy with the physical conditioning of a jogger seems appropriate. The unconditioned runner does not "feel" like jogging; to him it is a burden; however, if he persists and overcomes the "this just isn't the real me" resistance and keeps on practicing, he changes. The first time his change is noticeable is when he cannot run on a given day and he feels uncomfortable and sluggish because he cannot run! He is now a conditioned runner and he feels different. People become psychologically conditioned by exercising previously weak areas.

APPLICATIONS

Problems

Because TA begins with the observation of what goes on between human beings, theoretically, all problems can be ana-

lyzed. Being a contractual treatment, TA requires the cooperation and willingness of the client to seek and participate in treatment. A distinction is made between what is primarily a "caring" relationship between therapist and client as compared to actual "curing" TA treatment. In "caring" the client receives support and nurturing from the therapist as *the* major activity. The therapist is a primary source of strokes and the relationship is not working toward the attainment of an ultimate goal, or as time goes by, the early goals are forgotten or neglected. This is labeled *care* and not TA psychotherapy. (Certainly care is often an important and desirable activity.)

In contrast, TA treatment, although emphasizing the importance of the nurturing and caring personality of the therapist, primarily focuses on change as defined by the treatment contract based on an Adult to Adult agreement between the therapist and the client about what will be the process and the desired goal. Rather than being a primary source of strokes, except temporarily, the TA therapist is a catalyst for the client's own efforts.

TA is devised for those who will exert enough responsibility to undertake a contract. However, TA has been applied to severely disturbed individuals who are not able to make an Adult contract at the time of onset of treatment. Jacqui and Aaron Schiff (J. Schiff, 1969) represent a special group of TA therapists who have developed an alternative, yet compatible, theory with specific techniques that encourage clients to regress to earlier infantlike states, which may be preverbal. Although the client is expected to be as responsible as possible, the expectation during this phase of treatment is different from expectation of chronologically mature, nonregressed individuals. The approach is controversial, not accepted by all TA therapists, and is considered an offshoot of TA.

TA is effectively used with both couples and family relationships in that TA's game theory focuses on the common, predictable, destructive game patterns of behavior that occur among individuals. These patterns can be easily recognized, dealt with, and ultimately changed to strengthen the relationship. Berne chose the game *If It Weren't For You* to illustrate game principles in his work, *Games People Play* (1964), and stated that this is the most commonly occurring game among married couples. By the maneuvers in the game, the wife complains that, "If it weren't for my husband, then I would be a princess . . ." and so on. In his initial uncovering of this game, Berne discovered that the wife was actually struggling from fears of being active in public life, but justified her position by choosing a controlling man as a mate, who expected her to stay in the home. Thus, she was protected from her fear and habitually justified her position by claiming that it was her husband's fault. She was only one-half of the game. Her husband chose a "stay-at-home wife" and was tyrannical in his part of the game system, thus protecting himself from his deep fear of abandonment. TA is especially useful in relationship problems as games are interrupted; thus basic fears are bared and script redecision can be approached. The tendency for different people to polarize and lock themselves into positions in relationships is explained by egograms, that is, husband (Critical Parent) overbalance; wife (Adapted Child) overbalance. Unfortunately, in both the home as well as on the job, people will maintain the same balances on their egograms; therefore, people will be continu-

ally reacted to in predictable ways based upon their egograms. Persons frequently are given nicknames that represent their particular egograms; "pushover," "dictator," "snob," "crazy," "dumb," and "sulky" are a few examples of the large assortment of nicknames.

Difficulties with authority figures are special applications of TA in human relationships. Most frequent is the *Kick Me* player, who at an early age decides he is not OK and then develops a personality with a high Adapted Child and routinely gets kicked. Fanny, previously mentioned, is a classical example of a person with authority conflicts. Also noted is that the same patterns that occur with the boss, school authorities, and others also tend to occur with the therapist or other group members.

The problem of self-concept has two special considerations. First, the client may not actually see himself the way others do, being psychologically blind. When an entire TA group constructs an egogram and they agree, this is potent feedback about how one appears to others. By increasing perception and sharpening intuition about others, self-perception tends to become more acute. The second problem of self-concept is the resistance to change even if someone does not like what they see in themselves. Basic script redecisions to review early decisions of not being OK and game interruption that halts the process of reinforcement of basic script acceptance of what has become a self-belief, are employed.

Fears of a crippling or phobic nature may be treated at the level of personality identity as portrayed by the egogram by exercising and strengthening underdeveloped ego states. People who fear abandonment cling to others and even to the therapist by playing *Do Me Something* (a game by which the client offers the therapist some bait in the nature of a potentially resolvable problem such as insomnia, then says, "That's not good enough," after the therapist tries drugs, interpretations, or other maneuvers). By structuring time and performing exercises such as nurturing or assertive exercises, the client takes on more Parent energy and is therefore not as frightened.

The client fearing abandonment is asked to join a TA group, not to talk about himself, but to focus on the needs of others, encouraging nurturing. When this force develops, it is easier to nurture oneself and decrease the fear. Script redecision may also be used in overcoming fears, for instance, when the client decided at an early age that life is scary (to him).

Maladjustments occur as a result of psychological blindness. For example, a high Free Child, low Adapted Child person may, in good spirits, take a job as an accountant, which requires lower Free Child (unless the corporation wants a creative accountant) and high Adapted Child, which encourages conformity. Recognizing strengths and weaknesses of personality forces allows one to choose jobs and relationships that are most compatible.

So-called *perversions* can best be understood at the script level. An individual may be told to be "normal" on the value level, but at the injunction (Child of mother or father to Child of the biological child) level, the message is, "You are different." Even though this message may be nonverbal and hidden, if the child accepts this injunction, *perverse* behavior later in life is seen as conformity not to values, but to injunctions. Social difficulties such as teenage drug problems, and what is commonly called rebel-

lious behavior, which may best be called pseudorebellion, is actually viewed as conformity to script (J. Dusay, 1977, pp. 194–202).

Personality trait problems are best understood by considering the egogram. Assertiveness is too much Critical Parent, and too little Critical Parent corresponds with the passive acceptance of oppression—getting psychologically pushed around by others. Too much Nurturing Parent is overbearing and actually inhibits the independent growth of children; too little Nurturing Parent makes one inconsiderate, and a low Nurturing Parent corresponds with loneliness. High Adult is technical but perhaps boring; with a low Adult, one lacks logic and orderly causal thinking and problem solving is difficult. Someone with too high a Free Child, although creative and zesty, may fail to pay the rent. Low Free Child is associated with depression. People who are too high in the Adapted Child trait overconform and are too accepting or compromising, but with too little, the problem is the opposite—too little compromise in human relationships. Personality trait disturbances are seen by looking not at one specific trait on the egogram but by looking at the balance or imbalance of the total mosaic. One's specific problems, trait disturbances, and specific egogram imbalances are directly related to one's early script decisions as well as the specific games the person developed to reinforce this script.

Delusions are structurally seen as a contaminated ego state where the boundaries between Parent, Adult, and Child are broken down (Figure 10.6). The subject of psychosis is quite involved and the controversy that rages between different academicians and therapists of many persuasions also occurs within the TA family.

Some mention that the basic lesion is genetic or biochemical and that psychotherapy should be directed toward better social adjustment. Others vigorously pursue the developmental motive of psychosis, structure a long-term (years) live-in environment, encourage regression in severe psychosis, and basically start over. This approach is naturally limited by the sheer amount of energy investment needed on the part of the therapist, but seems to have been effective in some cases. Basic expansion in TA theory has been necessitated by exploration in this area (Schiff, 1971).

Most of what was previously called neurosis is redefined by TA practitioners into more useful theory-related terms. The depressive neurotic, for example, would be seen as a person who made an existential life decision of I'm Not OK— You Are OK, in response to an injunction script message of "Get Lost" (or some specific variation). Then, after this, he played a long string of decision-justifying and reinforcing games such as *Kick Me* or *Reject Me* by gathering put-downs from others. His personality developed as a high Adapted Child and a low Free Child. A TA diagnosis will commonly state that the client has too much AC, too little A, too much CP, too little NP, and so on. This is more effective terminology than diagnosing "neurosis" or "psychosis" because the TA diagnosis immediately suggests the curative ways to proceed for treatment of the person's problems. Cures are accomplished when the clients strengthen and build up their underdeveloped ego states to achieve harmonious balances on their egograms. Criminal behavior that is traditionally labeled psychopathic or sociopathic may also be better understood by attention to the clients' long rap sheets that frequently elucidate their common games of either

Kick Me (for those who set it up continually to get both hurt and caught) or *NIGYYSOB* (for those who are intent on not getting caught as they hurt others).

Evaluation

TA, like most psychotherapies, was developed outside of the university setting and early in its history reported mainly anecdotal individual case histories. Although these early reports were enthusiastic, they lacked controls or comparison to other methods, a basic problem in most psychotherapy outcome research. The culmination of this type of reporting occurred in 1968, when Berne, Dusay, and Ray Poindexter reviewed their TA case loads and presented the results to the San Francisco TA Seminar of how many clients achieved their goals as stated in the TA treatment contract. The results were that 80 percent of the clients stated they got what they came for and their therapists agreed.

Following the first decade of TA, independent investigators began to review the outcome of TA treatment. One of the most important outcome studies ever made was a comparison of TA and behavior modification (McCormick, 1973). Behavior modification is generally also a contractual therapy based on research data. The project studied the effects of treatment on hard data changes in a population of 904 young men aged 15, 16, and 17 who were in two schools of the California Youth Authority. Almost all of the subjects had serious arrest records, most failed as probationers in the home community, and all had serious emotional or behavioral problems. More than 60 percent had used drugs (a third were heroin or LSD users). The average reading level was seventh grade; arithmetic level, sixth grade. There was random assignment to TA methods (460) and behavior modification (444). Both populations improved more than was expected in outcome; in math grade-equivalent scores, the TA group gained 0.91 and behavior modification 0.62. In reading, the average word improved was 1.48 in behavior modification and 1.16 in TA, far above ordinarily expected gains. Although both TA and behavior modification showed significant improvement over controls, the TA population was treated for 7.6 months at which time the TA program was completed (as defined by the goals of the therapists). To achieve similar improvement, the behavior modification subjects were treated for 8.7 months. TA achieved similar results in significantly less time, an early claim of TA enthusiasts.

Another hard data gain was in the area of parole success. Before the treatment project, parole revocation within a year was at the rate of 43 percent. After the project, the return rate had dropped to 33 percent for both TA and BM groups, but this decrease did not occur for two youth authority groups that served as controls.

Although both methods achieved significant positive results, the TA program took less time than the behavior modification program and the therapists, youth authority employees, and the subjects claimed that TA was more fun and enjoyable (McCormick, 1973).

The greatest research interest has been in the evaluation of the basic concepts of TA. The foundation of TA, the ego state, has been subjected to several investigations. Most important is the research project of George Thomson (1972), which established that ego states are observable, that trained TA experts have a high interrater agreement about which ego state is in operation in a given subject, and that naive observers can be trained to correctly

(in agreement with experts) identify ego states. Thomson used a tape recorder to preserve nine hours of group-therapy sessions. From these tapes, he extracted a research tape whereby each participant was heard to say a couple of words or phrases for a few seconds. When played back, there were varied words, tones, and inflections on each segment. These were presented to a panel of TA experts who were asked to judge between Parent, Adult, and Child. The experts had a 95 percent consensual agreement about the ego state classification. Naive listeners from various backgrounds were then presented the research tape and were found to do poorly; after a week's training, their proficiency at identifying ego states improved markedly. Thomson proved what Berne and early transactional analysts claimed: that ego states are observable and that people can spot ego states, classify them, mimic them, and actually improve upon their ability to do so by study and observation.

Thomson went further by hypothesizing that certain clinical problems would impair ego-state identification; that is, that "schizophrenics" and "depressives" would have more difficulty in identifying Parent ego states than normals. This seems to be the case on his research tape, but those people being diagnosed as psychopaths had a better than average ability (for normals) to identify Parent. This also seemed to be the case and he hypothesized that psychopaths need to be keenly aware of Parent-type people to be successful.

John Hurley and Howard Porter (1967) categorized 194 college students enrolled in a study-methods course, notable for immature academic behavior, into Adapted Child (AC) types and Natural Child (NC) types (this corresponds with FC) and found they were able to distinguish 47 as one or the other category during 20 twice-a-week, 50-minute class periods. AC is characterized by a general inhibition of impulse expression grounded on the fear of disturbing others; NC functioning is directed against external restraints and is expressed in openly self-indulgent or assertive acts. The construct validity of the AC versus NC distinction was tested by comparing the two groups to their performance on certain standard psychological tests. All completed the MMPI Psychopathic deviate (Pd) and the Marlowe-Crowne Social Desirability (SD) scales. A true-false version of the LaForge Interpersonal Checklist (ICL) provided scores on the orthogonal factors, LOV (love-hate continuum), and DOM (dominance-submissiveness continuum).

It was hypothesized that the AC functioning group would correspond with lower Pd and DOM scales (rebellious and dominating tendencies) and with higher SD and LOV scores (conforming and acceptant tendencies) than characterized by the NC functioning group. Confirmation was found for both sexes except on the SD measure, which failed to differentiate between the AC and NC categories. However, all group differences were in the hypothesized direction except for an insignificant Pd reversal among females. These findings not only support the construct validity of certain ego-state formulations, but indicated that relatively untrained raters (the observers) can effectively distinguish subgroups in the college classroom.

Five advanced members of the weekly San Francisco TA Seminars (now known as the Eric Berne Seminar of San Francisco) volunteered themselves as egogram subjects in 1971. Their egograms were drawn by 15 other seminar members who had known them for varying lengths of time. While the 15 persons drew each subject's personality profile privately, the subjects also drew their own. The result was 100 percent agreement on both the high and low columns of the five ego-state graph. This finding led to further formal and informal investigation.

John Kendra (1977) viewed a sample of Rorschach reports of various psychiatric patients. He constructed egograms from these projective tests and was able to distinguish a group of egograms different from the others that were characteristically low in Nurturing Parent and Free Child, while the Critical Parent, Adult, and Adapted Child were markedly high (the Adult slightly lower). These turned out to correspond with the successful suiciders (Figure 10.8).

While Kendra used intuition to construct his suicide egogram, Robert Heyer (1979) began to develop a concept-oriented written test. Heyer's ego-state profile questionnaire is still undergoing modification; at present it consists of 49 researched items of which the subject rank orders himself. Heyer's dissertation data was presented to the 2,000-subject sample of the California Poll (Field Poll) two weeks before the presidential election in 1976. The subjects were asked to rate themselves, as the item statements consciously applied to them, and then they were asked to construct a profile for the two presidential candidates, Jimmy Carter and Gerald Ford. The responses were not random; there occurred a distinct and significant difference between the two candidates (as they appeared to the voter through the media). There are some indications that the voters' self-perceived egogram has a correlation with candidate choice (they were also asked who they were voting for). Egogram profiles have now being constructed for various populations such as San Quentin prisoners, outpatient clinics, alcoholics, attendees at weekend growth-encounter groups, students, and government employees.

Ego states and egograms especially lend themselves to research, and with the development of a standard hard data test research, possibilities are expanding.

Treatment

TA historically and traditionally has been practiced in groups, although through the years, since its beginnings in the late 1950s, TA has been diversely applied by therapists from different backgrounds with varying levels of professional education and training, who have approached the entire gamut of psychological problems and challenges. Therefore, TA has been successfully practiced in almost all settings. The earlier observations in groups tend to hold up in dyadic, family, marathon, and other settings.

Berne (1966) distinguished between six possible ways that people spend their time with each other, in ascending order of stroke potential. They will be defined as they relate to therapy:

Withdrawal: Occasionally, people *withdraw* in the presence of others, either by fantasy or by delusion. The therapist discourages withdrawal by stroking and encouraging conversation.

Ritual: There are formal and informal *rituals.* Formal rituals are culturally determined and of little concern for psychotherapy; however, informal rituals are encouraged as a warmup. The greeting ritual of saying hello followed by a hello response is an example. This gives a stroke and also illustrates the almost syllable-for-syllable nature (stroke-for-stroke) quality. If one person says, "Hello, how are you? Haven't seen you in weeks," and gets a simple "Hello" in response a game

is developing. Overresponding likewise becomes a game; for example, one person says, "How are you?" The respondent replies, "I'm glad you asked. My hemorrhoids ache. I can't sleep," and so on. Again a game is started. Informal rituals are mainly social courtesies, not encouraged beyond a warmup and good-bye; however, the breaking of a mundane ritual is seen as a takeoff for possible game behavior.

Pastimes: These are an orderly series of transactions designed simply to while away the time in a socially acceptable, but nonmeaningful, manner. Unlike games, there is no distinct payoff of negative feelings. A popular *pastime* is called "General Motors" whereby one player says, "I like Chevy, Plymouth, Ford (choose one), better than Chevy, Plymouth, Ford because . . . (fill in with 25 words or less)." There is a tendency for therapy groups to play pastimes, sometimes for an entire session, to avoid more meaningful activity. This is called playing *Psychiatry.* The therapist breaks up pastimes to get to more meaningful work.

Work: This is goal-directed activity to solve problems or expand potentials. Much TA is at this level.

Games: Clients frequently slip into *games* to reinforce their basic script decisions and, by doing so, avoid both work and prevent intimacy. This is counteracted by the TA therapist.

Intimacy: This is a straightforward human interaction, and is none of the above. Intimacy is a desired goal in human relationships and is encouraged in TA treatment.

TA therapists as group leaders pay attention to the above possibilities, encouraging work and intimacy, interrupting games, and avoiding meaningless pastimes. Beyond attention to group functioning, Berne in observing himself and his trainees delineated eight specific therapeutic interventions (1966):

Interrogation: A TA therapist *interrogates* to document specific points that may be clinically useful in the future. "Did you actually hit her?" is directed to the client's Adult. Overinterrogation is to be avoided or the client will be prone to play *Psychiatric History.*

Specification: This is a declaration on the part of the therapist that categorizes certain information. "So you have always viewed yourself as having an excessive temper" is intended to fix *specifically* certain information about the client so it can be referred to later in therapy.

Confrontation: A TA therapist will use information previously elicited to disconcert the patient's Parent, Child, or contaminated Adult, by pointing out incongruencies. The client: "I can't stop smoking." The therapist: "Will you say, 'I *won't* stop smoking'?" This *confrontation* is intended to disturb one's egogram energy balance and hopefully cause a redistribution of energies. The client may insightfully say, "There I go giving away my power again," which indicates a switch from his Child to Adult.

Explanation: The therapist will encourage clear *explanations* to strengthen the client's Adult. The therapist may say, "Sometimes your Child becomes overactive and that's when your Adult fades out. Quite possibly you reach for a cigarette without thinking."

Interrogation, specification, confrontation, and explanation are *interventions.* The next operations are more than that. They are *interpositions* that are an attempt by the therapist to interpose something between the patient's Adult and his other ego states to stabilize his Adult and make it more difficult for him to slide into Parent or Child activity.

Illustration: This becomes an anecdote or comparison that follows a successful confrontation; the purpose is to reinforce the confrontation and avoid possibly undesirable effects. The therapist may interpose by saying, "You are saying *can't* just like Gladys does," as Gladys is listening. Some illustrations are remote, yet provide humor or meaning to the Child. "You're going to the party is similar to Little Red Riding Hood going to the woods—they both have a lot of wolves there."

Illustration is an artful form of psychotherapy that may be effectively used when both the client's Adult is listening and the Free Child is finding it humorous. When working with a self-righteous, literal Parent (as with many paranoids), the therapist may be chided for "making fun of me" if an illustration is attempted.

Confirmation: The interposition of a *confirmation* by the therapist is to stabilize the patient's Adult. The therapist encourages the client to offer further material to confirm the confrontation and this will reinforce the ego boundaries and the Adult functioning. If the client says, "I just can't do this—Oops, I mean, I *won't* do it," the therapist will immediately confirm and acknowledge the client's awareness.

Each of these operations has a primary objective to activate the client's functional Adult. The client will then possess a clear, defined, competent, uncontaminated Adult. When the client's Adult is in control, he is filled with positive choices and options for growth.

Interpretation: A psychodynamic *interpretation* may go into the realm of, "You have given away your power. Your Child has decided to remain powerless and helpless because your mother would say, 'Don't leave me.' " Interpretations are not necessary for treatment to be successful; in fact, occasionally the reverse is true. Overzealous therapists may interpret the games and symbols to their clients and receive a passive acceptance, which they will quickly forget. Each of the operations before this is employed to strengthen the client's Adult so a clear interpretation will be assimilated by an informed Adult. Little benefit accrues just by telling a person what is going on.

Crystallization: TA's technical aim is to facilitate the client to accept an effective crystallization statement from the therapist. This takes the form of an Adult-to-Adult statement: "So now you're in a position to stop playing that game if you choose."

Often the client will incorporate the statement, which may represent his readiness to terminate and begin an autonomous, choice-making existence. Berne himself would emphasize the importance of strengthening the client's Adult, which would enable the person to make better choices. Berne would interrupt the client's usual habitual patterns by directly confronting and intervening; rather than remaining passive and anonymous, he became an active therapist. Berne's active techniques of the mid-1960s are still used today; however, TA has developed into an even more active and dynamic system of psychotherapy since Berne's time. McNeel (1975) studied what was actually done in a weekend TA session conducted by Robert and Mary Goulding. The following techniques and attitudes are commonly employed by many TA therapists:

Emphasis on the client's personal power and responsibility: Each individual is *responsible* for his life and has adequate *power* to be in charge of his life. Clients may feel they are victims of events or circumstances, and confrontations will reinforce their feelings of responsibility. A client who says, "You make me feel . . ." will be confronted since this is a common ploy to deny one's responsibility for his own feelings. A person who habitually says "I can't" will be confronted and en-couraged to substitute "I won't," which illustrates that the person is making a choice not to do something.

Developing a nurturing environment: Nonjudgmental *nurturing* is an effective milieu, and persons are warmly stroked for taking personal responsibility for their actions and feelings. Likewise, the use of humor is prevalent, although there is an avoidance of laughing at gallows humor, which is encouraging others to laugh at pathological behavior (drinking, overeating, etc.).

Separating myth from reality: Many clients cherish myths about themselves; and the effective confrontation is, "Do you really believe that?" Clients then receive permission to question and discard their myths.

Confrontation of incongruity: When a client offers two *incongruent* communications at the same time (verbal and nonverbal), the therapist needs to recognize that both forms of communication are important. A "no" head shake that accompanies a "yes" verbal response, a smile that grins during a tragic story, are examples of the incongruous behaviors that therapists will interrupt.

Specific techniques: Analysis is used to raise a deficient Adult. Double-chair techniques aid a participant to "own" all of his psychological parts and reach the emotions of the Child ego state. Verbally saying good-bye to the past is also important in that people will drag their negative past experiences around with them, like a ball and chain. Techniques may involve role-playing a deceased parent and then saying good-bye. Fantasy techniques are used to raise the Free Child. Parent ego-state interviews are also useful in which the therapist interviews the client's Parent projections.

Procedural rules: During therapy, there is no small talk or gossip. An actual time limit is put on each client's work so it will not go on indefinitely. In effective therapy, there are specific rules such as no violence or threats of violence; sex only with attending partners in weekend functions; no alcohol or mind-altering drugs to be used. Persons also make a commitment to remain in therapy for a specific period.

The above observations already indicate what is done by leading TA therapists to create a milieu conducive to redecision and change.

MANAGEMENT

The Setting: TA therapy may effectively take place in a wide variety of settings. Certain TA therapists prefer a home-like atmosphere, comparable to a living room with the accompanying furniture, books, plants and artwork; some like a more traditional office setting; while others enjoy conducting therapy outdoors in retreat settings and at resorts. While some therapists utilize traditional couches and chairs, others prefer conducting therapy on the floor or cushions. An important commonality with TA therapists is that no tables or desks are used which could block the participants' full view of one another. Because body language, postures and other non-verbal clues to personality are important in doing TA therapy, there must be good lighting as well as non-obstructive seating arrangements.

The majority of TA treatment environments utilize the customary blackboards and giant paper pads that can be used by both the therapists and their clients to draw pictures, elucidate games and transactions, construct egograms, and also to engage in Adult ego state clarifications. (At this writing, not a single transference to a blackboard has been reported.) Some therapists may employ audio-visual aids which may aid in a client's feedback, awareness and understanding. Because of the wide and diverse backgrounds of professionally trained TA therapists (from office-practicing psychiatrists to inmates working within the confines of a prison), it becomes impossible to generalize about a typical TA therapeutic setting.

Relationships: A prevailing attitude exists among TA therapists with their clients—they provide a supportive, nurturing environment conducive for growth and change. An agreement of confidentiality is respected by both the therapist and the clients. The therapist provides permission for the client to maintain an active role in change and therapy process. The client is also given protection and encouragement from the therapist as one begins to change and validate a new way of thinking, feeling and behaving. For the therapist's permission and protection to be effective, the therapist must be potent, well-trained and competent to be in this role. Authentic TA therapists undergo years of required training, schooling and clinical experience under authorized clinical teaching members of the ITAA before they are endorsed as certified TA therapists by the ITAA. TA therapists may work independently or in co-therapy teams. They conduct therapy with individuals, couples, families, and group members according to the specific needs of the client.

The simple vocabulary of TA, as well as commonly understood words are used in therapeutic sessions so that time isn't wasted with unclear verbiage or confusing concepts. The client is viewed as an equal partner in the therapeutic process. The common goal of each TA therapist is to catalyze a cure—defined as their reaching therapy goals—and to do so as quickly as possible. A TA therapist is generally an active participant in the client's process and will frequently operate on intuitive perceptions and will invite clients to be open and intuitive as well.

Client Problems: Whenever there is a break from the agreed-upon treatment course of action, for instance, non-payment of the therapist's fee or missing scheduled appointments, the therapist will view these transactions as psychological games and will provide therapy from this standpoint. The simplest to the most severe human psychological problems have been successfully resolved through TA therapy.

CASE EXAMPLE

Judd was diagnosed as a hypochondriac by many physicians who had treated him. He complained about being weak, weary, headachey, and jittery as he displayed his collection of pills and remedies. Judd's belief that he was sick was seen to reach far back into his past as he nostalgically reminisced about his family's medicine cabinet and remembered his mother taking his temperature, giving him pills, and stroking him for being a weak, sickly child. He was able to repeat his early life-style with his wife, whose attitude toward Judd was similar to his mother's. Both wife and mother had high Nurturing Parents and high Adapted Childs on their own egograms.

At his first TA group session, the other members drew his egogram (Figure 10.18) and he established a treatment contract: to experience a full month without having a noticeable headache.

In a subsequent session, Judd was

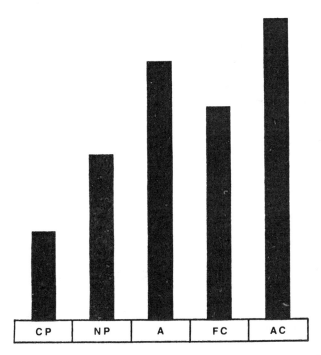

JUDD'S EGOGRAM (BEFORE TA)

Figure 10.18

habitually complaining of feeling "sick" and another group member, Wayne, who in contrast to Judd had a critical personality (high CP), told him to "stand up for yourself." Judd appeared especially frightened and the therapist, noticing this, asked him if he wanted to work on his feelings. Judd nodded affirmatively.

Knowing that this "feeling" was a repetitive racket, the therapist did not comfort Judd; rather, the negative feelings were enhanced by instructing Judd to exaggerate his tight jaw and tense wrinkled brow. When Judd was in obvious pain, the therapist asked him to close his eyes to enable him to leave the here-and-now of the group setting and begin to trace his racket feeling back to a childhood prototype episode of his script decision.

After pausing briefly at the reexperience of his wedding ceremony, then at school episodes, Judd began to quiver, and said, "I'm five years old, and I want

my Mommie to come to nursery school with me, but she won't. Please, Mommie, I'm not big enough. I'm scared . . . I'm sick!" Beads of perspiration formed on his forehead and he rubbed his stomach. He was instructed to place his fantasized "Mommie" in the empty chair and tell her what he was feeling. The role playing served to enhance his emotional state.

Judd [age five]: I'm scared. My tummy aches and my head aches, and I want to stay home with you.

Mommie [played by Judd]: I know you don't feel very good, so let me give you some pills for your head and tummy and then you can go to school.

Judd I feel so sick. I don't think the medicine will help.

Mommie: Well, then, I'll put you back to bed now, and I'll give you some pills, and by tomorrow you'll feel good enough to go to school.

Judd [very relieved]: Okay. If I'm sick

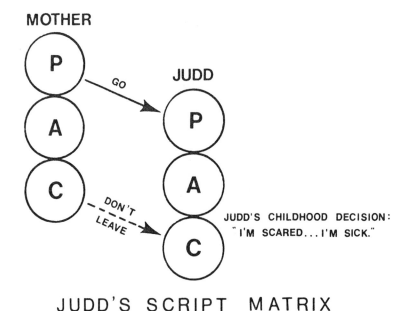

JUDD'S SCRIPT MATRIX

Figure 10.19

and stay home, at least I won't be so scared.

"What are you deciding about yourself now?" the therapist asked.

"I'm scared of people," Judd replied. "I'm scared of going to school and being with the other little boys. If I stay sick, I won't have to face them."

Judd's real mother, for her own psychological reasons, probably was nervous about having a healthy child who could someday leave her. She passed her anxiety and scared feelings on to Judd by the usual scripting process (see Figure 10.19). From her Parent, she sent him the life value, "Go to school." (Later in life, this expressed itself as "Be a man," and so on.) But her Child ego state sent him the incompatible injunction, "Don't leave me!" Eventually Judd's Adapted Child made his decision, "I'm scared and sick. I won't leave you." This basic childhood decision carried through his life. In treatment Judd was encouraged to reexperience his "little boy" ego state feeling and express it fully. By surfacing his early feelings and thoughts, he was able to view the original scene that set the tone for his life.

To change, one must redecide. Judd was soon reintroduced to his other powers by focusing on the other forces in his egogram. His Adult was chosen to oppose his scripted Adapted Child because this logical force was quite strong in him, and although his Nurturing Parent force would also be helpful, a conversation between his weak, conforming Adapted Child and his scientific, rational Adult was structured. As before, he switched chairs as he switched ego states:

Judd (*AC*): I feel sick and I'm scared to go to school by myself.
Judd (*A*): Why are you scared?
Judd (*AC*): Because I'm afraid I'll get lost and I can't take care of myself.

Judd (*A*): Little five-year-olds can't take care of themselves!
Judd (*AC*): I know! I'm so scared and I think my stomach hurts.
Judd (*A*): You said you *think* your stomach hurts?
Judd (*AC*): Well, it kind of hurts, and my mother thinks it hurts.
Judd (*A*): Do you think you might have talked yourself into this?
Judd (*AC*): Yes, I think so. My stomach doesn't hurt me any more than anyone else's stomach hurts, but it helps me forget about my scare.
Judd (*A*): How long do you want to keep scaring yourself and have stomach aches?
Judd (*AC*): No longer. I don't have anything to be scared of. I can take care of myself now. I'm not so little anymore.

The conversation was stopped and Judd said he felt great, as if he were healthy for the first time in his life. He no longer was dominated by the little boy in his head. Others in the group were happy for him and freely gave him hugs and congratulations. Judd, with tears in his eyes, spontaneously said, "There is one more thing I'm going to say to that little boy in me." He then went to another chair and said in a nurturing voice, "You're really an OK person."

Judd decided he would be OK, not scared, and thought that getting into good physical shape would be helpful in reinforcing outside of the group what he had redecided in therapy. He committed himself to jogging even though it did not feel right at first. He soon worked up to running at least two miles a day and exercised at the local gym. His legs and lungs felt better and he soon lost his craving for cigarettes. He chose a new set of friends at the office who shared his new interest in exercise and nourishing foods. The structures in his life supported his new healthy view of himself.

Unfortunately, when the redecision process is not successful, it is due to a resistance. The intrapsychic resistance occurs, in Judd's case, when he slips from his Adult or Nurturing Parent, into his Adapted Child. In this instance, he would be switching back and forth, from chair to chair commiserating with his Adapted Child. This occurs as follows in the example:

Judd (*AC*): I feel bad.
Judd (*A becoming AC*): Gulp! I feel bad, too.

When this occurs, the therapist quickly introduces a third observer chair, to combat the slippage. The chair is placed perpendicular to the ongoing dialogue chair and Judd is asked to switch and describe what he is observing. Usually this successfully allows Judd to confront his own resistance. If not, he is probably not ready for redecision and needs to have more group experience to strengthen his Adult and/or other curative ego state forces that are low on his egogram. Then he will reapproach the problem with increased strength.

In addition to his own internal resistance, Judd challenged the subtle resistances from outside himself: socially at home, institutionally at work, and even culturally in the rest of his environment. When Judd announced to his wife he was going to start jogging and was not going to have headaches anymore, she was outwardly full of joy, but somehow did not seem to know what to do with herself. She was used to the old Judd, whom she greeted every day with, "How are you feeling today?" His typical response had been, "Not so good." When he overcame his script injunction, his answer became, "Oh, I feel fine." This was met by a sickening smile from his wife and she would plead, "Are you sure?" The first few times this happened, Judd replied, "Well, now that you mention it, I think I do have a little ache in my neck." Temporarily he succumbed to this volley of social resistances from his wife. Soon he increased his awareness of these day-to-day hindrances and gathered support from those who had not vested interest in his being sick (the group members). As he insisted on being treated as a healthy person, his wife became more and more frantic. "It's about time to go to the doctor and get your prescription filled," she said. Judd's response was, "I don't need medicine anymore." It can be predicted in advance that close social contacts will resist the change at least as hard as the person undergoing it. Game analysis and group support were aids at this level.

Institutional resistances also confront the individual and usually involve economics. In Judd's case, the drug industry was involved. When Judd walked into the doctor's office, he was walking into an institution that, like his wife, did not give up easily. After multiple complaints, the frustrated doctor, hoping to do something beneficial, would reach for his prescription pad and give him one of the newer pills that had been advertised heavily in the medical journals.

Cultural resistances to personal change are subtle, ever present, and strongly influential. One of the Western civilization's "cultural truths" is that if you are feeling bad, the remedy is to open your mouth and put in some magic elixir, as did the Greek deity Bacchus. Television advertising abounds with graphically suffering men and women who are dramatically "cured" by ingesting the right product. Fairy tales passed from generation to generation reinforce the belief in the power of magic potions to influence life.

Just as Ponce de León wandered in search of the fountain of youth, Judd sought the elixir for "relief from his chronic pain and discomfort" and for everlasting health and vigor. Judd's mother also bought this mythology, as evidenced by her intriguing medicine cabinet. The commonly shared myths made it easy and culturally acceptable for Judd to avoid facing his real problems.

Judd's egogram, constructed again after more than a year of rigorous attention to change via diagnosis of weak areas, surfacing inner conflicts, confronting resistance, redeciding, practicing, exercising both psychologically and physically, overcoming resistances, showed his Critical Parent gained power as he was able to say "NO" to harmful outside influences and stop being a social patsy (see Figure 10.20). His Adult gained particularly in his ability to see himself more accurately. Also, he laughed more as his Free Child grew. The most dramatic change was the decrease in his Adapted Child as he lived his life with personal strength and freedom from psychological slavery.

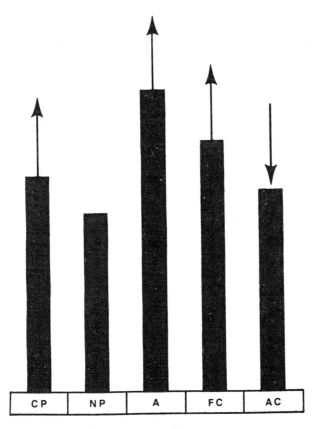

JUDD'S "AFTER" EGOGRAM

Figure 10.20

SUMMARY

Historically, transactional analysis developed in an exciting era for psychotherapies, between the mid-1950s when classical psychoanalysis, with its emphasis on therapist anonymity and client insight was supreme, through the early 1970s in which the "psychological revolution" erupted with the emphasis on emotional expression and experience. TA went through several phases and continues to evolve at the present. The first phase, ego states (1955–62), focused upon Eric Berne's discovery that the dynamic personality can be observed by paying attention to "here-and-now" phenomena. The therapist and client are able to predict future as well as infer past history by attention to things such as present attitude, gestures, voice, vocabulary, social response, and other observable criteria. Eric Berne at that time used these findings about ego states in group psychotherapy as an adjunct for his psychoanalytic approach but it soon became clear that the concept of the dynamic unconscious was not necessary for clients to gain insight and social control.

The second phase of transactional analysis focused on transactions and games (1962–66). This was when a totally fresh view of human interaction was made possible by the delineation of "games." Transactional analysis during this period was basically an intellectual approach, still imbued with the idea that insight or "catching onto" what is happening would be curative. This, of course, was true for many individuals, but certainly not for the majority. It was during this phase that TA became popular, because of its forthright and simple vocabulary and because people could readily identify their game patterns. The third phase, script analysis (1966–70), encouraged strong emotional reexperience in the practice of transactional analysis. Clients not only analyzed but relived those decisive moments in their lives with the emotions that accompanied childhood decisions. Transactional analysts began to incorporate other systems, especially by Robert Goulding's combination of Gestalt techniques with TA. The fourth phase, action (1970 onward), was stimulated by the action techniques of the human-potential movement, Gestalt, psychodrama, encounter, and many of the other explosive energy-liberating systems. The new model, the egogram, was developed to bridge the gap between the more structural definitions and theories of early transactional analysis and provide a model for the otherwise haphazard explosive action techniques.

TA has had a rather full history in a short time and has a remarkable amount of clinical and theoretical research for such a young psychotherapy movement (Blair & McGahey, 1974, 1975). Because of its easily understood vocabulary and because of the willingness of therapists to share ideas with clients, TA became a rapidly popular psychotherapy. As such TA has been used not only by psychiatrists, psychologists, social workers, and other traditional therapists, but also by paraprofessionals who found the theoretical aspects of TA were easy to learn and had direct applicability to their concerns. Indeed, street workers and prison inmates have become outstanding TA therapists. Effort for the TA therapist is in practical applications rather than in decoding mystical jargon.

The future of TA seems to be moving in the direction of action, emotive, and energy models to correct overconcentration upon "understanding," resulting in a balance between affect and cognition. The history of TA is a history of rapid change to new and more effective techniques rather than adherence to earlier models. The structural concepts of ego states, the transaction (the unit of social action), the script or games theory, will not be discarded; however, the techniques employed to bring about change have and will be distinctly shifted from the major reliance upon understanding and insight (which is still thought to be important) to an approach that is more experiential and emotive.

From eight early members in 1958, there are in 1979 over 10,000 members in the worldwide TA organization. Transactional analysis, unlike many of the "new psychologies," is amassing a large written literature. Like most of the newer approaches, TA has been applied gradually to a wider array of psychological and social problems, even to the analysis of destructive and oppressive social institutions.

ANNOTATED BIBLIOGRAPHY

Berne, E. *Games people play.* New York: Grove Press, 1964.
Written as a handbook for transactional group therapists, but because of its readability and forthright vocabulary, it became a best seller in 1965. This book summarizes the early phases of TA: ego states, transactions, and games. The theory of games opened an entirely new psychology of human relationships.

Berne, E. *Principles of group treatment.* New York: Oxford University Press, 1966.
This is a widely used textbook for those interested in the broad field of group interaction and treatment of individuals in a group setting. Although written from a TA standpoint, Berne provides an excellent comparative approach and a workable model for group structure and process.

Berne, E. *What do you say after you say hello?* New York: Grove Press, 1972.
This is Berne's final statement, published posthumously, and outlines the total theory of personality that evolved after 15 years of TA. The occurrence of *scripts* is the major focus.

Dusay, J. *Egograms: How I see you and you see me.* New York: Harper & Row, 1977.
An expansion of TA via a functional and energy model is presented for the first time. Egograms represent a growth model, which is specific and departs from a theory of a dynamic unconscious.

Steiner, C. *Scripts people live.* New York: Grove Press, 1974.
A comprehensive discussion of script theory by the creator of the script matrix. There is a special focus on political and social institutions; abuses of psychiatry and overcoming oppression are well described, and an era of social action is opened.

CASE READINGS

Berne, Eric. Case example. In *Sex in human loving.* New York: Simon & Schuster, 1970.
Dusay, John, & Steiner, Claude. Case example. In H. Kaplan & B. Sadock (Eds.), *Comprehensive group psychotherapy.* Baltimore: The Williams and Wilkins Company, 1971.
Dusay, John. Case example. In B. Ard, Jr. (Ed.), *Counseling and psychotherapy.* Palo Alto, Calif.: Science and Behavior Books, 1975.
Holland, Glen. Case example. In R. J. Corsini (Ed.), *Current psychotherapies.* Itasca, Ill.: F. E. Peacock Publishers, 1973.
Jongeward, Dorothy, & Scott, Dru. Case example. In *Affirmative action for women.* Reading, Mass.: Addison-Wesley, 1973.

REFERENCES

Abraham, K. *Selected papers.* London: Hogarth Press, 1948.
Adler, A. Individual psychology. In G. B. Levitas (Ed.), *The world of psychology.* New York: Braziller, 1963.
Bateson, G., & Ruesch, J. *Communication.* New York: Norton, 1951.
Bateson, G.; Jackson, D.; Haley, J.; & Weakland, J. Toward a communication theory of schizophrenia. *Behavior Science,* 1956, 1(1). Reprinted in D. Jackson (Ed.), *Communication, family and marriage.* Vol. 1. Palo Alto, Calif.: Science & Behavior Books, 1968.

Berne, E. The nature of intuition. *Psychiatric Quarterly,* 1949, 23, 203–26.

Berne, E. Intuition IV. Primal images and primal judgment. *Psychiatric Quarterly,* 1955, 29, 634.

Berne, E. Intuition v. the ego image. *Psychiatric Quarterly,* 1957, 31, 611–27.

Berne, E. *Transactional analysis in psychotherapy.* New York: Grove Press, 1961.

Berne, E. *Structure and dynamics of groups and organizations.* Philadelphia: Lippincott, 1963.

Berne, E. *Games people play.* New York: Grove Press, 1964.

Berne, E. *Principles of group treatment.* New York: Oxford University Press, 1966.

Berne, E. *What do you say after you say hello?* New York: Grove Press, 1972.

Berne, E. *Intuition and ego states.* San Francisco: Harper & Row, 1977.

Blair, M., & McGahey, C. *Transactional analysis research index, volumes I and II.* Tallahassee: Florida Institute for Transactional Analysis, 1974, 1975.

Breuer, J., & Freud, S. On the physical mechanism of hysterical phenomena. In J. Strachey (Ed.), *Standard edition of the complete psychological works of Sigmund Freud, vol. III.* London: Hogarth Press, 1962 (originally published 1893).

Campbell, J. *The hero with a thousand faces.* New York: Pantheon Books, 1949.

Chandler, A., & Hartman, M. Lysergic acid diethylamid (LSD-25) as a facilitating agent in psychotherapy. *A.M.A. Archives of General Psychiatry,* 1960, 2, 286–99.

Crossman, P. Permission and protection. *Transactional Analysis Bulletin,* 1966, 5, 152–53.

Dusay, J. Eric Berne's studies of intuition, 1949–1962. *Transactional Analysis Journal,* 1971, 1, 34–44.

Dusay, J. Egograms and the constancy hypothesis. *Transactional Analysis Journal,* 1972, 2, 37–41.

Dusay, J. Eric Berne. In A. Freedman; H. Kaplan; & B. Sadock (Eds.), *Comprehensive textbook of psychiatry/II.* Baltimore: Williams & Wilkins, 1975.

Dusay, J. Four phases of TA. In G. Barnes (Ed.), *Transactional analysis after Eric Berne.* New York: Harper's College Press, 1977(a).

Dusay, J. *Egograms: How I see you and you see me.* New York: Harper & Row, 1977(b).

Dusay, J. *TA treatment training manual* (in progress), 1978.

Dusay, K. The hero in your head (an analysis of the hero). Master's thesis in psychology. San Francisco: Lone Mountain College, 1975.

Dusay, K. Recurring themes throughout world literature: Persecutors, rescuers and victims. Master's thesis in English. San Francisco: San Francisco State University, 1976.

English, F. Episcript and the hot potato game. *Transactional Analysis Bulletin,* 8:32, October, 1962, 8, 77–82.

Federn, P. *Ego psychology and the psychosis.* New York: Basic Books, 1952.

Glasser, W., & Zunin, L. Reality therapy. In R. J. Corsini (Eds.), *Current psychotherapies.* Itasca, Ill.: F. E. Peacock Publishers, 1973.

Goulding, R. New directions in transactional analysis: Creating an environment for redecision and change. In C. Sager and H. Kaplan (Eds.), *Progress in group and family therapy.* New York: Brunner-Mazel, 1972, pp. 105–34.

Goulding, R. Thinking and feeling in psychotherapy (three impasses). *Voices,* 1974, 10(1), 11–13.

Goulding, R., & Goulding, M. Injunctions, decisions, and redecisions. *Transactional Analysis Journal,* 1976, 6, 41–48.

Harlow, H. The nature of love. *American Psychologist,* 1958, 13, 673–85.

Harris, T. *I'm OK, you're OK.* New York: Harper & Row, 1969.

Heyer, R. Development of questionnaire to measure ego states with some applications to social and comparative psychiatry. *TAJ,* 1979, 9(1).

Hurley, J., & Porter, H. Child ego state in the college classroom. *Transactional Analysis Bulletin,* 1967, 6, 28.

James, M., & Jongeward, D. *Born to win.* Reading, Mass.: Addison-Wesley, 1971.

Kahler, T. Scripts: Process and content. *Transactional Analysis Journal,* 1975, 5, 277–79.

Karpman, S. Script drama analysis. *Transactional Analysis Bulletin,* 1968, 26.

Kendra, J. Research presentation at ITAA Conference 1973. In J. Dusay, *Egograms: How I see you and you see me.* San Francisco: Harper & Row, 1977, 56–57.

McCormick, P. TA and behavior modification: A comparison study. *Transactional Analysis Journal,* 1973, 3(2), 10–14.

McNeel, J. Redecisions in psychotherapy: A study of the effects of an intensive weekend group workshop. Ph.D. dissertation. San Francisco: California School of Professional Psychology, 1975.

Penfield, W. Memory mechanisms. *Archives of Neurology and Psychiatry,* 1952, 67, 178-98.

Penfield, W., & Roberts, L. *Speech and brain mechanisms.* Princeton: Princeton University Press, 1959.

Perls, F. *Gestalt therapy verbatim.* Lafayette, Calif.: Real People Press, 1969.

Schiff, E., & Mellor, K. Discounting. *Transactional Analysis Journal,* 1975, 5(3), 303-11.

Schiff, J. Reparenting schizophrenics. *Transactional Analysis Bulletin,* 1969, 8, 47-62.

Schiff, J. *All my children.* New York: Evans, 1970.

Schiff, J., et al. *The cathexis reader.* New York: Harper & Row, 1975.

Schiff, J. and A. Passivity. *Transactional Analysis Journal,* 1971, 1(1), 71-78.

Spitz, R. Hospitalism: Genesis of psychiatric conditions in early childhood. *Psychoanalytic Study of the Child,* 1945, 1, 53.

Steiner, C. A script checklist. *Transactional Analysis Bulletin,* 1964, 6, 38-39.

Steiner, C. *Games alcoholics play.* New York: Grove Press, 1970.

Steiner, C. *Scripts people live.* New York: Grove Press, 1971.

Thomson, G. The identification of ego states. *Transactional Analysis Journal,* 1972, 2, 196-211.

Vernon, J., et al. The effect of human isolation upon some perceptual and motor skills. In Solomon, et al. (Ed.), *Sensory deprivation.* Cambridge, Mass.: Harvard University Press, 1961.

Weiss, E. *Principles of psychodynamics.* New York: Grune & Stratton, 1950.

11

Psychodrama

LEON J. FINE

OVERVIEW

Psychodrama is a method of psychotherapy which uses action methods that focus on the theory, philosophy, and methodology of J. L. Moreno. This approach employs dramatic interactions, sociometric measurements, group dynamics, and depends on role theory to facilitate changes in individuals and groups through the development of new perceptions and behaviors and/or reorganizations of old cognitive patterns. Current applications of psychodrama include but are not limited to clinical, social, educational, and research activities.

Basic Concepts

Moreno is generally recognized as one of the first initiators of group psychotherapy, a treatment procedure in which clients learn from and are supported by each other as well as by the therapist. As a therapist, he focused on the existential I-Thou encounter and on life processes of the immediate moment. Moreno was interested in the theatre and his methods and language were of the theatre. His therapeutic method was psychodrama (Moreno and Elefthery, 1975).

In psychodrama the therapist is called the *director*. The group members are the *audience*. Group members and specially trained co-therapists may serve as *auxiliaries*, or assistants, for the therapeutic drama in which the *protagonist* (the client) explores, expresses, and modifies elements of his existence. The therapeutic enactment takes place in any part of a room or on a specially designed *stage*. The auxiliaries are the therapeutic agents of the director who guides them in their functions. The director is in charge overall, directing all in collaboration with the protagonist, setting up the stage, getting the protagonist to give information to the group, helping to select auxiliaries, helping them to prepare for their roles, and starting action and ending it. After a psychodrama is finished, the protagonist, the auxiliaries, members of the audience, and the director generally engage in a nonjudgmental discussion known as *sharing,* which is an important part of the therapy for in it group members discover their communality. Sharing also provides support and confrontation, warms up other clients to their own personal issues, and increases interpersonal effectiveness.

In Western medicine, the "sick patient" is diagnosed, treated, and cured by a "doctor." Moreno rejected the medical model for helping people with psychological problems. He viewed his clients as people who had become damaged through social acculturation. To recapture their power to be spontaneous and self-directing was the cure.

At a Moreno therapy group, some group members were trainees, others outpatients, and some might be inpatients. Moreno introduced everyone by the title *Doctor* explaining that the word was derived from the Latin for teacher and that all were there to learn from one another. The word *protagonist* for the client was a nonstigmatizing label emphasizing that the person was there to learn about and improve his effectiveness in living in a social world.

Moreno's sociometric-spontaneity theory is based on the person in the context of other people. An existential system, it stresses that all that exists is here and now, at the moment of observation. For Moreno, the ideal person is the fully actualized genius: the spontaneous creator. Humans in society are seen as continually evolving. Each person who is open to his internal strengths meets external events in creative ways that continue the evolution of his society. Effective behavior is *spontaneous* (optimally adaptive). Pathological behavior is *conserved* (frozen, fixated). The malfunctioning individual is unable to meet each new moment in a fresh and adaptive way. Spontaneity implies good choice and is operationally manifested in successful behavior.

Any specific act is the result of one's somatic, psychodramatic, and social roles. A *somatic role* is a constellation of body states at the moment. A *psychodramatic role* is a constellation of role behaviors particular to the individual based upon all experiences up to and including the present moment. A *social role* is the constellation of role behaviors common to one's

subgroup passed on by parents and teachers. Body, psychological self, and the incorporations of society blend and are experienced as *self* and expressed in *behavior.*

Moreno's personality theory stresses normal functioning. An individual at birth is seen as having an innate, creative vitality to meet the continually changing environment encountered throughout a lifetime. By nature, humans are social; they learn and evolve in the context of others. To live fully, one must have reality based, reciprocal relationships. Prior learning and models from society are necessary as a supportive base. Ideally one is also open to the immediate moment and able to respond with novel, adaptive, and creative behaviors to each new event. Ideally each person is an actualizer, a creative growth seeker, and an ever developing, socially interactive person.

We take from society and we give to it. Each person has a network of others with whom he gives and receives. Being with others provides models for role behaviors and the opportunity for spontaneous and creative interaction. Psychotherapy ideally occurs best in a setting that allows for a holistic use of body and mind in interaction and co-action with other individuals. According to Moreno, each patient is the therapeutic agent of the other; consequently group members assist in treatment and are as important as the therapist. Therapy patterns itself after life and should be based on interpersonal encounter and feedback as in ordinary living.

Coping with problems and actualization of self are assumed to be natural functions of humanness. The primary goal of therapy is to reclaim one's innate ability to meet each moment in a fresh, optimally adaptive way—in short, to be spontaneous.

Psychodrama uses procedures from the

legitimate drama and some devised for the method itself (Z. T. Moreno, 1959; Starr, 1977). The timing and selection of dramatic procedures imply beliefs about how change occurs for an individual. The theory of psychotherapy is that a person usually has ability to be self-correcting when given accurate information about his behavior. When this ability is limited, guidance and support may be provided to encourage growth. Special psychodramatic procedures are used to facilitate expression, awareness, knowledge of the effects on others, and behavioral change. Some of these procedures are introduced here.

In *role presentation,* a person (1) presents self in a simple role play that demonstrates how the person is in everyday life or (2) presents self symbolically by dramatizing different aspects of his intrapsychic or interpersonal experience. Deciding how to represent the situation can be insightful in itself (Fine, 1959). For example, Maria complained she was in conflict with a fellow worker she supervised. She felt this employee was critical of her and looked down on her. Asked if she felt there were others in her life who fitted this critical pattern, she named her mother and a teaching nun from her school days. She was asked to take three volunteers and place them in space in relation to her. She placed herself on her knees looking up at these three figures. "Oh, I see," said Maria. Gaining insight through setting the scene she decided to stand up and face them and began her psychodrama.

Role reversal calls for exchanging roles with another person and seeing the relationship or conflict through the other person's eyes. In this case example, Maria changed places and became the employee looking down at the auxiliary who was now playing on her knees. She experienced a leveling in the relationship as the auxiliary gradually stood to her feet. Through the role reversal, she experienced the confirming power of her decision to "stand up for herself."

In *soliloquy* the protagonist pretends to be alone and that no one can hear the inner thoughts and feelings that are expressed aloud. Soliloquy is free association paired with expressive movement. The soliloquy can serve as a warm-up to other activities or to integrate thoughts after action has occurred. Soliloquy provides the director with information about the immediate status of the client, especially if the behavior is congruent or contradictory with the words.

Aside allows the protagonist to voice feelings that seem inappropriate to say out loud or that he did not say aloud in the real life event. As in the theatre, in psychodrama everyone acts as though the aside has not been heard. The aside may then lead to direct open expression or may simply serve as a method and rationale for saying the unspoken or unspeakable.

Doubling provides an alter-ego for the protagonist (Toeman, 1948). The auxiliary becomes as one with the protagonist by duplicating her movements, by subjectively identifying with the client, and by expressing herself as though she were the client. In the case example, the double got down next to Maria on her knees. She looked up and experienced the effect of the actors standing and looking down at her. She said, "I feel so small. I don't know what to do." Maria agreed: "Yes, I feel weak and helpless but I see that I must stand up now and face them as a grown-up person." The double is a supportive therapist who helps the protagonist towards fuller awareness and expression of self.

Amplifying is a simplified form of doubling. The auxiliary speaks loudly or even shouts the words that the client has spoken. This procedure is useful for shy people in large groups and especially for regressed patients who have given up hope of ever being heard (Ossorio & Fine, 1959).

The *mirror* is primarily a feedback method to let the client see a reflection of herself. She watches an auxiliary repeat the event she has just completed. It is like an instant reply on television. The psychological distance that comes from watching allows her to assess her behavior more objectively and to plan changes she wants to make when she resumes her own role in the drama. Mirroring also teaches group members observational skills and alerts them to perceptual distortions since several replays and discussions are often necessary before consensus about the replay of the event is reached. Carl Hollander (1967) uses the mirror to deal with resistance, confrontation, and to increase spontaneity.

Modeling is the demonstration of behavioral alternatives to the client by the group members. As a rule, other procedures are used first to allow the client to find her own way. Modeling does not mean showing the "correct" way to behave, but rather giving a broad spectrum of possibilities since often the "correct" way is stereotyped whereas the "wrong" way may be innovative.

Psychodrama is related to the concepts of *group psychotherapy* and *sociometry* emphasizing that the person's social roles and relationships are as important as intrapsychic processes and physical self. Sociometry refers to the research, measurement, and observation of interpersonal dynamics. It is a means of measuring attitudes of social acceptance or rejection among members of a social group. In clinical practice, a sociometric evaluation can alert the therapist to the changing structure of group relationships so he can intervene when this structure defeats the goals of its members. *Group psychotherapy* is defined as a method of treatment in which a group of patients participates with a therapist in an attempt to reestablish former levels of effective coping and/or to establish new levels of self-awareness, self-acceptance, emotional expressiveness, interpersonal effectiveness, and renewed spontaneity. Psychodrama is usually a group psychotherapy, but it may also be applied in one-to-one therapy, and in the monodrama form, the client takes all the roles by himself and can even apply the procedures when alone.

Other Systems

When Moreno introduced psychodrama, psychoanalysis was the primary form of psychotherapy. The patient reclined on a couch and did not have eye-to-eye contact with the therapist. The patient dealt with inner thoughts and feelings and his relationship with the therapist. The therapist was instructed to be a blank screen upon which the patient was to project. This process assumed that the patient's relationship with the therapist would be similar to those of other significant figures of his past. Releasing feelings, gaining insight, and working through the transferred relationship were the prime therapeutic goals. Feelings and thoughts were to be put into words and not acted out. The encounter was in essence with one's self, facilitated by a therapist who was to be as neutral as possible. Psychoanalysis was a very private matter and therapists usually had offices with two doors so a person leaving would not be seen by the next client.

Moreno's theory and procedures were quite different. In addition to the transference of the past, Moreno insisted that the realities of the present be recognized.

A therapist sitting behind a couch and making occasionally facilitative interventions was not really a neutral stimulus. Since a human is an acting and not just a verbal being, catharsis, awareness, and relationship were limited by the passive physical stance of the patient as required by psychoanalysis. Moreno postulated that engaging with one's muscles in movement increased intensity of memory and catharsis and did not reduce but enhanced awareness of one's thoughts, actions, and emotions. When working in a group, repeated patterns emerge not only with the therapist but with other members of the group. Patterns occur with women that are different than with men, or with younger people that are different than with older people. These emerging and varied transferential behaviors provide information about self to the client in an interpersonal context.

The client in psychodrama also encounters real, two-way relationships that include *tele,* defined as a reciprocal, emotional aspect between people. Working in groups permits participants to learn and to discover self through others. Behavior learned in this protected setting with other peer members is more directly generalized to everyday life than that learned on the psychoanalyst's couch.

In psychoanalysis the therapist is supposed to (a) experience his own feelings and emotions while (b) subjecting these feelings to the critical scrutiny of his own observing ego. He bases his interventions from the interplay of this event. In psychodrama these two therapist positions are split into separate roles taken by two or more persons. The director generally takes an objective view of the therapeutic process while the actors or auxiliary-egos are expected to give free reign to their emotions and allow themselves to express themselves fully, knowing that the director will provide control and limits if needed. The two "therapists" in concert are able to have a wider view of the patient since they view the situation from different observational stances. Theoretically this is more effective than using the one therapist who rigidly contains his spontaneity (Fine, 1967).

Howard Blatner (1971) addresses himself to reservations made about psychodrama. Blatner prefers to use the term *acting in* instead of *acting out.* He stresses that psychodrama is not "acting out" as in an antitherapeutic discharge of tensions without awareness. The enacting of psychodrama is done with words and actions in a supportive context in which one uses full powers of expression with awareness and with feedback from therapists and group members who serve as observers. It certainly is not "acting out" as used in psychoanalytic conceptualizations of violent behavior with little control based on discharges of drives as modified by transferences.

Gestalt therapy is theoretically compatible with psychodrama. Moreno and Fritz Perls shared concepts and goals even though they used different terminologies. Perls sought to help the client become more response-able through greater awareness. The client's goal was to function in a "mature" or self-directing manner in which he relied on his inner supports rather than on the environment. These notions are similar to Moreno's concepts of spontaneity and creativity as well as the human being as actor and director of his life who is to be creative in the moment of encounter with others. Fritz Perls used a dramatic technique, the "hot seat," in which the client enacted different aspects of himself moving from one chair to another and addressed aspects of himself in dialogue. The technique is Moreno's monodrama extended as the *auxiliary chair technique* (Lippitt, 1958) in which aspects of self are projected onto an empty chair and role reversals used so the individual experiences and reowns aspects of self.

Perls objected to psychodrama because he thought auxiliaries (the therapist's assistants) might contaminate the therapy and take away from the self-explorations of the individual. He was concerned that all the elements of the exploration would come from the patient and not from assistants who might affect his treatment with their own projections. Moreno also was concerned that the drama be the production of the protagonist. The therapist's task was to populate the world of the protagonist so he could see and experience it more fully as well as attempt new behaviors within it. The dilemma that Perls advanced of the actors projecting and contaminating therapy is of real concern. It is handled by the director training the auxiliaries to take their cues from the behavior of the protagonist and to base the dramatic production upon their perceptions of the protagonist's private logic. These auxiliaries must learn to use their eyes and ears to pick up cues in the ongoing enactment. This function is a critical construct of Gestalt therapy. The auxiliaries in the psychodrama are receiving therapy as well as the protagonist when they use their eyes and ears, voices and bodies, to attend to and recreate the fantasies and perceptions of the moment of the protagonist. Another check on accuracy is that clients are asked to correct or discard incorrect inputs from the auxiliaries.

Perls in Gestalt therapy was particularly concerned with an intrapsychic exploration. The client was to become more aware of his own processes and, through this awareness, more contactful in the world. Much of his work was intrapsychic and he gave less emphasis in Gestalt ther-

apy to the interpersonal process than psychodrama provides. Other Gestalt therapists such as Erving Polster (1973) pay more attention to the contact function and between-people process.

It is important to distinguish between *process* and *content* in therapy. Process is *how* and content is *what*. *Content* is the theme the client talks about. It is the subject matter discussed or dramatized. *Process* is the manner or sequence of events through which the content is presented. Process is less subject to conscious control in comparison to content. Most therapists attend closely to process cues, reflecting the saying that "actions speak louder than words." Process behaviors include switching content, blocking, showing anxiety at critical moments, and, in general, represent the pattern or configuration of the client's words and behavior. Learning to be observant of one's own processes (how one is) is central in Gestalt therapy. Attending to underlying process flow is critical to analytic therapy. Psychodrama by its nature attends richly to process. Enactment makes process events vivid and explicit as they occur. Process events can also become the theme (content) to be dramatized, discussed, or otherwise attended.

HISTORY

Precursors

We have all had experience with psychodrama. As children, one way we tested and mastered the world was to play roles. Lori put a coronet in her hair and became a queen and her girlfriend became her lady in waiting. Gary built satellites and took elaborate interstellar space explorations in his room. Children's play is an enactment of their fantasies in which they practice the social roles of their culture.

The action and enacting world of the child is full of energy, excitement, and social learning. Fantasy acting of the child is free and creative.

Primitive peoples engage in dance and dramatization as part of their preparation for war, birth, and death. Medicine men use movement and dramatic rituals to drive away evil spirits and to cure sickness. As individuals became more civilized, these enactments became ritualized or, in Moreno's term, *conserved*. Ancient Greek drama began as religious observation (Greenberg, 1968). Dionysus was identified with life, death, and immortality. Part of religious celebration was to portray and dramatize ritually the deity's experiences and to become one with God by invoking his spirit. Greek drama provided the audience with a cathartic opportunity. Identification was enhanced by an intermediary group called the chorus. Modern psychodrama is an extension of life in which catharsis and insight are available not only to the audience but to the players as well.

Ihara Saikaku (1964, p. 161–62) gives an illustration of the therapeutic use of an informal psychodrama in seventeenth-century Japan. After an afternoon of sports, something seemed to cross the mind of the mistress of the castle. Her face grew fierce and there was no humoring her. Her attendants lapsed into silence. One of the ladies who had been in service for many a year approached: "Would madame be pleased," said she, "to hold a Jealousy Meeting again this evening, until the candle burns itself out?" Hearing this, the Lady instantly recovered her good humor. "Yes, indeed, yes indeed!" said she in high spirits. A bell was rung and 36 women including kitchenmaids and serving girls seated themselves without ceremony in a great circle. "Each of you may speak without reserve and confess your troubles openly. Pour forth your hate, revile men with your bitter jealousy, tell of loves which went awry." The Lady took out a female doll that was the image of a living person. The women, in turn, began to speak of what lay on their minds. After a while, one of the women speaking as though she were the Lady of the house, said to the doll: "You came as a concubine and found favor with my Lord and you share his bed with him every night and you have made him set his true wife aside." So saying, she glared at the doll, gnashed her teeth, and acted with rancor. Her words hit the very core of the Lady's concern, and she said, "That's it. That's why I made the doll. Though I ever be at my lord's disposal, he is pleased to treat me as though I were not here." This is a clear example of a psychodrama including doubling and catharsis for members of the group.

J. L. Moreno credited Henri Bergson for bringing the concept of spontaneity to philosophy through his metaphors of *donneés immédiate, élan vital,* and *durée.* He credits Charles Sanders Peirce, the founder of pragmatism, as defining spontaneity as newness, freshness, and diversity (J. L. Moreno, 1974, p. 73–74). He also felt influenced by Jesus "that improvising saint," and by Socrates who pioneered the psychodramatic format with dialogues that were like reports of therapeutic sessions (Yablonsky, 1976, p. 276).

Beginnings

Jacob Levy Moreno was born in Bucharest, Romania, in 1889. His family moved to Vienna when he was five. Entering college as a student and later a teacher of philosophy, he graduated from medical school in 1917. While in Vienna, he published a literary magazine, *Daimon,* and published books on philosophy and poetry including *The Words of the Father,* which considered man's relationship to God, his creativity, and godlikeness. He first came to the United States in 1925 to continue work on an invention he called "radio film," which recorded both sound and optical images (Z. T. Moreno, 1976).

> To the psychiatric fraternity, he was a problem: his views of man and his interpersonal and intergroup relations flew in the face of all that was being taught. He was just too controversial, too personally difficult to accept: a maverick, a loner, a narcissistic leader, charismatic but aloof, gregarious but selective, loveable but eccentric, unlovable and appealing . . . he found a fatherly, protective figure in William Alanson White . . . Superintendent of St. Elizabeth's Hospital, Washington, D.C. (who) made it possible for the theatre of psychodrama to be constructed. . . . (Z. T. Moreno, 1976, p. 132)

Moreno opened a private mental hospital at Beacon, New York, in 1936, which operated for 30 years. In 1937 he founded, edited, and published *Sociometry, a Journal of Interpersonal Relations.* In 1942 he established institutes in New York City and at Beacon, New York, for the training of psychodramatists and group psychotherapists. In 1947 he began to publish *Sociatry,* which in 1950 changed its name to *Group Psychotherapy* which in 1976 became *Group Psychotherapy, Psychodrama and Sociometry,* the official organ of the American Society of Group Psychotherapy and Psychodrama. Moreno toured Europe at regular intervals beginning in the 1950s and set up training opportunities throughout Europe. He organized the first International Committee of Group Psychotherapy in 1951, which sponsored international congresses and led to the establishment of the International Association of Group Psy-

chotherapy in 1973. Translations of his works have appeared in many languages. In his last years, he was the recipient of many awards and recognitions, but he never was fully accepted by his peers in American psychiatry.

While attending the University of Vienna, Moreno encouraged children to improvise plays in the city parks. He invited children to choose new "parents" to act out stories about their families. Certain parents were chosen and others were rejected and Moreno began to form his ideas about the reasons for these selections and rejections, which became the basis for sociometry. In exploring the reasons for patterns of choice, he had the children role reverse by playing the parts of their parents. These enactments and reversals eventually led to therapeutic psychodrama (Siroka, 1971). "During the years 1914 to 1921, Moreno continued his creative activities in the realm of poetry, philosophy, theology and literature . . . his philosophy was closely related to interpersonal themes. Terms such as 'here and now' and 'encounter' so popular today in the human potential movement, were to be found as key ideas in Moreno's poetic writings of this period" (Blatner, 1973, pp. 140–41). From 1921 to 1923, Moreno ran a public Theater of Spontaneity in which events from the daily newspaper were enacted as an entertainment with involvement by the audience. The personal effects noted on members of the cast as they enacted roles was another step that led toward the development of therapeutic theater. In the United States, Moreno progressively developed the use of improvisation in the treatment of individuals, couples, and small groups. Moreno laid claim to being first to do and use the terms *group psychotherapy, psychodrama,* and *encounter* with its therapeutic meaning.

In 1929 he began his first regular program of large-scale, open psychodramas in America with a three-times-a-week Impromptu Group Theater at Carnegie Hall. Moreno made sociometric studies of the social structure of prisoners at Sing Sing Prison in 1931 and 1932 and with Helen Jennings experimented in modifying the environment (milieu therapy or therapeutic community) at the New York State Training School for Delinquent Girls from 1932 to 1938. *Who Shall Survive?* originally published in 1932, was revised in 1953 with Lewis Yablonsky assisting in the editing. Yablonsky (1976, p. 282) writes:

in 1952, Moreno invited me to accompany him to lecture on psychodrama and the group method . . . to a group of New York's psychotherapists. . . . I have never forgotten the hatred and chastisement that Moreno encountered that afternoon in response to his belief in the *primacy of group* concepts in all types of therapy. He was openly denounced, ridiculed and even laughed at by members of the group during the brutal questioning. . . . At the end of his presentation . . . I said, "How can you take these insults?" He smiled, "First, Lew, I know I'm right. Secondly, I may be crazy like they say, but I'm making a lot of other people, like you, crazy with me; and each year as more and more people join our movement, I will be considered less crazy."

When Moreno decided to die, he went out with style. He had an agreement with his wife that if he had a terminal illness, he should not be artificially maintained. He suffered a stroke and when he could not retain food or function at capacity, he decided it was time for him to die. He stopped eating and only took water. He let his friends and students know of his decision. People from throughout the world came to visit him and he survived through the annual April 1974 meeting of the society he had started. Confined to bed and in and out of sensorial contact, he visited and said his good-byes with those who came to see him. Moreno approached death with dignity, creativity, and control. At 85 years of age, he had led a full and vigorous life and now, as his body and senses were failing him, he elected to finish in his own way. His wife and medical colleagues, paying him deep respect, allowed him to have his wish. Still the actor and director of his fate, he died in his own way at his own pace.

Current Status

Zerka Moreno told a story that when Moreno was a medical student, he encountered Sigmund Freud. Freud invited the members of the class to study with him and become his followers. Moreno implied that he did not want to be a son but rather a father and to have his own followers. As was true of Freud, Moreno preferred to have followers about him rather than peers. He was very generous to young students and would help to train them, but as they became men and women with power of their own, he often pushed them away, or they left him.

The American Society of Group Psychotherapy and Psychodrama, which Moreno founded and tightly monitored, has grown progressively more democratic and now encourages a wide variety of psychotherapeutic methods. Continuing development has occurred under the recent presidencies of James Sacks, Robert Siroka, and Dean Elefthery. Membership in the society is open to mental-health professionals as well as those who have evidenced special talents and contributions to the fields of group psychotherapy and psychodrama. Information may be secured by writing to the American Society of Group Psychotherapy and Psychodrama, 39 East 20th Street, New York, New York 10003.

In 1975 the American Board of Examiners in Psychodrama, Sociometry and Group Psychotherapy was formed to accredit individual practitioners, trainers, and training centers. This independent board certifies competence in the field. Until a few years ago, only the Moreno Institute of Beacon, New York, trained and accredited people in psychodrama. In the last few years, there has been an increase in the number of training institutes. A Federation of Training Institutes has been formed to promote and develop training.

The Morenos with A. Ancelin-Schutzenberger of France, organized the first International Congress of Psychodrama in Paris in 1964. Meetings were held in Spain, Brazil and Austria in ensuing years. In 1973 they helped form the International Association of Group Psychotherapy whose membership is worldwide.

One of the growing list of master's degree programs in psychodrama is headed by Joseph W. Hart at the University of Arkansas Graduate School of Social Work. Leslie College of Cambridge, Massachusetts, where Joseph Powers and Peter Rowen are on the faculty, grants a master of arts in psychodrama. Missouri and Colorado have had civil service positions in psychodrama.

The action methods Moreno fostered permeate the field of therapy. They are so pervasive that credit often is no longer accorded. Eric Berne wrote: "In his selection of specific techniques, Dr. Perls shares with other *active* psychotherapists the Moreno problem: the fact that nearly all known *active* techniques were first tried out by Dr. J. L. Moreno in psychodrama so it is difficult to come up with an original idea in this regard" (Berne, 1970,

p. 126). William Schutz stated that most of the action procedures about which he has written were anticipated 40 years earlier by Moreno (Schutz, 1971, p. 201).

Psychodrama is now practiced with many points of view. There are as many varieties of psychodrama as there are personalities and backgrounds of the therapists who direct the therapies. In addition to the classical psychodrama of J. L. Moreno (1946, 1959, 1969), there is psychodrama with a psychoanalytic frame of reference (Sacks, 1960), psychodramatic group therapy (Corsini, 1957), psychodrama with an Adlerian emphasis (Starr, 1977), transactional analysis, primal therapy, and reality therapy models (Yablonsky, 1976), a social learning mode (Haskell, 1975) and even for the timid clinician (Leveton, 1977). Moreno's philosophy and method have also influenced the separately derived systems of Gestalt therapy (Perls, 1969) and Psychomotor therapy (Pesso, 1969).

Bibliography lists on psychodrama have been prepared by R. J. Corsini and L. J. Putzey (1956), B. Lubin and A. Lubin (1964), R. J. Corsini (1966, 133 annotated items), and V. J. Greer and J. M. Sacks (1973). Additional bibliographies may be found in the doctoral dissertations on psychodrama by A. R. Anderson (1965), D. C. Daly (1961), J. M. Dysart (1952), L. J. Fine (1967), I. A. Greenberg (1967), J. P. Maas (1964), P. P. Rosenberg (1952), and J. N. Shapiro (1964). John Mann (1966) reviewed the research to that time in group psychotherapy including psychodrama.

Psychodrama is practiced world-wide. In France there are two primary trends: Analytic Psychodrama as represented by Anzier (1956) and triadic psychodrama, an amalgam of psychodrama, group dynamics and non-verbal communication as taught by Schutzenberger (1970). There are active psychodrama programs in most European countries and in Japan as well. Weil (1967) of Brazil and Rojas-Bermudez (1970) of Argentina represent psychodrama as it is used in South America.

PERSONALITY

Theory of Personality

Psychodrama presently is used by practitioners who subscribe to a variety of personality theories. Theory guides the therapist in organizing the clinical data in therapy and helps determine the nature and timing of interventions. The therapist operating with a psychoanalytic frame of reference might direct the psychodrama to emphasize transference or insight into the origin of the problem. The therapist operating from a Gestalt frame of reference might stress the client's awareness of his immediate process and confront him psychodramatically with the options and choices he has regarding his behavior of the moment. Some therapists use Moreno's theories as their cognitive support system to direct their therapeutic interventions. But even those who do not rigorously subscribe to Moreno's thinking owe him a debt in his espousal of man as a responsible, creative actor and growth seeker who has the potential for increasing self-actualization.

J. L. Moreno (1946) developed his system from observations of normal behavior. The child develops in the context of important and vital others. An individual exists in the context of his relationships to other people, real and imagined, present and absent. Moreno operationally defined personality as a unified and consistent cluster of observable role behaviors an individual learns to identify as *self.*

The tangible aspects of what is known as "ego" or "self" are the roles in which it oper-

ates. Role and relationship between roles are the most significant development within any specific culture. Working with the "role" as a point of reference appears to be a methodological advantage as compared with "personality," "self," or "ego" (which) are less concrete. . . . Roles do not emerge from the self, but the self can emerge from the roles. . . . The genesis of roles goes through two stages, role perception and role enactment (J. L. Moreno, 1960, p. 81).

Some roles, such as sleeper, eater, and eliminator, are born with the individual. These natural roles are influenced early in life by mother and others who interact with the growing child. They model role behaviors (social roles) that influence the child and that at first he takes in an undifferentiated manner. When old enough to differentiate between fantasy and reality, and self and other, he begins to form his own psychic roles, which are called the psychodramatic roles.

Man has an innate capacity to cope: Moreno's spontaneity factor. To the newborn, all is new and original and every first response is spontaneous. In Moreno's language, *spontaneous* means optimally adaptive: to find a new effective response for a situation or to use old behaviors in novel ways. The child is influenced by the behaviors of others. The hungry newborn has a somatic starter. Hunger leads to restlessness and to crying. Mother picks up her child in her own particular fashion and brings breast or bottle in accordance with the cultural norms in which she has been raised. Initially, the child's sucking is random and instinctive but soon it becomes patterned and that which was new and spontaneous becomes part of the *conserved* or habituated behavior.

The child lives within a matrix of others. One's *social atom* is ever changing as people come and go in one's life. These people are carriers of cultural norms. They bring reinforcers for role behaviors and define that which is and which is not acceptable. The cultural system shapes individuals and is in turn changed by its members. The ideal culture encourages growth and creativity while providing the advantages of past history and learning. Too often, those who selectively reinforce society's norms discourage the spontaneity and creativity of the child. When a person is fixated and not able to meet the demands of a situation in an optimally adaptive, spontaneous, and creative fashion, that individual suffers from a pathological defect. Spontaneity has been lost.

Moreno hypothesized two types of memory: *content* (mind) and *action* (body). Content memory is stored as thoughts, recollections, feelings, and facts. Act memory is stored in the brain but also in the musculature as tension, holding, tingling, warmth, incipient movement, and the like. The best route to recapturing act memory is through expressive methods that use the whole person (body and mind) in action, movement, dance, and dramatization. So, too, preparation for the future is most effectively generalized when the patient practices the actions he intends rather than just reviews these plans in words and thoughts. Therapy seeks to help the patient to be congruent and integrated in behavior (acts), intentions and beliefs (mind), and emotions (body-mind). Internal and external forces are continually changing and adjustments must be made for optimal adaptivity. To act in accord with the demands of moment rather than from habit is the essence of *spontaneity*.

Variety of Concepts

Ledford Bischof (1964) reviewed the primary concepts of Moreno's personality theory including: social atom, tele, warming up, role playing, spontaneity, creativ-

ity, and conserve. The *social atom* is the smallest living social unit, such as a family, which cannot be further subdivided, in which there is reciprocity of relationship. A social atom exists in the *now*. It may have a long history and intense feelings (as a parent and child) or minimal feeling and short history (as with a storekeeper and customer). The social atom describes the states of relationship between people and is a value-free structural concept. Having adequate connections with others is a requisite for *sociostasis* (social balance or equilibrium). A collection of social atoms is a social structure. The ideal social structure is permeable. It allows for development and change and provides support and reciprocity of feeling. It is an open, supportive, balanced system. Pathology occurs (1) with too rigid a social structure where the individual is unable to grow and change or (2) when relationships are not balanced. A cultural atom is an irreducible role defined by society that can support or oppose the social atom. For example, in our culture it has been the model that the woman stays at home and takes care of the child and the man works outside and provides for the family. This cultural role is in the process of evolution. A married couple wishing to reverse their roles together needs strength to counter this cultural norm. In this instance, the roles defined by society are in opposition rather than in support of the roles that the spouses elect to take with each other.

Tele describes the emotional aspect between people. Tele is conceived of as a two-way process as basic as hunger, breathing, and elimination. It is a fundamental factor underlying one's perception of another in relationship to one's self. Tele describes the process of action and affection or disaffection between individuals. Tele is usually an aspect of a relationship between people. Tele is the simplest unit of feeling transmitted from one person to another. Its intensity varies from relationship to relationship. Tele has the characteristic of sensitivity in being able to penetrate and understand another person. It may have positive or negative loading. Tele is not due to symbolic transference but "to certain realities which (the) other embodies and represents. Even when the affinity is not mutual . . . as long as an individual is attracted towards a reality (it is tele)." (Moreno, 1946, p. 229). Transference is a one-way projection or fantasy about a relationship or a perception of a person. Empathy is a one-way, real, here-and-now, emotional recognition of the other. Transference and empathy are one-way relationships. Tele is a two-way function and is the basis for realistic relationship. Normally, tele is self-starting in that an individual not only reacts to another but can initiate action. Pathological function implies transference, which is a delusional process of reacting to a current person as though he were a figure from one's past or another person from the present. Tele, a theoretical construct, is the process aspect of the social atom.

A *warm-up* is the process of getting ready for action. The shorter the warm-up period, the more effective one is in meeting life's situations. Warming-up is essential to effective action or behavior. The runner exercises to get his muscles ready for the race, knowing he will run better if his body is tuned to the coming event. Progressive warm-up is seen in sexual foreplay behavior. Warming-up continues during the act and is the development of readiness to switch to a new set of behaviors. An individual has innate physical self-starters such as breathing and sucking but learned starting mechanisms are also integral to the warm-up process. An example of a learned starter are the cues learned by the baby when the mother lifts the newborn to her breast to suckle. Interpersonal modeling and the development of language and concepts leads to the establishment of mental starters. The warming-up process becomes associated not only with contact zones of mouth, anus, and genitals, but with the musculature and skin as well, and with persons, places, and objects outside the body. In the adult, warming-up has physical *(somatic),* psychological, and social aspects. Warming-up implies an energizing (or deenergizing), a moving toward or away from arousal and alertness, and a readiness of the system to act or to respond. Pathology in the warming-up process occurs when an individual has not developed self-starters and is dependent upon external events for initiation.

Role playing is a characteristic set of institutional behaviors defined both by the individual and by the group. Not only does an individual strive for *homeostasis* (internal balance) but he also strives for *sociostasis* (social balance through having well-established social atoms). *Personality* may be defined as the constellation of all role behaviors one has learned. Roles are usually learned early in childhood through observation and play behavior. The child assumes parental and societal models that he sees about him and plays these roles as a way of mastering them. One's spontaneity and creativity is supported by all that one has learned plus attention to the forces of the immediate movement. The wider the variety of role experiences and models that have been accepted, incorporated, and are available for action, the greater are the chances that the individual can meet the exigencies of life in an optimally adaptive and creative fashion. Pathology stems from a person having a paucity of roles due to a deprived environment, from incorporating incongruent or ineffective role models, and/or from inhibiting the expression of roles that are in the person's repertoire but blocked at an expressive level. Therapy for the deprived or maladaptive person means to learn and practice a wide array of possible role behaviors and to integrate these models into everyday behavior. Therapy for the blocked person might mean looking at the fears or inhibitions about a blockage and then practicing new behaviors in the safe and controlled circumstances where the threat of negative consequences in everyday life is reduced. For the impulsive person, therapy may teach constraint and inhibition.

Taking roles in play is a natural way by which the child explores and gains mastery of its world. Psychodrama is a formal process in which a person can experiment with, develop, and expand role repertoires. Roles integrated into the self reduce the warming-up period required to meet novel situations. If a person is limited in his roles, or if his role behavior does not meet the requirements of the moment, he is *fixated* or *conserved*. Habitual behavior, fixed to a set pattern, when not responsive to the context of the moment, is pathological. The past provides role repertoire, the future provides goals for the roles and the present situation defines the effective action within the role. Integrated behavior simultaneously attends to past, present, and future so immediate behavior is optimally adaptive when it attends to the cultural context and the goals that give one's life direction.

Spontaneity describes a response to a situation that is immediately appropriate. Anxiety is a symptom of inhibited spontaneity. Spontaneity implies a moving to engage and enact with one's environment. It also implies a trial-and-error learning or learning through observation of effective models. Spontaneity includes both innate readiness to meet the moment and the learned body of knowledge of how to meet the moment effectively. Pathology occurs when one's response is novel but not adaptive or adequate to the situation.

Spontaneity is a readiness to act and respond. It occurs when one is physiologically, emotionally, and socially warmed up to meet needs of the moment. Three forms of resistance to spontaneity are: (1) resistance against one's own bodily actions and sensations when engaging in a role; (2) resistance due to one's value system; and (3) resistances that arise as a response to the body actions, ideas, and emotions of the person with whom one is in contact (interpersonal resistance). Spontaneity cannot be conserved. It must emerge to be spent and must be spent to be replenished. Spontaneity functions in the present and "propels the individual towards an adequate response to a new situation or a new response to an old situation"(Moreno, 1974, p. 76).

Creativity is a result of spontaneity. In this sense, Moreno uses spontaneity as a synonym for energy or *élan vital*. The implication is that when one puts emerging, bubbling, warmed-up spontaneity into action, one may bring something new to life. The new may not be new for others, but is new for the individual.

When evolving creations of society or of individuals become established, good or bad, they make up the *cultural conserve,* which gives support for continuity and growth. In its pathological form, it limits and constrains. The vital person not only meets new situations but creates new situations. The cultural conserve is the preservation of values, knowledge, and arts of a particular culture. It is an end product of earlier creative moments now frozen that provide a supportive base from which to evolve. Stagnation or conflict occurs when the society or the individual makes final the current state of affairs and prohibits creative evolution. When an individual fixates himself, therapy is to help him return to his natural flowing process of a spontaneous and creative state. We can say he moves from a static, frozen state to a dynamic, open state.

PSYCHOTHERAPY

Theory of Psychotherapy

Each new moment in life has novelty, calls for the exercise of choice, and has the potential for inventiveness. For all of us, there exists a great reservoir of potential, dormant capabilities and skills (Clayton, 1975). New behaviors and new roles occur in novel contexts that call for spontaneous action in a specific situation at a specific time. For the very young child, each new event in life is a major opportunity for spontaneous response and expansion of self. Opportunities for growth continue throughout life.

Ideally, the child has a protected environment in which to grow. His parents are his auxiliary egos who provide for him in ways he cannot provide for himself. In early infancy, they do almost everything for him. They carry, protect, and nurture him. As he grows, he becomes more self-sufficient and wants and does more and more for himself. Wise parents keep him from danger while at the same time they progressively step back and allow him to expand and master life for himself. Ideally, the parent does for the child only that which the child cannot do for himself, allowing the child to experience his own growing power. Eventually, the normal child grows to autonomy where he is in full charge of his life. Psychotherapy in theory follows this analogy.

Psychodrama is usually conducted in a group since the theory underlying psychodrama is socially interactive. The therapy group is a social network providing a supportive, protective climate in which the learner can test and expand his limits in the presence of the group's members and therapists. In psychodramatic therapy, each patient is the therapeutic agent of the other. The group provides a setting for the development of new relationships. Tele replaces transference. Group members are taught to distinguish between spontaneous interpersonal interaction and habituated or maladaptive interpersonal behavior. In the psychodrama group, honest, here-and-now relationships are established, examined, enhanced, and expanded. Here, a person can examine his intrapsychic world and distinguish between reality and fantasy.

The past, the present, and the future are available on the psychodrama stage as here-and-now events. Enactment of the past, whether for catharsis, or insight, or understanding of relationships, or for releasing behavior is done now in a present-tense enactment that becomes the real world of the moment. The psychodramatic enactment shows the protagonist as he perceives himself in this time and place. It is the subjective reality of the client in the moment.

In psychodramatic enactment, the future and the past become the present. As the protagonist engages in an anticipated event, or deals with what was, he engages in a drama with full use of body and mind in the here-and-now.

Dramatizing promotes self-awareness of feelings, behaviors, and impact on others. Group members also increase the protagonist's awareness when they give information or demonstrate alternatives. Group members have opportunities to be altruistic, to improve their interpersonal skills, to expand their role repertoires as they engage in each other's psychodrama, to learn how they inhibit spontaneous behavior, and to learn to own their power so they become self-starting initiators as well as responders.

Moreno shares with Fritz Perls and Carl Rogers the notion that to be aware of one's immediate process is to have the power of choice and self-direction. Such awakened options can be practiced immediately in social reality or on the psychodramatic stage. Enactment with figures from the past allows finishing incomplete acts. Engaging with figures in the future allows for successful later encounters. Enactment of future events is not intended to develop practiced role behavior but rather to expand the repertoire of role possibilities of the person so when real events are met, one may tap a richer pool of prior experience than if the role playing had not occurred. Psychodrama also stresses spontaneity training, that is, learning or relearning the process skill of responding to present events as they occur.

The protagonist is like the composer of an opera. He writes the score and the lyrics. The therapist, like the conductor of the opera, follows the notes written by the client, facilitating the interpretation of the drama. The auxiliaries are like the supernumeraries and the musicians, for although they inject their own emotionality or emphasis, basically they follow the protagonist's scripts. In the enactment of the psychodrama, they populate his world as he sees it. They are his extensions. They bring his memories, fears, and fantasies to life but they do so within his design allowing him to modify his own intrapsychic and interpersonal processes.

Some therapists would add to this analogy that the director and auxiliaries should modify or correct the client's script, spotting deficiencies and directing the protagonist's attention to points that need to be strengthened or changed. Some therapists would even tell the client how his piece is to be rewritten. Directiveness might be useful for a deprived or intellectually deficient client. For neurotic clients, however, directiveness gets in the way. If the therapist takes over, the client is no longer the creative composer of his life's opera. This type of client needs to learn to be his own orchestrator so he may function fully away from the guidance of the therapists.

In working with patients, the therapist must evaluate the point at which he enters the client's life. If the client has full functioning capacities, the therapy is directed towards self-realization. On the other hand, if the client is symbolically but an infant, he must be symbolically carried and guided until he can begin to crawl, then totter, walk, and run. In short, therapy is designed to the client's capacities as viewed by the therapist and is most effective when the goals and pace of therapy accord to the reality of the client's limitations. When in doubt, the therapist should assume more capacity and more readiness rather than less capacity and less readiness.

Psychodrama requires the therapist to be spontaneous and creative. The therapist expands his own self through real experiences with clients. When his procedures prove effective, he adds them to his role repertoire, and when they prove inappropriate, he learns to discriminate in making better future therapeutic interventions. The psychodramatic therapist engages with the client in a human, personal way to help the client recognize how each relationship unit contributes to making life rich and meaningful. The therapist also guides group members towards increasingly effective human interaction with each other. Psychodrama is the richest of the therapeutic modalities since it engages in a dynamic, holistic way with the individual and his social network. The challenge to the therapist is to use his own personhood, including his theoretical and therapeutic models, to attend to the immediate personal and interpersonal happenings within the group.

Process of Psychotherapy

From an outsider's point of view, psychodrama may appear as a consistent and unified method having a generally consistent theoretical frame of reference. Actually psychodrama varies widely with the personality, training, and belief system of the therapist as well as the capacities of the client population. Psychodrama can be used in one-to-one therapy or for mass audiences wherein a protagonist is the catalyst for reaching and influencing huge numbers of people. Lewis Yablonsky's (1976) presentation of a 12-week series of television psychodrama programs using real people and real issues, which were broadcast over a public broadcasting network, is such an example.

A psychodrama has beginning *(warm-up),* middle *(development),* and closing *(integration* and *sharing)* phases. A therapy session could be devoted entirely to one individual but more typically several clients will take turns. Sometimes an entire session is devoted to the group as a whole, working through interpersonal issues among group members or in identifying and modifying norms that have been developing in the group. Sometimes a common theme such as "loneliness" touches everyone in the group. A series of short dramatic presentations about each person's loneliness intensifies involvement and leads to real, here-and-now encounter among group members.

Some therapists prefer that each pro-

tagonist experience a classical psychodrama with warm-up, a thorough enactment and development of his therapeutic issue, and a closure with group sharing before any other work is done. Other therapists work with the emerging events; one client's psychodrama serves as the warm-up for another and sharing may be invited at any point or saved for the end of the session.

Group size, duration of treatment, and length of session vary widely, dependent upon the patient population and the therapist's orientation. Some groups have limited goals and meet for a fixed number of sessions. A vocational rehabilitation counselor might run a series of meetings designed to prepare clients for job interviews and employment. Role training in which specific skills are identified, defined, and practiced is done. Each session progressively builds towards the goal of employment. Early sessions might dramatize events such as buying a newspaper, looking up want ads, and initiating employer contact through mock and later real telephone calls. Later sessions might involve job interviews. A businessman from the community might be brought in to be the interviewer with everyone knowing that no actual hiring will be done. Later, members might play employers and interview each other in role reversals. The final steps would be actually going into the community to participate in real interviews, reporting back to the group for refinement and ultimately securing employment.

Some groups are open-ended and run for years with a flow of patients entering and leaving the group. Sessions usually run a minimum of one and one-half hours and a maximum of three hours, and it is typical for groups to meet once and sometimes twice a week. The size of an ongoing therapy group usually runs between 6 and

14 people. A group of this relatively small size has enough people to take roles in dramas and is small enough that the therapist can attend to emerging interpersonal issues among members.

In a new group, the director may provide guided warm-ups to get the group comfortable and moving. A guided warm-up could be a discussion topic like "What are your goals in this group?" or a series of short dramas on a theme such as "Portray a meaningful incident that you have had with some significant others." After a group has become established, it is typical to start with a nondirective warm-up where the therapist remains quiet and allows initiative to generate from group members.

Through a warm-up, group attention becomes focused and a protagonist is selected. The director listens to the protagonist's account of his issue and also listens for metaphorical language (such as "there is a wall between me and my wife"). The director looks for nonverbal process cues, for example, say every time the protagonist mentions his wife, his eyes tear up, he stops talking, and wraps his arms about himself as though holding himself tenderly. At the same time, the director also watches the group and is attentive to how individuals in the group respond or withdraw from the presentation. The director filters and integrates this information and also taps into his own affective and cognitive responses to the situation. Together with the protagonist, he chooses an entry point for the therapeutic drama. In this example, an entry scene might reproduce a real event that has occurred between the protagonist and his wife, or the metaphor of "the wall between them" might be constructed with the protagonist occasionally playing the wall and occasionally playing the wife and occasionally playing himself. Or the non-

verbal cue of holding himself tenderly might be attended to with an interview to determine whether the protagonist envisions himself holding someone or being held by someone. This can be enacted.

A creative moment for the director occurs in the selection of auxiliary egos for the drama. Frequently, the protagonist makes his own selections for roles in his drama. The way he chooses contains information. The director can also use the selection of the auxiliaries as a therapeutic intervention. For example, suppose that the wife is a very expressive and angry person. This role could be taken by a trained auxiliary; or the "wife" could be a person in the group who finds it easy to be expressive and angry; or, for therapeutic reasons, the director could select someone for whom this role is difficult. In this instance, accepting the role to help another group member allows a shy client to expand her role repertoire since she has permission to engage in behaviors she has either not learned or not allowed into expression.

The director guides the protagonist in establishing the scene, be it a realistic portrayal of the room in which the event took place or a symbolic representation of the wall between the protagonist and his wife. As the protagonist sets the scene, warm-up occurs. He typically gives information about himself and his relationship to his wife in the way in which he describes the setting. Say that the protagonist describes a living room with a wall of books. He is asked, in fantasy, to take a book from the shelf. The book's title, he says, is "Helter-Skelter," the story of the Manson murders, which may give an indication as to his mood about the forthcoming scene.

Once an enactment has started, the protagonist and actors talk in the present tense. That which is happening on the stage in the enactment is happening here-

and-now. It is an observable event that all in the room can see and share. Whether the event repeats reality is not important. What is important is that the event grows out of what he does at this moment.

The final phase of the psychodrama session is *sharing*. Group members relate how they were affected during the session. Most psychodramatists stress that in the sharing time, one should avoid giving advice, criticism, or praise. Sharing is not a judgmental event. Sharing helps all in the group to further their own growth and transparency. Meanwhile, the protagonist can review his own behavior or attend to the sharing of group members, identifying with statements that impact meaningfully for him but not having to defend or explain himself.

A short chapter can only begin to describe the subtleties of psychodrama. The following discussion expands on some of the procedures, described in the Overview section, which the director and the auxiliary egos use to facilitate the therapeutic work.

The *auxiliaries* are therapeutic assistants who may be trained co-therapists or client members of the group. In a drama, the auxiliary may: (1) represent an absent person or become the concrete, externalization of a belief, body part, resistance, hallucination, and so on; (2) be a social investigator exploring the perceptions and dimensions of the protagonist, not through interview, but through innovative role playing cued to the protagonist's information; (3) interpret an absent other by expanding the role with "as if" possibilities based on his perception of the role subject to correction by the protagonist; (4) test and expand the protagonist's limits by maximizing the expression, feelings, and acts of the protagonist especially in role reversal; and (5) provide guidance with role models of alternative behaviors.

Role reversal has many uses: (1) It allows a perceptual shift so the client (protagonist) can see the situation in a fresh way. (2) It instructs the auxiliary how to play roles according to the client's perceptions. (3) It permits expansion of the client's awareness and behavior. (For example, a man plays his own role as "tough guy." When he switches and plays the role of his wife, he portrays her as a "tender" person. The experience may give him permission to experience and express his own tenderness when he returns to his own role.) (4) It may show how the client defines his "self." (For example, a diabetic man was in a psychodrama with an auxiliary who represented his father. As the drama progressed, it seemed as though the client was suffering from hypoglycemia—lack of sugar—as he became weak and shaky. Repeated role reversals revealed a startling pattern for he was only shaky when he played self but he was strong and vigorous when he switched to the father's role. This then became the issue of his psychodrama.) (5) It reduces internal dissonance as when the client reverses with different aspects of self or an internalized other. (For example, the protagonist says to his dead mother: "Do you forgive me?" This question is a signal for role reversal so forgiveness or lack of forgiveness of self is initiated by the client.) (6) It encourages the client to take responsibility for his behavior and decisions. (For example, "What should I do?" signals a role reversal so the protagonist can answer his own question and thereby become self-directing.) (7) It controls the intensity of a scene, so if the client is about to hit out, he may be reversed to a more passive role. (8) It serves as a confirmation or confrontation to self when the reversal is timed to give the protagonist feedback about his immediate interpersonal behavior.

The *double,* one of the most potent of auxiliary positions, helps the protagonist express himself. Doubling facilitates the client's awareness of his internal processes and his expression of unvoiced thoughts and feelings. The activity level of the double depends upon the functional capacity of the client. The double may do all the talking for a catatonic patient or, at the other extreme, be mute with a protagonist who is free-flowing, articulate, and insightful. Directors with different philosophies of treatment differentially shape the way in which the double functions. One therapist would encourage the double to be interpretative and to enlarge upon and extend from cues given by the protagonist. Another therapist would require that the doubling be more reflective of the immediate state of the client. A third therapist might stress the description of movements and process events.

All doubles attempt to identify with the protagonist and to use their subjective experiences as a first approximation of the status of the client, which are sharpened as increasing information becomes available. The client who learns to become a double receives indirect personal therapy by (1) increasing skills in observing other and self, and (2) expanding role repertoires when playing unfamiliar patterns of behavior of various protagonists.

Informally, *modeling* actually occurs at all times as group members demonstrate their variety of styles of being with each other. In psychodrama a *model* is the intentional use of other persons to demonstrate alternative behaviors. The director's goal is to facilitate the protagonist to find his own ways. Modeling sometimes frees the blocked client by giving him permission to express that which he has held back until someone else has voiced his thoughts, or by teaching him how to search for alternatives so he creates his own creative coping strategy. If the client simply lacks knowledge because he has not had a variety of experiences in his upbringing, modeling can directly teach emotional expressiveness, interpersonal communications, and professional skills.

Mechanisms of Psychotherapy

Three dimensions of therapeutic work to aid the client toward more effective functioning are (1) *cognitive* (thought processes), (2) *affective* (emotional processes), and (3) *behavior* (actional processes). Most therapeutic approaches stress one of these but psychodrama can attend to all three with equal strength. *Cognitive therapy* stresses that change will occur and be long lasting if the client modifies his belief system and ways of conceptualizing about self and others, and if he makes rational decisions to alter the course of his life. *Affective therapy* stresses the release of blocked feelings so one may freely experience emotions and be able to express feelings to self and others. A *behavioral therapy* stresses that behavior may be modified directly with the focus on identifying one's patterns of behavior and correcting these patterns by acting differently. Psychodrama is effective and efficient because a dramatic representation of self includes one's behavior, beliefs, and feelings. In addition, group psychodrama takes place in a social context. The learning that occurs is therefore more easily carried over to everyday living.

Some therapists theorize that insight and change in self-concept leads to new and more effective behaviors. Other therapists insist that behavior change leads to new self-concepts. It is the chicken-egg paradox. Each can lead to the other. Insight or cognitive understanding of past events is important for some clients but not to others. Change of behavior is more important than insight. If a cognitive structure or insight facilitates or anchors behavioral change, it is worth its while, but insight without behavior change or without change in self-concept is worthless.

One aspect of psychodramatic therapy is *role training,* which assumes that behavior can be directly modified when a person who wants to change unsatisfactory behavior is presented with feedback about his behavior and allowed to search out, identify, and practice new behaviors. The modeling of alternatives expands the possibilities of better behavior patterns. The practice of new behaviors can be designed in a particular sequence to insure success. New behavior can be practiced in small bits until the individual incorporates them in his role repertoire and gains mastery through practice.

Moreno believed in the wisdom of the organism. Solutions to effective coping are available if one is open to his spontaneity and creativity. Therapy is most successful and long lasting if the client learns the process of effectively meeting new moment-to-moment events. Spontaneity training prepares the client to meet any problem since what is learned is the way or process of meeting all events freshly and effectively. One form of spontaneity training is to provide difficult surprise situations in the protected setting of the therapy group. Spontaneity is tested and developed by novelty. It is important to keep the degree of difficulty and surprise within the tolerance of the protagonist so success is assured from step to step. If simple behavioral training methods are not sufficient to reach the patient's goals, a more psychodynamic or psychosocial depth therapy is required.

An important change mechanism is for the client to learn how to deal with, main-

tain, and even change his social atoms. A long-term group becomes a support system and provides a change for the client to build and maintain intense, intimate, personal relationships. The group is also a place to discover transference distortions to be replaced by realistic two-way relationship.

Different client issues call for different therapeutic interventions. The resistive client needs support through which to confront his fears and avoidances. The blocked client may require release of the musculature perhaps through expressive movements or attention to breathing. The person who has narrowed his world and lives in fantasy must test reality and develop realistic relationships. For the psychodramatist using a Gestalt philosophy, process awareness is stressed. Psychodrama, since it focuses on observable behavior, has developed a rich range of feedback techniques and is an excellent way of helping an individual become response-able or in Moreno's terms, spontaneous.

Perhaps most important of all in psychodramatic therapy is that the client has the opportunity for corrective emotional experiences. The group is like a new family that provides protection, values, and behavioral models that encourage experimentation in alternate styles of living leading to spontaneity.

APPLICATIONS

Problems

Although psychodrama can be used with a vast array of clients, it must be modified according to the goals, intelligence level, attention span, ego strength, and psychological sophistication of the client population. Adeline Starr (1977) has special sections in her book dealing with psychodrama, with marital therapy, children, drug abuse, alcoholism, psychoses, depression, and outpatient groups. Psychodrama has been used in family therapy (Allen, 1954), in prison settings (Haskell, 1960), with drug addicts (Eliasoph, 1955), to train psychiatric residents (Fine, 1971), in training the handicapped (Brandzel, 1963), and as an adjunct in autogenic training (Rothman, 1961). It has been used with a therapeutic community (J. L. Moreno, 1953) and with regressed psychiatric patients (Fine, Daly, & Fine, 1962). A series of monographs detail J. L. Moreno's work with different patient problems including the treatment of a performance neurosis (1944), psychosis (1945a), marriage problems (1945b), and the integration of dissociative episodes into consciousness (1939). Called *role playing,* psychodrama is used in business and industry (Corsini, Shaw, & Blake, 1961), and in education and decision making (Shaftel, 1967).

Illustrations of psychodrama presented earlier in this chapter have been of clients who were functional in everyday life. Psychodrama has also been found useful for those more troubled. Hannah Weiner (1965) reviews the literature and discusses the use of psychodrama in the treatment and management of alcoholism. Weiner worked with 300 alcoholics in over 400 sessions and saw spouses in 50 additional sessions. The psychodrama group was used to get interaction, feedback, open discussion, and the interest of other participants. After three years in her treatment program, the clients were more accepted by others, more secure, and more self-accepting. Weiner lists 33 benefits that different authors report for alcoholics in psychodrama and describes case-study material on her own work.

S. M. Tawadros (1956) conducted a treatment and research program to determine if spontaneity training changed the level of functioning for the severely retarded person. Role-training and spontaneity-training methods were used, including (1) role playing everyday life situations with peers, parents, and hospital staff, (2) role taking of community roles such as workers, tradesmen, and professionals, and (3) creative role playing in which clients had a choice of roles and selected the dramas for themselves. Although there was no change in intelligence quotients, the children did show an increase in their social effectiveness and social adjustment.

Working with a backward, regressed group, Abel Ossorio and Leon Fine (1959) found they had to modify their usual approach to meet the short attention spans and remoteness of a group of older women who had been hospitalized an average of 30 years each. Simple social skills such as introducing oneself to a fellow diner or asking the nurse for permission to see the doctor or dealing with a hallucinated voice were the bits and pieces of psychodrama. The project was successful in meeting the goals set for the group, which were to reduce the number of problems the ward was causing the hospital including increasing staff and patient morale, decreasing staff absenteeism, and decreasing the use of wet sheet packs, medication, and patient injury. Patients did not become rehabilitated to the community, but their institutional adjustment was much improved and the ward ceased to be a "trouble spot" for the hospital.

Evaluation

Patients are best worked in heterogeneous groups from a homogeneous population. There should be differences among group members to allow for variation of role behaviors and emotions and group members should have sufficient similarity so they may identify with one another to achieve group cohesion. People who vary too much in age, intelligence, cultural background, or ego strength either will be driven from the group by other members or will feel so isolated they will remove themselves. The therapist should seek people of a common functional level and then introduce differences within the group to increase the opportunity of their learning from each other.

Traditional methods of screening include the individual interview, studying case material, and receiving recommendations from people with whom the client has previously engaged. One method of assigning a client to a psychodrama group is to have the person participate in an intake group in which the person's group behavior can be assessed. This way people who, by their behavior, show capacity to handle confrontation, insight, and catharsis may be grouped together whereas those who are more in need of support, guidance, and instruction can be put in a different group. Periodic review sessions of group members are useful to assess current status and growth. New mutual, intermediate goals can be formulated to guide the therapy. Feedback from the patient about his outside behavior and feelings is also important as a gauge of movement, regression, or stasis.

Psychodrama is perhaps the most difficult of the group psychotherapies since the therapist must attend to the individual patient, to the interaction among them, to group-centered themes, to the application of dramatic and actional principles, and to verbal exchanges. Those seeking training in psychodrama usually go through a four-step process leading towards full certification as a practitioner of the method. Full training requires close to 1,000 hours of experiential training, personal growth

experiences, and seminars with a senior therapist, as well as supervised practice, a written thesis, a successful oral examination on knowledge of theory and concepts, and a demonstration of ability to use the theory and concepts in an actual performance of the psychodramatic therapy. There are also three earlier levels of training for assistant therapists.

Treatment

We have covered therapy with individuals and with groups. We now consider psychodrama in natural groups such as the intimate pair, the family, and the work group. These three groups are real-life, ongoing social atoms or social networks. Such groups exist before therapy, exist during therapy, and usually will continue to exist after therapy is completed. Sometimes, a natural group functions within a formed group. For example, an individual was having marital difficulties. He was feeling suicidal recognizing that he was repeating a self-defeating pattern. He had been married before and had disrupted his marriage with a blatant affair. Now, he was doing it again. He was distressed that he was automatically replaying the same behavior that had previously led him to a suicide attempt. He felt unable to control himself. At first, his therapy was done in the group with an auxiliary playing his wife. Later, the therapist, with the patient's permission, telephoned the wife and found that the wife was willing to cooperate in the therapy. When they were both ready, his psychodramatic therapy resumed with his real significant other (the wife) included.

An intimate pair may be seen by the therapist in couples therapy. Another option is to form a group composed of intimate pairs. In this instance, not only does one deal with individuals, but with pair relationships or social atoms, as basic units within the group. A third possibility is to have the couple within a group otherwise made up of single individuals. Similar designs are possible in working with families.

In working with couples or families, role reversal is a potent procedure. Imagine the impactfulness of a role reversal between a parent and a small child where the parent gets small on the floor, perhaps kneeling, and the child gets tall as she stands on a chair and looks big and talks to the parent as the parent talks to her. Such physical enactment vividly demonstrates their role relationship and often leads to dramatic change by itself.

A couple may learn from viewing how other people see them functioning through the mirror technique. They may practice new behaviors with each other, discovered as they observe the behavior and therapy of other couples, or models of alternatives may be specifically provided for them. The therapist can treat homogeneous subgroups as units. All of the women, or all of the dominant persons in the marriage, can work as clusters in opposition to their partners' subgroup. It is especially useful in working with couples or families to examine their social structure through an *action sociogram,* an enactment or display of the relationships of each individual to the other as seen by each person in the network (Seabourne, 1963). Thus, a husband shows that he and his wife are close and that she is superior when he puts her on a pedestal while he is on his knees looking admiringly up at her. Her point of view of the relationship is different. When she establishes the tableau, she sets herself and her husband ten feet apart with his back toward her as she reaches out to him. These action sociograms become entry points for therapeutic work. Setting up an action sociogram

of one's family of origin may identify repeated patterns or a repeated role relationship in the marriage that had earlier occurred in the primary family.

Another type of social atom is the working group whose role relationships are specified in job descriptions and the organization's structure. There are also informal pairings and networks that enhance or bypass the formal networks. Psychodramatic procedures may be used with work groups, sometimes focusing simply upon here-and-now events and other times using the full range of psychodramatic exploration so individuals may grasp how transference elements may be contaminating relationships in the work situation. As with an individual client, the level at which one works with an institutional "family" depends upon their capacity and goals. The stress may be on direct behavior modification or on a depth therapy but this needs to be negotiated and contracted with the client rather than imposed by the therapist.

Management

Psychodrama is typically practiced as a form of group therapy. Mental-health centers, outpatient clinics, mental hospitals, and college counseling centers often have programs that use psychodramatic therapy.

Private-practice clients are usually self-referred or referred by prior patients or by professionals in the community. They usually know what they are looking for. They have heard of the therapist or of the method used and so initiate contact for themselves. Typically, a client telephones the therapist and is given information about screening procedures and fees. One method is to see a client individually long enough to establish a relationship and to assess whether the client seems suitable for the psychodrama group and the group suitable for the client. Since dropouts usually occur in the first six sessions, it is preferable to see the client individually for at least that number of meetings to insure that the group will not be bothered by a flow of people who stay for only a short time.

If the therapist believes in long-term therapy, the client is advised that treatment usually takes from one to three or more years and that initial enrollment in the group is for a three-month trial period to see if the client and group are suitable for each other. He may be asked not to accept the three-month trial period unless he is really seeking a long-term treatment situation. Other therapists accept and welcome a flow of patients in open groups. J. L. Moreno used to have open groups in New York where people would come in off the streets for a session, paying a fee as though going to the theater. People could continue in this open group, coming when they wanted. The participants in the group were not viewed as patients but rather as students or audience. Those who wanted extended therapy could elect to go into closed groups that met on a regular basis. The large open group served to screen clients for the closed groups.

Written guidelines about treatment and group norms are often provided and further reviewed in individual screening sessions. When available, movies or television tapes serve to orient new members. New clients usually learn the method from the older group members. When a new group begins, group norm behavior is taught by the therapist in early sessions and selectively reinforced in later group life.

Clients are given information about the group norms desired. For instance, in one model used in private practice, clients are encouraged to have social contact outside of the group. A dyad rotation pattern is established so each person may visit one hour a week with some other member of the group. They are asked to consider that anything that happens with anyone in the group anywhere is group business. They are encouraged to engage openly in the group about their wants, fantasies, and attractions. They are reminded that the group is an artifical, protected, learning community where they can experiment to expand their self-system for the everyday world. To insure that the learning climate is optimal, they are advised to avoid the complications of engaging sexually with one another. If they abide by this, they can then feel safe in expressing attraction without demand and can physically show affection without conflict or contamination. They are told that should they choose to break this norm, it is group business.

In this private-practice model, the clients are told they are in a long-term group and that it is open-ended. There will be people who finish and leave and others who come and begin during their course of treatment. They are told of the limits of the group size; of the hours of the meeting, usually two and one-half hours an evening; and they are asked to give at least one month's notice before leaving to allow them and members of the group to deal with their feelings about termination. They are alerted that some people consider terminating when they are finished and ready to move on. Others use talk of termination as a stepping stone to dealing with resistances or as first steps to communicating. Talk of termination may be a way of testing the group's interest in them, avoidance of confrontation, an indirect statement to the therapist or other group members about their anger or disenchantment, or from a basic assumption that they do not have the power to change the structure when they do not like what is happening. Alerting the client to give plenty of time to this issue allows for effective attention to the underlying dynamics.

Clinics typically charge fees according to ability to pay. In private practice, some have variable fees and others a fixed fee. Some charge by the session but there is an advantage to having a prepaid flat monthly fee in that the ambivalent client is more likely to attend regularly. Collateral individual sessions are generally useful in enhancing the client's use of group time. Individual sessions may be used to integrate group experiences. The group may be used to represent the "real world of others" and be a place to practice issues opened or clarified in individual sessions. The individual sessions provide closer relationship with the therapist and attention to intrapsychic self. The group sessions provide contact with peers, auxiliaries for psychodrama, and a social world in which to refine one's capacity for long-term intimacy. Attention is paid to generalizing from the therapy session to daily behavior since the goal for most patients is to reach self-actualization in everyday life.

CASE EXAMPLE

The case example describes three sessions with George, age 30. Three years, physical distance, and a pending divorce of his choice separate him from his wife and small daughter. George keeps pictures of his young daughter in his room and dreams of the time when she will be old enough so he may tell her of his love and longing for her and explain why he left the family. George is handsome, bright, articulate, energetic, and affectionate. He is an adventurer and doer. He has learned to take care of himself and to

get what he wants. George easily establishes relationships with women but then, not wanting to be trapped, he moves away when he feels he is getting too involved. He says he is distressed by his repetitive behavior. He feels his attachment to people is shallow and he states that he brings the potential for great hurt to a deep relationship. George wants to continue with his new love, Jessica, without moving away when he feels engulfed by her.

On the first day of a five-day intensive workshop, participants introduced themselves by portraying their family relationship at some moment in childhood. George chose to show his family when he was six years old, just before his father died. George (6) his mother, and his younger brother (3) are on one side of the room. All are touching and George is in the middle like a "little father" who will protect and take care of mother and younger brother. Father is at the other side of the room with oldest brother (9) kneeling and clutching father's leg. Father knows he is going to die. Observing the tableau, George gets emotional. Crying, he crosses the room, embraces "father" and tells him it is important that they talk before father dies and leaves him. He promises he will spend more workshop therapy time with father later in the week.

On the first night of the workshop, the group met as a peer group without the formal leader. The reason for this is that different issues generally surface when a leader is not present. Some individuals feel an increased freedom of expression and there is opportunity to relate, take responsibility, and practice skills with peers. This evening, the group bogged down trying to decide whether Martha should be permitted to smoke in the room. The smoking issue went on for a long time. People left the session dissatisfied and their morning reports indicated further group process work was needed to get the group to cooperate. Each member of the group was asked to have a fantasy about the group. Several of these fantasies were enacted. George imagined an adventurous trip across a great desert in a caravan of three Land Rovers, sufficient to carry the 11 group members comfortably.

There is food and water for two weeks and plenty of gasoline. The caravan stops in the midst of a desert because the center car breaks down and cannot be repaired. The group is now in dangerous territory and help is far away.

This is a rich projective opportunity. It is as though a Thematic Apperception Test card has been provided to the group. Pillows were laid out to represent seats in each of the cars. The group members closed their eyes and assessed which place each had in the first, second, or third car to symbolize the role they saw themselves having in the group. They signaled readiness to begin by opening their eyes.

When all were ready, they were asked to go to their places (pillows) in the cars. Martha, the "smoker member," immediately went to the second car, which had broken down. She insisted she be the driver. Another woman, Grace, also wanted to be the driver of the same car but yielded to Martha's demand.

Grace typically yields to people who are "more needy" and allows them to get what they want rather than fighting for what she wants. She will work on this later in the group when her yielding pattern becomes obvious. Others, however, compete for places as driver or navigator or passenger. The way each selects, asserts, or yields for position serves as behavioral evidence about his everyday functioning, which can then be investigated later.

George immediately headed for the broken car intending to be of service to the driver. Martha was so insistent that she drive and be in charge of that vehicle that George decided he would leave the car. He then went to the first car. He asked if any of the four members there would like to transfer to another vehicle. George was a popular member of the group and two of the people in the first vehicle wanted to include him. As they argued about the ways in which he might be included, he turned away and went to the last car where he found complete acceptance. The people in the first car voiced disappointment. One member said he was about to allow George to be in the car. The two women members indicated how they wanted very much to have George in the first car and would have made room for him. He had suddenly left after making his inquiry. They felt surprised, frustrated, and disappointed that although he initiated contact, he did not maintain it, and he seemed insensitive to what was happening to them. In this very short psychodrama, George had visited and had been accepted in three cars but had rejected members in two cars. George was stunned as he recognized that his behavior was a repetition of what was happening in real life regarding his attachments with women.

On the third day of the workshop, George became the protagonist of a psychodrama. He chose four women in the group to represent women with whom he had had an intimate relationship. He lined them up in chronological order. Jessica, with whom he was now involved, was last in the line. George presented a series of descriptions of these women and then used role reversals with each of the women to establish their characters and behaviors for the benefit of the auxiliary egos. He engaged with them one by one, searching for his usual pattern. One key phrase he used was: "If I love you, you will leave me." Another was: "If I love you, I will have to take care of you." His statements were like those he had made in his first-day psychodrama as a child to father ("Don't die and leave me") and to mother ("Don't worry, I will love and take care of you"). Reminded by the director, he agreed to add them to the line placing father first and mother next as first of the series of women in the line. He was asked to say the key phrases to each of the people in line. He found the phrases valid for his current girl friend and mother but his greatest emotional reaction occurred when he talked to his father.

The strength of his tearfulness and agitation served as a signal to focus the therapeutic work. Soon George's associations returned to age six before his father died. George wanted to be held in his father's lap. This was dramatized. The auxiliary had been trained to play the role of George's father by George on the first day of the workshop. George, as a child, crawled into his "father's" lap and was held. He cried intensely in the warm recollections of his closeness with his father, which he had all but forgotten. After about five minutes, when George was beyond the peak of his emotion, the director signaled the "father" to die suddenly. This was a representation of an event that had occurred to George in real life. The actor went limp with George still in his arms. George's first impulse was to take care of his mother. He related that he had only one memory of being in his father's lap and that he was surprised by the depth of warm feelings that he had rediscovered for his father. He also became aware of his anger at being left as the responsible member of the family.

After dealing with traumatic past events,

it is important to return to the present to help the person move toward establishing a realistic, two-way tele in current relationship. George turned his attention to "Jessica," and through direct dramatization and role reversals, he recognized that she was special. She was different from the other women in his life in that she allowed him to struggle with coming and going and accepted him back when he would return. He said that he could allow himself to be a baby with her. His statement had great impact for him against the background of his psychodrama with "father" where he allowed himself to be a baby in "father's" arms. He was very moved and repeated to "Jessica" that he could again be a baby with her, that is, he could be trusting, open, and vulnerable and allow her to care for him. At the end of the week, George was feeling good about himself and his discoveries and he was ready to return to the real Jessica to see how they would continue their relationship. He had increased self-awareness, relief and integration from catharsis, and a readiness to engage in a fresh way with Jessica.

SUMMARY

J. L. Moreno, a seminal thinker, had great impact in the field of group psychotherapy, encounter, behavioral therapy, family therapy, sociometric investigation, and psychodrama. He was first in many of the activities and ideas now accepted as cultural norms. Although a worldwide figure, with his writings published in many languages and followers of his methods throughout the world, he is still relatively uncredited and unrecognized. He espoused creativity and spontaneity and described as ideal the spiral effect of each individual adding to and changing the cultural conserve while at the same time receiving support from the consistency of the culture for the next move up the spiral.

However, in his operations, he tended to act as Freud did, exerting strong control over his students. He was the only one who knew the extent of the full psychodramatic network and he was not eager to share this knowledge. Many who developed power or exercised their creativity away from him were pushed from the nest or left of their own accord. Those pushed away tended to ignore him but not what he taught them. Psychodramatists today are expanding their role repertoires by becoming learned in other psychotherapy systems and philosophies and thereby enriching psychodrama and other systems. Psychodrama is an evolving method that is rich and exciting for therapist and client alike.

Since Moreno's death in 1974, there has been a blossoming of training centers by his students and three major books have appeared (Haskell, 1975; Yablonsky, 1976; Starr, 1977). The American Society of Group Psychotherapy & Psychodrama, which he founded, has survived him with new strength and leadership and national certification is now possible for those who are proficient in the field.

Dramatization, role playing, and dramatic enactments are frequently found in other therapy modalities whether or not credited to Moreno. The central concept in psychodrama is spontaneity and creativity, which calls for the continuing evolution of the method. Psychodrama is holistic. It attends to behavior. It attends to the person in the moment. It focuses upon the I-Thou encounter. It is exciting. It is creative. Psychodrama is becoming a new method that will have great appeal to the professionals who are now early in their development. They will take it and

modify it so it continues to evolve richly and it in turn will build a new step in the cultural conserve.

ANNOTATED BIBLIOGRAPHY

Blatner, H. A. *Acting in: Practical applications of psychodramatic method.* New York: Springer, 1973.

This is a simple and short guidebook to the structure and use of psychodramatic techniques in a group setting. It has been a popular how-to-do-it source of information, especially for beginners.

Corsini, R.; Shaw, M.; & Blake, R. *Roleplaying in business and industry.* Glencoe, Ill.: Crowell-Collier, 1961.

This is an excellent book on the use of role playing in a nonpsychotherapy setting. There is no better text in describing how to structure and use psychodrama for feedback and teaching. The material is easily translated to the therapy situation. It includes an annotated bibliography and case material.

Haskell, M. R. *Socioanalysis: Self direction via sociometry and psychodrama.* Long Beach: Calif.: Role Training Associates, 1975.

This book is directed towards normal development and the enhancement of interpersonal relationships. It is a how-to-do-it description of Dr. Haskell's variation of psychodrama and includes methods of analyzing social networks and examples of exercises, training sessions, and charts used to teach his method.

Moreno, J. L. *Psychodrama: Volumes I, II, III.* New York: Beacon House, 1946, 1959, 1969.

These are collections of original papers by Dr. Moreno describing his philosophy, theories, and methods of psychotherapy. Moreno, a genius and foreign-born, is somewhat difficult to read. However, this is the original source and it is important to anyone interested in the method to dig around and find the rich treasure troves that exist.

Starr, A. *Psychodrama: Rehearsal for living.* Chicago, Ill.: Nelson Hall, 1977.

This is an easy-to-read book, which is heavy on method and includes theoretical underpinnings. Especially useful are case examples and annotations about how doubling works. The book has special sections on working with different kinds of patient populations.

CASE READINGS

Corsini, Raymond J. Psychodramatic treatment of a pedophile. *Group Psychotherapy,* 1951, 4, 166–71.

This is a case study of a prisoner in a psychodrama group at San Quentin who had committed a senseless sexual crime against a young child openly in front of others, who in psychodrama had a violent reaction at the reenactment of the discovery of his father being dead, which apparently was related to the sexual crime.

Garber, A. Psychodramatic treatment of a stutterer. *Group Psychotherapy and Psychodrama,* 1973, 26, 34–47.

This case study presents the successful treatment of a stutterer aged 30. The client began to stutter at age 5 after an unexpected operation for a hernia. Speech therapy at age 14 and a year in an inpatient facility for stutterers at age 18 did not prove as successful as his first psychodramatic session in establishing his self-concept as a fluent and effective communicator. The initial session, which was mostly nonverbal and with nonword sounds, led to the discovery of the functional use of the client's stuttering. Twenty-one subsequent sessions over a six months' period are also briefly described.

Moreno, J. L. *Psychodramatic shock therapy.* Psychodrama monograph No. 5. New York: Beacon House, 1939.

Moreno believes that psychotic episodes should be integrated into the client's experience rather than repressed or expunged through electric-shock treatment. This monograph gives three case studies of controlled reentry into psychotic experience and integration of the experience through psychodrama. A rationale for the method and an analysis of each case study is also presented.

Moreno, J. L. *Psychodramatic treatment of marriage problems.* Psychodrama monograph No. 7. New York: Beacon House, 1945.

This monograph describes Moreno's general approach and illustrates the issues through a specific case of a marriage triangle including catharsis, investigation of the social structure, and guidance through the coaching of an auxiliary ego as a role model.

Moreno, J. L., & Enneis, J. M. *Hypnodrama and psychodrama.* New York: Beacon House, 1950.

This small book gives two lengthy case studies by Enneis and introduction and commentary by Moreno. Induction procedures and the use of hypnosis in psychodrama are described including the use of auxiliary egos and dramatization while the client is in an altered state of consciousness. The first illustration is about a 24-year-old, male hospitalized patient who was much more expressive of himself while in hypnosis about problems in relating with women. The second protocol describes a session with a young black woman and the enhancement of her catharsis through hypnodrama regarding a traumatic life incident.

REFERENCES

Allen, D. T. Psychodrama in the family. *Group Psychotherapy,* 1954, 7, 167–77.

Ancelin-Schutzenberger, Anne. *Precis de psychodrame.* Introduction aux aspects techniques avec glossaire et biblographie. Paris: Editions Universitaires, 1966 (rev. ed. 1970).

Anderson, A. R. An experimental evaluation of roleplaying in group counseling. Doctoral dissertation, Brigham Young University, 1965.

Anzier, Didier. *Le psychodrame analytque chez l'enfant.* Paris: Presses Universitaires de France, 1956.

Berne, E. Gestalt therapy verbatim (a review). *American Journal of Psychiatry,* 1970, 10, 1519.

Bischof, L. *Interpreting personality theories.* New York: Harper & Row, 1964, pp. 355–419.

Blatner, H. A. Comments on some commonly held reservations about psychodrama. In R. W. Siroka; E. R. Siroka; & G. A. Schloss, *Sensitivity training and group encounter.* New York: Grosset and Dunlap, 1971, pp. 118–24.

Blatner, H. A. *Acting in: Practical applications of psychodramatic method.* New York: Springer, 1973.

Brandzel, R. Role playing as a training device in preparing multiple-handicapped youth for employment. *Group Psychotherapy,* 1963, 16, 16–21.

Clayton, L. The personality theory of J. L. Moreno. *Group Psychotherapy and Psychodrama,* 1975, 28, 144–51.

Corsini, R. J. Psychodramatic group psychotherapy. In *Methods of group psychotherapy.* New York: McGraw-Hill, 1957.

Corsini, R. J. *Roleplaying in psychotherapy.* Chicago: Aldine, 1966.

Corsini, R. J., & Putzey, L. J. Bibliography of group psychotherapy. *Group Psychotherapy,* 1956, 9, 178–249.

Corsini, R. J.; Shaw, M. E.; & Blake, R. R. *Roleplaying in business and industry.* Glencoe, Ill.: Crowell-Collier, 1961.

Daly, D. C. Psychodrama as a core technique in milieu therapy. Doctoral dissertation, St. Louis University, 1961.

Dysart, J. M. A study of the effect of in-service training in sociometry and sociodrama on teacher-pupil rapport and social climate in the classroom. Doctoral dissertation, New York University, 1952.

Eliasoph, E. A group therapy and psychodrama approach with adolescent drug addicts. *Group Psychotherapy,* 1955, 8, 161–67.

Fine, L. J. Nonverbal aspects of psychodrama. In J. L. Moreno (Ed.), *Progress in psychotherapy: Vol. IV.* New York: Grune & Stratton, 1959, 212–18.

Fine, L. J. Therapist position report in psychodrama as a function of frame of reference and behavioral stance. Doctoral dissertation, Washington University, 1967.

Fine, L. J. Actional group processes and psychodrama in residency training. In Gene M. Abrams & Norman S. Greenfield (Eds.), *The new hospital psychiatry.* New York: Academic Press, 1971.

Fine, R.; Daly, D. C.; & Fine, L. J. Psychodance, an experiment in psychotherapy and training. *Group Psychotherapy,* 1962, 15, 203–23.

Greenberg, I. A. Psychodrama and audience attitude change. Doctoral dissertation, Claremont Graduate School, Claremont, Calif., 1967.

Greenberg, I. A. *Psychodrama and audience change.* Beverly Hills, Calif.: Thyrsus, 1968.

Greer, V. J., & Sacks, J. M. *Bibliography of psychodrama.* New York: Greer, 1973.

Haskell, M. R. Group psychotherapy and psychodrama in prison. *Group Psychotherapy,* 1960, 13, 22–33.

Haskell, M. R. *Socioanalysis: Self direction via sociometry and psychodrama.* Los Angeles, Calif.: Role Training Associates, 1975.

Hollander, C. The mirror technique as a psychodramatic encounter. *Group Psychotherapy,* 1967, 20, 103–12.

Leveton, Eva. *Psychodrama for the timid clinician.* New York: Springer Publishing Co., 1977.

Lippett, R. The auxiliary chair technique. *Group Psychotherapy,* 1958, 11, 8–23.

Lubin, B., & Lubin A. Bibliography of group psychotherapy 1956–1963. *Group Psychotherapy,* 1964, 17, 177–230.

Mann, J. Evaluation of group psychotherapy: A review in evidence. In J. L. Moreno (Ed.), *The international handbook of group psychotherapy.* New York: Philosophical Library, 1966, pp. 129–48.

Maas, J. P. Ego diffusion in women with behavioral disorders and the integrating effects of psychodrama in identity consolidation. Doctoral dissertation, University of Southern California, 1964.

Moreno, J. L. *Psychodramatic shock therapy.* New York: Beacon House, 1939.

Moreno, J. L. *Psychodramatic treatment of performance neurosis.* New York: Beacon House, 1944.

Moreno, J. L. *Psychodramatic treatment of marriage problems.* New York: Beacon House, 1945 (a).

Moreno, J. L. *Psychodramatic treatment of psychosis.* New York: Beacon House, 1945 (b).

Moreno, J. L. *Psychodrama: Volume I.* New York: Beacon House, 1946.

Moreno, J. L. *Who shall survive?* New York: Beacon House, 1953.

Moreno, J. L. *Psychodrama: Volume II.* New York: Beacon House, 1959.

Moreno, J. L. (Ed.) *The sociometry reader.* Glencoe, Ill.: The Free Press of Glencoe, 1960.

Moreno, J. L. *Psychodrama: Volume III.* New York: Beacon House, 1969.

Moreno, J. L. The creative theory of personality. In I. A. Greenberg (Ed.), *Psychodrama: Theory and therapy.* New York: Behavioral Publications, 1974, pp. 73–84.

Moreno, J. L., & Elefthery, D. G. An introduction to group psychodrama. In G. Gazda (Ed.), *Basic approaches to group psychotherapy and group counseling.* Springfield, Ill.: C. C Thomas, 1975.

Moreno, Z. T. A survey of psychodramatic techniques. *Group Psychotherapy,* 1959, 12, 5–14.

Moreno, Z. T. In memorium: Jacob Levy Moreno. *Group Psychotherapy, Psychodrama and Sociometry,* 1976, 29, 130–35.

Ossorio, A. G., & Fine, L. J. Psychodrama as a catalyst for social change in a mental hospital. In J. L. Moreno (Ed.), *Progress in psychotherapy: Vol. V.* New York: Grune & Stratton, 1959, pp. 212–18.

Perls, F. *Gestalt therapy verbatim.* Big Sur, Calif.: Real People Press, 1969.

Pesso, A. *Movement in psychotherapy: Psychomotor techniques and training.* New York: New York University Press, 1969.

Polster, E., & Polster, M. *Gestalt therapy integrated.* New York: Brunner/Mazel, 1973.

Rojas-Bermudez, Jaime. *Titeres y psicodrama: el objecto intermediano.* Buenos Aires: Ediciones Genitor, 1970.

Rosenberg, P. P. An experimental analysis of psychodrama. Doctoral dissertation, Harvard University, 1952.

Rothman, G. Psychodrama and autogenic relaxation. *Group Psychotherapy,* 1961, 14, 26–29.

Sacks, J. M. Psychodrama and psychoanalysis. *Group Psychotherapy,* 1960, 13, 199.

Saikaku, I. *The life of an amorous woman,* edited and translated by I. Morris. London: Corgi Books, 1964, pp. 156–63.

Schutz, W. C. *Here comes everybody: Body-mind and encounter culture.* New York: Harper & Row, 1971.

Seabourne, B. The action sociogram. *Group Psychotherapy,* 1963, 16, 145–55.

Shaftel, F. R., & Shaftel, G. *Roleplaying for social values: Decision making in the social studies.* Englewood Cliffs, N.J.: Prentice-Hall, 1967.

Shapiro, J. N. A comparison of certain Rorschach score patterns with psychodrama action patterns. Doctoral dissertation, University of Arizona, 1964.

Siroka, R. W.; Siroka, E. K.; & Schloss, G. A. (Eds.), *Sensitivity training and group encounter.* New York: Grossett and Dunlop, 1971.

Starr, A. *Psychodrama: Rehearsal for living.* Chicago: Nelson-Hall, 1977.

Tawadros, S. M. Spontaneity training at the Darra Institute, Alexandria, Egypt. *Group Psychotherapy,* 1956, 9, 164–67.

Toeman, Z. The "double situation" in psychodrama. *Sociatry,* 1948, 1, 436–48.

Weiner, H. B. Treating the alcoholic with psychodrama. *Group Psychotherapy,* 1965, 18, 27–49.

Yablonsky, L. *Psychodrama.* New York: Basic Books, 1976.

FILMS & TV TAPES

Fine, L., & Pauly, I. *Psychodrama in group processes: A problem of acceptance* (psychodramatic treatment of an adolescent girl). University of Oregon Medical School, 1966; distributed by New York University Film Library.

Fine, L.; Pauly, I.; & Owens, W. *Psychodrama in group processes: Interstaff communications.* University of Oregon Medical School, 1965; distributed by New York University Film Library.

Moreno, J. L. 1. *Introduction to psychodrama (1949);* 2. *Psychodrama of a marriage (1964);* 3. *Group psychotherapy and psychodrama in action (1964).* Beacon, N.Y.: Moreno Institute.

Fink, A. K. 1. *A gift from the magic shop;* 2. *An encounter with blindness;* 3. *Being oneself in a group;* 4. *Do opposites attract?* 5. *Essence of encounter: The signs of love;* 6. *Generation gap;* 7. *Jesus in Buffalo* (three parts); 8. *Showing emotions in a group: A trilogy;* 9. *Situational test as warm-up;* 10. *The context of individual behavior in a group;* 11. *The importance of feedback: A trilogy;* 12. *Warm-up to psychodrama.* State University College; distributed by State University College, Media Library, Communications Center-Room 102, 1300 Elmwood Avenue, Buffalo, New York 14222, available in video tape and 16 mm film.

Siroka, R. W. *The experience of psychodrama.* 230 Park Avenue, New York: Forum III Films, 1975. Available in 16 mm color and video cassette.

12

Family Therapy

VINCENT D. FOLEY

OVERVIEW

Family Therapy as the name clearly states, is the theory of families. The focus is not on an individual, identified patient, but rather is on the family as a whole. The basic concept of this form of treatment is that it is more logical, faster, more satisfactory and more economical to treat all members of a system of relationships—in this case, the primary nuclear family—than to concentrate on the person who is supposed to be in need of treatment. The task of the family therapist is to change relationships between members of the troubled family, so that symptomatic behavior disappears. To accomplish this, family therapists have developed a variety of different strategies and techniques, based on somewhat different theories, for the ultimate goals of realigning relationships in the family to achieve better adjustment of all individuals in the family, including the so-called identified patient.

Basic Concepts

Family therapy may be def' ed broadly as the attempt to modify the re. nships in a family to achieve harmony A family is seen as an open system, reated by interlocking triangles, maintained or changed by means of feedback. Therefore, there are three basic concepts in family therapy: *system, triangles,* and *feedback.*

According to Thomas Kuhn (1962), a *paradigm* is a way of looking at scientific data and is the critical dimension in how one goes about investigating evidence. Family therapy offers a new paradigm that brings with it new concepts and new ways of making interventions (Haley & Hoffman, 1967; Levenson, 1972). Family therapy is a quantum leap from (a) the prior paradigm of viewing people as individuals apart from one another to (b) seeing them strictly in their relationships with others. As a result, the locus of pathology is shifted from the *individual* to the *system.* The attention of the therapist shifts from the "disturbed" individual to the dysfunctional system. In family therapy, the "identified patient" is seen as but a symptom, and the system itself (the family) is viewed as the client.

Concept of System. A *system* (Buckley, 1967) is made up of sets of different parts with two things in common: (1) the parts are interconnected and interdependent with mutual causality each affecting the other; and (2) each part is related to the other in a stable manner over time. A heating unit in a house is a system, whereas people traveling to work on a bus are not. If a system has a continuous flow of elements entering and leaving, it is an *open* system. If it lacks such a flow, as in the case of a heating system, it is a closed system (Von Bertalanffy, 1974). An open system, such as a family, has three important properties: wholeness, relationship, and equifinality.

Wholeness means the system is not just the sum of its parts taken separately, but also includes their interaction. It follows from this that one cannot understand a given part unless one understands its connection to the other parts. Therapeutically, this means a client must be seen in the context of his life, especially his relationship to his family. Wholeness, therefore, refers to the interdependence between the parts of the system. This wholeness represents a Gestalt conception since the whole is more than and different from the sum of its parts. So the family consists of the people in it *and* also the relationships between the individuals.

Relationship refers to the property of a system that considers what is happening between the parts and examines interactions. It puts an emphasis on *what* is happening rather than *why* it is happening. This shift results from the use of a paradigm based on the system concept rather than a paradigm based on a collection of separated and separable individuals. *What* becomes more important than *why*. The family therapist asks, *"What is the family doing?"* rather than, *"Why is the family doing this?"* If the ongoing patterns of interaction can be seen and understood, the therapist believes an ameliorative change can be made in the system without uncovering the *why* of the pattern. We shift our attention from what is going on *inside* family members to what is going on *between* them.

Equifinality, or the self-perpetuation of

structures, means that if interventions are made here and now, changes can be produced since open systems are not governed by their initial conditions. A system has no "memory." This concept has enormous importance for family therapy because it justifies concentrating on the here-and-now. Regardless of the origin of a problem, any difficulty can be removed if a change is made at any point in time in the system. Silvano Arieti (1969) suggests that avoiding getting involved in the past, what he calls the "genetic fallacy," might be the most important contribution system thinking has made to therapy. Almost all other therapeutic systems, especially psychodynamically oriented ones, concentrate on the past, seeking for underlying causes, making interpretations about past events, implying that the "real problem" is in the past. The family therapist does not deny the importance of the past, but emphasizes that what perpetuates the problem is the current interaction within the system. For example, say that a man began heavy drinking 20 years ago because he had unresolved problems with his mother, but if he drinks now it may be because of the present relationships with his wife. If the interaction between husband and wife can be altered, the drinking may be changed without ever getting involved in the why or in the past. Equifinality has many practical ramifications in the way in which a therapist will make interventions into a family system.

Interlocking Triangles. A series of *interlocking triangles* are the basic building blocks of the family relationship system (Bowen, 1971). An emotional network such as a family is composed of a series of interlocking triangles that lend stability to the system. They are a means of reducing or increasing the emotional intensity of a system. One can formulate an axiom as follows: *Whenever the emotional balance between two people becomes too intense or too distant, a third person or thing can be introduced to restore equilibrium to the system and give it stability.* This is why frequently marriages in trouble have presenting problems such as husbands having affairs or becoming "workaholics" or alcoholics and wives becoming overinvolved with children, clubs, or family. These troubling behaviors can be viewed either (a) as the result of problems of the individuals or (b) as tactics for gaining closeness or distance within the context of the marriage or the family. Family therapy takes this latter view. To repeat the basic point of view: family therapy is therapy of the family and not of the individuals.

Analyzing the various triangles in a system and making interventions to change the system are the primary tasks of the family therapist. Murray Bowen and his associates of the *family-system* school of thought (See Liebman, et al. 1976) are particularly concerned with triangles over three generations involving grandparents, parents, and children. Salvadore Minuchin (1974) and *structuralists* in general are more concerned with triangles in the nuclear family of father, mother, and child. Both, however, work on the triangles as a way of producing change and not with individuals in the system.

Feedback. In system theory, *feedback* refers to the process whereby a system adjusts itself. *Negative feedback* is the process by which the deviation in a system is corrected and previous equilibrium is restored. *Positive feedback* destroys a system by forcing it to change, not allowing it to return to its former state.

A frequently observed clinical pattern illustrating the concept of negative feedback would be the following. John's parents ask for help with their son who is labeled "school phobic." The therapist views John's problem as a response to the family system; he is overclose with his mother and too distant from his father. He sees John, the identified patient, as a "coverup" for parental problems. The counselor works with the parents and their marriage. John is thereby relieved and begins to go to school. The marriage, however, worsens as more and more problems between husband and wife are uncovered. John senses their worsening relationship and begins to become phobic again. The parents now unite and stay together "for the sake of the child." John's school phobia can be labeled as "negative feedback" needed to maintain the old system.

Positive feedback has been aptly described by Carl Whitaker (1975) as the "leaning tower of Pisa" approach. A therapist instead of correcting a symptom pushes the problem in the other direction so the system falls of its own weight. This approach uses the absurdity of a symptom, and instead of restoring balance, moves it into further chaos to its ultimate destruction. Positive feedback is an indispensable clinical tool for the family therapist and is an example of the use of paradox in psychotherapy.

Other Systems

Many early pioneers in family therapy such as Murray Bowen and Nathan Ackerman were trained as psychoanalysts and, consequently, there are similarities between their ideas and those of psychoanalysis. There are many interfaces between family therapy and psychoanalytic thinking, and some family therapists, such as Ivan Boszormenyi-Nagy and Geraldine Spark (1973), and Helm Stierlin (1974) in particular, work on these. A major difference between psychoanalysis and family therapy is that in psychoanalysis, parental involvement is excluded as a hindrance to the development of the transference neurosis, which is seen as necessary to successful therapy; whereas, in family therapy all members of the family are brought into the therapy sessions.

Adlerian psychotherapeutic theory shares much with family therapy. Its emphasis on family constellation is a major concept borrowed by family therapists. Adler's approach was holistic and so is family therapy. The use of paradox, a major weapon in family therapy, has its roots in Alfred Adler (Mozdzierz, Macchitelli, & Lisiecki, 1976). Likewise, an emphasis on the conscious and the present are Adlerian concepts. The freedom to improvise is a feature of family therapy and it, too, has its roots in Adler. Adler died in 1937 before the full impact of system thinking so, although he took the family system into account in therapy, he did not give it the same importance as do family therapists. The basic concepts of family therapy are found in a latent state in Adler's thinking (Christensen, 1971).

Client-centered therapy, similarly to family therapy, stresses the here-and-now, puts responsibility for behavior on the person, and views man holistically. However, client-centered therapy is totally individual and does not use system thinking. Its basic model is alien to the family therapist.

Rational-emotive therapy (RET), too, uses a different model. The similarities between it and family therapy are superficial: sharing here-and-now emphasis and taking responsibility. Its differences are major. RET stresses rugged individualism and overemphasizes the cognitive; whereas family therapy strives to strike a balance between being an independent self and relating to others in the family.

Behavior therapy has been used by several family therapists (Lieberman, 1976;

Engeln et al., 1976). The frequently used technique known as "prescribing the symptom" has aspects of behavior modification. However, there is a critical difference between behavior therapy and family therapy. Behavior therapy regards the "problem" as the symptomatic client; family therapy sees the "problem" as a response to a system, as a notice that something is wrong in the system. Behavior therapy puts the burden of change on the individual; family therapy on the system, not the individual.

Gestalt therapy clearly shares a common base with family therapy. Its concern for the present and its emphasis on behavior and active participation by the therapist are common to both approaches. However, with families, Gestalt gives more importance to feelings and confrontation than do most family therapists (Kempler, 1974).

Reality therapy, likewise, stresses responsibility and the present, but places more of a burden on the individual than does family therapy. Reality therapy is too individualistic and does not take into account the influence of the family system. Family members, especially children, are not totally aware of the system in which they live. Escaping from one's family of origin is not easily done and physical distance does not necessarily bring emotional peace. Reality therapy grants too much freedom to the individual and fails to take into account the power of the family system. In addition, it is too cognitive. Family systems are powerful precisely because they "hook" an individual in his "guts" more than in his head.

Transactional analysis (TA) uses an interpersonal model and tends to emphasize the "why" rather than the "what" as in family therapy. TA recognizes the importance of triangles in its concept of games (Berne, 1964) and shares the belief that symptoms are strategies to control the behavior of others, especially in alcoholics (Steiner, 1971). Nevertheless, TA rarely uses the family as the unit of treatment, preferring to deal with the individuals either alone or in therapeutic groups.

Psychodrama is the basis for a technique known as *family sculpting,* widely used in family therapy, in which a family member recreates his family of origin in space and position. For example, does Mr. Jones place his mother next to his father or at his feet looking up at him? Does he put his sister equidistant between them or close to his father? Where does John himself fit in the family? Sculpting is a way of visualizing the closeness or distance experienced in a family. The difference between sculpting and psychodrama, however, is that the latter is used to relive and resolve a traumatic event, whereas sculpting is more concerned with closeness and space as a means of understanding emotional involvement (see Papp, Silverstein, & Carter, 1973). Sculpting is also known as role presentation.

Group therapy bears some resemblance to family therapy in that it takes into account the importance of others, but there are two major differences. First, the group does not have a history. It has no past and no future. The family has both. Second, the agent of the change is the group with the therapist in the role of facilitator (Yalom, 1975). The family therapist, on the other hand, serves more as a model or teacher than facilitator.

In summary, family therapy has similarities to most active therapies and borrows techniques liberally from many. The critical difference between family therapy and other approaches is the role given to the family system. Other therapies deal either with the individual, the dyadic unit, or the group, but only family therapy sees

the family system as the "client." The family is treated, not the individuals. Family therapy is concerned with *how* family members interact and not with *why* they so act. It is a therapy of the family as a system of relationships and not the treatment of maladjusted persons as individuals. We may even say it is concerned with the "spaces" between people—their relationships—rather than the individual processes. As such, it has much in common with Asian personality theory (Pedersen, 1977).

HISTORY

Precursors

A humanistic approach to the alleviation of suffering due to relationship problems began with the psychological discoveries of Freud. In addition, with reference to the precursors of family therapy as we know it today, two other therapists were important: Alfred Adler and Harry Stack Sullivan.

Sigmund Freud. There are two discernible threads in the thinking of Freud. The first, coming from his early training in the physical sciences, is his theory of instincts. The second, going beyond instinct to a more psychological explanation, culminated in the theory of the Oedipus complex. Most of Freud's life was spent in examining instincts; and it was left to others, especially Sullivan and other object-relational thinkers or ego analysts such as Melanie Klein, Ronald Fairbairn, and Heinz Hartmann, to elaborate on the more purely psychological aspects (Guntrip, 1971).

As early as 1909, Freud (1964) saw the connection between a young boy's phobic symptoms and his relationship with his father. Nevertheless, Freud chose to treat young Hans independently of the father, and this choice was to influence therapists in that direction. Freud was probably bound to the mechanical model he had inherited from his early teachers.

Alfred Adler. Adler has had an important but indirect influence on family therapy in a number of ways. The most influential of the so-called social thinkers in therapy, Adler saw context and environment as essential. Man was not primarily an instinctual being but rather a social, purposeful being motivated not by drives but by goals. He was, in brief, a responsible agent able to make choices. Change in the here-and-now, despite one's past, was not only possible but attainable. Virginia Satir (1972) says it simply, "All of the ingredients in a family that count are changeable and correctable" (p. XI).

Second, Adler stressed the importance of the family constellation. It was not just a case of looking at the interaction of child and parent—the concept had to be widened to include siblings and their relationships. Adler's emphasis on sibling position has become one of the essential concepts in the thinking of a school of family therapy associated with Murray Bowen (1971).

Adler emphasized the conscious, the positive, and one's ability to change. This typifies family therapy. The family therapist is less concerned with the past than with the present. He looks at the positive in family relations, its communication, and at the "growing edge" of the family, as well as its dysfunction. Oscar Christensen (1971), an Adlerian family therapist, says, "Adler would view behavior as movement, communication, movement toward others, and the desire to belong—the desire to be part of" (p. 19). This is a description of family therapy.

Harry Stack Sullivan. Sullivan's contribution to family therapy lies in his investigation of schizophrenia. His interpersonal theory is a development of that psychological thread mentioned above in Freud. Sullivan moved away from a biological answer and toward a psychological one, sensing that the primitive relationship between mother and child was critical in schizophrenia. Sullivan's thinking shifted the focus of therapy from a purely intrapsychic to the interpersonal. Therapy was moving toward a system concept.

Sullivan's thinking entered family therapy through Don Jackson who, while a resident at Chestnut Lodge in Maryland, was under the influence of Sullivan's disciple, Frieda Fromm-Reichmann. Jackson later moved to the West Coast and began a school of family therapy at Palo Alto that stressed the importance of communication.

Beginnings

The beginnings of the modern family-therapy movement started in the mid-1950s and focused largely on research into schizophrenia. This produced a series of concepts known under various labels that became the core ideas in family therapy. The following are some major concepts.

The Double Bind. In 1956 a paper on communication, "Toward a Theory of Schizophrenia," combined the thinking of Gregory Bateson, Don Jackson, Jay Haley, and John Weakland (1956). They discovered that in schizophrenic families, a process known as *double binding* occurred regularly. This means a person is put into a situation in which he cannot make a correct choice, because whatever choice he makes, it is unacceptable. "He is damned if he does and damned if he doesn't." No real choice can be made because, in fact, no good choice is possible. The "victim" in a double bind, however, is not aware of his dilemma. A child, for example, is told, "Mommy loves you." On the verbal level, such a message shows love and concern. However, in a double-bind situation, the message is delivered in a cold, distant manner. Consequently, he is told (verbally), "I love you," and is informed (nonverbally), "I don't love you." If the child cannot deal with the two contradictory messages, he cannot deal effectively with this problem. The authors of the paper suggested that such double binding is frequently found in the communication of schizophrenic families. Repeated episodes of double binding produce bewilderment and ultimately withdrawal. Such behavior is then labeled "abnormal" and the person in question is "put away."

Stuck-Togetherness. Bowen (1971) used this term to describe a process he observed in schizophrenic families. By this he meant that various family members are related to each other in such a way that none of them has a true sense of self as an independent individual. The boundaries between the family members tend to be blurred, and the family forms into an amorphous mass without distinguishing characteristics. Family members can neither gain true intimacy, nor can they separate and become persons. They have a quality of *stuck-togetherness* that gives them no freedom or option to move closer or to get away.

Schism and Skew. Theodore Lidz, Alice Cornelison, Stephen Fleck, and Dorothy Terry (1957) at Yale observed two processes in particular in families. One pattern involved a dominant spouse who took control of the relationship. This pattern was labeled *marital skew,* meaning the marital relationship was not an equal partnership. Another pattern involved a marriage in which the husband and wife could not attain role reciprocity or in which there was an overattachment

to the parental home of one of the spouses. This pattern called *marital schism* was particularly evident in marriages in which there was a schizophrenic member. The primary alliance that should exist between a husband and wife in their role as parents was noticeably absent and in its place was a violation of the boundaries between husband and wife brought about by an alliance between one parent and that parent's parent.

Pseudomutuality. Lyman Wynne, Irving Ryckoff, Juliana Day, and Stanley Hirsch (1958) coined the phrase *pseudomutuality* to describe a false kind of closeness they observed in schizophrenic families. This they defined as "a predominant absorption in fitting together at the expense of the differentiation of the identities of the persons in the relations" (p. 207). To be in such a family is to lose one's boundaries, to become disoriented. The consequence of this process of confusion is to lead one into a state of dependency on the family. Family members are caught and cannot leave. There is no true intimacy or closeness, only a pseudo-love or caring. The family becomes all not by choice but by necessity.

Mystification. R. D. Laing in England, in doing research with the families of hospitalized schizophrenic teenage girls, noted a process of confusion and obfuscation that he called *mystification,* defined as, "One person (p) seeks to induce in the other some change necessary for his (p's) security" (1965, p. 349). He found this process to be rampant in these families, what in popular language might be called "double talk," a blatant form of manipulation. Laing came to the conclusion that frequently such girls identified as patients by their parents and others were, in fact, often the healthiest members of the family.

Interlocking Pathologies. Nathan

Ackerman began his career as an orthodox child psychiatrist who did not see
parents of patients. In time, however, he
realized it was impossible to understand
children without getting some idea of the
family environment and dynamics. His
book *The Psychodynamics of Family Life*
(1958) was the first major work in the
field in which the relationships between
an individual and his family were investigated. Ackerman (1956) referred to the
difficulties in a family as *interlocking
pathologies,* in that the problems of one
member could not be understood apart
from those of other family members.

His contribution to family therapy is
special for two reasons. First, he did not
work with schizophrenic families exclusively and thus considered relationship
processes in less disturbed families. Second, he brought family therapy to the attention of a largely hostile community of
psychodynamically oriented therapists
and acted as a go-between for many years
between the more traditional approach
and that of family therapy.

These various ideas and concepts began
to jell into a more coherent form when in
1962 Ackerman and Don Jackson united
to found *Family Process,* a journal dedicated to examining family research and
treatment. The family-therapy movement
now had a vehicle through which ideas
could be filtered and concepts developed.

Current Status

Since its beginning with Freud, psychotherapy has moved through a series of
paradigms from the individual to the interpersonal to the system. Although family therapy began with an interpersonal
model, it has now moved to a system concept. Some family therapists, although
using systems thinking, spend much time
on past relationships and so can be distin-

guished from those who deal more with
the here-and-now presenting problems
and current system functioning. We can
identify four schools of family therapy in
terms of the emphasis given to various
aspects of the treatment process. (Foley,
1974)

Object Relations. This viewpoint has
close connections with the traditional one
of ego psychology and in particular with
the theory of *object relations* as articulated by Ronald Fairbairn (Guntrip,
1971). Whereas Freud maintained that instinctual gratification was the fundamental need, others, such as Melanie Klein
and Ronald Fairbairn, opted for a satisfying object relationship as more basic. The
word *object* in this connection refers to
"people." The inability of a person to
work out such a relationship with the
family of origin carries over and "con-
taminates" the new family system in relation to one's mate and the children. Boszormenyi-Nagy (1965) states that family
pathology is ". . . a specialized multi-
person organization of shared fantasies
and complementary need gratification
patterns, maintained for the purpose of
handling past object loss experience" (p.
310). Others who use this kind of framework include James Framo (1970), Gerald
Zuk (1975), and Norman and Betty Paul
(1975). In an object-relations approach,
the identified patient is often seen as
the carrier of the split-off and unacceptable impulses of other family members
(Stewart et al., 1975). In therapy much
time will be spent on working with these
prior relationships for those who use an
object-relations theoretical viewpoint.
The main center for this approach is the
Eastern Pennsylvania Psychiatric Institute in Philadelphia.

Family Systems. This school of
thought has been called *family systems*
and by some *Bowen system theory* be-

cause of the influence of Murray Bowen.

The goal of this mode of family therapy is to teach people to *respond* and not merely to *react* to their system. Responding means taking into account the needs of the family but ultimately making a choice based on reason and not feeling. Reacting means acting on a feeling basis and being pulled into the system. Reacting eventuates in the twin dilemmas of anger and guilt. The goal of Bowen's theory is to enable a person to become a solid self differentiated from one's family system but remaining in touch with the system. Such a therapy tends to extend over a long period. Philip Guerin (1976) presents the best elaboration of Bowen's theory and practice.

At present it has two centers: Family Studies in the Department of Psychiatry at Georgetown University in Washington, D.C., where Bowen teaches, and at the *Center for Family Learning* in New Rochelle, New York.

Structural Family Therapy. This point of view is associated with the name of Salvador Minuchin (1967, 1974) and is a development of the concepts of "alignments and splits" introduced into family therapy by Lyman Wynne (1961). It is called *structural family therapy* because it seeks to change structures, that is, the alliances and splits in the family. The structural family therapist works on the boundaries between family subsystems,

emphasizing the boundary between parent and child. This approach also stresses the notion of triangles but tends to focus more on the parent-child relationship than on a three-generational analysis as does Bowen's procedure (1976). The main center for structural thinking in family therapy is the Philadelphia Child Guidance Clinic.

Strategic Intervention. This school of thought proceeded from the thinking of Don Jackson who clearly stated concepts relative to the formulation and resolution of problems. The main ideas are: (a) the symptom presented *is* the problem; (b) such problems are caused by faulty life adjustments, especially at critical points like birth and death; (c) problems continue because attempted solutions only intensify the problem; (d) the cure, paradoxically, is often found in an intensifying of the problem (Weakland et al., 1974).

The goal of therapy in strategic intervention is to devise tactics that will force people to behave differently. Paradox in the form of "prescribing the symptom" is often used. Prescribing the symptom means the client is asked to continue his life in such manner as to make the symptom worse—not better. However, his behavior is now under control of the therapist and is no longer involuntary. The most complete statement about this process with numerous examples can be

Figure 12.1. Four Schools of Family Therapy Schematized in Terms of Continuum Ranging from "Ego Psychology" of Psychoanalysis to the Objective Theory of Strategic Intervention.

found in Paul Watzlawick, John Weakland, and Richard Fisch (1974). The main center for strategic intervention is the Brief Therapy Center, Mental Research Institute, in Palo Alto, California.

Summary. The four schools mentioned share things in common; yet each has different approaches to time, level, and intensity of treatment. All agree that troubling, symptomatic behavior is the result of dysfunctional interaction in the family system. Schools 1 and 2 believe that more time and energy has to be spent on clarifying relationships from the past, and schools 3 and 4 (see Figure 12.1) take more literally the concept of equifinality and stress that if the present system can be changed, the past need not be an issue. The schools presented have the same basic concept of the family: a commonality of thought and approach that unites them, but at the same time, each school differentiates itself from the others in terms of their special viewpoints.

PERSONALITY

Family therapy is essentially an approach to psychotherapy that sees the family as the primary unit of treatment. It is not a personality theory in the traditional understanding of that term, but it implies essentially a unique theory of personality. This is true of any approach to therapy because underlying any treatment approach is a concept of what is human nature, what is health, what is sickness, and what can a therapist do to intervene.

Theory of Personality

Family personality theory states that the psychological development of any person results from his family system. The family is the basic source of health or sickness. Family theory focuses on the family system more than other psychotherapeutic systems, because things being equal, the major force in the development of an individual is his family. In terms of time and emotional force, the family is dominant. Other social systems compete with it but neither the school nor the church nor any other group has as much effect on a young person as does one's primary family.

Murray Bowen noted that an identified patient who functioned adequately in the hospital would often regress when sent back into his family. Bowen discovered that family forces often opposed the interventions of the therapist. The emotional pull of forces exerted by the family were extremely powerful and potent.

There can be little argument with the notion of the family as the most critical factor in the determination of personality. What we are genetically and how we look, think, feel, and act are all influenced by the family into which we are born.

Family therapy views man in a holistic manner considered not only in himself but in relation to his environment. Although it affirms the importance of heredity, it stresses more the importance of environment. A person is the net result of his interactions, and foremost among these is his family of origin. Therefore, the explanation of the development of an individual's personality, its growth, and its decline will be found by examining the family. From this arises the notion that making interventions that restructure the system is the method of choice in the therapy of people in families.

In family therapy, when one talks about personality theory, one is talking about the family nexus. Three issues must be discussed: (1) What is a family? (2) What is a "dysfunctional" family? (3) Why must a family change?

What Is a Family? Each individual

has basic needs: some physical, some emotional. The physical ones are easily recognized; the emotional ones are less obvious. Emotional needs can be reduced to three dimensions: *intimacy, power,* and *meaning.* People need to be close to others, to belong. They also need to express themselves, to be unique. Finally, there must be some meaning or purpose in their lives. For most people, the first dimension involves a heterosexual relationship; the second involves work; the third involves having children.

Although it can be argued that the family unit is not necessary to fulfill these goals, nevertheless, in very few instances is it possible to achieve these three needs without a family. A family is the social unit in which people by mutual choice attempt to attain their needs for these three dimensions.

People usually marry each other because they find that choice is the most satisfactory way of getting the things they need emotionally. The way in which they negotiate differences determines the success or failure of the marriage. *Can I be close to you and still remain myself? Can I avoid being swallowed up by you? Does our relationship make sense in my life?* The process of marriage answers these quesions.

What Is a "Dysfunctional" Family? Family therapists prefer talking about *dysfunction* rather than sickness because this states more clearly what they see as the fundamental problem—the inability of family members to attain the desired goals of closeness, self-expression, and meaning. When these goals cannot be attained, symptomatic behavior takes place. For example, the husband gets involved in an affair; the wife becomes depressed; a child becomes school phobic.

The difference between seeing symptoms as system oriented or as the property of an individual is not merely semantic. Working from a theoretical model of a system, the therapist believes the other members of the system are critically important if change is to be made in the identified patient. In the more traditional approach, family members are likely to be seen as obstacles to treatment who interfere with the transference process. In a family-system concept, however, the other members are an essential part of the therapeutic process.

A *functional family* is one in which the needs of various family members are met. In a *dysfunctional family,* such needs are not being met and therefore symptomatic behavior occurs. The important difference between a functional family system and a dysfunctional one is not the presence or absence of conflict, but rather the attainment of need satisfaction. In either case, there will be *conflict* in the family. Such conflict should be expected because the goals of various people or subsystems in the family rarely coincide.

For example, the father of a family may want his children at home on Christmas Eve with his wife and himself, feeling this will foster his goal of closeness for the family. His son John, however, wants to be with his friends at a basketball game. Mary and Jane, John's sisters, who form a family subsystem based on a common interest in ice skating, want to practice. The mother sides with the girls, pointing out they have spent the day decorating the tree and deserve some time to themselves. Clearly the goals of the father, mother, son, and daughters are in conflict. Their ability to solve such differences will answer the question regarding the functioning of the family. A functioning family will make compromises; a dysfunctional one will not.

It should be noted in the example given, the issues that ultimately are critical are those of closeness, self-expression, and meaning, especially meaning.

Why Must a Family Change? Just as an individual passes through a series of stages, so does the family. In the beginning of the family, the husband and wife need to unite into a functional system. They must form a functional "we" in addition to their own personalities.

The next step is opening the system, allowing others to enter: the children. This critical step presents the couple with a crisis situation. The presence of a third party means the possibility of alignments and splits. Husband and wife must assume a new role, that of parents. This is a much different role from that of spouse. The anxiety level of many people is aroused by becoming a parent, but society tends to emphasize the positive aspect of parenthood, playing down the doubt and anxiety of the new parent.

System thinking explains the difference and the difficulty in parenthood by the concept of feedback. If a husband displeases his wife, feedback can be instant and immediate correction can be made. This is not true in the role of parent. The parent must wonder about what he or she is doing. *Am I too strict? Am I too easy?* The answer will not be known for many years. Feedback is not immediate.

The birth of subsequent children likewise creates a change in the family system. A second child is not simply an addition but rather is a change in the family system. As noted earlier, in a system concept, one plus one does not equal two. An additional family member means the system is restructured.

A new stage in family process is introduced by children going to school. The family system must again open, this time to outsiders. This may prove traumatic in many instances. The phenomenon of school phobia is seen as the inability of the system to make a proper adjustment, to widen its boundaries, and not just as the inability of a child to leave his mother. It can be seen how a new paradigm leads to a new way of conceptualizing a problem and a new way of approaching treatment. The family therapist asks, "What is going on in the *family* that produces school phobia in this child?"

Adolescence brings a need for further freedom for children. Overcloseness between a parent and a child may result in symptomatic behavior in one of the family members. A mother, for example, may not be able to allow a child freedom because it means a loss of meaning in her life.

The separation of children and parents through marriage creates a crisis situation for the parents. It means, frequently, a loss of meaning in life, the so-called empty-nest syndrome. The unresolved problems of the beginning of marriage may now surface as children move away, creating the possibility of marital difficulties.

Variety of Concepts

In family therapy, an individual personality—how one thinks, feels, and acts—is seen as the result of myriad, complex relationships that go on in the family. What has been traditionally called *intrapsychic,* the depth dimension of personality, is the result of the process of the family system. Harry Stack Sullivan recognized this by emphasizing the importance of others, especially the mother, in personality development. Alfred Adler, likewise, gave the family constellation an important place in his thinking. He thought one's personality is affected by one's ordinal position in the family. Thus, older children tend to be more responsible as adults, more traditionally minded;

middle children are more likely to be difficult and moody; while younger children, who came into the family systems late, tend to be spoiled and remain relatively incapable as adults. (Adler, 1949) Family therapy has taken these insights and emphasized three dimensions: (a) the marital subsystem, (b) the sibling subsystem, and (c) homeostasis.

Marital Subsystem. Family therapists vary widely in their approach to both theory and practice, but all are agreed on the above three dimensions. The beginning of a family system whether functional or dysfunctional starts with the couple. They must form a "oneness" that places them squarely on one side of the fence, apart from others. The violation of generational boundaries in particular is the beginning of family dysfunction. The process of differentiation is one that must be made both by an individual and a couple. "Stuck-togetherness," or "enmeshment," is the result of an inability to separate from a family or origin with a concomitant overcloseness to a parent, spouse, or child. The boundaries are violated to the detriment of all.

Symbolically, the ability to "close a door," to shut out others, is vital for a healthy marriage in the thinking of family therapists. Husband and wife ought to have secrets from their parents and children. There should be an intimacy between them that maintains their privacy. Early researchers in schizophrenia noted the obtrusiveness of parents into their children's lives and vice versa.

Another way of saying this is that in a good marriage the spouse is first and any others are second. Children-oriented marriages are always dysfunctional. Children ought to add meaning to a marriage and express the creativity and warmth of the parents, but they must always be subservient to the marital relationship. A man should always be a husband first and then a father, and a woman a wife first and then a mother.

Perhaps, paradoxically, the most successful parents are those in which each partner is spouse first and parent second. The reason seems to be that a normal married person does not need the child for fulfillment or to give life or the marriage meaning. Being satisfied in himself or herself and with the marriage, the spouse can give children freedom of choice. The child is not caught in the bind of conforming to the parent and being angry—or of "doing his own thing" and feeling guilty.

The triangle that exists among husband, wife, and child is kept less activated when the spouses are united. If they have a coalition, this prevents the child from forming a permanent alliance with one of the parents. It requires the child to seek a relationship with others of his own generation, especially with brothers and sisters.

Sibling Subsystem. A natural consequence of the parental coalition is the formation of a sibling subsystem that affords each child a chance to build a closeness with his brothers and sisters. Family therapists insist that children should have secrets from parents: matters that pertain to their private lives. Each subsystem, like each person, should have appropriate boundaries. A rule for determining dysfunction in families is to look at the presence or absence of discernible boundaries. Are parents clearly separated from children? Are children differentiated among themselves? Older children should be treated differently from younger children. If given more responsibility, they should be given more privileges.

As children grow, individual differences should be respected. Privacy is important for the development of personality. Reading mail addressed to others and not knocking before entering another's room are not merely signs of discourtesy but represent essential issues in a family. How much freedom will be given to children in a family is determined by two factors: maturity and culture.

Children do not grow at the same speed physically or intellectually or emotionally. The pace will be unique in each case. Consequently, one cannot say that because A was given a privilege, B should get the same privilege at the same time. Obviously, this can become an area of difficulty. It certainly will be one of conflict. The willingness to discuss differences and to compromise are signs of a functional family system. The issue is one of negotiation and the ability to bring harmony among conflicting goals in the family.

Closely allied with the above are the norms of a given culture or subculture, such as a neighborhood. Perhaps the most neglected area in family therapy is the impact of culture. The concepts of the spouse subsystem and the sibling subsystem find general agreement among family therapists. How they will be worked out concretely, however, will differ from culture to culture. How affection is expressed, money used, time spent with others, and so on are issues that vary greatly (Papajohn & Spiegel, 1975).

Culture determines the kind of relationship the nuclear family has with the extended family. In traditional rural settings, this has been very close; in modern, urban ones, it is more diffuse. Which is more effective is open to dispute. How spouses should relate to each other is similarly a cultural issue. Until recently, the man has been considered to be the instrumental leader, and the woman the affectional-expressive one. Social changes currently in progress seem to be destructive to this way of thinking. Although there may be a greater exchange of roles

between husband and wife in the future, it seems safe to say that in any case, there will be no exchange of basic dependency between parent and child. The generational boundaries will probably remain intact.

Homeostasis. How the marital and the sibling subsystems interact results in what family therapists call the *homeostasis,* or balance, in a family. Any system operates within given limits, and when these are transgressed, the system experiences difficulty. If that difficulty cannot be corrected, the system will eventually disintegrate.

The family system operates within limits determined in part by its members and in part by its culture. Families coming to a new culture frequently encounter "cultural shock," which destroys the family balance if the changes dictated by the new culture cannot be absorbed into the old system.

In family therapy, one looks at the behavior patterns in the family as balance mechanisms of the system more than as individual properties of family members. An alcoholic, for example, in a family concept is seen differently than in other approaches. Traditionally, therapists have regarded such behavior as bad or destructive and have attempted to deal with the alcoholic and his drinking in that light. In family therapy, however, the therapist regards alcoholism as a property of the system that performs a *positive* role in the family by maintaining its homeostasis. Rather than deal with the alcoholic as an individual, the family therapist prefers looking at the system to understand better its need for this behavior.

The goal of family therapy is change in the system: the creation of a new homeostasis, a new way of relating. If *therapy* is defined as the process of working through resistance, *family therapy* means working through the resistance to creating new ways of interacting. The key issue in the conflict is homeostasis, with the family fighting to hold on to its old way of relating and the therapist trying to produce a new one. Sometimes the battle is overt, but more often it will be covert. In either case, there will be a conflict if the therapy is to be effective. Conflict cannot be avoided because the family will define the issue as this or that member's bad behavior, and the therapist will see it as involving the entire family. The ability to move the family from its prior point of view to the new one—the view of the therapist—is the measure of his skill and the success of the therapeutic process.

A family therapist is most concerned with the process by which the family system operates: How does a family maintain itself? Specifically, this is done by examining the marital subsystem and the sibling subsystem within the context of a given culture. How one will go about this, the process itself, will vary among therapists depending on the weight given to issues of power, communication, and meaning.

PSYCHOTHERAPY

Family therapy is essentially a unique way of viewing pathology that sees problems within the context of the family system. Historically, it is a development of a process that began with concentration on an individual, emphasizing intrapsychic aspects, and then moved to individuals as family members emphasizing interpersonal relationships and communication modalities. Family therapy focuses on the way a system is organized and structured. Pathology is viewed as the result of the incorrect way in which the system is organized. The system of relationships is to be changed to achieve

desirable changes in individuals, and not the intrapersonal aspects of the identified client. Or more exactly, it is the person who is to be changed—but indirectly through changing the structure and texture of family relationships.

Theory of Psychotherapy

The heart of therapy is change in behavior. Philosophers have broken down human behavior into three areas: the emotional, the cognitive, and the volitional. Therapists, following this pattern, talk about feeling, thinking, and action. These divisions are arbitrary because a human being cannot be divided into sections but must be regarded as an indivisible entity. Nevertheless, in individuals or groups, one of these modes tends to dominate. Change in family therapy is ultimately change in behavior, change in interaction. What one feels and how one thinks are important, but unless these get put into action, nothing really changes. A primary goal in family therapy therefore is producing overt behavior change, even if the family members are unaware of what is happening. Therapists who use paradox, in particular, are concerned mostly with altering the family behavioral system. If this can best be done apart from the family's awareness of the process, that goal takes precedence.

Insight is not important in family therapy. Getting the family to see what it is doing and why members are acting as they do is not a goal for most family therapists. Insight is considered an intellectual game that prevents real change from taking place or an epiphenomenon. It is not important for the family to understand the way it is structured; this is only important for the therapist. Jay Haley (1963) represents a large number of family therapists in maintaining that getting the family aware of its interaction is actually anti-therapeutic since real change is one of behavior and not just of thinking.

Family therapists see different dimensions of therapy as having varying degrees of importance.

History. How important for the therapist is a knowledge of the past to change the present? This is the question raised by the issue of the role of *history* in therapy.

Object-relations theory and family-systems theory regard a knowledge of the family's history as important for understanding the present structure of the family. The present family system is seen as a reflection of past structures and a transferencelike process operates in the here-and-now. For family-systems therapists, the triangles that constitute the system extend over several generations and must be examined. Structural-family and strategic-intervention therapists are less interested in family history since they believe the important dimension is the current structure, and this can be changed without an involved analysis of the family history. How things got the way they are is relatively unimportant. What to do about things the way they are now is what is important. The analogy is of a broken leg. Does it really matter to the doctor how it snapped? It is broken—and the issue is how to fix it. Setting the bone will be the same whether the bone was broken from a fall or a kick or from a blow.

Diagnosis. Traditional therapy pays much attention to getting a correct *diagnosis*. It is considered important to know if a client is neurotic, has a character disorder, or is psychotic. In family therapy, there is less concern for diagnosis. In part, this is due to a paucity of ways of measuring family dysfunction as it pertains to a system. One can talk about the specific feelings of a family member or the role one plays in the pathology of another, but an adequate nomenclature or classification system has not yet been developed. Some work has been done on how people solve problems in families or how they cooperate in performing a task. There has been a general resistance to diagnosis because many feel it better serves the needs of the therapist than it does the client or family.

Diagnosis, in a wide sense, as a way of evaluating the current functioning is used, but it is used more for clinical convenience than for research purposes. Diagnosis in family therapy does not have the same value as in more traditional approaches.

Affect. Feelings are thought by family therapists to be the result of behavior and therefore not given a primary position. Apart from Virginia Satir, and to a lesser degree Salvador Minuchin, most family therapists would not use family feelings to any great extent. This is one of the neglected aspects in family therapy due to an overwhelming emphasis on the concept of system, which tends to minimize the role and importance of emotion. This lack will probably change as more work is done with cultural dimensions.

Minuchin (1974) uses feelings but more as a technique to change the family interaction than by addressing himself to the feelings themselves. For example, he will become angry with a father who allows his son to make fun of him to get the father to make some changes in his relationship to the son. He will not concentrate on the lack of feeling that the father is experiencing as such, but rather on the way in which that lack can be used to move the system in another direction.

The Role of Learning. To some extent, all therapies use *learning*. The issue usually is how to make the client or family aware of the learning process. Object-relations therapists spend time analyzing past relationships and discussing how they influence the present. Teaching the family members new ways of relating will be a goal for object-relations therapists. The learning process, furthermore, tends to be conscious and deliberate. Likewise, family-systems therapists who regard themselves as teachers of self-differentiation underline the importance of learning new and effective ways of interacting. The other family therapists tend to play down the conscious aspect of learning, believing that an emphasis on this cognitive process slows the rate of change.

Transference and the Unconscious. In the psychodynamic model, the locus of pathology is thought to be deep in the client. The process of cure is said to depend on the development of a *transference* neurosis, which most analysts maintain is the critical step in therapy (Greenson, 1967). In family therapy, however, the locus of the pathology is the very structure itself and the critical step is restructuring the system. Transferencelike phenomena do occur between the therapist and the family, but no true transference is developed because the medium of therapy is not their relationship but the impact of the therapist's interventions, the force of the feedback into the system. Murray Bowen (1971) and Don Jackson and Jay Haley (1968) insisted that transference was not a necessary part of family therapy. This might be of some concern for those therapists in the object-relations group because they are generally concerned with the role of the *unconscious* on family process. This issue of transference is not one of great importance for other family therapists.

Therapist as Teacher and Model. Family therapists generally agree that the medium of change is the therapist not as an object of transference but as a model or teacher. He is either the model of com-

munication or the teacher of individuation. The family learns new ways of solving problems and of avoiding dead-end discussions. Behavior is analyzed and relabeled and seen in a new light. For example, a mother complains that her son is "impossible," by which she means that he has some problem inside of him that causes him to act in a certain manner. The therapist listens to her and patiently examines her interaction with the boy. In the light of this, he is able to relabel the behavior from another point of view such as the mother's inability to communicate with the child.

In the practice of family therapy, despite differences in approach, all therapists are active and not passive. They are not nondirective, reflecting feelings, but rather make interventions according to certain guidelines. In no way are they blank screens upon which projections are made. There is an attempt to be themselves and not to assume a role. This accounts for the wide divergence observed among family therapists as to therapeutic styles. Beneath these differences, however, is the striving to teach or to model behavior for the family.

Process of Psychotherapy

The course of family therapy varies widely with the goals of the therapist. It can range from several sessions to several years depending on a number of interconnected issues.

Families being treated by object-relations and family-systems therapists will tend to be seen over a longer period than those by structural or strategic-intervention therapists. This is due to a difference in goals. In the first group, deep changes in interactional patterns will be the goals; in the latter, the problem is more symptom oriented and treatment time will be shorter. This illustrates how important the way a problem is posed influences the treatment process.

Initial Interview. This is a most important session because it sets the tone for the therapy. Specifically, it will determine who will control the process. There are two goals in this interview: first to relabel the presenting problem; second, to engage the family.

Phases. The therapist, let us presume, has gathered all the family members for the initial session. He proceeds in a series of phases or stages in the treatment process.

Warm-Up. The therapist generally allows the family members who enter the room to sit where they choose. He should have more chairs present than people, giving them a freedom of placement. This is the first live contact with the family and how they arrange themselves tells much about how they relate to one another, how they feel about the therapist in relation to the family, and how successful therapy will be.

How does the family distribute itself? Do the parents sit next to each other? Does a child sit between them? Does a family member pull his chair back from the others? Do the girls sit close to each other? Do the boys sit far apart? Frequently, the way such sitting occurs gives the family therapist a clue to the underlying problems and to the alliances and splits in the family.

Typically, one of the children will be presented by a parent as the "problem." He is therefore the identified patient. It is best for the therapist to begin the session by saying something like, "Before we talk about some of the problems in the family, I'd like to say 'hello' to each of you and to find out something about you." He should then address the parent who made the initial contact saying something like,

"It's nice to meet you in person, Mrs. Jones." He should then address himself to the other parent. In this way, he is recognizing the existence and importance of the marital subsystem. He can then turn to the other members of the family. It is helpful to follow some sequence based on age. In this way, the sibling subsystem is acknowledged and the fact that there are differences among the children. This first meeting is a *warm-up* phase. It is important for two reasons: First, it shows the family the therapist's personality, which is something each of them has only been able to fantasize, and diminishes the "therapeutic mystique" by mitigating the transference phenomenon; second, it says indirectly that the "family problem" is not the only issue or fact of life in the family.

This simple first phase is important because the therapist is an outsider and he is being judged by the family as to his worthiness to be allowed inside the family boundaries. Accommodating himself to the family enables him to join the system, and anything he can to do accomplish this is important. He is showing himself to the family before he asks them to expose themselves.

Relabeling the "Problem." Phase two begins after all the family members have been met. The therapist initiates it by saying to the parent who made the contact, "I'm wondering, Mrs. Jones, if you would tell me what brings you to see me." Or "Could you tell me in what way you think I can help you?"

These simple statements communicate to the family certain important attitudes of the therapist. Asking Mrs. Jones to state her reason for seeking help makes her put her request into the specific form of defining a person or a feeling or a behavior as the family problem. For example, it is certain that other family members will not agree with the mother's formulation of the problem. Instead of making this obvious comment, the therapist can conclude this phase of the process by noting, "It seems that some of you have different ideas on what the problem is in this family." This second phase relabels or redefines the problem. By proceeding in this way, the therapist avoids painful hassles with family members about the "real" problem.

Spreading the Problem. Phase three heightens the conflict in the family by pointing out the different ways how the problem may be defined. The therapist, having listened to the parents or their formulation of the problem and perhaps also listened to the children's comments or objections, may simply reformulate the problem quite differently as a kind of hypothesis, getting all to think differently about the "real" issues. This is also a way of pointing out the family's need for outside help. It tends to reduce guilt and to enhance hope. Comments on the pain in the family, its frustration, unhappiness, and so on are useful in emphasizing the impotence of the family system to solve its own problems.

Need for Change. Phase four begins when the therapist asks the family what solutions have been tried in the past in dealing with its pain. The issue is getting the family to focus on change. The therapist may ask: "What have you done about this problem?" and "Have you done anything about this problem?" These statements are made to reinforce awareness of the inability of the family either (1) to find successful techniques for dealing with the problem, or (2) to point out that nothing constructive has been done about the problem so far. It stresses the need for new attempts to solve the problem or develop new techniques. In either case, the emphasis is on *change* among all the

family members. The therapist focuses on behavioral change and the inability up to this point of family members to make those changes. This narrows down the problem to behavior and keeps it within the boundaries of the family.

Changing Pathways. Phase five begins when the therapist begins to make his interventions into the family by means of suggestions. In more technical terms, he begins to try to change the pathways of communication by making interventions. To illustrate: he may request that an uninvolved parent take charge of a child's behavior, thus building an alliance between that parent and the child while putting some distance between the child and the overinvolved parent. He may ask the uninvolved parent to plan a day of fun with the child he cannot talk to and not to tell the other parent about it. Or he may ask the mother to teach the child how to light matches with the help of a child who plays mother's helper (Minuchin, 1974). The possibilities are endless.

These suggestions for how the initial interview should go follow most closely the procedures of the structural school but are similar for the other family approaches as well. More family background information, or more concentration on family of origin, or more use of specific tactics such as paradoxical injunctions might be features by other schools of family therapy. However, in all schools, the therapist informs the family that each member is part of the process and that any problem is never to be seen as the personal property of that person, but always involves two or more family members, and that the behavior of the family in the here-and-now is either creating or perpetuating the problem.

The first interview is important in family therapy as in other approaches because it concerns the issue of the therapeutic

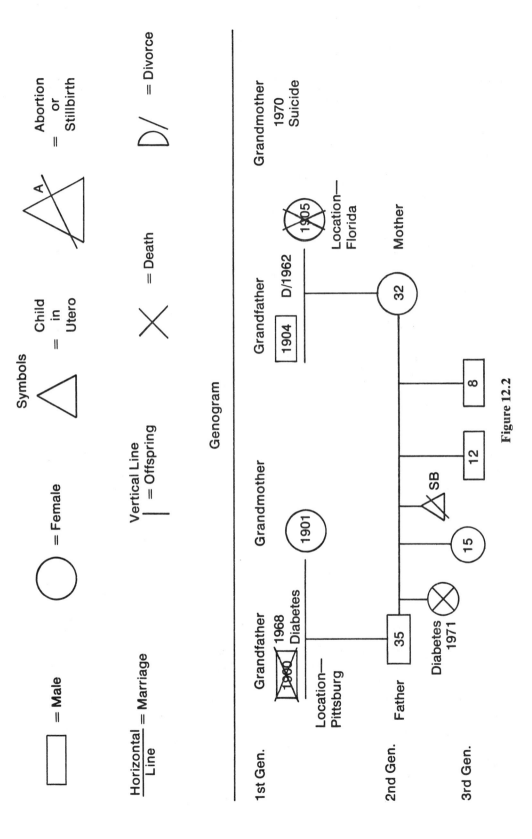

Symbols

◯ = Female

▢ = Male

△ = Child in Utero

Vertical Line | = Offspring

△ with A = Abortion or Stillbirth

✕ = Death

Horizontal Line ――― = Marriage

⌒/ = Divorce

Genogram

1st Gen.

Grandfather 1960 1968 Diabetes
Location— Pittsburg

Grandmother 1901

Grandfather 1904 D/1962

Grandmother 1970 Suicide

1905 Location— Florida

2nd Gen.

Father 35

Diabetes 1971

Mother 32

3rd Gen.

15   SB   12   8

Figure 12.2

contract. It should state in a clear manner what family therapy is. In addition to these theoretical goals, it should begin the process, if possible, in the session itself by not only talking about the process but reenacting it.

Use of Techniques. Some techniques employed by family therapists include the following:

Reenactment. If a presenting problem is the inability of a father and son to talk to each other, instead of asking for an example, the therapist might request that the two talk to each other in the session. If the father complains that when he tries to talk to his son, his wife interferes, the therapist might ask them to begin talking and then have her intrude into their conversation. If a problem can be reenacted in the therapy session, this is frequently done. The obvious advantage of this approach is that the therapist can see for himself what is happening in the family and he does not have to rely on reports. This is an effective technique, what Moreno called "psychodrama *in situ,*" because so many complaints relate to the inability of two people to talk with each other. Communication problems can become the major substance of the sessions.

Homework. As the name indicates, this refers to actions the therapist asks family members to perform between sessions. It has the value of making the therapy sessions places where solutions to problems are found and not just where talking takes place. In addition, it accustoms family members to understand that if they change their behavior, they can change how they feel and think as well. The homework assignments restructure family pathways by building coalitions and changing the intimacy-distance lines between members.

Family sculpting. As mentioned previously (page 464), this is the name given to a process by which the dimensions of closeness and power within the family are examined in a nonverbal manner. For example, a father is asked to describe his parents and his place in the family not by words but by using space. Family sculpting has the advantage of making visible feelings about family structures. It also explains to current family members reasons why their parents may act in a certain way, as one of the concepts underlying family sculpting is that people tend to repeat earlier patterns (Papp, Silverstein, & Carter, 1973).

Genogram. Family-system theorists, in particular, are interested in the emotional climate of a family and how this exerts influence on the relationships within the family system. Boundaries within the family, between the family and the outside world, and membership within the family are some of the more pertinent issues that some believe can best be handled by using this approach. A *genogram* is "a structural diagram of a family's three-generational relationship system. This diagram is a road map of the family relationship system" (Guerin & Pendagast, 1976, p. 452). It is a means of getting at significant issues in a more graphic manner than simply talking about them. It is widely used by followers of Bowen's system although other schools of thought employ genograms also (see Figure 12.2).

Behavior-Modification Techniques. Some family therapists use techniques adapted from behavior modification. It should be noted, however, that in general, family therapists conceptualize these procedures differently. For example, a family therapist might use behavior-modification techniques with a family whose presenting problem was an encopretic child. Nevertheless, the therapist would still maintain that the child's problem was essentially an interpersonal one involving a nonverbal comment on some aspect of it, whereas a behavior-modification therapist might accept the presenting problem as the "problem."

Multiple-Family Therapy. This technique involves seeing several families at the same time. It has a long history in the field of family therapy (Laqueur, 1973). It has two advantages. First, it offers family members a glimpse of other families and allows them to see firsthand that there are similarities in problems, enabling family members to identify with others; second, by permitting others to participate in a quasi-therapist role, it tends to lessen the authority of the therapist, which at times may be most advantageous. Vincent Foley (1975), for example, has found that with black, disadvantaged families, multiple-family therapy helps hasten the therapeutic alliance by breaking down hostile feelings of the family for a white therapist.

The techniques of modifications mentioned above are only illustrative. Since family therapy is based on a model that sees pathology as the result of dysfunctional relationships, it is freer than other approaches in adopting techniques to help change the interactional system. Family therapy is open to any number of techniques as long as they serve to change family process.

Length of Treatment. Family-therapy treatment can last from a few sessions to a period of years. As mentioned previously, structural and strategic interventionists tend to be briefer than object-relationists and family-system therapists. Gerald Zuk (1975) sees the length of treatment as dependent on the goals presented by the family. If its main goal is to reduce tension, sessions tend to be 1 to 6 interviews. If symptom reduction is the aim, it more likely will be 10 to 15 sessions. If better

communication is sought, 25 to 30 sessions over a 6- to 8-month period are called for. If a restructuring of the family with better differentiation of family members is considered, the length will tend to be 40 more sessions over an extended period.

Zuk also relates goals and length of the therapy to socioeconomic factors as well as verbal ability. His analysis would seem to conform to the experience of many therapists outside as well as inside family therapy. Generally, better educated, highly verbal people with some financial resources are more attracted to long-range therapy than those who do not have these assets.

Indications and Contraindications. Lyman Wynne (1965) suggested that problems such as adolescent separation and interlocking problems, those one family member believes cannot be solved without the cooperation of another, were good indicators of the need for family therapy. In general, problems of paranoia and sexual acting out in the family are considered poor indicators for this kind of treatment.

It is difficult to make absolute statements about the issue of what problems are suitable for family therapy other than to say that therapists who incline more toward a system concept would tend to see most psychological adjustment problems as amenable to family therapy, and those coming from a more traditional psychoanalytic background are inclined to be less certain. The issue of what kinds of problems are amenable to family therapy is one that needs further investigation.

Mechanisms of Psychotherapy

Despite all the theoretical concepts any system uses to justify its existence, ultimately one question matters, "How does change take place?'' Within that question, one finds related ones such as: Can the process that one describes be analyzed into its component parts? Is it measurable? Is it teachable? In the final analysis, is it beyond articulation? Is it an art or a science?

At this point in family therapy, there is more speculation than hard data. Most therapists do not take pretests and post-tests either in individual or family therapy. Most of the data gathered are self-reports of the families. Unfortunately, self-reports can be unreliable. With these observations in mind, let us now proceed with some tentative answers.

Family therapists concentrate on changes in behavior as evidence of progress. Changes in feelings and thinking are considered less important. How is behavior change accomplished? There is a growing belief among family therapists that therapy is a power struggle between the therapist and the client. It is a battle of wills in which the stronger one prevails.

Jay Haley (1963) drew an analogy between the therapist and the hypnotist in that both seem to ask for change while at the same time denying it. Haley took the position that the therapist has the responsibility for change and that failure is always his failure. It is his responsibility to analyze problems correctly and to devise tactics that lead people into change. Feelings do not produce change nor does thinking. Empathy, although important for engaging the family, is not corrective. Insight is even less helpful because it can provide a convenient way of avoiding change, giving the family intellectual games to play. The name of the game is power. The therapist must create situations that force the family into a bind. Either it continues its behavior, but does so under the command of the therapist, or it rebels, thus producing the desired change. In either case, the family system is under assault.

Most family therapists, although perhaps not taking as extreme a position as Haley, would tend to accept his thinking, seeing all family therapy as a power struggle. Family therapists tend to be more open about the power element in therapy. Giving directives or telling people what to do can be either overt or covert. In either case, it is at the heart of therapy. The nondirective therapist, for example, is covertly giving directives by picking up on the client's comments about feelings. He is teaching him that a response is given when he approaches things in that manner. The cues are reinforced by other nonverbal comments, such as nods of the head and smiles.

Some family therapists might object to the emphasis Haley gives to the power struggle, but at some level, all will likely agree with the notion of relabeling as a critical step in the change process. To accept this concept is to agree with the idea of power as the main ingredient in change. To illustrate: a family comes for help with a child who will not go to school. A long story of the family's failure to be effective in dealing with this problem is recounted. Kindness has been tried and found wanting, punishment has followed and has not worked, and now the child is labeled as ''sick.'' He is labeled a problem to the family and has become an outcast or pariah. The therapist, however, may see the school phobia as the child's response to difficulties between husband and wife. This becomes clearer as the parents talk about the problem, the mother being overinvolved with the child and the father underinvolved. The therapist may suggest that the father spend more time with the child and that he should take command of the problem.

The therapist may have in his own mind relabeled the problem as a conflict between husband and wife, which is not being dealt with overtly in their roles as father and mother. Instead of bringing this redefinition or relabeling into the open where it can be denied, the therapist may shift the family balance about, in effect neutralizing the mother's power. This can be made even more effective if he then instructs the wife that she is to keep after the husband to make sure he carries out his job of being a good father.

Once the child's behavior has calmed down as a result of this power change, the covert conflict of husband and wife will surface as that of husband-and-wife rather than father-and-mother. At this point, the child might be dismissed from the sessions and work might be done with just the couple. Changes have been accomplished not by interpretation or insight or by improving communication but by making structural variations in the way in which the family operates. Thus, the therapist who covertly reinterprets the family's problem relabels the pathology and suggests changes without giving explanations, leading to new behaviors and affecting family relationships by his intervention.

At this point, a therapist might want to work with issues of closeness or meaning with the couple or investigate areas of differentiation of self.

This example of a school-phobia problem taken from a structural family model illustrates the process of relabeling, but similar examples could be given from any of the other schools as well. Change in family therapy begins with a shift from the way the family sees the problem to the way the therapist sees it. This is best done by maneuvers that realign the family rather than cognitive measures—by action, not talk.

Change in family therapy is accomplished by modifying the structures of the system. This means working on the triangles that compose it and producing new alignments. This in turn produces changes in behavior that influence feelings. Devising techniques that change existing structures is the major goal of psychotherapy for family therapy. Change in how the system operates produces change in individual members of the system.

APPLICATIONS

Problems

Family Problems. Problems labeled "family ones" by the family itself are most amenable to treatment. However, such presenting problems are rarely encountered. People with a disturbed member in their family rarely think the essential cause is that the family itself is in need of treatment. This should not be surprising since the idea of thinking in terms of systems—field psychology—has not filtered down to the public, and indeed the concept of restructuring the field is still a minority concept with psychotherapists. The general tendency in families and also among therapists is to locate and deal with the so-called identified patient who from the point of view of a family therapist is in reality the scapegoat for the family. However, from time to time, referring people, such as principals of schools or medical doctors, do realize that the symptomatic person is a function of a disordered family.

Marital Problems—Both Partners. Frequently family problems are labeled "marital problems" rather than "family problems." Marriage counseling is well known to most people, and columns on such problems are a staple in most magazines. Newspapers, too, carry columns such as *Ann Landers* and *Dear Abby,* and a large percent of their questions concern marriage. However, even though a client may call and state, "We are having some problems with our marriage," it is soon evident that one of the partners to the marriage believes the problem is the exclusive domain of the other. In an initial interview of a couple, the caller will often begin with, "My husband drinks too much," or "My wife is depressed," or "I know I'm not perfect, but my wife/husband *really* has problems." The clear implication is that the other one is the so-called identified patient.

Individual Problems. At times one encounters the isolated individual who is truly alone, not part of any family system. This, however, is rare. Most people in our society are married and have families. A spouse, children, parents, and siblings are relationships that are deepest and most lasting. Literally, we never get over them. They should be the context within which therapy takes place. Individual problems can be seen as the exclusive property of a person or as a response to the context of a family. Family therapy clearly opts for the latter.

Other Relationships. It should be clear that system thinking applies to any system, not just the family. This means that difficulties in meetings, PTA groups, and other social systems can be analyzed as individual problems or system difficulties. When seen in the former way, one concludes that some people are "difficult," or "destructive." If seen in the latter way, one looks at the process of the system as the cause of the behavior. The staff member who "messes up" and forgets can be considered as "dumb" or as responding to the system in a hostile nonverbal manner.

Family therapists state that all systems are built of interlocking triangles, not just family systems. Analyzing the structure of such triangles and learning how to deal with them by responding instead of reacting is a possibility open to all. Family therapy is system thinking and it involves a search to find ways to change the system. The first step is to analyze the structure of the system; the second, to see one's role in it; the third, to change one's behavior in that system. These concepts can be applied to any human-relations system whether it be a club, a factory, a team, a military unit, a congregation, a union, a partnership, and so on.

Evaluation

The most neglected aspect of any therapy is *evaluation.* Most therapists make unprovable claims for their system. This is due to the model chosen. To illustrate: if we follow a traditional model regarding the client as the problem, we use labels such as "schizophrenic," "schizoid problems," or "obsessive-compulsive." We then make interpretations on what is the "real" problem as distinguished from the presenting problem. In no way can these be evaluated because such labels say nothing about what is a soluble problem and how it might be cured.

The most obvious example is the label "schizophrenic." What does the word mean? Is it an entity observable in the same way as a physical problem? Clearly not. What then is a schizophrenic? Someone who is different from other people.

On the other hand, if we describe interaction in terms of behavior, we are able to make evaluations of effectiveness. If we can measure, count, or observe the phenomenon, we can measure the value of the therapeutic maneuvers. Thus, if in a family, the diagnosis is that a child is "maladjusted" and if attempts are made to "adjust" him, evaluating success can be difficult. However, if the issue is defined as "he does not do chores," evaluation is easy. If he now does do his chores, a clear-cut, easily evaluated goal has been achieved.

Family therapy attempts to use such an approach, specifying what therapy outcomes should be. This is mostly true of the structured and the strategic-intervention schools of thought because they are frankly symptom oriented and so more amenable to this kind of thinking.

Family therapists are aware of the need for research. In 1967 a group of distinguished family therapists met together with family researchers in Philadelphia for a dialogue in which they blended clinical expertise and sophisticated statistical thinking (Framo, 1972).

A brief account of research in the area of family interaction is by Jules Riskin and Elaine Faunce (1972). In addition to reviewing the literature of the 1960s, they add a valuable glossary of terms. A more recent evaluation of both marriage and family research is by Ronald Cronwell, David Olson, and D. Fournier (1976).

The most complete analysis in the area of marriage and family is published by the University of Minnesota (Aldous & Hill, 1967; Aldous & Dahl, 1974a, 1974b; Olson & Dahl, 1975). The first two volumes cover the field of research from 1900 to 1972. Volume 3 is an updating together with a summary of the literature in 1973–74. Each succeeding volume is to cover one year. These volumes are listings and are not critical reviews. Most of the listings do not pertain to family therapy, but to the sociology of the family, and are an invaluable source of information on the family.

The basic problem of research into the family focuses on the issue of methodology. A cursory glance at the literature shows a weakness in the methodological approach of most studies. In particular, selection of families has been poorly controlled, and the relationship between theory and definitions is at best tenuous.

The need for replication is obvious. Too many studies are made with limited populations and the results extrapolated. Above all, longitudinal studies are required, especially those dealing with symptom relief. The traditional response to change of symptom is that the symptom will appear elsewhere, that is, such change is not real and true change. It is not enough for a therapist to make the statement that the symptomatic behavior has disappeared, but he must also show that it has not returned and that the system is indeed functioning at a higher level of productivity.

The problems presented to a researcher looking at family therapy are more extensive because of the number of variables to be controlled. Designing studies in which this can be done is a fruitful field for exploration. If therapy, using any model whatever, wants to be taken seriously in the future, it will be absolutely necessary that research justify those results. In general, family therapists are probably more aware of this need than therapists from other schools.

Mention should be made briefly of the factors to be covered by such research. First, it must include basic structures of a family. What is biological? What is cultural? Second, the differences between the roles of husband-wife and father-mother must be covered. It was suggested previously that one way of looking at these is from the point of view of feedback; the husband-wife relationship is open to instant feedback, and father-mother roles have a delay in them. This observation is only one of many that might be made on such differences. The essence of research must be the relationship of family interaction to the development of the personality of the individual. This is the key to the future of family therapy because it will answer the question of the value of dealing with a system as opposed to seeing individuals. Most material produced in the field has been the work of clinicians. It is important and of great value but it is limited by the bias of the clinician.

It is imperative, therefore, that any research involving family therapy test its hypotheses in a way acceptable to scientists and investigate a most neglected area—the moral family, that is, the symptom-free family. Such studies must be carried out *longitudinally*. One is constantly reading about studies that produce instant cures. But do they last? On what basis are such judgments made? How rigid are the controls in the research? Researchers into family process need clinicians to bring them down from ivory towers of theory, and clinicians need researchers to stop them from building ivory towers of theory based on poor samples, contaminated variables, and extrapolated conclusions. Perhaps in the spirit of our times, one might suggest that, if a wedding were not in order, at least clinicians and researchers could consider living together for a time. The results would be invaluable for both.

Treatment

In family therapy, the mode, or the way treatment is carried on, will vary among therapists following their theoretical orientations and/or differences in personality. Therapy is always a blend of three factors that interact: (1) the theoretical stance of the therapist; (2) his personal style of relating; (3) the type of family he faces, its current state of functioning, and where it is developmentally.

Theoretical Stance. Therapists of the object-relations and family-system schools are concerned with issues that deal with generational conflict, intimacy or distance, and unresolved problems of the past, in particular, grief. Therapists who are more system oriented, those of the structural and the strategic-intervention schools, will be more symptom oriented and concerned with how the system boundaries are structured and what techniques may prove helpful in getting change to occur. If a therapist believes issues of the past are important, the therapy will tend to resemble a more traditional approach and be of a longer duration. If he is governed more by the notion of equifinality, his therapy will tend to be more situational and of shorter duration.

Personal Style. Personal style varies widely among family therapists. There are some basic concepts that one must accept to be classified as a family therapist, but the manner in which one works will be highly individualized. Unlike other training approaches, such as psychoanalysis, family therapy is not rigidly structured. Some therapists are warm and empathic; others tend to be more distant and cognitive; still others use a virtually idiosyncratic approach. What binds them together as family therapists is the way in which they conceptualize family interaction, not the way in which they operationalize it. Family therapy has long regarded this as its strength because it allows for the personality of the therapist to shine through so he can be himself and not play a role called "therapist." This is also why family therapy has not been controlled by any single group in the field of mental health but has been open to people from varied backgrounds.

Type of Family. The family the therapist meets also can be classified according to its (a) closeness or distance, (b) current state of functioning, and (c) where it is developmentally.

Whether a family can be classified as enmeshed-disengaged or open-closed will be important to the therapist in his evaluation. These classifications enable him to know how much the family will open up to admit an outsider or close to keep him out. More importantly, it will give him a good idea of the flexibility of the system and how much stress it can handle. This in turn will govern the tactics used to change the structure.

Current state of functioning refers to the amount of stress that presently exists. Is this a family under unusual pressure and about to "fall apart," or is it reporting minor chronic problems? The therapist is interested in finding out what therapeutic leverage he will have. Families in crisis are generally more open to outside inputs than those that are not in crisis. There is less resistance to the therapist. Some family therapists, such as Minuchin and Barcai (1969), argue for the necessity sometimes of creating a disturbance in the system if one is not present. The issue is one of homeostasis. The family frequently wants to maintain or reestablish the old balance and cannot accomplish this. They then call in a professional, one with expertise, to produce calm once again. This is often found in rigid families facing the problem of adolescence.

Developmental issues, too, cause constant family tensions. People are always undergoing change because of the need to adapt to ever-changing circumstances. Intimacy wanes between a husband and wife, economic changes affect the marriage, and above all, children grow into adolescents. Parents who tend to be overprotective and all-knowing often have problems with their growing children. The need of the family to open and allow the children to move out is absent and conflict follows between the generations. The behavior of such children is labeled as "bad" or "sick," and finally a therapist is summoned. The therapist must decide what are the developmental issues in the family. Some recent research indicates that such families are intrusive, overresponsive to each other, intolerant of change, and tend to produce family members who suffer psychosomatic symptoms, especially abdominal pain (Liebman et al., 1976). The therapist will seek to alleviate the presenting problems but more importantly strive to restructure the system to eliminate the need for such behavior.

Family therapy then is a blend of theory, style, and family structure. Theory will conceptualize the presenting problem as one of the system. It will be attacked in line with the style of the therapist using a variety of tactics. The depth of the problems will be determined in part by the factors mentioned: closeness or distance, crisis state or chronic state, and stage of development of the family, that is, a new family, school problems, adolescent problems, transition to marriage of the children, and so on.

Taking into account the three factors of therapy, the therapist then makes a choice of how to proceed. He is like a director of a drama. One might well liken family therapy to the theatre, in particular Brechtian theatre, with its use of paradox as a means of dramatizing family issues. The comparison is not bizarre but in line with what family therapists would consider the relationship of therapist to the client-family.

Therapy is a drama—a tension-filled process that takes place between a therapist and traditionally one person or, more recently, with a couple or a family. The focus may be on the past, present, or future, but in any event, the process of change, whether of feeling, thinking, or doing, is always in the present. Therapy means a change of one or all of these ways of speaking about human beings. How is it accomplished?

Family therapists in general would say that therapy begins by the therapist informing the client or clients that things are not what they seem to be. Psychoanalysts will interpret seemingly harmless dreams or actions into complex entities that are largely unconscious. Other therapies use similar ways of confounding clients. It is evident that therapy is a power struggle. Family therapists explain the struggle in terms of communication theory, which says that every communication is both a report and a command that attempts to define the relationship. To illustrate: if I talk about trivia, I am telling the other person I am not interested in getting serious about our relationship. If, however, he asks, "Why don't you ever say anything about how you feel?" he is attempting to change the relationship and move it to a more intense level.

This shift can be overt or covert. It is overt when the other says so in words; covert, when it is more subtle, when done behaviorally. This method, in fact, is a very powerful one because usually it is followed by the comment, "I can't help it." The person is saying that such behavior is involuntary. The child who "throws up," the wife who has "blinding headaches," the husband who "forgets," can be viewed as having problems in themselves but also as covertly commenting on the relationships within their family system. These behaviors or symptoms can be considered as tactics in the struggle to deal with the relationship.

In family therapy, the therapist sees them as control tactics, but instead of pointing to them and analyzing their purpose, he will often say, "Of course you can't help it," and then tell the person to continue doing voluntarily what he claims is involuntary. He thereby creates a *benign* "double bind," in which the person is faced with either (a) stopping the behavior, or (b) continuing the behavior but now doing it under control of the therapist. In either case, he is showing that it is voluntary. Frankl (1960) calls this process *paradoxical intention.*

The family therapist may attempt to change the *context* of the system so the previous undesired behavior is no longer possible. The literature abounds with examples of how this can be done (Haley, 1963; Bowen, 1971; Watzlawick, Weakland, & Fisch, 1974; Minuchin, 1974). In more technical terms, changing the context means producing not just a substitution of one thing for another (first-order change) but a change of the structure (second-order change) (Watzlawick, Weakland, & Fisch, 1974). One effective way of doing this is the aforementioned "prescribing the symptom," telling the person to continue doing what he has been doing. For example, a therapist may demand that an overinvolved woman become even more concerned about her children and even to set aside a special hour each day for "worrying." This use of paradox is an example of how one might prescribe a symptom to produce a second-order change.

Family therapists maintain that therapy is a power struggle for control of the relationship, and that this is true of all therapies. The "insight" the psychoanalyst talks about is in reality getting the analysand to see reality through the eyes of the analyst. The "positive unconditioned regard" of the Rogerian is the victory of the counselor over the client done in a benign, covert manner. The family therapist will argue that in all therapies, success depends upon the therapist winning the battle and that this struggle is best described in terms of changing the context in which the therapy takes place by changing the frame of reference.

Management

The Setting. Family therapists function in all traditional settings and add the possibility of working in the home and the probability of at least making one home visit during treatment. This, of course, is understandable in light of the emphasis given to the context in which treatment takes place. Some would go so far as to say, "The beginning family therapist should require this (home visits) of himself routinely, and *without exception*" (Bloch, 1973, p. 44).

Seeing people in their ordinary home conditions has two distinct advantages: (1) People tend to be more relaxed and open on their own turf; and (2) the important issue of nurturance is more easily observed in the home. *To whom does a child go for attention? How is the request handled? What kinds of interaction go on between the parents in relation to the children's immediate needs? With what warmth or lack of it are they nurtured?* Observing these things in an office or clinic setting is sometimes impossible and usually unsatisfactory. The therapist gets a better idea of what is going on by visiting the family.

Using the home as the setting for all or part of family therapy sessions is also effective when it is helpful to reduce the distance between the therapist and the family as, for example, when a white therapist is seeing a black family (Foley, 1975).

How Patients Come. Most referrals for family therapy come from mothers looking for help in dealing with either (a) adjustment problems in school for children making the transition from home to school; or (b) adolescent conflicts centering about how much freedom to give the growing child or parents' inability to maintain control. Experience has shown that the most effective way of dealing with such referrals is to ask the whole family to come in initially for three sessions as a way of getting to know each other. This is normally sufficient time to redefine the problem in terms of other family members as well as working on the present problem. Objections to bringing in other family members can be handled by saying, "Of course he's got a problem, but I can't do much about it without your help." Since most people like to think of themselves as being helpful, this usually will bring them into a session. If the therapist can get them physically present, he should be able to involve them in treatment.

Confidentiality. Murray Bowen (1975) believes the issue of confidentiality must be reevaluated in the light of family therapy. This does not mean the family therapist becomes an indiscriminate gossip, but that he uses his knowledge for the good of the system. The shift in perspective from seeing the individual as the client to seeing the family as the client necessitates a shift from viewing the relationship of an individual to a therapist to one in which the family is the center. How a therapist accomplishes his role in regard to confidentiality takes much sophistication and clinical skill. The family members are trying to set up an alliance between themselves and the therapist by triangling him into their relationships. This he must avoid or he will be pulled into the system. He must create a new context in which behavior will change, and he cannot do this if he gets pulled into the ways in which the family normally interacts.

There are several ways of handling confidentiality. One is to announce at the first session that the therapist is relating to the family as a whole and therefore will not see individuals alone, and any attempts at violating this rule, such as a telephone call, will be reported to the rest of the family. If it becomes necessary to see parts of the family alone, say, the parents alone or only the children, the therapist should inform all concerned that he or she will make the choice of sharing or not sharing what he finds out with other family members.

A second way of handling requests for secrets is to ask how others feel about the alliance between the therapist and a family member who asks for a private interview. For example, a husband asks to see the therapist alone. Before granting the request, the therapist inquires about how other family members feel. "Mrs. Jones, your husband wants to tell me something that he doesn't want you to know. Do you think that's helpful to you or to the family?" Such a question focuses on the value of secrets to the family process.

In family therapy, raising the question of confidentiality is a ploy to control the system. It is a way of tying the hands of the therapist and setting up an alliance between himself and another family member. These "secret" sessions are to be discouraged. This does not mean that each and every issue in a family should be talked about in front of all other members. Family therapy is particularly concerned about boundaries between the generations. The sexual life of the husband and wife is a private matter and need not be discussed in the presence of the children. Similarly, the privacy of a child must be preserved in enmeshed and intrusive families.

Family structure can be destroyed by collusion between a member of one generation and another. Here the legitimate boundaries are not observed, to the detriment of all. The family therapist must not become part of the destructive process by entering into separate secret pacts with some family members in the name of confidentiality. The most effective way for a therapist to avoid the problem is to make clear from the beginning that he will not tolerate such alliances. If that is clear, the problem will rarely arise.

Recordings. Family therapists have pioneered in the area of showing others what they do. Most therapies are arcane; the outsider has little knowledge of how sessions are conducted. This is not true in family therapy. Recordings, both video and audio, are common. The use of one-way mirrors is increasing. Live supervision, where the supervisor watches the session in progress and calls in his observations on a phone or even enters the therapy session, is also used. Of course, for all of these observations, permission must be given by the family.

Recordings are invaluable for family therapy. They serve a double purpose: First, they preserve the process of the family therapy sessions and can be used for teaching purposes; second, the material used with one family can be shared with another. For example, the Browns may have a problem similar to that of the Smiths. Showing them a videotape of the Smiths may provide the kind of feedback necessary for them to change. Showing the family themselves at earlier points can also be an enlightening experience. In particular, videotape is invaluable for getting at nonverbal communications that take place among the family members (Alger, 1973).

Family therapy has the most complete collection of films and videotapes of any therapeutic approach. Those offering material include:

Eastern Pennsylvania Psychiatric
Institute
Family Psychiatry Department
Henry Avenue and Abbottsford Road
Philadelphia, Pennsylvania 19129

Mental Research Institute
555 Middlefield Road
Palo Alto, California 94301

Nathan W. Ackerman Family Institute
149 East Seventy-eighth Street
New York, New York 10021

Philadelphia Child Guidance Clinic
Two Children's Center
34th Street and Civic Center Boulevard
Philadelphia, Pennsylvania 19104

Vincent D. Foley, Ph.D.
St. John's University
Department of Counselor Education
New York, New York 11439

CASE EXAMPLE

Background

Mr. Jones had been referred by a local minister who had seen him previously for a problem with drinking. The man subsequently quit drinking and joined AA. Shortly thereafter his wife went into a depression, and following that his son was arrested for stealing. The man called the minister, saying, "My son is in trouble." Sensing that the issue involved all the family members, the minister referred the man to a therapist who dealt with "family problems."

The family therapist on the telephone asked Mr. Jones to bring his wife and son to the initial session. After a brief introduction, Mr. Jones began by saying that about a year ago he decided, at the urging of his boss, to give up drinking and he also stated that he began drinking 19 years previously, shortly after the birth of his son. As a first corrective step, he had gone to his minister who had urged him to join AA and become active in the church. He continued seeing the minister for about three months. About that time, his wife complained of feeling "down." She went to a family doctor and was given medication. She became worse and was sent to a psychiatrist who suggested that at age 45 she was beginning to experience a change of life and a loss of feeling sexually attractive to her husband. She began seeing the psychiatrist weekly for private sessions. During this period, their son, who had been considered by all as a "model child," became more overtly hostile in his comments, careless about his appearance, and indifferent in his school work. Finally, he was arrested for stealing an automobile but was told he would not be charged with the crime if he got "help." The father sent him to the psychiatrist who referred him to a psychologist whose field of expertise was adolescent problems. The psychologist agreed to see the boy privately on a weekly basis.

The father stated he did not see any change in either his wife or son and was becoming more upset himself. The wife said she was not being helped but would continue in treatment; the son said his sessions were a waste of time and he wanted to quit. The father said he was tempted to return to drinking, and this fear finally drove him again to call his minister.

In retelling the story, the father mentioned his fear of "falling off the wagon," and the son, quiet until then, commented, "At least then we'd know what to do with you.'' The therapist asked the son to elaborate on the comment, and he said that since sobriety his father had become a "pompous ass." The mother smiled at this comment as she looked at the son approvingly.

The therapist then asked the wife to "tell me something about yourself.'' She began by mentioning the difference between life before and after her husband's drinking. It was clear that she had more roles while her husband was drinking and also more gratification. When the father was drinking, the son acted in the role of surrogate husband and had a closeness with the mother, which was inappropriate—a violation of the generational boundary.

The therapist began his first intervention by asking the son John to change places with him so the son could sit next to his father. The therapist then sat between the father and mother so the boundary between them might be visibly established. In moving his position, he commented to the mother, "As a good mother, Mrs. Jones, I'm sure you'd like to see your husband and son get along better.'' "Of course,'' she responded, although her face indicated otherwise. The therapist then asked the father and son to talk about interests they had in common.

Problem

The case is typical of many in that a number of different analyses of it can be given. For example, the father can be considered an orally dependent man as evidenced by his drinking. He could be seen alone in treatment. The drinking of the father and the depression of the mother can be viewed from a communication point of view as signs of their inability to express themselves in words. If this is the formulation of the problem, the therapist can work on their communication. Or the therapist can see the behavior of all three as related to each other and more importantly as contributing to the dysfunction in the here-and-now. From this viewpoint, one would want to work with all three members of the system. This last viewpoint is known as *field thinking* and represents family-therapy concepts in that each person is viewed in the context of the system.

Two observations may be made about the minister's role in Mr. Jones's sobriety. First, he failed to take into account the positive role of alcohol in the family system. Simply put: the drinking served a homeostatic function in the family. Mr. Jones was taken care of; Mrs. Jones had a meaning and purpose in doing this; John received special attention from his mother. When Mr. Jones stopped drinking, the position of everyone changed. Second, the initiative for change came less from Mr. Jones than from his boss who had promised him a substantial raise. The minister reinforced the passivity by being so active in moving Mr. Jones toward involvement in AA and the church. Mr. Jones went from a dependency on his wife to a dependency on the minister and then on AA.

The problem in this case is to understand how each of the family members is entangled in the system and to observe the ongoing patterns of interaction that keep the system dysfunctional. It is the role of the family therapist to see this interaction and to make interventions that will restructure the system.

One could analyze the family in terms of dysfunctional triangles. The wife by her overcloseness to the son prevented her husband from getting close. He in turn triangled in a "bottle." Having gotten rid of the bottle, he then triangled in work and the church. The son's growing up and wanting more distance from the mother, combined with the husband's distancing, produced depression in the wife as she was still isolated from her husband even when he was sober. She got depressed as a way of gaining recognition. This produced some sign of caring by the husband and guilt-induced caring by the son. However, the constant demands of his mother made the son angry, and he expressed this in his sullenness and eventually by stealing. The symptomatic response of all the family members can be regarded as tactics for survival and control of the system as well as properties of each person within it.

The therapist made the choice of intervening between father and son because he thought the best way of changing the system would be to get an alliance between them. At the same time, he put the mother in a bind by saying she should support such an alliance. Had he attacked the overcloseness by suggesting that the mother-son coalition was unhealthy, he probably would have met massive resistance. Rather than attacking, he felt a more effective strategy would be to create more closeness between father and son. This alliance, it is true, would produce more isolation for the mother, but instead of leading into a further depression, she could now bring this to the therapist who in turn could reintroduce it into the system.

At the initial session, father and son had agreed to go fishing, an activity they both enjoyed. It also gave them a time and place for talking. Predictably, such activity caused the wife to become upset. After several fishing weekends, the wife called the therapist saying she was very

happy about how things were going between her husband and son, but she now felt isolated. The therapist commented that he chose this alliance knowing it might cause her problems but did so because he knew she had great strength. He agreed, however, that it might be best to bring this problem up in the next session and further suggested that they leave John out of that session.

Mr. and Mrs. Jones came alone to the next session. Instead of dealing symptomatically with her isolation, she was able to verbalize it in the session. Mr. Jones at first was angry at his wife when she told him of her isolation. She responded to his anger by crying, and saying, "It's no use." The therapist commended Mr. Jones for his anger, interpreting it as a way of showing concern, but an ineffective way, because it turned off his wife. He then asked him if he wanted to take responsibility for moving toward his wife. The therapist continued probing the husband trying to find out how much commitment he wanted to make to the relationship and how much energy he wanted to invest. The delicate and tedious task of rebuilding their relationship was under way.

Treatment

In family therapy, as in other therapeutic approaches, one can discern various phases or stages. Three phases can be distinguished: (1) observation, (2) intervention, and (3) consolidation.

The initial interviews focus on observing patterns of interaction. What kinds of information are exchanged? By whom? And how? Can certain sequences be observed? What are the alliances and splits?

Although one can make interventions from the beginning, as noted in the case given, most family therapists tend to try out hypotheses before making interventions. These would be done to change the interaction of the system and constitute a second phase of treatment. Controlling the presence and absence of members at sessions, requesting people to dialogue with each other, and finding issues around which to build closeness, for example, fishing, are ways of intervening.

Consolidation is the last phase of treatment and most important. The presence of the therapist creates a new system; his absence may allow the old one to return. It is necessary, therefore, that he be sure his interventions are of such magnitude that they last after his removal from the system. The question to ask is, "Can the system function in my absence or will it again become dysfunctional?" Termination must be a process and not a sudden withdrawal from the family. The possibilities for growth and decline must be discussed and examined.

In the case of the Jones family, it was decided that the husband and wife would be seen twice a month, Mr. Jones and his son once a month, and the three together once a month. In this way, the marital subsystem, the father-son subsystem, and the family system itself would receive attention. The husband's tentative moves toward his wife diminished her feelings of isolation and, at the same time, made her less demanding of her son's attention. This removal of pressure enabled John to feel better toward his mother, which showed itself in his willingness to drive her to the store and to give other assistance. His father's attempts at moving closer made him feel more confidence in the father and his ability to take care of the needs of the mother. John then was able to move outside appropriately toward peers without either anger or guilt. Mr. Jones began to spend more time with

his wife because she was more responsive. His involvement in outside activities continued but in a more controlled way.

Resolution

In any family, there are individual problems usually seen in symptomatic ways, for example, feelings of depression; interpersonal problems seen in behavioral ways, such as husband overinvolved at work; family problems seen in the inability of family members to solve problems or to get closure on important issues.

The resolution of the Jones family meant restructuring the system so each member would have options other than the stereotyped ones they had shown. This was accomplished over a period of 24 sessions without getting involved in issues of why and when and staying with those of what and how.

Follow-up

After 24 sessions, the family was seen twice a month for a period of three months and then once a month for six months, at which time, on the basis of mutual consent, therapy was discontinued. In all, 36 sessions were held over a period of one and one-half years. Since that time (1972), no further help has been requested, and no symptomatic expressions of depression, drinking, or antisocial behavior have been reported.

Each family case is unique and has its own specifics. Treatment will be governed in part by the theories of the therapists and in part by the family. Some would work more on intergenerational issues and some more on symptoms. Some would hold fewer sessions, and some would hold more. In all cases, however, the focus would be on the system as the client and not on any single member in it.

SUMMARY

Family therapy started about the middle 1950s. The question must be asked about its future. Will it grow or will it decline? Its future looks bright for several reasons. First, the whole movement in therapy is away from a focus on the individual and toward the context in which one lives. Man is a social creature, and the more he is isolated from others, the less social and the more like animals he becomes. One need only look at the decay in our cities, produced in large measure by isolation, to see the truth of this proposition. Second, there is growing interest in family, in one's "roots." Interest in communal living is further evidence that if one cannot relate in the context into which one is born, one seeks a substitute family. These reasons give support to the feeling that family therapy will continue to grow in importance.

Family therapy is concerned with the most basic relationships in life, those of the family. Instead of dealing with the ghosts from the past, it brings them into the session itself. It teaches a person to be a self while remaining in touch with others. It attempts to hold on to both because each of them is of value. It strikes a balance between the self and the family because mental health requires a development of the self together with a meaningful relationship with others. Family therapy is more attuned to these needs than other approaches that emphasize one at the expense of the other.

George Mora (1974), a historian of psychiatry, notes, "Within the limits of psychiatry proper, there is no question that the field of family psychiatry will continue to develop, at the expense not only of individual psychotherapy but also of child and adolescent psychotherapy" (p. 71). This is due to the introduction of context into the process of therapy. No longer can the therapist lock himself into a room and shut out the world. If he is to produce change, it must begin by bringing significant others into the therapy.

This history of therapy in the movement from Freud to the present has gone from the individual to the interpersonal to the system. If therapy is to be viable in the future, it must become ecological since ecology studies organisms in relation to their environment, and family therapy is the most ecological of all therapies because it always looks at a person in his context, in relation to his environment. Health and sickness are not attributes of an individual alone but are produced by the world in which he lives. Change is contained within the system in which an individual lives. This power has only begun to be tapped, and those therapies that hope to survive must learn soon either to use the context of a client's life or cease to be effective.

ANNOTATED BIBLIOGRAPHY

Ackerman, Nathan; Lieb, Judith; Pearce, John (Eds.) *Family therapy in transition.* Boston: Little, Brown, 1970.
This is a collection of articles in which one finds Ackerman, Framo, and Paul among others. It represents to a large extent the thinking of what we have termed School 1 *(object relations),* especially Framo's *Symptoms from a Family Transactional Viewpoint.*

Foley, Vincent D. *An introduction to family therapy.* New York: Grune and Stratton, 1974.
This book is a primer meant for the beginning student in the field at a master's level. It is designed to be used for a one-semester course in family therapy. It is divided into four sections. Part one deals with the seminal ideas in the field: the double bind, pseudomutuality, schism and skew, mystification,

and general system theory. Part two treats the major historical figures: Nathan Ackerman, Virginia Satir, Don Jackson, Jay Haley, and Murray Bowen. Part three notes the similarities and differences in their concepts. Part four looks at the current state in the field and makes suggestions about the future.

This book provides the reader with a structure within which he can understand the evolution of thinking in family therapy from its beginnings to the present. In the light of it, he can read the works below with more understanding.

Guerin, Philip (Ed.) *Family therapy.* New York: Gardner Press, 1976.

This book contains Bowen's most recent thinking and numerous chapters by his followers. In addition to theoretical articles, there are sections on clinical issues and techniques that spell out theoretical concepts more concretely. Although the book represents School 2 *(family systems),* it also has articles by structuralist thinkers and strategic-intervention therapists that give the reader an overall view of the wide range of theory and practice in the field within the confines of one book.

Minuchin, Salvador. *Families and family therapy.* Cambridge: Harvard University Press, 1974.

This is the best explanation of the theory of the structural position by its major exponent. Most of the book is taken up with examples of how the *structural approach* (School 3) is used with functional and dysfunctional families at various points in the developmental process.

Watzlawick, Paul; Weakland, John; & Fisch, Richard. *Change: Principles of problem formation and problem resolution.* New York: Norton, 1974.

This book contains a complete explanation of the *strategic-intervention approach* (School 4) to therapy. It gives philosophical concepts upon which it is based together with excellent and detailed examples of how these concepts are applied. It explains the difference between first- and second-order change and the function of paradox in reframing messages.

CASE READINGS

Family therapy has an extensive amount of material on videotape, audiotape, and case studies. Two works in particular are devoted to cases. *Techniques of Family Therapy* (J. Haley & L. Hoffman [Eds.] New York: Basic Books, 1967) gives the transcripts of initial interviews with 5 family therapists and their comments. *Family Therapy: Full Length Case Studies* (P. Papp [Ed.] New York: Gardner Press, 1977) presents 12 therapists with varying approaches and their work with families in treatment.

Of special interest are two cases by Nathan Ackerman and Don Jackson since much of the current techniques in family therapy have their roots in their work.

Ackerman, N. Rescuing the scapegoat. In N. Ackerman (Ed.) *Treating the Troubled Family.* New York: Basic Books, 1966, pp. 210–36.

A good example of Ackerman's style, which he called "tickling the defenses." Ackerman redefines the family conflict, thus shifting the focus from Henry, 14, the identified patient, to the family system itself. This shift enables him to unearth the reason for his father's role as family martyr, namely, his way of dealing with the memory of his father who was an irresponsible gambler. The roots of the current object-relations approach can be seen in this case.

Jackson, D. The eternal triangle. In J. Haley & L. Hoffman (Eds.), *Techniques of family therapy.* New York: Basic Books, 1967, pp. 176–264.

This is a classic case in which Jackson demonstrates his ability to relabel a problem in terms of the family interaction rather than as that of the identified patient. He accomplishes this by "prescribing the symptom" rather than working toward insight.

Four examples illustrating the major approaches to family therapy currently being used are:

Framo, J. In-laws and out-laws: A marital case of kinship confusion. In P. Papp (Ed.), *Family therapy: Full length case studies.* New York: Gardner Press, 1977, pp. 167–81.

A good example of an object-relations approach to family therapy. Framo gives a clear demonstration of the connection between current family difficulties and unresolved issues of the past. He shows how a skilled clinician can use history in a way that makes it relevant in defining current family problems and more importantly in finding solutions for them.

Guerin, P. The use of the arts in family therapy: I never sang for my father. In P. Guerin (Ed.), *Family therapy: Theory and practice.* New York: Gardner Press, 1976, pp. 480-500.

This brief article examines the well-known play and movie, *I Never Sang for My Father*, by Robert Anderson, from the point of view of a therapist trained by Murray Bowen. The Garrison family becomes a case study for the therapist who examines the script in terms of interlocking triangles, the possibility of relationships, the conflictual issues in the system, and the critical incidents that might have moved the system in a more healthy and differentiated direction.

Aponte, H., & Hoffman, L. The open door: A structural approach to a family with an anorectic child. *Family Process,* 1973, 12, 1-44.

This article is a commentary on a videotape of an initial family interview conducted by Drs. Salvador Minuchin and Marriano Barragan with a family whose presenting problem is a 14-year-old girl diagnosed as anorectic. It is of special value because it can be read in conjunction with viewing the tape so one can get a clearer notion of the relationship of theory and practice in structural family therapy.

Fisch, R. Sometimes it's better for the right hand not to know what the left hand is doing. In P. Papp (Ed.), *Family therapy: Full length case studies.* New York: Gardner Press, 1977, pp. 199-210.

This case study is a good example of the brief therapy practiced by the Palo Alto school. It is an extension and development of the ideas of Don Jackson. The therapist defines an issue as *the problem* as a first, critical step. He then uses paradox, prescribing the symptom, and therapeutic double binding as means to resolving the problem in a time-limited setting.

Foley, V. Alcoholism and couple counseling. In R. Stahmann & W. Hiebert (Eds.), *Counseling in marital and sexual problems.* Baltimore: Williams & Wilkins, 1977, pp. 146-59.

An analysis of a case in which a system approach to the role of alcohol in the family is examined. Drinking is seen as a homeostatic balance in the family and not just as a dysfunction of the identified client. In addition, the manipulation of the therapist by the client is analyzed. Finally, three stages of treatment—observation, intervention, and consolidation—are suggested. The case illustrates a structural approach with emphasis on what is happening in the system rather than why it is happening.

REFERENCES

Ackerman, N. Interlocking pathologies in family relationships. In S. Rado & G. Daniels (Eds.), *Changing concepts in psychoanalytic medicine.* New York: Grune and Stratton, 1956.

Ackerman, N. *The psychodynamics of family life.* New York: Basic Books, 1958.

Adler, A. *Understanding human nature.* New York: Permabooks, 1949. (Originally published, 1918.)

Aldous, J., & Dahl, N. *International bibliography of research in marriage and the family, Vol. 2, 1965-1972.* Minneapolis: University of Minnesota Press, 1974(a).

Aldous, J., & Dahl, N. *Inventory of marriage and family literature, Vol. 3, 1973-1974.* Minneapolis: University of Minnesota Press, 1974(b).

Aldous, J., & Hill, R. *International bibliography of research in marriage and the family, Vol. 1, 1900-1964.* Minneapolis: University of Minnesota Press, 1967.

Alger, Ian. Audio-visual techniques in family therapy. In D. Bloch (Ed.), *Techniques of family psychotherapy.* New York: Grune and Stratton, 1973.

Arieti, S. General systems theory and psychiatry—An overview. In W. Gray; F. Duhl; and N. Rizzo (Eds.), *General systems theory and psychiatry.* Boston: Little Brown, 1969.

Bateson, G.; Jackson, D.; Haley, J.; & Weakland, J. Towards a theory of schizophrenia. *Behavioral Science,* 1956, 1, 251-64.

Berne, E. *Games people play.* New York: Grove Press, 1964.

Bloch, D. The clinical home visit. In D. Bloch (Ed.), *Techniques of family psychotherapy.* New York: Grune and Stratton, 1973.

Boszormenyi-Nagy, I. The concept of change in conjoint family therapy. In A. Friedman (Ed.), *Psychotherapy for the whole family.* New York: Springer, 1965.

Boszormenyi-Nagy, I., & Spark, G. *Invisible loyalties.* New York: Harper & Row, 1973.

Bowen, M. The use of family theory in clinical practice. In J. Haley (Ed.), *Changing families.* New York: Grune and Stratton, 1971.

Bowen, M. Family therapy after twenty years. In D. Friedman & K. Juzrud (Eds.), *American handbook of psychiatry, Vol. 5.* New York: Basic Books, 1975.

Bowen, M. Theory in the practice of psychotherapy. In P. Guerin (Ed.), *Family therapy.* New York: Gardner Press, 1976.

Buckley, W. *Sociology and modern systems theory.* Englewood Cliffs, N.J.: Prentice-Hall, 1967.

Christensen, O. Family counseling: An Adlerian orientation. In G. Gazda (Ed.), *Proceedings of a symposium of family counseling and therapy.* Athens, Ga.: University of Georgia Press, 1971.

Cronwell, R.; Olson, D.; & Fournier, D. Tools and techniques for diagnosis and evaluation in marital and family therapy. *Family Process,* 1976, 15, 1–49.

Engeln, R.; Knutson, J.; Laughy, L.; & Garlington, W. Behavior modification techniques applied to a family unit—A case study. In G. Erickson and T. Hogan (Eds.), *Family therapy: an introduction to theory and technique.* New York: Jason Aronson, 1976.

Foley, V. *An introduction to family therapy.* New York: Grune and Stratton, 1974.

Foley, V. Family therapy with black, disadvantaged families: Some observations on roles, communication and techniques. *Journal of Marriage and Family Counseling,* 1975, 1, 29–38.

Framo, J. Symptoms from a family transactional viewpoint. In N. Ackerman; J. Lieb; & J. Pearce (Eds.), *Family therapy in transition.* Boston: Little, Brown, 1970.

Framo, J. *Family interaction: A dialogue between family researchers and family therapists.* New York: Springer, 1972.

Frankl, V. Paradoxical intention: A logo-therapeutic technique. *American Journal of Psychotherapy,* 1960, 14, 520–35.

Freud, S. Analysis of phobia in a five-year-old boy. In J. Strachey (Ed.), *The complete works of Sigmund Freud.* London: Hogarth Press, 1964.

Greenson, R. *The technique and practice of psychoanalysis.* New York: International University Press, 1967.

Guerin, P. (Ed.) *Family therapy.* New York: Gardner Press, 1976.

Guerin, P., & Pendagast, E. Evaluation of family system and genogram. In P. Guerin (Ed.), *Family therapy.* New York: Gardner Press, 1976.

Guntrip, H. *Psychoanalytic theory, therapy and the self.* New York: Basic Books, 1971.

Haley, J. *Strategies of psychotherapy.* New York: Grune and Stratton, 1963.

Haley, J., & Hoffman, L. *Techniques of family therapy.* New York: Basic Books, 1967.

Jackson, D., & Haley, J. Transference revisited. In D. Jackson (Ed.), *Therapy, communication and change.* Palo Alto: Science and Behavior Books, 1968.

Kempler, W. *Principles of Gestalt family therapy.* Salt Lake City: Deseret Press, 1974.

Kuhn, T. *The structure of scientific revolutions.* Chicago: University of Chicago Press, 1962.

Laing, R. Mystification, confusion and conflict. In I. Boszormenyi-Nagy & J. Framo (Eds.), *Intensive family therapy.* New York: Harper & Row, 1965.

Laqueur, P. Multiple family therapy: Questions and answers. In D. Bloch (Ed.), *Techniques of family psychotherapy.* New York: Grune and Stratton, 1973.

Levenson, E. *The fallacy of understanding.* New York: Basic Books, 1972.

Lidz, T.; Cornelison, A.; Fleck, S.; & Terry, D. The intrafamilial environment of schizophrenic patients: II, Marital schism and marital skew. *American Journal of Psychiatry,* 1957, 114, 241–48.

Lieberman, R. Behavioral approaches to family and couple therapy. In G. Erickson & T. Hogan (Eds.), *Family therapy, an introduction to theory and technique.* New York: Jason Aronson, 1976.

Liebman, R., et al. An integrated treatment program for psychogenic pain. *Family Process,* 1976, 15, 397–405.

Minuchin, S. *Families and family therapy.* Cambridge: Harvard University Press, 1974.

Minuchin, S., & Barcai, A. Therapeutically induced family crisis. In J. Masserman (Ed.), *Science and psychoanalysis, Vol. 14.* New York: Grune and Stratton, 1969.

Minuchin, S., et al. *Families of the slum.* New York: Basic Books, 1967.

Mora, G. Recent psychiatric developments (since 1939). In S. Arieti (Ed.), *American handbook of psychiatry, Vol. 1.* New York: Basic Books, 1974.

Mozdzierz, G. J.; Macchitelli, F. J.; & Lisiecki, J. The paradox in psychotherapy: An Adlerian perspective. *Journal of Individual Psychology,* 1976, 32, 169–84.

Olson, D., & Dahl, N. *Inventory of marriage and family literature, Vol. 3, 1973–1974.* Minneapolis: University of Minnesota Press, 1975.

Papajohn, J., & Spiegel, J. *Transactions in families.* San Francisco: Jossey-Bass, 1975.

Papp, P.; Silverstein, O.; & Carter, E. Family sculpting in preventive work with "well families." *Family Process,* 1973, 12, 197–212.

Paul, N., & Paul, B. *A marital puzzle.* New York: Norton, 1975.

Pedersen, P. B. Asian personality theories. In R. J. Corsini (Ed.), *Current personality theories.* Itasca, Ill.: F. E. Peacock Publishers, 1977.

Riskin, J., & Faunce, E. An evaluative review of family interaction research. *Family Process,* 1972, 11, 365–455.

Satir, V. *Peoplemaking.* Palo Alto: Science and Behavior Books, 1972.

Steiner, C. *Games alcoholics play.* New York: Ballantine Books, 1971.

Stewart, R.; Peters, T.; Marsh, S.; & Peters, M. An object-relations approach to psychotherapy with marital couples, families and children. *Family Process,* 1975, 14, 161–77.

Stierlin, H. *Separating parents and adolescents.* New York: Quadrangle, 1974.

Von Bertalanffy, L. General system theory and psychiatry. In S. Arieti (Ed.), *American handbook of psychiatry, Vol. 1.* New York: Basic Books, 1974.

Watzlawick, P.; Weakland, J.; & Fisch, R. *Change: Principles of problem formation and problem resolution.* New York: Norton, 1974.

Weakland, J.; Fisch, R.; Watzlawick, P.; & Bodin, A. Brief therapy: Focused problem resolution. *Family Process,* 1974, 13, 141–68.

Whitaker, C. Psychotherapy of the absurd: With a special emphasis on the psychotherapy of aggression. *Family Process,* 1975, 14, 1–16.

Wynne, L. The study of intrafamilial alignments and splits in exploratory family therapy. In N. Ackerman; F. Beatman; & S. Sherman (Eds.), *Exploring the base for family therapy.* New York: Family Service Association, 1961.

Wynne, L. Some indications and contraindications for exploratory family therapy. In I. Boszormenyi-Nagy & J. Framo (Eds.), *Intensive family therapy.* New York: Harper & Row, 1965.

Wynne, L.; Ryckoff, I.; Day, J.; & Hirsch, S. Pseudomutuality in the family relations of schizophrenics. *Psychiatry,* 1958, 21, 205–20.

Yalom, I. *The theory and practice of group psychotherapy.* 2nd ed. New York: Basic Books, 1975.

Zuk, G. *Process and practice in family therapy.* Haverford, Pa.: Psychiatry and Behavioral Science Books, 1975.

13

Human Potential

JOHN H. MANN

OVERVIEW

Human Potential (HP) is a global term that reflects a common conviction among a highly diverse group of practitioners that the average human being uses a very small part of his capabilities. They further agree that an extraordinarily broad spectrum of approaches, methods, and techniques exist for releasing this potential. Collectively, these practitioners and methods constitute what has come to be known as the *human-potential movement*.

Basic Concepts

The fundamental principle upon which the human-potential approach is based is that the normal individual represents a point of departure, rather than an objective. Other schools of psychotherapy take a different view. They assume that therapy is given because an individual is in personal difficulty. The treatment is designed to restore normal functions. In the process, it may be viewed as desirable for the individual to fulfill himself, but the criterion of success is usually socially oriented, for example, having friends, attaining good family relationships, holding a productive job, and so on. HP methods are essentially for those who

have satisfied the requirements of society, but who remain themselves dissatisfied. This underlying lack of fulfillment is viewed as productive if its motivates the individual to seek further in the pursuit of his own development.

A second contrast between HP methods and other approaches is in the complexity of therapeutic modalities. All forms of psychotherapy are complex. If they appear simple, it is only because they are familiar. Any attempt to reduce the processes involved to a researchable formulation quickly reveals the bewildering array of variables that must be considered and appropriately controlled.

Nevertheless, the complexity of HP methods considered as a whole are of a different order because they do not represent a single system. The HP practitioner employs a variety of approaches, using every conceivable means. The only common element within this diversity is that each technique must meet the criterion of helping the individual to develop further some aspect of his functioning beyond socially acceptable levels.

Although one perhaps should not attempt to deal with such a bewildering state of affairs within the context of the present volume, the author at least hopes to reduce the confusion. Similarly, although methods such as behavior therapy, transactional analysis, and Gestalt therapy perhaps should be included here, at least in passing, the main criterion for selecting methods to be included was the population to which they are customarily applied, rather than the method itself. Thus psychoanalysis is usually given to neurotics. It is clearly psychotherapy. However, brainstorming is not. It occurs in industry, government, or wherever there is a need to generate creative and productive ideas in a problem-solving context. Thus, even though it uses "free association," it would more logically be classified as a human-potential approach. It helps individuals exceed their ordinary level of performance.

The distinction is similar to that made in education between the normal curriculum and remedial work. The typical curriculum gradually develops existing human capacities. Remedial work helps to correct personal difficulties. This analogy breaks down, however, because of its limited focus. Psychotherapy is primarily concerned with emotional reeducation. The human-potential approach is much broader. It develops emotions, sensations, physical expression, creativity, mystical capacities—virtually any human function. Emotion is viewed as an important driving force, but work on emotions is only one segment of a complete approach.

In parallel with this multidimensional outlook is the assumption that individuals are fundamentally different in their overall profile of capacities. Thus, one person is superior emotionally, another in intellectual analysis, a third in the use of his body, a fourth in creative expression. An emotional method used with a physically oriented person is not likely to be productive. By using a broad spectrum of approaches, the HP practitioner assumes

that something will work. An individual who cannot freely associate may be able to fantasize. One who cannot move freely in creative dance may be able to draw. In more limited therapeutic approaches, the individual either fits or is out of luck. He is cut to size or eventually leaves. This is not efficient, or humane, since a client is not in a good position to judge his own condition when he is inwardly disturbed. If a variety of alternatives is available, he can find out through experience which he relates to most easily and which give the most productive results. This orientation runs the danger of substituting variety for depth, but all approaches have their inherent weaknesses. The best protection is to be aware of them in advance.

From a social point of view, the human-potential orientation contains a basic ambiguity. To society as a whole, human potential is often viewed as irrelevant. Things work well enough as they are. Society is not interested in basic social and individual change except as a means of preserving the existing status quo. Releasing human potential is therefore essentially an individual concern except in special instances, such as the training program for astronauts.

However, within the human-potential orientation is a utopian vision of a social order that truly serves the development of the individuals who constitute its membership. Of course, this is precisely the ideal upon which the United States and various other democracies and nondemocracies were founded. However, ideals and social reality correspond only coincidentally, and the view of what Abraham Maslow (1961) called "Eupsychia—the good society" remains a vision, realized only occasionally in partial form, on a small scale, and under special conditions.

The widespread development of free universities and communes during the

1960s was in direct response to this vision. They represented alternative educational and life-styles better suited to the needs of the individuals who were willing to temporarily delay or abandon the more traditional pursuits of society in the search for their own fulfillment.

It is natural that a threatened society should focus on the inefficiencies of such experiments, but their significance was in the possibilities they suggested, not their mortality rate. As such, their importance is hard to overestimate. The very willingness of youth to abandon the relative luxury and security of their familiar environment to participate in such a new way of life offers the best evidence of the underlying need for personal growth and fulfillment that motivates such developments and indicates the extent to which society has failed to meet these needs in the normal course of socialization.

One of the social experiments closely associated with the human-potential movement is the "Growth Center." There have been historical antecedents, but it is essentially a uniquely American development in its particular combinations of elements. A *growth center* is a social structure that provides a setting for the discussion and application of human-potential methods. It is independent of all large-scale social influences, such as government, industry, or education. The criterion for the successful functioning of such a center is quite simple. It must be self-sustaining; that is, it must offer a continuing series of programs sufficiently appealing in themselves to attract an audience. Because of this practical need, these centers not only tolerate but positively encourage every new method, idea, and development in human potential. This may produce a certain superficiality, but it delays or avoids commitment to a particular approach and leaves the door

open for whatever may emerge in the near future. Perhaps universities should perform such a function, but if they did, growth centers would not have continued. Universities are too intellectually oriented and too specialized to encourage such a wide open atmosphere of exchange and experimentation.

Other Systems

It is not feasible to contrast any particular system of psychotherapy discussed in this book to human-potential methods considered as a whole. It would be like comparing apples with pears, grapes, peaches, and pineapples—all considered together. However, there are certain basic effects produced by an HP orientation that differentiate it from other approaches.

Proponents of any system of psychotherapy tend to go overboard. Not only are ego factors involved, but also selective perception, the effect of faith, and so on. Ultimately, one's economic well-being is at stake. When one is identified with a particular approach, to leave it behind is tantamount to a divorce. A somewhat similar problem is found in the area of religion. If a person is devoted to a particular faith, he cannot reasonably be expected to be detached either in relation to criticisms of the system he follows or in responding positively to productive aspects of other systems.

Proponents of particular human-potential approaches may have a similar problem. For example, if a person has spent much of his adult life developing and teaching a special approach to sensory awareness, he may be quite biased in its favor. Although such specialized pioneers are prominent, they are relatively few. The more typical practitioner in the area is relatively open to new alternatives. He has less need to build a theoretical cathedral to protect his beliefs, because he is less attached to any method than to the ideal of human perfectability. As long as there is an untried approach he can use, he will try it. The failure or success of a particular approach is not a direct threat to his professional image.

This not only creates a favorable climate for clinical experimentation, but makes it difficult for the politics of power, which operate in all areas of professional life, to flourish. Professionals in human potential do not function on certificates and degrees so much as on their capacity to deliver something that is real and useful to potential consumers. This is a relative distinction, but a real one. In most systems of psychotherapy, one is concerned with the qualifications of the individual therapist as determined by some certification process, but as Carl Rogers (1973) so clearly points out, such an emphasis does not necessarily produce therapeutic excellence and certainly eliminates creativity.

Some of the people working at growth centers are highly qualified in a professional sense. Others are not. Their backgrounds are extremely varied. They may be gym instructors, art teachers, industrial consultants, classical Chinese scholars, almost anything. As long as they have some kind of relevant background for the work they do, it is sufficient. The marketplace provides the criterion for success, a concept totally out of keeping with our professional standards, but very much in keeping with the economic system in which we function.

The research implication of these factors is considerable. The problems involved in evaluating any approach to psychotherapy are compounded by the vested interest the practitioner has in the method he employs. Since HP practitioners are less committed to any particular method, they are, in principle, more open to research. They can always discard one method to take on another. However, the complexity of the activity occurring in a growth center is such that it does not lend itself to simple research efforts, since so many methods are being applied simultaneously. Openness to evaluation is not enough. An appropriate design must be used. The problem is further complicated because the needs and methods of the researcher are quite different from those of the client, which are very different from those of the practitioner. The client wants to feel or act better. He does not really care how this is accomplished as long as it happens. The scientist, on the other hand, is somewhat obsessively concerned with the purity and predictability of the process, so all relevant variables are controlled. The therapist hopes to be vindicated, but given the conservative spirit of science, he has more to lose than to gain.

A human-potential specialist approaches the basic research situation partially free from any assumptions. He knows that if he is to succeed in using the full capacities of those who come to him, improvements must be made in the methods he uses. His predilection is to experiment in an eclectic manner. His criterion is primarily practical, whereas an individual wedded to a particular system of psychotherapy has not only the method, but the theory and the social structure developed around the method, to defend. He has much more to lose by evaluation and many more obstacles to overcome.

Similarly, a client who comes to a human-potential experience is also more open to experimentation. He is experimenting just by attending a workshop and views himself as a participant, not a patient. Thus, he is in a position to accept the role of experimental subject and co-worker more readily than someone who is looking for traditional treatment.

In comparing other systems with the present orientation, one runs the risk of falling into the trap of attempting to demonstrate conclusively how one's own system is obviously better than any other. Identification produces prejudice. It is inevitable. The scientist and therapist, each in his own area, does what he can to avoid bias, but in the end attempts to correct for it, knowing that human beings are inherently subject to error. In general, the HP practitioner recognizes that it is important to remain open-minded and experimentally oriented in an area in which people's emotions notoriously tend to mold their beliefs.

At this point in the evolution of our understanding of human development, it seems reasonable to suppose that a multidimensional approach to personal growth is likely to work more effectively than a limited one. Therefore, a climate that encourages such approaches is useful. At the same time, the advantage of a highly developed form of psychotherapy, complete with concepts, theory, and fairly rigid details of practice, is also considerable. One can achieve more lasting results. The danger of the human-potential orientation is that it may lead initially to excitement, but produce a superficial result. It does not have to. Many of the methods employed have been used in depth by their developers. However, the consumer would rather seek novelty than hard inner work, and this is a weakness to which this approach is prone. What needs to be clearly understood is that the smorgasbord stage of searching and sampling many HP methods is only phase one. It needs to be followed by a more focused and intensive period of therapeutic work, using the most effective methods discovered in phase one as the individual pursues his search for personal growth.

HISTORY

Precursors

Almost every culture has some ancient ties to the human-potential theme, usually within its mystical religious tradition. Perhaps the most familiar is in Genesis when God creates man in his own image. The implication of such an action is that man is of the nature of God. Since his historical behavior does not bear out such a belief, this possibility must lie in his potential development rather than his everyday functioning.

A parallel tradition is found in the Upanishads of India, those early mystical books of the forest philosophers. The basic message in this work is contained in the three-word formula: "Thou Art That." The individual is the cosmic. All of yoga and much of Eastern religion is designed to actualize the possibility contained in those three words. These beliefs are extremely old, predating the written record that bears them testimony (sixth to eighth century B.C.) by more years than scholars can establish.

A third example is the Greek tradition from which the pagan world draws its roots. It emphasizes the need to examine and celebrate life to appreciate it. Further, in such teachings as the Platonic cave myth, the notion of the evolution of man from the comparative darkness of his present condition to a new form of consciousness and understanding is clearly supported.

Within this general context, the Christian tradition clearly focuses on the central role of rebirth in the attainment of a higher state of being. This idea predates Christianity, but receives its most dramatic expression in the life of Christ. The basic notion that the change of human condition depends on a fundamental transition rather than on minor alterations or cosmetic psychic surgery is fundamental to any cosmic conception of human possibilities.

The parallel but totally independent tradition of Zen Buddhism emphasizes the abrupt nature of such a transition, preceded by a long period of effort designed to create the inner conditions from which "satori" (i.e., enlightenment and true understanding) can come.

Man has always needed to relate to the natural and cosmic forces surrounding the structure of the society he has created. In most cultures, this has been done through the religious development of a divine hierarchy that is personalized in varying degrees. It is the insight and contribution of the human-potential orientation to see in these divine beings an expression of man's own higher possibilities.

Beginnings

On several levels, the original impetus for what has become the human-potential movement can be traced to William James, the American philosopher and psychologist. Although James is best known as a developer of pragmatism and as a classical psychologist who helped define the shape and nature of the field, he laid the groundwork for three separate developments that only now are bearing fruit within the human-potential context.

The first is his belief in the significance of what has come to be called "parapsychology." As early as 1901, he predicted: "Hardly, as yet, has the surface of the facts called 'psychic' begun to be scratched for scientific purposes. It is through following these facts, I am persuaded, that the greatest scientific conquests of the coming generations will be achieved" (James, 1909). Subsequent events have certainly not supported his early enthusiasm, but almost 70 years later, the tide is slowly turning.

The second area for which his studies were clearly the precursor is the alteration of consciousness. His study of religious experience, published in 1902, directly led him to hypothesize a series of alternate states of consciousness that could become available under special conditions.

Our normal waking consciousness, rational consciousness as we call it, is but one special type of consciousness, whilst all about it, parted from it by the filmiest of screens, there lie potential forms of consciousness entirely different. We may go through life without suspecting their existence; but apply the requisite stimulus, and at a touch they are there in all their completeness, definite types of mentality which probably somewhere have their field of application and adaptation. No account of this universe in its totality can be final which leaves these other forms of consciousness quite disregarded. . . . (James, 1902).

During the last six months of his life, James (1910) wrote: "But we know so little of the noetic value of abnormal mental states of any kind that in my opinion, we had better keep an open mind and collect facts sympathetically for a long time to come. We shall not *understand* these alterations of consciousness either in this generation or in the next."

The most important and directly relevant material to the development of the human-potential movement is contained in a short, little-known monograph entitled, "The Energies of Men." In this study, James (1907) discusses how special conditions in the life of ordinary people reveal them to possess unsuspected sources of strength, courage, endurance, love, and creativity. He discusses methods for developing these powers, concluding with the prophetic statement:

The two questions, first, that of the possible extent of our powers; and second, that of the various avenues of approach to them, the various keys for unlocking them in diverse individuals, dominate the whole problem of individual and national education. We need a topography of the limits of human power, similar to the chart which oculists use for the field of human vision. We need also a study of the various types of human beings with reference to the different ways in which their energy-reserves may be appealed to and set loose. Biographies and individual experiences of every kind may be drawn upon for evidence here.

This would be an absolutely concrete study. . . . The limits of power must be limits that have been realized in actual persons, and the various ways of unlocking the reserves of power must have been exemplified in individual lives. . . . So here is a program of individual psychology. . . . It is replete with interesting facts, and points to practical issues superior in importance to anything we know.

In a very real sense, this call to action was answered most clearly by the early work of Maslow (1950, 1954), focusing on what he called the "peak experience." One might say a *peak experience* is a moment in time when potential becomes actual. It is the concrete evidence for vastness of untapped human resources, about which the whole human-potential enterprise is organized.

Maslow is a modern figure, generally viewed as a founding father of the human-potential movement, rather than a precursor. He has, however, helped to clarify the importance of the work of another pioneer, Dr. J. L. Moreno, from whose earlier efforts the human-potential movement partially arose. In a letter written to *Life* magazine, regarding their extensive article on HP, Maslow (1968)

said: "Many of the techniques set forth in the article were originally invented by Dr. Jacob Moreno, who is still functioning vigorously and probably still inventing new techniques and ideas."

Moreno is largely known as the creator of psychodrama, role playing, and sociometry. He was also one of the founders of group psychotherapy. He was not primarily either a philosopher or practical psychologist like James, but, rather, a practicing psychiatrist like Freud. Here the resemblance ended. Moreno's work constitutes an almost total antithesis of psychoanalysis: emphasizing the here-and-now, openness, the importance of social forces, and the limitless creative expression of the individual.

His least known contributions are contained in his earliest works, some of which were published anonymously. Two, in particular, *The Words of the Father* (1920) and *The Theater of Spontaneity* (1923), contain many of the principles upon which the human-potential movement is based.

As documented in *The Words of the Father,* Moreno began as a religious, not a therapeutic figure. He believed that humans were co-creators of the universe with God; that by fulfilling their potential, they were helping to create the universe. His emphasis was not on theory, philosophy, or principle, but on action. During the first decade of this century, he wandered around the streets and parks of Vienna in a long white robe, calling on people to be true to their own inner natures, and creating various street dramas and confrontations that were totally spontaneous and helped to focus on the inherent dilemmas of the times. From this basic orientation, he began to devise various methods to help people express the totality of their needs and aspirations, which he first described in *The Theater of Spontaneity* and then later developed in the various forms more familiar today. Although he was a medical doctor, his interest was not in treatment, but in personal fulfillment. Toward this end, he used the stage as a culturally neutral space in which anything could happen. It offered a very natural setting for the profusion of methods that were to surface and collectively become associated with the human-potential movement.

Current Status

Assessing the current status of HP work is not easy, because it resembles a large unpruned plant, each stalk of which represents a different field of endeavor. The vigor of the expression can be judged by the journals that are in varying degrees relevant, such as the *Journal of Humanistic Psychology, Journal of Mental Imagery, Journal of Creative Behavior, Journal of Transpersonal Psychology, Journal of Parapsychology,* and literally 20 to 30 others in which articles of relevance regularly appear.

Another indicator of current activity is the overall number of growth centers established throughout the United States. This figure is somewhat difficult to establish because of their high birth and death rate, but it is generally held to be from 150 to 200 throughout the United States (Schutz, 1973). When the classification is extended to include centers devoted to specific types of HP methods such as psychodrama, yoga, or creative problem solving, the number is much greater.

Within this diverse and sometimes furious activity, has come a basic change in orientation, as an interview with Michael Murphy (1976), the president of Esalen, has documented. The history of the HP movement is directly related to the development of Esalen, since it was the original growth center. Murphy himself went to India after graduation from Berkeley, staying for 18 months at the Ashram of Sri Aurobindo. While there, he began to conceive of a marriage of Eastern and Western wisdom in the service of human development, which led him to the founding of Esalen. The early years emphasized the group aspect of this enterprise, which paralleled the revolutionary social focus of the 1960s. It is evident to Murphy, however, that the balance has swung back toward the inner person, with an increasing interest in mysticism, yoga, and transpersonal experience.

This trend has been brilliantly described by Tom Wolfe (1976) in an essay entitled: "The Me Decade and the Third Great Awakening." Wolfe makes the basic point that the encounter ethic of total self-expression, both within various HP methods and outside in communes and other social experiments, has given rise in the seventies to a new religious revival. The emphasis is still on self-expression, but the thrust of the third religious awakening in America is to raise the level of the personal search for fulfillment to a cosmic plane and in the process to create what Wolfe describes as "the greatest age of individualism in American history!"

Further evidence of a strong turn toward mystical experience is provided in a recent book by Daniel Goleman (1977), in which he compares 14 types of meditation. In certain respects, he offers a consumer's guide to different teachers and teachings, but at the same time, he seeks to establish the underlying principles shared by different schools and to clarify the basic differences that do exist.

As interest in alternative states of consciousness and mystical experiences has grown, the growth center has to some extent been supplanted by another recent development in the arena of social experiments, the *ashram*. It is strange that they should follow each other historically because they could hardly be more different. The growth center is typically American in outlook and design. The ashram is an import from India. The growth center is intended to be a forum for new ideas. The ashram is the forum for one teacher and one teaching. It is a form of group living organized around the guru who controls all phases of social life. His control is more theocratic than autocratic. He derives his position from his contact with higher power and constitutes for his students and disciples an intermediary to such power.

In the classical Indian model, the guru is held dearer than one's parents. He is a spiritual parent. The American version has been influenced by our own traditions and democratic orientation, but the startling contrast remains between the wide-open atmosphere of most growth centers and the highly disciplined religious atmosphere of most ashrams. However enduring it proves to be as a social institution, the ashram offers striking confirmation of the extent to which people are turning inward in their search for fulfillment and their willingness to look toward unfamiliar paths and to accept teachers who claim, rightly or wrongly, to be divinely inspired. As Wolfe points out, the members of the new left communes of the sixties have become the followers of teachers and gurus of the seventies, without the total contradiction of the shift appearing to bother them.

PERSONALITY

Theory of Personality

The most significant moment in the development of the individual is the moment of conception. All but one cell, the zygote, is in the realm of potential. From a more realistic viewpoint, the most important stage of personality development begins at birth. The newborn child represents potential in the purest form that we commonly observe it. Although in one sense, he is closely tied to his instincts, in another, he experiences a cosmic state not unlike those sought by mystics. The world and the universe are one. But more important, beyond certain global aspects of temperament that may reveal themselves in the first days, each baby ever born is capable of incredible modification. This only becomes evident when a child born in one culture is brought up in another or in such highly unlikely incidents as a child brought up by animals or in isolated conditions.

As far as we know, any child can successfully grow up in any culture as long as his physical appearance does not create special problems for him and he is accepted by members of that culture as a normal infant. This is a very remarkable fact. He can learn any language, adopt any system of morality, learn to look at the world in any of the extraordinarily rich, varied, and complex ways that humans have devised or will ever devise in the future.

It cannot be said that such a conclusion has been proven through controlled experiment because of the humanitarian considerations involved, but the evidence is certainly quite strong, and most anthropologists would subscribe to such a view.

Of interest in this regard is the study of the Manus, made over a 25-year period by Margaret Mead (1956). In this investigation, she reports on an isolated group of people who successfully made the transformation from stone age to modern culture in two decades. In this case, not only was the flexibility of human nature demonstrated, but also the capacity of social institutions to adapt to an extraordinary degree.

A parallel instance of human adaptability on an individual scale was reported by C. Turnbull (1962). He described an individual who successfully led the life of an African chief, complete with three wives, when at home in his native village, while following all of the expected behaviors of a Western official when living in the city as an important member of his nation's government.

If such changes can occur in adults after they have been socialized, infants are surely capable of much greater feats of adaptability, limited more by our imagination to conceive than their capacity to perform.

The extraordinary potential of the infant is largely overlooked by those responsible for the socialization process, because they are overly familiar with the society the child is entering. They are primarily concerned with the success of their efforts, since failure to socialize creates a potential threat to society. If an individual meets the standards and expectations of society, he is accepted as normal and receives suitable rewards and responsibilities. When he does not, appropriate treatment is instituted.

Socialization is a purely relative term. It is defined by the institutions within which it is embedded. The actual behavior and attitudes vary widely from culture to culture. For example, in Japan, hissing is a means of showing deference. In England, it is rude. In the Orient, kissing is a strictly private act and is censored from Western movies. The variations are endless.

What never changes is the assumption that one should do what is expected, performing the appropriate social role. When this does not occur, the person is labeled

sick or deviant and appropriate remedial action is taken. This may take the form of reeducation, psychotherapy, medicine, social work, or a vast array of other procedures that can be introduced formally or informally, depending on the severity of the deviance, the age of the individual, and the nature of the culture.

The concept of sickness is, of course, also culturally relative. At one end of the scale are fatal illnesses that cannot be ignored or wished away. At the other end are fairly subtle symptoms that might or might not be recognized as signs of illness or deviance in a given culture. In extreme instances, such as the practice of voodoo, people become ill simply because they are supposed to.

Within certain fairly obvious physical limits, a person is sick when he believes he is sick and when others agree with him. Since so much of one's inner experience and physiological functioning are influenced by psychosocial factors, particularly as these act over an extended period, it can be said that sickness represents the outcome of a failure to socialize, that is, a failure to accept the norms of one's society as identical with one's own needs.

There are various ways in which a person can manifest such sickness. He can experience a breakdown in physical functions. He can develop neurotic or psychotic behaviors. He can attack those he feels are threatening his own integrity. All of these behaviors represent a failure in socialization. In the broad sense, he is not doing what he should be doing.

Although this view may be thought "oversocialized" by some, the more important issue is the fate of other possible avenues of development the individual might have undertaken if he had grown up in a different culture. The obvious answer is that they remain unfulfilled. Eventually, sickness may occur because the individual does not actualize his potential. This is the general human-potential viewpoint. It does not apply to every situation. A person can be born with birth defects of various kinds. These must be corrected. His intelligence may be low. This will require special educational approaches. In general, however, people become ill because of a failure to fulfill their capacities due to limits placed on them by social institutions. From this viewpoint, illnesses are an inevitable by-product of the existence of society. They may or may not represent a struggle between the individual and society as Freud believed, but they certainly represent an inevitable outcome of society's limited model of the individual.

In general, theorists associated with the HP viewpoint have not emphasized the social limits on individual development, although they certainly recognize its existence. Their focus has usually been on the positive aspects of human capabilities, partially as a reaction to the more pessimistic orientation of psychoanalysis. Although they use somewhat different language and have distinctly different backgrounds, theorists such as the sociologist P. A. Sorokin (1954) in his study of altruism, the psychiatrist R. Assagioli (1971) in his development of psychosynthesis, and the psychologist Abraham Maslow (1950, 1954, 1968) in his studies of being needs and peak experiences all agree that in addition to ego and unconscious aspects of human behavior, there is a higher level of conscious experience that is possible. They postulate a three-level model of human personality. The first is *instinctive*. The second involves *ego functions*. The third level contains the *cosmic aspects* of individual experience. In some respects, Jung's "collective un-

conscious" represents a partial step in this direction, but in another sense, the third level of human personality is much closer to the fourth stage of human consciousness described in early Indian literature as *turiya* and referred to in many mystical and religious traditions in various ways. Although theorists in the human-potential movement emphasize the higher possibility of human awareness, this does not mean they in any way deny the more familiar ones. It is done to counteract the previous emphasis within the behavioral sciences on man's animal heritage.

Variety of Concepts

The basic contrast between human-potential concepts and others found in more traditional forms of psychotherapy is clearly expressed within Maslow's third-force psychology (Goble, 1970). The first force in psychology, according to Maslow, was scientific objectivity, most clearly illustrated by behaviorism and classical learning theory. The second force was Freudian with its emphasis on the unconscious determinants of behavior and an essentially pessimistic view of existence. The third force was humanistic in orientation, emphasizing positive human capabilities. It would be difficult to prove or disprove any of these positions. They simply constitute different approaches to the complex nature of human behavior.

Scientific psychology was originally a reaction against the close connection between psychology and philosophy in the late nineteenth century. Freudian psychoanalysis was a reaction to scientific objectivity that tended to become more and more precise, but have less and less significance. Third-force psychology was a reaction to the previous two, emphasizing an openness to new approaches and experiences, a quality not emphasized in either of the other alternatives.

There are so many different methods used within a human-potential context, each based on different concepts, that it is difficult to single out a few for special treatment. Encounter, for example, uses concepts such as "inclusion," "control," and "affection" (Schutz, 1973); sensory-awareness training emphasizes "awareness," "contact," and "flow" (Gunther, 1976); meditation uses categories such as "concentration," "insight," and "creative possession" (Naranjo & Ornstein, 1971).

Some of these concepts overlap, but the proliferation that occurs in adjacent areas of interest, although natural, is also confusing. This is no more than one would expect in a field whose essential quality is the iconoclastic inclusion of anything that might be relevant to extended human development.

Certain concepts are, however, sufficiently broad to cross-cut most, but probably not all, HP methods. Of these, perhaps the most widely known is the *peak experience*. Maslow used this concept as an organizing principle of a good deal of his work in this area. He defined it as follows: "The word peak experience is a generalization for the best moments of life, for experiences of ecstasy, rapture, bliss or greatest joy" (Maslow, 1963). Using this concept, it was possible for him to identify individuals in whom such experiences tended to occur or isolate conditions tending to produce such experiences. Underlying such investigations was the assumption that a peak experience was desirable in itself. But even more important, it served to indicate what was possible for the individual, a measure of his potential. As such, the peak experience was like a flag on a mountain top, left by a successful climber.

Confusion arises if it is assumed that the purpose of life is to achieve such experiences. Persons in the human-potential movement have sometimes acted as if they believe this to be the case. However, that is a partial perversion of the concept. One studies the best examples of a phenomenon, not because it is typical, or even desirable as a steady diet, but because it represents a high-water mark and indicates the inherent possibilities involved.

A second concept found in diverse HP methods is *life force*. Different words are used to express the energy or energies involved, but the emphasis on the release and flow of vitality frequently recurs.

This view is central, for example, to bio-energetic analysis based on the work of Wilhelm Reich, who emphasized the concept of orgone energy well before it was popular to do so. A similar concept is found in various forms in Indian yoga under the term *prana,* which is generally translated as "life force." The basic purpose of yoga is to contact and absorb prana in ever increasing quantities. Certain forms of yoga are specifically directed toward the channeling of energy in a very direct manner. Kundalini yoga, for example, is described in classical texts as "the Yoga of Psychic Force" (Evans-Wentz, 1968). Energy flow is basic to sensory-awareness work, and W. C. Schutz (1973) has described energy cycles as crucial to encounter work. A very similar concept appears in modified form in a number of the Oriental martial arts. The "ki" in aikido, and "chi" in tai chi chuan are both vital energies the student learns to cultivate and direct.

Of course, one finds a similar emphasis in psychoanalysis in the concept of "libido." The difference appears on the level of methodology. Psychoanalysis, at least in its classical form, is essentially a passive and verbal experience. Neither the patient nor the analyst move, nor do they make physical contact. Thus, the energy exchange is limited in certain distinct ways.

The methodology of human-potential methods requires movement and involvement on all levels: verbal, intellectual, emotional, physical, psychic, and cosmic. The whole thrust of the effort is either to increase the flow of energy on all planes or to remove the blocks to such flow.

The experience of energy flow in HP methods is viewed as good in itself, as well as a sign of physical well-being. It is also recognized that one must be able to control the flow when it occurs, if any lasting benefit is to come from it, but the tendency has been to emphasize the flow, rather than the control, since that is what most individuals lack.

A third concept that appears in rather diverse approaches, is that *people are more similar than different.* It is not necessary to make elaborate distinctions between them. This is seen quite clearly in encounter groups. The main criterion for membership is simply wanting to belong. The assumption is that the differences in the members really do not matter, or that they can be dealt with by the multidimensional methods employed in the group setting.

Finally, it should be emphasized that there may be a basic contradiction between the methods employed in human-potential workshops and the context from which they are drawn. This can be formulated as a fourth concept that states that *different methods can be successfully combined out of context.* For example, a workshop may employ a Zen form of meditation as a means of clearing the mind. What is going on during the rest of the workshop may in no way represent the monastic Zen ideal of living. More than

likely, it may directly contradict it. Zen is not eclectic. It represents a pure and rather rigid tradition that has maintained its identity over several thousand years. An HP workshop is likely to be wildly eclectic, bringing together concepts and means developed by people who have never heard of each other, working in different fields, countries, and historical periods. It is precisely this quality that characterizes the experience.

A Zen master might be horrified, but the HP practitioner views such cross-fertilization as the original contribution he is making to the growth process. The obvious danger of such an approach is that the technique, when used out of context, will lose its effectiveness. The great advantage is that it helps to clarify the extent to which a technique is valid in itself and is not just a reflection of its cultural and situational context. From a scientific and applied viewpoint, such information is invaluable if we are to attain a more rational approach to human development.

PSYCHOTHERAPY

Theory of Psychotherapy

The meaning of psychotherapy in a human-potential context is radically different from almost any other. In a sense, there is no psychotherapy. The client is assumed to be normal. In another sense, there is a religious orientation. Mystical systems generally suggest that man, as we know him, is a seed capable of a total transformation under the right conditions. Most HP practitioners agree with this view, but are too eclectic to be religious in any formal sense.

Irrespective of these overtones, the basis of HP psychotherapy could be described as a willingness to do anything to

TABLE 13.1
A Classification of Human-Potential Methods

Modality	Methods
Physiological manipulation	Acupuncture, psychedelic drugs, rolfing
Sensory awareness	Sensory awakening, hatha yoga, biofeedback
Emotional expression	Primal therapy
Personal behavior	Behavior therapy, role playing, role-construct therapy
Creativity	Creative problem solving, synectics
Self-image	Who am I (Maharshi), Gestalt, hypnosis
Interaction	Encounter
Social restructuring	Communes, altered life-styles, free universities
Transpersonal	Meditation, parapsychology altered states of consciousness

help the interested individual actualize his capabilities. The only limit imposed is that the development should be positive. When the positive or negative aspect of the development is not entirely clear, the tendency is to proceed in the belief that growth is self-corrective in the long run.

A willingness to do anything (within the legal and professional limits imposed by society) covers a lot of territory. It may be useful to outline some of the possibilities involved and to indicate how various forms of therapeutic work fit within an overall design.

Table 13.1 outlines a systematic approach to HP therapeutic methods by placing examples of such methods in appropriate categories. To clarify this system, each of these illustrative examples will be briefly discussed. Before becoming involved with specifics, however, there are several general points that should be made.

First, each of these methods is quite distinct. They have been developed by individuals with different backgrounds, interests, and beliefs who are each as limited in their view as proponents of any method tend to be. What they generally have in common is that they are func-

tioning outside of the mainstream of psychotherapy as it is currently practiced.

Second, when the methods are used in an HP context, it is generally within a highly eclectic environment, such as a growth center. They follow each other week by week and inevitably interact in a statistical sense, which complicates the problem of judging their individual effectiveness.

Third, their presence in the following discussion in no way indicates their scientific validity. Often, little or nothing is known of their effectiveness. Research has not begun to catch up with the proliferation of the methods themselves, nor, for the most part, have their proponents been particularly interested in encouraging research at the expense of either teaching or practice. There are some partial exceptions, however, such as in the areas of biofeedback and meditation.

The methods selected in Table 13.1 were chosen to illustrate the categories in which they appear. Other methods that might otherwise be mentioned do not clearly illustrate a particular category. For example, a martial art such as aikido is partially a "personal behavior"; that is, it is definitely something one does. At the same time, it is a form of inner awareness of cosmic energy so it could be classified under both "transpersonal" and "sensory awareness." The methods that have been listed are less complex than this, at least in their mode of action. The theory behind them may be quite elaborate.

For example, *acupuncture* is an ancient form of Chinese medicine, having little or no theoretical similarity to the principles of modern Western medicine. It is based on an elaborate system of quasi-physiology and philosophy. The method itself consists of direct intervention in the body of the subject, using special needles designed for the purpose. Thus, it fits nicely into the category of physical manipulation.

Similarly, *psychedelic drugs* are also introduced into the organism from the outside as a form of physiological manipulation. These two methods, although widely differing in outcome, share the same basic approach. The subject is passive. He does not have to do anything but allow the manipulation to occur. The intense and somewhat painful system of *massage* developed by the physiologist Ida Rolf (1972) also falls into the same category. The client does nothing except pay for the treatment and withstand the pain.

Sensory awareness refers to the inner flow of sensation to which a person can relate, if his attention is directed to it by his own will or the suggestion of others. This involves mental effort on his part. If he does not stay with the inner experience, very little will happen. In its purest form, this category is illustrated by the work of Charlotte Selver (1957). Her basic purpose is to cultivate such awareness as a basis of personal growth.

Hatha yoga can also be placed in this general category. It is precisely because of its emphasis on sensory awareness that it differs most clearly from any Western system of physical culture. This point is not made clear in most books on the subject. The emphasis is usually placed on the physical positions involved in the practice of hatha yoga, rather than the inner conditions that must accompany them.

The importance of *sensory awareness* is clearly indicated by the results obtained in *biofeedback* work. The more objective technical considerations of biofeedback are what usually catch our attention. The effectiveness of these methods, however, depends on their capacity to help the individual relate his awareness of an inner condition to some objective indicator of the same condition. The fundamental purpose is to help him gain control over his autonomic nervous system through such awareness.

The significance of these efforts has been well documented. A. Turin and R. M. Nideffer (1976) have recently reviewed and abstracted 50 studies of the clinical application of biofeedback. B. B. Brown (1977) has also reviewed the clinical effectiveness of such work. In both cases, the overall conclusions are positive, although, of course, the scientific quality of the work on biofeedback shows great variability.

Most forms of psychotherapy emphasize emotional expression more than any other category. Psychotherapy is, in fact, often described as emotional reeducation. *Primal therapy* is a recent development that has many classical aspects. It is associated with a charismatic founder and has developed its own theoretical statement with a particularly striking concept around which all else is organized. It exhibits a tendency to attempt to explain and cure everything, which is typical of new methods in their earlier stages. It has also generated its own system of training and specialized forms of treatment procedures (Janov, 1971).

Whatever the refinements, the primal-therapy approach provides an excellent illustration of a strong emphasis on emotional expression as the basis of psychotherapy. Until the patient can emit a primal scream, nothing fundamental has happened. That in itself is not enough, but it is certainly the pivotal experience, somewhat analogous to the obtaining of a secular satori.

Primary emphasis on personal behavior is most clearly seen in the approaches used in behavior therapy and role playing, but these methods are dealt with elsewhere in this volume. A further example of this orientation is provided in *role-construct therapy* developed by George A. Kelly (1955). Although this approach is accompanied by a comprehensive and complex theoretical statement, it is basically directed at systematically creating a new identity for the client by a restructuring of his role performances. Thus, central emphasis is put on behavior change, rather than inner dynamics and insight.

The category of *creativity* is primarily oriented toward problem solving. It contains strong intellectual elements, but goes beyond them in the systematic use of insight. Various processes and procedures have been developed for heightening the creative process. Some, such as *creative problem solving* (Parnes, 1967), emphasize careful and systematic analysis of alternatives, combined with the use of unlikely or unexpected solutions. Others such as *synectics* (Gordon, 1961) use various methods, such as brainstorming, or the use of analogies within a group setting.

The *self-image* is a psychological construct that is useful in organizing the elements in the individual's awareness with which he particularly identifies. No method limits itself exclusively to work on the self-image, but the construct is central to a number of them. The Hindu saint Ramana Maharshi (1962) based his teaching on the single question: "Who am I?" His students used the question much in the spirit of a Hindu *Koan,* continually repeating it until a new understanding emerged, that is, until their self-image began to alter.

In hypnosis, also, the self-image is altered. The nature of the experience involves a transference of the individual's will to the hypnotist, and a resulting expansion of his behavioral possibilities. This can certainly be interpreted as a change in self-concept.

The Gestalt emphasis on reintegrating the fragmented aspect of personal experience is also related to expanding and resolving the sense of self in a very direct and immediate manner.

Social restructuring is a familiar aspect of our lives in modern society, but in most instances, the individual is more likely to be the victim than the beneficiary of such efforts. However, within this framework, the availability of alternate life-styles, particularly in urban settings, and the spread of communes across the country provide the opportunity for individuals to change the pattern of their existence in a fundamental manner. The bases of these opportunities vary widely, as do their power to endure and the reactions they produce in the environment immediately surrounding them. However, their importance is far beyond their size or number. They offer the opportunity to experiment with utopian hopes and, in a different sense, clarify the scope of human potential in the social sphere.

In the last decade, the transpersonal aspect of human potential has received increasing emphasis. Approached from different directions by seekers, scientists, gurus, and clinicians, the varied areas of meditation, altered states of consciousness, and parapsychology all help the individual to relate to a more cosmic level of experience. In some respects, many of the methods employed are ancient, but the context is new and from a modern Western viewpoint, it is all new to us.

Process of Psychotherapy

For reasons already made evident, many of the typical considerations relating to the process of psychotherapy simply do not hold when applied to the complexity and even partial contradictions of different HP methods. Almost anything that might be said in relation to the first interview, type of patients, length of treatment, termination of treatment, and so on would hold only for certain methods and not for others, leading to a confusing situation. Thus, the Rolf method of *structural reintegration* is typically given in a series of 10 individual treatments, each session focusing on a different part of the body; whereas *sensory awareness* as practiced by Charlotte Selver may be given in 1 1/2 hour group sessions, twice a week, for as long as the individual wants to continue.

On the other hand, as one studies human-potential approaches, one is gradually struck by the fact that the practitioners make their methods sound more unique than they actually are. The reason for this is largely economic. Methods are in competition, just like breakfast foods. One does not succeed by proving that what one does is similar to what everyone else is doing. One emphasizes the difference. This may make good business sense,

but from an objective point of view, it is quite misleading. One tends to overlook the basic similarities involved.

For example, all methods depend, in varying degrees, on the presence of a leader. All methods work better if the practitioner and client have faith in them. Almost all methods attempt to create a nonthreatening climate in which experimentation with new behaviors is possible and in which old fears can be revived and successfully overcome. These common components of the psychotherapeutic process have been analyzed and described by various authors, such as J. D. Frank (1961) and J. H. Mann (1965).

Behind the specifics of any technique lies the general assumption that any form of human experience can be subdivided into more fundamental components, much as any physical substance can be broken down into the elements of which it is composed. On the chemical level, this process is realistic. On the psychosocial level, the distinctions are less clear, but this type of approach is still possible. The great advantage to viewing psychotherapy in this way is that the building blocks shared by highly diverse methods are more or less identical. If these can be identified, the whole area of behavior change processes can be investigated in a more rational and systematic manner.

In 1968 the Educational Policy Research Center, located at the Stanford Research Institute, initiated a project to study human-potential methods. Fifty-one different HP methods were carefully reviewed within a common descriptive framework. The results of this research were reported by Peterson (1971) in *A Catalog of Ways People Grow*. A more detailed study of the common components of these methods was conducted by Mann (1972) and reported in the

TABLE 13.2
Clusters of Strategies

Found: Human = Potential Methods
1. Letting go
2. Concretizing
3. Variation of a significant element
4. Communications
5. Redistribution of energy
6. Increasing personal involvement
7. Manipulation
8. Testing the limits
9. Merging with a larger collectivity
10. Controlling attention
11. Problem solving
12. Enhancing creativity
13. Alteration of self-image
14. Environmental reorganization

volume *Learning to Be.* The basic approach was to identify as many components as possible within each of the 51 methods. These were then subjected to an impressionistic cluster analysis that isolated the 14 change strategies listed in Table 13.2.

Although such an approach has certain important research advantages to be discussed later, its immediate relevance is that it provides the basis for generating a common, descriptive framework that can be used to analyze a variety of different methods. Since HP methods are extremely diverse, such simplified means of describing them are helpful. The crucial step in any scientific approach is to isolate the relevant variables.

The utility of these categories in describing the process involved in any particular HP method can be judged by several examples. The Rolf method, already mentioned, principally involves *manipulation.* One person works on another directly. It also uses *testing the limits,* since it is a process that can be very painful, and *concretizing,* since the individual becomes very aware of specific areas of his body as they are worked on.

In contrast, sensory-awareness methods

principally involve *letting go. Concretizing* is also used as the teacher draws the subject's attention to various parts of the body through verbal instructions. Usually, when one person talks to another, it produces an external interaction. To the extent that this process is reversed in the present case, it provides an example of the *variation of a significant element.*

This type of analysis is helpful in clarifying the nature of any particular method, but more important, it heightens the nature of the similarities and differences between methods. In the above example, both methods employ concretizing, but otherwise use quite different strategies.

A contrast of a different type is supplied by comparing encounter with biofeedback. Encounter principally involves *communication.* Other relevant components are *concretizing, increasing personal involvement, testing the limits, merging with a larger collectivity, problem solving, alteration of self-image,* and perhaps *environmental reorganization.* Encounter is clearly a multidimensional approach.

Biofeedback also principally involves *communication.* In addition, emphasis is placed on *controlling attention, concretizing,* and, of course, *variation of a significant element;* that is, one becomes aware of physiological signals that would ordinarily pass unnoticed. In this case, the distinguishing features are not in the principal component, but among the lesser ones.

If this approach is valid, it may simplify not only the descriptive problem of what is occurring in varied methods, but also have direct implications for training persons in HP approaches. Instead of having to learn hundreds of partially overlapping methods, one might master a small number of components.

Mechanisms of Psychotherapy

The difficulty in discussing the mechanisms of therapeutic change and cure employed in HP methods is that they are not basically different from those associated with other forms of psychotherapy. Most therapists agree on their basic definition of mental health. They further agree that the individual must gradually face and resolve the difficulties and dilemmas of his life in a guided and partially protected therapeutic environment where emotional relearning is possible. Defense mechanisms and sources of resistance are also generally viewed in similar terms. If there is a major difference, it arises out of the portion of the spectrum of human development to which their efforts are directed.

As already stressed, HP methods are for normal persons seeking to further their personal growth. In pursuing this goal, their sense of human possibility verges on the religious as already mentioned. Using nontheological language and coming from diverse traditions, one can detect a tendency to believe in and work toward a death and rebirth experience in various HP approaches. It is not simply change, modification, or minor alteration of the personality structure that is sought, but, more fundamentally, something that existed begins to die. Something that did not exist (or if it did, only in a potential form like the oak in the acorn) comes into being. How does this occur? Two answers are possible. It happens very gradually; and it happens very abruptly. Although these answers are directly contradictory, they actually refer to two aspects of a total process.

When a bird breaks out of an egg, or a butterfly emerges from a cocoon, it is an unprecedented event. It constitutes the beginning of a new form of life, but at the same time, it is preceded by a long period of preparation that set the stage for this dramatic breakthrough.

It is natural that scientists, therapists, and the general public should be interested in the dramatic emergence of the new and unexpected, rather than the lengthy period of gestation that preceded it. This is reflected in the continuing fascination with areas such as parapsychology, hypnotism, alternate states of consciousness, and drugs.

Parapsychology has had a long and mostly frustrating history. It seems to bring out the worst in both its critics and its proponents. Nevertheless, results continue to accrue. A typical example is in studies of the relationship between personality and extrasensory perception (ESP) scores. Dozens of experiments involving sheep-goat effects on ESP ability were recently reviewed by J. Palmer (1971, 1972). Although the precise interpretation of the findings presented some difficulties, the overall trend in the results was clearly positive, suggesting that high ESP scores are positively related to a friendly acceptance of, and interest in, the ESP task situation and its demands. Any such experiments that directly or indirectly support paranormal abilities are interesting in themselves. More important, to the extent that they are taken seriously, they require a fundamental restructuring of our view of the individual and his relation to the universe within which he functions. Such a step is, of course, congenial to an HP orientation, which tends to assume that our current view of almost anything is extremely limited.

Similarly, *hypnosis,* although still confusing as a phenomenon, suggests a vast and significant set of human possibilities that can be made to function in an almost effortless manner. The phenomena are familiar, but their basic implications are usually ignored. Hallucinations can be caused in normal people, age regression produced, amnesia induced, pain reduced or eliminated, and the sympathetic nervous system controlled in varying degrees (Nideffer, 1975). Since none of these experiences is under the individual's control under ordinary circumstances, it is astonishing that hypnotism, which is essentially a limited form of social influence, can produce them all. It is as if the individual requires external permission to use powers that lie unbidden and unexplored within him, waiting only for the proper command.

Drugs are perhaps the most striking instance of the effortless creation of extraordinary experiences. Although the effects are unpredictable in any given individual, the remarkable nature of these effects is certainly evident. Although drugs are not a substitute for growth, they can undeniably provide the individual with a glimpse of his potential and, from a scientific viewpoint, help to establish the further limits of human experience, although they may not provide much insight into the attainment of these conditions on a permanent basis.

Interest in the alteration of consciousness produced by drugs is not as new as we sometimes like to think. James (1902) discussed the effects of nitrous oxide in his analysis of religious and mystical experience.

Some years ago I myself made some observations on this aspect of nitrous oxide intoxication. . . . Looking back on my own experiences, they all converge towards a kind of insight to which I cannot help ascribing some metaphysical significance. The keynote of it is invariably a reconciliation. It is as if the opposites of the world, whose contradictoriness and conflict make all our difficulties and troubles, were melted into unity. . . .

He followed in a long line of scientific and personal accounts of such experiences. The main difference between these accounts and our modern position is that the range of drugs available to us has greatly increased. Human nature is still much the same.

All of this material and other forms of inner experience such as meditation have found a convenient focusing point in the area known as *altered states of consciousness*. The hallmark of studies in this area is that they attempt to relate inner states of awareness to observable physiological indicators, thus providing an objective verification of material that could previously only be dealt with by subjective report. This is largely a technical innovation, but important nevertheless. It opens some of the more subtle and evanescent aspects of consciousness to respectable scientific study.

An example of what may be possible is suggested by studies of various techniques of meditation that have recently been reviewed by V. F. Emerson (1972).

Much of the early work focused on the physiological correlates of *transcendental meditation* (TM). Numerous investigators reported findings such as decreased oxygen consumption and lowered carbon dioxide elimination, a decrease in blood lactate, an increase in skin resistance, and high alpha rhythm. All of these indicators suggest a state of deep relaxation. These results were widely used by TM practitioners to promote the method. Some of this enthusiasm was spiked, however, when it was found that virtually the same results were obtained by having subjects repeat the number "one" to themselves (Benson, 1975). No special mantra or other instruction was necessary.

However, further studies of meditation have shown some highly differentiated results. Measures of alpha blocking, the tendency of alpha waves to be curtailed abruptly in the presence of a sudden, unexpected stimulus, such as a strong light or loud noise, have been extremely interesting in this regard.

When Indian yogis were studied, alpha blocking was found before, but not during, meditation (Bagchi & Wenger, 1957). This suggests that while meditating, the yogis were removed from environmental influences, which is precisely the condition of detachment from the phenomenal world that yoga is supposed to produce (Akishige, 1970).

Studies of Zen masters have shown a different pattern. Alpha blocking did not occur during meditation, nor did this pattern change as it did for a group of controls who gradually became accustomed to the external stimulus. In short, no matter how many times the stimulus was suddenly administered, the Zen masters continued to react to it. This is totally in keeping with Zen philosophy, which does not involve turning from the world of illusion as in yoga, but advocates a passionless awareness of the world.

Studies of *kriya yoga,* where the overall purpose has been the arousal of *kundalini* energy at the base of the spine, rather than withdrawal or passionless involvement, have produced quite different patterns in brain wave activity and other physiological indicators. In this case, beta activity (associated with high states of internal arousal) was greatly increased and heart activity accelerated (Das & Gastaut, 1957).

All of these results are based on relatively few subjects, but they are extremely suggestive. For the first time, it may be possible to begin to obtain objective proof of what were previously assumed to be purely subjective phenomena of a relatively subtle nature. Although the practitioners of these methods may not themselves be terribly impressed, the long-range implications for the validation of meditative approaches and their eventual application to a variety of social situations their originators had never conceived, such as survival in emergency situations or self-control under various normative conditions of social interaction, are very important.

A note of caution must be introduced, however. Early work on the correlation of alpha rhythm with the relaxed awareness produced by some forms of meditation led to an instant enlightenment fad, in which biofeedback was used to train persons to increase their alpha rate. In itself, this was a perfectly reasonable activity. However, the tendency for American culture to emphasize anything new, particularly if something electrical or mechanical can be related to it, produced claims and involved economic considerations that quickly got out of control as countless people rushed to turn on with alpha.

As this experience suggests, the danger in this type of investigation is that it lends credence to the notion of easy enlightenment. This is not the way it really happens. Even in the Zen tradition, which emphasizes sudden and unexpected insight, such experiences are preceded by a very lengthy preparation and a degree of effort and discipline that most Westerners would shun. This is typical in any well-developed tradition. There is a long period of introductory work before the breakthrough. This is seen not only in mystical experiences, but also in classical studies of creativity.

The average individual who lives successfully in his society has developed his ego gradually through a lengthy process of socialization. This *ego* is an artificial creation developed to protect the individual from various threatening forces in the environment and in himself. The fundamental change that HP methods produce, if they are successful, generally involves an alteration in the experience of the ego. This alteration occurs through breaking down the barriers created by normal psychological defenses, so the individual is able to redefine and reexperience his own boundaries. In varying degrees, he becomes one with a larger collectivity. Eventually, he may feel one with the universe. Such an experience cannot come without a lengthy preparation because the strength of a healthy person's defenses is too great to permit it. If it should occur due to artificial means, such as drugs or an external emergency, it is likely to be extremely disorienting and may lead to a psychotic episode as the individual attempts to flee from experience that appears to engulf him.

It takes great flexibility and inner security to surrender one's familiar identity to allow something of a greater nature to begin to manifest itself. It is precisely such a rare and wonderful possibility that HP methods in their strongest form seek to encourage. If they succeed, the human experience is transferred onto a cosmic stage.

APPLICATIONS

Problems

The major distinctive quality in individuals best suited for HP experiences is that they are self-selected. They are not referred by professionals but come precisely because they are dissatisfied with what professionals have to offer. They may, in some cases, have been exposed to various psychotherapies. Now they wish to extend their experience and functioning.

For this reason, one cannot isolate a particular client group for whom HP methods are most suitable, because presumably all such categories have been passed through before HP methods become relevant.

Of course, in any practical situation, it is never that clear-cut. Everyone is a little neurotic. Even if this were not the case, as the individual delves deeper, he realizes the positive potential that comes to light is balanced by negative potential that hopefully remains in the dark. Part of sanity is to understand one's potential for insanity and transcend it. The individual who has to deny such tendencies in himself must devote a great deal of his awareness and energy to maintaining his defenses intact. That, in itself, is not particularly healthy.

It may sound like a gross simplification to say that HP methods are most suited to people who want them, but it is true. There are so many different types of HP methods that individuals can find something to which they relate on some level. If emotional catharsis is not fruitful, they can try sensory awareness. If that does not affect them, they can shift to guided imagery, biofeedback, or creative problem solving. They are sure to find one or more types of approaches to which they respond easily and effectively.

However, it would be naive to suggest that a person is automatically drawn to what he necessarily needs. The opposite may be true. The individual may be shy, but excellent at daydreaming and imagery work. For him to do what is already easy will not affect his shyness very much. Sooner or later, he must have some type of socially oriented experience, if he is to grow in a balanced manner.

To the extent that HP experiences are highly focused on one or two approaches, the selection process represents an important issue. If people refer themselves, will they have the insight and the courage to do what is good for them as distinct from what feels good?

In practice, however, this problem is not too serious. Most HP programs are extremely varied. In fact, practitioners seem to vie with each other to make their programs continually more novel and comprehensive.

At times, as one reviews the catalogues for various growth centers, one has the impression that one is reading the advertisements for new cars. Everyone is looking for something different to catch the attention of the public. In fact, all cars do about the same thing, and all workshops try to give the participants a varied interdisciplinary experience of methods drawn from various levels and backgrounds, limited mainly by the previous experience, competence, and confidence of the practitioner involved.

Although the persons coming to such experiences may be fairly normal as compared to the general run of the population, they do not stay normal. It is the nature of any growth experience to make people crazier as a function of the experience itself. This is a little dismaying to one who is unfamiliar with the process, but it is no different than the TB patient who promptly gets worse once he is in the sanatorium. The open conditions in an HP workshop allow any potential difficulty to reveal itself. This is necessary and useful. Such tendencies are ordinarily hidden and controlled, but they represent limitations and a source of future difficulties if they are not faced and resolved. As one begins to open internally and allows defenses to loosen, it is natural that what emerges is not always pretty, but this is a familiar experience in psychotherapy. The difference is that in therapy, people are expected to act strangely or they would not be there in the first place. We fail to realize it is normal to be crazy at times if one is trying to grow. The process is inherently stressful and threatening to the ego that is being stretched and slowly transcended.

Evaluation

In the long run, evaluation is crucial in determining the significance of any development, particularly new ones. At the same time, one must recognize that it is very difficult to establish the value of any form of psychotherapy because of the variables that need to be controlled, special methodological problems that occur, extensive bias that exists, and the lack of motivation that practitioners have toward such an undertaking, regardless of the method being studied.

Specifically, any form of evaluation must face a series of technical problems associated with the measuring instruments employed, the subjects, the practitioner, and the method. Such evaluations must employ instruments that measure relevant outcome variables. These instruments are all subject to various sources of bias and error. For example, subjects can give "socially desirable" rather than true answers, that is, give the responses they think the practitioner or experimenter wants. Further, there may be an interaction between the instrument and the method. The nature of the instrument may sensitize the subjects to certain aspects of the method and produce effects that would not have occurred if the instrument had not been used.

Further, there are a number of characteristics of any practitioner that must be controlled, including his faith in the method, the degree of training and competence he possesses, his personality, and so on. All of these factors may influence outcome, but are in no way related to the validity of the method in its own right.

The subjects of the study also present a number of characteristics that must be controlled. By virtue of being experimental subjects, they receive special attention. This attention may produce change, irrespective of the method. The attitude of the subjects toward the method is an important variable. Faith in the absence of any method can produce change.

Finally, the method itself is a source of possible confusion. Most forms of psychotherapy are exceedingly complex. However, any responsible scientific study must be reproducible. For this to be possible, the method must be clear and precise. This can create a basic dilemma, in which precision must be traded off for realism. Further, it is naive to assume that just because a practitioner says he is using a particular method that this is necessarily true. It requires independent confirmation from an observer.

There are, in addition to these technical considerations, a series of social difficulties that occur if research is carried out under field conditions, which is generally the case.

For the sake of the research, it is desirable to keep the program under evaluation as isolated as possible from the institution in which it is being conducted, so the process does not become contaminated by outside influence. However, institutions depend on open channels of communication for their effective functioning, so the scientist and the administrator find themselves at cross-purposes.

The use of a control group of patients who do not receive the treatment under investigation goes counter to the psychotherapeutic ethic that says treatment should be provided in accordance with need. Although this is no longer a serious problem in practice, it still constitutes a direct contradiction in principle.

Further, it is desirable to use as many practitioners in the study as possible. The greater the sample of practitioners, the more generalizable the results. However, from an administrative viewpoint, the fewer the practitioners involved, the less disruptive it will be to the normal program of activities.

The professionals in most mental-health settings work regular and long hours, subject to the supervision of their superiors. Researchers generally supervise themselves and constitute an isolated island within the total institution. They can come and go as they please and follow a different ethic and work code. This can lead to misunderstanding, particularly since the practitioners involved in the study may be somewhat threatened by the process. It is hard for them to separate the effectiveness of the method they use from their personal impact on the subjects. If the evaluation fails, it is a personal failure to them.

Evaluation has a tendency to spread. What starts as an isolated activity slowly permeates the institution, creating a sense of threat among workers and administrators in other programs that have been proceeding without evaluation or objective accountability. If the climate becomes hostile, the conduct of the study can become almost impossible, particularly since it takes years, not months, for most evaluative research to be conducted.

This leads to a final point. The general time lapse between inception of a study design and the use of its final conclusions is about five years. It takes a year to conceive of and secure funds for the study, three years to conduct and write the results, and a final year to digest and apply the conclusions. It is quite likely that whatever administrative actions must be taken in regard to the particular method under investigation will have occurred long before the five-year period has elapsed. Thus, the study serves no immediate purpose, except to employ the staff involved.

Even more serious, however, is the question of what is learned in such a process, even when it is successfully carried out. The answer unfortunately is, "Not much." The information can be summarized in one or two conclusions. The method produces demonstrable effects, or it does not. Since the methods that are evaluated are constructed of a complicated set of interacting variables that are very difficult to describe and almost impossible to control, the more crucial question of why change occurs is not clarified. This is the kind of information that must be obtained if our understanding of the relative contribution different variables make to the change process is ever to improve.

Treatment

In principle, HP methods were developed for working with normal people and what W. C. Schutz (1973) calls "normal neurotics," that is, people who do not require traditional forms of psychotherapy. Thus, the very concept of treatment does not really apply. One "treats" a "problem." One educates a capacity.

Under everyday conditions there is no particular necessity for most people to function at high performance levels, but when the level of expectation is raised, HP treatment methods become pertinent. This may occur in the context of executive development, leadership training, or survival experiences of various types. But more typically, as previously indicated, the individual selects himself as a subject for HP treatment. He wants to function at a higher level of efficiency and to experience a greater degree of personal fulfillment.

TABLE 13.3
Human Capacities

1. Sensory awareness (on inner stimuli)
2. Perceiving the environment
3. Moving in space
4. Emotional expression
5. Visualization and imagination
6. Empathy
7. Paranormal abilities
8. Creative expression
9. Intelligence
10. Ethical values
11. Concentration and will power
12. Meditation
13. Role behavior
14. Conditioning
15. Environmental reorganization

In any discussion of HP methods as a form of treatment, one cannot talk in familiar categories. The treatment is not problem oriented. Rather, one must organize the experience around the cultivation of particular capacities. There are as many ways to define human capacities as there are theories of individual development. The particular categories that are used matter less than the clarity of the divisions and the degree of completeness of the coverage. One set of categories is given in Table 13.3.

Workshops exist that clearly relate to one of these categories. Consider the following titles, taken from a recent growth-center catalogue (Entayant, 1977). "The Use of Poetry in Personal Growth" falls clearly into the creative expression category. "The Magic of Movement" is primarily concerned with moving in space. "Interior Design Awareness" focuses on environmental reorganization. The "Isolation Tank Experience" emphasizes sensory awareness.

More typically, one finds workshops that cover a number of capacities. Examples are endless: "Transcendental Sex. . . . In this workshop, we'll explore a meditative approach to human sexuality." "Gestalt Bio-energetics Workshop. . . . The focus will be on the here and now. . . . You will experience how your body is the best clue to your problems and limitations." "Guided Imagery and Music . . . new techniques to facilitate deep relaxation, affect-release, music and symbolic imagery as an approach in healing and as an effective treatment in therapy."

At the other end of the scale are open encounter groups, such as those developed by Schutz (1973) that consciously attempt to use methods from virtually every aspect of human performance within the context of a group experience. Whether a highly eclectic approach is better than a clearly focused one depends on many factors: the needs and attitudes of the participants, the skills of the leader, the time available, and the nature of the setting. This is an issue that must ultimately be settled by comparative research. For purposes of description, the simplified workshop is useful in clarifying the methods most typically associated with the cultivation of particular abilities.

The profusion and complexity of such methods make the situation appear almost hopeless to the social scientist interested in studying behavior change. There are, of course, exceptions. Areas such as biofeedback, hypnotism, and alteration of consciousness have occasionally been the subjects of fairly accurate scientific exploration. The reason in each case is that the nature of the method permits the use of physiological indicators, such as EEG, EKG, skin resistance, and heart rate, to measure effects. These measures provide accurate results, which are always an attractive feature to scientific investigators looking for topics that are both interesting and precise. Further, the independent variable can also be clearly

described. Thus, in studies of hypnotism, the induction procedure can be written out or recorded on tape so reapplication is possible. Studies of altered states of consciousness use physiological, psychological, or pharmacological stimuli that can be precisely specified.

If one has any faith in the scientific method as a guide to the improvement of human performance, the difficulties presented by experimental studies of human-potential methods must be resolved. As already suggested in the section Process of Psychotherapy, any HP method can be reduced to the component strategies of which it is composed. These strategies are simple building blocks of human experience that can be accurately described and consequently lend themselves to scientific testing more easily than the complex methods from which they were derived. Even more important, when a component strategy is tested, something is learned about all methods in which the component appears. When the complex method is tested, almost nothing is learned about anything, except whether the total experience produces any measurable effect.

One means of studying component strategies in an efficient multivariable design has been described by Mann (1972). Other possibilities exist. What is needed is a more general recognition that the question of treatment effectiveness must be asked in the right way if meaningful and useful answers are to be obtained.

Management

The major management features of HP experiences are produced by the structure of the growth center in which they are often conducted. To the extent that the methods lend themselves to a workshop format, many of the traditional forms of intake, office structure, billing, and role relationships between practitioner and client are dramatically altered.

A recent growth-center brochure deals with these familiar issues in the following terms (Entayant, 1977):

1. Leaders do workshops in their current interest and where their energy is.
2. Leaders lay no trips on participants. That participants be allowed to come to their own awareness in their own time. Facilitation to that end is a leader's job.
3. In any experimental work, the participants takes responsibility to say stop when they want to. The leader fully accepts that.

Although the above principles leave something to be desired from a legal and linguistic standpoint, they document some typical practices in the HP movement. First, the participant is fundamentally responsible for his own behavior. If something goes wrong, he cannot blame the leader unless he can prove he was forced to do something he really did not want to do. Since the above statement indicates he should not allow that to happen if the work is experimental, the situation is inherently ambiguous.

Second, although leaders are, by inference, paid professionals, they are doing what they want to do, not carrying through some professional function just for the money. Third, some of the activities are explicitly recognized as experimental. The purpose of a growth center is precisely to allow such activities to occur. In this respect, it clearly differs from most therapeutic work. The average patient would be wary of anything marked "experimental," unless he was desperate and did not know where else to turn.

Payment and intake procedures are equally atypical. In most therapeutic situations, one pays after services are received. In the same growth-center bulletin, the question of payment and intake are handled as follows:

> Your registration must be *received* . . . ten days before the date of the workshop you wish to attend. . . . Full payment is required before workshop starts. If after registering, you decide to cancel, you must notify us 10 days or more prior to the scheduled event. One half of your deposit will be refunded, the other half applied to another workshop of your choice. . . .

With open registration, it is difficult or impossible to exercise much control over the intake procedure. There is typically no attempt to have any preliminary screening interview. However, neither are long-term services being offered. The assumption is that the individual assumes responsibility for selecting the activities he wants, and that any problems that occur can be dealt with during the workshop experience. To some extent, this is a realistic position, since the purpose of any therapeutic experience is to deal with current difficulties. However, it is also increasingly recognized that special provision must be made for unusual situations. The previously quoted catalogue states in this connection: "We ask that anyone involved in a program of psychological counseling therapy consult with their counselor or therapist before enrolling in a Workshop. Our Workshops are designed for emotional enrichment (a learning experience) and not as a substitute for on-going therapeutic experience." It is further stated that: "Counseling service available on selection of workshops."

A clear distinction is drawn between traditional therapeutic practices and the growth-center experience. This distinction is not only useful in theory, but also helps to establish a working relation between more traditional therapists and the practitioners in the growth center. Further, inasmuch as some advice is available in relation to programs offered, the participant can, at least potentially, make an informed choice. This would be very difficult from the catalogue alone, since all activities are made to sound as interesting as possible.

Any form of group work (and almost all workshops fall into this category) must contend with the problem of confidentiality. A professional in charge of the activity may feel bound to secrecy, but this in no way limits the participants. They may or may not agree to keep the contents of the experience within the group setting. However, there is no legal means of enforcing such a decision when it is made, particularly when the participants are only together for a few days and then scatter to different communities. The participant must assume that no binding pledge of confidentiality exists and act accordingly. Since traditional therapy is not being conducted, this is not often a serious problem. Sharing of previously hidden material may, in part, have a therapeutic effect. The public confession of one's deficiencies is a vital element in many group methods.

The typical growth center convenes in two different types of settings: urban and rural. The urban center functions mainly during the colder seasons and makes up in convenience what it lacks in beauty. The major requirement is that it have sufficient space for the activities that may be involved, such as creative movement, and sufficient privacy so hideous screams will not bring the police.

The rural settings are what most people have in mind when they think of growth centers. These are usually located as far from civilization as possible, in as beautiful a location as is available, and constitute a therapeutic cultural island in

which participants can temporarily lose themselves. These locations operate during the summer, unless the climate of the region permits a more extended season.

On entering most growth centers, one is immediately struck by their nonprofessional aspects. All of the familiar accoutrements of the doctor and clinician are gone: diplomas on the wall, formal furniture, nurses in uniform, and so on. In their place are lots of people, in varying stages of uncertainty, with the emphasis on informality, letting go, and trying new forms of behavior. In that respect, growth centers are like resorts. They are by no means luxurious, however. Living conditions can be relatively primitive. They may be primitive for practical reasons, but it is also in keeping with the spirit of the experience. One goes to the workshop to get in touch with one's more natural, childlike, spontaneous aspects. Simple living arrangements bring back one's childhood and help to level all the participants and take them out of their familiar living patterns.

All of these factors—the informality, the responsibility each person takes for himself, the educational rather than therapeutic orientation, the nature of the setting, the expectation of the participants—interact to produce a tension and excitement that is hard to describe unless one has felt the effect. It is this more than any particular element that leads to the unique impact of the growth-center experience.

CASE EXAMPLE

(In the following history, events are described by the therapist as if he were present although, in fact, he heard about most of them after they had occurred.)

Bob came to an open group encounter, partly in ignorance of what the experience might be. Within the first five minutes of the group meeting, he was mildly terrorized by a wrestling match that started between two men. This fear grew during the course of the experience, as the intensity of the emotions expressed were more than he could either accept or encompass. His outward behavior was one of silence or flight. Considerable effort was exerted both by the group leader and other members to include him in the encounter, but it was not successful. He engaged in a series of evasive maneuvers until the focus of the group shifted elsewhere.

Nevertheless, the fear he felt caused him to reach out for comfort to one of the shyer women present. They gave each other mutual support as the events of the group continued on their intense path with different people taking the center stage, working as needed under the general guidance of the leader, using a variety of approaches: fantasy, psychodrama, personal confrontation, and even a touch of psychoanalysis. Inwardly, Bob had one objective: to survive the experience.

The 48-hour period during which the group met became, in retrospect, a turning point in his life. On the drive home to his wife and family, he went through a personal crisis. His point of first concentration was staying on the road, since he was physically shaking. His second was facing the life he had made for himself. Whichever way he looked, the truth was there to see. He had an interesting, secure job. He was married and had several children. Society was satisfied with him. But he realized he had never really become a man. This was a somewhat shattering insight coming as it did in his late thirties, but emerging from the brutal intensity of the encounter-group experience, he could not deny it. There were two central features within him that rose up and stared back at him with hollow eyes. One was his fear of aggressive contact with

men. The second was that he had never really had a satisfactory relation with a woman. He had never grown up and no one really cared, except, temporarily, himself. He knew he must make a choice, and that it must occur before he got home, or he would lose the insight and the courage. He chose to become a man.

He proceeded to pursue this goal by attending a number of encounter-group weekends during the next six months. Each of these experiences, although complete in itself and seemingly endless at the time, provided opportunities for confrontation with his weaknesses. He had to physically break out of a circle of group members who tried their best to hold him in. He was ultimately forced to wrestle with the group leader. During the emotional battles that occurred, he became closer to several of the women present. At the end of the period, he climaxed his progress by temporarily becoming co-leader of the group.

This phase concluded when the leader left the area and moved west. At that point, Bob had another choice to make. He could cash in his chips and go about his normal life or he could continue to pursue his own maturity. He realized that to continue might disrupt his relationship with his wife, since living out the adolescence he had never really had increased his attraction to other women. He thought it over and decided to continue. He had only taken the first steps.

The next phase of his search carried him to Esalen. It was here that his vision of what might be possible took on expanded dimensions. As he drove along the highway from the Monterey airport, the mountain road cut into the cliffs overlooking the Pacific took him away from all familiar landmarks. Arriving at Esalen, he was surrounded by people in search of themselves, by leaders reveling in the freedom of the environment, and by a strange group of hippie caretakers, cooks, and waiters. The natural scenery and the unique social situation were unlike anything he had previously known.

He immersed himself in the environment. His first experience was in a workshop on creativity. It was comparatively mild. At one point, a Chinese girl asked everyone to sit in a circle, close their eyes, and visualize a seed being put in the ground. "For the next 20 minutes," she said, "I want you to watch the seed grow." Bob thought he had heard wrong. He opened his eyes, but everyone seemed to be taking her seriously. He started to visualize putting the seed in the ground. To his amazement, he discovered it was possible. Time passed. Days passed. The seasons passed. The seed sprouted. It grew into a tree. People came and went. The sun, the stars, the wind. When the 20 minutes were up he was surprised, but also dissatisfied.

"It would have been better," he said to the group leader, "if we could have acted it out."

"What do you mean?" asked the leader, mildly intrigued.

"Just *become* a tree," said Bob.

"Why don't you show us?" said the leader.

For the next 15 minutes, Bob became a tree. He acted out its gradual growth, the effect of the wind and the sun and the air. He became completely immersed in the experience, forgetting that anyone was watching. At the end, there was applause. He was surprised. The leader was impressed. For the first time, he thought something he had done was successful and not just tolerated because he was learning.

It gave him courage to approach the hot sulphur springs for which Esalen was famous, but which he had avoided during the first few days. He did not know what

he would find, except he had heard that people went nude and that sometimes it was co-ed. He was overweight and felt awkward. Everyone seemed to take the baths for granted, and consequently he could not find out too much about them without appearing slightly ridiculous.

When the creativity workshop was over, Bob gathered together his courage and his towel and walked down the steep hill to the baths. They were almost deserted, which was both a relief and an anticlimax. Lying in the hot sulphur water and listening to the waves of the Pacific break on the rocks far below, his life seemed very strange and suddenly much more unpredictable.

As he lay there, others came in. It was co-ed, but he was already in the water. It all seemed quite natural even though he did not know the people.

Later he emerged. There was another workshop to come. He walked back up the path. Halfway up, he paused. There was a girl he had never seen before coming down. At that point, the path widened so they could pass each other. There was a moment's pause. Suddenly, to his amazement, he took her in his arms and they held each other for what seemed a very long time, two total strangers in a familiar land. . . .

The next workshop was an open encounter experience that went on for five days. It followed its familiar course of gathering intensity, but because it was familiar, he could relax without trying to avoid or predict the outcome.

Surrounding Esalen was a remarkable redwood forest owned by neighbors, but used by workshop participants when they needed to get away. After several days, Bob felt impelled to go out into this forest, partly to be alone and mostly to let something out that needed isolation. As he walked, he began to mutter to himself.

Then he talked in a German accent. He was aware that he must look crazy to anyone who was watching him. He did not care. Whatever was inside had to emerge. His voice grew louder. He realized it was a Nazi talking, who wanted to kill, destroy, and rule the world. The voice kept pouring out of him for a half hour. It was horrifying and thrilling at the same time. When it had run its course, he collapsed on the forest floor, listened to the sound of the wind and the forest stream, and felt the aftereffects of the passing insanity. He left the woods feeling stronger, wilder, and with a new sense of freedom.

Part of the encounter experience was to meet in pairs. During one of these intervals, he and a woman, named Ann, got together on the front lawn.

They sat there very relaxed. Bob was struck by the fact that he felt totally at home.

"You know," he said, "I've hardly said two words to you before this, but I feel like I've known you all my life."

"I feel the same," she said.

In the course of a 15-minute exchange, they became extremely close. It was very natural but almost unbelievable. It went against every expectation. It should have taken months.

During the workshop, Bob had his first Esalen massage, an experience that had been developed by the staff over a several-year period to combine massage, sensory awareness, and meditation. The massage itself was preceded by a long soak in the sulphur baths. Then he lay down on a table in the sunshine, nude, with only the sound of wind and the ocean waves in the background. The girl giving the massage said only, "Relax and experience what I am doing as deeply as you can. And enjoy it."

For the next one and one-half hours, Bob soaked in the impressions created in his own body. He emerged from the experience not quite sure what had happened until he returned to the encounter group. Then he quickly realized he was totally defenseless. This was wonderful in itself, but not a very good position to be in when other people were arguing and attacking each other. He blended into the background until the effect of the massage wore off.

A day later, while he was eating supper, a young man who was sitting next to him asked, "How are you feeling?" It seemed like an innocent question.

"I feel great," said Bob, "Or I did until you asked the question."

"I noticed a change in you about five minutes ago," said the young man. "In about two minutes you should be really sad."

Bob was understandably dubious.

"Come on in the next room before it hits," said the young man. "There's a rocking chair there."

Bob followed meekly, beginning to feel a great sense of loss. In the next five minutes, he began to enact one of the stranger scenes of his life. The young man sat on the rocking chair. Bob began to cry. The young man motioned Bob to sit on his lap. With some reluctance, he did and then started to bawl his head off. Although he felt very peculiar, Bob had sense enough not to allow anything to stop the experience. It lasted for almost a half hour. During that period, the group formed again, totally at a loss whether to do something or ignore what was happening.

After it was over, Bob did not want to talk about it, beyond expressing his gratitude to the young man. Later, it was very evident to him that he had become one or two years old and was back in his mother's arms. It proved to be a very healing experience.

Bob continued to grow closer to Ann. During this period, he was loaned a small house in the woods in a beautiful and romantic location. He thought about asking Ann to spend the night. But the workshop was coming to an end. There was very little time. It was something he wanted to do, but more than that, something he felt he had to do. He had no idea how she felt. Finally, on the last night of the group, he decided to approach the matter out in the open. He talked with her in the group, the two of them facing each other with everyone else watching.

"I want to spend the night with you, Ann."

"I'm really flattered."

"I'm not trying to flatter you. I mean it."

She smiled. . . .

After a time, various group members made comments. Much to his surprise, the group leader gave Bob his support. But the whole situation was a little ambiguous. It seemed like an understanding had been reached, but not absolutely.

The group continued until 1:30 in the morning. After that, Bob asked Ann to go for a walk. The night was dark. They walked back toward the house in the woods.

"What's going to happen?" he asked.

"What do you mean?"

"I mean," he said, "are we going to stay together?"

"I can't. Don't you understand?"

"No, not really."

"I'm married," she said.

"So what? I'm married, too."

"I'd like to, but I can't. How can you ask me?"

Bob became more intense as she became more evasive.

Finally, the truth emerged.

"Don't you understand? My husband is here with me at Esalen. He's in a different group. How could I explain to him where I was?"

After that, Bob had nothing to say. They kissed goodnight, and he went on alone to his little house in the woods. He threw himself on the bed and began to cry. It was quite different from any other tears. He felt like he was being ripped open. He did not fight. He did not want anything to be different. He just shed tears that had been held in for decades. It did not matter how things turned out. All that mattered was that he was alive and that a deep source of sorrow had been tapped and was surfacing.

The next day, the participants left, and Bob had the pleasure of watching Ann depart with her husband. But it no longer mattered. The process that had begun about nine months before was completing itself. He knew it would take some time to digest the impressions and experiences that had been condensed into a 10-day period at Esalen. He also knew he could not emerge from the incredible personal intensity the same person. He could no longer accept the life he had known or the weakness in himself that had led him to accept it. Wherever he looked, he could see work for him to do on himself. But he had the rest of his life to do it, and it would be worth the effort.

The preceding emphasizes certain therapeutic experiences occurring during a significant period in Bob's life. Many of these events might have occurred in other therapeutic approaches. What is unusual is the way in which the HP experiences interacted within the encounter group and growth-center environment to produce a therapeutic impact that escalated beyond the control of any single individual or situation.

It is traditional to conclude any case example with a brief statement indicating that the problem was resolved, and that five years later, progress continues. This is not quite adequate to the present situation, although it is true. Bob did develop a new life, which was more or less inevitable. What was not so inevitable was his attitude toward himself and his future life. This can best be described in terms of a dream he reported.

I was climbing a mountain. I walked and walked. I scaled cliffs. I did whatever I had to do to get to the top. When I got there, what I saw was another mountain range, higher than the one I was standing on. Behind that was mist. I knew that the mist concealed an even greater range, and that it went on that way forever. The only question was how far I wanted to go. There was no limit, nothing on the earth would hold me back if I was willing to make the effort. . . .

SUMMARY

The human-potential movement differs from other forms of current and traditional psychotherapies in a number of fundamental ways.

First, it is not a particular type of therapy. It is a diverse collection of approaches drawn from different areas, traditions, historical periods, and cultures.

Second, it is probably not psychotherapy at all. The major concern of the human-potential movement is personal growth. It is not intended for persons who are mentally disturbed, but for normal individuals who are successfully socialized, but remain dissatisfied with their existence. In this sense, it is more like education than therapy.

Third, it is not education in the usual sense, because its interests are much broader. The ordinary educational curriculum limits itself to intellectual pursuits. Other human capacities, such as physical performance and creative behavior, are relegated to sports, theater, or extracurricular activities.

Human potential is interested in all human capacities. It includes every method that can extend, cultivate, and develop these capacities. These include sensory awareness, perceiving the environment, moving in space, emotional expression, visualization and imagination, empathy, paranormal abilities, creative expression, intelligence, ethical values, attention and the will, meditation, conditioning, role behavior, and environmental reorganization.

Fourth, it is remarkably unconcerned with issues of certification and professionalization. It views these tendencies as regrettable necessities that interfere with productivity and limit the definition of the field.

Fifth, it has developed its own social structure, the growth center, which is relatively independent of the major institutions of society such as schools, industry, and the government. Growth centers are self-sustaining and exist only to present the latest and best in human-potential approaches. They are totally eclectic and to be distinguished from workshops and institutes developed by particular forms of therapy that may on superficial inspection appear somewhat similar.

Sixth, the human-potential approach is a source of creative ferment, rather than a clearly articulated system. Certain individuals have been prominent in bringing early recognition to the area, but it is marked by a continuous turnover of practitioners and approaches.

Seventh, although it is notably apolitical, the human-potential movement is very closely connected with ethos of the times. In the 1960s, it embodied personal struggle for fulfillment, offering the psychological equivalent of the social revolution that was occurring at the same time. During this period, the encounter group was its most visible symbol. In the 1970s, the focus has become more intrapersonal and transpersonal. Increasing interest has been focused on altered states of consciousness, not only because of recent breakthroughs in the availability of subtle physiological measurement techniques, but also as part of a general religious revival in America that places primary emphasis on personal experience. Although this is a broad social phenomenon, it is clearly reflected in the maturing and redirection of much human-potential work from a group to an individual emphasis. A new social form has been adopted for this purpose: the ashram.

In many respects, the ashram is the antithesis of the growth center. It is run by one person who has religious rather than political sources of authority and power. It is devoted to one outlook. It encourages a disciplined manner of life. It embodies a clearly defined sense of direction as an alternative to the smorgasbord approach to human-potential methods that the growth center has offered and continues to offer.

The human-potential movement is the visible expression of what Abraham Maslow called "Third Force Psychology." It is the antidote to the scientific and Freudian excesses of the past. As with any movement, it develops its own excesses, such as a tendency toward novelty for its own sake, a lack of differentiation between methods, a relative indifference to long-range effects, and an overemphasis on immediate experience. All of these tendencies are potential sources of difficulty. None of them are inevitable, but they must be recognized by those who are responsible for this work if they are to be successfully corrected. If this occurs, the initial enthusiasm of the HP movement can be integrated into the longer reach of scientific humanism where it truly belongs.

ANNOTATED BIBLIOGRAPHY

Barber, T. X. (Ed.) *Advances in altered states of consciousness & human potentialities, Volume 1.* New York: Psychological Dimensions, 1976.

This is the first in a projected series of volumes containing articles and studies in the varied fields of altered states of consciousness and human potential. The specific topics covered include: awareness, consciousness, and mental functions; biofeedback; mind-altering drugs; hypnosis; acupuncture; dreams and sleep, parapsychology; and human potentialities. The general quality of the selections included is high and the level of interest broad. If the series continues, it should represent an important resource in the field.

James, W. The energies of men. *Philosophical Review,* January, 1907.

This early paper is the classic statement of the human-potential position. It appeared at least 50 years before the human-potential movement began to form, but would hardly need to be rewritten for a modern audience. William James was the model scientific humanist. He maintained an open mind in areas where other psychologists refused even to look; balanced his intellectual understanding with his personal experience; and more than any of his contemporaries, and few who came later, was able to develop models for future developments that others only now are beginning to use.

Mann, J. H. *Learning to be.* New York: Free Press, 1972.

William James, in "The Energies of Men," stated that the cultivation of human powers and capacities held the highest priority in the formulation of the educational goals for the individual and the nation. This volume is directed toward that end, attempting to relate the methods evolved by the human-potential movement to the education of various human functions. This book is based on the Stanford Research Institute study of human-potential approaches. In addition to providing an analysis of HP methods, it discusses research strategies for studying these methods and provides a visionary statement of the school of the future in which they are actually applied.

Miller, S. *Hot springs.* New York: Viking Press, 1971.

A personal account of what it was like to live for an extended period in a growth center. The book is written with unusual style by a former English professor who left his academic life behind to enter the enchanted, threatening, bewildering, but never dull cultural island of Esalen. It captures not only the impact of particular experiences, but the longer range influence of the environment on the maturation of a New York intellectual who really did not know what he was getting into when he went west.

Otto, H., & Mann, J. H. (Eds.) *Ways of growth.* New York: Penguin, 1976.

This book was originally outlined by Michael Murphy of Esalen and Herbert Otto, but finally appeared as indicated above. It constitutes the first collection of articles on human-potential methods in book form. When it was first issued in 1968 in hard cover, it produced remarkably little interest. But since that time, it has gone through 3 softcover publications in 10 editions. It contains the early statements of a number of practitioners in the field who have subsequently written at much greater length in their areas of interest, including Sydney Jourard, Harold Greenwald, Magda Proskauer, Herbert Otto, Jack Gibb, Claudio Naranjo, George Brown, and Willis Harman.

CASE READINGS

Haigh, G. The residential encounter group. In H. A. Otto & J. H. Mann (Eds.), *Ways of growth.* New York: Grossman, 1968, pp. 86–100.

An account of an intensive crisis in the life of an encounter-group participant that illustrates the integration of therapeutic functioning and group member support.

Krippner, S. The plateau experience: A. H. Maslow & others. *Journal of Transpersonal Psychology,* Spring, 1973, 11–33.

A transcript of a discussion between experts on altered states of consciousness, revealing both the personalities of the participants and their thoughts.

Moreno, J. L. Psychodrama of a pre-marital couple. *Sociatry,* 1947, 2, 103–20.

Moreno presents the protocol of a session involving an engaged couple illustrating the self-directed form of psychodrama in which subjects initiate practically all ideas and actions.

Schutz, Will. A guided fantasy: Nora's account. In W. G. Schutz, *Joy.* New York: Grove Press, 1967.

An example of the use of guided fantasy in the treatment of a disturbed young woman.

REFERENCES

Akishige, Y. A historical survey of the psychological studies of Zen. In Y. Akishige (Ed.), *Psychological studies on Zen.* Bulletin of the Faculty of Literature of Kyushu University, No. 11 (V), Fukuoka, 1970.

Assagioli, R. *Psychosynthesis.* New York: Viking Press, 1971.

Bagchi, B. K., & Wenger, M. A. Electro-physiological correlates of some yogi exercises. In L. van Bogaert & J. Radermecker (Eds.), *First International Congress of Neurological Sciences, III.* New York: Pergamon Press, 1957.

Benson, H. *The relaxation response.* New York: Avon, 1975.

Brown, B. B. *Stress and the art of biofeedback.* New York: Harper & Row, 1977.

Das, N. N., & Gastaut, H. Variations de l'activité électrique du cerveau, du coeur, et des muscles squelettiques au cours de la méditation et de l'extase Yogique. *Electroencephalography and Clinical Neurophysiology,* 1957, Supplement 6, 211–19.

Emerson, V. F. Can belief systems influence neurophysiology? Some implications of research on meditation. *Newsletter-Review,* Spring, 1972, 5.

Entayant Institute. Workshops and Seminars. 1977.

Evans-Wentz, W. *Tibetan yoga and secret doctrines.* London: Oxford University Press, 1968.

Frank, J. D. *Persuasion and healing.* Baltimore: Johns Hopkins Press, 1961.

Goble, F. *The third force.* New York: Grossman, 1970.

Goleman, D. *The varieties of meditative experience.* New York: Dutton, 1977.

Gordon, W. J. *Synectics.* New York: Colliers, 1961.

Gunther, B. Sensory awareness and relaxation. In H. Otto & J. Mann (Eds.), *Ways of growth.* New York: Penguin, 1976.

James, W. *The varieties of religious experience.* New York and London: Longmans, Green & Co., 1902.

James, W. The energies of men. *Philosophical Review,* January, 1907.

James, W. The final impressions of a psychical researcher. *American Magazine,* October, 1909.

James, W. A suggestion about mysticism. *Journal of Philosophical, Psychological and Scientific Methods,* 1910, 7, 85–92.

Janov, A. *Primal scream.* New York: Dell, 1971.

Kelly, G. A. *The psychology of personal constructs: A theory of personality.* (2 vols.) New York: W. W. Norton, 1955.

Maharshi, R. *Maharshi's gospel, 1 and 2.* Tiruvanna Malai, India: Sri Ramanasram, 1962.

Mann, J. H. *Changing human behavior.* New York: Scribner's, 1965.

Mann, J. H. *Learning to be.* New York: Free Press, 1972.

Maslow, A. H. Self actualizing people: A study of psychological health. In *Personality symposia: Symposium no. 1 on values.* New York: Grune & Stratton, 1950.

Maslow, A. H. *Motivation and personality.* New York: Harper, 1954.

Maslow, A. H. Fusion of facts and values. *American Journal of Psychoanalysis.* 1963, 23, 117–31.

Maslow, A. H. Letters to the editor. *Life Magazine.* August, 1968.

Maslow, A. H. *Eupsychian management.* Homewood, Ill.: Irwin, 1973.

Mead, M. *New lives for old: A cultural transformation. Manus, 1929–1953.* New York: Morrow, 1956.

Moreno, J. L. *The words of the father.* Berlin: Kiepenheuer Verlag, 1920.

Moreno, J. L. *The theater of spontaneity.* Berlin: Kiepenheuer Verlag, 1923.

Murphy, M. Profiles by C. Tomkins. *New Yorker Magazine,* January 5, 1976.

Naranjo, C., & Ornstein, R. *On the psychology of meditation.* New York: Viking, 1971.

Nideffer, R. M. Altered states of consciousness. In L. Wheeler; R. Goodale; & J. Deese, *General psychology.* Boston, Mass.: Allyn and Bacon, 1975.

Palmer, J. Scoring in ESP tests as a function of belief in ESP. Part I. The sheep-goat effect. *American Journal of Psychical Research,* 1971, 65, 373–408.

Palmer, J. Scoring in ESP tests as a function of belief in ESP. Part II. Beyond the sheep-goat effect. *American Journal of Psychical Research,* 1972, 66, 1–26.

Parnes, S. *Creative behavior workbook.* New York: Scribner's, 1967.

Rogers, C. Some new challenges. *American Psychologist,* 1973, 28, 379–89.

Rolf, I. *Structural integration.* New York: Viking, 1972.

Schutz, W. C. Encounter. In R. J. Corsini (Ed.), *Current psychotherapies.* 1st ed. Itasca, Ill.: F.E. Peacock Publishers, 1973.

Selver, C. Sensory awareness and total functioning. *General Semantics Bulletin,* 1957, 21–22.

Sorokin, P. A. *The ways and power of love.* Chicago: Regnery. 1954.

Turnbull, C. *The lonely African.* New York: Simon & Schuster, 1962.

Turin, A., & Nideffer, R. M. Biofeedback: Clinical applications. In T. X. Barber (Ed.), *Advances in altered states of consciousness & human potentialities, Vol. I.* New York: Psychological Dimensions, 1976.

Wolfe, T. *Mauve gloves & madmen, clutter & vine.* New York: Farrar, Straus and Giroux, 1976.

Name Index

Subject Index

A-B-C theory of emotional disturbance, 190
Abreaction, 191, 193
Acceptance, 116–117, 189, 221
Action sociogram, 451
Active-directive therapy, 186, 192, 193, 206
Activating event, 185, 187, 193, 215
Active imagination, 116
Actualizing tendency, 145
Acupuncture, 514
Adlerian psychotherapy, 44; dreams, 68–69, 70; insight, 69–70; interpretation, 70–71; life style investigation, 67–69; relationship between patient and therapist, 64–67; re-orientation, 69; RET compared, 188, 201; setting, 77–79; task setting, 71–72; testing, 79; therapist, 79–80
Adolescence, 16
Advice, 70
Aggression: dental, 284; drive, 12; instinct, 53, 96; self-directed, 8
Agoraphobia, 24
Alfred Adler Institute of Chicago, 54, 75, 77
Alfred Adler Mental Hygiene Clinic, 55
Altered states of consciousness, 519
American Psychoanalytic Association, 11, 25
American Psychological Association, 10, 77
American Society of Adlerian Psychology, 54
American Society of Group Psychotherapy and Psychodrama, 435, 436
Anal phase of libidinal drive, 13
Analytical psychotherapy, 95; contrasted with traditional psychotherapy, 98; dream-work, 113–116; guidance of unconscious, 111–112; inner world, 117–118; interpretation, 112; relationship of patient with analyst, 116, 122; setting, 122; termination, 120; training institutes, 103; transference, 118
Anima and animus, 104, 105–107; collective unconscious, 106
Anonymous therapist, 80
Antisuggestion, 72
Anxiety, 9, 16, 144, 148, 230, 353
Archetype, 98, 100, 101, 104, 384; collective unconscious, 108; energy field, 107;

formulation of theory, 102; hero, 104; mother, 121; religion, 119; victim, 109
Archetype of adaptation, 104
Art, 119
Assertiveness training, 251–252, 256, 259, 262
Ashram, 507–508
Association, 113, 114
Association for Advancement of Behavior Therapy, 236
Association test, 101
Autoerotism, 14
Autonomy, 145
Aversion therapy, 235, 252–253, 256, 260
Awareness, 146; distortion, 148; Gestalt therapy, 274, 276; sensory, *see* Sensory awareness

Basic mistakes, 67
Behavior, 44; conscious and unconscious motivation, 96; conserved, 429, 438; spontaneous, 429, 438
Behavioral psychotherapy, 5, 230; ancillary personnel, 263; assertiveness training, 251–252, 256, 258; aversion techniques, 252–253, 256, 260; change process, 233; cognitive behavior modification techniques, 254–255; 261; cognitive restructuring, 192; family, 480–481; flooding, 250–251, 255–256, 258; functional analysis, 243–249; learning, 230; operant conditioning, 230, 239; RET, 204; setting, 262; systematic desensitization, 249–250, 255, 258; token economy, 253–254, 258–259; validation, 233
Behavior change, 135, 165; Process Scale, 166; stages, 165–166
Behaviorism, 135, 234
Behavior modification theory, 62, 189, 230, 231, 354; civil liberties, 232
Behind-the-back technique, 71
Belief system, 185, 193; anxiety, 198; unrealistic, *see* Irrational beliefs
Beyond the Pleasure Principle, 8
Bibliotherapy, 186, 221
Binet tests, 79

THE BOOK MANUFACTURE

Current Psychotherapies, Second Edition was typeset at Fox Valley Typesetting, Menasha, Wisconsin. Printing and binding was at George Banta Company, Menasha, Wisconsin. Cover design was by Charles Kling and Associates. Internal design was by F. E. Peacock Publishers art department. The type is Times Roman.